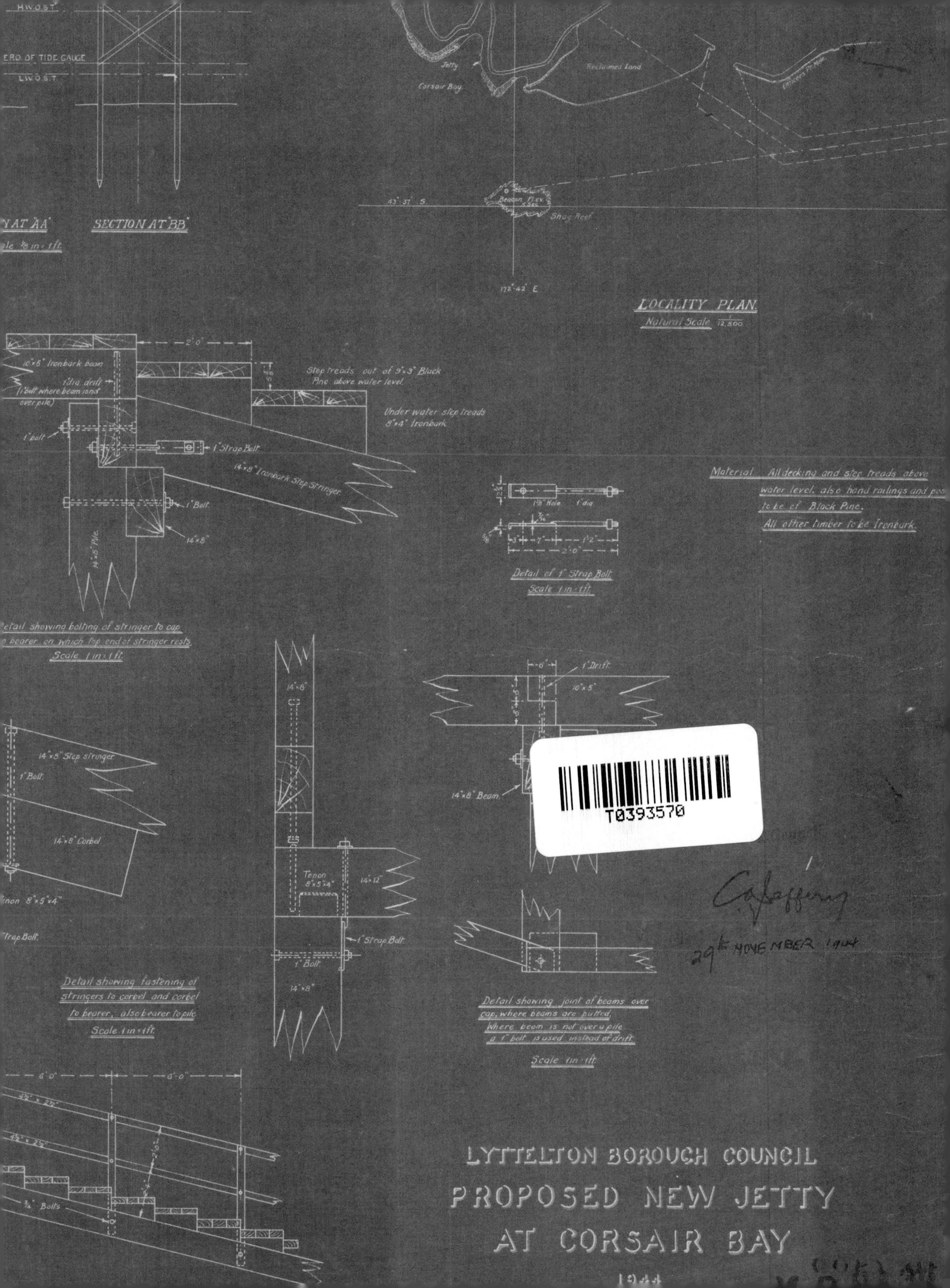
H.W.O.S.T.
ERO OF TIDE GAUGE
L.W.O.S.T.
Y AT "AA"
SECTION AT "BB"
le 1/8 in = 1 ft.
Jetty
Corsair Bay
Reclaimed Land
Officers Pt.
43° 31' S
Beacon
Shag Reef
172° 42' E
LOCALITY PLAN.
Natural Scale 1/12,500
2'0"
10"x5" Ironbark beam
1" dia drift
(1" bolt where beam is not over pile)
Step treads out of 9"x3" Black Pine above water level.
Under water step treads 8"x4" Ironbark.
1" bolt
1" Strap Bolt
14"x8" Ironbark Step Stringer
1" Bolt
14"x8"
14"x8" Pile
Detail showing bolting of stringer to cap
to bearer on which top end of stringer rests.
Scale 1 in = 1 ft.
1 3/8" Hole
1" dia
3"
7"
1'2"
2'0"
Detail of 1" Strap Bolt
Scale 1 in = 1 ft.
Material. All decking and step treads above water level, also hand railings and posts to be of Black Pine.
All other timber to be Ironbark.
14"x8" Step stringer
1" Bolt
14"x8" Corbel
Tenon 8"x5"x4"
Strap Bolt
14"x8"
Tenon 8"x5"x4"
14"x12"
1" Strap Bolt
1" Bolt
14"x8"
Detail showing fastening of stringers to corbel and corbel to bearer, also bearer to pile.
Scale 1 in = 1 ft.
6"
1" Drift
10"x5"
14"x8" Beam
Detail showing joint of beams over cap, where beams are butted.
Where beam is not over a pile a 1" bolt is used instead of drift.
Scale 1 in = 1 ft.
6'0"
6'0"
4½" x 2½"
4½" x 2½"
2'0"
¾" Bolts
T0393570
29th NOVEMBER 1944
LYTTELTON BOROUGH COUNCIL
PROPOSED NEW JETTY
AT CORSAIR BAY
1944

Living Between Land & Sea

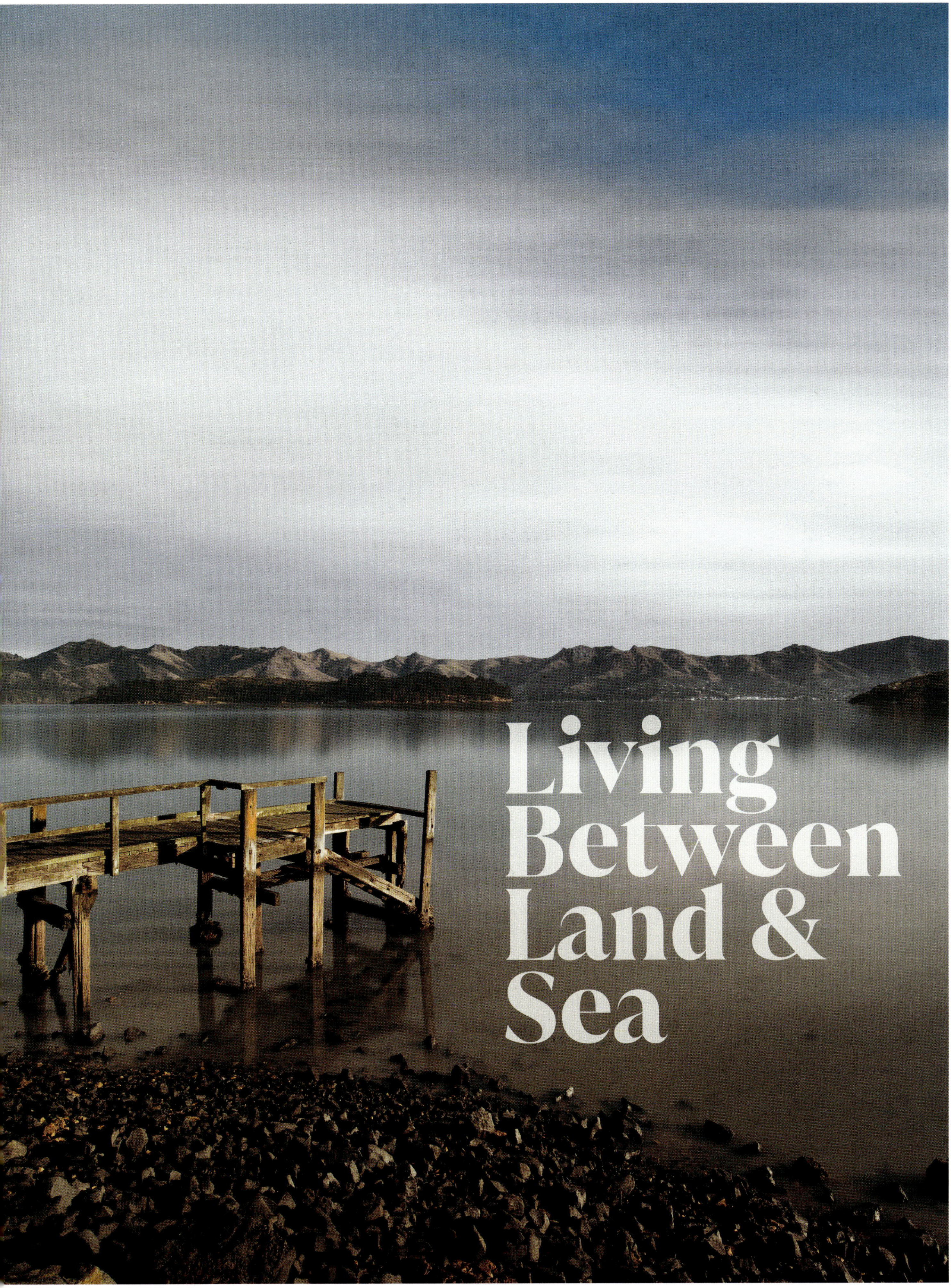

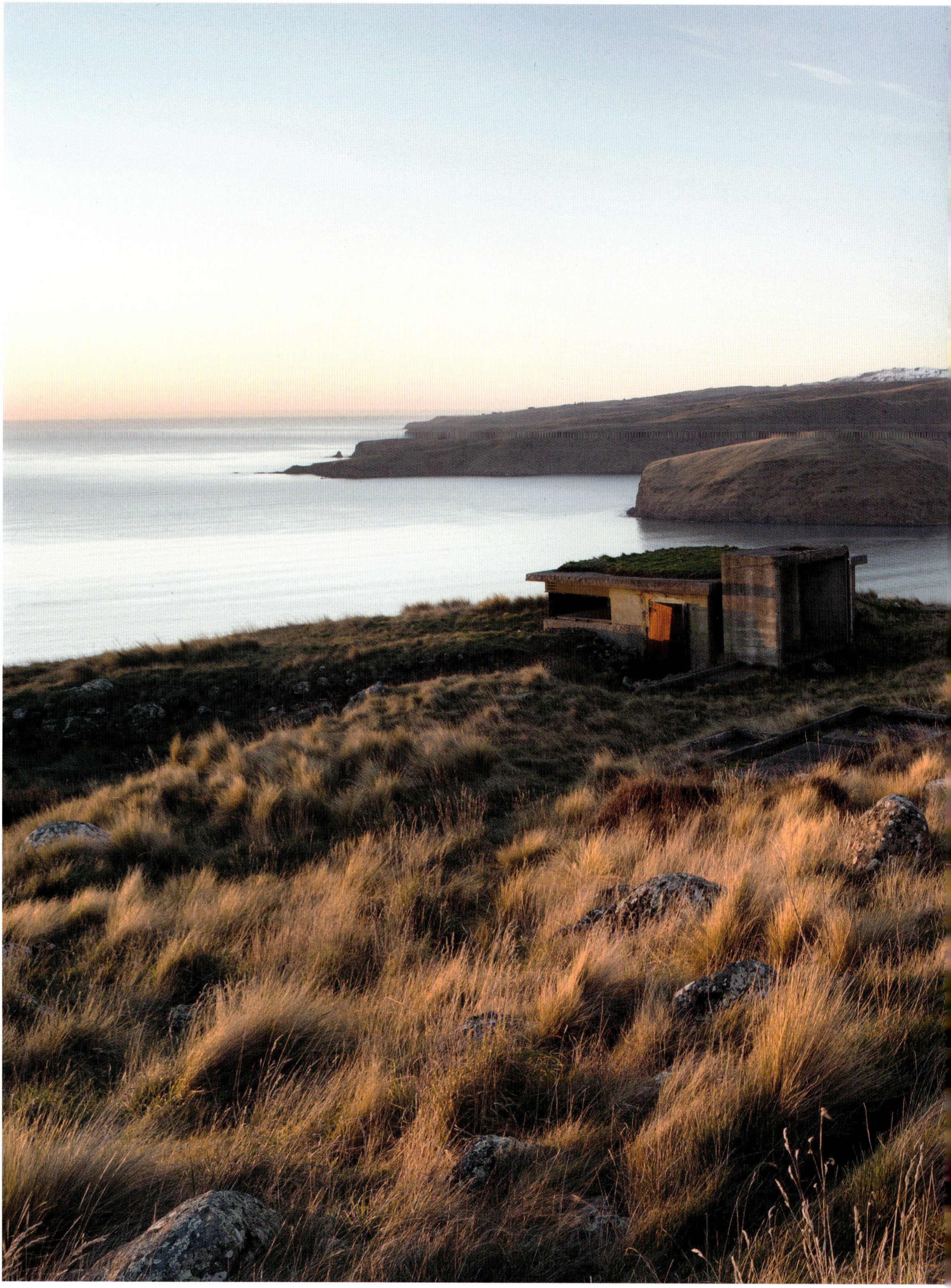

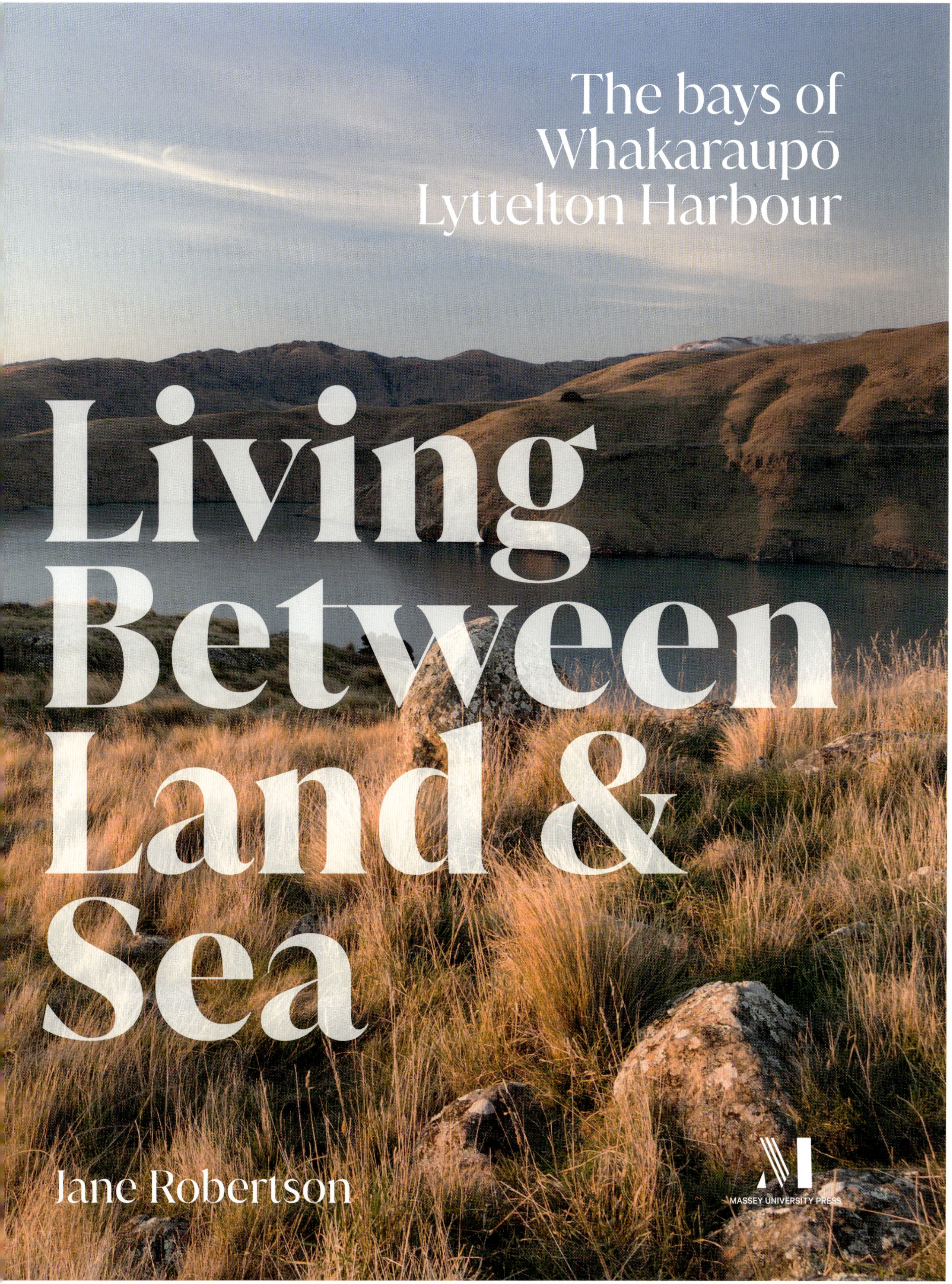

The bays of
Whakaraupō
Lyttelton Harbour

Living Between Land & Sea

Jane Robertson

MASSEY UNIVERSITY PRESS

Contents

Introduction 7

1 | Living on the edge 15

2 | Waitata Little Port Cooper 31

3 | Te Pōhue Camp Bay 45

4 | Rīpapa Island 63

5 | Pūrau 81

6 | Te Waipapa Diamond Harbour 105

7 | Kaioruru Church Bay 127

8 | Te Wharau Charteris Bay 145

9 | Tauwharepaka Teddington 165

10 | Allandale and Ōhinetahi 181

11 | Ōtoromiro Governors Bay, Pukekaroro Sandy Bay, Māori Gardens 197

12 | Ōtamahua Quail Island 219

13 | Te Rāpaki-o-Te Rakiwhakaputa 245

14 | Motukauatirahi Cass Bay 265

15 | Motukauatiiti Corsair Bay 279

16 | Magazine Bay 295

17 | Te Awaparahi Buckleys Bay and Ōtokitoki Gollans Bay 313

18 | Awaroa Godley Head 331

19 | Connecting the harbour 347

Afterword 367
Notes 370
Bibliography 377
Glossary 380
Image credits 381
Acknowledgements 382
Index 383

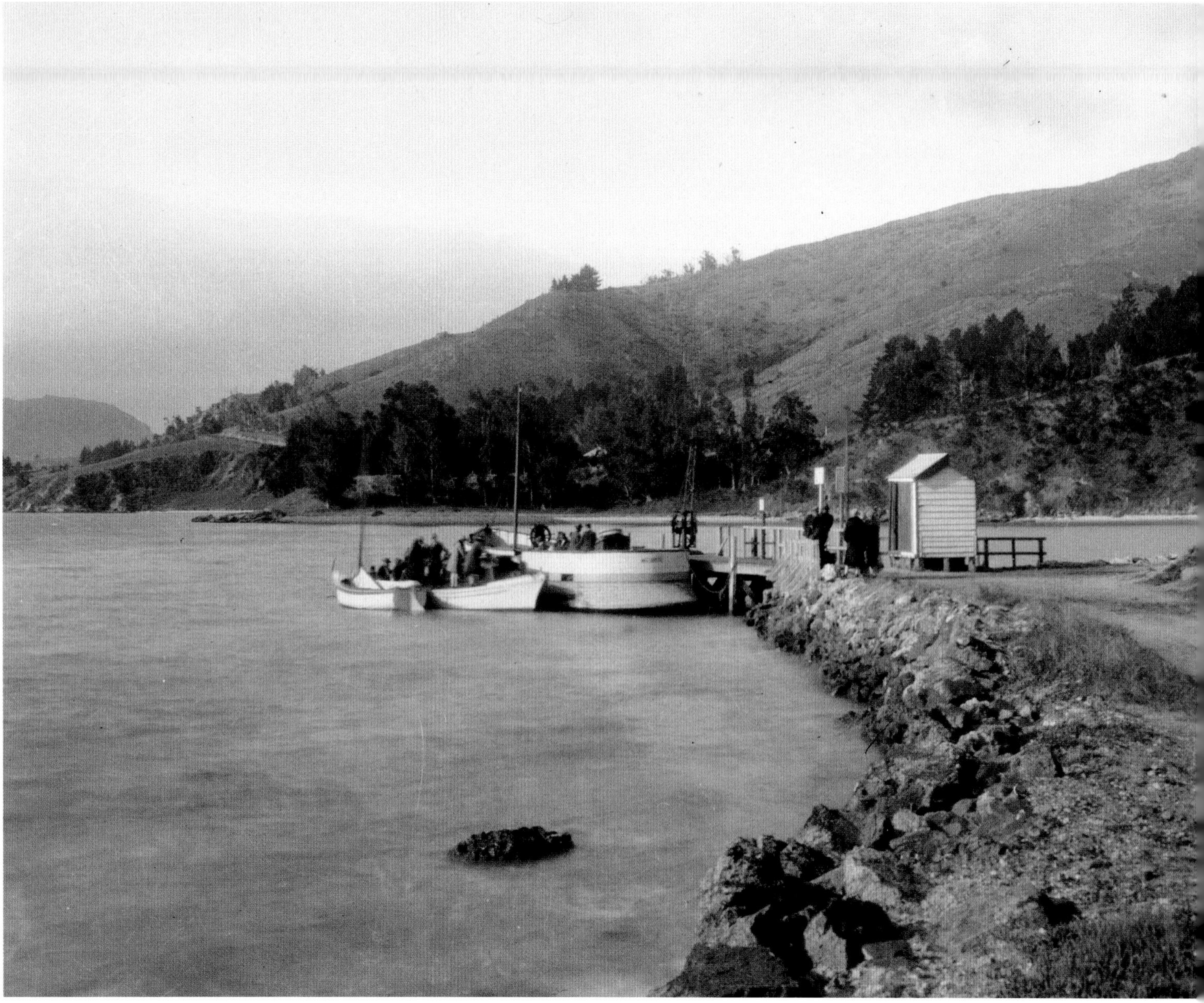

Introduction

This book began life as a blog in which I wrote and posted images about the jetties of Whakaraupō Lyttelton Harbour and the small settlements serviced by those jetties. The blog posts went out on local social media, triggering responses from those who lived — or used to live — in the harbour. Those responses and other conversations with harbour residents fed into what was to become this book.

The focus on jetties grew out of my research for *Head of the Harbour: A History of Governors Bay, Ōhinetahi, Allandale and Teddington*. While working on that book I found myself particularly engaged in, and challenged by, the mysteries of the various jetty structures, past and present. I decided to extend my research to embrace all the jetties in Whakaraupō.

The tidal zone or takutai moana, which jetties inhabit, is both land and sea, a place where the two coexist in an intimate relationship. The sea constantly caresses or pounds the edge of the land, changing it slowly and relentlessly or, sometimes (and increasingly), suddenly and devastatingly. In this zone of ebb and flow we build structures that enable easier access to the ever-shifting sea. Jetties, wharves, piers, quays, slipways — such projections shape 'a relationship of familiar into unfamiliar . . . making an inaccessible environment accessible'.[1] The sea becomes a highway, an extension of land routes, with those coastal structures acting as a hinge or threshold between land and sea.

I like jetties, particularly those in varying states of decay. I find them both beautiful and poignant — beautiful because of their wonderful textures and shapes, poignant because they represent a way of life that is largely gone. Throughout Whakaraupō there are jetties in various states of dereliction: some have been reduced to piles or dismantled, others have been swallowed by the sea. While jetties denote settlement and suggest a degree of permanence, they are, in themselves, anything but permanent. Without maintenance, such sea structures degrade inexorably in their unforgiving marine environment.

Although jetties were the physical starting point for this book, it rapidly

Three boats tied up at the Bradley/Charteris Bay jetty with what is now known as 'Traffic Cops Bay' behind. The jetty still stands but has been closed to the public since the 2010/11 Canterbury earthquakes.
CANTERBURY MUSEUM, W. A. TAYLOR COLLECTION, 1968.213.392

became clear that these pathways over the water were just a portal — a way of stepping back into harbour communities whose reliance on the sea was so much greater than ours is today. I wanted to write more broadly about the relationship between land and sea and how that relationship changed over time for those who made the harbour their home.

Each chapter in this book tells the story of one settlement or a small cluster of settlements. Structurally, I have followed the U shape of Whakaraupō's shoreline, starting in the south-east adjacent to Te Piaka Adderley Head and working in a clockwise direction. The settlements are: Waitata Little Port Cooper, Te Pōhue Camp Bay, Rīpapa Island, Pūrau, Te Waipapa Diamond Harbour, Kaioruru Church Bay, Te Wharau Charteris Bay (including Hays Bay), Tauwharepaka Teddington, Allandale, Ōhinetahi, Otoromiro Governors Bay, Pukekaroro Sandy Bay, Māori Gardens, Ōtamahua Quail Island, Te Rāpaki-o-Te Rakiwhakaputa, Motukauatirahi Cass Bay, Motukauatiiti Corsair Bay, Magazine Bay, Te Awaparahi Buckleys Bay, Ōtokitoki Gollans Bay and Awaroa Godley Head. I have not included the port of Lyttelton except where it affects neighbouring settlements. That would be a project in its own right and awaits another author.

Long before any jetties were built in Whakaraupō, Māori navigated its bays, selected sites for settlement, understood the vagaries of the harbour weather and gathered the plentiful kaimoana to feed whānau and manuhiri (visitors). Every part of the harbour bore a Māori name which described its role or significance within te ao Māori. Since colonisation, many harbour settlements and features have been better known to all but a few by their European titles, which supplanted the earlier Waitaha, Ngāti Māmoe and Ngāi Tahu names. In this book, when a place name is introduced for the first time I use both its Māori and English names, regardless of whether the dual naming is official or not. Thereafter I use either name, with context generally determining my choice. Over the years in which a place would generally have been referred to by its European name, I follow that convention. However, I hope this book will contribute to the growing use by all of us of the beautifully descriptive Māori names that graced our harbour for centuries and are increasingly receiving official recognition.

The terms 'jetty' and 'wharf' tend to be used interchangeably to refer to fixed structures that project out from the land into water. 'Jetty' is derived from the French word *jetée* or 'thrown'. 'Wharf' comes from the Old English *hwearf*, meaning 'bank' or 'shore'. Both terms are used for such structures in Whakaraupō. I have chosen to use the term 'jetty' throughout the book, referring to 'wharf' only when it is quoted in source material.

The first jetties in Whakaraupō were built by private individuals to facilitate the transport of farm produce to Lyttelton and markets further afield. Household supplies were carried on the return journey. Such jetties were essential to surviving and thriving in the eroded caldera of an ancient volcano, flooded by the sea. As the nineteenth century gave way to the twentieth, and more public jetties were built by the Lyttelton Harbour Board, their recreational value increased, with motor launches criss-crossing the harbour bringing day trippers and holidaymakers to 'resorts' such as Corsair Bay, Governors Bay and Diamond Harbour. Thereafter the construction of better roads around the harbour, the use of trucks to transport farm produce and the growth in private vehicle ownership meant a slow decline in the use of jetties, although they continued to serve yachties and other boat owners.

The foreshore, with its marine structures, was and is a gathering place, a site of community activity and identity, a place of arrivals and departures, a liminal space. It was also a contested political space. As the need for facilities increased and privately built jetties gave way to publicly funded structures, the Lyttelton Harbour Board and the Mount Herbert County Council locked horns over the ownership, construction and maintenance of jetties. Farmers and boat owners were caught in the financial crossfire. The continual silting of the harbour, which

Mark Stoddart arrived in Port Cooper (Lyttelton Harbour) in January 1851 and purchased land in Diamond Harbour. In the late 1850s he built one of the first private jetties. The present-day Diamond Harbour Jetty is the direct descendant of the Stoddart Jetty seen in this pre-First World War photo.
DHHA, STODDART ALBUM

increasingly impeded access, was often blamed, fairly or not, on the actions of the harbour board. In the twenty-first century, climate change with its associated sea-level rise may alter familiar shorelines and pose further political challenges.

The stories of the harbour settlements and their jetties are also the stories of the dinghies, whaleboats, ballast craft, lighters, barges, yachts and steam launches that carried people and produce around the harbour. These tough little craft provided a vital service for isolated harbour families and a much-anticipated recreational opportunity for townies. They were involved in accidents and rescues. Some craft, like the steamer *John Anderson*, were in service for decades and were much loved by harbour residents. Boats and jetties enjoyed a symbiotic relationship. As reliance on the former decreased, so, too, did the need for the latter. This book is also a tribute to all those hard-working harbour craft and those who skippered them.

When people asked me how 'the jetty book' was going, I wanted to say, 'It's not just about jetties.' But generally I didn't, because that's where it started. Tracing the stories of the jetties has required a lot of fruitful and fruitless archival work. Some mysteries, especially around the Teddington jetties, remain. The long-disappeared ghost jetties, especially, have been both challenging and exciting to 'surface'. The discoveries that surprised and delighted me most were perhaps the long jetty built for the signal station settlement at Little Port Cooper and the very short jetty in Mechanics Bay that, incredibly, serviced the lighthouse at Godley Head. Neither of those I knew about before beginning this book. I tried to visit the site of every jetty, whether extant or in skeleton or ghost form. Two were beyond my reach: the jetty at Godley Head, inaccessible except to amphibious mountain goats because of its location at the bottom of a much-eroded cliff, and the jetty at Buckleys Bay, since the bay has long since disappeared beneath rubble quarried from the crater wall to form Cashin Quay.

In recent years, the Department of Conservation and the Lyttelton Harbour Board (subsequently the Lyttelton Port Company) have partnered to rebuild or restore jetties on Ōtamahua Quail Island and Rīpapa Island. Te Hapū o Ngāti Wheke at Te Rāpaki-o-Te Rakiwhakaputa carried out extensive repairs to their Gallipoli Jetty in the 1970s, and after the 2010/11 Canterbury earthquakes Church Bay residents worked hard, using voluntary labour and expertise, to restore their jetty. A private jetty in Charteris Bay remains in excellent repair. The Governors Bay long jetty, built initially as a short jetty in 1874, is being rebuilt by a community that sees historical, cultural and recreational value in retaining such a structure. Perhaps we might even, one day, see launches return, on special occasions, to the upper harbour.

Passengers disembark from the steam pinnace *Canterbury* at Governors Bay, c.1905. This was the second public jetty in the bay, built in 1874 and extended significantly in 1913. Despite the remarkable length of the jetty — 300 metres — silting in the upper harbour meant that access at low tide continued to be a problem.
CANTERBURY MUSEUM, F. C. BISHOP COLLECTION, 1923.86.2

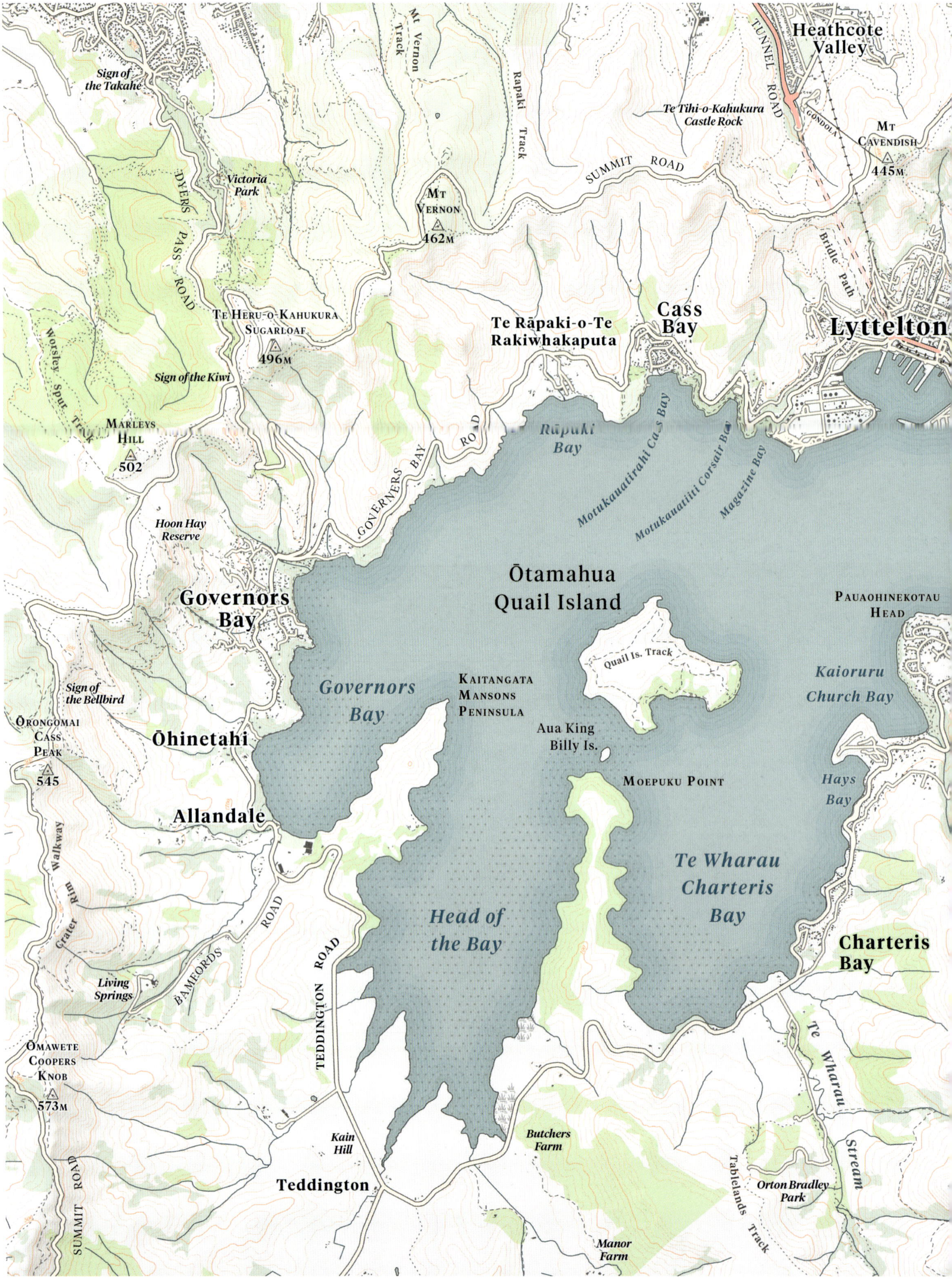
Heathcote Valley
Mt Vernon Track
Sign of the Takahe
Rapaki Track
Te Tihi-o-Kahukura Castle Rock
Tunnel Road
Gondola
Mt Cavendish 445m
Summit Road
Victoria Park
Dyers Pass Road
Mt Vernon 462m
Bridle Path
Worsley Spur Track
Te Heru-o-Kahukura Sugarloaf 496m
Te Rāpaki-o-Te Rakiwhakaputa
Cass Bay
Lyttelton
Sign of the Kiwi
Marleys Hill 502
Rāpaki Bay
Governers Bay Road
Motukauatirahi Cass Bay
Motukauatiiti Corsair Bay
Magazine Bay
Hoon Hay Reserve
Ōtamahua Quail Island
Governors Bay
Pauaohinekotau Head
Quail Is. Track
Sign of the Bellbird
Governors Bay
Kaitangata Mansons Peninsula
Kaioruru Church Bay
Ōrongomai Cass Peak 545
Ōhinetahi
Aua King Billy Is.
Moepuku Point
Hays Bay
Allandale
Crater Rim Walkway
Te Wharau Charteris Bay
Head of the Bay
Bamfords Road
Teddington Road
Charteris Bay
Living Springs
Omawete Coopers Knob 573m
Te Wharau Stream
Kain Hill
Butchers Farm
Summit Road
Teddington
Tablelands Track
Orton Bradley Park
Manor Farm

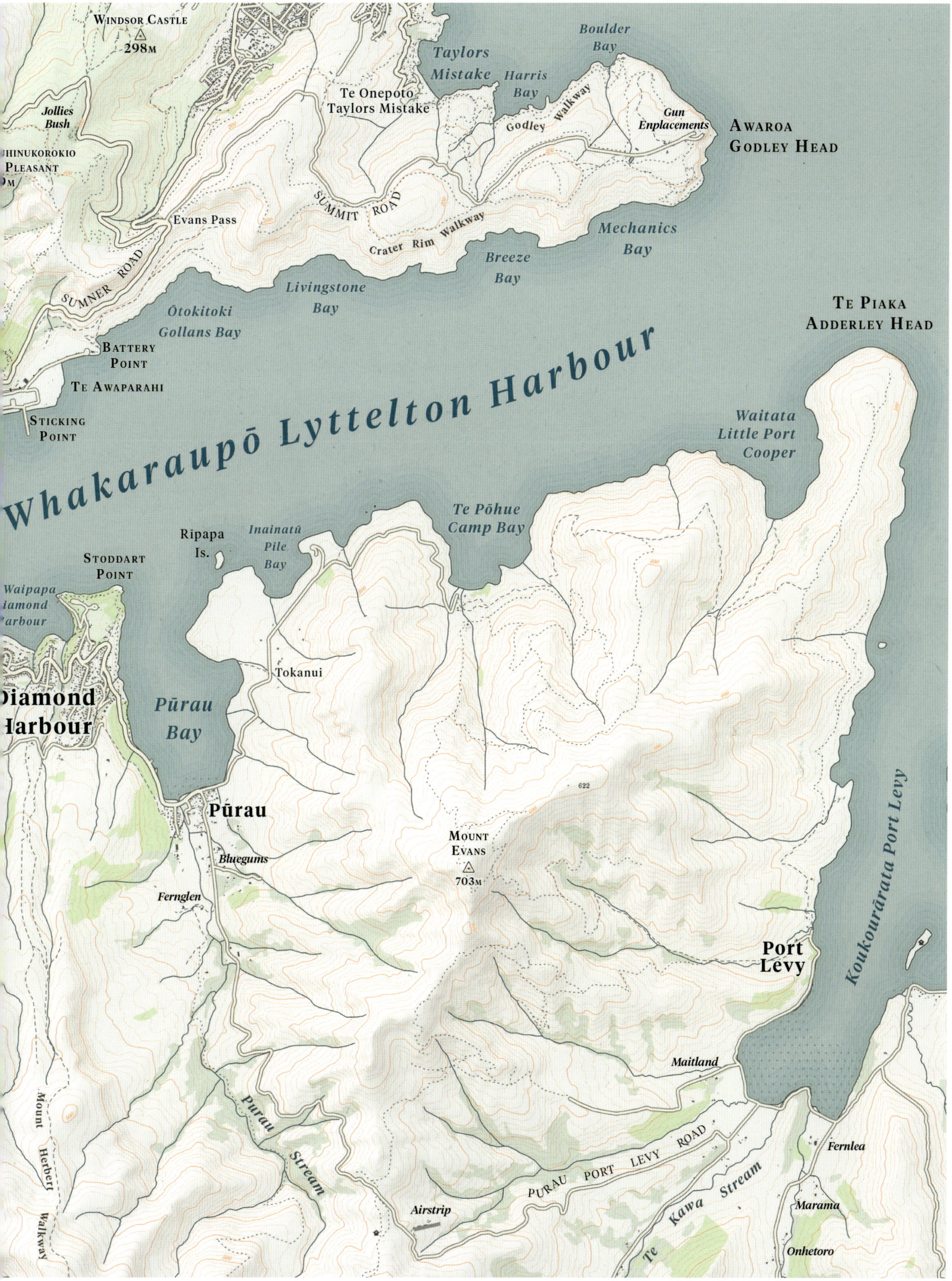

Windsor Castle
298m
Jollies Bush
Evans Pass
Sumner Road
Te Onepoto
Taylors Mistake
Taylors Mistake
Harris Bay
Boulder Bay
Godley Walkway
Gun Enplacements
Awaroa
Godley Head
Summit Road
Crater Rim Walkway
Mechanics Bay
Breeze Bay
Livingstone Bay
Ōtokitoki
Gollans Bay
Battery Point
Te Awaparahi
Sticking Point
Te Piaka
Adderley Head
Whakaraupō Lyttelton Harbour
Waitata
Little Port Cooper
Te Pōhue
Camp Bay
Ripapa Is.
Inainatū
Pile Bay
Stoddart Point
Tokanui
Diamond Harbour
Pūrau Bay
Pūrau
Bluegums
Fernglen
622
Mount Evans
703m
Port Levy
Koukourārata Port Levy
Maitland
Mount Herbert Walkway
Pūrau Stream
Purau Port Levy Road
Airstrip
Te Kawa Stream
Fernlea
Marama
Onhetoro

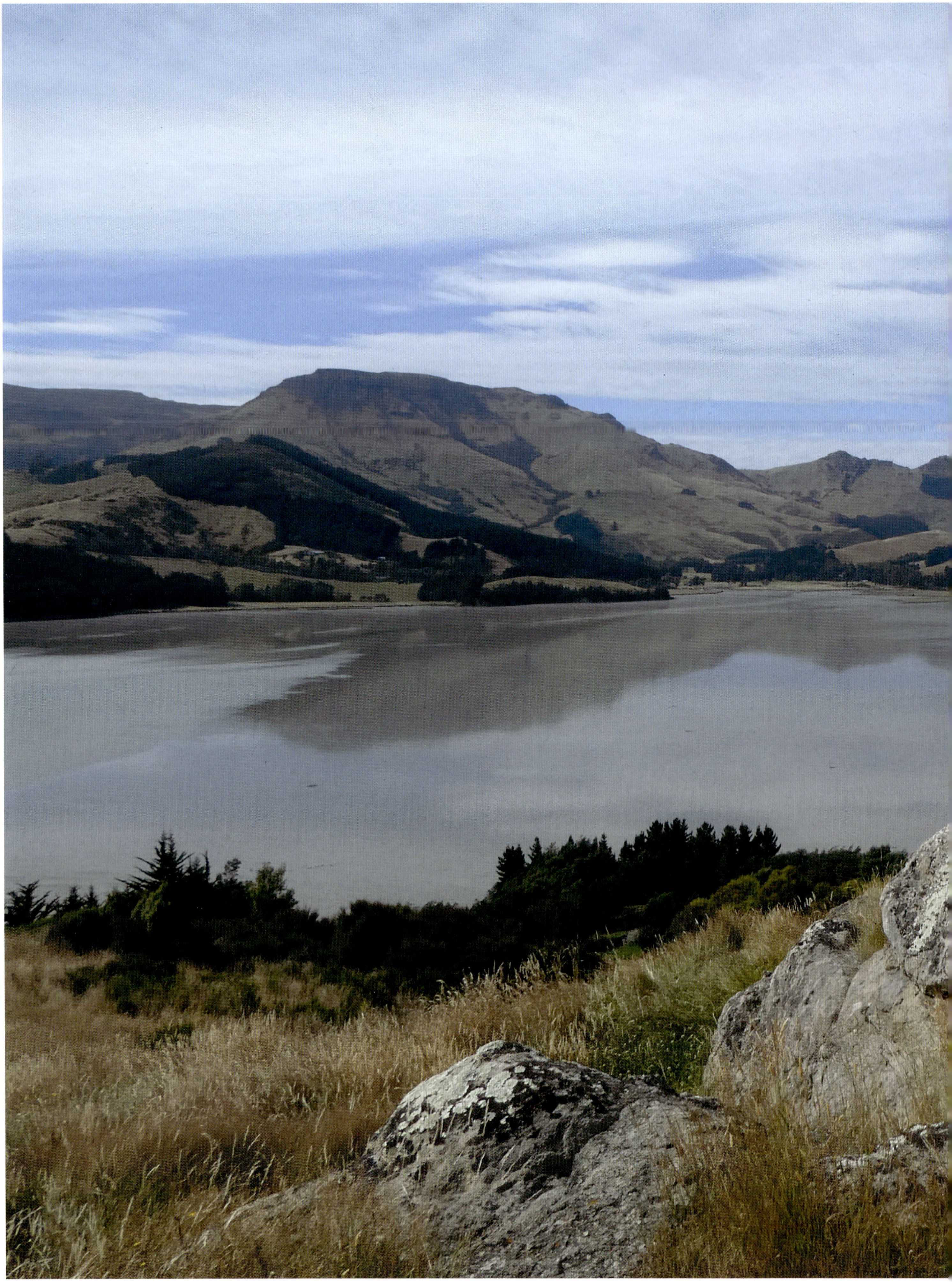

1 | Living on the edge

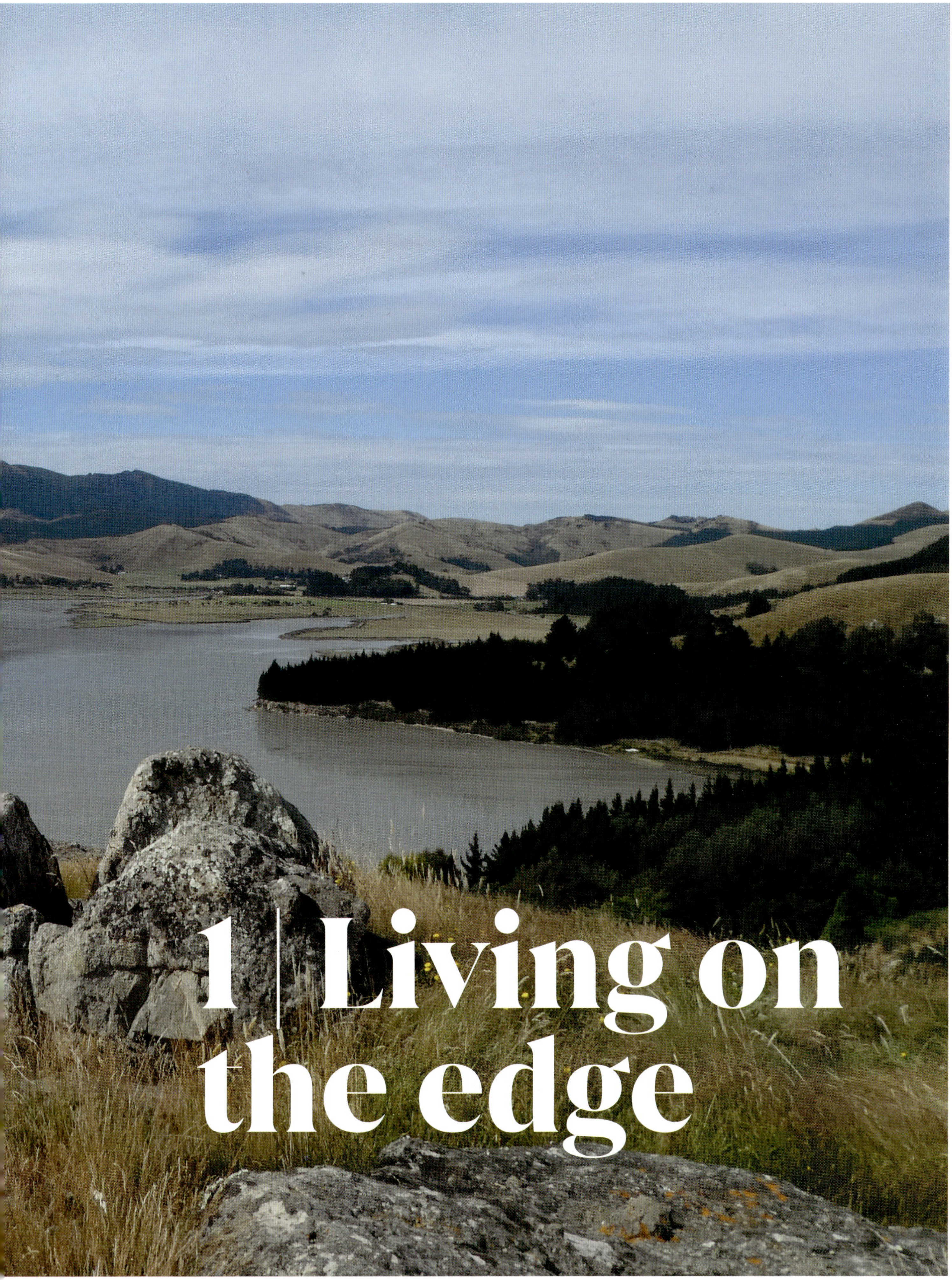

In Aotearoa New Zealand we are never far from the sea. Most of us live on, or very near, bodies of water that connect to the huge expanses of the Tasman Sea or Pacific Ocean. We swim, fish, sail, kayak on the sea, holiday beside it and gain sustenance from it in terms of kaimoana and spiritual renewal. We all, tangata whenua and those of us who arrived later, came to Aotearoa by or over sea. Even in an age of flight when most parts of the globe are accessible, New Zealand remains somewhat isolated in the swirl of the southern oceans. Were our planet flat, we would be clinging to a watery edge.

✻

On the otherwise fairly featureless east coast of Te Waipounamu the South Island, backed by Kā Pākihi Whakatekateka o Waitaha ('the great flat lands of the Waitaha', or Canterbury Plains), a bulbous nose protrudes into the South Pacific Ocean. This is Te Pātaka o Rākaihautū or Horomaka, commonly known today as Banks Peninsula. If Aotearoa is on the edge, then Te Pātaka o Rākaihautū is the edge of the edge. For most of its existence the peninsula was an island, formed between eleven and eight million years ago by the violent eruptions of two main volcanoes. At its tallest, the island towered some 1500 metres above sea level. Gradually the volcanic complex eroded and deep valleys formed. Over time, huge quantities of outwash debris flowed down from the Southern Alps and coalesced in shingle fans, eventually joining Te Pātaka o Rākaihautū to Te Waipounamu. Windblown silt (loess) from the west covered the peninsula hills and valley floors. As the sea level rose, the low-lying terrain flooded, creating the natural harbours that now serve Akaroa and Lyttelton. Even when it finally became a part of the mainland, the mountainous peninsula remained all but cut off from the plains by swamps, lagoons and streams.

Today, the volcanic rocks of the peninsula are covered by deposits of loess up to 20 metres thick, blown from the Canterbury Plains. This fine sediment is easily and constantly eroded from the hill slopes around Whakaraupō Lyttelton Harbour. The eroded material has infilled the harbour basin to depths of up to 47 metres, creating extensive tidal flats in Governors Bay, Head of the Bay and Charteris Bay.[1] This natural geological process, speeded up by human intervention, plays a part in the stories of the harbour settlements.

In the Māori legends of Te Waipounamu, Rākaihautū (a Polynesian ariki or high chief, and captain of the canoe *Uruao* which brought the Waitaha tribe to Aotearoa) and his son Rokohouia explored the southern island and named its lakes and lagoons. When Rākaihautū first saw Banks Peninsula, almost all parts of it were covered in dense podocarp forest, home to many native birds. The mudflats were fringed with salt-grass, jointed rush and shrubby ribbonwood, while native flax flourished in wet areas and on shady rocky spurs. The bays and harbours teemed with fish and shellfish. Rākaihautū named the peninsula his pātaka, or great food storehouse.

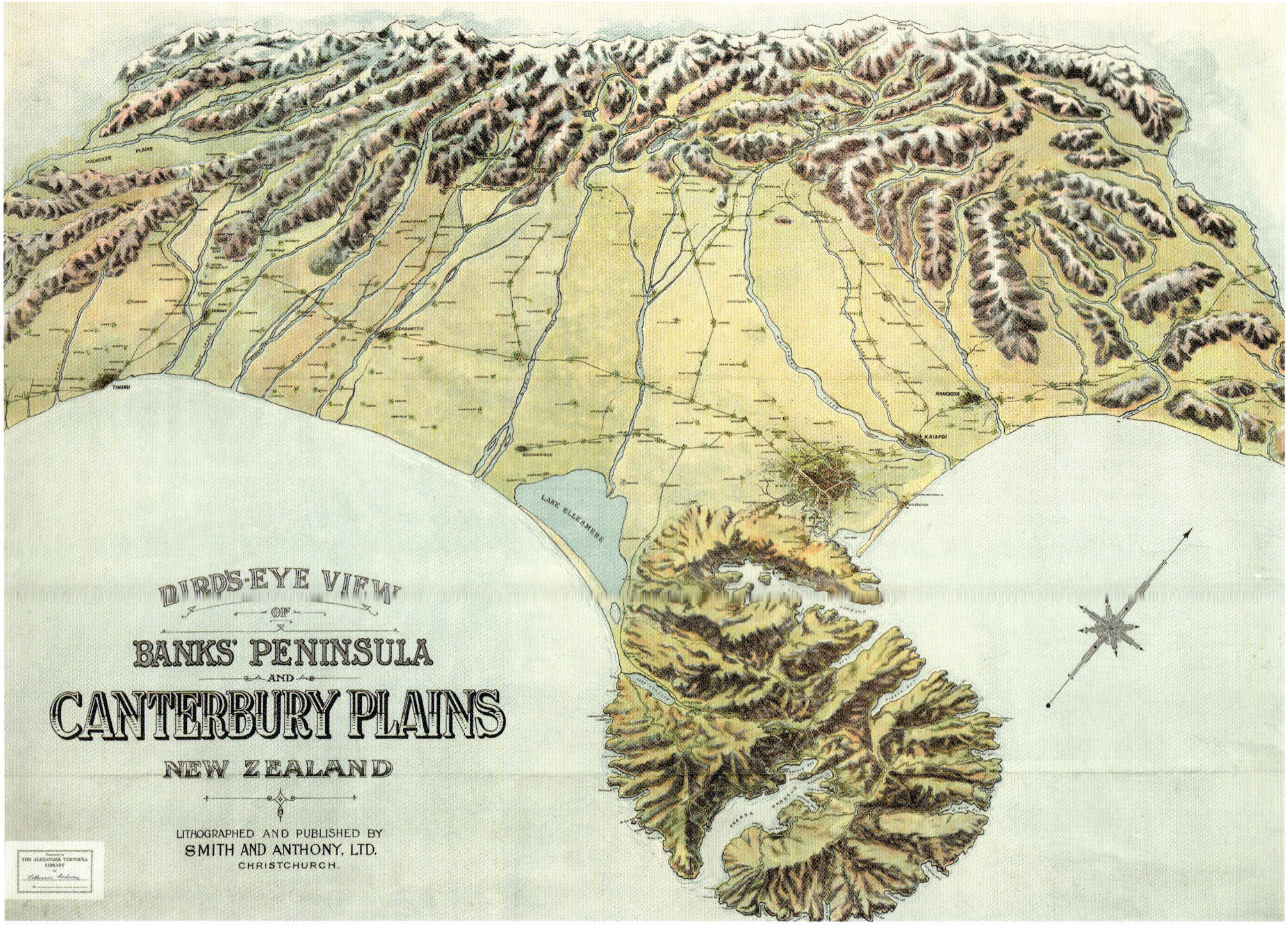
BIRD'S-EYE VIEW
OF
BANKS' PENINSULA
AND
CANTERBURY PLAINS
NEW ZEALAND
LITHOGRAPHED AND PUBLISHED BY
SMITH AND ANTHONY, LTD.
CHRISTCHURCH.
LAKE ELLESMERE
TIMARU
THE ALEXANDER TURNBULL LIBRARY

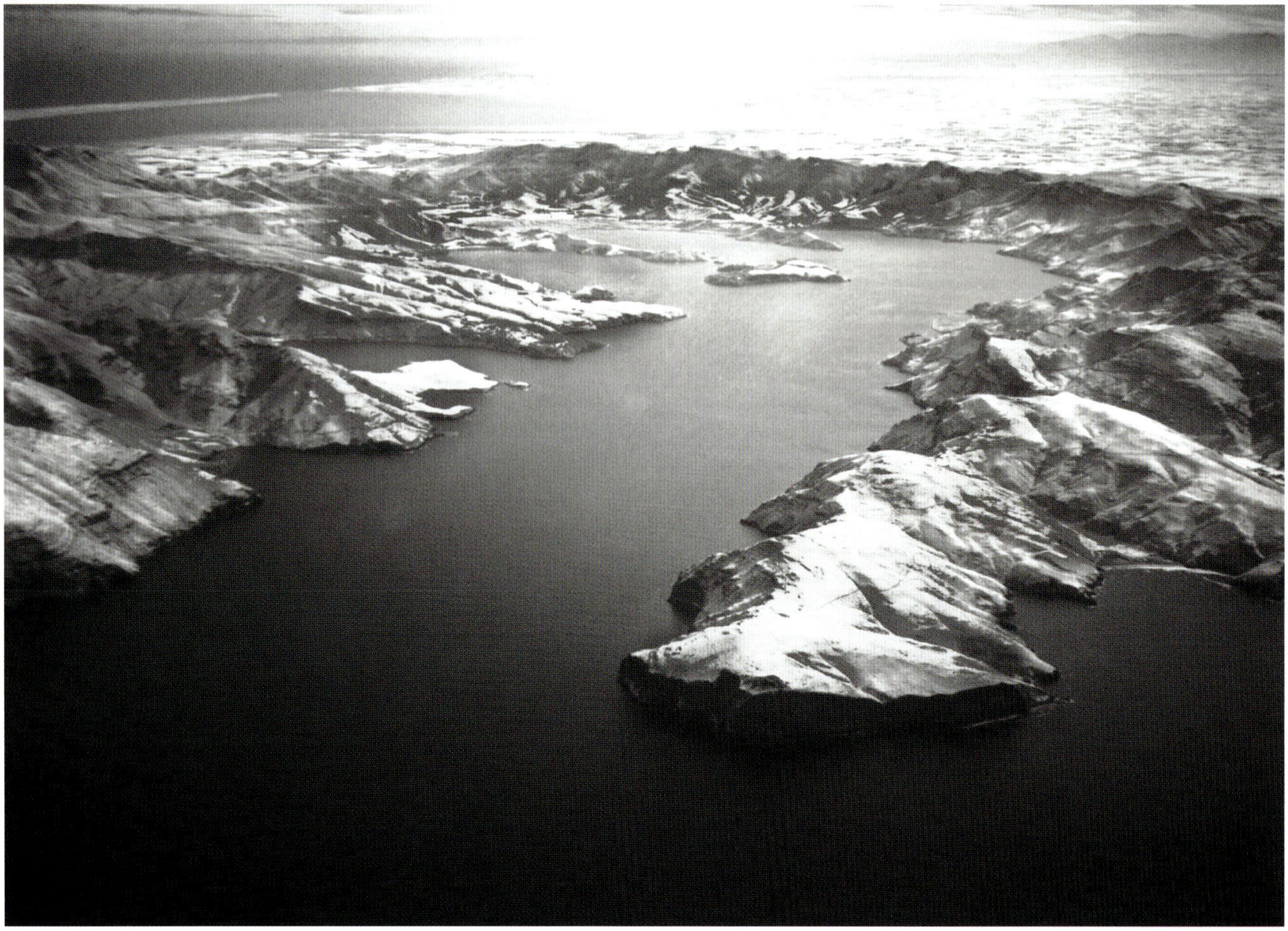

Tamatea Pōkai Whenua, descendant of Tamatea Ariki Nui, who commanded *Tākitimu* from Hawaiki to Aotearoa, also explored Te Waipounamu. When Tamatea came to Te Pātaka o Rākaihautū he named the large and relatively sheltered harbour on its north-eastern side Whakaraupō, after the raupō reeds that were once plentiful at the head of the long bay. This harbour was to sustain, in succession, Waitaha, Ngāti Māmoe and Ngāi Tahu, with its kaimoana and native birds providing an intricate network of mahinga kai (food resources and locations).[2]

But the impact of human occupation on Te Pātaka o Rākaihautū generally, and on Whakaraupō in particular, was devastating. About a third of the peninsula's forest cover was lost during the period of Polynesian settlement. The rapid removal of almost all the remaining blanket of vegetation following European occupation opened up the deep layers of loess covering the hills to the erosive effects of wind and rain. The silting of Whakaraupō, already a natural phenomenon, increased.

Before the development of reasonable road access — or any roads at all — the sea was a highway on which Māori and, later, early European settlers depended. Māori used a variety of waka to traverse ara moana (water-based trails) within Whakaraupō, between peninsula settlements and along the east coast. Tauranga waka (canoe landing points) were common and were associated with nohoanga (temporary settlements), linking a sea trail to a land trail. Māori could easily beach their waka on sandy shores or flat, rocky platforms. However, by the early 1840s Assistant Protector of Aborigines Edward Shortland reported that for Māori, 'whaling and sealing boats have superseded canoes, in the management of which they show great skill and boldness'. In addition, 'they have become expert whalers, and obtain employment at the fisheries often on the same terms as Europeans'.[3] According to Charlotte Godley, early colonist, astute observer and author, the whaleboats had five, seven, nine or eleven oars, were peaked and high at both ends, and were steered by a man standing with an 18-foot oar.[4]

The waters around Banks Peninsula attracted whaling ships from the 1820s onwards. By the mid-1830s, Port Cooper (as Lyttelton Harbour was known then),[5] with its sheltered anchorages at Little Port Cooper, Camp Bay and Pūrau, had become a significant rendezvous point for the whalers, evidenced by the nine whaling ships using Little Port Cooper as a base or a refuge in 1836. A Prussian whaler, Captain George Hempleman, brought the brig *Bee* into Little Port Cooper and beached her for much-needed repairs in February 1836. Boats were sent up the harbour, probably to the Māori settlement at Rāpaki, for potatoes.

In his role as the first surveyor general for the New Zealand Company, Captain

ABOVE The unusual aspect of this map illustrates the island-like nature of Banks Peninsula and how the Port Hills isolate Lyttelton Harbour from the Canterbury Plains.
ALEXANDER TURNBULL LIBRARY, 834.44A/ACC.6638

BELOW Whakaraupō Lyttelton Harbour looking west from the heads, with Awaroa Godley Head in the foreground, Te Waihora Lake Ellesmere and the Canterbury Plains in the distance. The volcanic crater rim of the Port Hills is also visible.
V. C. BROWNE & SON, PB0904-7

William Mein Smith was tasked in September 1842 with mapping the harbours on the South Island's east coast. He favoured the inlet of Koukourārata Port Ashley (later Port Levy) over Port Cooper 'because the most prevailing and violent winds draw through it [Port Cooper], producing a considerable swell'.[6] Despite this disadvantage, the 1840s saw the arrival of the Greenwood brothers, followed by the Rhodes brothers at Pūrau and the Gebbie and Manson families at Head of the Bay (Teddington). The Deans brothers were farming at Pūtaringamotu Riccarton on the Canterbury Plains, while the Hay and Sinclair families settled at Wakaroa Pigeon Bay. These men and their families used the waters of Port Cooper as a roadway. The Deanses crossed the harbour to Pūrau and walked or rode to Port Levy to collect mail. The Greenwoods, Rhodeses, Gebbies and Mansons took their farm produce across the water to provision visiting ships. The ships then took the butter and cheese produced in Port Cooper to the new settlement in Wellington and further afield to markets in Australia. In fact, until the early decades of the twentieth century, many farmers and families in the bays around Banks Peninsula relied almost wholly on sea transport to get their produce to market.[7]

Thomas Cass arrived at the end of 1848 to take up the role of assistant surveyor for the Canterbury Association. He was joined by Charles Torlesse and Henry Cridland, the three young surveyors initially camping out at what became known as Cass Bay. While permanent settlers built or acquired their own boats, the surveyors were dependent on hired transport. For four or five shillings, Māori at Rāpaki would take Cass, Torlesse or Cridland across the harbour to Pūrau or up to the Manson and Gebbie farms at Head of the Bay. By 1851 the Ward brothers added to the growing harbour traffic as they rowed or sailed to Ōtamahua Quail Island, where they were developing a farm and building a house.

In Lyttelton Harbour, the first jetties were built by private individuals of some means. The Rhodes brothers built a jetty (now just a scatter of piles) on the east side of Pūrau Bay. Mark Stoddart's private jetty in Diamond Harbour, built about 1856, eventually became the public jetty still in use today. The Bradley family built a jetty in Charteris Bay, and the Manson and Gebbie families in Teddington constructed a 300-foot jetty (on account of the mudflats) that was promptly destroyed in the tsunami of 1868. (On 15 August that year, a powerful earthquake off the Pacific coast of Peru and Chile generated the largest recorded distant tsunami to strike New Zealand.) Governors Bay had a scattering of private jetties and also two very early public jetties, one built in Sandy Bay in 1860 and the other, where the long jetty now stands, in 1874. In the absence of a jetty, goods could travel by lighters, which would run up onto the beach to be offloaded, then refloat on the next high tide.

The behaviour of the waters in Lyttelton Harbour vexed early settlers. The harbour was open to the ocean swell that swept around Banks Peninsula. This swell, from the east and north-east, could at times travel up the harbour 'with great violence and in very long undulations'.[8] The harbour was also subject to sou'westerly gales which, in only two or three fathoms of water, could raise a short, choppy sea. In between the nor'easterlies and the sou'westerlies was the northwest wind, which blew down off the hills 'in furious eddying squalls or "williewas"'.[9] Criss-crossing the harbour in small vessels was frequently challenging and sometimes fatal.

Land transport gradually supplanted transport by sea as the road network around the harbour improved and trucks capable of carrying large loads came into service. As sea transport declined, jetties took on a more recreational purpose. Launch trips to Corsair Bay, Governors Bay, Charteris Bay, Diamond Harbour and Pūrau had always been popular. In the early decades of the twentieth century, hundreds of day trippers might disembark daily at any one of these bays. As yacht and motor boat ownership increased, the jetties became popular with boaties.

The annual Lyttelton regatta attracted sailors from all around the harbour and well beyond. The first, held in May 1851 to celebrate the Queen's Birthday, included a race for vessels from 8 to 15 tons; a rowing match for four-oared boats; a rowing match for five-oared whaleboats; a race for open sailing boats under 5 tons; and a sculling dinghy match. There was also a 'duck hunt', with a dinghy to be chased by two four-oared boats without a steersman. The duck had a five-minute start and had to be caught by the bow oarsman.

By 1858 the regatta had been shifted to New Year's Day, when the weather was more settled and people were in holiday mode. It became Lyttelton's big show day when city folk visited the harbour, and it grew so popular that by 1896 approximately 25,000 people travelled to the port for the day by road or rail. Festivities continued into the evening when, about 9.00 p.m., the popular steamer *John Anderson* left the wharf crowded with excursionists. 'She was illuminated with coloured lanterns, and after making a round of the inner harbour, she took a procession of boats in tow, all of which were brilliantly illuminated with Roman candles.'[10]

Yacht clubs at Lyttelton/Magazine Bay and Charteris Bay gave generations of children their introduction to sailing. The development of a 14-foot centreboard, clinker-built, dinghy-style yacht suitable for younger sailors coincided with the arrival in 1920 of Admiral Lord Jellicoe, who had been appointed Governor General. A keen yachtsman, Jellicoe championed the new design, which came to be known as the Jellicoe Class or X-class.

When the Sanders Memorial Cup was donated in memory of Lieutenant Commander W. E. Sanders, VC, DSO, for interprovincial competition amongst boats of the 14-foot, one-design class, interest really took off. Only one entry was allowed from each province and competition was intense.[11]

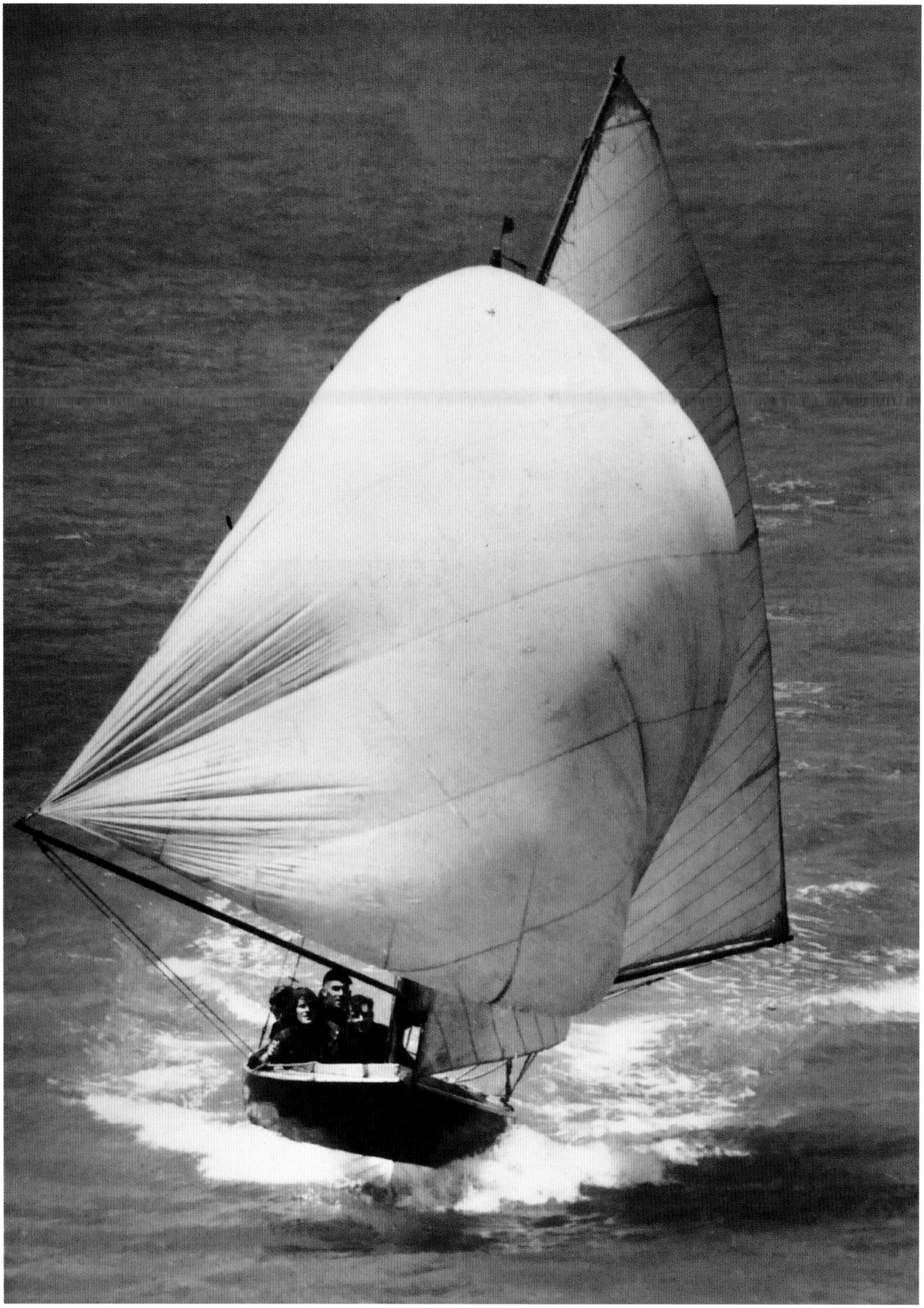

While the harbour was a popular playground, its foreshore was politically contentious. It was an area of interest to both the Lyttelton Harbour Board, established in 1877 with a responsibility for the management of the harbour's commercial and recreational facilities, and the Mount Herbert County Council, formed in 1902 with a particular focus on the county's roads and infrastructure.

Jetties in particular were objects of dispute. Initially, the port of Lyttelton and any outlying public jetties came under the control of the Provincial Government of Canterbury, but the provincial governments were disestablished in 1876 and jurisdiction passed to the fledgling harbour board. One of the sticking points for the harbour board was the fact that the foreshore was not vested in the board — meaning it could not recoup the cost of constructing and maintaining jetties by charging for their use. In April 1880 the harbour board first discussed the desirability of its gaining jurisdiction over the beach or foreshore reserve around the harbour. In 1905 the Lyttelton Harbour Board Land Act vested 'certain parcels of land being portions of the foreshore in the Port of Lyttelton used as sites for jetties and wharves' in the harbour board.[12] The New Brighton and Sumner Borough Councils and the Heathcote Road Board raised no objection. The Mount Herbert County Council, within whose jurisdiction Lyttelton Harbour fell, unsuccessfully opposed the Act, believing that the harbour board was really seeking to control privately owned wharves, which would then be charged levies.

The Harbour Board Land Act gave the Lyttelton Harbour Board jurisdiction over foreshore land in Governors Bay, Sandy Bay (Percivals Point), Heathcote, Port Levy, New Brighton, Charteris Bay, Sumner, Diamond Harbour, Pūrau (two areas) and Rāpaki. This legislation eased the way for the construction of further outlying jetties and the maintenance of existing structures. Between 1905 and 1915 new jetties were built, rebuilt or significantly altered at Little Port Cooper, Pūrau, Diamond Harbour, Church Bay, Charteris Bay, Governors Bay and Corsair Bay. Rāpaki, Camp Bay and probably Teddington followed, during and after the First World War. It was a golden age for public water transport in Lyttelton Harbour.

The Lyttelton Harbour Board, seeking to recoup costs from jetty users, had to decide on a revenue-raising mechanism. Its engineer, Cyrus Williams, outlined the options in a 1909 memo. The 'outlying' jetties in Lyttelton Harbour under the board's jurisdiction included those listed above plus two at Governors Bay and an extra one at Pūrau. Williams estimated the lifespan of the older jetties at about 30 years, since they were constructed of 'inferior timbers which had previously been used for temporary purposes in connection with the Dock etc.'[13] The more recently built jetties could be expected to survive at least 40 years. Several of the older jetties were nearing the end of their useful lives.

Williams calculated that the amount of revenue that would accrue to the harbour board from wharf charges would not justify any elaborate collection

Eliot Sinclair and Barry Bowater in *Genie*, c.1954. Sinclair retained the Sanders Cup for Lyttelton sailing *Irene* in 1934 and 1935 and *Avenger* in 1936.
NAVAL POINT CLUB

mechanism. He consulted other harbour boards to see how they were handling the matter. Mr Clibborn, the Lyttelton Harbour Board's watchhouseman and collector, suggested that 'shipmasters or owners when collecting their freight be asked to collect the wharfage on goods, at a commission of, say, 2½ percent'. Williams thought this would not be a 'vexatious charge' and that it would establish the custom and principle that 'special conveniences should be paid for by those benefiting by them'.[14]

Maintenance of the outlying jetties continued to be an issue for the Lyttelton Harbour Board. 'It was to be regretted that the local bodies interested had met with legal difficulties in the way of contributing towards the cost of the upkeep of these, to them, great conveniences.'[15] In August 1912 the Lyttelton Harbour Board adopted the Outlying Jetties By-law, which required all licensed vessels using the outlying jetties to pay one shilling per ton on cargo landed or shipped from the jetties and one penny per head on each passenger landing or embarking. The harbour community was having none of it. Farmers already paid wharf fees when their produce was offloaded in Lyttelton. This additional fee would mean they were taxed twice. A stand-off ensued. Port Levy farmer R. J. Fleming told the harbour board that if the charge went ahead he would ship his wool clip out 'the old way', by lighter run up onto the beach, rather than via the jetty. 'I have already told the agents of the SS *John Anderson* that if they pay wharfage on any of my stuff at this end that they do so at their own risk for I shall strike it off my bills . . .'[16]

The Lyttelton Harbour Board sent out reminders to launch operators regarding charges due for the use of outlying jetties. This also met with passive resistance. Launch owners simply refused to submit their freight lists. The harbour board referred to the 'deliberate evasion' of the payment of charges, but was at a loss to do anything about it. Eventually, in November 1920, the system of charging goods and passengers was replaced by a scale of annual fees. The annual rates for boats plying the harbour would be: *John Anderson* £75 10s, *Onawe* £32 10s, *Toi Toi* £15, *Matariki* £15, *Zephyr* £10.[17]

In 1913, a bill was tabled which would give the harbour board complete control of the foreshore and surrounding bays of the harbour. In the end the board was granted authority over the beach up to the high-water mark. In May 1914, a deputation from the Mount Herbert County Council requested that the harbour board remit its charges for the use of outlying jetties. The council 'would be quite happy to pay for maintenance and repairs if the wharfage rates were abolished'.[18] In response to a board question, the deputation spokesman said he considered it fair that the residents of the bays should pay for the construction of their own wharves.

Eight years later, in September 1921, the Harbour Improvement Committee recommended that the harbour board pass control of the outlying jetties to the various local bodies concerned. The local bodies (in the case of Lyttelton Harbour,

Governors Bay Transport trucks parked on the main road in Governors Bay. Transport by sea was gradually supplanted by vehicles as the road network around the harbour improved.
LACHIE GRIFFIN ARCHIVE

the Mount Herbert County Council) would be responsible for maintenance and minor repairs, while major repairs resulting from weather conditions and general depreciation would be carried out by the harbour board. The jetties would be brought up to scratch and, where necessary (Pūrau, Charteris Bay and Camp Bay), equipped with cranes by the harbour board before the handover. The troubled saga of ownership and revenue collection suggests that the harbour board would have been mightily relieved to relinquish day-to-day management of the jetties. In February 1922, the county council resolved that, under the agreed conditions, it would take charge of all wharves and jetties within the county for a term of three years. Whether this change in jurisdiction continued beyond the agreed three years is unclear but, in light of later events, it seems the harbour board retained control.

As more farmers took advantage of trucking services, subsequent years saw a gradual decline in the harbour launch fleet.[19] This meant that passenger traffic became the main income-earner for the launch operators, especially on public holidays, when the launches could be overwhelmed by excited day trippers. The harbour board decided in 1933 to abolish licences for use of the outlying jetties and instead to increase general harbour passenger licences to between £1 and £5 per annum. Another ongoing frustration for the harbour board was the vandalism or theft of life-saving gear placed on jetties for the safety of the public. Offenders could be fined up to £200 or imprisoned for up to a year.

One of the biggest problems for harbour residents and the harbour board was the gradual silting of the harbour, caused primarily by topsoil washing into the sea from the surrounding catchment. Over time, once-functional jetties were left high and dry at low tide. A graphic example was the 'long' jetty at Governors Bay. Beginning life in 1874 as a 'short' jetty, it was extended in 1913 to accommodate launches bringing holidaymakers. A second jetty was built in the bay in 1883 to provide launch access at all tides.

The jetty built at Little Port Cooper in 1909 to service the Adderley Head Signal Station was built exceptionally long to deal with the gently sloping beach and the fact that the harbour board had been dumping dredged sediment there for many years. In Charteris Bay access to the official jetty at low tide became increasingly uncertain, and a second jetty was built in deeper water to enable golfers from Lyttelton to play at the Charteris Bay Golf Course. At Teddington the effectiveness of any jetty was dependent on a channel winding across the mudflats. Dredging would have enabled easier sea access to many harbour settlements, but it was a process deemed too expensive for servicing only small numbers of residents.

Arguments about the cause of silting in the upper harbour seem never to have been fully resolved. Locals regularly wrote to the papers blaming Lyttelton Harbour Board's dredging and dumping of spoil in the lower harbour. They claimed that this spoil was redistributed around the harbour by tidal action. Charteris Bay resident Robert Anderson pointed out in 1897 that he and others used to dredge for oysters in a line between Church Bay and Cass Bay when the harbour bottom was hard live shell. 'But soon after dredging began the bottom gradually got softer, and at the present time it is a dungeon of soft mud.'[20] Head of the Bay resident Bruce Gebbie recalled 'an often repeated comment from around the late 1800s–early 1900s . . . that the silt beat the dredge back to port'.[21] Writing to the *Press* in 1930, John Hadfield was 'astonished to see the mud-flats extending almost to the long jetty that was built by the Harbour Board some years ago and which now can only be used by a launch at high tide'.[22]

The harbour board vigorously denied these anecdotal claims. In 1934 its chairman, W. G. Gallagher, reported that engineer Percy Fryer's plans of soundings taken in Governors Bay in 1849, 1903, 1927 and 1934 indicated no changes in the depth of water.

Claims from residents continue to this day. Some believe the construction of the breakwater at Cashin Quay in the 1960s altered the flow of water in the harbour and contributed to further silting in certain areas.[23] Certainly, the altered flow of water meant that the foreshore at Pūrau was much more actively eroded. However, Bruce Gebbie does not believe that silting has got worse, nor that the upper reaches of the harbour have become shallower since the 1960s. 'I've always been aware of how long you have each side of high tide to launch or retrieve at both Sandy Beach and Charteris Bay. Back in the seventies we considered it safe to water-ski for two hours either side of high tide between Walkers Beach and King Billy Island.'[24] Today, it seems that the mudflats at Allandale and Governors Bay may in fact be in retreat.[25]

Lyttelton Port Company's engineering services manager Neil McLennan observed that when he started at the harbour board in 1975 and for much of the decade after, Malcolm Jones, resident engineer at the port company's Lyttelton office, managed the outlying boatsheds with associated slipways and often small jetties. 'Many of these were in serious disrepair and a safety issue, but Malcolm took a constructive approach to assisting the owners to make them safe.'[26] Nevertheless, underused and disused public jetties continued to deteriorate.

In 1989, the creation of the commercially driven Lyttelton Port Company saw control of the outlying jetties pass to the newly formed Banks Peninsula District Council. When this council amalgamated with the Christchurch City Council in 2006, the city council took over management of the jetties in Lyttelton Harbour. An assessment of the condition of marine structures in 2009 revealed that many of the jetties were in poor condition, reflecting years of limited, reactive maintenance and renewal. Following the Christchurch earthquakes of 2010 and 2011, the jetties at Church Bay, Charteris Bay and Governors Bay were deemed unsafe and closed to the public. In 2013/14 the amount of deferred work totalled roughly a million dollars.

In 2014, the Christchurch City Council published an Activity Management Plan for its harbours and marine structures.[27] The council's user survey revealed that boating, sightseeing, walking, jumping and swimming were common jetty activities. Over the long term, the council aimed to rationalise the number of marine structures that it provided to an 'affordable level'. This meant reducing reactive work with a steady programme of maintenance and renewal. Funding constraints meant that some structures could be closed and not renewed. Others might be renewed in a form different to their current design. Still others could benefit from a different model of ownership and management. Community involvement could relieve the council of unsustainable expense while extending the life of marine structures valued by their communities.

Historically, self-reliance and resilience have been hallmarks of communities in Lyttelton Harbour and on the peninsula generally. So it is not surprising that the residents of Te Rāpaki-o-Te Rakiwhakaputa, Church Bay and Governors Bay have, in turn, taken on the restoration of their bay's jetty. The latest, and most ambitious, project is the virtual rebuild of the 300-metre Governors Bay jetty, spearheaded by the locally constituted Governors Bay Jetty Restoration Trust and drawing on a wide range of local expertise. A common thread running through harbour community projects over time has been the recycling and repurposing of materials, and this is very evident in jetty restoration.

Currently Black Cat operates a regular and popular launch service between Lyttelton and Diamond Harbour, enabling day trippers from Christchurch to enjoy the seaside. During summer, Black Cat also runs a daily launch service to Ōtamahua Quail Island, now a Department of Conservation (DOC) reserve and the site of a major ecological restoration project, popular with swimmers, walkers and those interested in harbour history. Rīpapa Island, also a DOC reserve with a colourful history, is once again accessible by sea following the repair of its jetty after the 2010/11 earthquakes. Perhaps, in the future, launches might also operate between Lyttelton and some of the other harbour bays, linking with the Head-to-Head Walkway (under construction at the time of writing) and offering a recreational experience that recalls the harbour's early history.

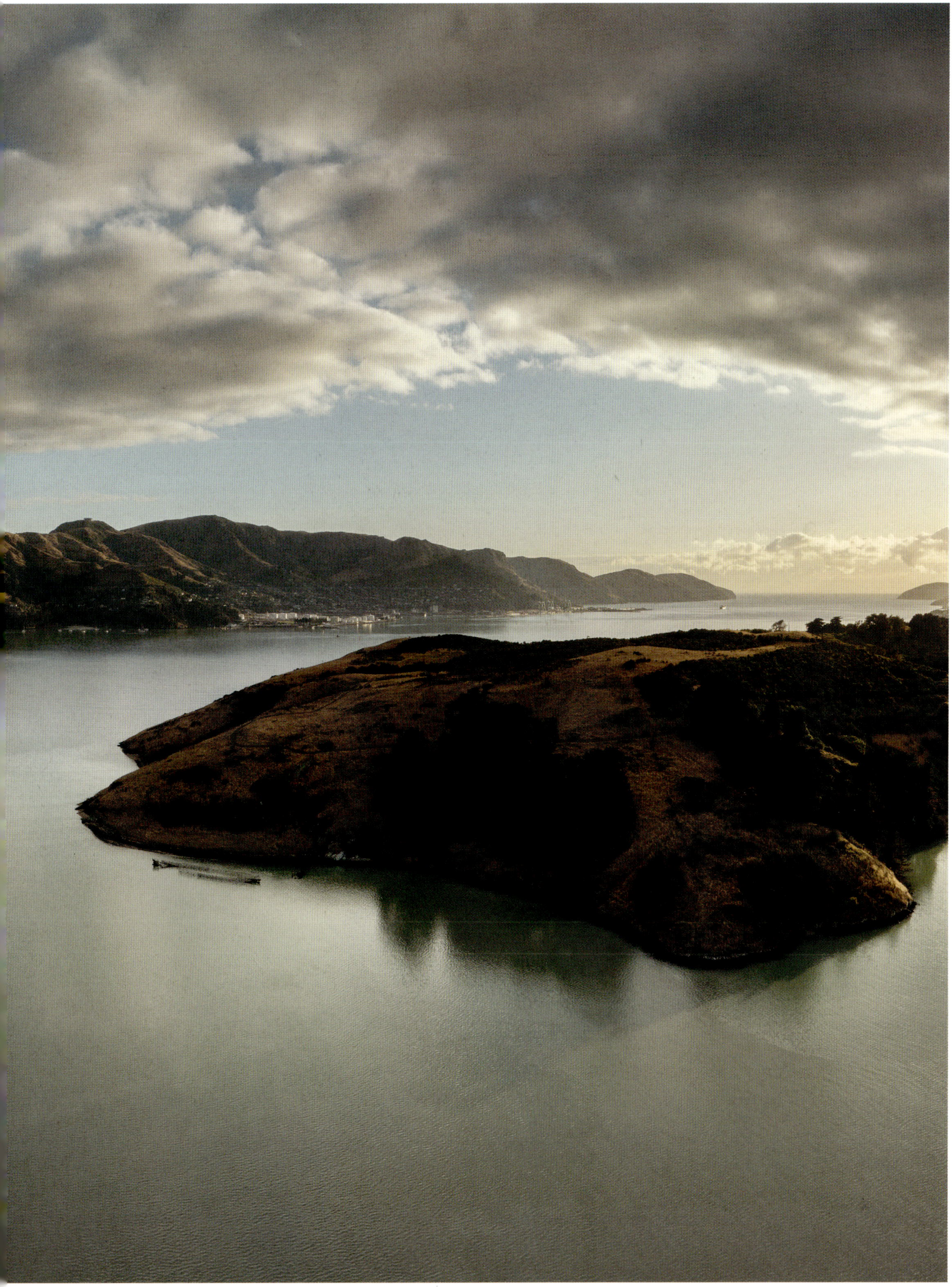

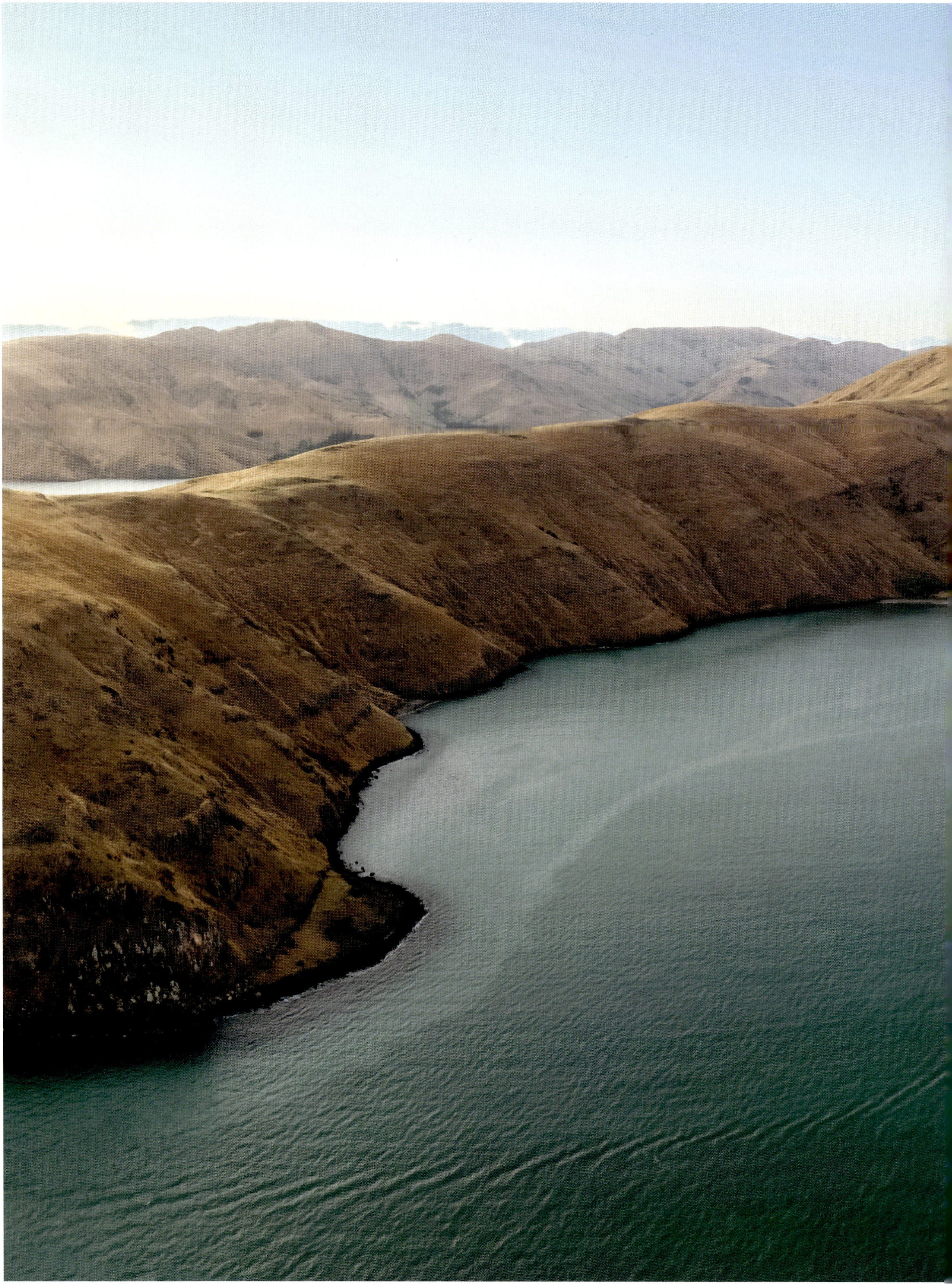

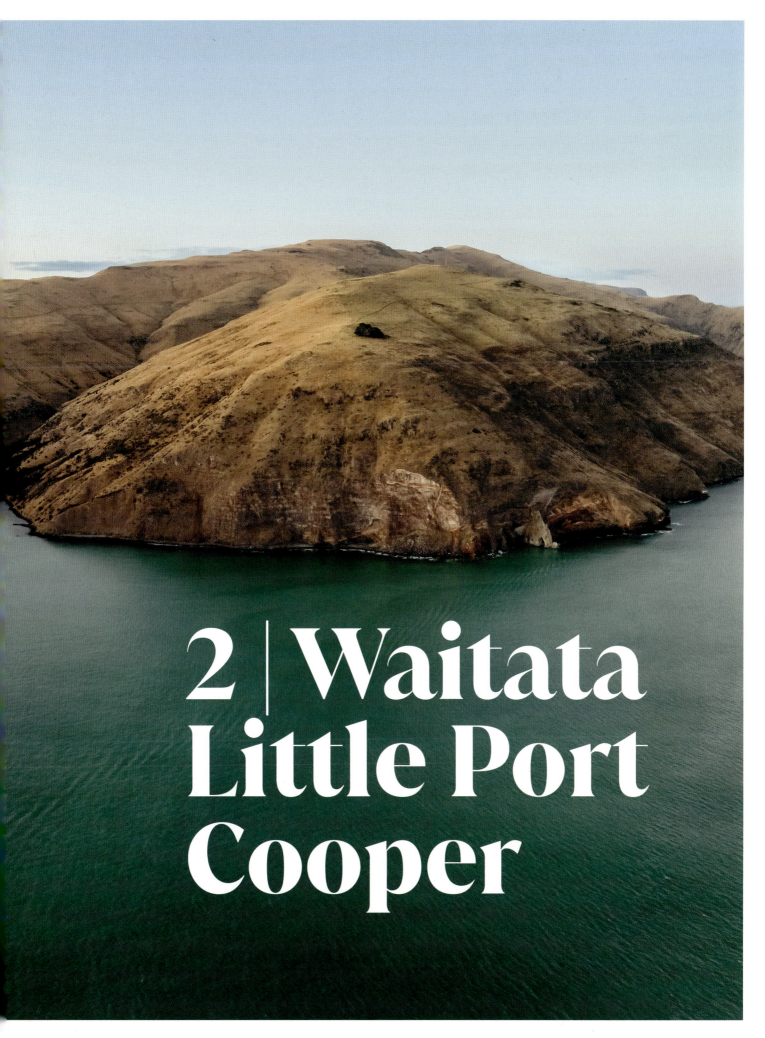

2 | Waitata Little Port Cooper

If you drive west from the Sign of the Kiwi along the Port Hills Summit Road, you will find the car park opposite the Sign of the Bellbird. From here you can gaze down on the full glory of Whakaraupō from 'head' to 'heads'. The most distant, blunt-nosed headland to your right, guarding the entrance to Whakaraupō, is Te Piaka, renamed Adderley Head after Charles Adderley, friend of Canterbury settlement founder John Robert Godley, and member of the Canterbury Association's management committee.

✶

The summit of Te Piaka affords superb views up and down the coastline and into Whakaraupō. For Ngāti Māmoe and Ngāi Tahu in the days before European settlement, the headland was important for nautical navigation, signalling the entrances to both Whakaraupō and Te Ara Whānui o Makawhiua (now Port Levy Harbour). Later it was used by whalers as a strategic lookout. Sheltered by Adderley Head is the still-remote bay named Waitata ('water beating down'), renamed Little Port Cooper in 1849 to commemorate the Sydney merchant Daniel Cooper (after whom the larger harbour of Port Cooper was named). Waitata was an outpost settlement and significant mahinga kai for Māori, whose home base was around the headland in Koukourārata Port Levy. Evidence of Māori use of Waitata is captured in the names of two caves: on the east side of the bay, Papa Kōiro (kōiro means conger eel), and on the west side, Te Ana Ngāti Māmoe.[1]

The journal of French surgeon Dr Félix Maynard, who visited Whakaraupō and, in particular, Waitata on a whaling boat in 1837–38 and again in 1845–46, gives us a unique insight into the Māori camp. There were huts covered and panelled with yellow leaves. Platforms on wooden posts protected sweet potatoes, bundles of dried fish and cakes of fern from the dogs that roamed the settlement. Canoes were hauled high and dry on the beach. Maynard noted 'women washing or beating between two stones the phormium [flax] soaking in a stream'.[2] Children 'daubed with red ochre' played by the sea amidst the whale bones. The men wore flax mats or coverings of white wool. Māori from Koukourārata and Akaroa inhabited this outpost in the winter when the whaling boats visited and there were opportunities for trade.

By the 1830s Waitata was home to the only whaling station on the north side of Te Pātaka-o-Rākaihautū Banks Peninsula. Early whalers in search of the southern right whale favoured the bay because it offered the only safe harbour in the area. This was where Captain George Hempleman beached the brig *Bee* for repairs and to build a whaling boat in February 1836. Repairing *Bee*'s leaks involved stripping copper plates from around its port bow and took nearly a month, during which time the captain went further up the harbour to cut spars for the brig and to obtain potatoes from Māori at Rāpaki. According to early settler James Hay, a baby was born to the Hemplemans on board *Bee*.[3]

ABOVE Two houses were initially built for the pilot and signal personnel on the narrow, flat space at the base of Long Point, below Adderley Head. The men built four more small houses for their families. A dry stone wall is still visible at the rear of the flat land. In 1875 the signalmen moved their homes to the sheltered area above the beach at Little Port Cooper.
JANE ROBERTSON

BELOW In 1875 the pilot station boatshed was relocated from Adderley Head to the more sheltered bay known as Little Port Cooper. A broad pathway led around to the houses above the beach. The remains of the concrete boatshed, the iron rails of the slipway and a boulder breakwater can still be seen on the west side of the bay.
JANE ROBERTSON

Hempleman then set up a tryworks on the shore to render oil from whale blubber, along with a flax-roofed house for the whaling party who were to winter over. Harpooned whales, explains historian Gordon Ogilvie, 'were towed back to the bay and flensed either on the beach or alongside the *Bee*, which was now anchored in the bay and had its own tryworks on deck'.[4] A second shore works, operated by another whaler, was likely set up at much the same time, and by the end of the year there were nine whaling ships using Little Port Cooper as a base or refuge. For a short time from 1839 a shore station was operated by Captain Swift of the *Favourite*, while in 1844–45 the station owner was James Ames, who had 30 men working with four boats.

Maynard described a graveyard at Waitata for the mariners who died in the dangerous work of slaughtering whales. The graves were marked by wooden crosses. Each year when the whalers returned to the bay, they would tend the graves and repair the crosses. By the time of early settler William Pratt's arrival in Lyttelton Harbour in 1849, the whaling station and the little cemetery had been abandoned, but large piles of whalebones still lay whitening in the sun.[5]

There is no evidence that the whalers built a jetty of any sort. Rather, they would anchor their boats offshore, bringing them up the gently sloping beach only when repairs were necessary. Nevertheless, the almost deserted Little Port Cooper of today must have been a busy, noisy place with men working hard in the confined space and peninsula Māori arriving with items to trade.

Offering a sheltered proximity to Adderley Head, with its great view of the coastline, Little Port Cooper was used as a pilot base from 1853 onwards. From March to May 1859, six highly experienced boatmen from Deal in Kent camped in Little Port Cooper and provided the rowing manpower.

The Adderley Head Signal Station was established in 1867 when the provincial government invited tenders for the removal of the pilot's house and boat shed from Sumner to Little Port Cooper. Duties included keeping a four-hour watch (later extended to six hours) day and night for approaching ships, acknowledging requests for a pilot, and relaying shipping movements to the Timeball Station (where a ball dropping down the station's mast on its stone tower signalled the time to ships in Lyttelton Harbour) at Officers Point above Ōhinehou Lyttelton township. Messages were sent by code flags flown from the flagstaff during the day and by carbide Morse lamp at night. Communications with Lyttelton improved with the introduction of a telegraph line in 1876 and a telephone system in 1880 — the first submarine telephone service in New Zealand.[6]

Initially a single men's house of two rooms and a pilot's residence of five

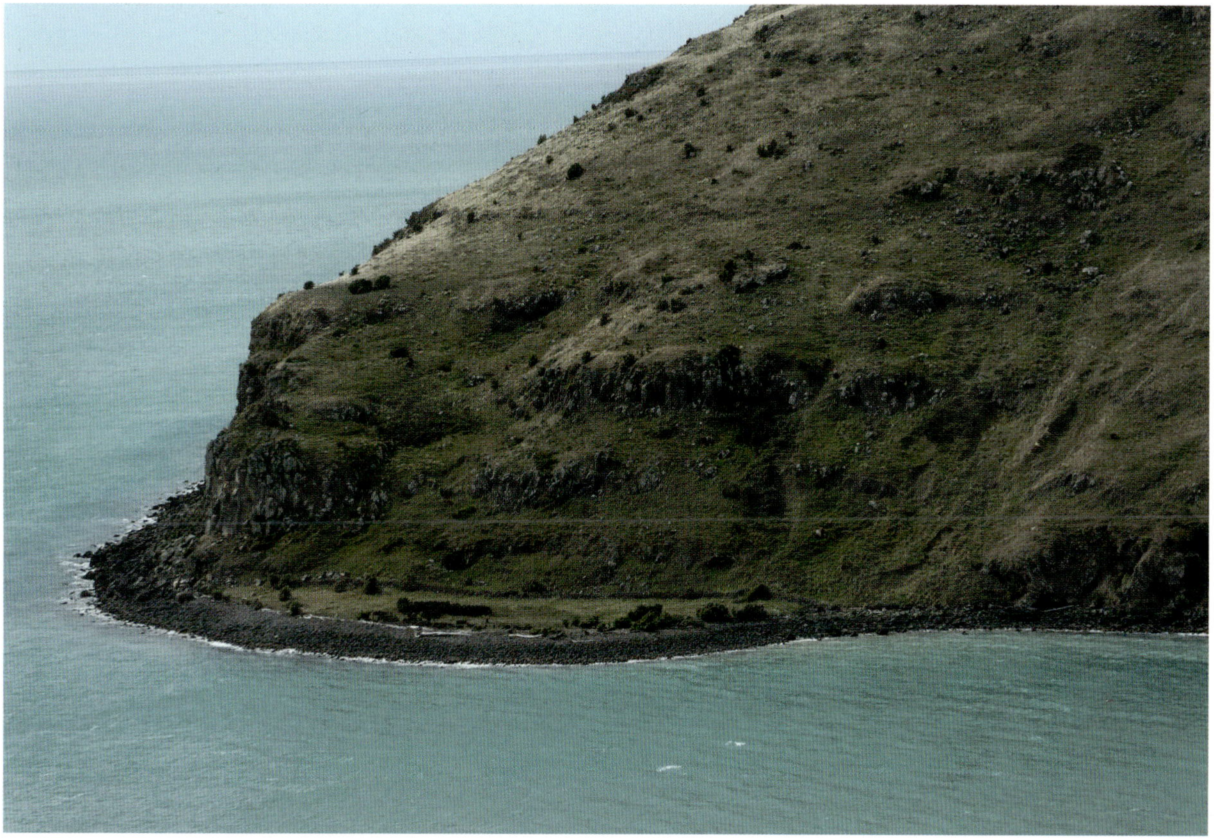

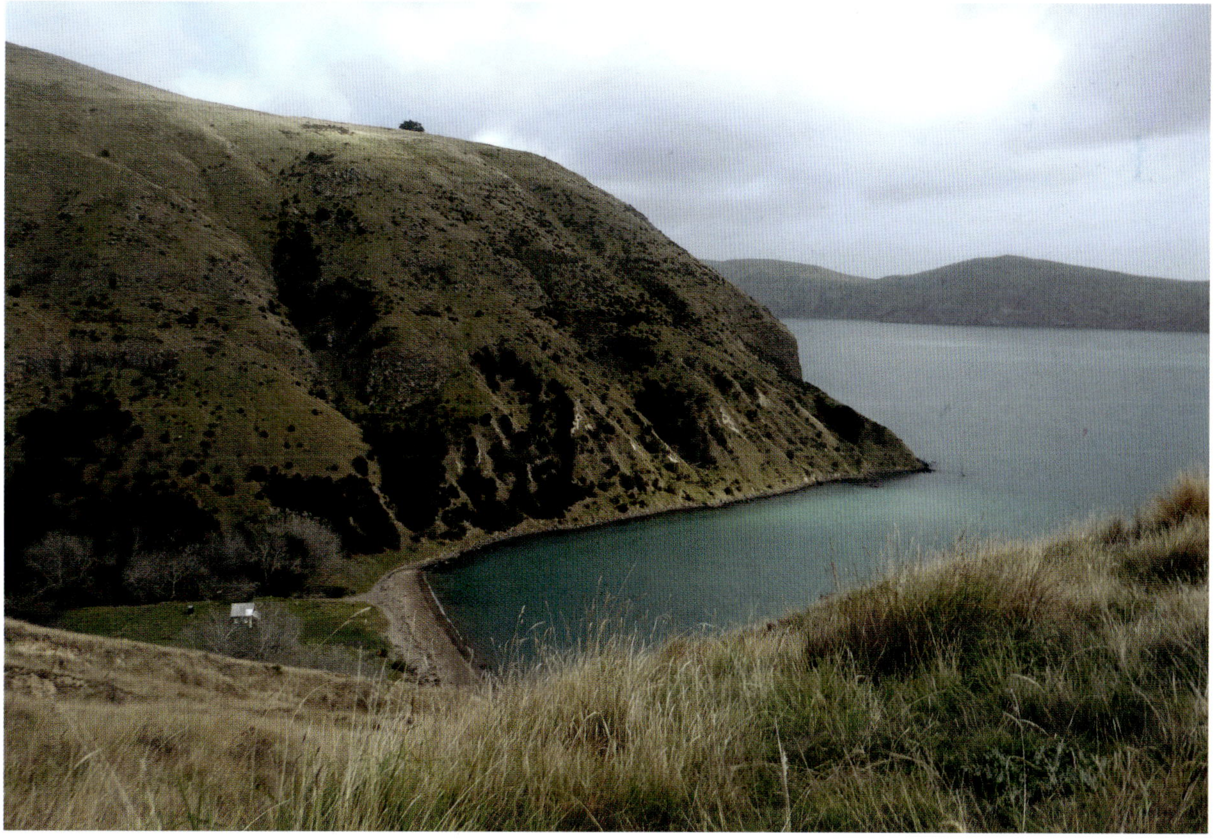

rooms were built on Long Point (Cabbage Tree Point), below Adderley Head. Here, on a very exposed site with little flat space, the pilot boat would be launched. The accommodation proved insufficient and the men, 'on sufferance',[7] built four two-roomed houses for their families. By 1873 these extra structures were home to four wives and a total of 14 children, with two more on the way. According to a *Star* newspaper reporter who visited the site a few years later, the families must have felt like 'so many rats in a trap'.[8]

In May 1873, a large boulder rolled down the hill behind the settlement and struck one of the boatmen's children, leaving the little girl with a broken thigh and other injuries. An official report determined that either the loose boulders on the precipitous cliff should be dislodged (which would require moving the houses 20–25 yards forward while the work was undertaken) and then formed into a stone wall to intercept further rock fall — or the settlement should be moved to the flat area at the head of the bay.[9] Because the Long Point site was regarded as the best situation for launching the pilot boat, the houses were duly moved forward, the rocks dislodged and the houses returned to their original location. The resulting rock wall can still be seen today.

Despite all this effort and expense, in 1875 the houses were indeed dismantled and moved to the far more sheltered area above the beach. The pilot station boatshed was relocated to the west side of the bay. A third house and a school were built in 1883. In 1885 the pilots relocated to Lyttelton Port, leaving only the signalmen and their families — a community of up to 20 adults and children.

We can only imagine the challenges involved in living in such a remote community where the only really viable access was by sea. A small, sad notice in the *Star* offers a glimpse of the potential difficulties. 'Galbraith. — Oct 16, at the Pilot Station, Little Port Cooper, the wife of Captain John Galbraith, of a daughter. Stillborn.'[10] There was no electricity and no proper water supply. In September 1877 the harbour master reported to the Lyttelton Harbour Board that a further three iron tanks should be installed to meet the need for water in summer. To fetch food and other necessities the signalmen would row the dinghy across the harbour to Lyttelton — not an easy task given the distance and the often turbulent waters.

Just how dangerous the harbour seas could be was apparent when the schooner *Randolph*, on its way to port from Pigeon Bay with a load of firewood in March 1874, was becalmed off Little Port Cooper. A sudden squall blew up and *Randolph* capsized. The crew eventually made it into the dinghy as the schooner went down in the deep water. With the squall now a gale, and the pilot boat away assisting another vessel, the men set out for the pilot station a quarter of a mile away. It took them two exhausting hours to reach the station, the captain bailing out the dinghy with his sou'wester.[11]

Nevertheless, the bay did attract visitors. Patients from Sunnyside Asylum were taken by the steamer *Titan* to Little Port Cooper for their annual picnic in March 1877. The day was beautifully fine and the Sunnyside band went along to provide entertainment. No doubt the Port Cooper families welcomed the visitors and enjoyed the entertainment. The patients must have been ferried ashore in small craft since there was no jetty there at this time.

In 1880 a *Lyttelton Times* reporter made a special visit to Little Port Cooper to witness the new telegraph and telephone system in action. The visitors were transferred from the tug to 'a big white boat' and rowed over to inspect the pilot station boatshed. This was a substantial structure built of concrete with an iron roof, its entranceway protected by a boulder breakwater. A large winch hauled up or launched the boats easily and quickly. From the boatshed a 'broad pathway' led round to the houses.[12]

The 'big white boat' was a lifeboat that had been built on the Isle of Wight. It was solid, with stout planking, a thick diagonal lining and a number of watertight compartments along each side, as well as fore and aft. It accommodated two or three rowers and could also hoist a sail if required. A reporter from the *Star* described the scene three years later in more tabloid terms: 'The bronzed boatman runs his vessel into the little stone jetty thrown up to make the pilot-men a secure landing place. Under the shed lies their great whaleboat, a model of neatness and order, ready to launch down the gridiron at a moment's notice.'[13]

The boat featured in the news. In November 1899, aeronaut Captain Charles Lorraine (the stage name of Auckland-born David Mahoney) was to make a much-publicised ascent in the balloon *Empress*. At Little Port Cooper signalman John Toomey watched the balloon sail over the hills towards the sea. All went well until the silk parachute came adrift; when the balloon was about half a mile from the shore, near the entrance to Port Levy, it collapsed and fell like a stone. Toomey could see Captain Lorraine sitting on the floating balloon until it sank and then attempting to swim to shore. In the meantime, signalmen Balfour Toomey and Tommy Carter launched the lifeboat and rounded Adderley Head to search for Lorraine. Despite all efforts, no trace of him was found.

In May 1883, when the little school was newly opened, there were just under 30 men, women and children living at Little Port Cooper. Other buildings included the head pilot's house and the men's quarters. The Little Port Cooper School was listed by the Education Board as an 'aided school' and as such received £5 per annum for every child taught there. On the opening day, when a *Star* reporter visited the settlement, the schoolroom was hung with flags for an evening party.

The Deal boatmen

Goodwin Sands is a large sandbank rising out of deep water several miles off the port town of Deal in southeast England. Between Goodwin Sands and Deal is a stretch of deep water, known as the Downs, which provides a naturally sheltered anchorage. Although Deal did not have a harbour as such, it became a significant port for merchant ships and for the Royal Navy. Reaching the shelter of the Downs, however, required navigating the ever-shifting, 'shippe-swallowing' sands, which are believed to have caused more than 2000 wrecks.

Deal was famous for its boatmen, who ferried goods to and from ships, helped sailing vessels over the treacherous Goodwin Sands and swept the seabed for anchors left by visiting vessels. The work was competitive — first crew to a ship got the job — so the boatmen had to be exceptionally tough and skilled. Their legendary reputation was earned in the saving of countless lives.

By the mid-nineteenth century, with the advent of steam power, the services of the several hundred Deal boatmen were no longer in demand, leaving them destitute. It was decided that jobs might be found for the younger boatmen elsewhere. James Edward Fitzgerald, the first superintendent for the new province of Canterbury in New Zealand, returned to England in 1857 and acted as the province's immigration agent for the next three years. He offered six Deal boatmen and their families free passage to establish a fishery in Lyttelton Harbour. 'The harbour is six or seven miles long. In the neighbouring rivers and rocks are plaice and cod, very similar to ours, but the deep waters have not yet been tried, and that is what I wish you to do.'[15] There would be a good boat and fishing gear waiting for the boatmen.

Thirteen boatmen (six government-funded and seven self-funded) and their families, plus a Deal fishing boat, sailed on the *Mystery*, leaving London in December 1858 and arriving in Lyttelton on 20 March 1859. All the men were married and 10 of them had young children. Fifteen deaths on board from smallpox and scarlet fever meant that the ship was quarantined on arrival.[16] It was reported that the provincial government had offered the men the option of occupying the reserve at Little Port Cooper — a location from which they could fish and supply the Lyttelton market. Their presence would also facilitate the establishment of a pilot or signal station.

Just what happened next is a little unclear. It seems that the self-funded men found employment at the port doing the sort of work they did in Deal, while the six government-funded boatmen camped at Little Port Cooper from March to May 1859, manning the pilot boat and endeavouring to start a fishery business (their families would have remained in Lyttelton, given the lack of accommodation in the bay at that early stage). Unaccustomed to fishing, the men soon accepted a better offer from Henry John Le Cren, an early settler and merchant in Lyttelton, who suggested the boatmen might work in his landing service in Timaru, where he had settled in 1856. By September 1859 the Deal boatmen and their families were settled in Timaru.

In October 1860 a 'furious gale' and high running sea put the schooner *Wellington* in danger off Timaru. The Deal boatmen launched their surfboat to go to its rescue, but the rough sea swamped the boat. Of the crew of six, two drowned, one leaving a widow and five children. Another man was severely pounded by the waves on the beach, and the *Lyttelton Times* reported that hopes for his recovery were slight.[17]

A sad ending to an interesting story with its small connection to Little Port Cooper.

G. B. Toomey and T. T. Carter launching the pilot boat at Little Port Cooper, November 1899. They were going to the aid of Captain Lorraine, who had been giving a display at Lancaster Park when his parachute came adrift from the rapidly ascending balloon. The parachute fell off and Lorraine was left clinging to the balloon, which headed over the Port Hills and out to sea. Signalmen at Adderley Head saw the balloon land in the sea about 10 miles from Lyttelton and set out to search for him. No body was found.
CHRISTCHURCH CITY LIBRARIES, PHOTOCD 3, IMG0094

In the school porch was a neat row of bookshelves containing a small library belonging to 'the men'. Books included 'well thumbed copies of Dickens, Marryatt [sic], Thackeray, George Eliott [sic] and Blackmore'.[14] Given that the books had never been added to since the pilot station was established, the reporter suggested that readers might like to donate any unwanted 'light and readable books' to the pilot station library.

An insufficient number of pupils meant the school was closed for some years. In 1917 the Education Board agreed once again to subsidise a teacher's salary, and Elizabeth Ryan from Kumara moved to Little Port Cooper. She had five students, with other children approaching school age. The isolation meant that it was always difficult to get teachers to stay for any length of time.

The staff in 1883 comprised head pilot Captain Galbraith, four men and the cockswain. According to the *Star*, the signal station high on Adderley Head was a 20-minute uphill walk from the settlement. A later account, from the first decade of the twentieth century, has the signalman coming on watch riding a horse up to the station; the signalman going off-duty would then ride back down. The horse spent most of its time in a paddock behind the houses. For much of the signal station's existence the signalmen worked in an approximately 10-foot square stone hut. There was a large fireplace at one end to help keep the howling winter winds at bay. In 1937 a more modern wooden outlook building was constructed alongside the stone one, but was accidentally burnt down in 1967 by a group of Scouts.

One man was always on watch at the signal station. When the bell rang in the men's quarters and the pilot house to signal the arrival of a ship (or any other need for a pilot boat), the men would make their way round the waterfront to the boathouse and could be out on the water within 10 minutes. With all hands at sea, the man on watch had to remain there until relieved — and in the event of a drop in the wind, that could be a very long time. On the day of the reporter's visit, the man who went up to the lookout at 4 a.m. was only relieved 12 hours later. He would then have to return to his lookout at midnight. It was not unusual for the boatmen to be away for 20 hours at a stretch, piloting vessels in and out of the harbour.

Remarkably, the pilot boat was *rowed* across to Lyttelton and out to meet arriving ships. Given the rough seas that can be experienced in the harbour, and especially at the heads, this required strength and level-headed expertise. In July 1895, however, it wasn't rough seas that caused a problem. Little Port Cooper signalman Balfour Toomey set off on a calm, sunny morning to row to Lyttelton. He made excellent time until suddenly his boat was unaccountably stopped in its tracks. The barrier was a sheet of ice, half an inch and more thick, extending 7 miles from Officers Point across to Rīpapa Island and up to Head of the Bay. Toomey had to force the boat through the ice to reach the port — and very nearly gave up. Such an ice layer can form on the sea surface in the Whakaraupō bays

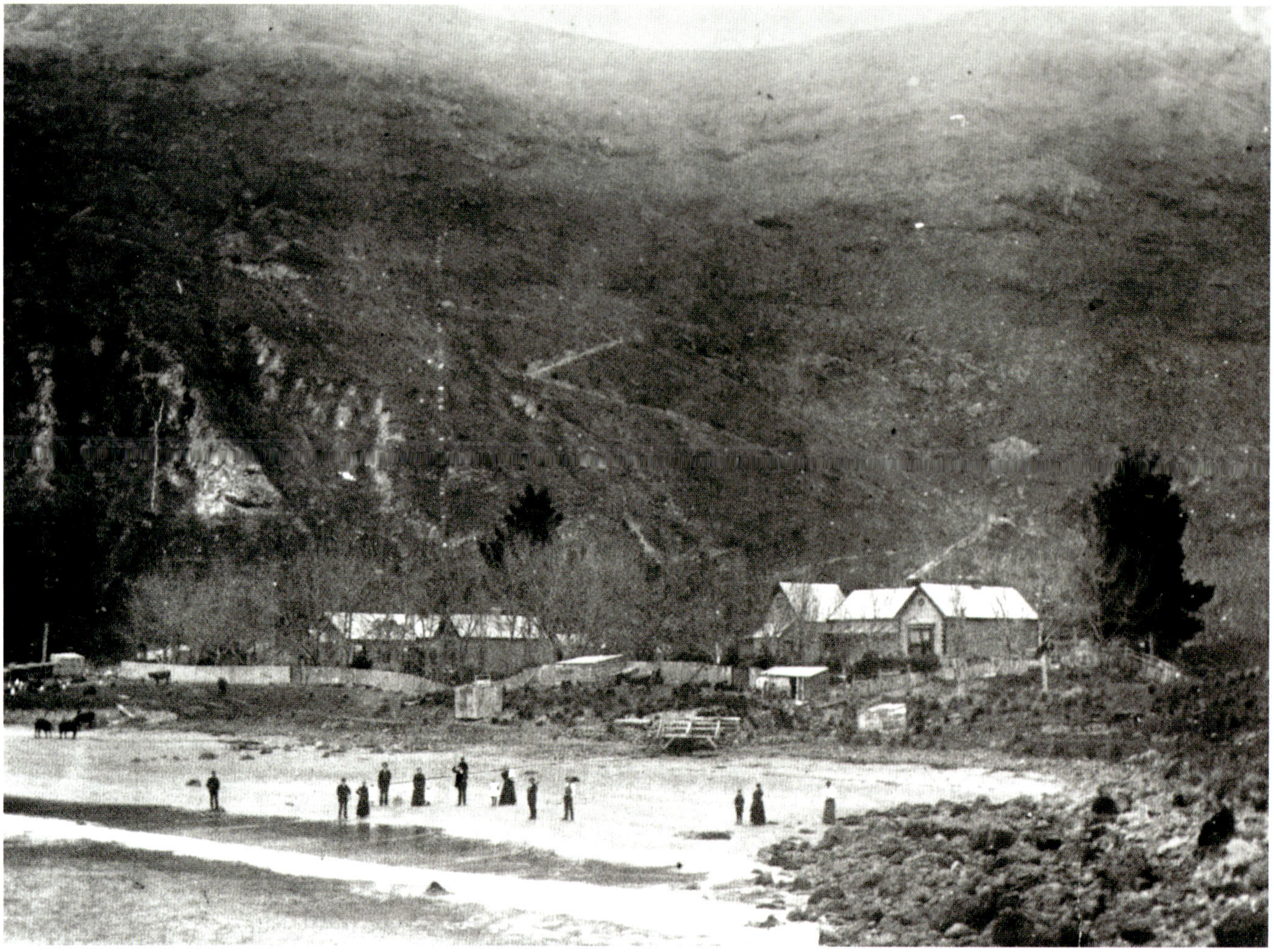

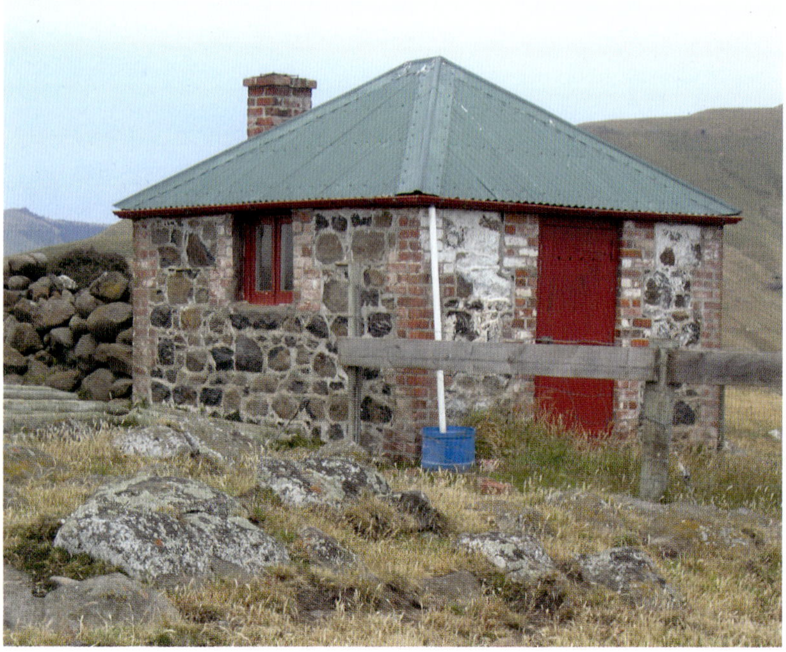

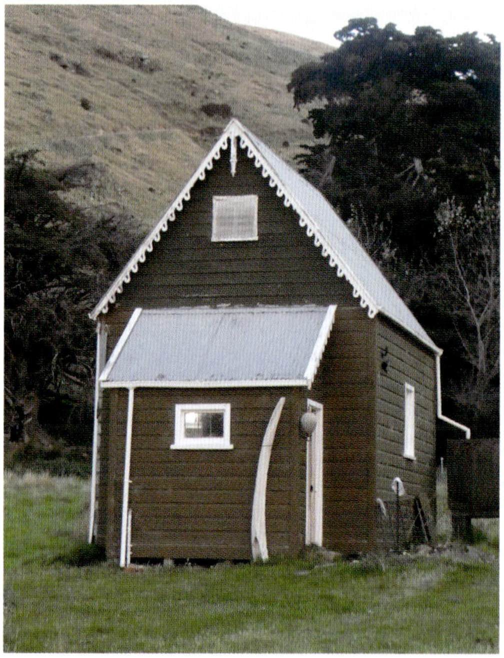

in winter when rain follows frosts and the freshwater inflow is not mixed with seawater. If an onshore wind then develops, the ice accumulates at the mudflat tide margin and can persist there for days.[18]

Despite potential dangers, sometimes rowing was the safest option. In May 1908, chief signalman Thomas Carter and his assistant Paddy Nolan were returning to Little Port Cooper in the tug *Canterbury* with their dinghy being towed astern. Once in the bay, the tug stopped and Nolan clambered over its stern into the dinghy. Carter was on the point of pulling the dinghy alongside when one of the tug's propellers started up again. Nolan leapt into the water just in time as the damaged dinghy capsized, its bottom smashed by the propeller. A line was thrown to Nolan, who was hauled to safety on the tug.[19]

Carter retired five years later, after 40 years living at Little Port Cooper and working as boatman, pilot and head lookout man.

Life for the women in the settlement must have been challenging. We have some small insights. For example, in 1904, Oliver Archibald Nolan married Elizabeth Mary Pascoe and was appointed signalman at Adderley Head. The couple lived at Little Port Cooper until 1910, occupying the middle of the three dwellings. Four children were born in that time and it is quite possible that they were delivered in the bay, given that Elizabeth's mother, Elizabeth Jane Pascoe, was a midwife.[20] If something went wrong there was little hope of timely intervention from outside the bay. The women no doubt tended the gardens in the settlement. 'So little are wind and cold felt here,' reported the *Star*, 'that green peas can be picked two full months before the Christchurch greengrocer is able to offer them to his customers . . . Geraniums grow out all the year round, flowering in profusion.'[21] Potatoes and peas were ready for harvesting in October. Early photos indicate plenty of hens and hen houses — a degree of self-sufficiency must have been a priority.

❋

Access in and out of Little Port Cooper for the signalmen and their families was seldom by land. It was a long and steep walk or ride through remote farmland to Camp Bay, Pūrau, Diamond Harbour or Port Levy. Rather, their links were mostly with Lyttelton and were by sea. All supplies came across the harbour by mail boat, or by the harbour board dredges and tugs that regularly dumped spoil from Lyttelton in Little Port Cooper and Camp Bay, to the consternation of many residents.[22]

In March 1908, the Harbour Improvement Committee recommended that the Lyttelton Harbour Board approve the construction of a jetty at Little Port Cooper at a cost of £475.[23] Progress was slow, but by August about 250 feet of the intended 475 feet had been completed and the work was expected to be finished in another

ABOVE The signalmen's cottages and schoolhouse, Little Port Cooper, c.1890, before the construction of the jetty. The steep track up to the signal station is visible in the hillside behind.
CANTERBURY MUSEUM, 8333

BELOW LEFT The original signal station on Adderley Head, established in 1867. It was closed in 1949 and badly damaged in the 2010/11 Canterbury earthquakes.
IAN LOCHEAD

BELOW RIGHT The old schoolhouse, opened in 1883, was restored and is available as basic accommodation for those wanting to stay in a stunning landscape. The whale bone at the entrance is a reminder of whaling days.
JANE ROBERTSON

This photograph shows the length of the jetty at Little Port Cooper, designed to accommodate the gentle slope of the beach and also the large quantities of spoil from harbour dredging dumped in the bay over many decades.
LYTTELTON MUSEUM. 12806.1

month.[24] Despite its impressive length, a signalman pointed out in late 1927 that access from the sea was difficult. The build-up of spoil from the dredge *Canterbury* made it harder to keep a channel clear for the tug or other 'fair draught vessel' calling at the Little Port Cooper wharf.[25]

Raised in Little Port Cooper, Helen Condon recalled 'many hairy, scary boat trips to Lyttelton'.[26] Enid Keenan tells the story of her mum 'travelling back to Lyttelton with me sitting in the pram up on the deck'. The boat broke down and a tow was called for. When the rescue vessel took up the slack of the towline, it caused the boat to jerk forward and the pram to jerk back. 'Mum said if it wasn't for some woman on board grabbing me and the pram we would've gone overboard.'[27]

Over the decades the residents of Little Port Cooper were witness to, and involved in, a number of sea rescues. In 1924, five children from the Burns family (Jack Burns was the chief signalman at the time) had gone for a row in fine, calm weather. The children, aged between two and thirteen years, paddled about in the

14-foot dinghy, never more than two or three hundred yards from the jetty. Then, as it can do in Lyttelton Harbour, the weather changed suddenly and the boat was blown offshore into more fierce seas. The older children rowed hard, making for the lee of the cliffs at Adderley Head. They dropped the anchor, but it wouldn't hold, and an oar was lost. Isabel, the oldest child, tried to swim to the shore beneath the cliffs to attach a rope to the rocks, but the task proved impossible. In the meantime, the Lyttelton tug had been alerted. It steamed down the harbour and spotted the dinghy heaving close to the rocks. With great difficulty and not before a crewman went overboard, the five half-frozen children were finally hauled on board the tug.

> The tug is feeling her way into Little Port Cooper. It is nearly low tide, and she cannot make the jetty. On the end of the jetty are seen a few figures, the parents of the children and one or two other adults who comprise the little community. They are plainly tense with anxiety. 'All safe' comes the megaphone voice from the tug, and there is an answering wave from the jetty. The children are brought up from below. There is another boat journey to be made, this time in charge of two seamen. Soon they are being hurried up to the house, to warm beds and a hot meal, no doubt.[28]

By 1949 there was no longer any need for a manned signal station. The men were redeployed, and the houses, with the exception of the small but exceptionally robust school building, were dismantled, as was the jetty. In 1999, the Lyttelton Port Company invited the surviving Little Port Cooper signalmen and their families to mark the fiftieth anniversary of the closing of the signal station with a return visit. The old tug *Lyttelton* took the party of nearly a hundred across. In the absence of a jetty, the tug's crew rigged up a gangplank, enabling smaller boats to come alongside and ferry the visitors ashore. Frailer members of the group were then carried through the surf by volunteers. Elsie Eagle, whose family shifted to the signal station when she was eight, recalled: 'It was a lovely place to bring up kids. I reckon I had as good a teenage life as you could get.'[29]

Owners of Keirangi Farm at Camp Bay hire out the restored old schoolhouse in Little Port Cooper to those seeking basic accommodation in a remote and magnificent location. From the schoolhouse you can walk around the foreshore to the site of the pilot boat shelter and slipway and climb up to the remains of the signal station on Adderley Head.

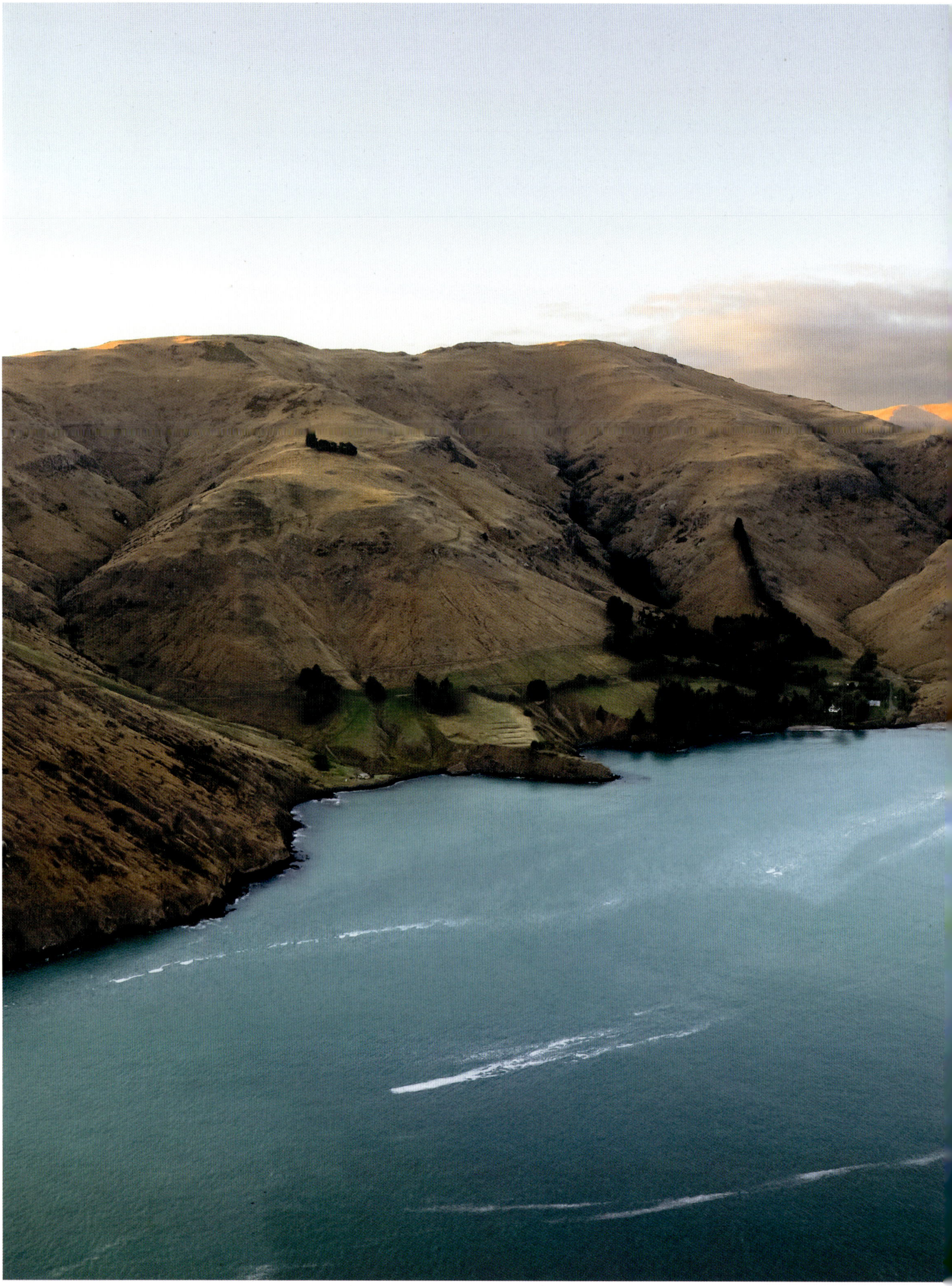

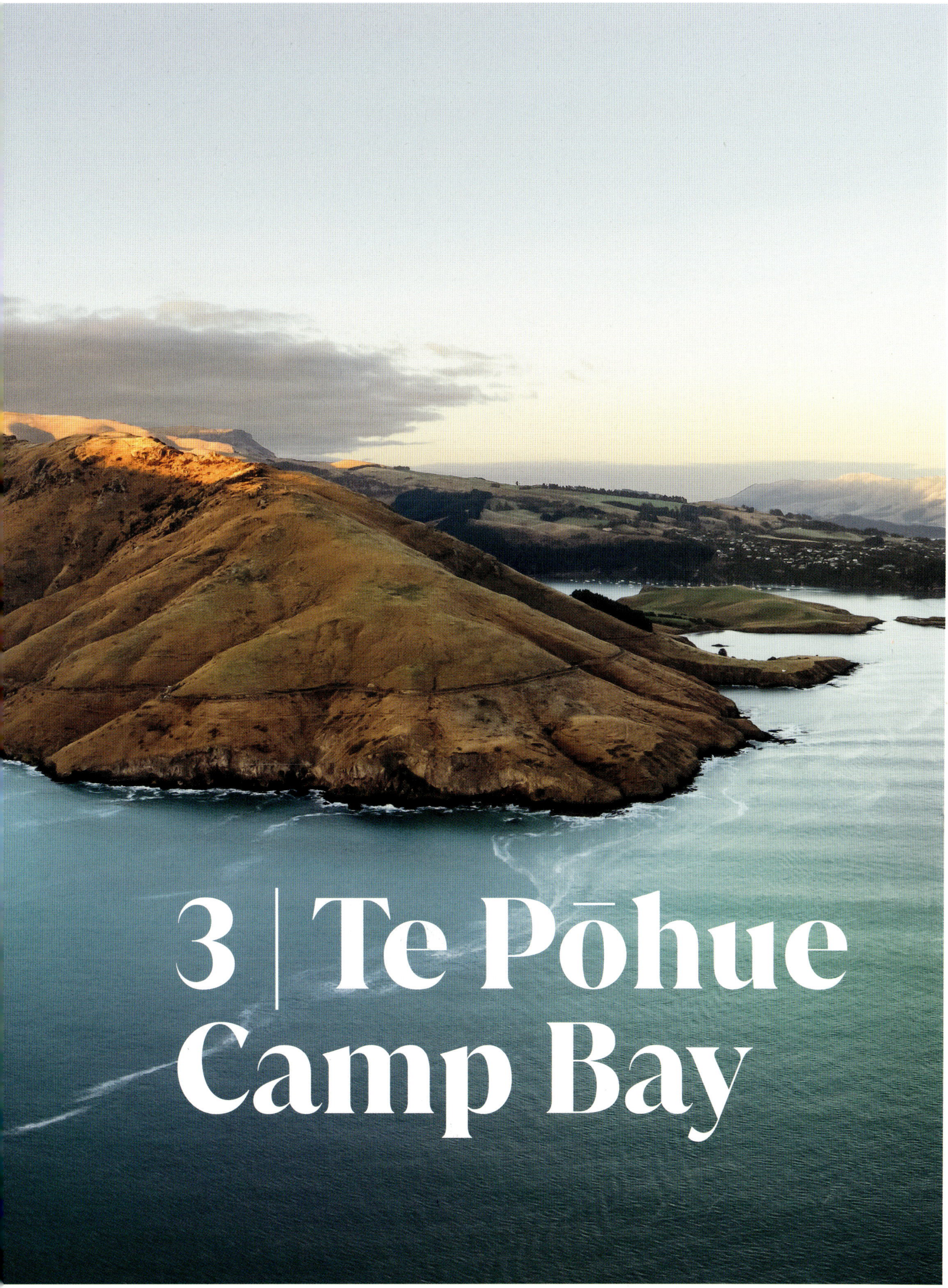

3 | Te Pōhue Camp Bay

At the end of the road that snakes around Whakaraupō from the Port of Lyttelton is beautiful Te Pōhue Camp Bay. The last part of the road, from just beyond Pūrau, is shingled and narrow. It is potentially hazardous, not so much on account of the road itself but because the driver's gaze is constantly distracted by the stunning views of the harbour. Around the last bend, and way below, is a smattering of houses and farm buildings and two small sandy beaches open to the north-easterly swells from the harbour heads. This is where the road ends.

✺

Māori named Te Pōhue after the small, tough native climber pōhuehue (*Muehlenbeckia complexa*), which must once have been more prolific but even now thrives in its fairly inhospitable environment. As with all the bays in Whakaraupō where waka can be beached, Te Pōhue must have provided shelter, food and perhaps a site for temporary, if not permanent, residence. Kūtai (mussels) grew prolifically on the rocks and were a staple kaimoana. Māori preserved kūtai and pāua by splitting seaweed, putting the mollusks in the pouch and filling it with hot bird fat. There is evidence of several Māori middens and a former rock shelter. Pounamu artefacts have also been found at the beach.

In the years just prior to and immediately after the arrival of the first Canterbury Association settlers in 1850, land in Camp Bay changed hands frequently. The first Europeans to occupy Māori land in Whakaraupō were the Greenwood brothers, who made their home in Pūrau. In 1847, the Greenwoods sold part of their Māori land lease of a whopping 25,000 hectares of Port Cooper hill country to the Rhodes brothers: William Barnard, Robert Heaton and George. Gordon Ogilvie notes that 'Camp Bay's western flank marked the eastern boundary of the brothers' 7000-acre Pūrau station. In 1850 a 50-acre section in Camp Bay itself . . . was sold to the Lee brothers, who speedily on-sold it to the Rhodes brothers in 1852.'[1] Since the bay's sandy beach and gently sloping valley would have provided a handy camp site for Greenwood or Rhodes farm staff, the name 'Camp Bay' may well have described its early European use.

It was Camp Bay's relative isolation that determined the next, sad phase of its history. Death in crowded immigrant ships from diseases such as smallpox, typhoid and scarlet fever was relatively common, and there was a high risk of infecting the new settlements of Lyttelton and Christchurch. Despite the Crown setting aside 30 acres in Camp Bay for quarantine purposes in 1850 (this was extended in 1855 to 2533 acres, to be held in trust as a quarantine reserve for sheep), the Canterbury Association initially gave little attention to the quarantine of infected ships. The options for the first 13 years of organised settlement were to confine all immigrants, healthy and sick, on board the infected ship — an intolerable situation for the healthy, whose only desire after three or more months at sea was to get ashore — or to land all new arrivals, including those infected.

It wasn't until 1863 that the authorities acknowledged the need for a designated quarantine area. By May of that year the barracks used to house new immigrants in Lyttelton were in need of replacement and it was proposed that new barracks, erected at Camp Bay, could address the urgent issue of quarantine. The attitude to infection, of both the health authorities and the general public, is apparent in a telling few words. 'Camp Bay is a healthy spot — out of the way of mischief — and offers great facilities for carrying out so useful a system of quarantine.'[2] Such 'facilities', according to the *Lyttelton Times*, included a good supply of fresh water, protection from the prevailing winds, easy access and good landing from a deep-water bay.[3] (Anyone who knows the headland at Camp Bay might challenge all of these attributes.) The plans drawn up included a jetty at which immigrants and supplies would be landed.

In October 1863 the health and immigration officer, Dr Donald, travelled to Camp Bay in the harbour master's boat to inspect the land and new buildings prior to their occupation. In getting from the boat to the shore he fell on slippery rocks and bruised his leg severely. This suggests no safe landing facilities. There is no evidence that the planned jetty was ever built, and yet it seems highly unlikely that large numbers of weary immigrants could have been landed by any other means. Bodies ferried for burial at Camp Bay from the later quarantine station at Rīpapa Island also had to be brought ashore. This would have been extremely challenging in easterly swells, with or without a designated landing place.

When *Captain Cook* arrived in Lyttelton Harbour on 5 September 1863 with 498 passengers, 11 deaths at sea, including two very recent ones from typhoid, required the ship to be quarantined. About 200 immigrants were landed at Camp Bay and accommodated in tents since the quarantine buildings had not yet been completed.[4] 'Portable huts' were on their way. Two hundred men, women and children, weary from a months-long voyage and possibly sick, were living under canvas on an exposed headland (which also served as a burial area) in still-chilly early September with likely only rudimentary, if any, sanitary facilities. The tents were pitched on the hill slope in such a way that the drainage from

Looking down into Te Pōhue Camp Bay from the farm track out to Adderley Head. The Quarantine Station headland is in the foreground (the levels on which the quarantine buildings and the cemetery were constructed are just visible) and the road to Pūrau can be seen centre right.
JANE ROBERTSON

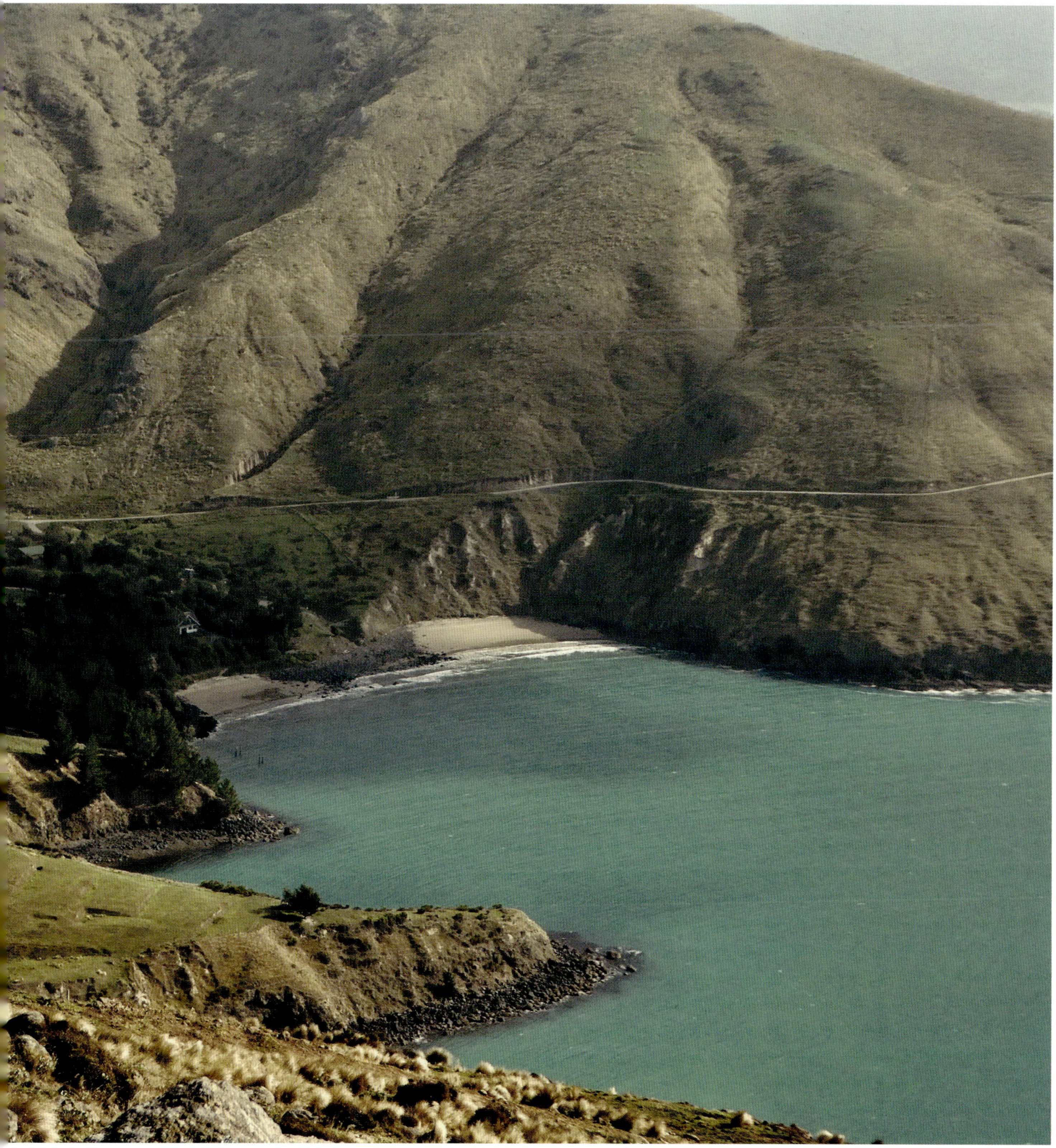

QUARANTINE STATION
CAMP BAY

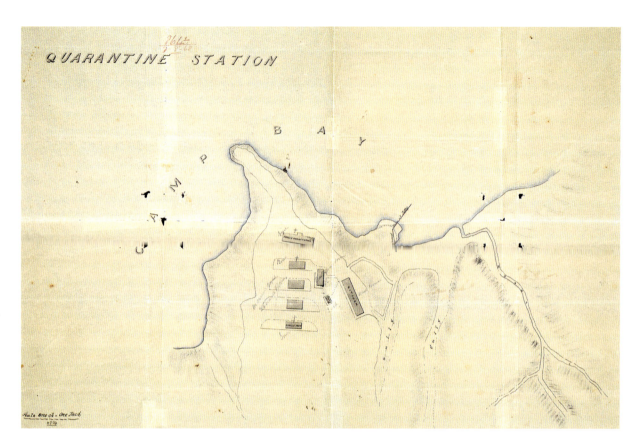

Sketch of the quarantine station buildings at Camp Bay, drawn by assistant provincial engineer G. Thornton, 6 June 1864. Single dormitories and single men's accommodation are marked, also the kitchen and cook house. The line of a proposed jetty (possibly never built) is indicated to the east of the station headland.
ARCHIVES NEW ZEALAND, DEPARTMENT OF LANDS AND SURVEY, CAAR, CH287, ICPW 705/1870, R8418486

the upper row of tents soaked the lower part of the encampment. Maria Rye, a social reformer and promoter of emigration from England, especially for young working-class women, observed the conditions and accused the government of being more interested in building 'magnificent roads and bridges' than in spending the money necessary to ensure the well-being of immigrants in quarantine, who were left to shift for themselves 'like so many savages'.[5]

Hard on the heels of *Captain Cook* came *Lancashire Witch*. Of its 420 passengers, three adults and 23 children had died en route. A group of 15 men went ashore at Camp Bay but found the place deserted, with buildings still unfinished, no one in charge to receive them and no provisions. Warned by the advance party, the remaining immigrants refused to go ashore. The men who had landed walked around the coast to Rhodes Bay (Pūrau) and finally reached Lyttelton on foot in very poor condition.

According to the *Lyttelton Times*, 'the indifference of the authorities amounts almost to cruelty, when it is remembered how ardent are the longings of every landsman to get on shore after a three months' voyage'.[6] The same report observed of the buildings erected thus far that 'no man with a regard for his horse would think of using them for stables'. The health officer himself condemned the existing buildings as not suitable for the purpose intended.

On 10 December 1863, *Brothers' Pride* arrived in Lyttelton after an awful 138-day voyage during which 44 of the 371 passengers had died of scarlet fever, typhus and 'low fever' (the modern-day equivalent of low fever is unclear). The ship's surgeon, Fitzherbert Dermott, who was both exhausted and traumatised by the experience, offered an insight into events. Early during the voyage a large number of children went down with scarlet fever. All recovered bar one. Then a typhus fever spread amongst the passengers. 'The fever was truly of an appalling character, and a panic reigned throughout the ship.'[7] By the time *Brothers' Pride* reached Cape Town, 84 days out from London, four adults and 10 children had died.

> On the fourth day out [from Cape Town], a fine boy, thirteen years of age, one of the second-cabin passengers, became affected with Scarlatina Malinga, he died; the disease spread with rapidity until indeed the ship was like a hospital, whole families, parents and all, being prostrated. Children in seeming health would in a few hours subsequently be dead, they were suffocated. Typhus fever also prevailed.[8]

The immigration commissioners found *Brothers' Pride* to be in 'a very unhealthy and disgraceful state' and directed the ship to anchor off Camp Bay. The captain continued up the harbour amongst other shipping and was warned by the harbour master to return to Camp Bay. According to the *Press*, 'the change of air and diet, and the general addition of comfort which will ensue even from increased facilities for exercise, will soon have a beneficial effect on those who are ill at present'.[9]

'Comfort' is a relative term given that the passengers were detained at Camp Bay until 5 January 1864. Early that year Thomas Woods of Pūrau complained bitterly about the management of the immigrants at the quarantine station. They were, he said, allowed to run loose over the whole peninsula, whose residents, as a consequence, were at risk of disease and were suffering much from 'wanton and mischievous depredations'. When stores for Woods were landed on the beach at Pūrau, a 'gang' of quarantine station detainees 'seized upon and plundered . . . almost the entire contents of four cases of bottle ale and two cases of whiskey'.[10]

Nonetheless, Woods wasn't averse to selling alcohol to people from the quarantine station at his accommodation house in Pūrau. He was warned in the magistrates' court that it was his duty not to admit them into his house but to place them under arrest. Passenger John Whitelaw escaped quarantine and found carpentry work at Diamond Harbour, returning to the quarantine station each evening. Given the dire situation of the Camp Bay 'detainees', it is hardly surprising that the 'gang' seized on grog or that Whitelaw regularly left the station. Newspaper reports and letters to the editor of the time reveal the tension

Camp Bay 4 July 1865

Stone Piles of Single Mens' House

Wreck of same

Married Couples House No 1 shifted 20ft from piles at one end

Sketch 1

NB Married Couples House No 2 is uninjured

Wreck of Single Womens House

Sketch 2

Top of Chimney Shaft from inside of Wash House

Sketch 3

Chimney Flue displaced in Barrack Masters Sitting Room

Sketch 4

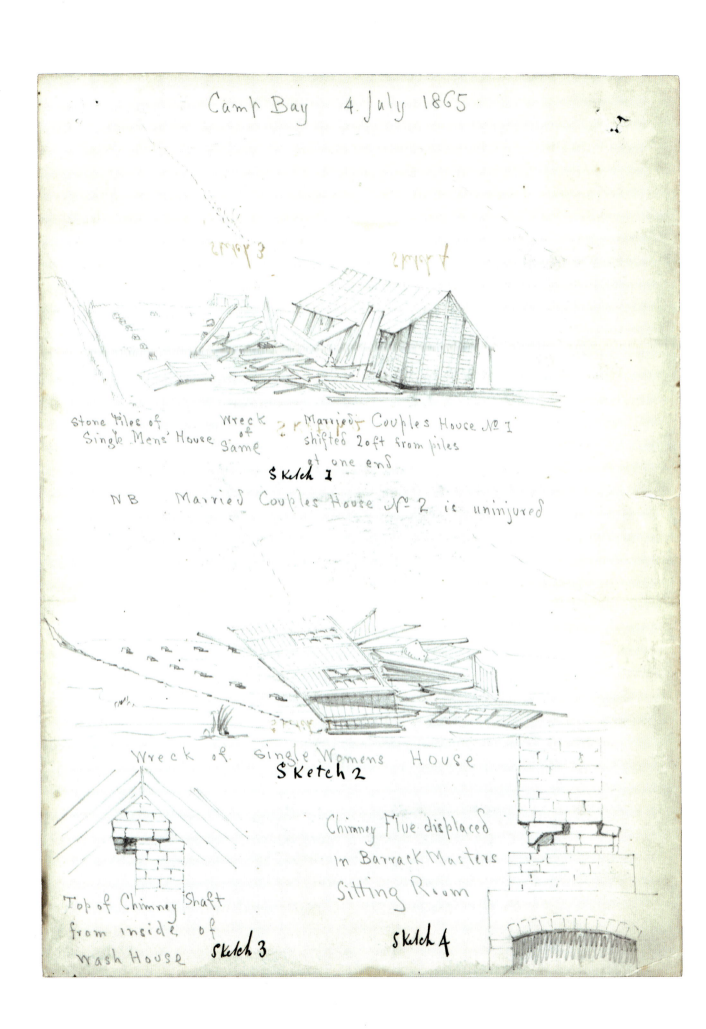

between those advocating a humane approach to the infected immigrants and those whose only concern was for the welfare of healthy residents. Fear and economy prevailed.

The assistant provincial engineer, G. Thornton, wrote to the provincial secretary on 15 January 1864 expressing concern that no burial ground had been set aside for those who died in quarantine. The graves were scattered about and, worse still, quarantine buildings had been erected on top of two graves. No water closets or urinals had been provided.[11] An inspection at the end of January found the buildings to be constructed of inferior, unseasoned board which had already decayed and shrunk. The roofing was defective and the barracks were in no fit state to house invalids. There was no hospital accommodation.[12]

Finally, in September 1864 Camp Bay was officially gazetted as a 'Quarantine Station and Lazaret'.[13] Permanent buildings capable of housing up to 300 people were completed on the terraced headland, and Captain James Daymond and his wife, Mary, were appointed master and matron in charge. There were nine buildings in all — quarters for single men and for single women, male and female infirmaries, two buildings for married couples (and, presumably, their children), a master's house and store plus two kitchens and washhouses.[14] A plan from 1864 detailing the layout of the buildings also indicates the proposed line of a jetty, east of the headland, to service the quarantine station. There is no record of this jetty ever being built.

Unfortunately, in July 1865, not even a year after their construction, a gale destroyed the single men's and women's barracks, blowing part of the materials out to sea. One of the married couples' barracks was shifted 20 feet (6 metres) from its piles at the south end, while the infirmary was twisted from its original position by about 8 feet (2.5 metres). The force of the gale was evident in pieces of timber, each weighing upwards of 100 kilograms, which were picked up on the beach at low water. An article in the *Press* suggested that the complex had been built without the input of an architect, to save expense.[15]

When *Blue Jacket* arrived on 18 November, little had been done to repair the damage. Only the single men were landed at Camp Bay while the women and children and all the saloon passengers remained on the infected ship — a situation described in a letter to the *Lyttelton Times* as 'cruel and unjust'[16] — until they, too, were landed at the 'very imperfect and insufficient shelter'.[17] The healthy stayed in the derelict buildings while the infected were forced to live under canvas in a gully opposite. The two groups were not allowed to communicate, and three special constables were appointed to prevent absconding.[18] One passenger penned a ditty that was published in the *Press* on 28 November. Two of its eight verses, sung to 'King of the Cannibal Islands', went like this:

Sketches of damage done to the Camp Bay quarantine station buildings during the gale of July 1865. The single men's and single women's houses were completely destroyed and the married couples' house was shifted 6 metres from its piles.
ARCHIVES NEW ZEALAND, DEPARTMENT OF LANDS AND SURVEY, CAAR, CH287, ICPW 705/1870, R8418486

> Why, what's the use of keeping us here,
> With a station on shore so very near,
> We shan't be crowded, and will breath freer
> On shore at the Quarantine Station.
> Then away they went a council to hold;
> And though it's unpleasant, the truth must be told —
> The houses are not large enough to hold
> Us all at the Quarantine Station.
>
> So whilst they are thinking and making a fuss
> Two more of our passengers are taken wuss;
> Which looks like a judgement on someone, not us
> For *not* having a Quarantine Station:
> And threat'ning curses, deep and loud,
> Were uttered by our complaining crowd;
> As everyone the Government row'd,
> For not having a Quarantine Station.

In late June 1866, another gale destroyed one of the infirmary buildings and blew the wreckage out to sea. Five years later, immigration officer John Galbraith reported that the bank at the back of the buildings had fallen in against the wash houses, and that rainwater was over the floor in the single girls' barrack and had undermined the blocks beneath the store. The buildings had still not been lined despite their exposed position and were very dirty.[19] There was also concern about the fire risk posed by the long, dry grass around the complex.

Some repairs must have been made because the station, despite its apparently unsuitable location, continued to be used for quarantine purposes until 1873 or 1874, when Rīpapa Island was selected and developed as the new site. Quarantined passengers who died were buried at Camp Bay until 1878. On the immigrant ship *Punjaub*, which arrived in September 1873, 'forty passengers were lost at sea with the fever and ten died at Ripa Island', noted the *Star*. 'Their bodies were taken around in a small boat to Camp Bay, the cemetery being on a small jutting headland.'[20] Once landed at the beach, bodies had to be carried uphill to the graveyard.

No one knows exactly how many immigrants were buried on the windy Camp Bay headland, but it would have been somewhere between 60 and 74. Two of the confirmed burials hint at the personal tragedies linked to the site, in particular the deaths of tiny babies. A baby with the surname Hathaway, born on the ship *Brothers' Pride* on 3 October 1863, died on 16 December at Camp Bay quarantine station. A week later, the same fate befell a six-week-old son of Absalom and Hannah (Anna), one of twin brothers.[21]

As early as 1916, Oliver Hunter of Church Bay, adjacent to Diamond Harbour, bemoaned the fact that the graveyard was unprotected and untended. The sandstone headstones were crumbling and the inscriptions were increasingly indecipherable. The post and rail fence had largely been destroyed and sheep grazed in the graveyard. Hunter urged that this desolate spot, 'so sacred and historical', was worthy of better keeping.[22] Three years later, the *Press* again mentioned the neglected condition of the cemetery. There was no fence to contain it, no railing around the graves, which were overgrown with grass and weeds. Even today the only on-site acknowledgement of the Camp Bay quarantine station and cemetery is a small, privately erected plaque.

Once the quarantine station was moved to Rīpapa Island, the land designated for that purpose at Camp Bay became an education reserve. A fisherman by the name of Koskella lived with his family in one of the ex-quarantine houses. Later, Pūrau farmer H. D. Gardiner took up the lease and transported by sea (there was no road) the best of the surviving barracks buildings for reuse as farm buildings.

Fisherman Koskella and family had a scare in March 1887 when a fire raging over the hills around Little Port Cooper also threatened Camp Bay. With the ex-quarantine houses almost surrounded by flames, the tug *Lyttelton*, which had already called in to Little Port Cooper to check on the signalmen and their families, approached the bay and sent a boat ashore to pick up Koskella's wife and children. Shortly after, the wind shifted and diverted the fire up the hill, away from the houses.

Danger at sea was ever-present. On 26 January 1888, the iron barque *May Queen* was coming up the harbour at the end of a 92-day voyage from London when it was caught well into shore by a squally wind and ran aground on a small ledge of reef at Red Head, between Little Port Cooper and Camp Bay. *Lyttelton* attempted to haul it off the reef, but the tide had dropped a foot or so and *May Queen* stuck fast. The following day, a gang of 20 men started unloading the vessel onto ballast lighters in hopes that it could be floated off. Ten more men with additional lighters relieved the first gang at midnight. About 150 tons of goods were taken off. However, the after-hatch was filled with water and any idea of floating the ship had to be abandoned. It was left to the underwriters.

Much more cargo was salvaged from *May Queen* in the following days, with the salvage gang quartering in the old Camp Bay quarantine buildings. The ship was stripped of all moveable fixtures. Meanwhile, *Jane Douglas*, *Canterbury* and *Waiwera* ran excursion trips down the harbour to view the wreck and the salvage operations. Early on 22 June, having been stuck fast for six months, *May Queen* was found with just its spars showing above water, heavy seas having finally dislodged it into deep water.

In January 1919, the big troopship *Briton*, carrying 1165 returning soldiers, anchored just off Camp Bay. The worldwide influenza pandemic meant that the ship was placed in 24-hour quarantine. An inhalation chamber was installed and the vessel was fumigated. An observer on the cliffs at Camp Bay would have seen the launch *Ruahine* draw alongside *Briton* in a heavy sea. Doctors, customs officials and military officers had to grasp a rope attached to the gangway at the steamer's side at the exact moment when the roll of the launch brought the gangway to a convenient position to jump. Each tricky manoeuvre was greeted with cheers and some laughter from the soldiers watching at the rails.

At the end of the First World War the government divided the education reserve into four blocks to provide farms for four returned servicemen. The two who drew blocks 1 and 4, facing Lyttelton Harbour, were Richard Candy and Cedric Smith (later Stapylton-Smith). Candy and Smith had no houses, no road, no wharf and few fences. The land was bare, dry and steep. Timber for two small two-roomed houses had to be landed on the beach and carried uphill. Not surprisingly, the men lobbied the Lyttelton Harbour Board for a jetty. The harbour board engineer estimated the cost of a jetty 100 feet long, exclusive of a tee head, at about £250. Such a jetty would be 'a great comfort and assistance to the returned soldiers who were settling in the neighbourhood of the bay, would

Camp Bay, c.1935, with the jetty and Richard Candy's house just above the beach.
CANTERBURY MUSEUM, W. A. TAYLOR COLLECTION, 1968.213.47

add to the attraction of Lyttelton Harbour, and would make available to the public a historic spot used by the first settlers'.[23] The harbour board agreed to build a wharf as speedily as possible and to more generous specifications than originally indicated. A large gang of men was employed and a pile-driver on the Lyttelton Harbour Board's punt was put to use.

The jetty itself was built by December 1918. To complete the structure, men from the Public Works Department had to blast a cutting through heavy rock adjacent to the foreshore. In the hot, dry late summer of 1919, a spark from the blasting or a billy fire ignited the long grass at the back of the beach. Fanned by a nor'westerly, the flames raced up the hillside, eventually burning at least 2000 acres of pasture between Adderley Head, Pūrau and Port Levy.[24] Dick Candy lost an estimated 1500 newly acquired sheep and all his grazing, while Cedric Smith lost 170 sheep and most of his grazing. The surviving stock had to be driven all the way to the Addington saleyards in Christchurch, where they were sold for less than the two farmers had paid for them.

Candy and Smith persevered, gradually transforming their farms with fences, stockyards, farm buildings, trees, water-supply systems, a jointly owned woolshed and, eventually, family houses. In the process they had to cope with 'grass fires, floods, washouts, droughts, isolation and a precipitous terrain'.[25] Driving stock to the Addington market involved a three-day marathon with stopovers at Charteris Bay and Governors Bay, followed by a final push over steep Dyers Pass. In 1925 the Lyttelton Harbour Board authorised the installation of a half-ton crane on the jetty, to assist in loading and unloading.

Another bonus was the construction of a clay road from Camp Bay to Pūrau in 1932. The road was cut by Depression relief workers, some based in Pūrau and others in Camp Bay, using picks, shovels, wheelbarrows and blasting powder. It was 'narrow, steep and dangerous' with no base core or shingle surface. Even after the construction of the road, groceries still came from Lyttelton to Camp Bay by the service boat to the wharf. If someone forgot to load the groceries in Lyttelton, or the sea was too rough for the service boat to run, the Camp Bay families had to make do.[26]

Telephone and electric power reached Camp Bay in the 1920s. Cedric Smith built a larger house in the Camp Bay valley and married Grace Gardiner in 1928. Shortly after, Dick Candy built his new house just above the beach and married Marjorie Pearson. The opening of a school in Diamond Harbour in 1945 meant that Pamela Stapylton-Smith could ride her pony to school in the summer months. In winter she had Correspondence School lessons at home. The shingling of the road in 1947 meant that wool could finally be taken out by truck, instead of being hauled to the jetty by horse-drawn sledge.

When the signal station at Little Port Cooper closed in 1949, Dick Candy purchased the 12 hectares from the harbour board. Several years later he sold the farm to Colin Acland, who then on-sold to Douglas McCready. In 1965, when Cedric Smith's son Paul and his wife, Mary, acquired the McCready farm, they became the proprietors of all the farmland between Camp Bay and Little Port Cooper, stretching back to Mount Evans. Mary has documented the history of the farm and her experiences living there in books such as *The Other End of the Harbour* and *Adderley to Bradley*. In 2014 the farm was purchased by Peter May and Sam Yeatman, who ran Perendale sheep and Angus and Hereford cattle over the 305 hectares. The farm changed hands again in 2020, with Wendy and Alex Keir the new proprietors.

ABOVE Camp Bay jetty with the harbour heads beyond.
CANTERBURY MUSEUM, W. A. TAYLOR COLLECTION, 1968.213.326

BELOW Camp Bay in 1954. Little had changed since the 1930s.
V. C. BROWNE & SON, 1509

A few piles are all that remain of the jetty at Camp Bay, the sea having taken its toll over the decades. Just how rough the sea could be right in the bay was illustrated in 1936 when Mr L. Toomey and some friends tied up the 27-foot launch *Seamew* at the Camp Bay jetty. The heavy swell carried away the lines and drove *Seamew* onto the rocks alongside the jetty. Toomey's foot was crushed as he tried to keep the launch off the shore. Following a phone call from Camp Bay the passenger launch *Onawe* arrived from Lyttelton to take the party back to port and medical attention.

Heavy seas in early 1954 prompted an inspection of the jetty and a report to the Lyttelton Harbour Board. The sea had lifted about 50 decking planks and loosened a great many more. Three 40-foot piles, most of the beams, and about 15 per cent of the decking would have to be replaced, and the head of the jetty would need to be braced — all for an estimated cost of £1274.[27] The harbour board was reluctant to maintain a fading structure. A letter from the Mount Herbert County Council to the harbour board sealed the jetty's fate and it was demolished some years later. Ironically, a reminder of the relative isolation of Camp Bay and the value of sea transport came in April 1968 when Cyclone Giselle (in which the ferry *Wahine* sank) took out power and telephone communication in Camp Bay. Slips took out trees, stock and kilometres of farm fences, and the road was closed to all but tractors.

There is another reminder of the ever-changing relationship between land and sea in the little bay to the east of the quarantine station headland. Standing alone is a small fisherman's cottage, the last of three built with materials brought in by sea. Without a jetty or slipway, the boats used to access the cottages were pulled up over the beach. Trevor and Noel Rogers and their family spent their summer holidays at the cottage they called 'Wee-Ona' in the decade from 1949 onwards, as their son Paul recalled:

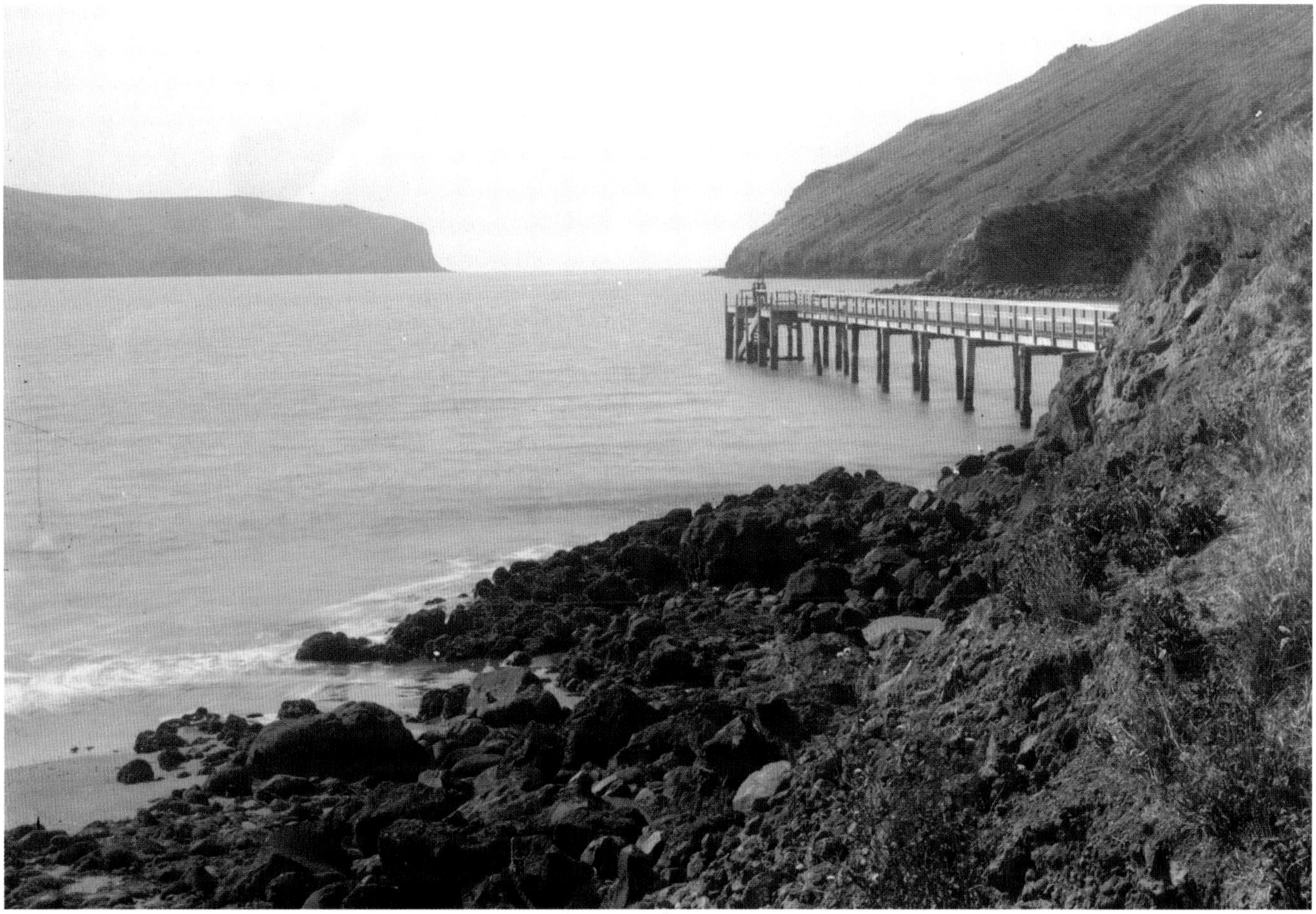

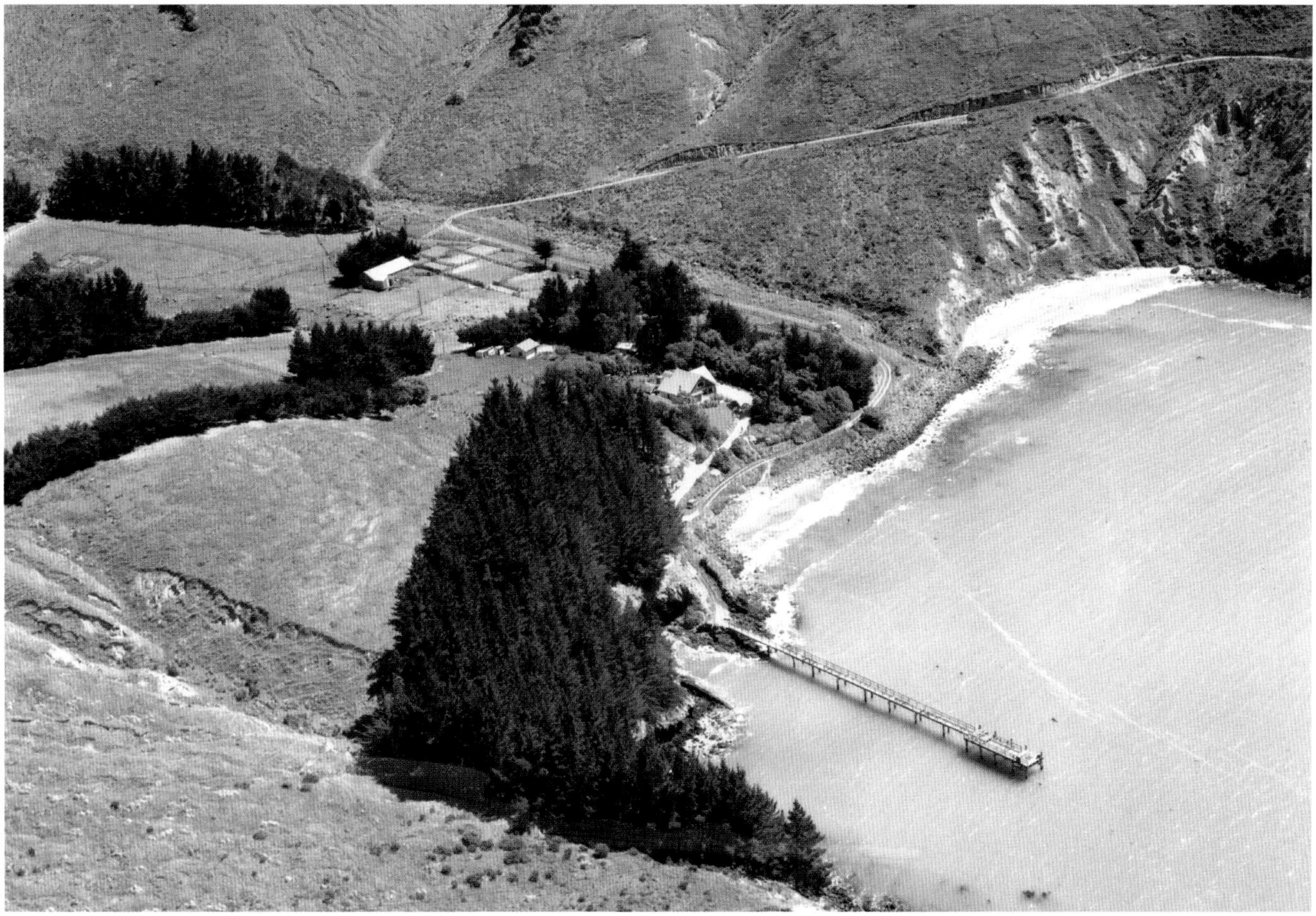

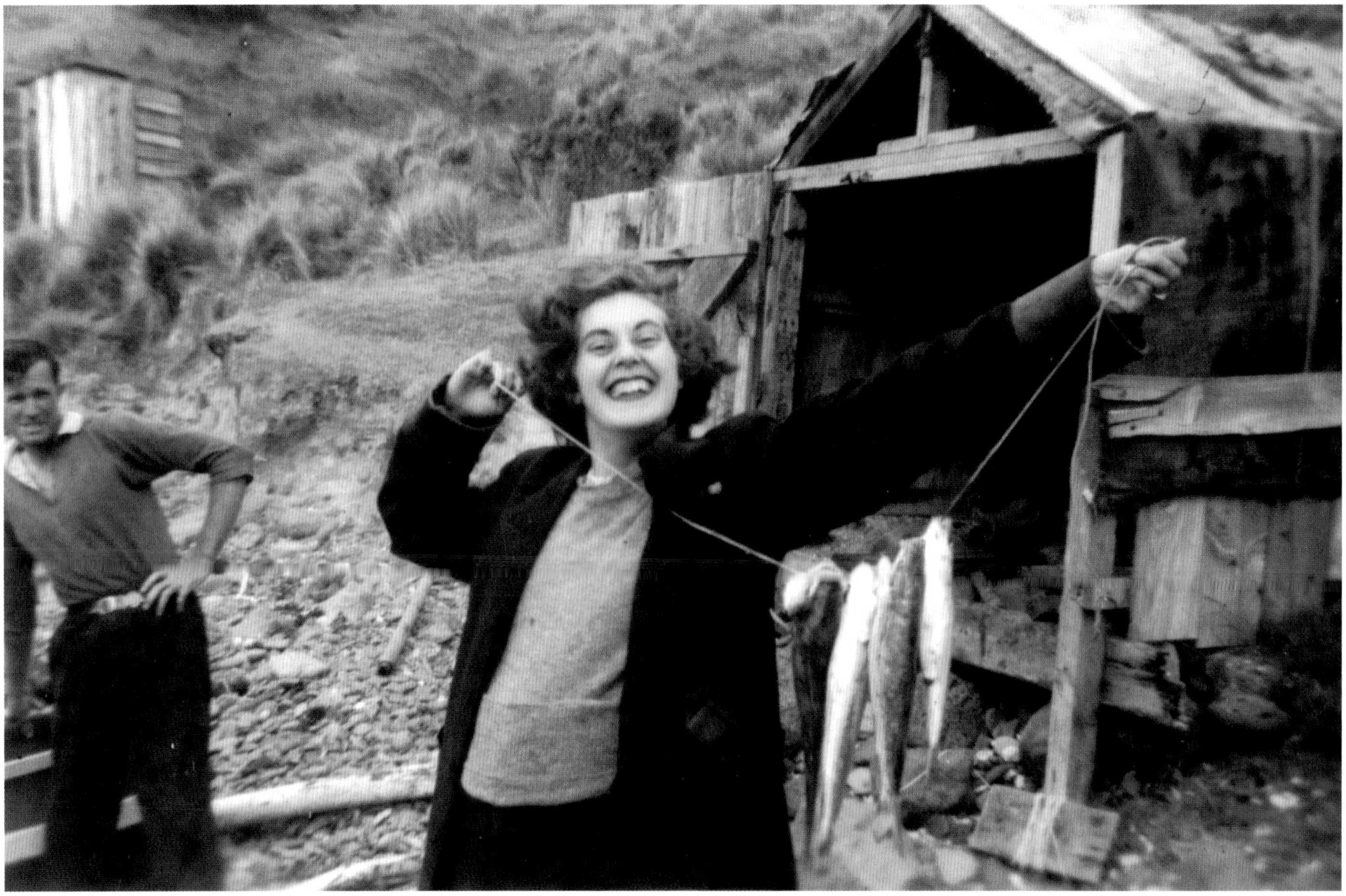

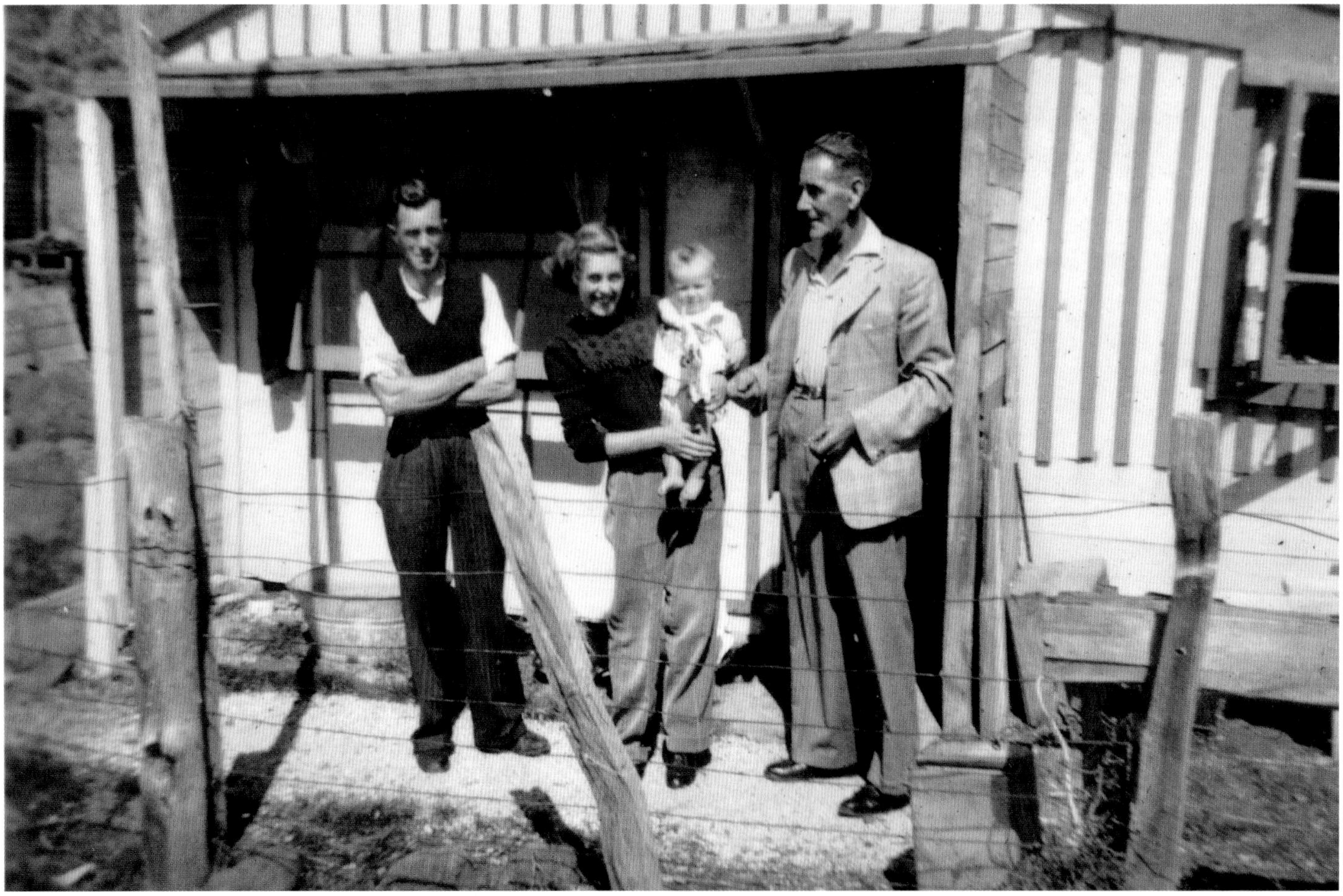

There was no electricity; cooking was done on a kerosene stove and lighting provided by a kerosene lamp and candles. There was no running water apart from a single tap above the kitchen sink that was supplied by a 44-gallon drum on the outside wall, which collected rainwater from the roof. And, of course, there was no bathroom; we just used a metal bowl on a bench outside the bedroom window.[28]

To fish, the children used a length of string wrapped around a stick, with a lead sinker and one or two hooks. For bait, they took mussels from the rocks. 'Our favourite fishing spot was at the eastern head of the bay where the steep hillside plunged directly into the sea.'[29]

Today, the cottage, lovingly restored, is available to holidaymakers. The peaceful foreshore is shared with seagulls, shags, oystercatchers, Canada geese, cattle, sheep and horses. Those staying in the cottage can watch container ships and tankers making their way up the newly deepened channel to and from the port and the regular passage of the little boat carrying mussels from Port Levy. It is a picturesque, serene spot surrounded by visible reminders of violent volcanics and almost invisible reminders of human tragedy.

ABOVE Trevor and Noel Rogers at Camp Bay, 1949. This is in the little bay where one of the three fishermen's cottages still stands. The old boat shed behind Noel was situated east of the remaining hut.
COURTESY OF NOEL ROGERS

BELOW Trevor, Noel and Paul Rogers with Jack Gatehouse outside 'Wee-Ona' in 1950.
COURTESY OF NOEL ROGERS

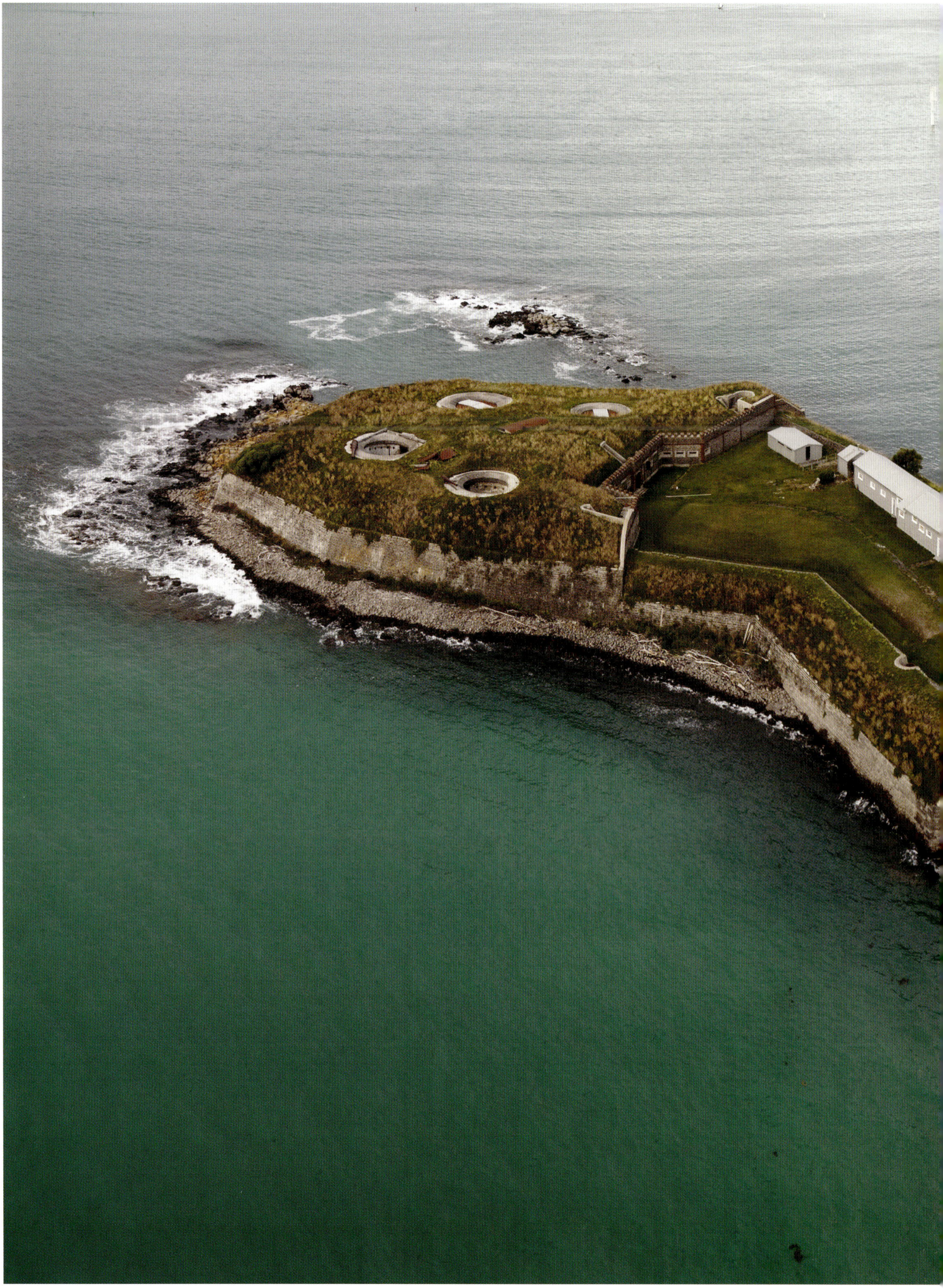

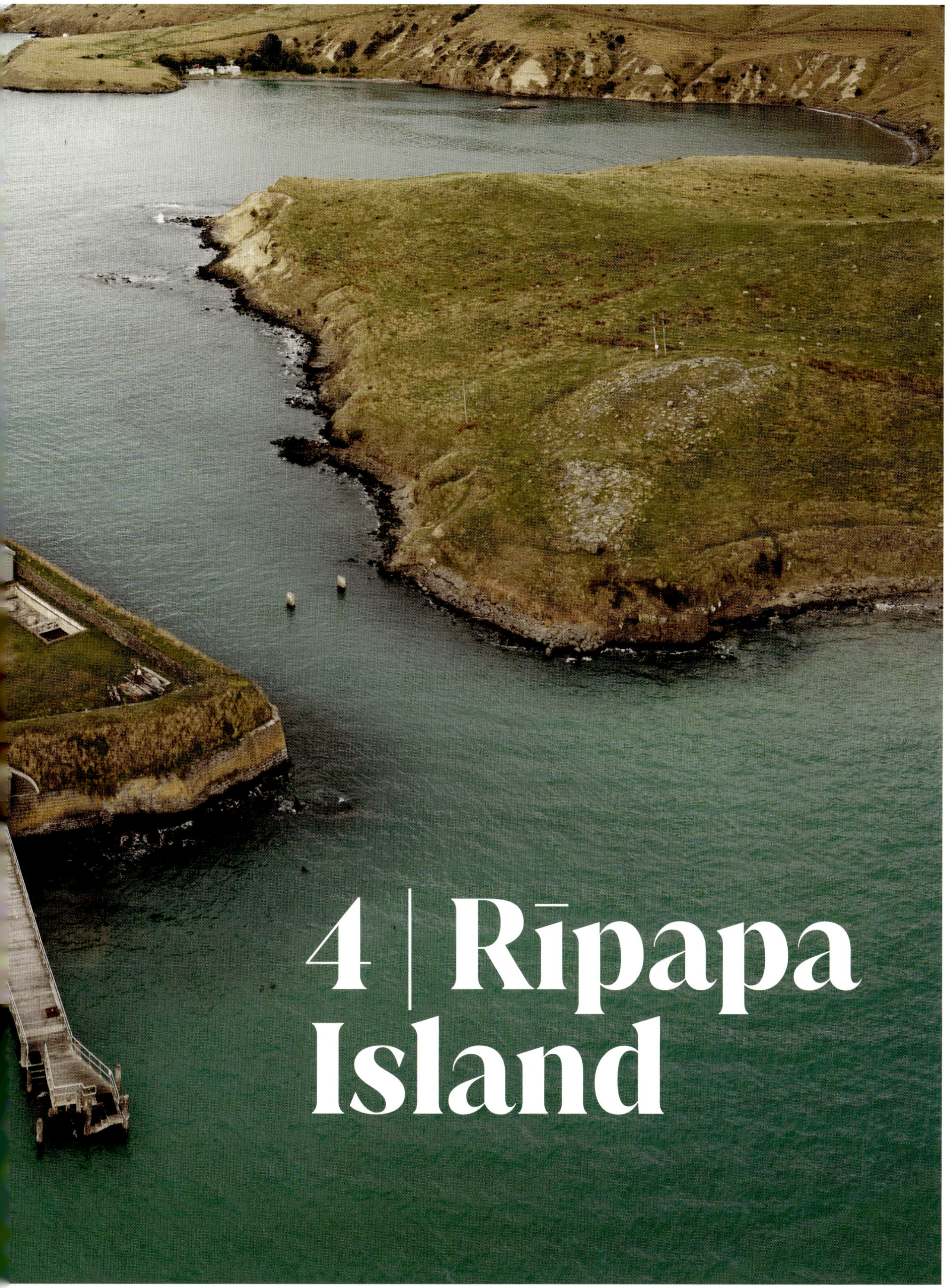

4 | Rīpapa Island

Rhodes Island. Ripa Island. Ripper Island. Rīpapa. Even Humanity Island. What's in a name? The Māori name Rīpapa (not the anglicised version Ripa) tells us much about the early use of the island. 'Rī' means a flax rope used to drag a waka ashore, and 'papa' a flat rock. A mooring rock. This small, much modified island, close to the headland separating Pūrau from Inainatu Pile Bay, has a dramatic history.

✳

Rīpapa Island was variously a fortified pā, a quarantine station, a place of incarceration and then, as Fort Jervois, part of New Zealand's nationwide coastal defence scheme. In other words, it was a place that needed to be accessed, but not too easily and only by those in control, those seeking a place of retreat, or those who were being removed from society for a time. The island's points of entry were a jetty, built in 1874, and a narrow bridge connecting it to the mainland, built sometime after 1914.

Early on, Ngāti Māmoe had a small village on the island, defended by a palisade. However, Rīpapa Island's strategic position, roughly halfway down the navigable harbour of Whakaraupō and jutting out just enough to afford a clear view to the heads, made it an obvious choice for a subsequent Ngāi Tahu pā site. The Ngāi Tahu chief principally associated with Rīpapa Island was Taununu, who migrated from Kaikōura and took possession of family lands in Whakaraupō.

Taununu established his pā on Rīpapa in the early nineteenth century. According to archaeologist Barry Brailsford, it may have been the first pā in Te Waipounamu specifically designed for the musket warfare era, and it demonstrated how rapidly Māori adapted pā designs to meet the threat posed by a new war technology: 'Seven bastions project out from the walls in a style reminiscent of the towers of medieval times. This gave the defending marksmen a clear field of fire along the line of the walls or palisades.'[1] Anyone attempting to scale the defences would be caught in a deadly crossfire. However, despite the fact that it appeared to have been designed as a musket pā, Rīpapa had no guns.

The story is a tragic one. In the 1820s, Rīpapa was drawn into the Kaihuānga feud between the peninsula subtribes when Taununu's nephew was killed by Kaiapoi Māori. In response, Taununu launched a surprise attack on Whakaepa — a small pā at Colgate, in mid-Canterbury, populated by Kaiapoi people — and slaughtered all the inhabitants. Kaiapoi countered by putting together a large fighting force armed with muskets. Rīpapa was caught in a two-pronged attack. One war party went overland via Koukourārata to Pūrau. Another went by waka around the peninsula to meet up with the land party. Warned just in time, Taununu crossed the harbour to safety. As his followers tried to flee the island in waka, Te Whakataupuka and his warriors, who had come north from Foveaux

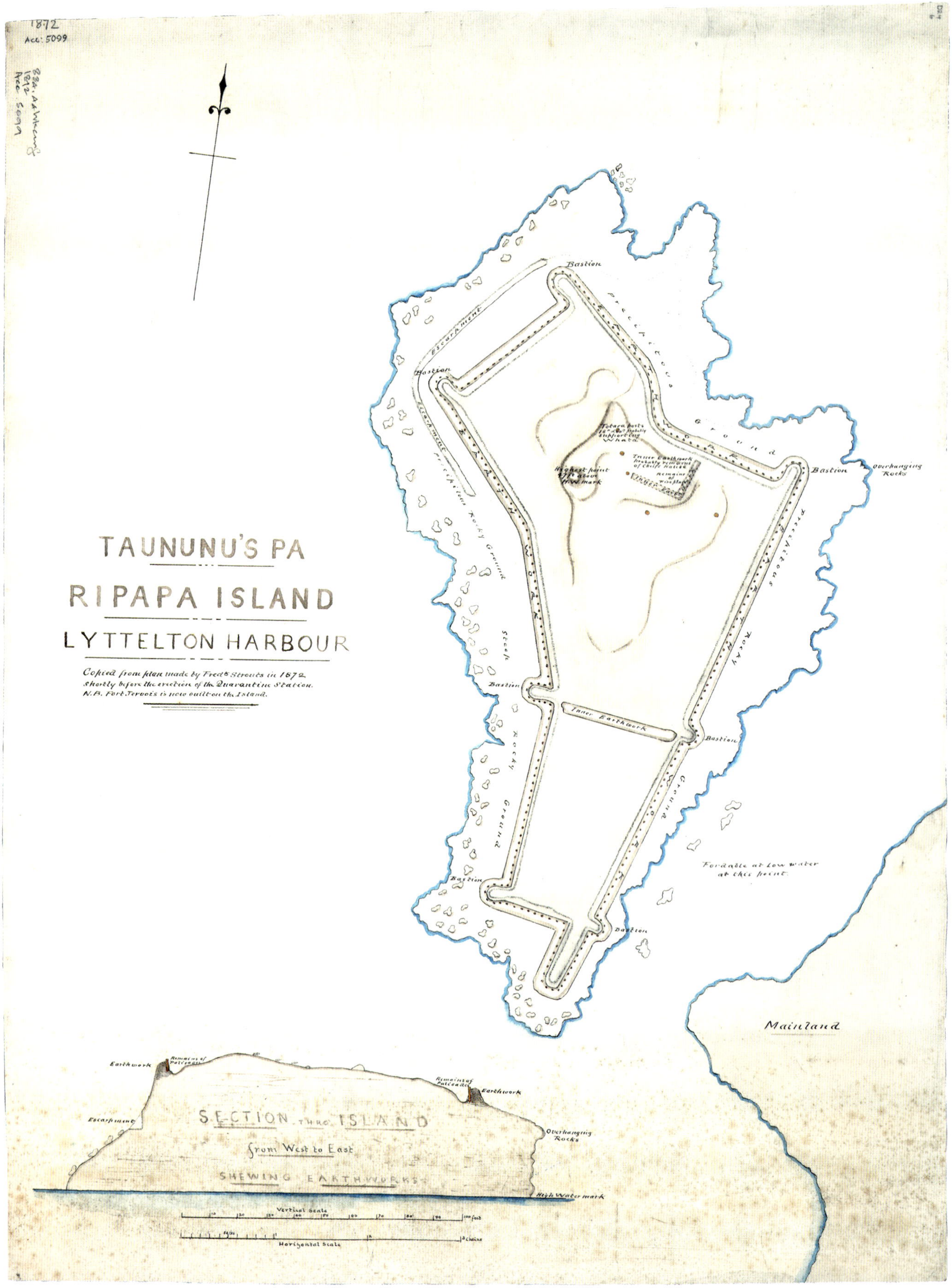
1872
Acc: 5099
TAUNUNU'S PA
RIPAPA ISLAND
LYTTELTON HARBOUR
Copied from plan made by Fred. Strouts in 1872
shortly before the erection of the Quarantine Station.
N.B. Fort Jervois is now built on the Island.
Bastion
Escarpment
Precipitous Ground
Overhanging Rocks
Precipitous Rocky Ground
Steep
Totara posts
supporting Whata
Highest point
H.W. mark
Inner Earthwork
probably remains of Chiefs House
Remains of Fireplace
Inner Earthwork
Rocky Ground
Fordable at low water at this point
Mainland
Earthwork
Remains of Palisade
Escarpment
SECTION THRO ISLAND
from West to East
SHEWING EARTHWORKS
Overhanging Rocks
High Water mark
Vertical Scale
100 feet
Horizontal Scale
3 chains

Strait to support the Ōtākou chief Taiaroa, rounded the headland from Te Pōhue Camp Bay and headed them off. All were slaughtered. Other Rīpapa residents, fleeing the pā on foot, were able to escape through the ranks of the attackers and scramble up the slopes of Mount Evans, from where they rolled big rocks down on their pursuers. The pā was plundered and the fortifications destroyed. Taununu was eventually clubbed to death at the Wairewa Lake Forsyth outlet.

Ngāi Tahu continued to occupy Rīpapa until about 1832, when chief Te Whakarukeruke left to help defend Kaiapoi against Te Rauparaha. After the fall of Kaiapoi, Te Rauparaha overran a number of pā on Banks Peninsula, including Rīpapa, which was never again occupied as a pā. The island is of special significance to Ngāi Tahu. The urupā on Rīpapa and nearby, and the island's status in tribal history, were acknowledged by the designation of Rīpapa as a Tōpuni site in the Ngāi Tahu Deed of Settlement with the Crown in 1998.[2] Today, Te Hapū o Ngāti Wheke at Te Rāpaki-o-Te Rakiwhakaputa are the guardians of Rīpapa.

In the early 1870s, central government took control of immigration from the provincial governments and ramped up the programme across the country. The almost complete failure of the immigrant facilities at Camp Bay forced the authorities to build a new quarantine station. Rīpapa was selected on the grounds that immigrants quarantined offshore would be less likely to abscond, or to pose a health threat to peninsula residents. In preparation for the new facilities, the site was levelled and the remains of Taununu's pā obliterated.

The new buildings, designed by architect Frederick Strouts, were officially handed over on 5 June 1873, with the steamer *Halcyon* conveying officials to the island. A *Press* account of the opening describes Rīpapa Island before the excavations of the 1880s transformed its geography:

> The island is of a mound-like form, rather steeply rising on all sides from a belt of rocks that encircle it, washed by the sea, the highest ground being of course chosen as the site of the sanitorium . . . The landing yesterday was made at the south-west corner of the island, where a permanent jetty will be built running in that direction, the flat slab-like rocks gradually forming a natural ascent to the higher level of the ground.[3]

On 24 April that year, tenders were called for the construction of a 'small landing jetty', and the job was awarded to John Sandford of Heathcote.[4] However, there was a delay in procuring the necessary piles and it was a year before work began.[5]

This plan of Taununu's pā on Rīpapa Island was drawn by the architect of the quarantine station buildings, Frederick Strouts, just prior to the destruction of the pā. It shows the butts of the palisade posts inside the high earth walls and the 1.5-metre-deep trenches behind the walls. An inner earthwork created the opportunity for a second stand against the enemy if one section of the pā fell. The cross-section shows the original height of the island.
ALEXANDER TURNBULL LIBRARY, 23027745

The Rīpapa Island quarantine station included barracks, a hospital, service buildings, a barrack master's cottage and a jetty. This sketch by Mary Catherine Medley gives an idea of just how built-up and crowded the island was prior to its being levelled for military purposes in the 1880s. What is not visible in this sketch is the jetty.
ALEXANDER TURNBULL LIBRARY, E-346-2-096/097

In 1876 the jetty was lengthened and steps were added to enable easy access at all tides.

Today's harbour residents, who see a flat, uninhabited island, would scarcely recognise the Rīpapa Island of the 1870s and 1880s. There were a sufficient number of timber and corrugated-iron buildings rising from the steepish cliffs to constitute a small township. On landing, immigrants or visitors would first pass the kitchen, followed by the 100-foot-long hospital, designed with a two-storey centre and one-storey wings. On the ground floor were a nurse's room, a surgeon's room, two storerooms, two bathrooms and two patent water closets. The wings contained separate wards for male and female patients, and the upper floor was divided into two dormitories, which opened onto a balcony, for convalescent patients.

Beyond the hospital were separate quarters for single women, single men and families. These were substantial two-storeyed buildings. Applying the lessons learned from the Camp Bay fiasco, the authorities ensured the buildings were firmly anchored down to large blocks of Governors Bay stone. Overall the barracks were capable of housing an extraordinary (for such a small island) 300 people, plus another hundred should the need arise. Since the only water available on Rīpapa Island was from rainfall, two brick underground tanks and 15 400-gallon iron tanks were installed.[6] John Edwin March was appointed superintendent of the quarantine station in July 1873, with George Plimmer joining the staff as assistant superintendent in September the following year.

The first immigrants to be landed at Rīpapa Island were passengers from *Edwin Fox*, which arrived at the end of August 1873. They were towed in to the jetty by the local steamer SS *Mullogh*. They were, apparently, very pleased with the living conditions. The following month the barque *Punjaub*, carrying 200 British and 112 Danish emigrants, arrived in Lyttelton. As noted above, it had lost 40 passengers to various fevers, and 10 more died in quarantine. In one family of four, the elder daughter died during the voyage and the mother and other daughter died at the hospital on Rīpapa Island, leaving a son, aged 19, alone in the new colony. In the midst of all the sadness a baby was born in the quarantine hospital to the wife of Soren Neilsen, mother and child reported as doing well.[7]

Access to the quarantine station was strictly prohibited. A penalty of £200 could be imposed on any unauthorised person found anywhere near the barracks. Ironically, the quarantine buildings on Rīpapa Island, though much superior to those in Camp Bay, were not used for long. Space was limited on the small island, and the close proximity of the wooden buildings constituted a fire risk. By the beginning of October 1874, several quarantine buildings on the much larger Quail Island, 5.8 kilometres further up the harbour, had nearly been completed, and on 11 February 1875 the whole of Quail Island was officially proclaimed a quarantine station. While immigrants continued to be quarantined on Rīpapa Island, those in their convalescent phase were often accommodated on Quail Island. The introduction of steamers on the voyage from England to New Zealand in the 1880s significantly reduced voyage times and consequently the risk of disease transmission. In late 1886 the *Press* noted that the quarantine station on Rīpapa Island had been unused for some years.

From May 1879 the people of Parihaka in Taranaki, led by Te Whiti o Rongomai and Tohu Kākahi, mounted a campaign of passive resistance to the large-scale confiscation of their land. Arrested without trial through 1879 and 1880 for activities such as removing survey pegs, erecting fences and ploughing, 405 men were transported far from home to gaols in Dunedin, Hokitika and Christchurch. Those in Christchurch were imprisoned in the Addington and Lyttelton gaols. Approximately 160 of the Parihaka Māori were eventually taken by the government ship SS *Hinemoa* from Lyttelton to Rīpapa Island, where they were held for six months.

Reporting on the arrival in Lyttelton of one group of 26 prisoners, the *Lyttelton Times* described them as 'chiefly young, powerful-looking men [who] do not seem to have lost their faith in Te Whiti through their arrest and confinement'.[8] Clearly their presence in a province whose Māori population was comparatively small created quite a stir. 'An immense crowd congregated on the wharf, all eager to see the Maoris land, the wagons being used as grand stands.'[9] The harbour launches ran special trips down the harbour and past Rīpapa Island in the expectation of sighting the prisoners.

The 'spectacle' was short-lived, with the prisoners on Rīpapa Island returning to Parihaka having served their sentence. (Leaders Te Whiti and Tohu were never on Rīpapa, as has sometimes been suggested; in 1881 they were incarcerated in the Addington Gaol in Christchurch.) By 31 March 1881 Rīpapa's quarantine station, which had been considerably altered to accommodate the prisoners, was undergoing a thorough renovation. As it happened, however, Rīpapa Island was shortly to be transformed and put to a whole new use.

On 17 February 1873, Aucklanders woke to news that a Russian warship had entered Auckland Harbour undetected and landed troops. Although the report was a hoax, conflicts between Britain and Russia in the nineteenth century inclined many in the new and undefended colony to take the threat seriously. A full-blown Russian scare in 1885, triggered by Anglo–Russian rivalry in Afghanistan, led to the building of major fortifications to protect New Zealand's coastal cities. The New Zealand government invited Lieutenant Colonel Peter Scratchley of the British Royal Engineers to assess the colony's coastal defences. In his report, Scratchley recommended that the four main ports be protected by a three-tiered defensive system comprising shore-based artillery, submarine mines and torpedo boats. With regard to artillery, guns on Rīpapa Island, Tapoa Erskine Point (adjacent to Magazine Bay), Spur Point (below Sumner Road heading east from Lyttelton port) and Battery Point (separating the port reclamation at Te Awaparahi and Ōtokitoki Gollans Bay) would provide protective coverage of the whole of Lyttelton Harbour in the event of a Russian invasion.

The strategic location of Rīpapa Island, already recognised by Māori, made it an obvious choice. Plans were drawn up by Lieutenant Colonel Boddam, following recommendations made by Lieutenant Colonel Scratchley and Sir William Jervois, and with the aid of drawings provided by the manufacturer of the 'disappearing guns' (so named because they recoiled into the emplacement between shots) to be mounted on the island.[10] Work began in 1886. The quarantine station, built only 13 years before and still used but only as 'overflow' accommodation, was dismantled and removed to Quail Island by Hollis and Williams of Lyttelton. The top 4.5 metres of the island were levelled, using unemployed and military labour. A submarine mine depot was completed in 1886, but funding cuts slowed other work. In September 1888 it was announced that what had, until then, been known as Fort Ripa would henceforth be known as Fort Jervois (after Sir William Jervois, Governor of New Zealand and an ex-military engineer).

To push the construction along, the government decided to use prisoners from the Lyttelton Gaol. This decision was unsuccessfully challenged by the

United States-founded Order of the Knights of Labour, which had become active in Christchurch in the late 1880s, representing the unemployed. Initially the prisoners were transported daily to and from Rīpapa Island by steam launch, via the jetty constructed for the quarantine station. But in 1889 the mining depot buildings were altered and the prisoners were then housed on the island for six days each week, guarded by warders and Permanent Artillery men. The work would have been hard and the conditions spartan.

The most famous and successful escape from the island was made by Jonathan Roberts in June 1888. Roberts, who had already escaped once from police custody in Timaru, joined the 40-strong labour gang on Rīpapa Island. With only one sentry on duty to cover the island, Roberts made his getaway when prisoners and warders were eating their midday meal in the mess-shed. Prisoners in the know shielded him from view as he prised open a section of galvanised iron. Once outside, Roberts slid down the 12-foot parapet wall and into the sea. It was high tide when he swam the narrow but potentially treacherous channel on the mainland side of the island. Later, his abandoned wet coat was discovered about 50 yards up the hill. From there he climbed high up into the snowline in his soggy, heavy clothes and dropped down into Kaituna Valley. There was a lot of public sympathy for Roberts, who rapidly became a local celebrity. He was never caught. Much later, he published a diary of his exploits.[11]

The prisoners built a bluestone masonry sea wall that encircled the island. A second wall retained the embankment surrounding the parade ground and outbuildings. The sea wall was pierced by a single entrance opening off a drawbridge and jetty.[12] According to David Gee, prisoners worked up to their waists in water at low tide to clear the seabed for jetty piles.[13] In addition to the drawbridge, the jetty, measuring some 100 feet long, had a removable centre portion to discourage people coming onto the island. At the south end of the island there were facilities to house and handle submarine mines and torpedoes. At the northern end concrete gun pits, ammunition stores and connecting tunnels were built in the solid bedrock. Soil from the tunnelling was then used to cover over the fort. A narrow-gauge railway shifted mines to and from the island's wharf.

The two quick-firing Nordenfelt guns and four hydro-pneumatic Armstrong disappearing guns were in place by 1889. The disappearing guns were designed to use the energy generated from their recoil to return to the firing position. However, it was suspected that if all four guns fired simultaneously the fort would collapse. The logistics of getting building materials and hardware to the island are mind-boggling. The big guns were barged over from Lyttelton, their barrels alone weighing 12 tons apiece. Teams of men had to drag each barrel up from the sea along a specially constructed earthen ramp. (When convict labour was abolished in 1913, work on the fort finally stopped.)[14]

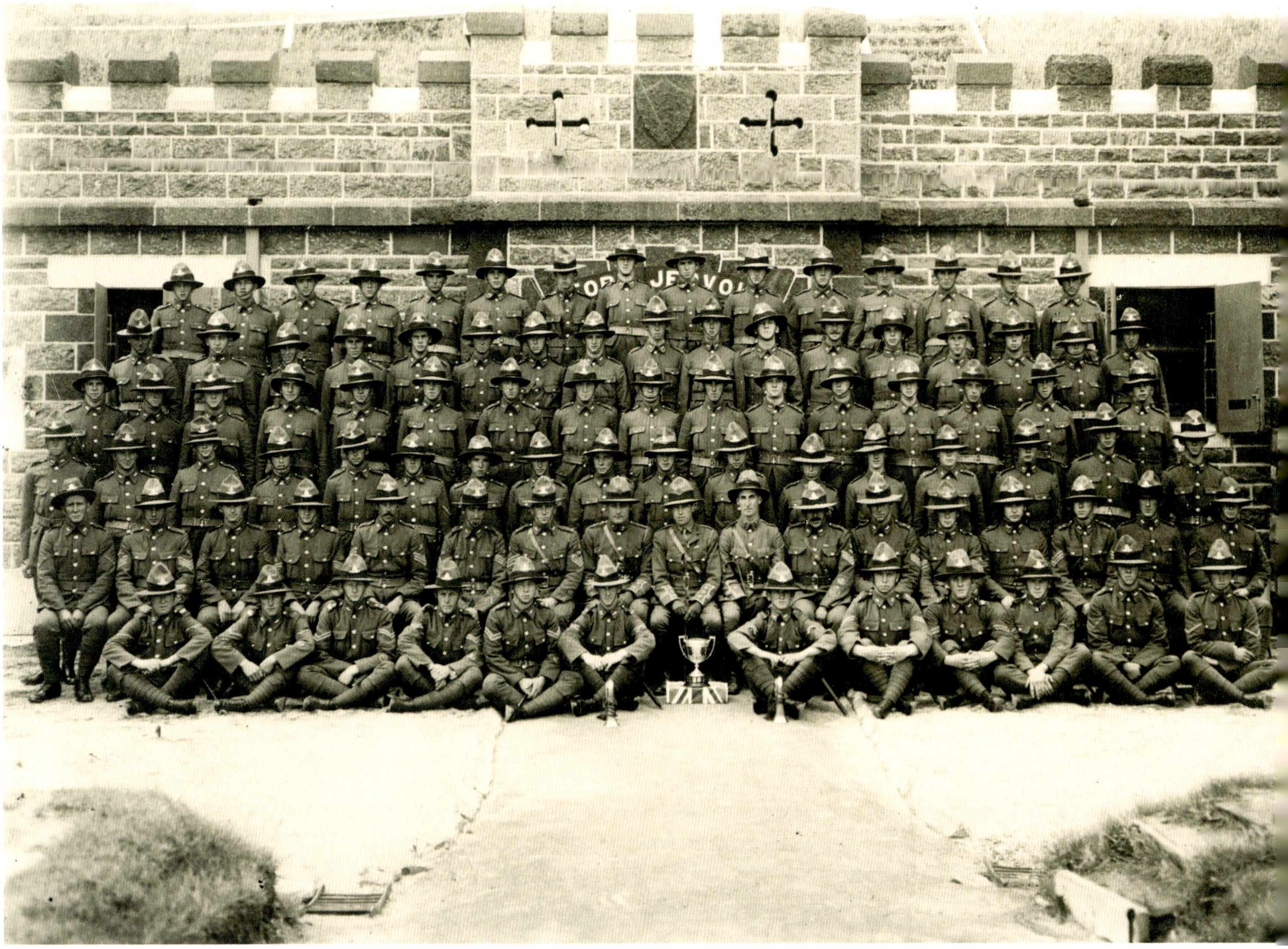

Fort Jervois was more impressive in appearance than in execution. The fort was not declared operational until 1895, well after the Russian scare was over. Meanwhile, with the first test-firing of the guns in the 1880s, cracks appeared in the concrete command centre, and ice plants (presumably used for camouflage) were tossed as much as 100 metres into the air, somewhat diminishing the effect of the 'disappearing' guns. A popular story from the Second World War, possibly an urban myth, has a shell from one of the 8-inch guns overshooting the Port Hills and landing in a suburban Christchurch garden, an incident that was hushed up by the military until after the war's end.[15] The lighthouse at Godley Head certainly received unwanted shrapnel from the Rīpapa Island guns.

Getting men (it was almost always men, although women visited on annual camp open days) onto the island usually involved a 20-minute steamer trip from Lyttelton, followed by transfer into a smaller vessel that could navigate the shallower waters around the island and jetty. This was not without its challenges. In April 1889 'a sixteen-stone member of the navals, not getting fairly in the bottom of the small craft, she refused to uphold him, sending the sixteen-stone member and three others, with a quantity of the Naval officers' baggage, and a couple of carbines, overboard'.[16]

Arrivals could be much more formal. In 1910, British Army Field Marshal Lord Kitchener visited Canterbury and was taken to view the harbour defences. Kitchener's party was conveyed to Rīpapa Island in the tug *Canterbury* and then transferred to defence launch *Te Whaka* in order to land at the shallow-water jetty, which was lined with men from the No. 1 and No. 2 Companies of the Garrison Artillery Volunteers. About 150 men paraded at the fort.[17]

Accessing Fort Jervois could also end tragically. In November 1893 the government steam launch had just left the jetty when the strong north-easterly swell caused it to lurch heavily. James McKenzie and Fitzroy George Hamilton, both members of the Torpedo Corps, were thrown overboard. The launch travelled another 200 yards before it could be stopped. Two men on the launch jumped overboard to help and a small boat was sent out from Rīpapa Island, but neither McKenzie nor Hamilton survived.[18]

Fort Jervois was constructed to defend Lyttelton Harbour from an unlikely invader at a time when the rapid rate of artillery development meant that almost any weapon or system was out of date by the time it was operational. The fort was used by volunteers for camps, gun drill and firing practice, and as part of the harbour examination system during the First World War, when arriving ships might have warning shots fired across their bows if they failed to respond correctly to signals from Adderley Head or Rīpapa Island. In 1914, No. 1 Field Company Engineers built a narrow bridge connecting the island with the mainland. Four years later, additional footing for the concrete pier supporting the bridge was

No. 4 Company, New Zealand Garrison Artillery, on Fort Jervois, Rīpapa Island (undated).
LYTTELTON MUSEUM, 8718.1

required following a severe gale. The bridge was washed away by Cyclone Giselle in 1968, and only the concrete foundations remain.

The island continued to serve as a prison. In June 1913, 13 young men from Christchurch and the West Coast were transported to Fort Jervois. The men, aged between 18 and 20, were Reg Williams, James Nuttall, Tom Nuttall, Bill Robson, Bob and Jack McTaggart, James Worrall, Ted Edwards, Edward Hannam, Walter Hooper, J. Coppersmith, Henry Guthardt and H. W. Thackwell.[19] They were passive resisters or, as we would term it now, conscientious objectors, sentenced to 28 days' incarceration on Rīpapa Island.

The Defence Act 1909 introduced a general training requirement for males 12 to 14 years old (Junior Cadets), 14 to 18 (Senior Cadets), 18 to 21 (General Training Section) and 21 to 30 (the Reserve). Men and boys could be exempted on religious grounds so long as they carried out non-combatant duties within the military. Refusal to comply could result in fines, and potentially imprisonment for those who did not pay. This was regarded as a possible forerunner to full conscription. Groups such as the Passive Resisters Union, the Peace Council and the 'We Wont's' rapidly formed, the main centres of resistance being Christchurch and the coal-mining towns of the West Coast.

The detention of the young men on Rīpapa Island went relatively smoothly at first. They refused to drill and were not forced to do so. But when they refused to clean weapons, they were placed on half rations. The men responded with a hunger strike. In the cold winter conditions they rapidly sickened. A court was convened on the island; the men were charged with insubordination and sentenced to another week's detention. Prime Minister William Massey refused to include conscientious objectors in any exemption to the Defence Act because he thought 'shirkers' might pose as conscientious objectors.

There was little support for the men in the local or national press. They were regarded as 'malingerers, trouble-makers and notoriety-craving youths' who were using their incarceration on Rīpapa Island to broadcast the pacifist cause (which of course they were). However, to others they were heroes. On 4 July a letter from the prisoners was read at the Labour Congress sitting in Wellington. The delegates resolved that 'this Congress strenuously protests against the wicked and barbarous method of imposing solitary confinement on the boys now incarcerated on Ripa Island', and called on the government to release them immediately.[20]

Four hundred members of the Congress marched to Parliament. A deputation met with the prime minister and minister of defence. However, the in-house inquiry that followed absolved the military and concluded that the young men were only 'out for misrule'. On 23 July another court was held, this time in the courthouse at Lyttelton. The magistrate dismissed all the charges. Some of the men were released at the end of July, others in late September. James Nuttall, who served three and a half months, wrote in a letter: 'We are fighting here, and hope you are doing likewise outside, because we realize that New Zealand must at all costs be freed from the clutches of this jingoistic monster, conscription.'[21]

Another very high-profile prisoner in Fort Jervois was Count Felix von Luckner who, in SMS *Seeadler*, sank 14 Allied merchant ships in a four-month spree during the First World War before his ship was grounded on the Society Islands. Von Luckner made it in a small boat to the Cook Islands and then on to Fiji (an epic journey under the circumstances), where he and his men were arrested. Brought to New Zealand as a prisoner-of-war, von Luckner was imprisoned on Motuihe Island in the Hauraki Gulf, from where he escaped; he was then rearrested in the Kermadec Islands and sent to Fort Jervois along with second-in-command Lieutenant Kirscheiss and a third man to act as an orderly. The three remained on the island for 119 days until the Armistice in November 1918.

Rīpapa Island was regarded as the most secure spot in New Zealand for von Luckner and his companions. On 12 January 1918 the *Press* reported that 'the island, a very appropriate one, is to be especially prepared for the reception of its visitors. A stockade is to protect its edges, and an armed guard . . . is to be placed on the island sufficiently strong to guard the prisoners night and day.'[22]

Thanks to press coverage of his daring escapades, the 'colourful, charismatic and enigmatic' von Luckner enjoyed (and no doubt encouraged) celebrity status.

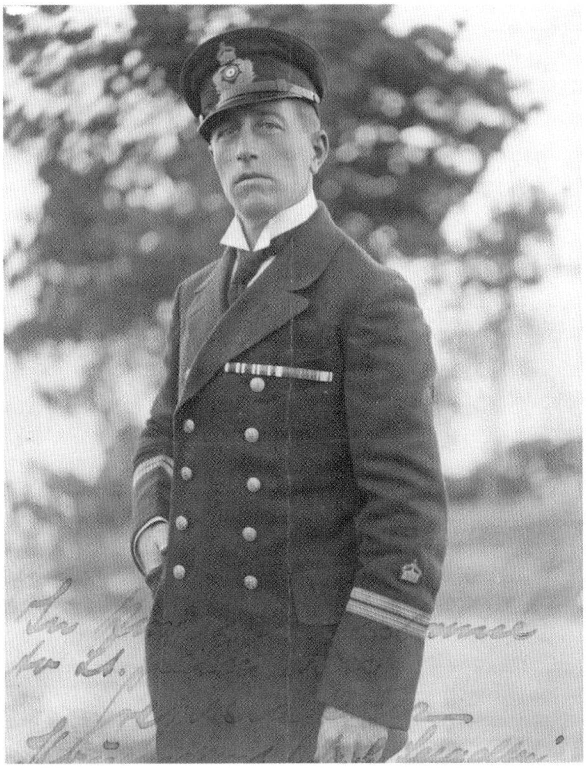

LEFT Count Felix von Luckner.
NATIONAL MUSEUM OF THE ROYAL NEW ZEALAND NAVY, APO 0001

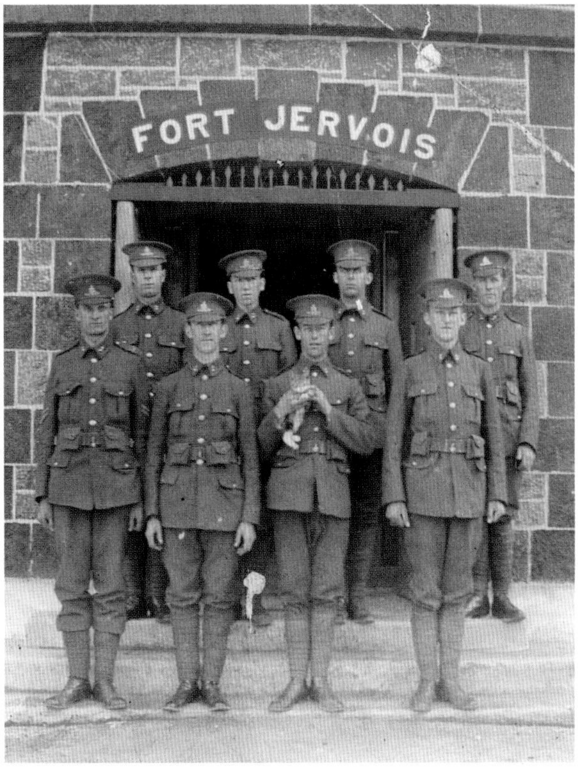
FORT JERVOIS

RIGHT Felix von Luckner's guard with kitten, Rīpapa Island, 1918. Von Luckner described his guards as 'good boys', and they do indeed seem to be not much more than lads. The presence of the kitten suggests a certain homeliness.
LYTTELTON MUSEUM, 7935.1

ABOVE The Banks Peninsula Cruising Club celebrated its season opening day with a picnic on Rīpapa Island, October 1934.
LYTTELTON MUSEUM, 7938.1

BELOW The restored jetty at Rīpapa Island. Following the 2010/11 Canterbury earthquakes the historic reserve was closed to the public. A $100,000 rebuild of the wharf, undertaken by the Department of Conservation and the Lyttelton Port Company, enabled Rīpapa Island to be reopened in 2019.
JANE ROBERTSON

'The Count, by the way, is said by those who know him, to be of very powerful physique. So strong are his hands in fact that it is possible for him to bend a copper coin between his thumb and forefinger.'[23] It was reported that he was to write a book during his detention on the island about his voyage in *Seeadler*.

There was concern that von Luckner and Kirscheiss were being treated too leniently on the island, especially given their track record of daring escape. The commander of the Canterbury Military District, Colonel Chaffey, protested that there was 'absolutely no foundation' to such claims. The prisoners were given the same food as the soldiers on the island. In their hut on the parade ground at the southwest end of the main fort building they had a stretcher, a wooden chair and a table in each room.[24] They were allowed to read censored newspapers and to write two letters a week each on a single sheet of paper. None of the prisoners was allowed on to the mainland. They had been allowed, however, to have an occasional bathe in the sea under the escort of two sentries with loaded rifles; that was the only luxury they received.[25] Given his colourful history, the greatest threat to von Luckner's well-being on Rīpapa Island was likely to be boredom.

As a little girl, Lynley Galbraith (née Jackson), who grew up at Fern Glen in Pūrau, would ride the big cattle horse Darkie on the front of her father's saddle ('a long way down from on top'). 'Once we were riding past the fort and a man was walking on the top of the fort. Father said this was Count von Luckner, the prisoner, so I must have been about four then.'[26]

Repatriated to Germany after the war, von Luckner revisited New Zealand on a lecture tour in 1938. He recalled 'the 119 weary days' spent in Fort Jervois but also acknowledged that Major Leeming, who was in charge of the fortress, was a gentleman, and the guards were 'good boys'. 'We liked them and so did they us.'[27] During his visit to Christchurch von Luckner expressed an interest in revisiting 'Ripa Island', but permission was refused for security reasons. This prompted a lively exchange in the local papers between those who applauded the decision and those who regarded it as an affront to the count. One letter writer pointed out that there was scarcely anything of security value to hide. The guns were in such a bad state of disrepair that they could not be raised from their mountings in the pits, and 'the only occasion the drawbridge was raised was in order to prevent the dog on the island straying and worrying the sheep on the mainland'.[28]

In fact Rīpapa Island had been downgraded to a magazine in 1922 and abandoned in 1925 without a shot ever having been fired in anger. Thereafter the island was used for a variety of purposes. In December 1929 the Royal Naval Volunteer Reserve training cutter *Deveron* was officially commissioned with a ceremony at Fort Jervois. From 1929 to 1936 Lyttelton shipping agents Rhind and Co. leased the island and took visitors across in their ferries.

In December 1932 the Banks Peninsula Cruising Club held a 'flannel dance' to

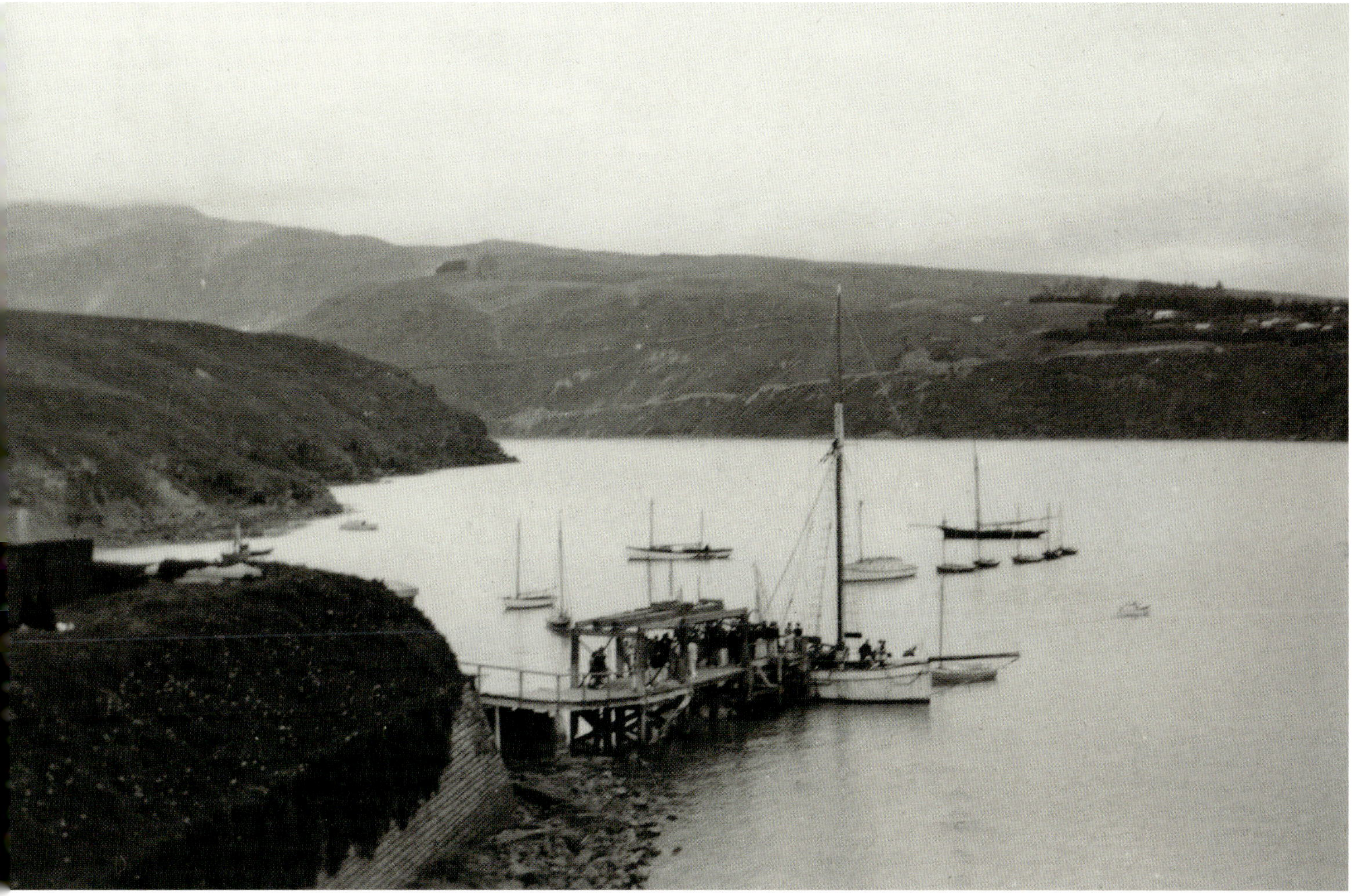

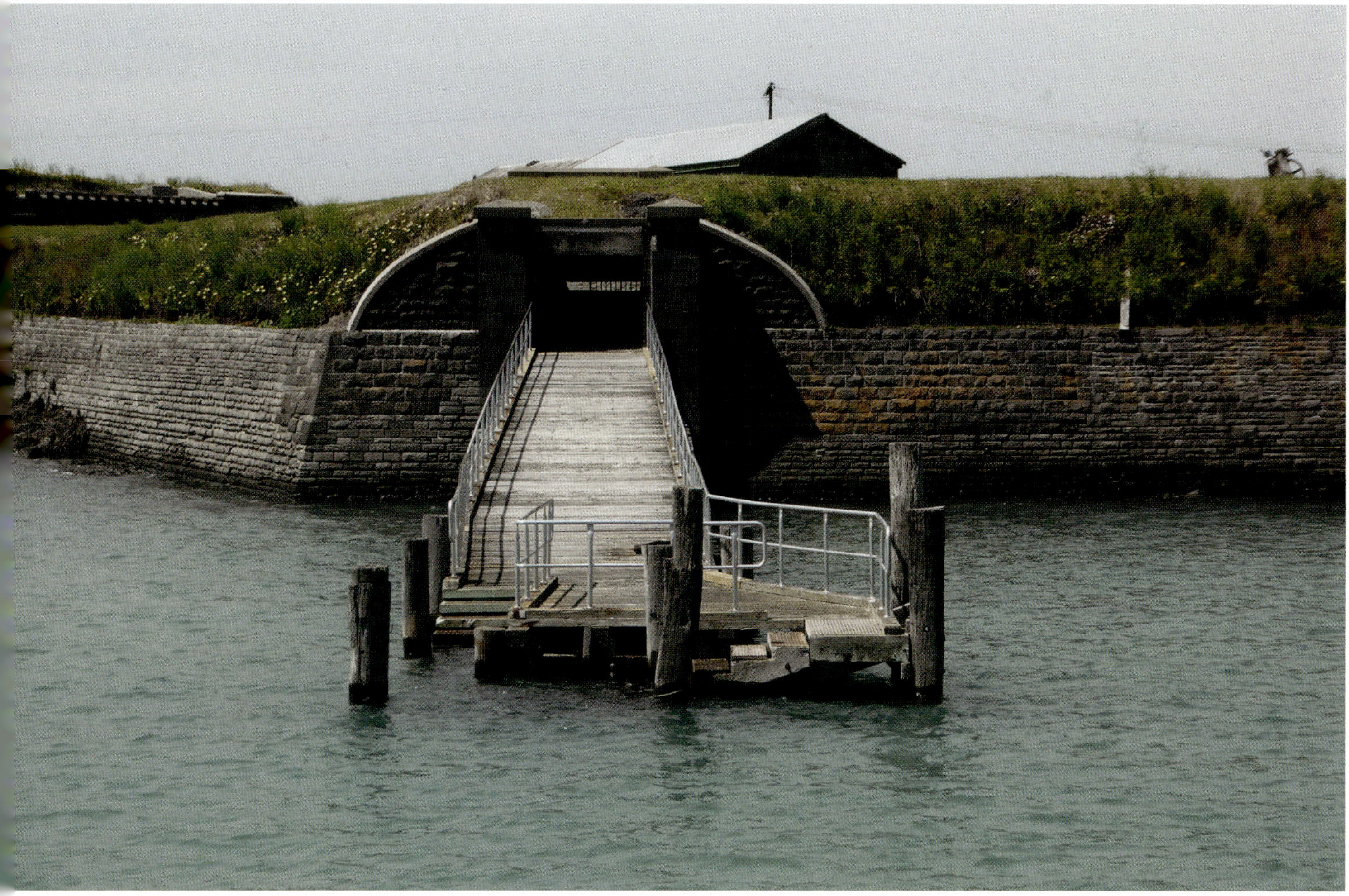

Pile Bay

Just east of Rīpapa Island and accessible from the Pūrau–Camp Bay road is the tiny settlement of Inainatu Pile Bay.[29] Almost completely sheltered from easterly and southerly winds, it would have provided a sheltered, sandy beach in close proximity to Taununu's rock-girt pā on Rīpapa Island. Today, baches huddle together on the foreshore.

Pile Bay's name comes from what was once a circle of piles offshore, which was used to adjust the compasses of small vessels. Each pile marked a cardinal compass point when lined up with a master or 'dolphin' pile placed in the centre of the circle. A vessel would run a line from its stern to the master pile and a line to one of the outer piles from the bow. When the master pile and the outer pile were aligned, the compass was checked and adjusted if necessary. Then, with its stern still tied to the master pile, the vessel would be warped around to the next pile and the procedure repeated until the circle was completed. By the 1930s the swinging of ships in Pile Bay had long been abandoned and shipping firms were arguing for the speedy licensing of a competent compass adjuster.[30] The bay was also used at times to careen boats for hull inspection.

Pile Bay became part of the Gardiner family's Pūrau property in 1874, with pine trees planted on the foreshore providing much-needed shelter and shade. In the 1920s the Norris family from Lyttelton acquired permission to camp in the bay. Since there was no road or track access, the wider family plus provisions, including drinking water in kerosene tins, came across the harbour in the launch *Helene*. Six weeks of camping life was basic but idyllic. The children enjoyed walks to get water for domestic use from a spring about a kilometre away above Rīpapa Island, and milk from the Candy farm at Camp Bay. Large red cod, attracted to the rotting piles of the compass adjuster, provided great eating. Most evenings the campers engaged in dragnetting off the beach.

Pile Bay was also a favoured destination for picnic groups including the Canterbury Yacht and Motor Boat Club, the Lyttelton Fanciers' Club, the Lyttelton Boxing and Sports Club and the Young Men's Christian Association. In October 1932 the Banks Peninsula Cruising Club planned to celebrate its inaugural opening day picnic at Rīpapa Island. A fierce southerly battering the harbour prevented crews and passengers from landing at the exposed Rīpapa Island jetty. Instead, the fleet anchored in Pile Bay. Even in the shelter of the bay, larger craft had trouble hanging on. With better weather in the afternoon, races, novelty races, a tug-of-war and a treasure hunt were held on the Pile Bay beach. This was the first of many season opening day gatherings in Pile Bay.

In the mid-1930s regular visitors began building baches on the foreshore. The first of these was constructed by Len Anderson out of dismantled Massey-Harris tractor cases, brought across on *Helene* from Lyttelton. Nine baches now cluster together at the top of the small beach. A track was cut down to the bay from Camp Bay Road in 1993 and replaced with a private road in 2002.

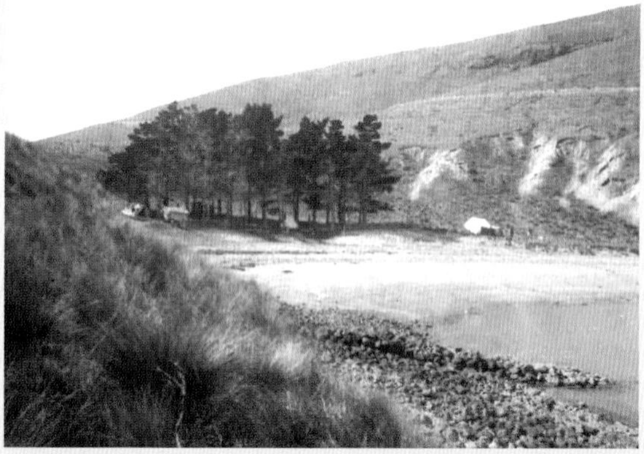

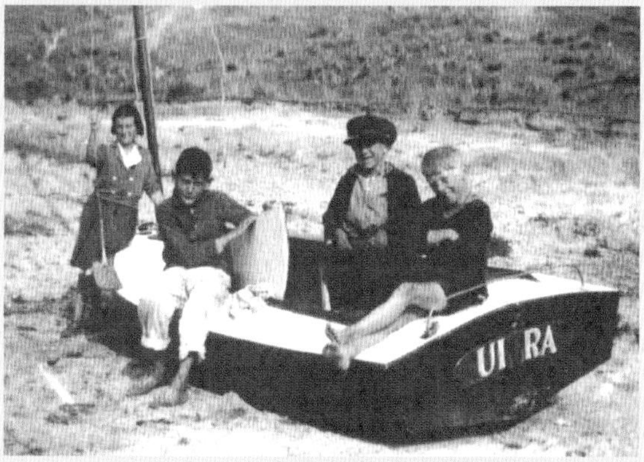
UI RA

From 1958, Navy League Sea Cadets trained on Rīpapa Island. This photo was taken at a summer camp, c.1962.
COURTESY OF MICK HORGAN

raise funds for the Sanders Cup yachting contest. Two hundred dancers arrived at Rīpapa Island in private launches and yachts and in the large passenger launch *Owaka*, which made two trips. The barrack room was transformed into a dance hall, and the tennis court outside accommodated the spillover of dancers. The dance raised £27, of which at least £10 went to the fund-raising cause. A special train left Lyttelton at 1.00 a.m. taking happy revellers back to the city.[31] The numbers were even greater a couple of years later when approximately 300 people crossed the harbour in passenger launches, boats and yachts for a Canterbury Yacht and Motor Boat Club picnic on Rīpapa Island.

The Navy League Sea Cadets also trained on Rīpapa Island. After being reinstated as a magazine in 1936, the island was manned by members of the Defence Reserve during the Second World War. Later, a contract was let to remove the guns as scrap, but the scrap-metal dealer gave up and two guns were left partially intact. From 1947 to 1956, the island reopened for visits and picnics under the administration of the Lyttelton Harbour Board. The Navy League was then appointed to control and manage the island in 1958, and sea cadets from TS *Cornwell* used the island for camps and training. National camps would be held there in the summer when over 100 cadets would sling their hammocks in the Fort Jervois tunnels. Supplies for the cadet camps were transferred from the mainland to the island via flying fox. The New Zealand Army upgraded the jetty in 1980.

In 1986 Rīpapa Island became a historic reserve, and in 1990 it came under the care of the Department of Conservation (DOC). The following year, Fort Jervois was classified with the Historic Places Trust (now Heritage New Zealand Pouhere Taonga) as a Category A site (now a Category I listed site). From the time of the Canterbury earthquakes of 2010 and 2011 until late 2019, the island was closed to the public while DOC carried out restoration work. For example, large cracks in the bearers under the main deck of the jetty needed attention before the public could access the island safely. Following a $100,000 rebuild of the wharf, undertaken by DOC and the Lyttelton Port Company, and the removal of a damaged building on its eastern side, Rīpapa reopened to the public in November 2019.

OPPOSITE ABOVE Camping on the foreshore at Pile Bay, 1936. The newly constructed road between Pūrau and Camp Bay is visible top right.
CANTERBURY MUSEUM, W. A. TAYLOR COLLECTION, 1968.213.4108, WAT221

OPPOSITE BELOW Fun on the foreshore at Pile Bay. Baden Norris, who established and acted as curator of the Lyttelton Museum, is the one wearing the hat.
COURTESY OF DAPHNE DAWSON

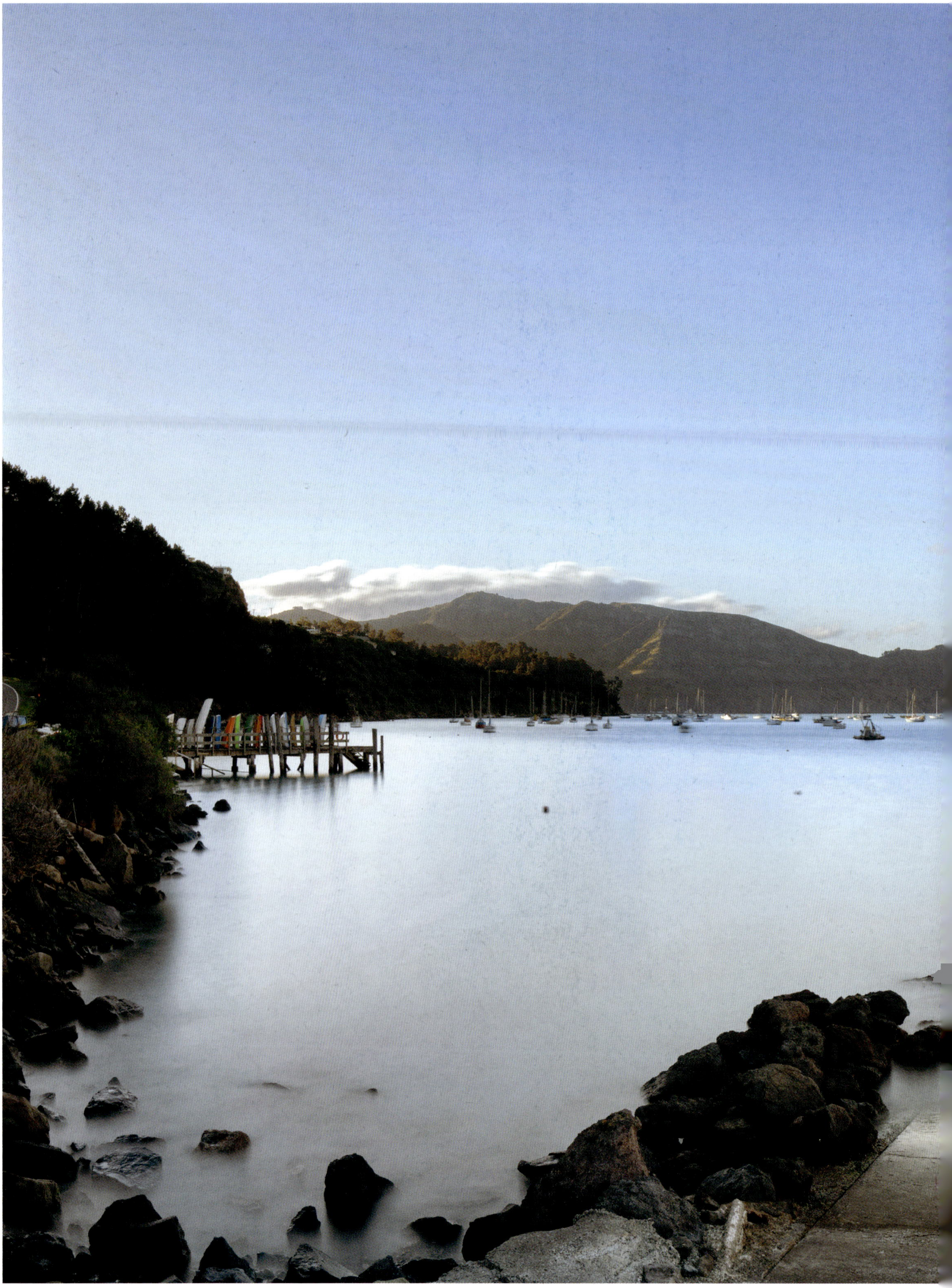

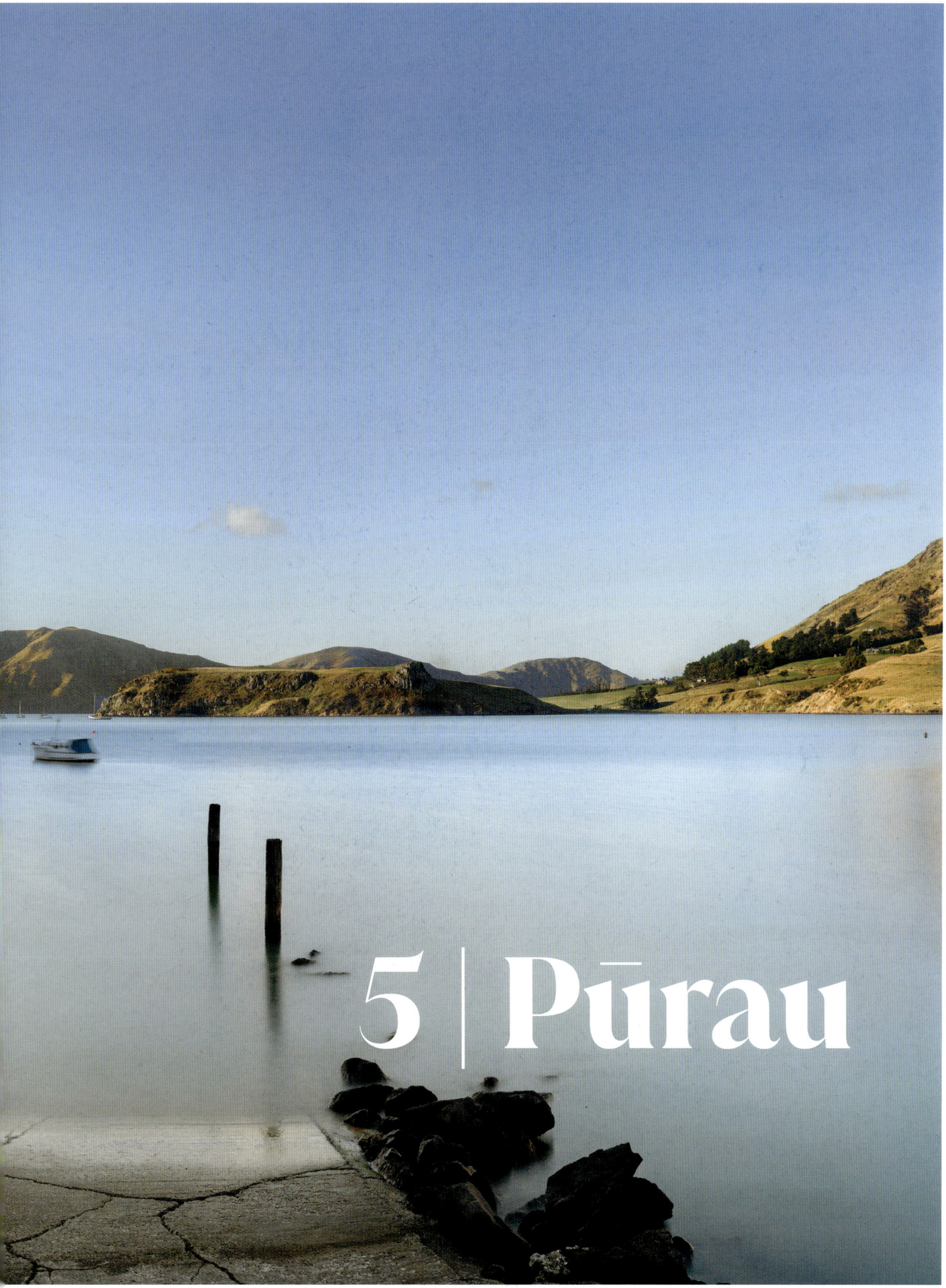

5 | Pūrau

West of Rīpapa Island and east of Te Waipapa Diamond Harbour lies sparkling, sheltered Pūrau. The bay has had many names over the years — Pūrau, Poulao, Port Greenwood, Acheron Bay and Rhodes Bay — finally coming full circle back to Pūrau, translated variously as a 'two-barbed spear', 'mussel basket', 'sea urchin', 'raking implement' or 'pointed stick with which to take food'.

❋

Long favoured by Māori, Pūrau was the choice for the first permanent European settlement in Whakaraupō. With easy access to kaimoana, more gently sloping land than most harbour bays, relative protection from the nor'east and sou'west winds, an original rich bush covering and a plentiful supply of fresh water, it must have seemed very beguiling. The setting was perhaps marred only by the presence of a gigantic, Loch Ness monster–rivalling eel named Tuna Tuoro who, according to the native assessor at Rāpaki, was a veritable taniwha.

Māori lived at Pūrau from the fourteenth century to the twentieth.[1] The discovery of necklace parts, stone adzes, bone fishhooks and Māori ovens containing bones from three different species of moa indicates the presence of Ngāti Māmoe kāinga. Later, Ngāi Tahu settled on the western side of Pūrau between the creek and Te Waipapa spur. The bay has many urupā, a legacy of its long history of occupation. Today there is a memorial marking the burial site of Tiemi Nohomutu, senior Port Cooper chief and a signatory to the French 'purchase' of Banks Peninsula in 1840, the Greenwood brothers' Māori lease at the end of 1846 and the Port Cooper Deed in 1849.

Chief Nohomutu and his whānau were resident in Pūrau when Yorkshiremen James, Joseph and Edward Greenwood arrived at Port Levy in December 1843 and proceeded to squat at Pūrau. They struck problems early on. James bought cattle in Australia but mistakenly offloaded them at Port Levy. The cattle and sheep scattered over the hills, and it took Joseph and five station hands a month to round them up and drive them to Pūrau. Gordon Ogilvie describes the brothers as 'courageous, enterprising and very hard-working but hard-nosed, short-tempered and not especially diplomatic'.[2] They asserted ownership by naming the bay 'Port Greenwood' and Rīpapa Island 'Greenwood's Island'. The brothers seem to have assumed a right to the land without payment. In the middle of January 1844, Joseph noted that 'the natives threaten what they will do if we do not pay them for the ground'. Two days later, 'the natives came from Port Levi for payment for the ground and as we would not give them what they wanted they prevented us from landing the goods'.[3] The Greenwood brothers enlisted the help of Police Magistrate Robinson at Akaroa, who championed the European settler cause.

Assistant Protector of Aborigines Edward Shortland went to Pūrau at the end of January 1844 to assess the situation. He noted that new settlers in general saw 'large spaces of what they termed waste and unreclaimed land, on which their cattle and flocks might roam at pleasure'. These settlers assumed a better right to the land 'than those whose ancestors had lived there, fished there, and hunted there; and had, moreover, long ago given names to every stream, hill, and valley of the neighbourhood'.[4] In Shortland's presence the Greenwoods agreed to an annual payment of £3 to £4 in goods if they could also occupy the next bay. After his departure, Joseph Greenwood determined to pay the rental only for as long as he deemed proper. In the meantime, Greenwood stock continued to roam across the unfenced terrain and destroy the Māori gardens, while the brothers helped themselves to timber and firewood from the bush up the valley and built stockyards.

Initially the Greenwoods lived under upturned whaleboats, then in a cottage near the beach built by Māori workmen (whom they refused to recompense), and finally in a home, built by Samuel Manson from Head of the Bay, high up a gully under Mount Evans, close to timber and fresh water but a long, weary trek from the sea. The brothers may have seemed isolated, but in fact there was considerable activity on the waters of the harbour during their residence. In 1844, for example, 23 vessels visited Port Cooper from America, Sydney and Hobart. In August *Murian*, *Terror* and *Fortitude* were all in the harbour at the same time. Whaling ships sent boats into Pūrau for fresh water. The Wellington traders *Emma*, *Eliza*, *Eleanor* and *Richmond* visited frequently.

When a vessel called, one of the Deans brothers from Riccarton usually stayed with the Greenwoods en route to collect mail at Port Levy. The Greenwood brothers themselves kept a whaleboat on the beach which they used to move about the harbour and sail around the peninsula to Akaroa when mail ships called in there.[5] A fairly common way of accessing the plains was to take the boat to the Māori settlement at Rāpaki and then cross the Port Hills on foot. There were visits to and from the Gebbies and the Mansons when they settled at Head of the Bay in 1845. The Greenwoods took cows up harbour in their whaleboat for Gebbie and Manson. Carpenters working on the Gebbie house gathered timber above Pūrau to raft up to Head of the Bay. In May 1845, Joseph Greenwood recorded in his diary that 'Hay, Sinclair came AM in the boat from Gibbies [*sic*]. It was so very foggy that they had lost their way and were unable to get here till about 9.00am having been about 4 hours on the way.'[6]

The Greenwood brothers cleared bush, developed gardens and stocked the land with sheep and cattle. They had 50 cattle by 1844. Their dairy produce was sent to Akaroa and Wellington, and they traded with the whaling boats visiting Port Cooper. Bringing in supplies and sending out produce must have been a challenge in the absence of a jetty, which was only constructed under the next ownership.

Looking across Whakaraupō Lyttelton Harbour to Pile Bay (at left), Pūrau (the large, indented bay), and Te Waipapa Diamond Harbour with Kaiorurū Church Bay on the far right, 1972.
V. C. BROWNE & SON, 14028

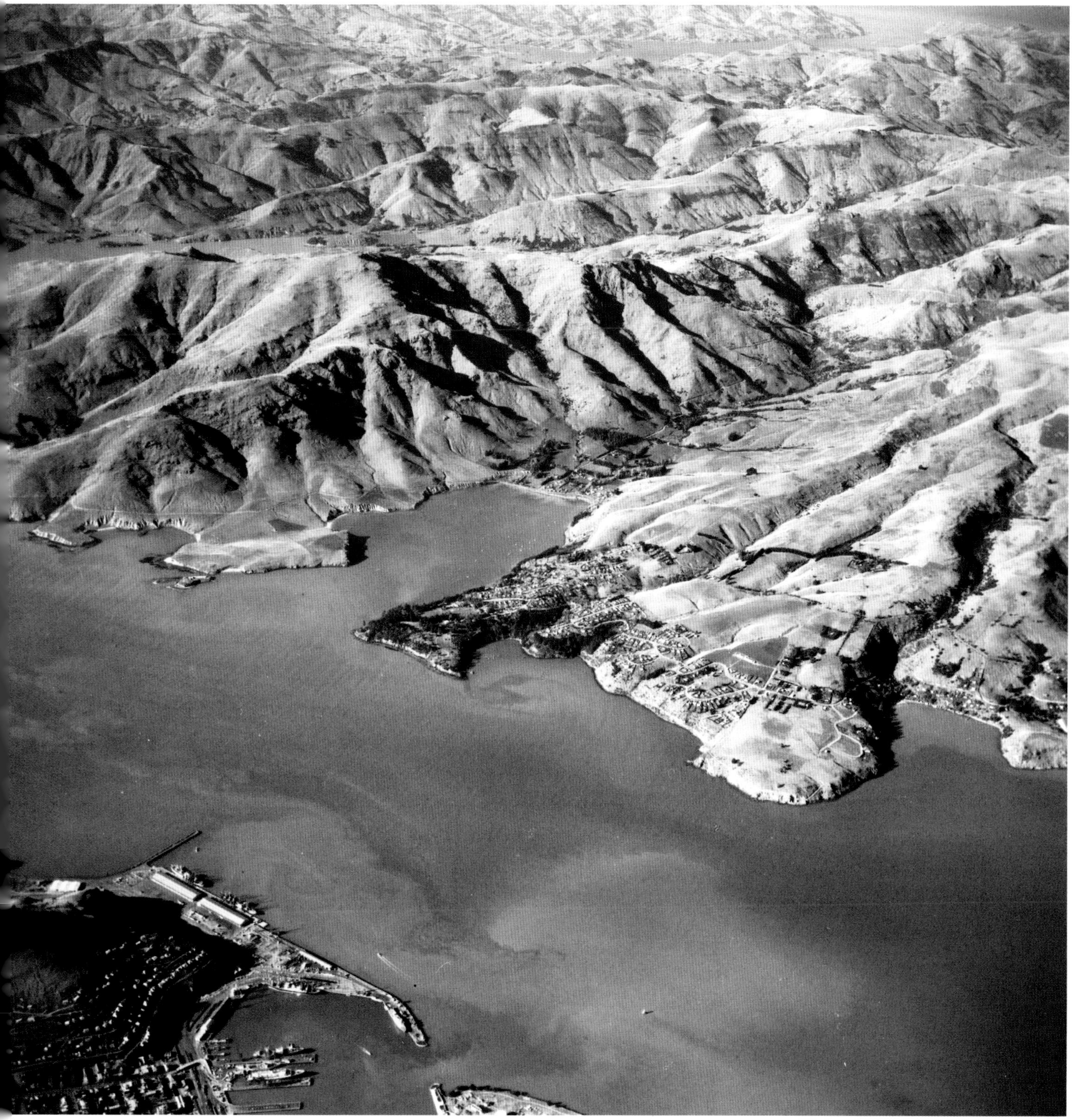

One of the brothers' biggest problems was locating stray stock. Joseph Greenwood seemed to spend much of his days searching fruitlessly for sheep and cattle. The brothers appear to have used Quail Island as a place where they could contain some of their stock, although beasts still managed to cross the tidal flats between Quail Island, Aua King Billy Island and the mainland.

Any hard-won success was undermined by an unnerving experience with the infamous Bluecap Gang. Convicts from Hobart, they arrived at Akaroa in 1846 and roamed around Banks Peninsula, eventually reaching Pūrau in July, where the Greenwood brothers gave them shelter in their own home and work sawing timber. As a reward for this hospitality, on their second evening one of the gang suddenly pointed a loaded gun at Edward Greenwood and threatened to blow his brains out. The other two gang members then pulled out pistols. They tied up James Greenwood and two servants, Joseph being absent that night. The gang then ransacked the house, drank some of the Greenwoods' wine, stole the whaleboat, which they loaded with booty, and made their getaway in the direction of Ōtokitoki Gollans Bay across the harbour. They were eventually captured in Otago, tried and sentenced to 15 years' transportation.[7] Decades later, the extended family of the Gardiner and Jackson children would get together 'to form blue cap gangs and stalk one another on the hillside'.[8]

In October 1846 Police Magistrate Robinson wrote out and witnessed a Māori lease for the brothers. Tiemi Nohomutu was the lead signatory. Robinson's successor extended the lease far beyond Pūrau to include about 25,000 hectares of the hill country around Port Cooper — for an annual rental of £8. This included the right to farm all of the Port Hills, the Whakaraupō catchment and the whole of the Te Ahu Pātiki Mount Herbert divide.[9] The Greenwoods then on-sold the lease to the Rhodes brothers of Lincolnshire — William Barnard, Robert Heaton and George — for £1710 and moved their stock north to Motunau. Joseph Greenwood was drowned off the coast shortly after the move, and James died in Sydney while buying stock. Edward, not surprisingly, returned to England.

There are many urupā or burial sites at Pūrau, a legacy of its long history of Māori occupation from the fourteenth to the twentieth centuries. This painting by Richard Aldworth Oliver from 1850 shows three dwellings and waka on the flat land just above the beach. The 1857 census showed 12 Māori living at Pūrau, growing wheat and potatoes, as well as three horses, two horned cattle and 43 pigs.
CHRISTCHURCH ART GALLERY TE PUNA O WAIWHETŪ, 83/49

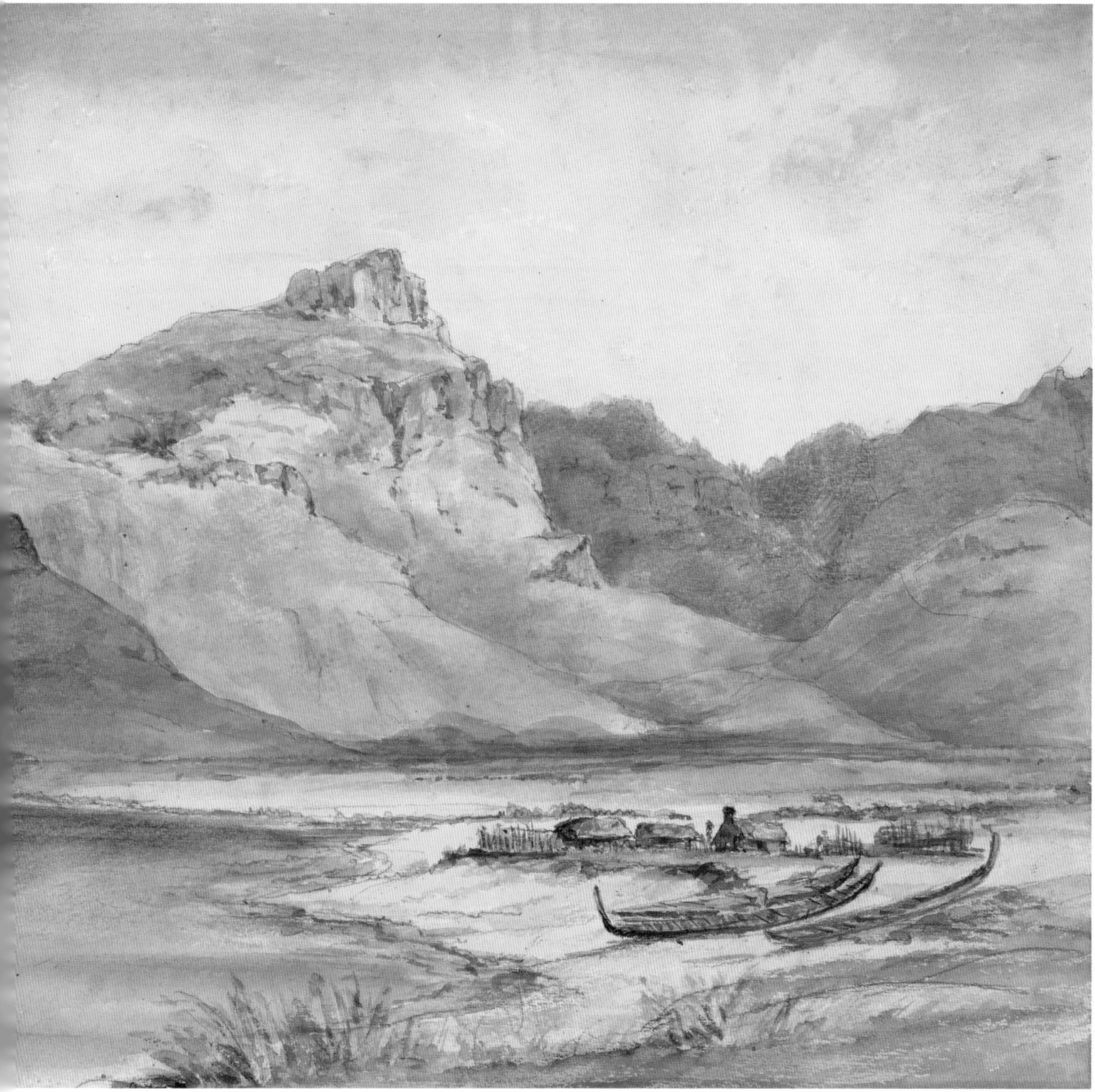

7.T

Plan of Native Reserve No 1

Situated at Purau "Acheron Bay"

Port Cooper

scale

0 1 2 3 4 5 10 15

Contents. about, 10 acres.

Octa Carrington
Surveyor,
Cavendish Bay. Port Cooper
2th July 1849.

ACHERON BAY
Kowatu
Pou

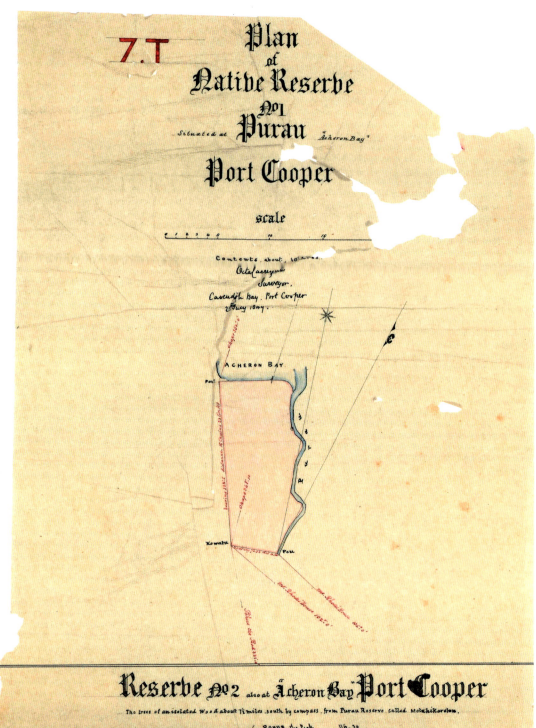

Reserve No 2 also at "Acheron Bay" Port Cooper

The trees of an isolated Wood about 1½ miles. south by compass. from Purau Reserve called Motahikarehu.

Bearings from Cairn on the Spur

POHUE, the Peak	116..30
STOMP	128°..15
OBELISK	188°..30
OHOPE, Peninsula.	351°..0

(Roll 140)

Octa Carrington
Surveyor
Cavendish Bay. Port Cooper
26th July 1849

At much the same time, the New Zealand Company was seeking suitable land for a new company settlement to be known as 'Canterbury'. Banks Peninsula and the adjacent plains fulfilled many of the necessary criteria, but for the New Zealand Company to acquire the land Māori title had to be 'extinguished' by purchase. Walter Mantell, formerly the superintendent of military roads at Porirua, was appointed commissioner for extinguishment of native claims, with the power to dictate what payment and reserves Ngāi Tahu would receive. In July 1849 Mantell arrived in Port Cooper from Wellington and joined the surveyors' camp at Cass's Bay (as it was known then). Local chief Nohomutu came to see Mantell and requested £2 million for Port Cooper with large reserves for Māori. In response Mantell offered £160 with two small reserves on a non-negotiable basis.

On 10 August 1849 the Port Cooper Deed was signed by Chief Nohomutu and 17 others. For the sum of £200, the deed transferred 'all the land and all belonging thereto' in the Port Cooper District to the queen, with the exception of 850 acres at Rāpaki and 9 acres at Pūrau. All the Pūrau gardens beyond the allotted area were to be abandoned after the current crops had been harvested. It wasn't until 1870 that the 9 acres was legally confirmed as 'Native Reserve 876 Pūrau'.[10] Ngāi Tahu not only received inadequate reserve land to support their needs, but also lost control of, and access to, their traditional mahinga kai.

According to a census in 1857 the 12 Ngāi Tahu residents in Pūrau were growing wheat and potatoes and raising three horses, two horned cattle and 43 pigs. A Survey Office map of 1860 showed five dwellings fronting the Pūrau beach to the west of the western creek. Fifty years later, only the Rāpaki kāinga remained in Whakaraupō. Tiemi Nohomutu died in 1850 and is buried in the public reserve in Pūrau along with at least 11 other Ngāi Tahu. That the reserve contains an urupā is the basis for repeated requests over the past 100 years that it come under the ownership and management of Ngāi Tahu.

Even before the Port Cooper Deed was signed, the Rhodes brothers received a grant of 450 acres in Pūrau from the New Zealand Company, plus an entitlement to graze their stock on 'unoccupied lands'.[11] The brothers farmed Pūrau from 1847 until 1874. They were astute businessmen with large land holdings on Banks Peninsula, in Timaru and in Hawke's Bay. Eventually, William Barnard Rhodes directed the family's land interests from Wellington, and George took over the running of the Levels at Timaru, while Robert Heaton Rhodes, who married Sophia Latter in 1858, remained at Pūrau — the headquarters for the brothers' peninsula operation.

In March 1848 the survey ship *Acheron* anchored at Pūrau and purchased fresh mutton from the Rhodeses' farm. The *Acheron* captain named the bay after his ship (a name only very briefly held) and Mount Evans after one of his officers (a name that stuck). Several months later, the three Canterbury Association surveyors — Captain Joseph Thomas, Thomas Cass and Charles Torlesse — arrived

A plan of the Native Reserve No. 1 situated at Pūrau (also named as Acheron Bay), Port Cooper, drawn 25 July 1849.
ARCHIVES NEW ZEALAND, CAYN 23142 CH1031 RM 149 R22857839

at Port Cooper. Torlesse noted in his journal that, having entered Port Cooper at 5.00 a.m. and anchored at 'Puru' or Rhodes Bay, the surveyors breakfasted at the Rhodeses.[12] The next morning, William Fox (by then principal agent of the New Zealand Company with a consequent interest in the Canterbury Association's choice of site for its planned settlement) and Charles Torlesse 'bathed in the stream at Puru' before heading off to walk to John Gebbie's farm at the head of the harbour. Torlesse noted that the men who did the shearing for the Rhodeses doubled as whalers during the season. Two years later, when Torlesse crossed the harbour to watch the sheep shearing at the Rhodeses' farm, the falling tide left his boat stranded and he and two friends had considerable trouble launching it.

Attracted by the prospect of a career in the new colony, young Irish lawyer Edward Ward 'became a member of the committee of the Society of Canterbury Colonists, formed in London to represent the buyers of land in dealings with the Association'.[13] Ward arrived in Lyttelton on 16 December 1850 aboard *Charlotte Jane*. Six days later, he wrote in his journal:

ABOVE The Greenwood brothers' house in Pūrau built by Samuel Manson, c.1845. The farm was sold to the Rhodes brothers in 1847. Acheron Bay was its original name, then Rhodes Bay. It then reverted to its original Māori name, Pūrau.
HOCKEN COLLECTIONS UARE TAOKA O HĀKENA, A782

BELOW The gracious Pūrau Homestead, built of reddish-brown volcanic stone in 1853/4 for Robert Heaton Rhodes and still occupied today.
JACKSON FAMILY ARCHIVE

> After service Wortley and I went in his little boat across the harbour to Pulao [Pūrau] Bay, a beautiful little land-locked inlet. There was a little level land at the upper end, but all round were high and wall-shaped hills . . . We landed and found the beach strewn with oysters, mussels and cockles. The oysters were sticking fast to the large stones. We gathered about a couple of dozen in five minutes and might easily have loaded the boat with them. We then beached the boat higher up, close by a Maori village, and walked up the hill to Mr Rhodes' station.

George Rhodes, at that time still living at Pūrau, was away, but 'his man' provided the visitors with a lunch of bread, milk and mutton. The garden was luxurious — full of thriving vegetables and fruit trees; even Indian corn and tobacco. At the end of a very hot, windless day, Wortley and Ward returned to the beach. They were grateful to the local Māori who had 'done us a real service, for as we had tied our boat, the tide had come in upon it, lifted it, and thumped it against the shore stones. They saw it bumping, unfastened it and anchored it in the sand safely.'[14]

In 1853 the Pūrau station workmen built a whare for their own accommodation using timber cut from the bush up the valley. At the end of the same year, Robert Heaton Rhodes commissioned architects Samuel Farr and C. E. Fooks to design a family home. The result was a handsome two-storeyed, gabled homestead using reddish-brown volcanic stone quarried from the surrounding hillsides and hauled down in a bullock sledge. The first house in Canterbury to be built of permanent materials, it is still occupied today. The Rhodeses also built a jetty on the east side

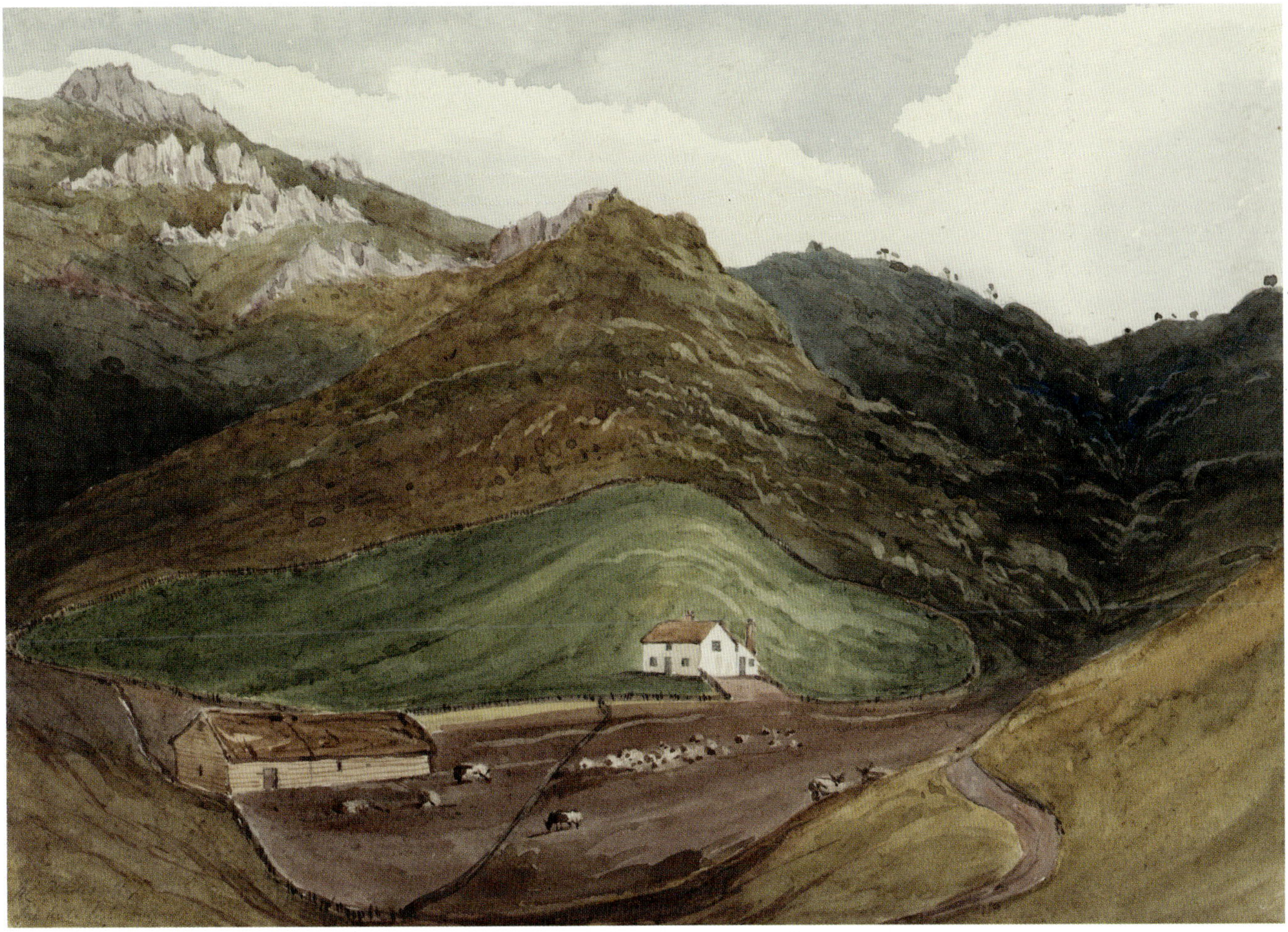

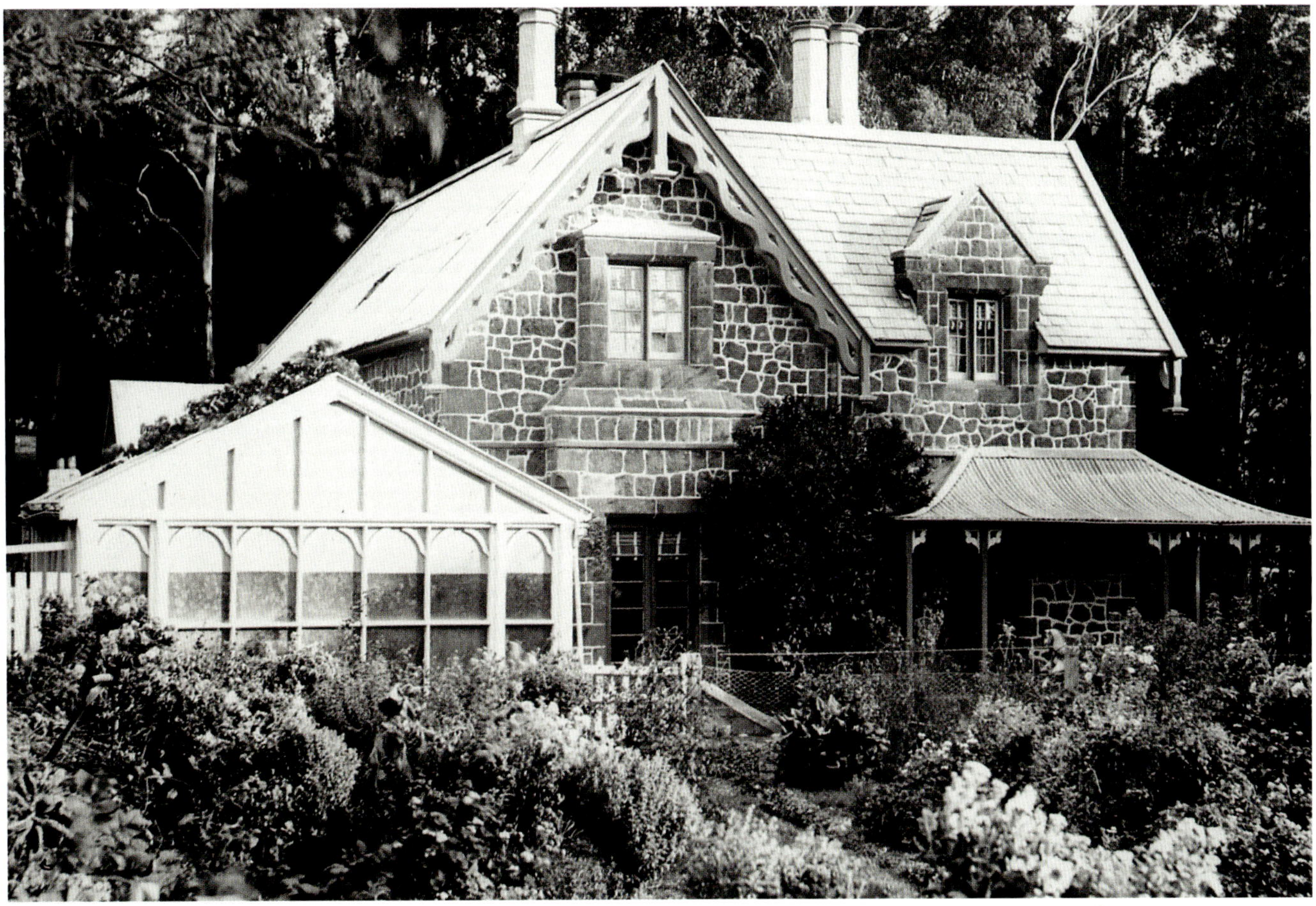

of Pūrau Bay. Unfortunately, this jetty was carried away in the 1868 tsunami that also destroyed the Mansons' 300-foot jetty at Head of the Bay. The tsunami wrecked the ketch *Georgina* in Rhodes Bay (Pūrau). The jetty must have been rebuilt, since the *Lyttelton Times* referred to it in 1882,[15] and it appears intact in a 1925 photo. The few remaining piles of this jetty are still visible today.

By 1864, with Robert Rhodes living in his newly built homestead, the Greenwood brothers' house further up the valley was rented from the Rhodeses by Thomas Woods and set up as Woods' Purau Accommodation House to service overland travellers. Travelling by horse or foot was not easy. Charles Perry Cox and his new bride planned a ride to Akaroa for their honeymoon. They travelled through Governors Bay and Head of the Bay to Pūrau, taking much longer than they had anticipated. The following day they continued on a track newly cut through the dense bush that still clothed much of the peninsula. The birds were so tame that 'a robin having hopped round us in a friendly way finally alighted on the bride's boot and had a good tug at a button there, under the impression that it was a new kind of berry!'[16]

James Ashworth drove cattle between Kaituna and Pūrau. The route took him up the back of Pūrau, over the flat plateau known as Tableland, adjacent to Mount Herbert, along the ridge and down into Kaituna Valley. 'The bush and undergrowth were so thick and tall that it joined overhead all the way.'[17] The tracks through this dense bush were mostly formed by cattle. Travellers had to watch out for wild cattle and wild pigs charging unexpectedly across the track. No wonder travel by sea was preferred.

By the late 1850s there were enough families living at Pūrau to warrant the running of a small school. George Dean took up duties as schoolmaster. George had been a silk weaver and piecer in Macclesfield. When his wife Mary Ann died in 1848, leaving George with eight children, he married Hannah Rathbone. Three years later, George and Hannah, together with seven of George's children, left England on the *Canterbury*, and arrived in Lyttelton in June 1851, taking up employment with the Rhodes brothers. George and Hannah were to have eight children of their own. With so many dependents, the 51-year-old George turned his hand to anything and everything. At various stages he was a boatman, dairy farmer, schoolteacher, hotel-keeper, store-keeper and gardener. (Despite all his income-earning efforts, George would be declared bankrupt in 1873.)

From 1851, George Dean and Charlie Walter ran a daily boat service out of Pūrau to Lyttelton. The whaleboat carried mutton or beef, dairy supplies and vegetables from the Rhodeses' garden and fresh fish caught by Māori from the Pūrau kāinga.

According to a Lyttelton resident, 'their whaleboat would cross the harbour to us from Purau laden with beef as heavily as the harbour seas allowed'. The meat was unloaded and sold on the quay. The men would then 'make the rounds of our huts and tents with fish bought from the Maoris earlier that morning and strung on flax'.[18] James Ashworth recalled:

> When the sea was calm two men were sufficient to work the boat from Purau with the meat and two experienced boatmen were kept for that purpose, but when it was rough three of Rhodes' men had to go and assist the boatmen . . . I remember one particularly rough trip when the boat got nearly swamped and I put in about two hours bailing out water with my boots.[19]

On one occasion, George Dean and Robert Ashworth were not far from the government jetty in Lyttelton when an unexpected nor'westerly gust capsized their boat. Laden with ballast, it sank with its cargo of live sheep and milk, and the men, one of whom couldn't swim, were rescued thanks only to the speedy action of local boaties.

Up to 20,000 sheep could be shorn at Pūrau, mustered and driven from as far away as Wairewa Lake Forsyth, Kaituna, and off the heights of Mount Herbert. The shearing was done by Māori from Pūrau, Port Levy, Rāpaki and elsewhere when required. James Ashworth recalled seeing as many as 200 Māori at Pūrau at one time, probably during shearing. According to Edward Dobson the wool could be delivered on board ship very cheaply. When the big wool store on the beach was full, a small craft would come in at high tide and run as far ashore as it could. The small boat would be loaded and the wool taken straight to the ship with no wharfage to pay.[20]

During the Rhodeses' tenure, Pūrau, with its gently sloping beach, became a very popular picnic spot. In January 1862, over 300 Lyttelton Sunday School children went across to Rhodes Bay by steamer and then were landed in whaleboats on the beach. They had games followed by a picnic — 'huge baskets of sandwiches, cut in the most solid proportions . . . followed by equally gigantic platters of bread and cheese, and mountains of gooseberries and currants, assisted by countless buckets of tea and fresh, sweet milk'.[21]

Not everyone had a good time at Pūrau. In 1863, brother George took up residence while Robert and his wife, Sophia, visited England. Mrs George Rhodes's sister, Mary Jane Wood, stayed with them. 'A most miserable place it is to live at. No-one ever comes near us, we can only get away by boat, and that is not pleasant at all times.'[22] Had Mary Jane Wood been staying at Pūrau in January 1872 she might have felt differently about access by sea. The fire that began in Camp Bay and threatened the settlement at Little Port Cooper came within 200 yards of the

Rhodeses' house in Pūrau. While the house was saved, the fire travelled up the valley and destroyed much of the remaining bush. From Little Port Cooper to Pūrau there was not a blade of grass left.[23]

In 1874, the Rhodes brothers, by then the foremost run-holders in New Zealand, sold Pūrau for £20,000 to Henry Dent Gardiner. Son of an Essex farmer, Henry had done well on the Australian goldfields. He arrived in New Zealand in 1855, purchasing land at Harewood, Irwell and Leeston before acquiring Pūrau as a going concern with all stock included.

Henry and his wife, Mary Ann, moved into the Rhodes homestead with nine of their children, leaving oldest son Herbert in charge at Irwell. Enterprisingly, Henry Gardiner purchased timber from the old Camp Bay quarantine station and freighted it around to Pūrau by sea in the Deanses' boat. The timber was likely used to enlarge the woolshed down at the beach. A wooden addition to the stone house was designed by Christchurch architect Alfred Luttrell in 1910. The Pūrau estate thrived. Henry added to his acreage by leasing the Adderley Head Reserve from the Education Department. Soon there were at least six dairies on Gardiner land. With his sons Herbert, Linton, Harold and Frank, Henry also cleared what remained of the bush at the head of the valley and planted cocksfoot.

Waterman Charlie Walter lived in a hut near the Pūrau homestead yards. Travellers from Port Levy and the eastern peninsula bays would leave their horses in the paddock by the wharf and be taken across to Lyttelton in Charlie's boat. Later Frank Gardiner recalled seeing up to 40 horses in the paddock at one time.

Meanwhile, access to still relatively isolated Pūrau continued to improve. A steep stock route to Charteris Bay (present-day Bay View Road) was built by George Stinson and his team in the 1870s. In the early 1890s the old track from Pūrau over the hill to Port Levy was upgraded to a road. As early as 1873, Thomas Potts had presented a petition from the residents of Banks Peninsula to the provincial council asking for a public jetty at Pūrau. Finally a new, deeper-water wharf was built on the Diamond Harbour side of the bay in the early 1890s. This was welcome because the only land route out of Pūrau around the harbour continued to be the old, high stock route, which could be treacherous in wet weather.

The new wharf enabled better transportation of farm produce and people. A regular service from Pūrau to Lyttelton began, with the steam launches *Purau*, *Canterbury*, *Waiwera*, *Monica*, *Cygnet*, *John Anderson* and later *Matariki* all working the route. Each summer, *John Anderson* would bring workers across to help cut the large quantities of cocksfoot grown in the Upper Gully at Pūrau. At the end of the season, bagged cocksfoot seed would be piled high on the decks of the steamer for the trip to Lyttelton. Andrew Anderson, the boat proprietor, used to bring parties over by launch for the dances in the woolshed. He would sleep on the boat at the wharf and in the early hours of the morning would return them to

Lyttelton. He ran *Matariki* twice a week to Pūrau in the later years when *Purau* and *John Anderson* were no longer used.[24]

The dances were legendary. In August 1919, the *Press* reported that the 'bachelors of Purau and Camp Bay gave a most enjoyable dance on Friday night in Mr F. R. H. Gardiner's wool store at Purau'.[25] The hall was decorated with orange and red streamers, native greenery and Chinese lanterns. In the sitting area, two large tree ferns suspended from the ceiling were 'most effective'. Romantic bowers were created using wool twined with flowers and shrubs. All the houses in the bay were full of overnighting guests, who would enjoy a big picnic the following day. 'There were always people staying at Purau. Shooting parties, cards and talk, boating and picnicking and dances. People stayed for weeks, sometimes for years.'[26]

On much-anticipated 'boat night' (Wednesday and Saturday) the Pūrau gigs, plus the Hunters' from Church Bay, would gather at the wharf to collect mail, newspapers and a variety of goods and provisions. The steam launch would return to Lyttelton with wool, cheese, sheepskins and livestock. School teacher Eleanor Isherwood recalled driving 'Lincoln, faithful, useful, ancient steed, in the "shandydan" loaded with gory, dirty, smelly sheepskins'.[27] On arrival at the wharf she helped transfer them into the boat.

Frank Jackson, who was born in 1919, recalled:

> The mail launch used to sail into Purau jetty at about 8.20 each weekday morning, to deliver mail, bread and papers and to pick up passengers. Also on three days a week to take the residents boxes to Bundy's at Lyttelton. These boxes were locked and Bundy's held the second key to each. Inside would be a list of requirements such as meat, fruit and groceries, toiletries from the chemist etc and these would all be assembled and come back in the box on the evening sailing at 5.00 p.m.

'Boat night' at Pūrau. Gigs from the Pūrau Homestead, The Kaik and Fern Glen would wait at the jetty to collect mail, goods and visitors. On the left is Eleanor Isherwood with Lynley Jackson waiting to collect the mail.
JACKSON FAMILY ARCHIVE

> On box days everyone arrived at the wharf in their buggies, wagons and gigs and this was an exciting occasion. These were also the days when town or the Addington sale was visited and people arrived and departed. There always seemed to be plenty of visitors as the homes in the Bay were noted for their hospitality, the girls for their beauty and friendliness and the young men for their eligibility.[28]

The boxes were carefully transferred from the carts onto a trolley, which ran on rails to the end of the jetty. The Jackson box was full of layers of eggs, each in a frame, and pounds of fresh butter to balance the grocery bill.

As the Rhodeses had been, the Gardiners were very generous with recreational access to the bay. Big retail firms in Christchurch organised annual picnics for their staff, chartering a boat to take them to Pūrau for the day. Christchurch schools went to Pūrau for their annual picnic. The logistics were startling. For example, in December 1899, 750 students, teachers and friends of Sydenham School travelled across to Pūrau on *Jane Douglas* and *John Anderson*. The 250 employees of the *Press*, with their families and the Stanmore Band, travelled across on *Canterbury* and *Waiwera* in March 1900. The band entertained the picnickers throughout the day. Large gum trees at the beach provided shade, and coppers and tanks to hold water were set up under the trees. George Dean and Jack Harris were the custodians of the coppers.

Sometimes the little boats that plied the harbour served a sad purpose. Lynley Galbraith (née Jackson) recalled her father's sudden death in 1923:

> When my father died, Aunt Emily came up to take me home to stay at Purau house. I can never forget their kindness in helping me over those days. I was up in the top garden when I saw the launch carrying my father on his last journey out of Purau. The flag was flying at half-mast and it was a calm, sunny day. The two waves from the wake spread right out across the bay and touched the headlands as it passed out into the harbour. Just as we had watched it many times together.[29]

Pūrau was also a base for army manoeuvres, involving groups such as the Christchurch Volunteers, Mounted Rifles and Naval Volunteers. The high country between Pūrau, Camp Bay and Rhodes Monument was used for reconnoitring, outpost duty and mock battles, with gun practice at Fort Jervois on nearby Rīpapa Island. A camp would be pitched on the Gardiner estate, within a chain of the high water mark. At the 1893 Easter encampment, between 70 and 80 bell tents stood in rows, with the brigade officers' and company officers' tents at the rear. The camp was sheltered by walnut and gum trees and had easy access to the freshwater stream.

ABOVE A crowded SS *John Anderson* approaching the 'new' Pūrau wharf built in the early 1890s on the west side of the bay.
CANTERBURY MUSEUM, CHARLES BEKEN COLLECTION, 1980.244.1

BELOW Pūrau became a popular destination for large picnic parties. Mature trees near the beach provided shade, and coppers and tanks were set up underneath them to hold water. Here members of the Lyttelton Fire Brigade and their families enjoy a picnic in the bay.
MACMILLAN BROWN LIBRARY, WISHA AND BARRY BOWATER AND HELEN MCKELVEY, 157287

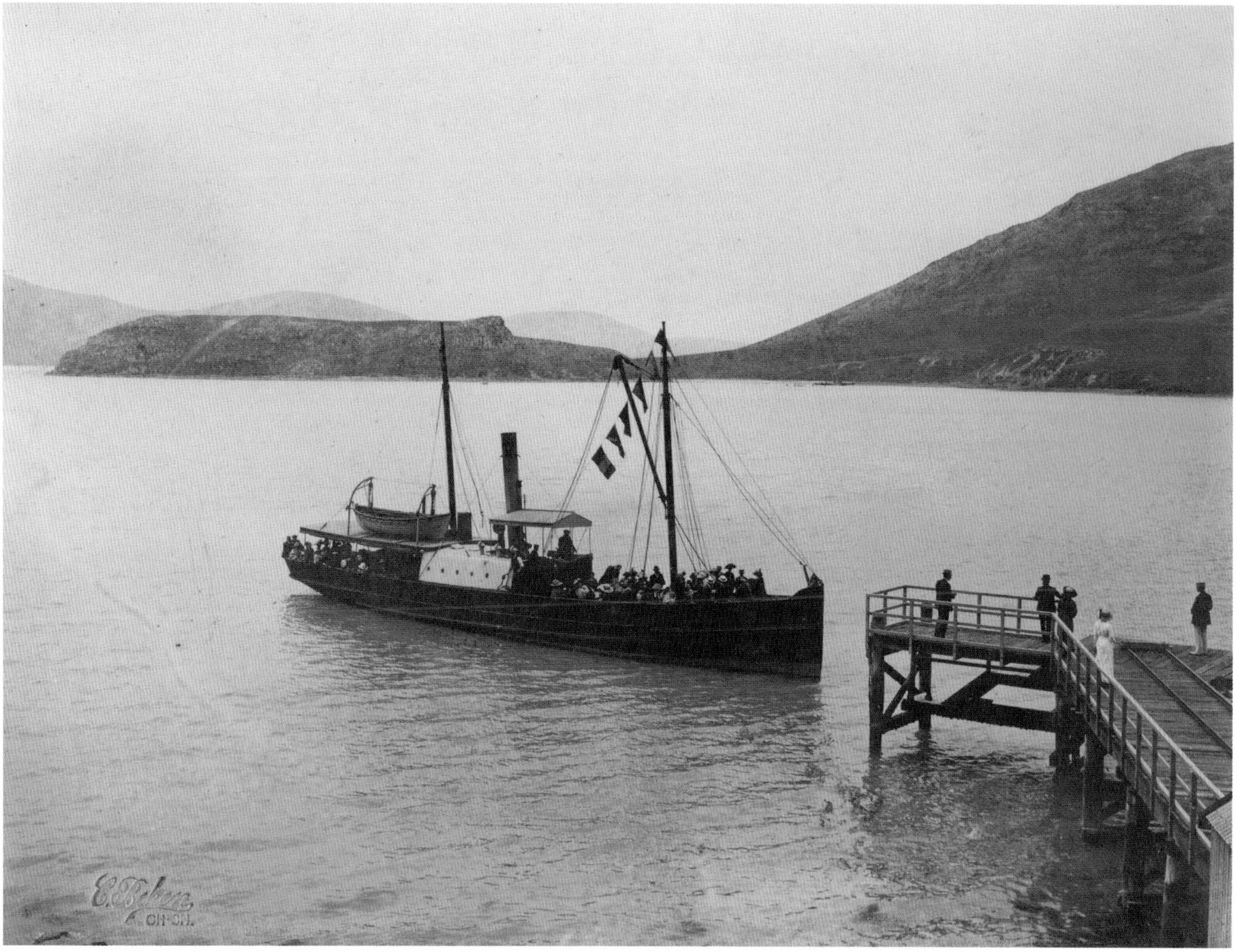

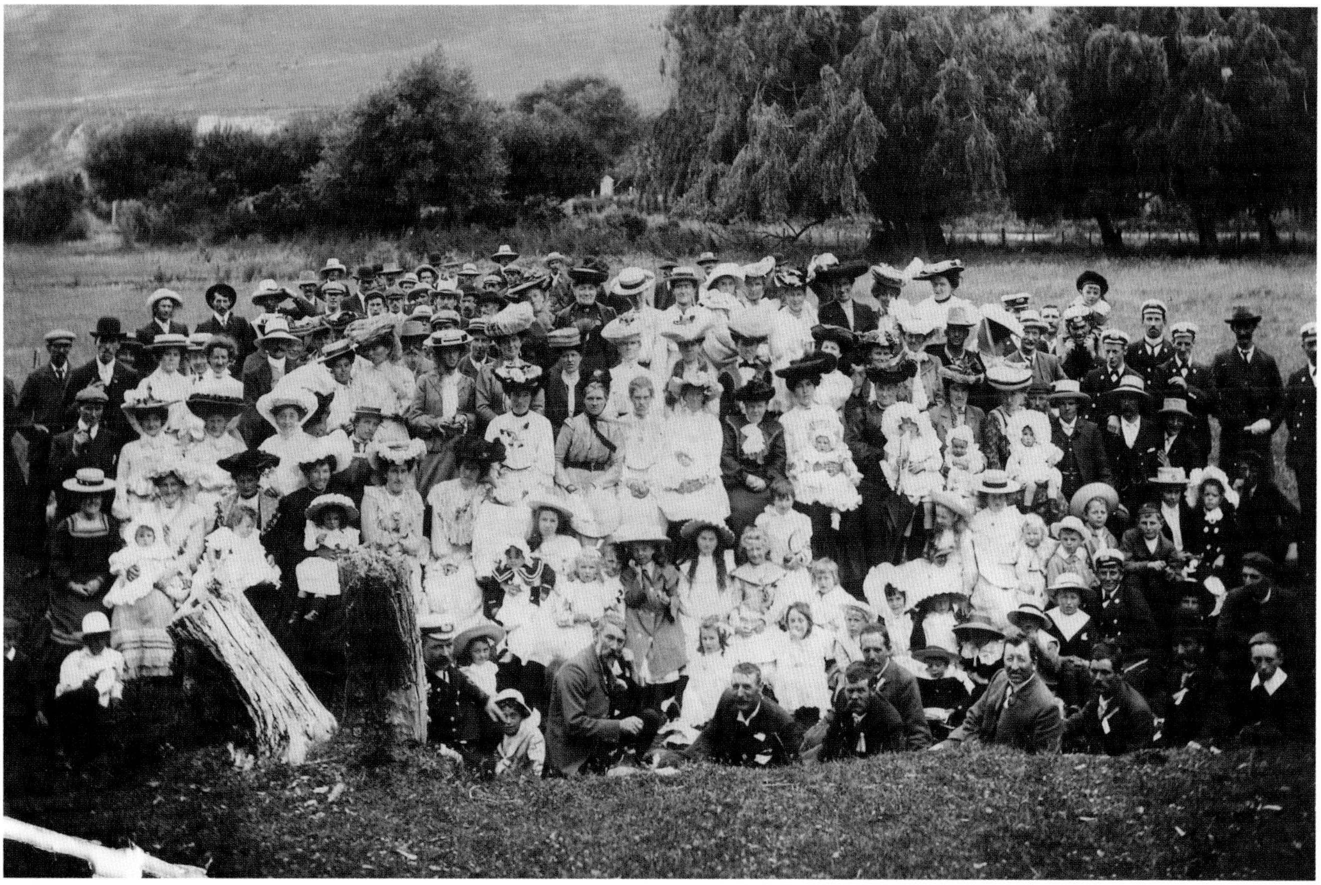

The logistics of getting 650 men to Pūrau (or Rhodes Bay as it was still sometimes called) were interesting. As always, the tide determined access. The Lyttelton Navals and the N. Battery Artillery crossed the harbour in the defence launch, arriving in camp shortly before 9 p.m. However, the main body of troops, along with their baggage, had to be transhipped from the tug to launches in order to access the jetty in a falling tide. It was midnight before all the men were in camp.[30]

The tide also affected recreational pursuits. On 16 April 1892, members of the Wharf Labourers' and Lumpers' Association of Lyttelton held a monster picnic on the Gardiner estate. Over 800 mostly women and children were taken across to 'Rhodes Bay' by the steam tug *Lyttelton* (lent by the harbour board). 'The tug had to make two trips, and upon the last was compelled to land her freight at Diamond Harbour owing to the tide being out.'[31]

Henry Gardiner retired to Christchurch in 1890, and Pūrau was divided into three blocks. Frank took over the homestead block, and Harold farmed the block known as The Kaik. Linton took the block named Fern Glen, but moved to a run in north Canterbury after his marriage, leaving Fern Glen to be worked by managers, with John Hunter from Church Bay filling this position between 1905 and 1918. In 1905, Harry Jackson and his wife, Henrietta (Henry Gardiner's youngest daughter), moved into Fern Glen homestead and, in partnership with Linton Gardiner, farmed the 2300 acres of reserve land at Adderley Head. When the Education Reserve was divided into four farms for returned servicemen, Harry Jackson bought Linton Gardiner's block at Pūrau.[32]

In the early twentieth century, Pūrau had its own school purpose-built by Mark Dean on land donated by Harold Gardiner. Eleanor Isherwood was appointed schoolmistress in 1905, a position she held for 20 years. Her pupils included children from the Jackson and Gardiner families, children of local farm workers, and John Hunter's children, who walked around the old stock road from Church Bay.

Miss Isherwood, an inspired teacher decades ahead of her time, raised money to build a bathing shed and shark-proof swimming enclosure at the beach for the children. On warm summer afternoons classes were held in the summerhouse at the corner of the garden, and nature studies dominated the curriculum. At shearing time the children could see, from the school, thousands of sheep milling about on the beach road waiting to be shorn at the woolshed and later, at the jetty, the wool bales being loaded onto *Matariki* for the trip to Lyttelton. Fat lambs were taken out on *John Anderson*. On Sundays the schoolroom was used for a church service. The Reverend T. M. Curnow would travel across by steamer from Lyttelton, take the service, and then walk up the old road to Diamond Harbour or set off on horseback to repeat the process at Port Levy. With the closure of the school in 1925, children at Pūrau were taught by the Correspondence School until 1945, when a school opened at Diamond Harbour.

ABOVE Teacher Eleanor Isherwood outside the Pūrau School. Miss Isherwood was appointed teacher in 1905 and remained there for 20 years, much loved by all her pupils and highly valued by their parents.
JACKSON FAMILY ARCHIVE

BELOW Pupils at Pūrau School in 1906. From left: Alan, Ada, unknown, Edna, Bessie, Beattie, Ted Henderson, Buller and Thelma.
JACKSON FAMILY ARCHIVE

Lynley Galbraith, daughter of Harry and Henrietta Jackson, remembered returning home to Pūrau following a visit to a farm near Ashburton. Lynley, who was five, and her brother Alan were put on the train to Christchurch. From there they caught the train to Lyttelton, where they crossed the rail tracks to the boat. However, something had gone wrong with the arrangements and the two children were stranded on the wharf at night with no one to take them across the harbour. Finally, a Mr Grennell, who was on his way by sea to Port Levy, offered to drop Lynley and Alan at Pūrau. From the jetty they had a long walk home in pitch dark.[33]

In January 1916 Frank and Harold Gardiner approached Lyttelton Harbour Board about the possibility of installing a sheep race at the Pūrau jetty. The brothers wanted to ship their sheep by boat and train instead of driving them overland as previously.[34] At the time, they were using a portable race made in sections to lay along the jetty. Whether the harbour board acted on this request is unclear. The advent of a truck service from Christchurch to the peninsula in the 1920s meant the end of double handling by sea and the beginning of a decline in the demand for the steam launches.

Land transport was boosted in the 1930s when Depression workmen built the roads eastwards from Pūrau to Camp Bay and westwards to Diamond Harbour and Charteris Bay. The men were housed in a large encampment above the beach at Pūrau. Their meals were prepared in the Pūrau House cookshop by the beach. Meanwhile, the twice-weekly launch service to Pūrau ceased in the 1930s. However, petrol rationing during the Second World War meant that once again most visitors arrived at the Diamond Harbour jetty and walked down to Pūrau.

As the condition of the Pūrau jetty deteriorated, the harbour board questioned its future usefulness. A report from the harbour master in October 1952 recommended that the jetty be demolished or its use discontinued.[35] The Mount Herbert County Council expressed its 'dismay' at the proposal. Pūrau residents challenged the assertion that the jetty was little used.

The road connecting Pūrau and Diamond Harbour was constructed in the 1930s. The 'second' jetty, built in the early 1890s, is just visible in the foreground.
CANTERBURY MUSEUM, W. A. TAYLOR COLLECTION, 1968.213.4114

> I can assure you that in the summer months it is a very popular spot
> for small craft and I am sure there would be many disappointed
> Sportsmen were this facility taken from them. We ourselves have
> at least four large parties of Scouts and Sea Cadets camping on our
> property each year — their gear always coming via Pūrau wharf.
> Hiking parties are also frequently landed or picked up there.[36]

Early the following year, the secretary for marine informed the Mount Herbert County Council that the estimated cost of repairing the Pūrau jetty would be £1860. The harbour board decided that the expenditure was not warranted and the wharf would be demolished. However, if the council were to take over responsibility for

the jetty, which would include ensuring the structure was safe, then its use could be continued; as the board put in a letter to the council, 'It is apparent there is still quite substantial use of both wharves' (the other wharf being Port Levy, which was also under demolition order).[37] Despite their dismay, the county council must have declined the offer. However, no demolition occurred, because a memo dated 16 January 1962 from the harbour board engineer-in-chief reads, 'Pūrau Jetty: The Board has confirmed its decision, made in February 1953, that Pūrau jetty be demolished. Please complete this work as early as convenient.'[38]

Somewhere during 1962 the jetty gained a reprieve, because in November that year plans were drawn up for its repair. Pūrau was becoming a sought-after location for mooring yachts, with the new harbour board swing moorings preferred to the early pole moorings near Stoddart Point. About 1970, a concrete boat ramp was constructed, enabling boaties to launch their craft from trailers. Despite its deceptively sheltered aspect, Pūrau was not immune from the vagaries of the harbour seas. In 1974 a huge sea surge struck the bay, tearing 13 boats from their moorings and driving them ashore. Yacht owners who moored their craft in the bay also needed a place to store and launch their dinghies. It seems that plans for a dinghy shelter and floating pontoon were abandoned in favour of a now much-photographed dinghy ramp constructed on the repaired jetty around 1980.

In the meantime, the foreshore land was subdivided for cottages. The old picnic grounds were sold to Fred Mackey from Church Bay. Fred burned the remains of the old gum trees on the site, cleared the land and grew tomatoes, strawberries, asparagus and daffodils. One year the creek flooded and buried all the tomatoes. During one of the many storms, Fred's daughter Mary remembers her dad rowing the children up the drive in a dinghy. Daughter Marion remembers hurrying to complete jobs at home in the morning in order to go water skiing with friends at Wreck Bay, near Rīpapa Island, later in the day. The popular Purau Motor Camp was established by the Gullifords in the early 1960s, offering families an affordable holiday that was not far from Christchurch and adjacent to a sheltered, child-safe beach. By 2008 it could accommodate up to 500 people; but sadly, in 2009, rising costs forced Ric and Aileen Ginders to close the business.

Today, because many visitors go no further than the café at Diamond Harbour, Pūrau remains a charming, peaceful and unspoiled bay in which to enjoy the harbour hills and sea.

Pūrau jetty with its much-photographed dinghies.
JANE ROBERTSON

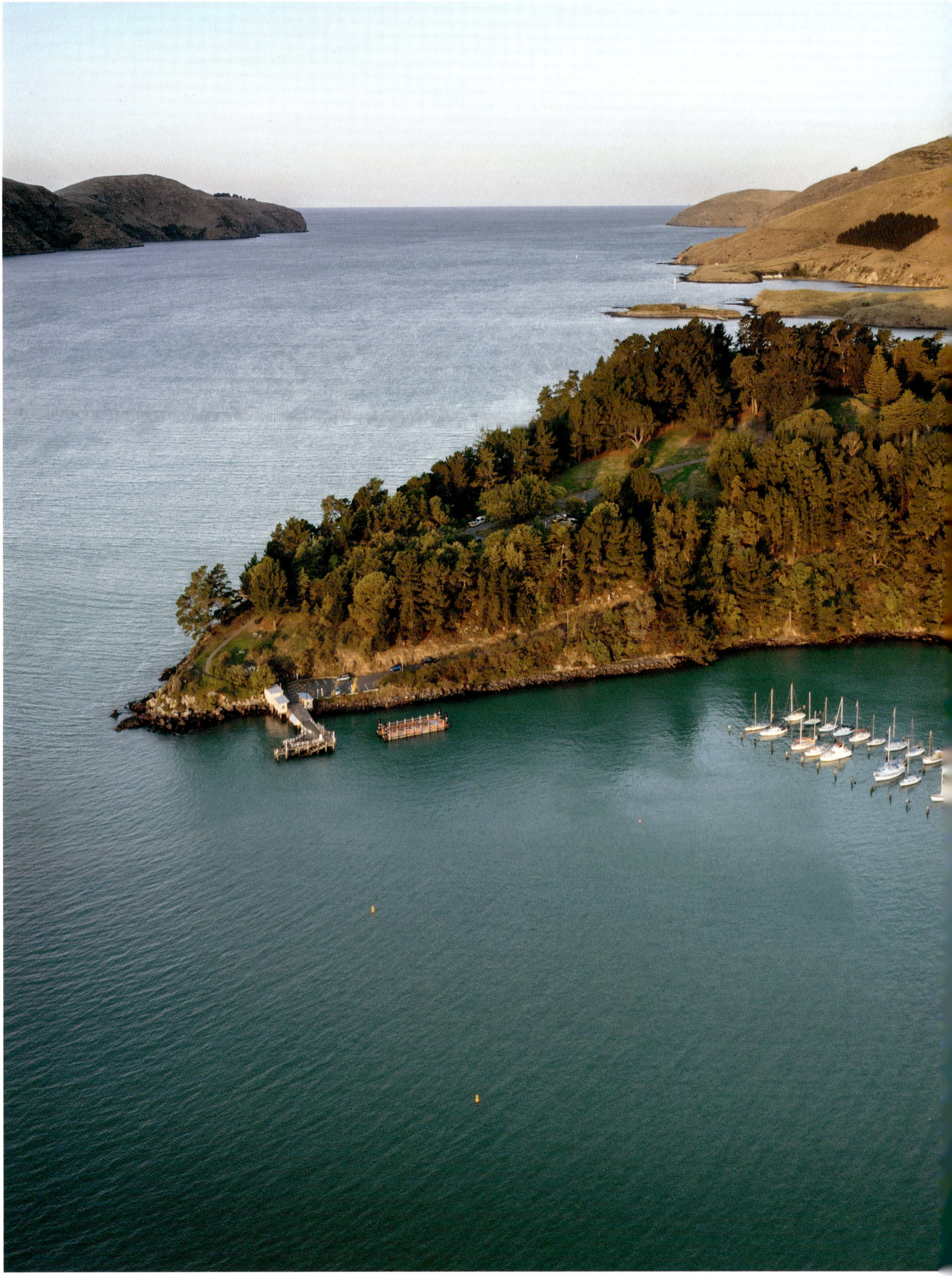

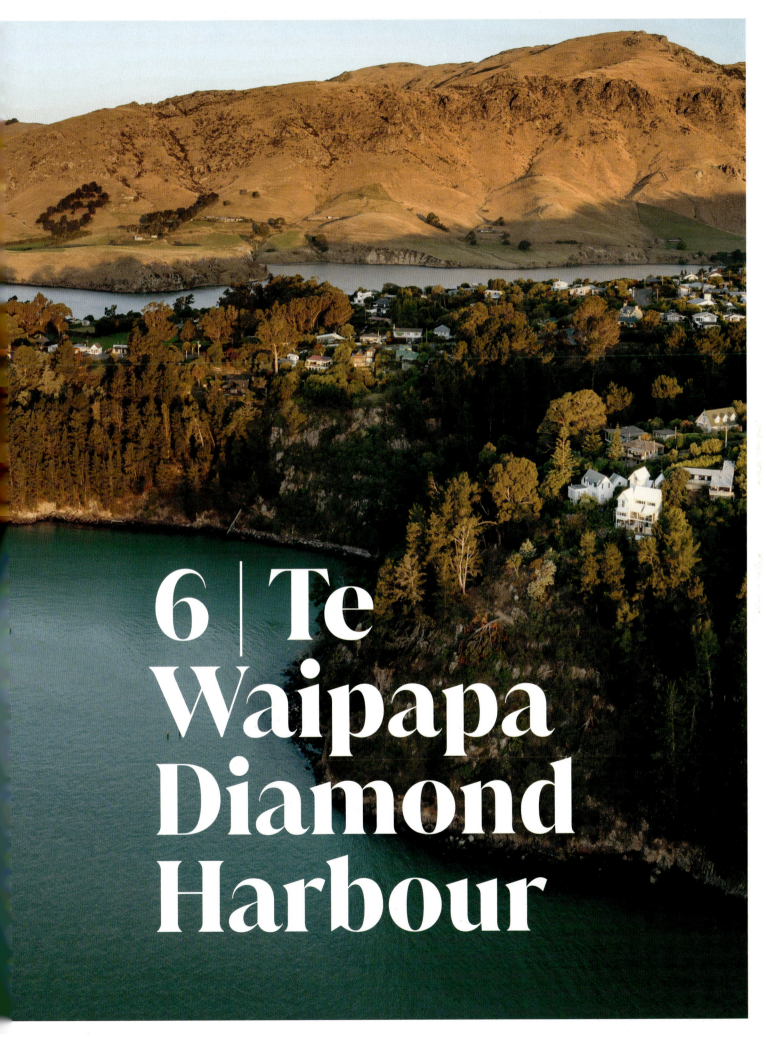

6 | Te Waipapa Diamond Harbour

Once, steam launches criss-crossed Whakaraupō Lyttelton Harbour servicing the little settlements on its southern and western fringes. Today, with the exception of summer trips to Ōtamahua Quail Island, Te Waipapa Diamond Harbour is the only settlement with a regular ferry service catering for local residents and visitors. Diamond Harbour can also boast the longest-surviving, albeit very heavily modified, outlying jetty in continuous use.

*

Recognising how sheltered it was from the south and east, Māori named the little bay Te Waipapa or 'flat water'. With the significant Māori settlement just over Upoko o Kurī Stoddart Point at Pūrau, the steep and rocky shores of Te Waipapa must have been a good place for gathering kūtai or toretore (mussels) and pāua.

From 1844 till 1847, the Greenwood brothers rented Upoko o Kurī from the Pūrau Māori. In September 1850, as part of the Canterbury Association settlement, The Reverend Robert Bateman Paul purchased 50 acres in the area, promptly reselling it to Mark Pringle Stoddart in 1852. Youngest son of an admiral, Stoddart was born and educated in Edinburgh. He went to sea at age 18 and eventually bought a sheep station in Victoria, Australia, before choosing to move to a more temperate climate. Stoddart's friend E. M. Templar had already chartered the ship *Australasia* to carry 2000 sheep to New Zealand. Stoddart joined him with his own mob of sheep, arriving in Port Cooper in January 1851, when the first four Canterbury Association ships bringing settlers to the colony were still at anchor in the harbour.

Stoddart gradually added freehold blocks to his original 50-acre landholding. These purchases included Ōtamahua, Aua King Billy Island, and the adjacent peninsula, Moepuku. Stoddart sold Ōtamahua to friend Thomas Potts of Governors Bay in 1862. Diamond Harbour holdings were managed by Stoddart's cousin Mark Sprot for some years, with Stoddart himself taking up residence probably in the late 1850s. We can date the construction of the original Diamond Harbour jetty with reasonable accuracy because, invited to the bay in April 1857, Dr Matthew Morris described tying up at 'a decent little pier'.[1] This simple jetty was built by John Grubb, at Mark Stoddart's expense, though it was used as much by the local public as by the Stoddart family.

It seems Stoddart and Sprot lived initially in a small cottage on the western point of Upoko o Kurī, just above this jetty. The cottage was close to a signal staff and the two men provided an important service for the port before the signal station was built on Adderley Head.

The cottage built for Mark Sprot and Mark Stoddart and later home to waterman Tom Wyman, who sold vegetables and fruit to ships moored off Diamond Harbour and provided a boat service when needed. The photo was taken in 1897 shortly before the derelict cottage was dismantled. Margaret Stoddart sits in the foreground.
CANTERBURY MUSEUM, STODDART ALBUM, 2015.114.6

To his Honor the Superintendent . . .

We have now for upwards of four years performed the duties of Signal Masters communicating to the public and the Harbour Master the appearance of vessels off the Heads . . . using our own telescopes and keeping in repair the flags &c. From this date [14 May 1862] it will be impossible for us to do these duties . . . having removed to a considerable distance from the Signal Staff to a situation commanding a very indifferent view of the entrance to the Harbour . . . We would let the house at the Signal Staff to the Government . . . The rent of the house would be £60 a year — the use of a jetty-crane, moorings &c included.

Stoddart and Sprot.[2]

Instead of government signal staff, waterman Thomas Wyman moved into the cottage. Operating a one-man rowing and sailing boat, Wyman took goods and people to and from Diamond Harbour. He supplied fresh fruit and vegetables to the newly arrived ships that sheltered from sou'westerly gales in 'Mr Stoddart's Bay'. He also did labouring and carting jobs for the Stoddart family. 'Waterman's

Cottage', as it became known, was demolished in the late 1890s and its timber reused by the Hunter family in Church Bay.

In November 1864 a road to the jetty, connecting it to higher, flat land at the top of Stoddart Point, replaced what must previously have been an informal track, the scene of a near-fatal accident in March 1861. The steamer *Avon* had discharged its load at the jetty and a man named Eaglesome was carting some iron gates and fencing up the track for Stoddart and Sprot. Agitated by the rattling of the iron, the horse started towards the cliff edge. Eaglesome was knocked over by the cart, which ran over his chest, breaking ribs. The horse, cart and load were 'precipitated over the cliff, and were at once crushed and shattered into atoms beneath'. The driver was said to be 'in a fair way of recovery'.[3]

This account highlights just how difficult it must have been to transport the building materials required for Mark Stoddart's family home. On a stock-buying trip to Australia in 1861, Stoddart had purchased a prefabricated cottage (to which he later added a front section built from local matai and tōtara). The cottage was assembled in time for his wedding to Anna Barbara Schjott in February 1862. Anna was a Norwegian clergyman's daughter who had come to New Zealand as a companion/governess. The wedding was in Okains Bay, where Anna was living. Local — though somewhat unlikely — legend has 43-year-old Stoddart and best man Thomas Potts walking from Lyttelton Harbour to Okains Bay on the day of the wedding. Fortunately, Mark and Anna sailed back to Diamond Harbour for their honeymoon.

The Stoddarts planted an extensive vegetable garden and orchard at their new cottage. They used kelp from the bay to fertilise their fruit trees, and shells from Pūrau to pave the garden paths. They also dredged oysters at Pūrau, fished from the Diamond Harbour jetty and gathered shellfish nearby. Like most of the early settler families in the harbour they would have been largely self-sufficient in terms of food. Water for the garden and house was captured in two dams constructed by Mark Stoddart and in a brick storage tank.

Produce from the orchard and vegetable gardens was sold at Lyttelton, shipped to Dunedin or sold to passing ships. The family also sold wool, sheepskins, live fat lambs and slaughtered sheep and cross-bred Cotswold rams. Eucalypts for fencing and hurdles were grown and sold at Lyttelton.[4] All of these goods would have gone out by sea, so Stoddart's jetty would have been a busy point of departure and arrival.

Mark and Anna Stoddart had seven children: Mark (who died aged two), Frances, Margaret, James, Mary, Agnes and John. Even with a young family, Mark continued to travel. In April 1866 he, Anna, Frances and Margaret sailed to Britain and stayed for at least 18 months. Stoddart Cottage was advertised for rent, with James Allen in charge of the estate. Prospective tenants were assured that 'the market boat, from Lyttelton, calls two or three times a week'.[5]

ABOVE Mark Stoddart, his wife, Anna, and children Frances, Margaret and James in Diamond Harbour, 10 March 1871.
CANTERBURY MUSEUM, STODDART COLLECTION, 1991.113.3

BELOW View of the Camerons' ballast jetty, Diamond Harbour. The quarry supplied ballast for ships visiting Lyttelton, and operated between the 1860s and the 1880s.
CANTERBURY MUSEUM, STODDART ALBUM, 2015.114.88

There was a second jetty in Diamond Harbour. Today all that remains of the Cameron brothers' ballast quarry and jetty are a couple of wharf piles, a hollowed-out cliff face and a narrow, rock-strewn foreshore — all visible, if you know where to look, from the present Diamond Harbour jetty.

In the early decades of the new Canterbury settlement, sailing ships that discharged their cargo at Lyttelton port might not have a return cargo to load. Empty or lightly cargoed ships had to load up with rocks to keep themselves stable on return journeys. There was no shortage of potential ballast in rocky Whakaraupō; it just had to be extracted. Diamond Harbour and Church Bay, sheltered from southerly gales and ground swell, became the first main sources of ballast.

On Mark Stoddart's land there was the seaward end of a broad lava stream flowing down from the summit of Te Ahu Pātiki Mount Herbert. The rock, known as trachyte dolerite, broke partly in flakes and partly in prismatic blocks and was much in demand for ballast. At some point Lyttelton businessmen and brothers John and Peter Cameron opened a wide, hard-rock quarry at this cliff face. The Cameron brothers had fingers in several colonial pies. In January 1861 they enlarged their already thriving retail business by opening a drapery, clothing and provision store, known as 'The Exhibition Mart', on Lyttelton's Norwich Quay.[6] In 1869 they expanded their lighter fleet, made up of the schooners *Streamlet* and *William*, by purchasing the steam lighters *Mullogh* and *Novelty*. The lighters transported goods between larger ships and the wharves.[7] In a complementary business, the Camerons began, in the early 1860s, supplying visiting ships with ballast from 'Mr Stoddart's quarry', which soon became known as 'Cameron's quarry'. In 1876 they purchased the paddle tug SS *Titan* to carry passengers to and from harbour bays. Peter Cameron was also publican of the Robin Hood Hotel, which from 1859 onwards was pretty much the employment agency for waterfront labour.

Quarrymen often worked high up on cliff faces in the ballast quarries, balancing on a rope-suspended board. They would blast the rock, which then had to be broken down to manageable size on the ground, lifted into barrows and wheeled out (in the case of Cameron's quarry) along the jetty to a waiting ballast craft. It was a slow, heavy and dangerous job. Whether a result of the danger inherent in the job or because the Cameron brothers, with their multiple business interests, were not the most assiduous employers, there were two deaths at the quarry in close succession in 1879.

The first accident, on 30 July, involved quarryman James Payne (whose name was associated with another quarry on the headland between Diamond Harbour and Church Bay). Payne was working with two others making a hole for blasting

Born in the Shetland Islands in 1836, whaler Gideon Henderson emigrated to New Zealand in 1874 with his second wife, Barbara, and seven children. He worked hard to establish a farm high above Diamond Harbour, rowing farm produce to the port in all weathers. Four more children were born in New Zealand.
DHHA

a large block of stone. Without warning the stone came adrift and crashed down on him, crushing his legs and lower body. He died almost immediately, leaving a large family.[8] (Payne's widow, Christina, gave birth to a daughter a few months later.) The second accident happened just a week after the first. Charles Plasted, a new arrival in the country, was quarrying stone with a bar when a rock on which he was standing slipped and carried him down with it. As he fell, a second stone rolled onto the lower part of his body, crushing him badly. His fellow workmen got him into a boat to take him across to Lyttelton, but he died on the water. He left a widow and five children.[9] It may have been that these deaths, as well as changes in the nature of shipping and cargoes, precipitated the closure of the quarry, since the wharf was little used after the 1880s.

The ballast craft that took the rock from the quarry jetty to ships at the port were solidly built, ketch-rigged vessels of up to 25 tons. About 30 feet long and 10 feet in beam, they were built of hardwood coated with coal tar.[10] Though poorly regarded by those with 'superior' boats, the tough little ballast craft had their own moment of glory in the New Year's Day Lyttelton Regatta. The sailing race for ballast boats offered a first prize of £20, no small sum. In January 1875, James Payne's cutter *Christina* came first by about six minutes, with C. Fisher's ketch *Rambler* second and the ketch *Diligent* third.[11]

The Henderson family followed the pattern of other Shetland Islanders (accustomed to a life dominated by the sea) who had already settled in and around Lyttelton Harbour. Gideon Henderson was born in 1836 at the Biggins on Papa Stour in the remote Shetland Islands. Life on Shetland was hard, with some 8000 islanders emigrating between 1861 and 1881. Gideon, who was a whaler, joined this exodus in 1874 with his second wife, Barbara (sister to Eliza Hunter of Church Bay), and their four children, as well as Gideon's three children from his first marriage to Christina Tait. A further four children were born in New Zealand.

Gideon initially worked in Lyttelton on the construction of Gladstone Pier and a breakwater for the port. But the confines of Lyttelton's west side were unappealing, and the family moved to make a living off the land on the other side of the harbour. Living first in Thomas Woods' old accommodation house at Pūrau and then in Stoddart's Cottage, Gideon built his own home high on the hillside midway between Diamond Harbour and Pūrau. The thick walls of the two-storey cottage, built of rammed clay reinforced with supplejack and mānuka, provided warmth in winter and a cool interior in summer.

The Hendersons sold butter, milk and other produce from their farm. Taking it to market in Lyttelton was hard work. Goods had to be got down the hill to the

The Hendersons' cottage at Diamond Harbour. Initially Gideon built his family a cottage made of rammed clay reinforced with supplejack and mānuka. Later he purchased this wooden worker's cottage located even higher up the hill and known as Pleasant View.
DHHA

foreshore and loaded into a boat, which Gideon then rowed, in all weathers, to the port, where he was well known and well liked. Supplies for the household were brought back the same way, often arriving the worse for wear in high seas. By the 1890s, regular ferry services spared Gideon from rowing across the harbour. Produce could be sledded down to the Pūrau wharf and loaded there. Perhaps then he could spend more time fishing, gathering oysters and crabs and even finding the occasional muttonbird on the cliffs around Camp Bay and Port Levy.

It was a hard life initially, not only for Gideon and Barbara but also for their children who, after farm tasks, had to walk every day to the school in Charteris Bay. Likely the children met up along the way with their Hunter cousins from Church Bay. Despite this demanding regime, 'I never saw a happier lot than the Henderson boys and girls — the old people were just the same.'[12] Eventually Gideon and Barbara purchased Samuel Tait's wooden worker's cottage located even higher up the hill and known as Pleasant View. Here the family would gather for New Year's Eve parties, when the men would dance the Papa Stour Sword Dance and the Highland Fling to the accompaniment of a fiddle. Eldest son John was the fiddle maker. He used native black kōnini, beech, ribbonwood, white pine and rimu. When the Cameron brothers' quarry wharf was no longer needed, John, in the spirit of reuse that was so common around the harbour, bought the wharf with the intention of using it for carving and fencing. However, when the time came to dismantle it, he discovered he had to remove the piles from the seabed, not just cut them off at sea level. He gave up on that idea.

In 1874 Mark Stoddart signalled his intention to subdivide his property. He advertised allotments to suit purchasers in an area 'unequalled in Canterbury with respect to the bracing purity of the atmosphere, the beauty of the scenery, the facilities for laying out gardens and pleasure grounds, and securing that drainage fall so necessary to the healthful occupation of any locality'.[13] There was a site marked out for a 'first-class Hotel'. Waterman Thomas Wyman could convey visitors across the harbour to a 'good landing jetty', and arrangements were pending 'for the establishment of regular communication by steamer to and from Lyttelton which would reduce the time for the journey from Christchurch Station to about forty minutes'.[14] In August of the same year, tenders were invited for repairs and additions to the roughly 15-year-old Diamond Harbour jetty. It seems ownership of the jetty had passed from Stoddart to the provincial government.

It is not clear what interest the subdivision proposal generated, but by April 1876 Lyttelton merchant Harvey Hawkins had purchased much of the Diamond Harbour estate. In 1877 the Stoddart family went to live in Scotland for several years. On their return in about 1880, Mark Stoddart bought a house in Papanui, Christchurch, where he died in 1885.

Harvey Hawkins was an ironmonger, a ships' chandler and a buyer and importer of cheese. It was his company that won the major contract to build the Lyttelton port moles (breakwaters), completed in 1877. Having secured the Diamond Harbour land, Hawkins built the lovely home that graced Stoddart headland until the 2010 and 2011 Christchurch earthquakes necessitated its demolition. Godley House (so named in 1913 after John Robert Godley, founder of the province of Canterbury) was built of brick, plastered to look like stone. The verandah was decorated with delicate iron lace.

The *Press* referred in October 1880 to the 'handsome seventeen roomed mansion to be seen opposite to the port, built for Mr Harvey Hawkins. It is not yet out of the builder's hands, but when finished there will be few private places in the province superior to it with respect to its design or the beauty of its surroundings.'[15] Transporting sufficient bricks and other building materials by sea to the little Diamond Harbour jetty and lugging them all uphill must have been a challenge. Once resident at Diamond Harbour, Harvey Hawkins commuted to and from the bay in *Waiwera*, a steam launch he purchased in 1881. On a trial trip around the harbour in October, *Waiwera* was said to move 'like a duck in the water'.[16] Hawkins also threw legendary parties, for which boatloads of guests would be ferried across the harbour. So the jetty, in the decade following 1877, continued to be a well-used structure.

Godley House in 1897, when ownership of the property reverted to the Stoddart family as secured creditors following Harvey Hawkins' bankruptcy. Between 1897 and 1913, when she wasn't painting and exhibiting in Europe, artist Margaret Stoddart called Godley House home.
CANTERBURY MUSEUM, STODDART ALBUM

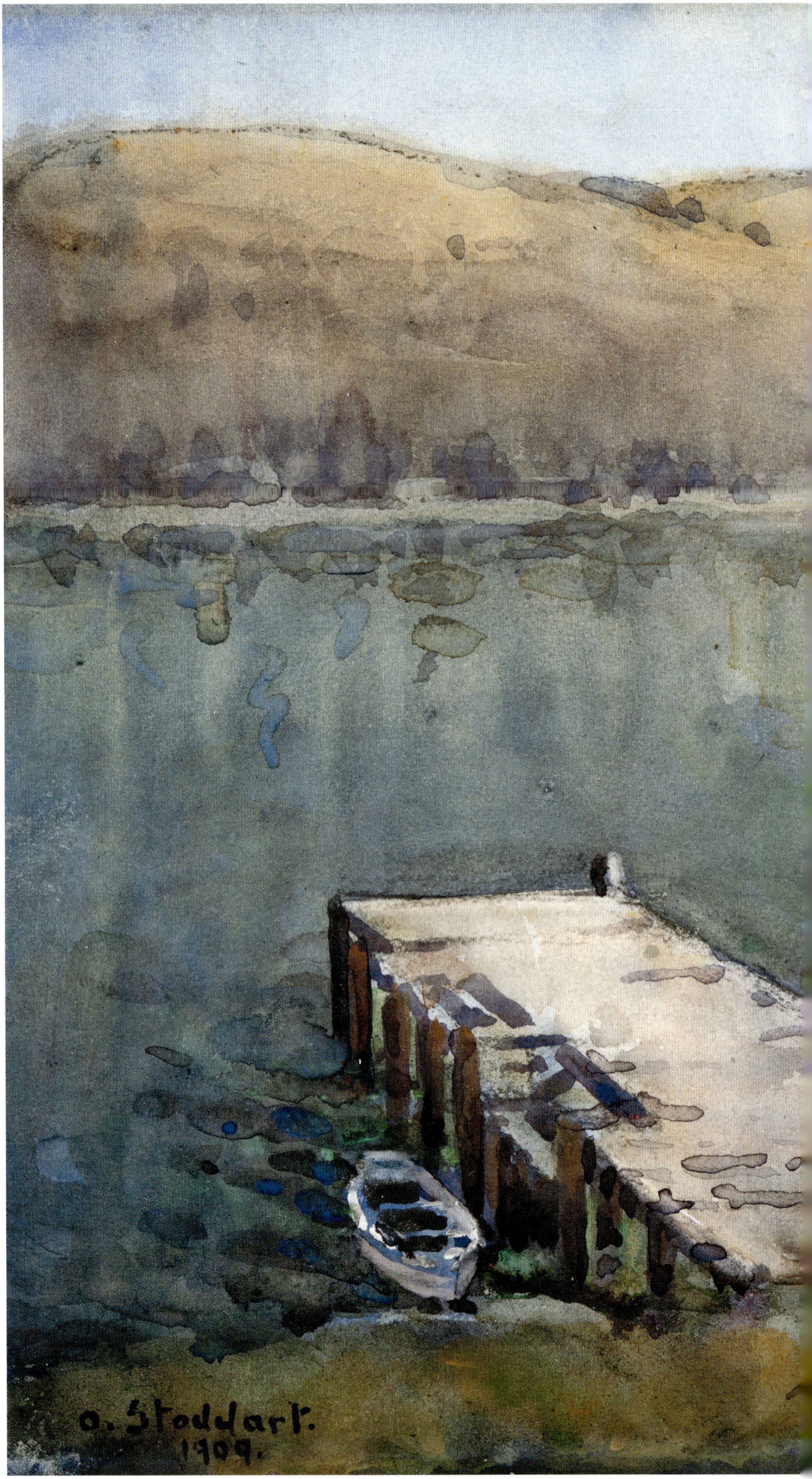
a. Stoddart.
1909.

Margaret Stoddart's painting of the old Diamond Harbour jetty and almond tree, 1909.
CHRISTCHURCH ART GALLERY TE PUNA O WAIWHETŪ, L86/93

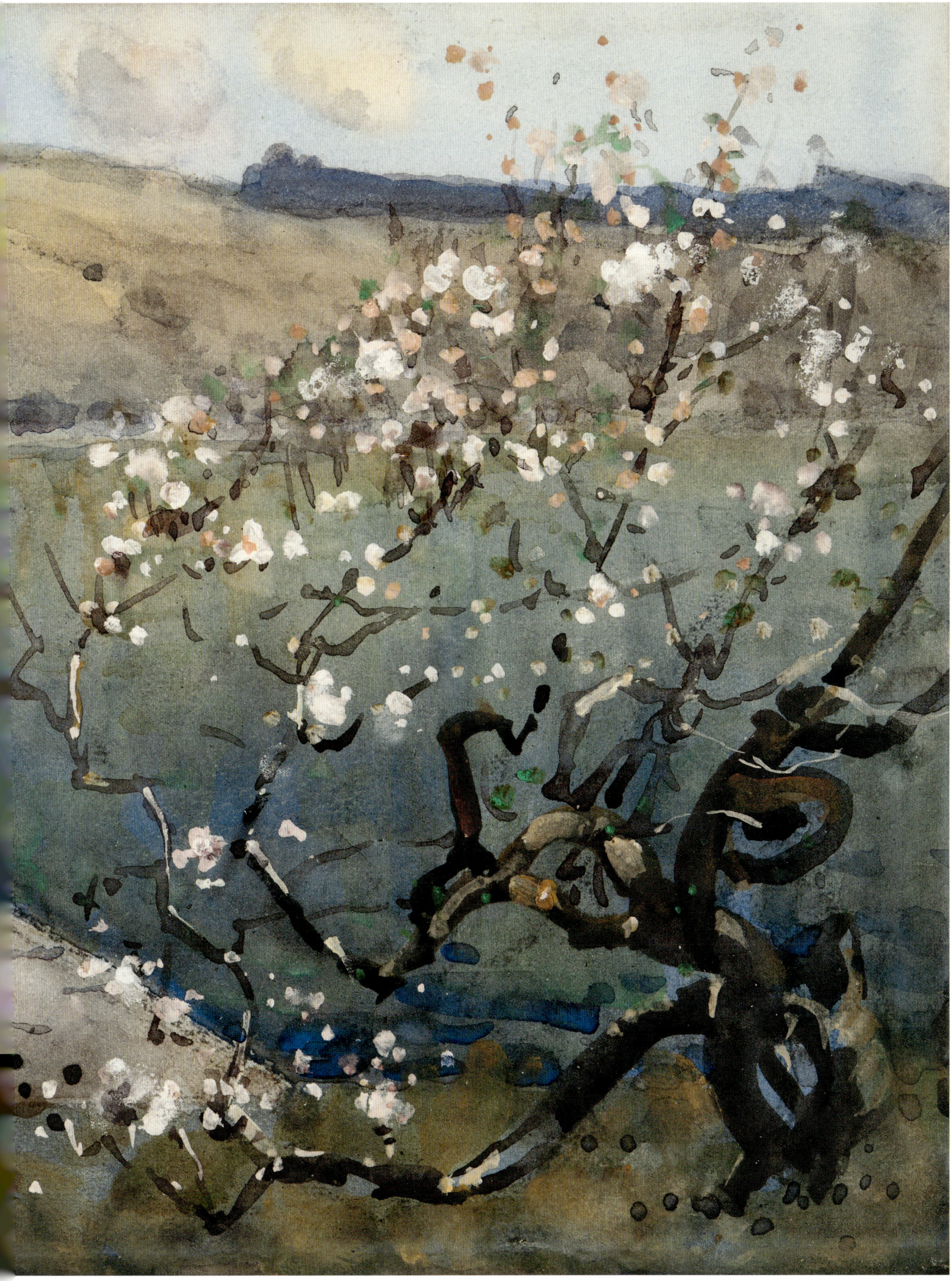

Sadly, Hawkins's ambitions exceeded his means. Through the 1880s he was borrowing money to pay off the Diamond Harbour land purchase and home-building costs. On top of that he lost money in various speculations. In 1891 he leased his gracious home and 33 acres of land to be transformed into 'Taylor's Private Family Hotel and Pleasure Gardens'. A year later, it changed hands to become 'Diamond Harbour Park', offering a recreation ground, picnic area and residence for convalescents. There were swings and swing boats, quoits and, closer to the edge of the headland, a social hall for dancing and roller-skating. Several leasees later, in 1894, Hawkins was declared bankrupt. His property was offered for sale, but it failed to attract any interest and reverted to the Stoddart family as secured creditors. The house was rented out until, in 1897, Anna Stoddart, with daughters Margaret, Mary and Agnes, returned to live there. The dance hall was dismantled and relocated to Sumner or New Brighton.

Margaret Stoddart (1865–1934) had spent her early years at Stoddart Cottage. With parents who farmed and were interested in the natural world, she and her sisters were encouraged to explore freely the land and seashore. Margaret left Diamond Harbour in 1876 aged 11. She enrolled in the Canterbury College School of Art in its opening year, 1882. In the following years she travelled widely, took lessons, painted and exhibited in Europe and became known as one of New Zealand's foremost flower painters.

Between 1897 and 1913, when she wasn't living and working in Britain and Europe, Margaret was based in Diamond Harbour. The sisters walked the hills, enjoyed botanising and took excellent photographs of the south harbour bays. This strong connection with the little settlement is captured in Margaret's paintings — of the homes, gardens, orchards, jetty and sea. Not only are these significant paintings in the history of New Zealand art, they are also important social records of a changing landscape and way of life.

Through a period of change and uncertainty, the Diamond Harbour jetty remained a key link with the outside world. In the mid-1890s the settlement of Diamond Harbour comprised 11 people living in the two houses (Stoddart Cottage and the 'Big House'). It was smaller than most of the other harbour settlements serviced by launches and, with road access difficult, was mostly dependent on sea transport.

In December 1891 the Lyttelton Harbour Board, ever keen to recoup expenditure on the outlying jetties, discussed the charging of sixpence on Boxing Day to people landing at Diamond Harbour. According to the commissioner of Crown lands the foreshore was vested in the people and they had a right to land there free of charge. The proprietors of the John Anderson Launch Company were advised that no legal charge could be made. It was also reported at the same meeting that the wharf was in poor condition but that the harbour board would not allow repairs to be made until a right of way to Pūrau was granted in perpetuity. This would put the onus for developing such a road on the landowner.[17]

The matter was still unresolved in 1899 when the Port Levy Road Board discussed a letter from Anna Stoddart expressing concern about the encroachment of the sea on the approach to the Diamond Harbour wharf. The board's reply to Mrs Stoddart was that it would not pay for any such work until a fairly graded road was available to convey them through the Diamond Harbour property.[18] By 1910 the harbour board was threatening to close the 'unsafe' Diamond Harbour jetty. A notice of closure would be placed on the jetty, visible from land and sea, since 'if such notices are posted and kept continuously on the jetties no action could successfully be taken against the Board for any injury that any person might sustain by going on them in their unsafe condition'.[19] In 1911 the jetty was closed for traffic, the harbour board stating that it would cost about £500 to repair.

Anna Stoddart died in June 1911, three years after the death of her daughter Mary in childbirth. The remaining members of the Stoddart family decided to move on from the large Diamond Harbour estate. At much the same time, the Lyttelton Borough Council was thinking of extending its boundaries to include a 'marine suburb' or 'trans-harbour township' which would offer Lyttelton workers the option of a warmer, healthier place to live while commuting by ferry to the port for work. By October 1911 the Lyttelton Borough Extension Act had been passed, enabling the council to purchase land outside the limits of the borough. Specifically the council was eyeing up the 350-acre Diamond Harbour estate for subdivision. This had immediate implications for the Diamond Harbour jetty, little changed since first built for Mark Stoddart around 1857. The act permitted the borough council to build and/or upkeep 'any wharf or jetty which may be required for the convenience of persons residing or proposing to reside on the south side of Lyttelton Harbour'.[20]

On 16 March 1912 the mayor of Lyttelton hosted a picnic on the Stoddart estate, offering an opportunity for locals to view the proposed new subdivision. The mayor, M. J. Millar, engaged the steamers *Purau*, *Canterbury* and *Monica* to take visitors across the harbour. Presumably the jetty closure was conveniently waived. Edward Chudleigh, son-in-law of Thomas Potts, was horrified at the behaviour of the visitors. 'The Stoddart gardens are lovely and should not have been entered but hundreds of the public rushed the grounds and stole all they could carry. I never saw anything like it, a disgrace to civilisation.'[21]

Since there was dissension in the ranks of the Lyttelton Borough Council over the cost of the proposed development, it was decided to hold a ratepayers' poll on the proposal to raise a loan of £15,000 for the purchase and development of

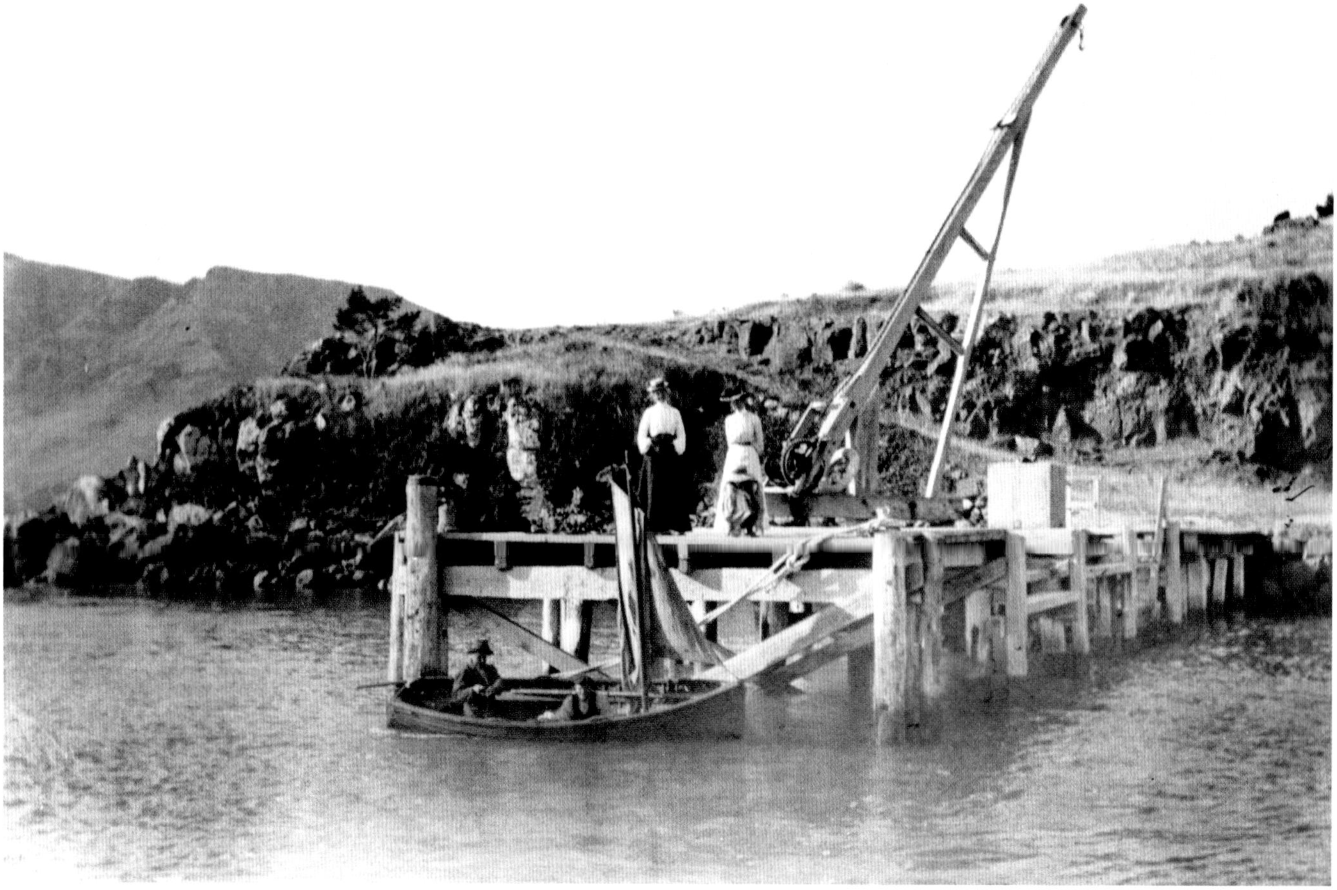

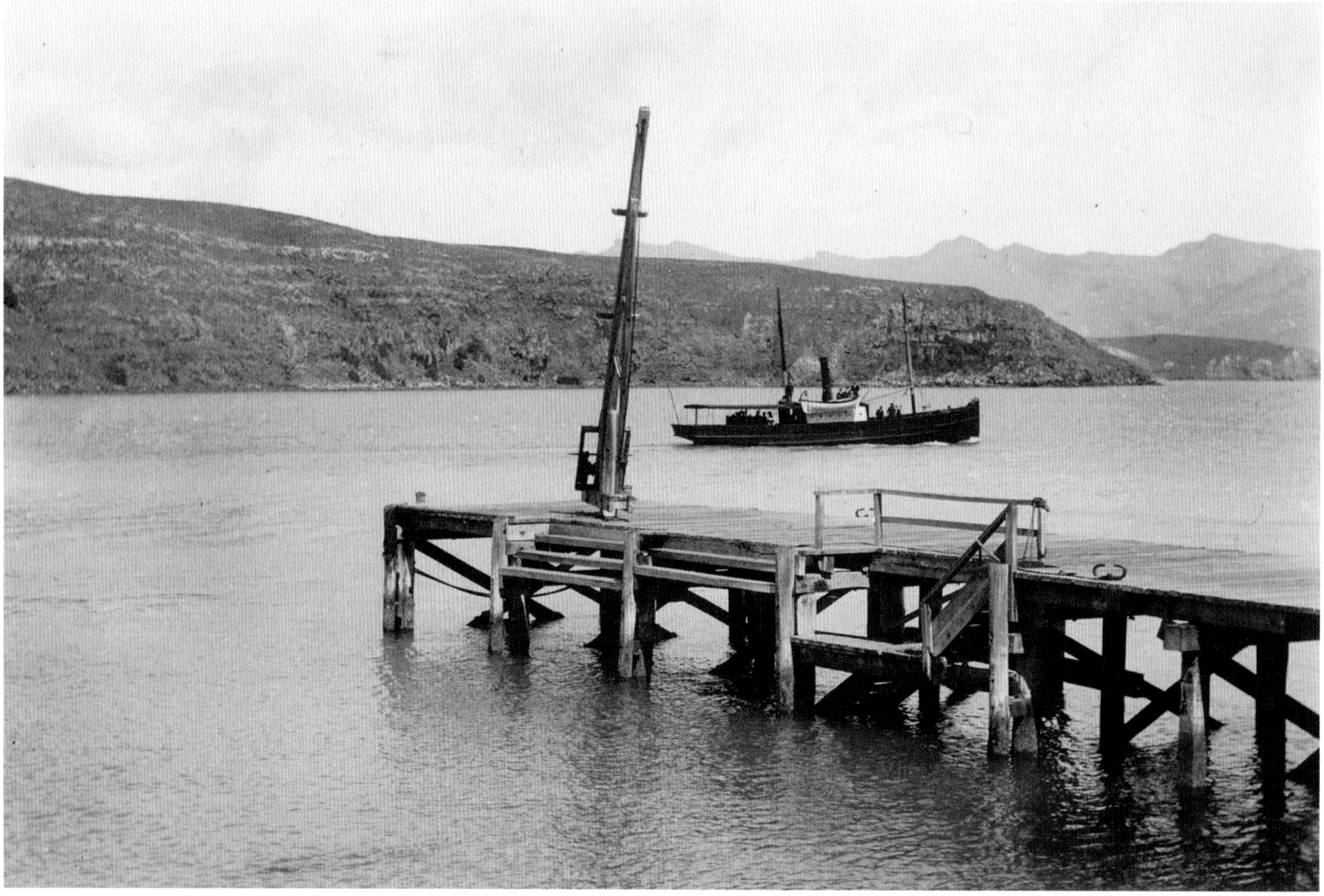

the Diamond Harbour estate (£7000 for the estate and the rest for roading, sea transport and other services). The polling, on 5 February 1913, was described as 'fairly heavy', with 478 votes being cast out of a roll of about 700. In a somewhat split vote, 250 voted for the proposal and 216 against.[22] The subdivision was then rolled out in stages. Seventy-six quarter-acre sections (eight of which were reserved for a water reservoir) were put up for auction in November 1914, with a further 35 being offered in February 1915.

The Lyttelton Borough Council reopened the jetty in November 1913. It chartered the launch *Canterbury* for six months, and then purchased *Ruahine* for £360 for the Diamond Harbour service. Godley House was renovated and opened for accommodation. However, both the ferry and, very soon, Godley House ran at a loss. Private launch owners were unhappy with the unfair competition from the municipal authority. The council decided to withdraw from running the ferry service and put it out to private tender. A. Rhind and Co., awarded the tender for a period of two years, then purchased *Ruahine* from the council.[23]

A purpose-built wharf was needed at Diamond Harbour to service an anticipated increase in passenger and freight traffic. By 1913 the Lyttelton mayor was talking optimistically about the possibility of two jetties, maybe three. However, the condition of the only existing jetty was a cause for concern. Among other mishaps, the *Press* reported a 'smart rescue' carried out at the jetty by a lad named Roland Stewart. A woman was walking down the jetty steps to the ferry launch *Ruahine*, leading a child by the hand. The child slipped on the steps and fell into the sea. Stewart dived in fully dressed, and got the youngster safely on board the launch.[24] Whether or not such accidents precipitated action or whether the reasons were purely economic, the rebuilding of the old jetty 'with enlargements and improvements' began on 21 June 1915 and was completed by August.[25] This activity coincided with the lease of the jetty site by the Lyttelton Borough Council on the understanding that the council would operate an efficient ferry service of at least five trips a day from Lyttelton and return.

The new, improved jetty was a hit with swimmers. Five months later, 'people [were] appearing on the landing jetty in costumes other than the regulation neck-to-knee suit'. Since this was deemed inappropriate, notices were put up stating that 'bathing would not be allowed about the jetty between the hours of 8.00 a.m. and 7.00 p.m.'[26] An old horse box was installed on the Diamond Harbour beach to serve as a changing shed for men and women.

The First World War put a temporary halt to development. Sunday trains from Christchurch to Lyttelton were stopped, meaning that fewer city residents had access to the Diamond Harbour ferry. Godley House was closed for some time and the ferry service was curtailed. An exception was made in October 1915 for a 'Patriotic Carnival in aid of the Canterbury Patriotic Fund'.[27] Stoddart Point

ABOVE Diamond Harbour jetty before its rebuild in 1915. A crane has been added but the flight of steps from the point is yet to be built.
CANTERBURY MUSEUM, STODDART COLLECTION, 1983.315.1

BELOW SS *John Anderson* in Diamond Harbour, 1897.
CANTERBURY MUSEUM, STODDART ALBUM, 2015.114.184

(then known as Pine Grove) was set up for a sports gathering and side shows. There was entertainment from the Māori Concert Party from Rāpaki, a minstrel troupe, members of the New Zealand Scottish Society, the Lyttelton Marine Band, Lyttelton Boy Scouts (demonstrating stretcher drill and a night camp alarm), a tug-of-war and a 'nail driving competition for ladies'. Motor boat, dinghy and punt races took place on the harbour, the punts propelled by coal shovels. Four steamers plus the tug *Lyttelton* carried visitors from the port to Diamond Harbour and back. All profits went to the war effort.

By 1918 things were looking up. Shelter sheds were erected on the jetty, and a further two sheds fitted with a water tank and fireplaces were built halfway between the jetty and Godley House — a welcome resting place for locals and visitors lugging goods uphill from the ferry. A dedicated ladies' bathing shed was built on the Diamond Harbour beach. The horse box, shifted and renovated, continued to service the men.

In December 1920, the *Press* reported that ferry traffic had increased beyond all expectation since the resumption of Sunday trains to Lyttelton and the opening of golf links in Diamond Harbour. A 6000-gallon concrete tank had been built to supplement the water supply since the settlement was dependent on rainwater. All of the sections in the first and second subdivisions had been sold, and the third subdivision was to open up in 1921. By now there were enough residents and visitors to warrant the construction of a dinghy slip on the foreshore between the jetty and the beach. The harbour board donated old decking timber, and the borough council provided concrete for the lower portion of the slip.

In 1924 the building of a flight of shallow steps leading down to the jetty improved access for campers on Stoddart Point. Heavy items, like dairy produce, were still sledged to and from the jetty. Sadly, the camping ground was closed at the end of the 1929–30 camping season with the onset of the Great Depression. Instead, a Public Works Camp was set up under canvas on the headland in September 1930, with about 30 men working on improving road access from Pūrau, through Diamond Harbour to Charteris Bay. In contrast with the high old stock route, the new road was lower, with gentler gradients.

Today we enjoy a speedy, relatively smooth trip across the harbour in the Black Cat catamarans. But the much slower ferries of previous years made heavy weather of blustery conditions. Betty Agar recalled growing up in Diamond Harbour in the 1930s:

> I went to school from Diamond Harbour to Lyttelton Main School and then to the Lyttelton District High School. I went on the ferries (which was the only way I could go). I remember using the *Onawe*, the *Reo Moana*, the *Owaka* and the *Tui*. I remember Tom Cleary and

Built in Port Chalmers in 1905, the steamer *Tarewai* was brought up to Lyttelton in early 1943 when wartime petrol shortages meant that it could be used on the Lyttelton–Diamond Harbour crossing. *Tarewai* was purchased by Wal Toy as part of Toy's Ferry Launches fleet. In this photo, taken by Leslie Agar from the Diamond Harbour wharf, the young man in uniform standing behind two women is Keith Trevor Agar, who was killed in action during the Battle for Casino in Italy in March 1944.
COURTESY OF SIMON AGAR

Demi-Kelly (Demeschelli) who owned the *Owaka* and Wal Toy — he ran the steam launch *Tarawai* during the war-time petrol shortages . . .

We'd try and do our homework on the ferry if it wasn't too rough . . . In really rough seas the boat would go 'thump, thump' into the waves as soon as we'd left the moles . . . We'd head for Payne's Quarry, and make our way along the shoreline where there was a bit of protection from the wind. The seats weren't bolted down so both seats and passengers slid about in the bad weather . . . At Diamond Harbour we'd often hitch a ride with Mr Paine's horse and cart.[28]

As a teenager, Maurie Agar and his friend would row a 9-foot dinghy from Diamond Harbour to Lyttelton to go to the pictures. The crossing took them 90 minutes and they would later row home, without lifejackets, in the dark. The boys were confident that 'our wooden dinghy would not sink even if full of water with two of us in it. We were very careful to watch the weather conditions.'[29]

Land had been earmarked for a school in Diamond Harbour when the settlement was first laid out in 1911. By 1935, some of the Lyttelton Borough councillors were asking for a school to be built, pointing out that the ferry timetable involved a lot of waiting around for the children and that sometimes the weather was so bad that the ferry crossing was suspended and children could not get to school at all. The Diamond Harbour School finally opened in 1945 with an initial roll of 17 students.

An interesting correspondence from 1937 details a disagreement between the Lyttelton Harbour Board and the Lyttelton Borough Council over ongoing

A busy Diamond Harbour jetty with lots of boating activity in the bay, c.1950s.
DHHA

responsibility for the Diamond Harbour jetty. The council had been granted a licence for the jetty 10 years previously, in return for a rent of £35 per annum. When the licence expired, the council clearly did not want to continue paying such rent. Equally, the harbour board was reluctant to maintain the jetty. 'The Board knows from its experience of the claim in respect of the loss of life by drowning from the Governors Bay jetty that these outlying jetties are liabilities rather than assets.'[30] The council declined to renew the licence.

Buried in the harbour board archives is a plan dated 25 November 1947 for a proposed jetty further around Diamond Harbour, to the west of the derelict Cameron's quarry jetty. The Diamond Harbour village was slowly expanding westwards, and the idea was to service residents further round the bay with an alternative jetty and also encourage yet more settlement. The more exposed site called for two sets of landing steps.[31] Nothing came of the idea. In a further effort to keep Diamond Harbour, and the harbour bays in general, growing as communities, the Mount Herbert County Council and the Governors Bay Progress League floated the idea of a vehicular ferry between Lyttelton and Diamond Harbour.[32] A letter in its archives indicates that the harbour board was actively exploring the possibility in the mid-1960s.[33] Nothing came of this either.

Also in the 1960s came letters from residents of Diamond Harbour seeking improved parking at the jetty and facilities for storing dinghies and launching small craft. There were similar requests at Pūrau and Port Levy. As the once-buoyant harbour ferry traffic declined, the interest in recreational boating had increased. As local postmaster and taxi driver Clarence Paine pointed out, 'Diamond Harbour is one of the oldest pleasure bays in the Lyttelton Harbour and yet the only boating amenity is an old inaccessible prehistoric boat slip that no one can use.'[34] A dinghy platform had been proposed in 1961 to the south-east of the jetty. In 1969, however, the harbour board drew up plans for the current dinghy shelter at the land end of the jetty.

With the sealing of the road between Christchurch and Diamond Harbour finally completed in 1967, travel around Lyttelton Harbour by car became more attractive. Rising private vehicle ownership also meant that families who might once have relied on ferry services for an annual holiday could take a break further afield. Harbour crossing by ferry became a choice, rather than a necessity, and the Diamond Harbour service faltered.[35]

In 2001, Black Cat Cruises launched the *Black Diamond*, purpose-built to operate as the new Diamond Harbour ferry, replacing the historic *Onawe*. The local community was apprehensive about this shift to private operation, but the Black Cat service has reduced the journey time between Lyttelton and Diamond Harbour to around eight minutes, with ferries departing at least every hour during the day.

The demolition of Godley House following the Christchurch earthquakes robbed Diamond Harbour of a gracious homestead and significant tourist attraction. However, new cafés and attractions in Diamond Harbour, plus the growing environmental constraints on car ownership, should ensure a secure future for an historic ferry service. In 2020 Black Cat Cruises was awarded the contract for the Diamond Harbour ferry service for a further 12 years, and options are being explored for a new, low-emission vessel to replace the current ferry. At the time of writing, work is under way to upgrade the wharf while retaining its heritage features and values,[36] and proposals are finally being sought for a building to replace Godley House.

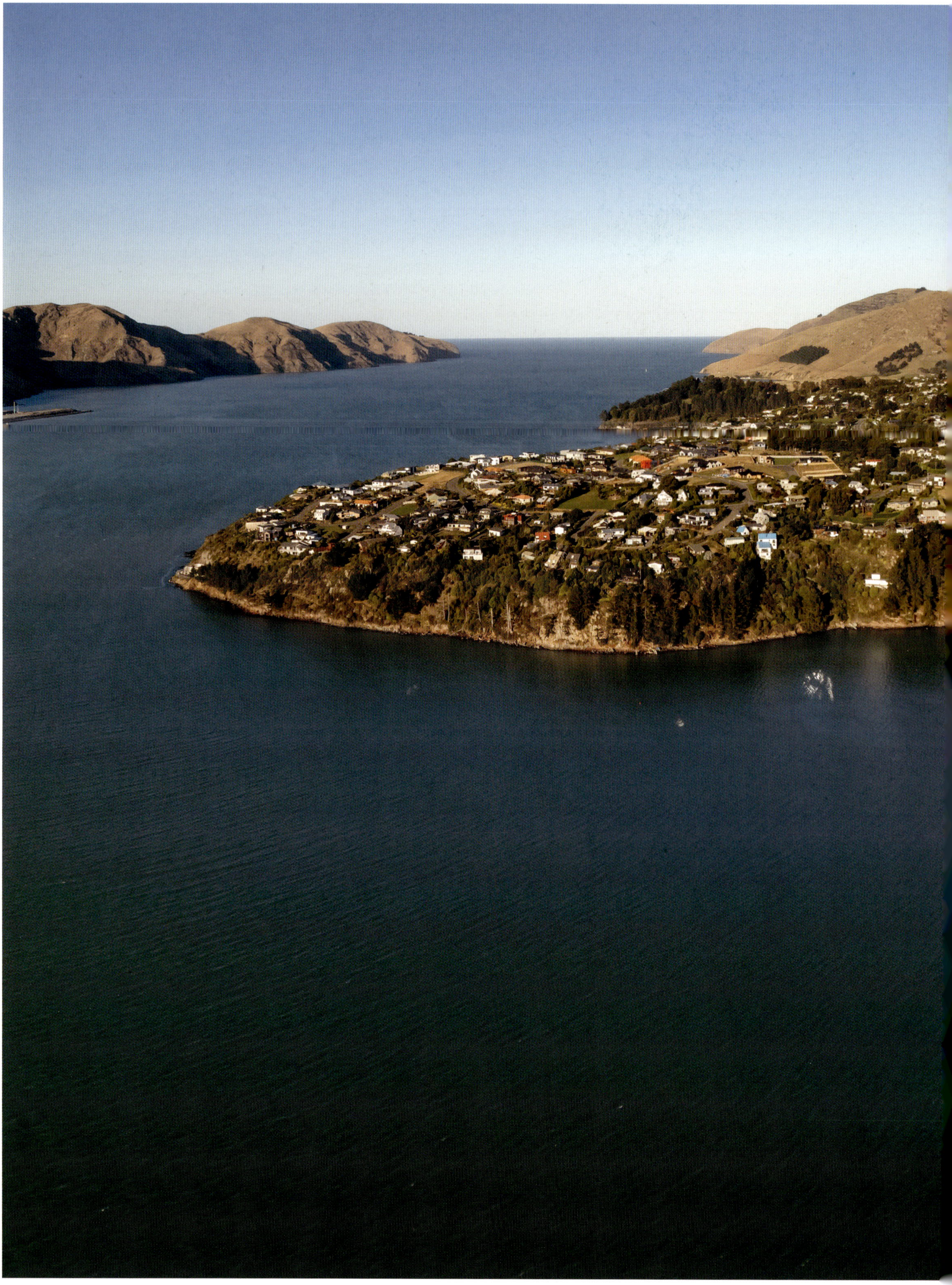

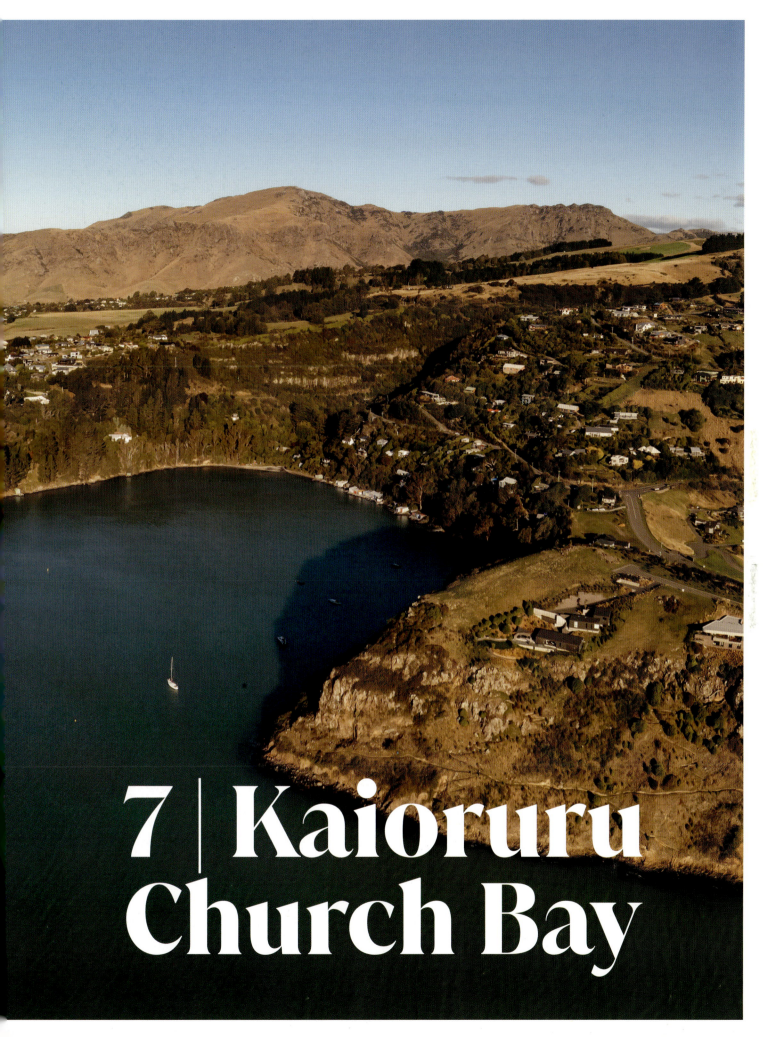

7 | Kaioruru Church Bay

Māori knew Church Bay as Kaioruru — variously translated as 'sheltered place' or 'food of the morepork'. The name might also refer to a Māori employee of Robert Rhodes named Ruru who lived at the bay. Tucked between Te Waipapa Diamond Harbour and Te Wharau Charteris Bay, Kaioruru is bounded by Pauaohinekotau Point to the north-east and Black Point to the west.

❋

Pauaohinekotau, which translates as 'the pāua-gathering place of the young girls', was also known in the early days of European settlement as Stormy Head. Stormy it can still be, but pāua are no longer commonly harvested there. Black Point was so named because of the low, dark mass of hardy native plants, in particular mānuka, matagouri, muehlenbeckia and prostrate kōwhai, that covered the headland before grazing razed most of the native flora.

Early on, land on the headland to the east of Church Bay was set aside to provide investment income for the Anglican Church — hence the name. Diamond Harbour's Mark Stoddart later purchased this land, while the Rhodes brothers from Pūrau owned most of the land above the old stock route — to which they added Church Bay Gully, with its guaranteed supply of fresh stream water. While today we see Kaioruru primarily as a place of holiday homes and permanent dwellings, the tranquil bay was once a hive of industry providing a base for various pioneering enterprises.

Māori had always valued the abundant kaimoana of Whakaraupō. Before European settlement, according to Church Bay farmer and conservationist Oliver Hunter, 'the heavily zostera-blanketed tidal flats of Charteris Bay were the main camouflaged spawning ground and nursery for fish frequenting the Canterbury coast'.[1] Unfortunately, with the arrival of Canterbury Association settlers this resource was rapidly plundered. Sharp-edged scraper-dredges were used to remove the long *Zostera* seagrass in order to access the oyster beds of Charteris Bay and Church Bay for the local market, and the loss of habitat exposed young fish to hungry seabirds.

Oyster farming, in turn, became an attractive option. In June 1867 an application was made to the chief commissioner of Crown lands 'to plant an artificial oyster bed on the shore adjacent to the Crown lands bordering on Church Bay on the southern side of the harbour'.[2] The area in question covered 70 acres and included the whole of Church Bay. The application received a rejection and a counter-proposal of 5 acres. It is not clear whether this reduced option was taken up, but in August 1898 the *Star* reported several days of phenomenally low tides during which 'the mud flats have been completely drained, and many residents of the southern side of the harbour have obtained plentiful supplies of oysters when the tide was out'.[3]

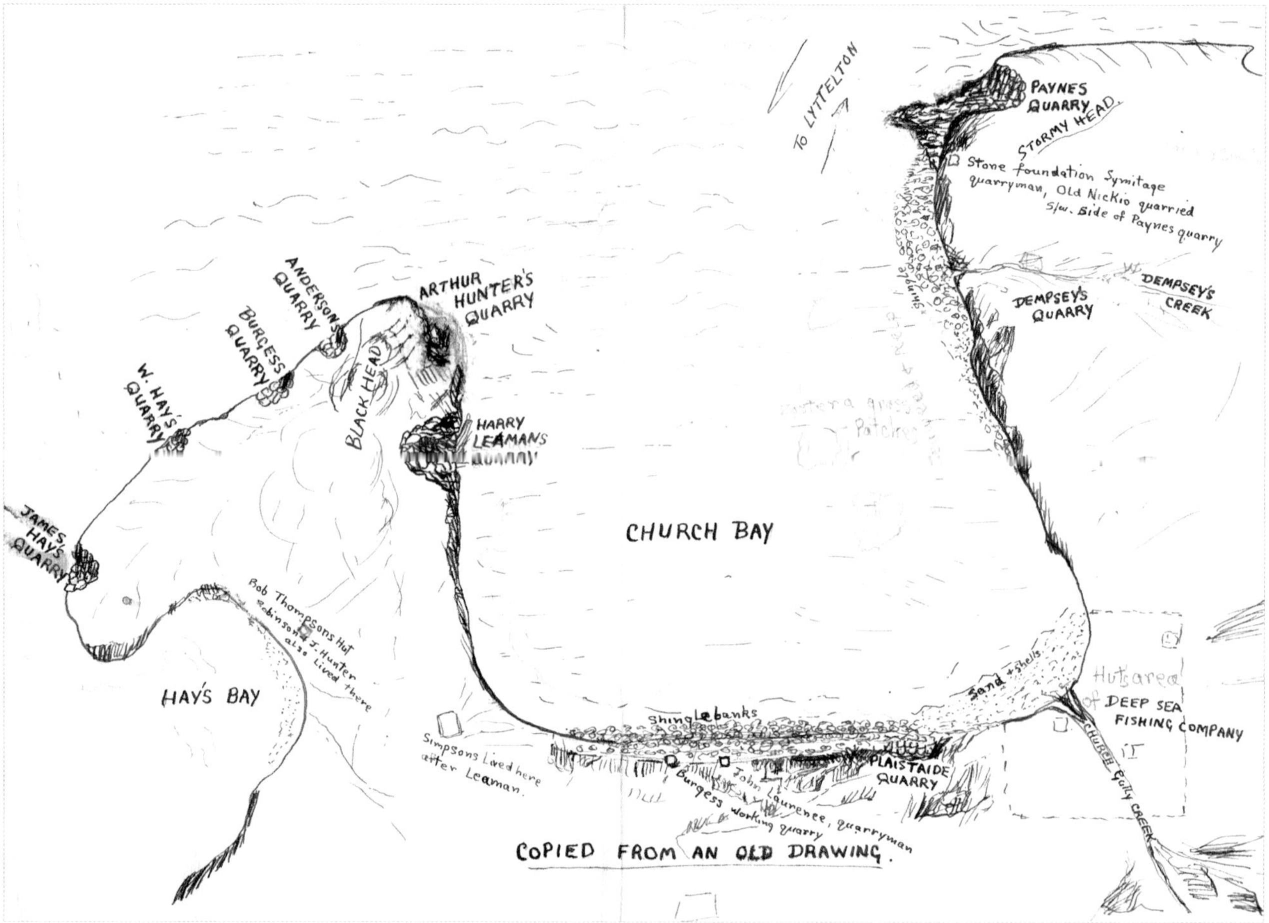
PAYNES QUARRY
STORMY HEAD
TO LYTTELTON
Stone foundation Symitage quarryman, Old Nickio quarried S/w. Side of Paynes quarry
DEMPSEY'S CREEK
DEMPSEY'S QUARRY
ANDERSON QUARRY
ARTHUR HUNTER'S QUARRY
BURGESS QUARRY
W. HAY'S QUARRY
BLACK HEAD
HARRY LEAMANS QUARRY
JAMES HAY'S QUARRY
CHURCH BAY
Bob Thompsons Hut
Robinson & J. Hunter also Lived there
HAY'S BAY
Shingle banks
Sand + Shells
Hut area of DEEP SEA FISHING COMPANY
Simpsons Lived here after Leaman.
John Laurence, quarryman
Burgess working quarry
PLAISTAIDE QUARRY
CHURCH Gully CREEK
COPIED FROM AN OLD DRAWING.

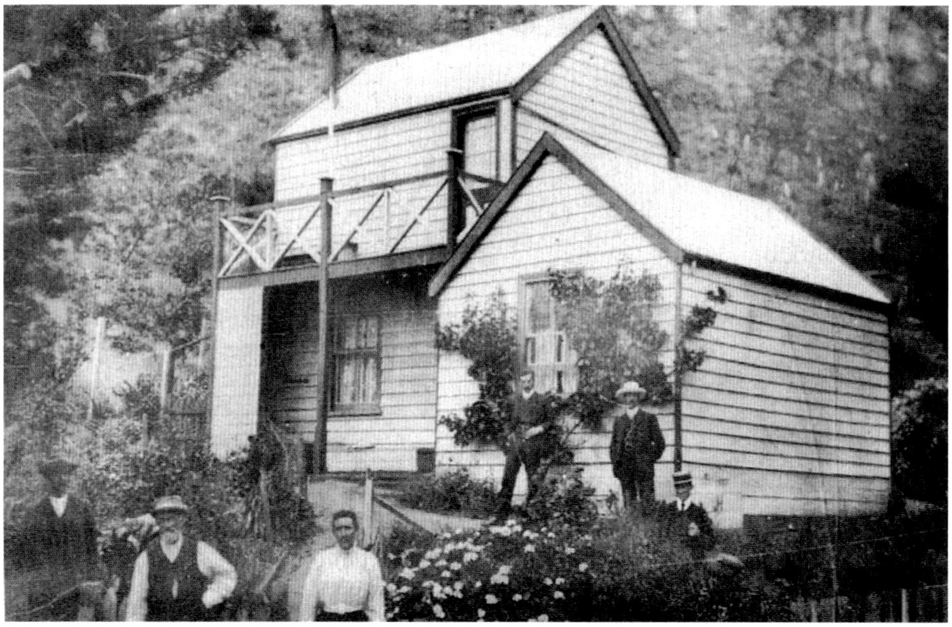

The Deep Sea Fishing Company, launched in 1872, purchased or leased 4 acres of land at the base of Church Bay Gully from Robert Rhodes with the aim of supplying the fast-growing town of Christchurch with fish and providing shareholders with a profitable return on their investment. The company established a fish-curing and smoking plant at the mouth of the Church Bay stream and built several huts on the foreshore for the fishermen. These men seem to have been the first Pākehā settlers in Kaioruru.

The company purchased *Nautilus* and, later, the schooner *Result* (which was promptly sold at a loss when it was found to be too small for purpose). Fish caught included trumpeter, sole, hāpuku, moki and crayfish. The *Press* reported in July 1873 that smoked trumpeter was becoming a favourite with the Christchurch public and that the company was planning to 'lay down a preserve in Church Bay, where fish can be kept alive, so that the market can be kept supplied two or three times a week with fresh fish'.[4]

However, by August there were signs that all was not well. The directors' report acknowledged a fair share of 'anticipated difficulties'. The original capital was far too small; the purchase of *Result* was an 'error of judgement'; the further prospecting required to discover good grounds for trawling for brill and sole would delay returns; the 'half-profit' system of remunerating crews had not been successful — instead crews were now paid wages and could be discharged at any time; and keeping the fish alive long enough to get them to market in a fresh state was proving difficult. Nevertheless, the directors concluded that 'the company will at no distant period become one of great importance'.[5]

Instead, the company folded in 1874. In May the fishing plant, consisting of seine and trawl nets, crayfish pots, oyster dredges and other items, was put up for public auction. The land owned by the Deep Sea Fishing Company was eventually purchased by Shetland Islander James Hay and his second wife, Jean. They added another level to the last fisherman's hut and retired there. After James's death in 1914, Jean lived on at Church Bay for many years. Their charming cottage sits just back from the beach and is still well cared for today.

Shortly after the Deep Sea Fishing Company wound up, 'Payne's quarry' (named after James Payne) opened on the north-east headland of Church Bay to meet the demand for ballast for sailing ships. The shingle beach west of Payne's quarry and the shingle banks in Church Bay were the first sources of ballast to be exploited. The sturdy ballast boats could be grounded at low tide and filled with shingle before the tide rose to refloat them.[6] Later, when the easy ballast had been lifted, rock was quarried from the cliffs and, as historian Colin Amodeo relates, 'men with huge wheelbarrows would struggle along grooved planks to load up before the tide turned. Anchors held the boats firmly on the seaward side while taut lines running to mooring bolts set in rocks on the beach kept them steady

ABOVE A map of the quarries at Church Bay drafted by Oliver Hunter from an earlier drawing. Ten quarries are marked, indicating the importance of access to rock for ballast and building purposes.
HUNTER ARCHIVE

BELOW The Deep Sea Fishing Company built several huts for their fishermen on the foreshore at Church Bay. Later, two of the huts were joined, modified and extended to become home to Shetland Islanders James and Jean Hay.
HUNTER ARCHIVE

and the loading planks secure.'[7] Quarrymen lived in the huts on the Church Bay beach left vacant by the Deep Sea Fishing Company.

Names associated with early ballast quarrying at Church Bay include Miller and Maughan, Haydon and Payne, and Payne as a sole operator. As early as 1859 Miller and Maughan were advertising ballast available from their wharf at Church Bay.[8] Where this wharf was is not clear and the advertisements appeared for only a few months. In 1870 John Stinson and Jim Hayden requested permission to build a small jetty on the south-west side of Church Bay,[9] for the purpose of loading their ballast boat. They assured the Canterbury superintendent that the jetty would not interfere with any existing interests and included with their request a letter, indicating permission to build, from Mark Stoddart, who owned the land fronting onto the proposed jetty. Superintendent William Rolleston and the harbour board approved the request, but it is unclear whether such a jetty was ever built.

The quarrying activity on this western side of Church Bay angered James Hay, who owned sections 13502 and 839 running between Church Bay and Charteris Bay and had his own quarry on the Black Point headland. Hay wrote to the secretary for public works claiming that the ballast men had broken up the chain reserve along his frontage and were encroaching on his land. The authorities could not identify any such damage. Oliver Hunter's hand-drawn map indicates just how many locals had small quarries from which they extracted stone for their own use.

The ballast business was not only dangerous, it was also highly competitive. In 1872 John Haydon took a case against James Payne, who was accused of maliciously damaging *Mystery*, jointly owned by Haydon, Stinson and Brown, by boring holes in the boat and scuttling her. Both Payne and Haydon had tendered for ballasting *Ben More*, with Payne apparently taking it upon himself to eliminate the opposition. Another altercation later in the decade involved James Payne and Thomas Holder jockeying for position in the quarry and rolling life-threatening stones down on each other in the process.

Later the *Mystery* hatchet must have been buried, because

Looking over Kaioruru Church Bay with Te Ahu Pātiki Mount Herbert at top right and Te Pōhue The Monument at top left. This image was taken in 1954 before the land above the main road was subdivided. The old stock route can be seen crossing the face of the hill and curving high up around the Church Bay Gully.
V. C. BROWNE & SON, 1473

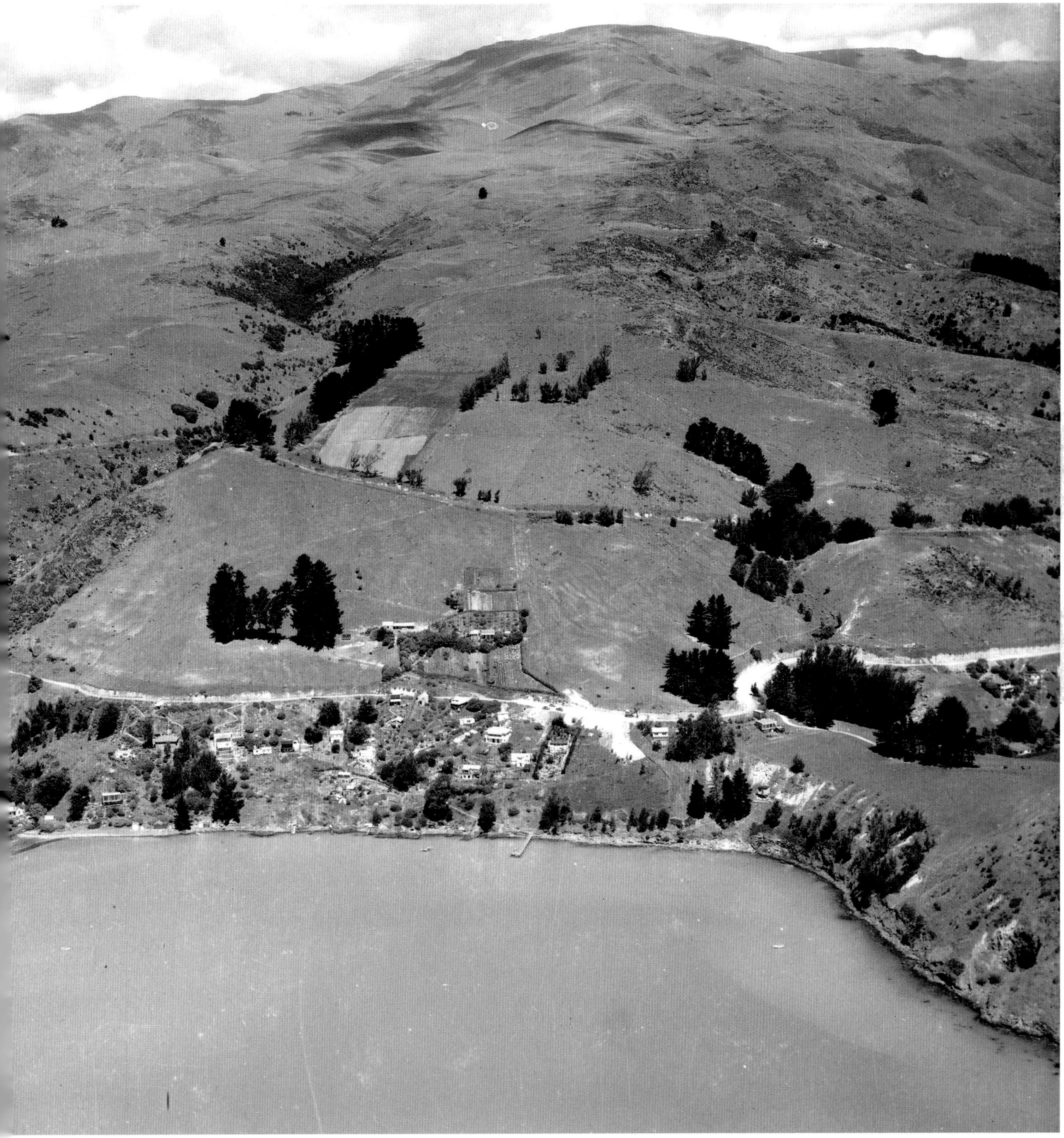

by 1876 Payne and Haydon advertised their services jointly. As noted earlier, it was in July 1879 that James Payne was killed by falling rock while working at the Cameron brothers' quarry in Diamond Harbour. We know Haydon continued to work the quarry at Church Bay because in December of 1879 the *Press* reported that John Burgess and John Laurence, quarrymen at Haydon's quarry in Church Bay, narrowly escaped being drowned in the harbour. They were heading for work late one morning when a squall capsized their boat. The men spent an hour in the water clinging to the boat before being rescued, 'numbed and exhausted'.[10]

Oliver Hunter evoked the sounds of the quarrymen at work.

> I vividly remember [a] carnival-like mixture of sounds when, on a bright moonlight night, I lay in bed in the attic of my parents' cottage home on the hillside above Church Bay: the crashing of rock being quarried and broken, the tapping and tinkling of steel drills, the constant squealing of the never-oiled axles of overloaded barrows, the rattle as the loads were tipped down a hatch, the flapping of canvas plus minor squeals from block and tackle. And through it all ran the clear call of human voices. Near at hand an irate quarry-man gave a spontaneous and unfavourable opinion of his amateur fellow-driller, while further out beyond the bay some old sailor, at the tiller of his craft, could be heard singing pleasantly 'Rolling home to dear old England'.[11]

The lives of the intrepid Hunter family were shaped by the sea and access to their property high on the hill above Church Bay. Arthur and Eliza Hunter came from Weisdale in the Shetland Islands, via the Victorian goldfields. When he was just 12 Arthur served as a cabin boy on a Greenland whaler. Later he worked in the Victorian and Canterbury West Coast goldfields before returning to Shetland to marry Eliza in 1867. Bringing his bride to New Zealand, Arthur was employed helping to build the Lyttelton breakwater.

Living somewhat unhappily in Lyttelton's west side, Eliza (who was sister to Barbara Henderson of Diamond Harbour) heard in 1874 that a cottage and 47 acres could be leased from John Stinson at Church Bay. Stinson had finished making the stock route from Charteris Bay to Pūrau (now Bay View Road) and no longer needed his property. Arthur and Eliza bought furniture and stores with the last money they had. Eliza then raised £2 on a ring in order to hire a ballast craft 'from which we and our belongings were dumped on the [Church Bay] beach. We carried up what we could that night and found that a dried-up landslide was covering

ABOVE From the Shetland Islands to Lyttelton Harbour: Arthur and Eliza Hunter at their home in Church Bay, 12 December 1911. Arthur would have been 72 and Eliza 66.
HUNTER ARCHIVE

BELOW The Hunter House, built of heart tōtara, above the road in Church Bay.
HUNTER ARCHIVE

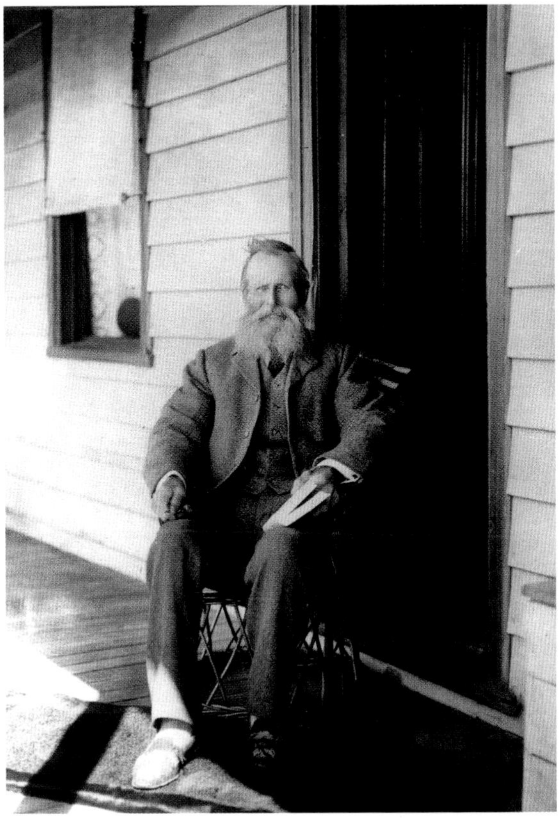

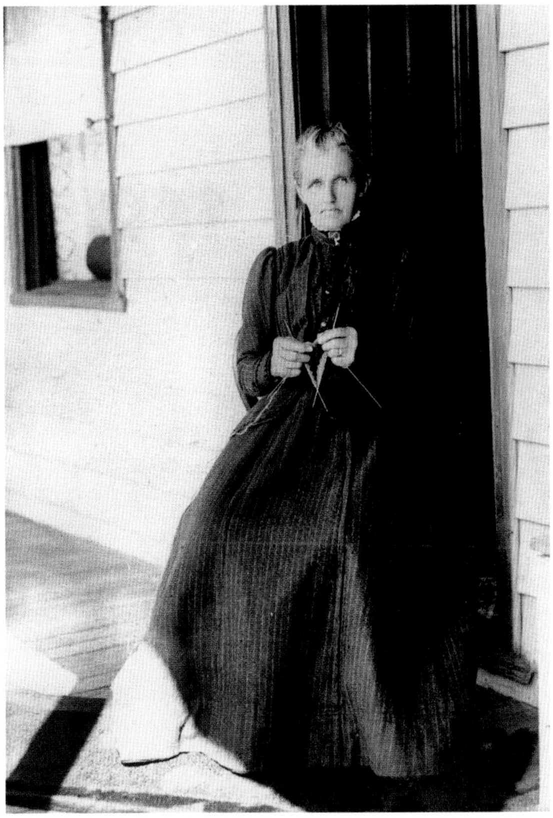

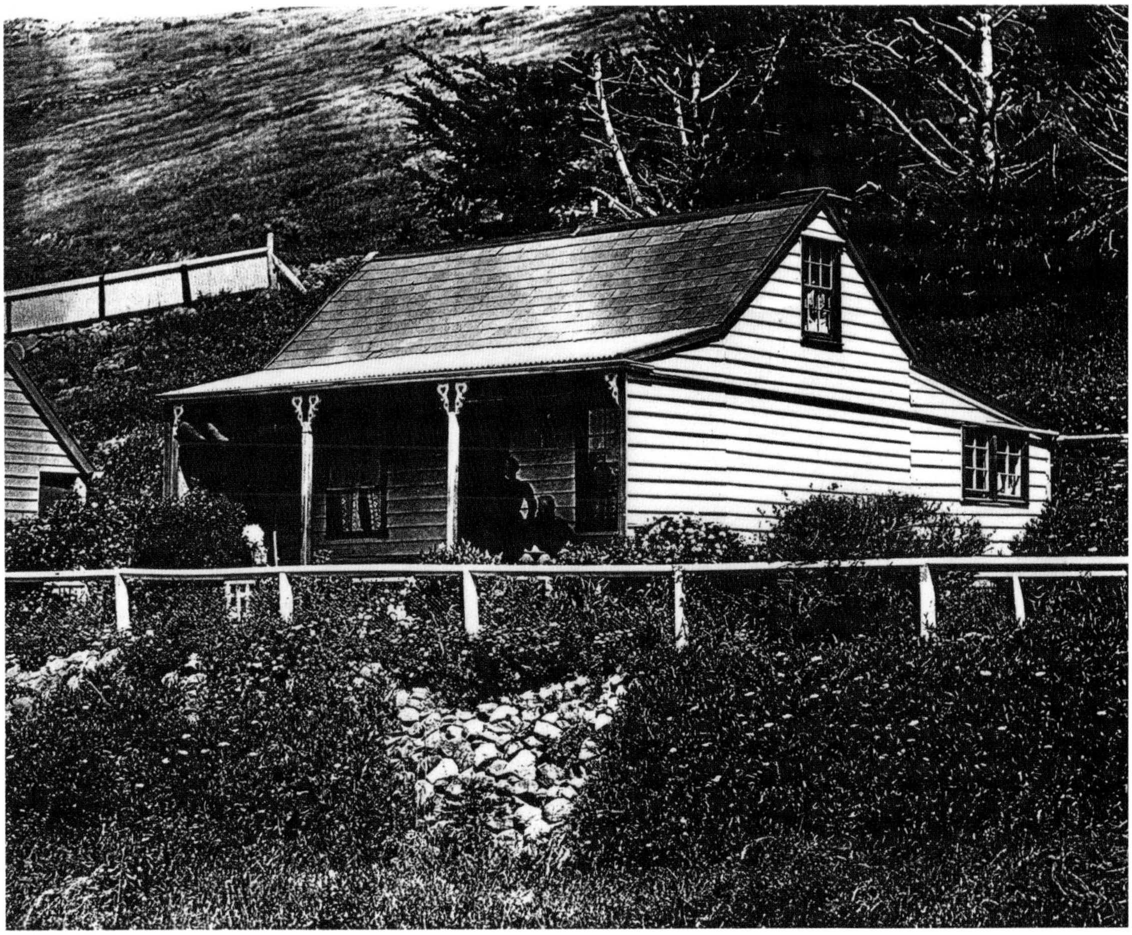

most of the back of the house.'[12] Eliza then had to go down to Church Gully to get water for tea. Despite starting from scratch (or, as Eliza put it, 'well behind scratch'), she was that night 'the happiest woman in New Zealand'.

Arthur took any job going, including fishing, farming and working as a ballast man at the Church Bay quarries. Reliance on rainwater meant Eliza went down to the Church Bay Gully to wash the family's clothes. The couple needed to fence their small farm. According to Eliza, 'a small sailing vessel brought 200 posts from Okain's Bay and landed them on the beach. Most of these posts were carried up in the moonlight. Arthur took three at a time and I took two.'[13] Eliza was indefatigable. 'Half a ton of potatoes had been landed at the beach and I did not want Arthur to have to carry them up when he came home from work, so I brought them up one afternoon . . . I carried up the half-ton in seven loads.'[14] Anyone who knows the distance between the Church Bay beach and the Hunter cottage, as well as the steepness of the climb, will appreciate just what a haul this was, not least since Eliza was five months' pregnant. Gradually the couple cleared land, ran a herd of cows (Eliza made butter and cheese) and grew early potatoes and strawberries. Eventually Arthur and Eliza were able to buy their land.

The poor condition of the stock route meant that access to the bay was still almost entirely by sea. Lyttelton doctors could be roused in the middle of the night by an anxious father-to-be who had rowed across the harbour to fetch medical help for his wife in labour. Supplies purchased at the Lyttelton Saturday market often arrived in the bay wet through. Farmers in Church Bay and Charteris Bay relied on two small oil launches to carry their garden and dairy produce to the port and bring back household supplies. In November 1913 the Lyttelton watersiders went on strike. Andrew Anderson brought a supply of cream across to port in *Matariki* and was met at the jetty by pickets, who would not allow the cream to be landed. A launch carrying garden produce from Church Bay was similarly held up. The pickets refused to allow coal and other household stores to be loaded for the return trip.[15]

Eliza and Arthur raised seven children in their small Church Bay cottage. Their son Arthur died of diphtheria at the age of four. From an early age, son Oliver was interested in the natural world, particularly native flora. When he later purchased his parents' farm, he painstakingly fenced off the Church Bay Gully and, over decades, with the help of his wife, Marion (and, much later in life, his second wife, Mabel), planted it in natives. Oliver was also responsible for scattering flower seed along the roadways through the southern bays, a tradition that continued down through the family, as granddaughter Mary recalls: 'Mum used to collect flower seeds in season then put them in flour bags. When we walked around the roads and gullies we would broadcast the seeds. It is always so rewarding to see the flowering treasures that were spread over 60 years ago.'[16]

Oliver Hunter with his children Hazel, Violet and Phyllis, their aunt Emily Turner and dog Pat.
HUNTER ARCHIVE

In 1966 Oliver Hunter received the Loader Cup for his significant contributions to plant conservation work in New Zealand. 'The area is a tribute to a man whose great love of the bush transformed a barren gully into a treasured reserve of New Zealand trees and plants for posterity.'[17] In 1977, two years before his death, he was awarded the British Empire Medal for services to conservation.

Prior to 1907 Church Bay had only private jetties, mostly servicing the ballast industry. A report from 30 July 1906 indicated that a public jetty could be built in the bay for about £120. In October a letter from Lyttelton Harbour Board member Robert Anderson to the Mount Herbert County Council requested the chairman's signature to a petition in favour of a landing stage at Church Bay. By December the wood was being prepared, and in early 1907 the *Press* reported that 'a small jetty at Church Bay, with 3ft of water at low tide at the head, had been constructed'.[18] This made life much easier for the Hunter family, who could now come and go in their own boat or in visiting launches rather than always have to travel to the jetties at Pūrau or Charteris Bay. The younger Hunter children travelled daily to school in Lyttelton, picked up at the jetty by Andrew Anderson's *Matariki*. In the late 1920s R. W. Godfrey and Johnny Hay pick-and-shovelled a track to the Church Bay jetty, running down the eastern side of the bay and wide enough to carry vehicles.

Godfrey used to take wool bales down by draught horse and sledge.[19]

Speedy access to Lyttelton by launch could be critical. Oliver Hunter was driving a horse-drawn sledge loaded with hay when the horse bolted and he was thrown to the ground and injured in the face by either the horse's hoofs or the sledge. Neighbour John Hay lost no time in crossing the harbour in his launch and bringing back Dr Newell, who treated the injured man. In May 1921 a Scripps-Booth car carrying seven members of the Hunter family, plus one on the running board, skidded in heavy rain on a narrow stretch of clay road at the summit of the spur between Diamond Harbour and Church Bay. All bar two of the passengers managed to jump clear before the car plunged almost 500 feet down the steep gully. Driver Robert Hunter and his sister Mary Jean Oakley, trapped in the car, ended up almost at sea level. Mrs Oakley died shortly after rescuers reached the car. Robert was badly injured. Despite a fierce southerly gale, John Hay crossed to Lyttelton and brought Dr Gilmour and Constable Mannix back to Church Bay in his launch.

In 1922 when she was 10, Oliver and Marion's daughter Florence Violet (known as Violet) wrote this striking account for a children's column in the *Sun* newspaper. Nothing captures the dependence on sea transport, or the uncertainty of employment on the Lyttelton wharves, better than Violet's description.

> I live on the south side of Lyttelton Harbour and my Father pays for the oil launch to call as there is no school nearer home. With my sister Phyllis I get aboard the *Matariki* at half past seven. We go to Quail Island, where two more children come aboard, and sometimes the doctor goes ashore to visit the leper colony. Some mornings we call at Charteris Bay, so we have quite a long trip. It is nice in fine weather, but in a gale the waves might be too high for us to see land over the top; still we do not get sick like the new passengers do. There are other launches and fishing boats, and big steamers passing the breakwater. When we get out at Lyttelton we have to go round or through the crowd of men waiting to be hired to unload the ships. The foreman stevedore stands up high and picks out the men he wants. The others have to go home. Engines and trucks are rushing to and fro and passengers on the station are waiting to go to the city.[20]

ABOVE Una Sinclair (later Una Herdman) and boyfriend Don Collins camping at Church Bay in the 1920s, well before any baches were built. Una's grandfather was Gideon Henderson of Diamond Harbour.
COURTESY OF STEPHEN MCKELVEY

BELOW Church Bay jetty at low tide.
HUNTER ARCHIVE

In the wool season, it was quite common for Violet and Phyllis not to arrive home on *Matariki* until 8 or 9 p.m.

Following the building of the jetty, Church Bay joined other harbour bays as a picnic destination. In January 1913, 120 seamen from the 'Home steamers' in port were taken across the harbour in three ship's boats towed by Andrew

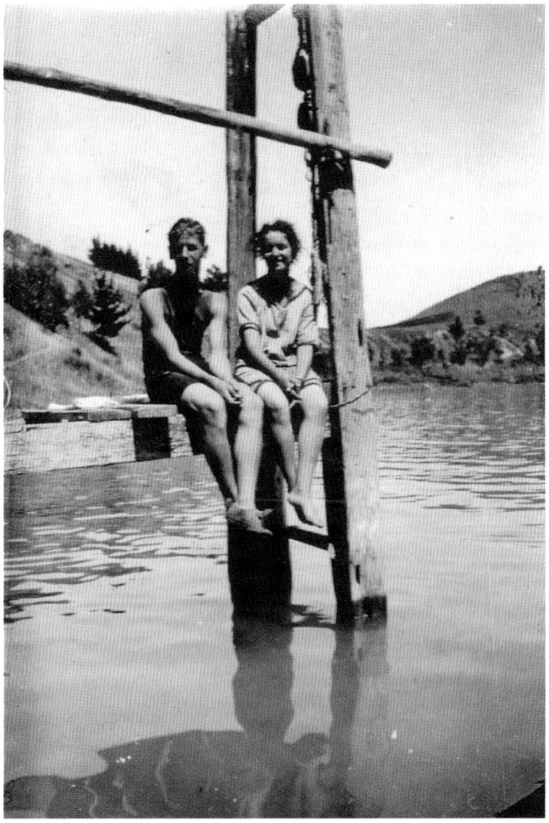

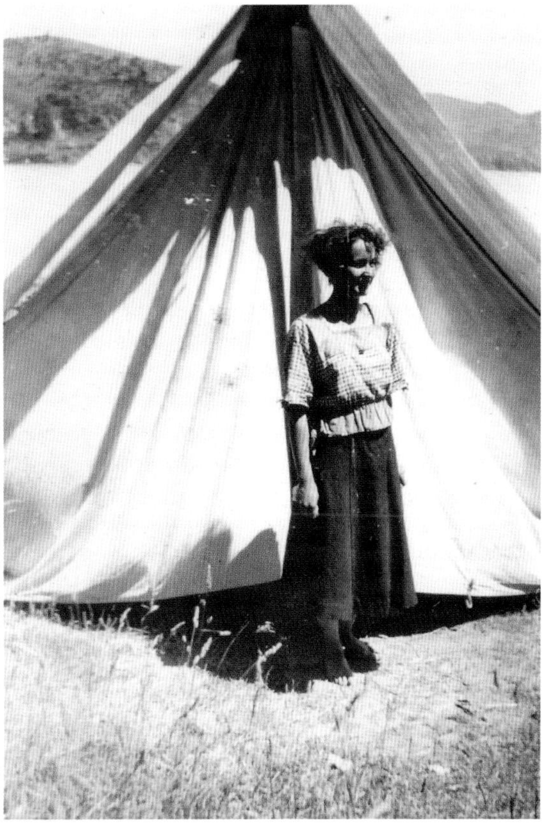

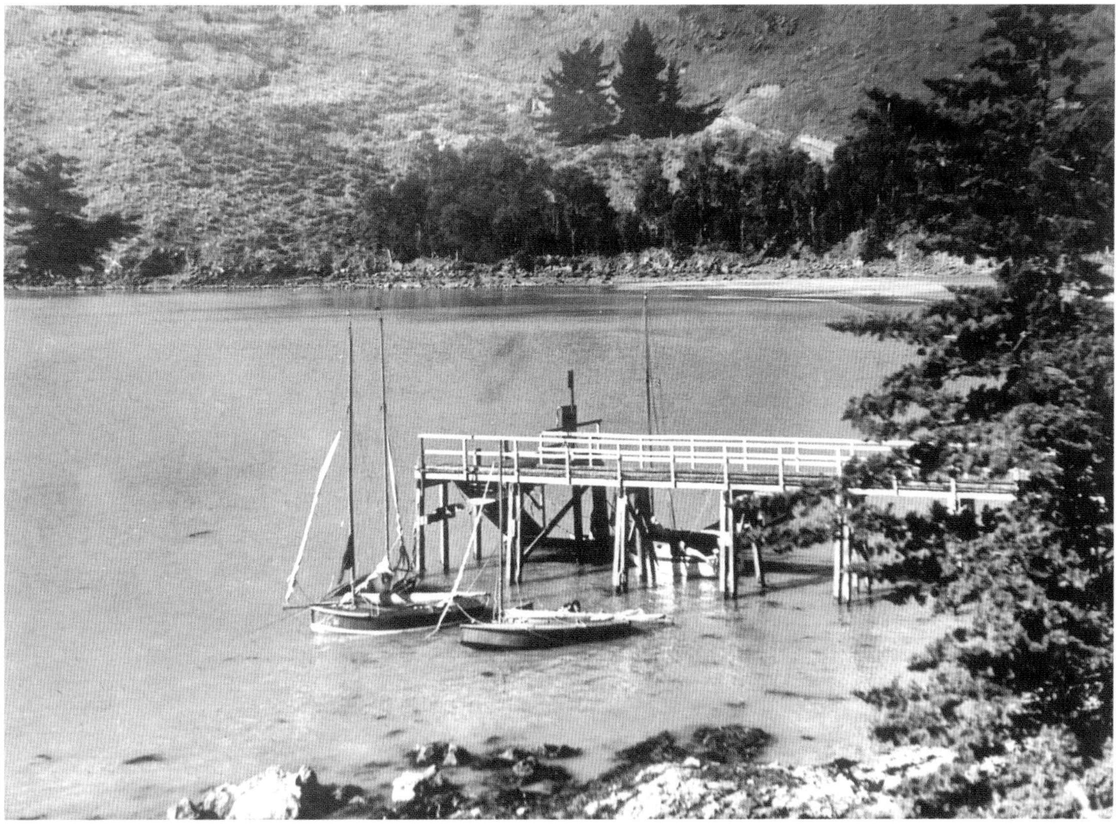

Anderson's *Matariki*. They took part in running and swimming races, played cricket and were treated to an excellent picnic tea.[21] The Hunter girls belonged to a club run by the *Sun* newspaper. Members of the club, known as 'Sunbeams', were given the treat of a holiday across Lyttelton Harbour at the cost of a shilling per day (waived for families who could not afford the charge), plus five pence each way for the train and a shilling for the ferry. A wagon and sledge hauled bags and provisions up the hill from the jetty while the children trudged uphill to their holiday home. (This was Pleasant View, once owned by the Henderson family but by 1925, according to author Elsie Locke, in the possession of Oliver Hunter.) The youngsters had picnic lunches down on the foreshore at Church Bay where old Mrs Hay, still living in the beach cottage that had once housed Deep Sea Fishing Company workers, provided drinks and thoroughly enjoyed the children's company.[22]

Gordon Ogilvie points out that Church Bay's population was given as eight in 1878, 16 in 1881, 12 in 1906 and five in 1911. Church Bay and Diamond Harbour, with their steeper frontages to the sea, were not favoured for early settlement to the extent that Pūrau or Charteris Bay were. However, with the new coast road built during the Depression, virtually completed by March 1933, the improved (and more scenic) access around the southern bays meant an increased demand for sections. As a result, Oliver Hunter subdivided some of his land below, and later above, the new road. In 1956 the land on the headland to the east of the bay was subdivided, though it took decades for any significant development to occur. The new Marine Drive, as the coast road was known, also reduced the dependence of both locals and visitors on the ferries, meaning that the relatively newly built Church Bay jetty was always patronised more by privately owned pleasure boats than by any sort of public launch service. Nonetheless, Church Bay did remain an excursion destination, with groups from Christchurch continuing to enjoy weekend picnics on the sandy beach.

During the postwar era, the sections below the road gradually filled with holiday homes. One in particular stood out amongst the timber constructions. Over seven years, between 1942 and 1949, Harold Sinclair, grandson of Barbara and Gideon Henderson, excavated stone from the foot of the cliff on his section and used it to construct a family holiday home. Another section, just above the beach, was purchased by a master builder who brought the timber for his house across from Lyttelton on a broad, shallow-draught barge. He successfully ran the barge up on the beach at high tide, unloaded the timber not far at all from the building site and constructed a modern cottage. Later, when the house had been purchased by architect Sir Miles Warren's father, the young Sir Miles offered to redesign the holiday home. The timber and steel pipes were to be brought over by launch from Lyttelton. In a reminder of that ever-present and sometimes fraught relationship between land and sea, 'we got the tides wrong: the launch was way down below the wharf, making loading difficult, and we arrived at Church Bay at dead low tide, far out on the mud flats.' Miles decided to throw the timber overboard and float it ashore. The treated timber sank into the mud.[23]

Oliver Hunter's grandchildren David, Marion, Ian and Mary grew up with their parents, Fred and Hazel, on the Church Bay farm, still the only permanent residents in the bay. As baches were built on the subdivided land below the road, the girls looked forward to other children arriving in the bay for summer holidays, as Marion recalled:

> They usually wanted to come up to see 'Mackey's farm' and we were quite happy to share (unbeknown to them), our vicious pet sheep or roosters. We always made certain we had a handy tree to climb or some other means of escape! It was quite an empty feeling when they all returned to Christchurch or wherever, after the holidays, but we readily made our own fun and soon became used to the 'normal' again.[24]

Later, when the family were living in Pūrau, David, Ian and Marion went to Linwood High School. This involved biking up the hill from Pūrau to Diamond Harbour, catching the 8.00 a.m. ferry (*Ngatiki* or *Onawe*), connecting with the train in Lyttelton, getting off at Opawa or Linwood Railway Station and biking or walking the remaining distance to school. On several occasions 'The Boat' failed to arrive at Diamond Harbour because of high winds and rough seas. The waiting adults might be picked up by the pilot launch, but this was not permitted to carry

Church Bay before subdivision began below the road in the later 1950s and 1960s. Hay Cottage is to the left on the beach, with Old Mac's Hut to the right and, above the road, the Hunter Cottage and farm. This shows how far Eliza had to carry the half ton of potatoes from the beach.
HUNTER ARCHIVE

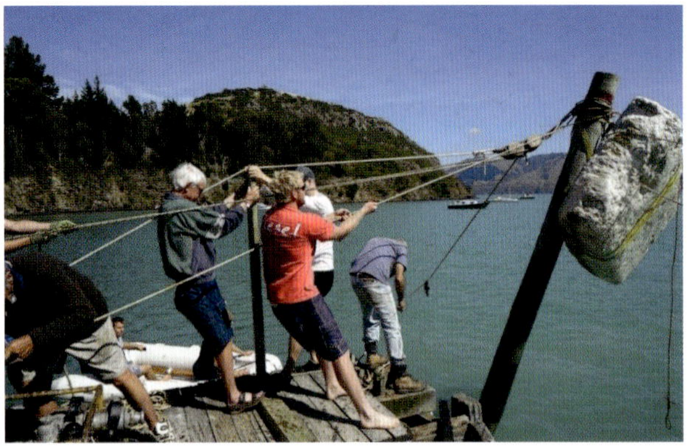

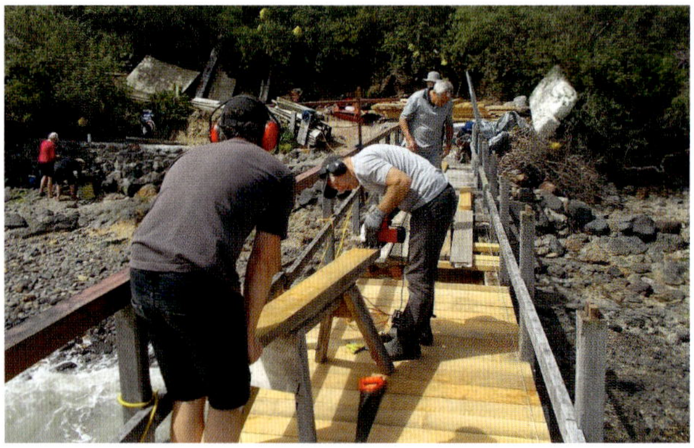

ABOVE Repairing the Church Bay jetty was a community effort. Three 600-kilogram vertical piles were brought around from Charteris Bay Yacht Club, floated behind a boat on a large polystyrene block.
PETER HARDING

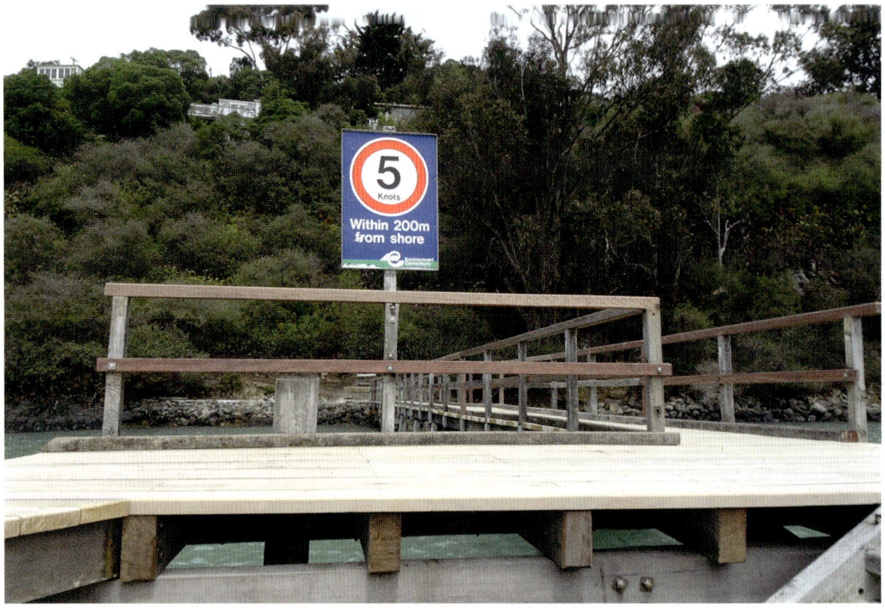
5
Knots
Within 200m
from shore

RIGHT Church Bay jetty after its repair and reopening to the public.
JANE ROBERTSON

children. This meant a day, or on one occasion two days, off school. 'The Boats used to tack almost to Quail Island or Rīpapa Island — depending on the wind direction, before finding an opportunity to turn in the huge swells. There were indeed some gut-wrenching moments!'[25]

Marion remembers the tsunami of 23 May 1960. For five minutes there was no water in Church Bay at all. The girls ran down to the beach, where Marion saw seahorses, but when the water returned they had to beat a hasty retreat. She recalls, too, how Johnny Hay taught them how to make bouncy balls and slippers out of kelp.

Sailing was another popular local activity. At one stage Oliver Hunter was the patron of the Charteris Bay Yacht Club, Fred was the commodore and Hazel the secretary. A Lyttelton lad who began sailing at about the age of 12, Eliot Sinclair, became a highly successful competitive yachtsman, representing Canterbury seven times in the prestigious Sanders Cup, and skippering boats to three consecutive wins. Eliot later built a bach in Church Bay on former Hunter land below Marine Drive, and the bay became a much-loved holiday destination for Eliot, his wife, Connie, and children Marton, Bruce and Bronwyn. They took advantage of all the recreational opportunities the harbour had to offer. Eliot purchased the 16-foot clinker-built motor boat *Elaine*, from which he could support the young in their own sailing efforts. 'The sturdy little *Elaine* was used to regularly tow a fleet of up to 10 kids in P class dinghies around to Charteris Bay for races and must have looked like a mother duck with a paddling of ducklings.'[26] The Sinclairs, too, were stalwarts of the Charteris Bay Yacht Club on and off the water — Connie always busy with the other mums preparing hot food for the cold and hungry young sailors.

Following the Christchurch earthquakes, the Church Bay jetty suffered extensive damage to horizontal beams and vertical piles. It was closed in 2011, and there was a risk that the cash-strapped city council would not repair it. The local residents' association resolved to take the project in hand and restore an important facility. In the spirit of partnership the council offered to pay for the materials, and about 40 locals volunteered a collective 1000 hours of expertise and labour, saving about $65,000 in labour costs. In December 2016 the jetty was proudly reopened. The partnership model between local community and council has paved the way for other jetty repairs in Robinsons Bay, Akaroa Harbour and Governors Bay.

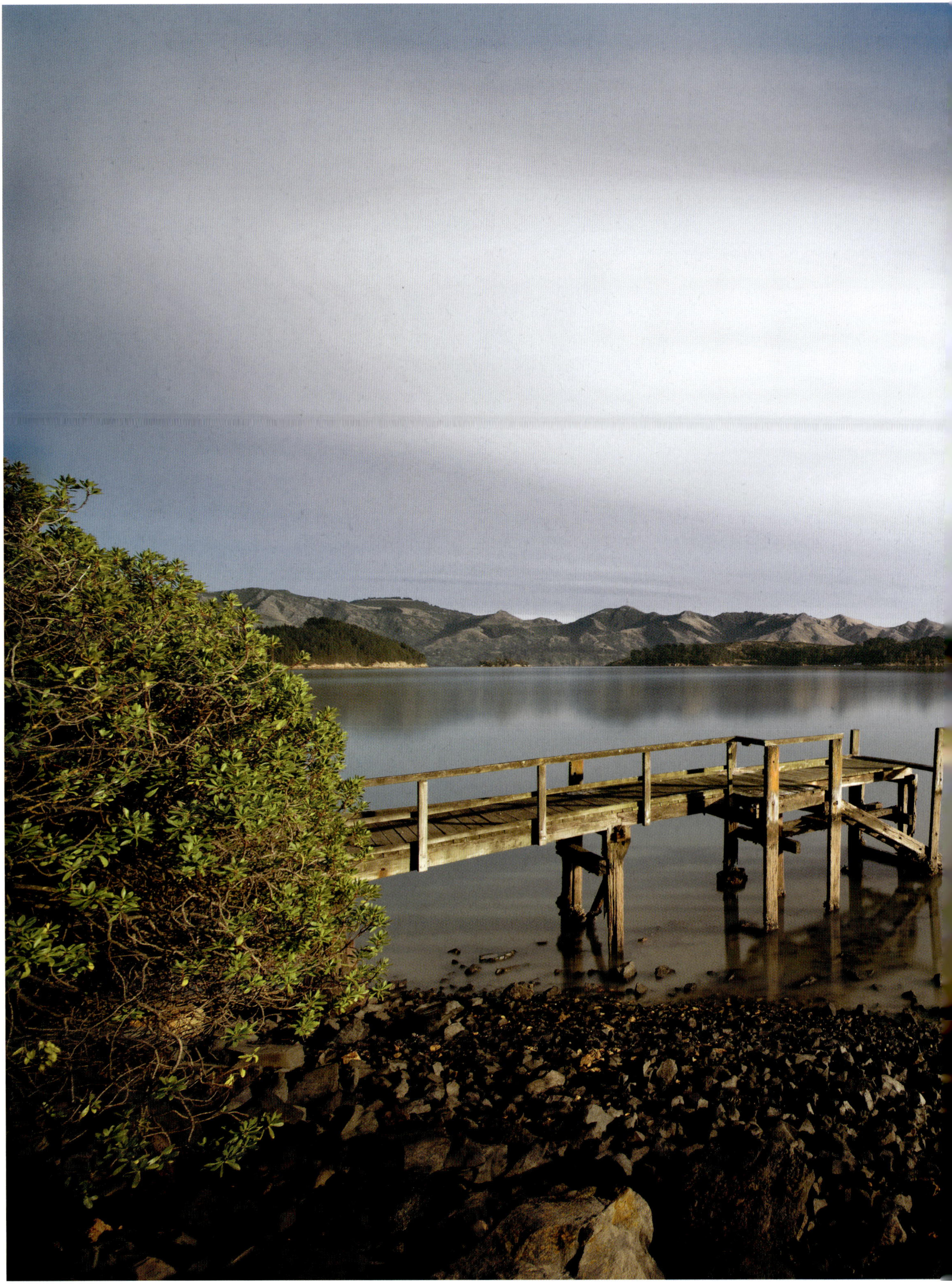

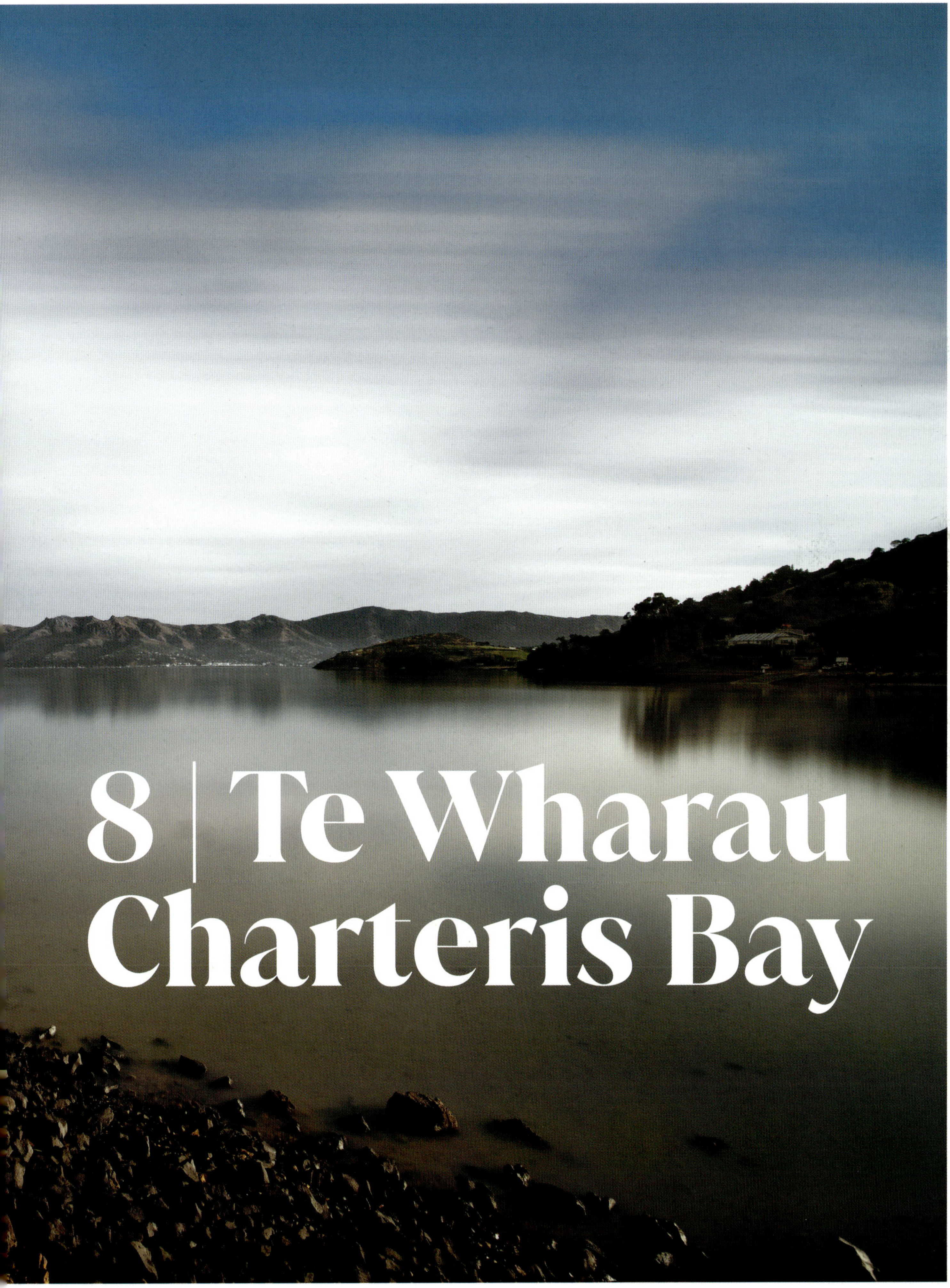

8 | Te Wharau Charteris Bay

The last of the 'southern' bays in Whakaraupō, Te Wharau Charteris Bay is nestled between Black Point to the east and the long, sheltering peninsula of Moepuku to the north-west, with the bulk of Mount Bradley rising directly behind. The area's Māori name refers to a 'hut' or 'shelter'. Waitaha, Ngāti Māmoe and Ngāi Tahu must have established kāinga in the bay over the centuries, attracted by the extensive oyster beds and fish spawning grounds. European settlers renamed it Charteris Bay after The Honourable Francis Richard Charteris MP, member of the management committee of the Canterbury Association.

*

In the early years, Charteris Bay residents could walk out on the oyster bank at low tide and gather oysters, small fish and crabs. But as oyster dredges ripped away the seagrass and damaged the bank, and as bush was felled, roads were built and land ploughed around the harbour, the resulting run-off covered the once-productive marine habitat, creating a 500-acre expanse of mudflat.

Early settlers Samuel Manson and John Gebbie (Head of the Bay) and the Rhodes brothers (Pūrau) leased land at Te Wharau from Ngāi Tahu before 1850. Manson built a stone shepherding hut (recently restored post-earthquake) in 1848 in what is now Orton Bradley Park. The initial plan for the organised Canterbury settlement was to situate Christchurch at the head of Lyttelton Harbour, with the town's botanical gardens at Charteris Bay and the prospect of increasing the town by up to 100 acres through reclamation of the mudflats. When the site of Christchurch was moved to the flat swamp over the hill at the last minute, the first Te Wharau sections were snapped up by The Reverend George Kingdon (chaplain on *Charlotte Jane*) and George Herbert Rowe (passenger on *Fatima*). Neither man ever occupied his land.

In November 1851 Dr Thomas Richard Moore arrived on *Sir George Pollock* with his wife, Ann, and six children. Moore had already purchased 50 acres in Charteris Bay before leaving England. With him came four cows, which became the basis for a highly regarded dairy herd.[1] While he continued to practise as a doctor in Lyttelton, Moore converted Manson's stone cottage into a dairy and employed the Ashworth family to manage the dairy farm. Cheeses from the dairy were sent over to Lyttelton by whaleboat. In 1853, Moore built a wooden cottage, a replica of which is now home to the Orton Bradley Park café. As well as adding to his land in Charteris Bay, Moore leased Ōtamahua Quail Island. He did not prosper financially, however, selling his entire property, of necessity, to The Reverend Robert Reginald Bradley in 1858.

Bradley, on the other hand, would farm at Charteris Bay until his death in 1892 (after which the farm passed to his eldest son, Orton, who continued to develop the property until his death in 1943). Robert Bradley had arrived in Christchurch with his wife, Frances, in 1856 to take up the position of vicar in the new parish of Papanui. He supplemented their income by growing vegetables and rearing stock

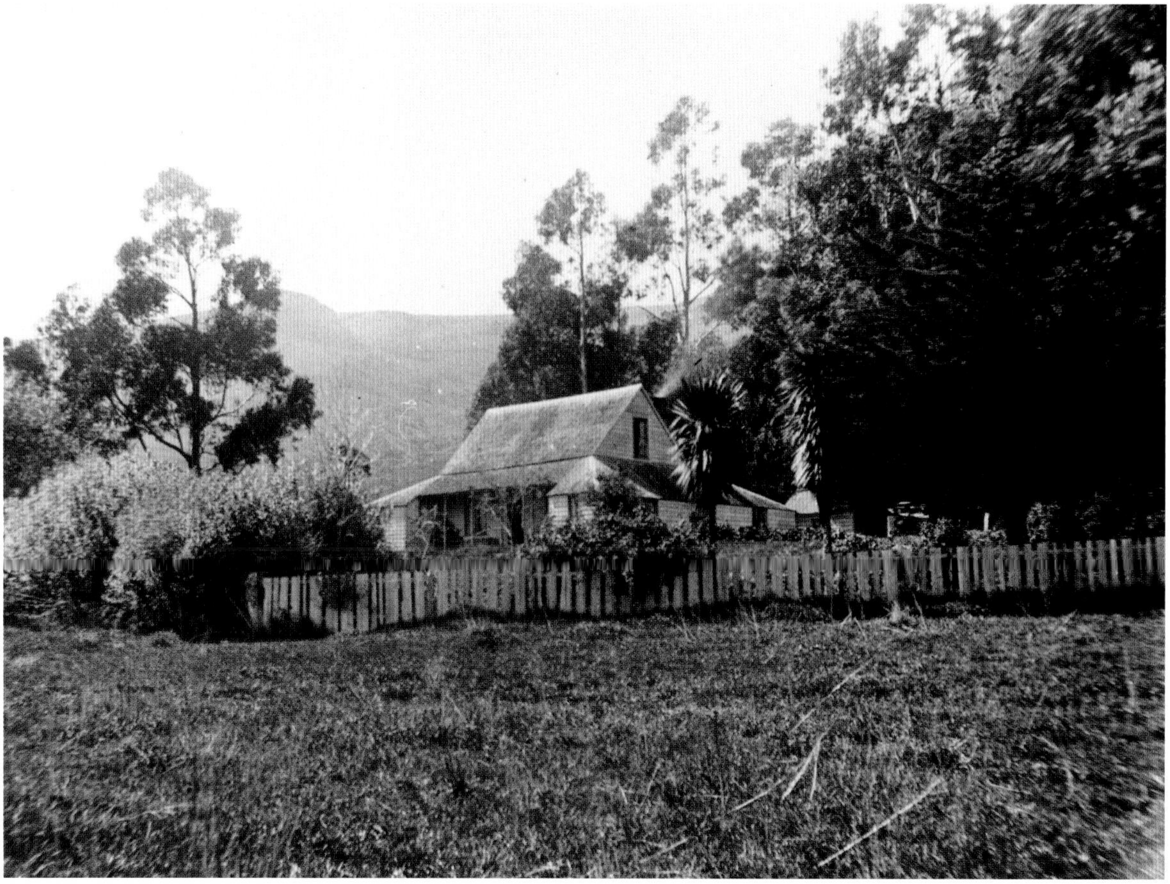

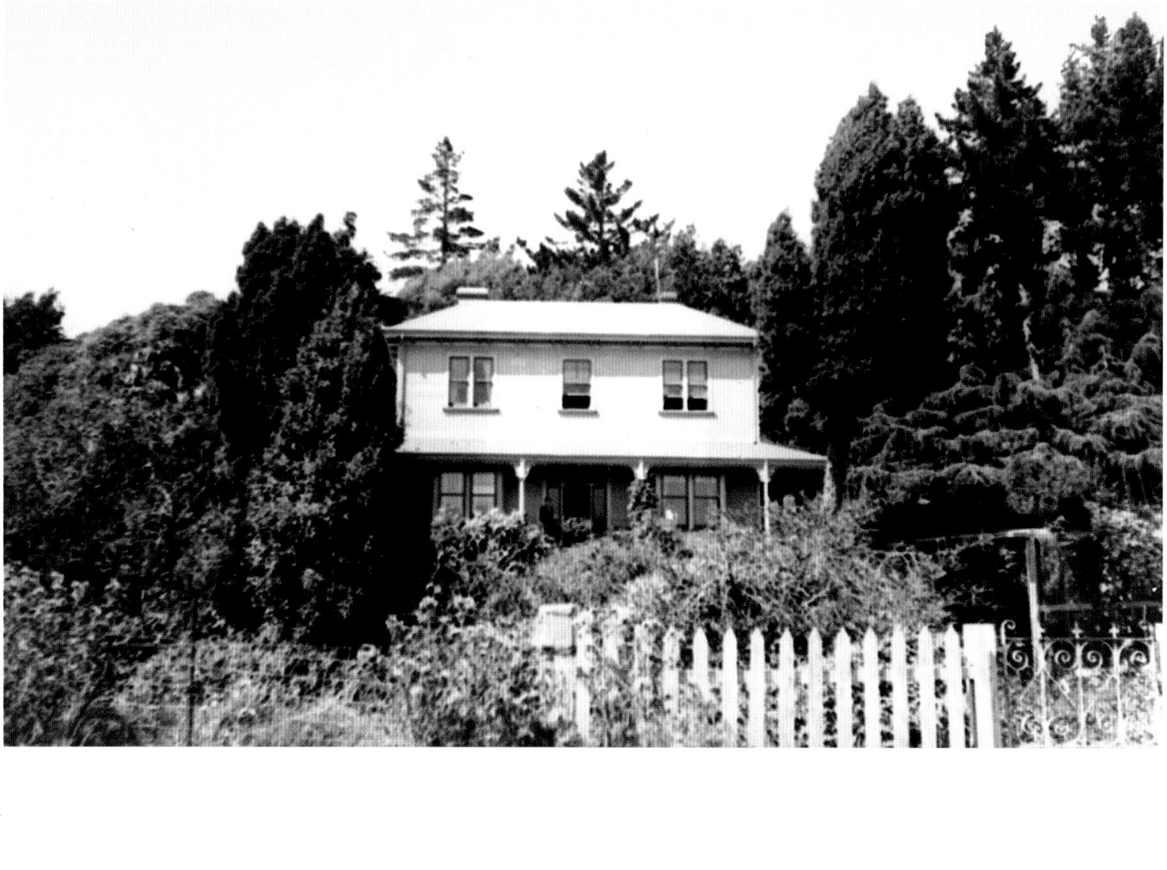

for fresh meat, and increasingly favoured his farming activities over his pastoral work. Services tended to be interrupted by Bradley's flock of guinea fowl, which roosted noisily among the piles under the church.[2]

So, in 1858 Bradley relinquished his vicar's duties at Papanui and moved to Charteris Bay. He and Frances had nine children, all of whom, with the exception of Orton, were born deaf. The children were well educated by governesses, who taught them sign language. Two of the children, Emma and Reginald, died young. Louis married teacher Alice Shailer and moved to a property in Cheviot. Orton, Frank, Alicia, Ada and Ethel remained all their lives on the Bradley estate. The eldest daughter, Kate Bowery Bradley, married Robert Anderson, and their two sons, Andrew Alexander and Robert, also lived and worked on the Bradley farm.

In 1900 or 1901 Orton Bradley shifted the building that had been home to the Moore and Bradley families since 1853 and commissioned Hollis and Brown of Lyttelton to build a two-storey, 14-room residence. Thanks to Orton's scientific and technical ingenuity, the new house boasted electric light in every room. The dynamo was driven by an overshot water wheel, still maintained in working order today at Orton Bradley Park. A number of visitors were invited to witness the electric light show in April 1901. They travelled across the harbour in the steam launch *Lyttelton* and noted that the house, 'with its many brilliantly lighted windows, made a highly effective spectacle'.[3]

Orton Bradley's other great passion, in addition to horses and matters technological, was trees, native and exotic. He planted approximately 150 species on the farm and seemed to have 'a deep understanding of the new science of ecology'.[4] Bradley generously shared his property with church groups, local families, and visitors from near and far. Through the 1920s, garden fêtes were held on the Bradley estate to raise funds for St Cuthbert's Church in Governors Bay. The fêtes were very popular, with many amateur gardeners from the wider region visiting the renowned arboretum. Special launches, connecting with trains from Christchurch, made the run from Lyttelton to Charteris Bay.[5]

Orton Bradley knew he had created something unique. His will ensured that following the deaths of his nephews Andrew and Robert the property would be gifted to the nation. In 1977, the park was formally handed over to the Orton Bradley Park Board to be maintained and developed for the enjoyment of the people of the harbour, Christchurch and further afield. In the years since, the farm park has been sympathetically developed, the old farm buildings well maintained and restored where necessary, and facilities added on an annual basis.

ABOVE The house built for Dr Thomas Richard Moore and family in Charteris Bay, 1853. A replica of this lovely cottage is now home to the Orton Bradley Park café. The photo is thought to have been taken by Mark Stoddart in about 1898.
CANTERBURY MUSEUM, 1983.315.3

BELOW The Bradley homestead on rising land 800 metres from the beach at Charteris Bay. It was built in 1901 by Hollis and Brown of Lyttelton. The house, constructed of kauri and lined with macrocarpa, burnt down in 1967.
HUNTER ARCHIVE

ABOVE The foreshore and mudflats below the Bradley estate, c.1898.
CANTERBURY MUSEUM, STODDART ALBUM, 8254.5

BELOW Pupils with teacher Alice Shailer outside the Charteris Bay School, possibly on the occasion of the school's closure in 1896.
HUNTER ARCHIVE

While the Bradley children (with the exception of Orton) were educated at home, by 1870 there were enough children in Diamond Harbour, Church Bay and Charteris Bay to warrant the opening of a school in Robert Anderson's shed. In 1879 a purpose-built school was constructed on land donated by The Rev. Robert Bradley, just over the road from the main gates of the Bradley homestead and, like all the harbour schools, very close to the sea. For its first few years Charteris Bay School shared a teacher with Teddington School. This proved to be a fraught arrangement — not only for the sole-charge teacher, who had to travel daily the 3 miles between the two schools, but also for the parents who expected their children to receive a full-time education. The solution was to open each school on alternate days, giving keen students the opportunity to have a full week of schooling if they were prepared to travel the extra distance. In 1884 there were about 40 children enrolled at Teddington School and 25 at Charteris Bay School. As a result of a petition signed by local residents and presented to the Board of Education in August of that year, a second teacher was appointed.

There was a fairly brisk turnover of teachers. At the beginning of September 1886, 19-year-old William Taylor was travelling by boat across the harbour with his father to take up the position of teacher at Charteris Bay School. A squall capsized the boat off the east point of Charteris Bay, and while Mr Taylor senior managed to swim to shore, young William drowned in his attempt to reach safety.[6]

The children mostly left school when they turned 12, the boys to work on the small family farms or for other local farmers, the girls to work in the house and dairy and perhaps later to go into service. All the children had to help out with morning milking before walking to school, returning home at the end of the school day to help again with the cows. Two boys rode an old white horse from as far away as Rhodes Bay (Pūrau).

The school committee in 1887 was a roll call of familiar local names. Its members were: James Hay, William Anderson, Arthur Hunter, Thomas Simpson, Robinson Hunter, William Hay and Robert Anderson, who was also appointed chairman. When the school finally closed in 1896 because of a falling roll, children had no option other than to travel the additional 3 miles to Teddington School or to board in town. The school building was used for church services (at which Robert Bradley officiated), social events and finally as a hay shed. In 1973 the dilapidated old building was jacked up and carefully shifted from its original site to a new position in the grounds of Orton Bradley Park. Local volunteers worked over nearly five years, gradually restoring the school building until, in February 1978, it was opened for the use and enjoyment of local groups and visitors.

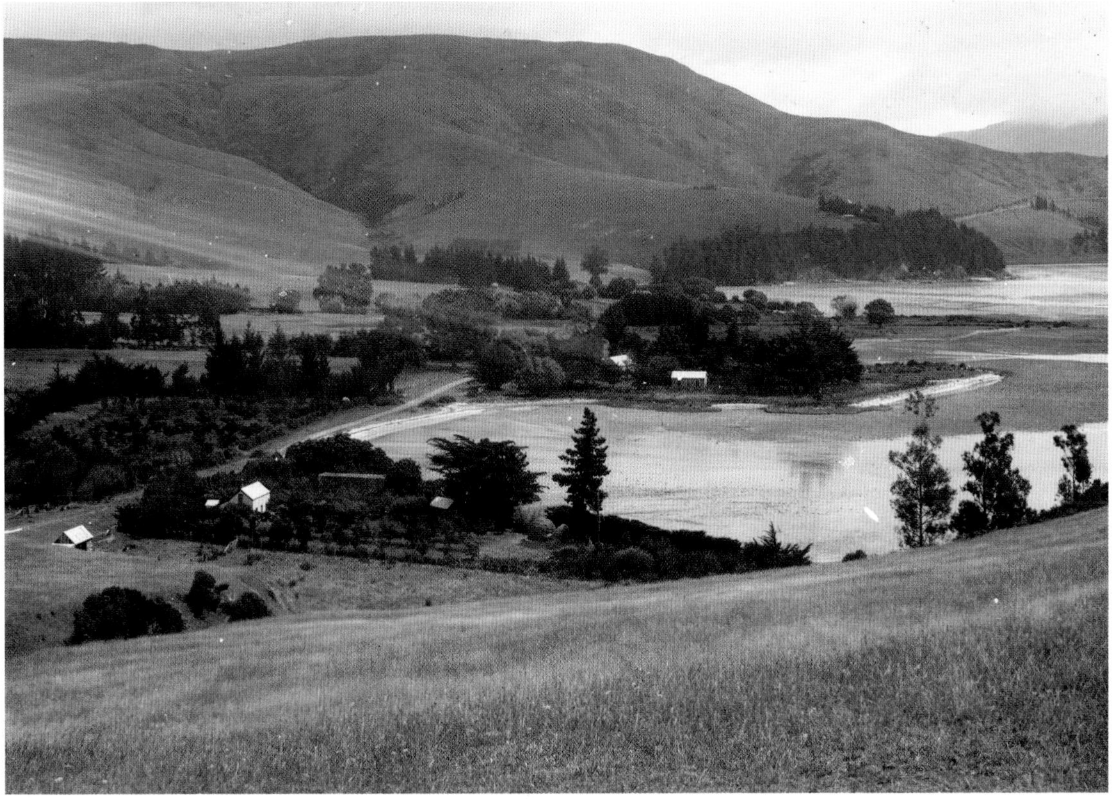

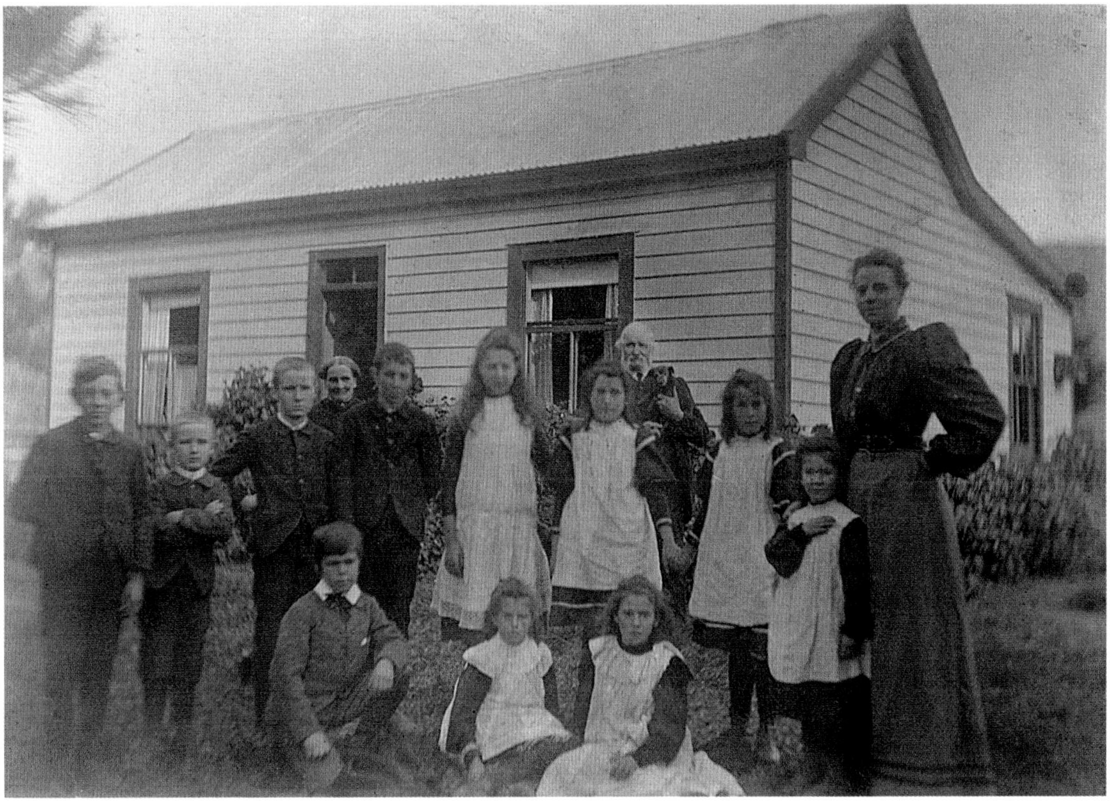

Charteris Bay resident Tom 'Seal' Simpson, his wife and children, all of whom worked at various times for the Bradley family. From left: Ivy Simpson (later married to Bill Manson), Mary-Ann, Emily, Tom Simpson, Martha, John (Jack) and Louisa.
HUNTER ARCHIVE

Shetlander Andrew William Anderson arrived on *Brothers' Pride* in 1863 and bought land in Charteris Bay before marrying Emma Metcalf. His brother Robert also settled in the bay, marrying Kate, the eldest Bradley daughter, in 1892. In 1905 Robert and Kate made their home in a handsome two-storey home, built by Hollis and Brown, near the sea in Charteris Bay. The house still stands today. Their two sons lived and worked on the Bradley estate.

The Simpson family initially lived in Church Bay, where Tom 'Seal' Simpson worked at one of the ballast quarries and his wife, Mary-Ann, acted as a local midwife. About 1880 the family moved to Charteris Bay, where Seal worked for the Bradley family for 42 years. The attachment between the Simpson and Bradley families was strong, and all the Simpson daughters worked at various stages in the Bradley household. Seal's daughter-in-law Ilma learned sign language so that she could better communicate with her deaf employers.[7]

The Moore, Bradley, Anderson, Simpson, Hay and Hunter (from Church Bay) families would have been almost entirely reliant on sea transport. There was no formed road connecting the southern bays with the rest of the harbour until 1875, and even then its condition was such that travel by sea was still the easier option. However, there is no evidence that the Moores, as the first family to settle in Charteris Bay, built a jetty. Maybe boats were simply run up on the mudflats and refloated at high tide. Since he leased Quail Island after the death of the Ward brothers, Dr Moore must have travelled across to the island quite frequently, as well as to Lyttelton to sell produce.

The Bradley family did construct a jetty, and maybe more than one. To support the nine children, their farm produced butter, cheese and meat, rope from a flax mill operated by Adam Chalmers, and stone from a quarry on the property. Most of this produce had to be transported to Lyttelton. The reverend used to boast how, 'in 33 years of travel by boat across the harbour, he had never met with an accident, despite some hair-raising journeys undertaken in appalling weather conditions'.[8]

In his diary, which spans the years 1879–80, the 22-year-old Orton Bradley noted: 'September 29 1879: Down with Bob Hunter and Gideon [Henderson] helping to put jetty up I was helping to put the outer trestle up, when the bottom slipped out & it nearly fell on us we were working up to our knees in water.'[9] In early January the following year, steam launch proprietor George Agar transported 24 bales of wool from the Bradley farm to Lyttelton. A couple of months later, 35 Bradley sheep and six pigs were picked up by the launch. In a diary entry for 16 March 1880, Orton Bradley noted that he had 'helped Hunters to take the old shears [sic] down that have stood at the jetty so long'. The tops of the 'shears' were rotten, but 'the bottoms were as sound as ever we took some of it to shellbay for props to the jetty there but the tide never went low enough for us to get to work'.[10]

This last excerpt hints at a possibility of two jetties. The structure in 'shellbay' or Shelly Bay (now Traffic Cops' Bay) was known early on as Bradleys jetty, or the 'Potato Jetty', since it was a transit point for the early new potatoes grown so successfully in and around Charteris Bay. Later it was known simply as the Charteris Bay jetty. It still stands today, earthquake-damaged and off-limits. As to the other jetty, that is a mystery.

In 1908 a young Oliver Hunter wrote in his journal:

> Went along to Bradleys Gully with the horse & sledge & after sorting & [???] up 14 cases of pears took them to Bradleys wharf. Mary helped me and we had dinner at W Hays then came home with sledge & father went back to Bradleys wharf & helped me to bring fruit to bay in boat. Arthur & I then took it to Port for shipment to Wellington by the Maori. Got back about 7o'c with light S.W. wind.[11]

The following month, the Hunters were still picking and transporting fruit to market:

> Went along to Bradleys Gully & picked & sorted fruit till 12 o'clock. Father sledged it to wharf. Came home & changed clothes then went to Bradley wharf & met J. Sinclairs oil launch & went to Port with fruit (28 cases to Wellington). After doing various business came home via steamer to Dia Hr.[12]

By the late 1880s, Charteris Bay farmers were keen to take advantage of more modern technology to improve access to Lyttelton and around the harbour. They petitioned the Lyttelton Harbour Improvement Committee for a new jetty for steam launches at Charteris Bay. The committee declined the request.[13] However, Lyttelton Harbour Board records indicate that the Charteris Bay jetty was entirely rebuilt in 1907. It may be that around this time the harbour board took over what had been Bradleys jetty. A half-ton crane was added to the jetty in September 1924. No doubt this would have been useful when Orton Bradley transported timber from the disbanded leper colony on Quail Island to Charteris Bay. The timber was used to build a sheep shed, which today houses a collection of old working farm machinery. Today, post-Canterbury earthquakes, the Charteris Bay jetty is permanently closed. It provides a handy resting place for shags.

Local resident Andrew Anderson took advantage of the Charteris Bay jetty rebuild when, in December 1908, he took possession of a new motor launch, built to order by Charles Bailey of Auckland. *Matariki* joined the growing fleet of launches that serviced harbour residents but also, and increasingly, catered for visitors to Lyttelton Harbour. It was a handsome boat, designed to offer passengers maximum comfort even at 9 knots.

Anderson built a slipway in what is now known as Paradise Bay, about two chains east of the current public launching ramp and next to the still existing Smarts jetty.[14] He used this to haul his launches out for painting and repairs. This ramp was passed on to Edgar Currie in the 1940s. Kororā little blue penguins used to nest every year under the Currie family bach just above the ramp. Anderson also built a stone jetty on a rocky outcrop three chains on from his slipway, out in front of the old Anderson house. Drays could drive out onto this jetty to load wool and other produce. To the north-east of this structure was Anderson's timber jetty, built of blue gum piles and planks, with a shed nearby measuring 60 by 70 feet. So the Paradise Bay foreshore, today favoured by swimmers for its gently sloping beach and sheltered privacy, was once a busy site of maritime enterprise.

Anderson's *Matariki* was in demand, helping the Church Bay and Charteris Bay farmers get their stores from Lyttelton and to ship their garden and dairy produce to the port. Anderson also ran a regular service to Pūrau and an on-demand excursion service to Diamond Harbour, Church Bay, Charteris Bay and Governors Bay. For example, the Lyttelton Golf Club commissioned *Matariki* to run regular trips at a fixed time on Thursdays, Saturdays and Sundays, with special trips as required. The Burwood branch of the Ministering Children's League took children to Governors Bay to see the site of the children's home to be built by Hugh Heber Cholmondeley. On their return to Lyttelton 'the children gave three hearty cheers for Mr Anderson, of the *Matariki*, who kindly took them to and from the bay

Andrew Anderson's launch *Matariki* heading for Lyttelton with Quail Island in the background. Built in 1908, *Matariki* was used to transport local produce to port, bring supplies back to the bays and carry visitors to Pūrau, Diamond Harbour, Church Bay, Charteris Bay and Governors Bay.
LYTTELTON MUSEUM, 11707.1

free of charge'.[15] The launch operators were well-known and well-regarded in the harbour.

When the Lyttelton Borough Council bought the Stoddart estate in Diamond Harbour for subdivision in 1911 it anticipated increased demand for ferry services. The council agreed to fund structural changes to *Matariki* and remove the engine to a position further forward in order to increase its carrying capacity. The nature of the relationship between private launch owner Anderson and the council that made such intervention possible is not clear.

The silting of the upper harbour posed an ongoing headache for launch proprietors and private boat owners. Oliver Hunter summed up the problem in a 1914 letter to the editor of the *Press*: 'When first seen at low tide, this structure [the Charteris Bay jetty] gives one the impression of having been erected far inland and driven to the shore, [where it] has baulked at sight of the water a quarter of a mile away, and been permanently abandoned.'[16] In 1919 it was proposed that a channel of 2 feet at standard low water be dug to the Charteris Bay jetty. This would mean the removal of about 5180 cubic yards of mud. If a small dredge were available to do the work, the Lyttelton Harbour Board estimated the cost at about £300. However, no such plant was available, and its construction would cost about £7000 with running costs of about £2200. The harbour board surmised that other harbour jetties would also appreciate the services of such a dredge, but could not see its way to funding such an item.[17]

In 1934 the harbour board refused an application from Andrew Anderson for the extension of the Charteris Bay jetty by two spans. Instead, the board's engineer suggested removing the loose stone at the shore end of the jetty, at a cost of £5.[18] Four years later, there was concern about the undermining of the sea wall near the jetty.

Charteris Bay was popular with campers in the early decades of the twentieth century. Tents were pitched on the hill facing the sea, and families swam, fished, climbed Mount Herbert and enjoyed trips out in the launch. The Bradley family would throw a garden party for residents and campers, with games for the children and afternoon tea on the homestead lawn. On 29 December 1930 the *Press* reported over 2000 visitors arriving by launch and car at Charteris Bay the previous day — a lot of people for a small settlement to accommodate, even if just for the day.

Ownership of the foreshore was challenged. 'Worker' wrote to the *Press* explaining that in summer he visited Charteris Bay, where 'there is a beach which gives good bathing when the tide is high, and a grassy bank on which it is pleasant to sun bathe'. During the most recent summers several weekend houses had been built on the sea front and, most recently, one holiday house had erected a fence which almost entirely enclosed the beach chain into his property. 'Worker' wanted to know 'by what rights this man has fenced in what I understood was public property, who has given him the right and what protection have working people like myself, who cannot afford to buy sections and erect houses?'[19] In response, Mr G. Anderson explained that he had fenced off newly planted ngaio and ribbonwood trees that were being eaten by hares. His section extended across the entrance to the bay, but it was not his intention to prohibit access to the public.

Jetties came and went within Paradise Bay, their purpose shifting over time from economic necessity to recreation. James Drewitt, Harold Smart and Fred Riley all had private jetties, in addition to the many slipways that serviced the boatsheds ringing the bay. The original Smarts jetty was built from blue gum felled directly onto the beach in the late 1930s by Harold Smart and Stan Rich. Before the building of the Charteris Bay Yacht Club, this jetty provided the base for yacht races. The jetty was rebuilt in the 1950s, and the shore end was rebuilt again by Barry Smart and his family following a massive landslide in 1975. In the late 1970s, yet another rebuild by Barry Smart and Brendon Leech added steps to the south side and a seat at the end, using treated timber. Over the past 25 years Carolyn (Barry's daughter) and Brendon Leech and family have kept up the maintenance, replacing posts, decking and general timber, as well as noting some eminent visitors: 'On a royal visit Prince Philip was brought over to Charteris Bay to go sailing with Ian White in his Flying Fifteen. They used the jetty to leave from and return to.'[20] Smarts jetty continues to be in constant summer use as a base for skiing and wakeboarding and as a favourite place for children to jump off. Carolyn and Brendon's daughter Sarah says that they 'intend to continue looking after the jetty and keeping it in the best condition'.[21]

A busy Smarts jetty in Paradise Bay, 1943. Before the building of the Charteris Bay Yacht Club in 1946, Smarts jetty provided a base for local yacht races.
COURTESY OF SUE CURRIE

Many people — even harbour dwellers — do not seem to know where Hays Bay is, perhaps because, for many years, access was only by sea or via a cliff track from the Charteris Bay Yacht Club. Today, the gently sloping, sandy beach at Hays Bay is more accessible and consequently popular with bathers during the summer holidays.

The land behind Hays Bay was farmed by James Hay (not related to the Hays of Pigeon Bay). Born in the Shetland Islands in 1838, James emigrated to Melbourne at age 20, seeking his fortune in the gold rush. He followed the gold to Gabriel's Gully in New Zealand, before returning to Shetland and then taking a passage on the same boat as Andrew William Anderson, the ill-fated *Brothers' Pride* (on which there were 44 deaths at sea out of 371 passengers), arriving in Lyttelton in 1863. He and his first wife had three sons, John, Gilbert and James.[22]

The dangers associated with dependence on sea transport were highlighted in November 1904 when son Gilbert Hay was leaving Lyttelton to return to Charteris Bay. A strong nor'westerly was blowing and Hay was just out of the harbour moles when a heavy squall capsized and sank his sailing boat. Two harbour board employees, C. Dobson and D. Sinclair, put out in their dinghy and picked up the young man. The boat disappeared without trace.[23]

To be living and farming in Hays Bay without water transport was inconceivable, and following the loss of Gilbert's boat a decision was made to take advantage of new technology. The following year the *Press* reported that 'a very handsome motor launch has just been completed by Messrs J. Sinclair and Son, of Lyttelton, to the order of Mr J. T. Hay, of Charteris Bay, who intends to use her on the run between the Bay and Lyttelton'.[24] The boat, 26 feet long with a 7-foot beam and depth of 4 feet, was constructed of kauri double planking. Hay then wrote to the Lyttelton Harbour Board requesting a landing place for passengers at Church Bay.[25] Whether in response to this or, more likely, as part of a spate of 'outer-jetty' building around the harbour in the first decade of the twentieth century, a jetty was duly built in Church Bay in 1907. In his diaries Oliver Hunter makes frequent reference to crossing the harbour in Hay's boat. At this time the Hays would presumably have used either the Church Bay jetty or the Bradley jetty further round Charteris Bay.

Due to ill health, John Hay (James's son) put the farm up for auction in 1935. It was described as a 'very warm, sweet piece of hill country, charmingly situated. The picturesque position of the homestead with its own little bay and beach, together with the beautiful outlook over Church Bay and its surroundings presents a unique opportunity . . .' The one-man farm with a practically new house carried 260 sheep and 15 cattle, and produced 'an abundance of early potatoes up to 10 tons to the acre'.[26]

In the 1940s Hays Bay and Charteris Bay joined the subdivision activity prompted by the building of Marine Drive in the 1930s but delayed by the war. After 1945, surplus army huts provided an excellent basis for inexpensive baches in the southern bays of Lyttelton Harbour. One of the first on the eastern side of Hays Bay had two army huts at its core.

At much the same time, a structure appeared in Hays Bay that more or less qualified as a jetty, though not one designed for launches. According to local yachtsman Paul Pritchett, the Hays Bay 'jetty' was a single plank that came from Payne's quarry. The plank had a groove running along its centre — once used for transporting barrows of rock from the quarry to the waiting ballast boats. Like so many structures around the harbour it was repurposed, in this case to create an access point to deeper water, enabling small craft to tie up and children to play. Photos from the late 1950s show normally quiet Hays Bay full of people and craft, enjoying one of the rowing regattas that were held out of the sheltered bay — and for which the flimsy jetty was maybe erected. There is no sign of it now.

The remains of yet another jetty can still be seen at Bakers Point, just to the south of the Charteris Bay Yacht Club. Lyttelton, in the early twentieth century, lacked a suitable space for a golf course. When, in 1912, Orton Bradley offered Lyttelton golfers rent-free land in Charteris Bay, the offer was keenly accepted and

Hays Bay was named after Shetland Islander James Hay, who farmed the land at the northern end of Charteris Bay below Black Point. This photo, taken during one of the popular rowing regattas, probably dates from the late 1950s or early 1960s. It shows baches and boat sheds (still there today), a woolshed and a 'jetty' (no longer there). CBYC

a golf club formed. Within 12 months, 60 men and women belonged. The only complication was getting there. Depending on the tide, *Matariki* would land golfers at the Charteris Bay jetty (very handy) or, if the tide was too low, at the Church Bay jetty (a long trudge with golf clubs to the golf course on the Bradley estate).

The launch trips could be unpredictable. One June evening in 1915, a party of golfers was returning to Lyttelton. The tide was out and the motor launch had to anchor some distance from the Bradley jetty. The six golfers requisitioned a small dinghy, designed for five passengers, to get out to the launch. As the sixth golfer got in, the dinghy sank, leaving the men waist-deep in water.[27] In August 1921 a motor boat carrying exceptionally keen Lyttelton golfers grounded about 800 yards short of the intended jetty. Some club members waded ashore in freezing conditions and secured a dinghy in which to transport the rest of the party. An hour into play, it began to snow. The game was abandoned in favour of a return home, but the motor boat engine wouldn't start. After a three-and-a-half-hour wait in heavy snow, a regular harbour launch finally rescued the stranded golfers.[28]

The following year a jetty was built at Bakers Point. This enabled more frequent access by sea than the mud-bound main jetty close to the Bradley estate, and it lessened the long trudge from Church Bay. The new structure was known as the Golf Jetty, Half-Way Jetty or Bakers jetty — Owen Baker owned the land and house above the structure. Long after golfers ceased accessing the Charteris Bay golf course by sea, the Charteris Bay Yacht Club continued to use Bakers jetty at times when its own jetty was too busy. Today only a few piles remain, although current owner Philippa Drayton has plans to resurrect the structure.

The Charteris Bay Yacht Club has offered countless youngsters and adults the opportunity to learn, compete and generally 'mess about in boats' for the past 80-plus years.

Competitive regattas were a feature of Lyttelton Harbour life from the early years of European settlement. In the late 1930s the Canterbury Yacht and Motor Boat Club, based in Lyttelton, ran New Year races at Church Bay and Charteris Bay. On New Year's Day in 1938, a particularly successful regatta was held from the jetty fronting James Drewitt's house in Charteris Bay, with more than 30 yachts and many launches gathering in the bay. As a result, in 1939 local residents decided to form the Charteris Bay Yacht and Power Boat Club, with Orton Bradley as club patron. The first race was sailed from Andersons jetty for a prize sum of 10 shillings. Until the end of the Second World War, private jetties in Paradise Bay were used, and competition was largely confined to the Idle-Along class.

The Idle-Along was designed in 1927 by Wellington resident Alf Harvey in response to the need for a cheap, one-class design that amateurs could easily build. Harvey's inspiration was a 12-foot 8-inch porpoise, which he captured, measured and released in Worser Bay. 'The curve of the porpoise's back inspired the keel profile, the back fin the centre plate, and the tail the rudder.'[29] A very broad beam gave the yacht stability, while airtight sections fore and aft lent extra buoyancy. Disparagingly nicknamed a 'butterbox', the Idle-Along was poorly regarded by many sailors until it proved its worth in very blustery conditions. The class was also within the reach of keen young sailors. In the early 1950s 'an Idle-Along could be built and completely rigged for £30'.[30]

Local yachtsmen Grant Anderson, Paul Pritchett and Fred Mackey took into account the particular conditions on Lyttelton Harbour when they designed the Skimmer class. These yachts had a very flat hull and a triangular bow and 'sailed particularly well when running with the wind or on the lead'.[31] They could be sailed and carried easily by two sailors and could be righted with ease following a capsize. Although yachting was mostly a men's sport up until the 1960s, with the women providing morning and afternoon teas in the clubhouse, the local ladies organised their own Ladies' Race as early as 1944.

In 1946 the decision was made to build a clubhouse and jetty in Charteris Bay. In the spirit so often evident in the harbour communities, a 40-foot by 30-foot shed, built by volunteers, and a 60-foot jetty, built by the Lyttelton Harbour Board, were ready for the opening in November that year. There was no storage area for boats in the early days. Yachts were kept on their own slipways, mostly in Charteris and Church Bays. According to Paul Pritchett, there was an intense rivalry between the adjacent bays. The Ferguson-Rich Trophy, awarded as the result of a teams' race between Charteris Bay and Church Bay sailors, was hotly

ABOVE New Year's Day Regatta, 1938. The success of this regatta led to the formation, the following year, of the Charteris Bay Yacht and Power Boat Club. Some of the young sailors included, from left: Des Irwin, Dick Morefield, Keith Hendry, Archie Childs, Bink Drewitt, Fred Mackey, Ian Stringer.
CBYC

BELOW Hazel Mackey launching Charteris Bay Yacht Club rescue launch *Te Wharau* at Lionel Jefcoate's boatbuilding shed in Governors Bay, 1958. Club patron Oliver Hunter is standing on the left and skipper J. A. White is at the helm.
HUNTER ARCHIVE

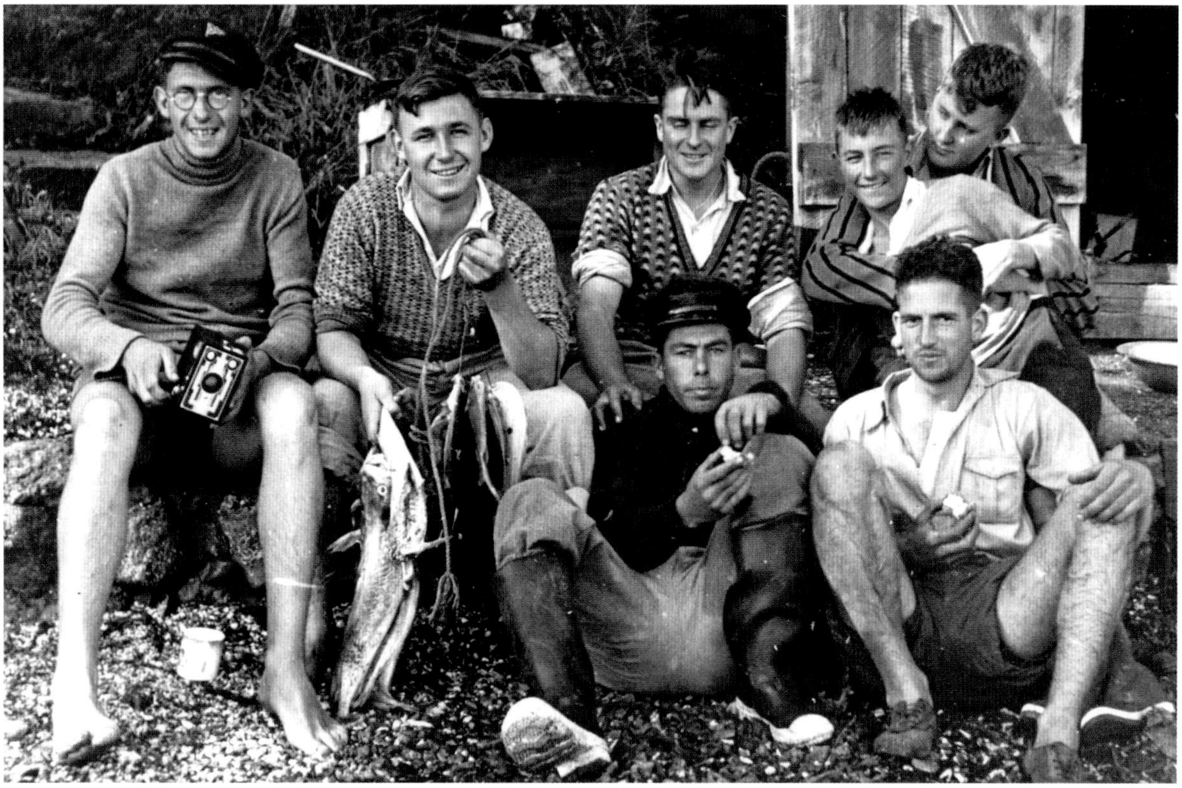

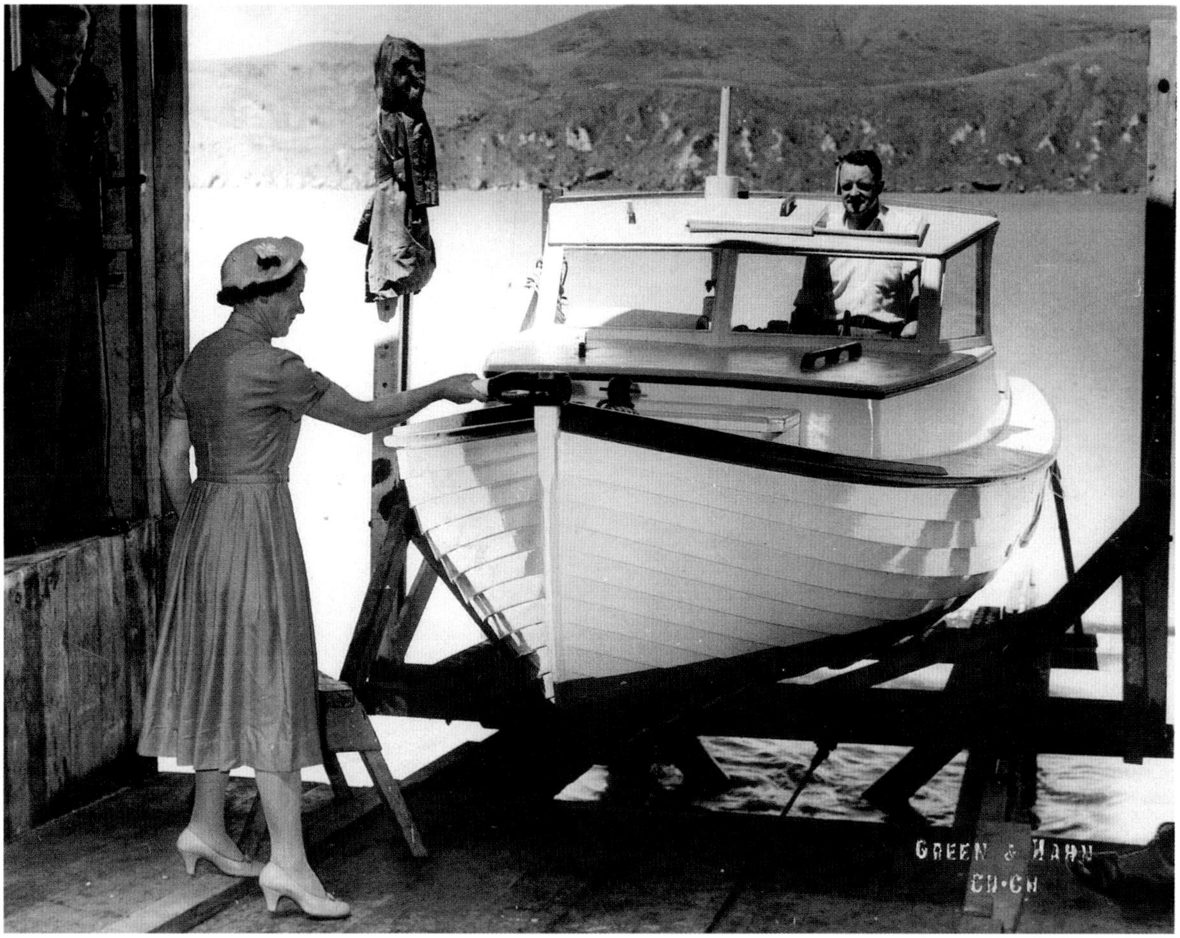
GREEN & HAHN
CH·CH

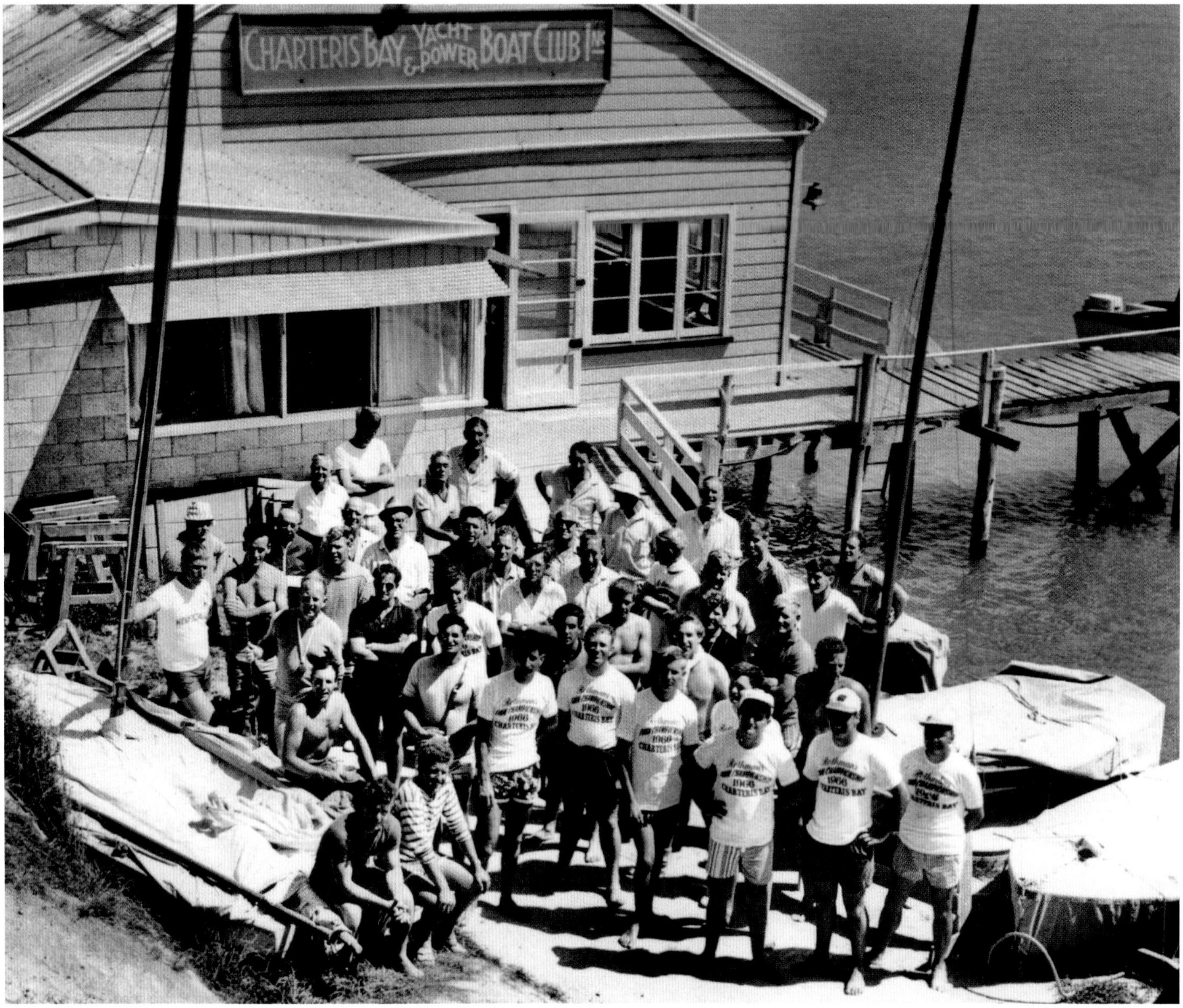
CHARTERIS BAY YACHT & POWER BOAT CLUB Inc

Colourful Optimists preparing to race from the Charteris Bay Yacht Club.
CBYC

contested and argued over. 'One night it mysteriously disappeared from the clubhouse and was not sailed for again.'[32]

The club needed a rescue launch for races. Its original boat, *Dolphin*, purchased in 1955, proved unreliable, and so a purpose-designed pick-up boat was crafted by Lionel Jefcoate at his new boatbuilding shed in Governors Bay. The 22-foot clinker rescue boat *Te Wharau* was launched on 22 November 1958 and is still in regular use today. One memorable rescue occurred in February 1964 when *Te Wharau* picked up an injured Charles Dudley from his capsized R Class. Charlie had been trying to right the yacht when, recalls Pritchett, 'he felt what he thought was a rope around his leg, put his hand down to push it away and found he had a finger missing and a bite out of his leg'.[33] *Te Wharau* radioed for an ambulance and got Charlie to the Lyttelton wharf, from where he was transferred to Christchurch Hospital.

The clubhouse became a centre of local social activity, including legendary dances. The shipwreck dances required those who attended to arrive by sea — home-made rafts (including a bath) took the place of the usual water craft. Fred Mackey steered his Second World War landing barge under the clubhouse to emerge up through the trapdoor. The club was also a magnet for youngsters from all over wanting to learn to sail and test their yachting skills. Membership in 1958 was a healthy 440, and the following year a jetty was built for the popular P Class yachts by staff of the Lyttelton Harbour Board.

Unfortunately, the tsunami in 1960 put the clubhouse under 14 inches of water and caused the floor to float up; it has never quite returned to its original level. Nonetheless, over the years, the clubhouse has been improved, largely through the work of enthusiastic volunteers, who have also been responsible for the many learn-to-sail programmes for young people.

OPPOSITE Charteris Bay Yacht and Power Boat Club Inc before the words 'power boat' were dropped in the mid-1960s.
CBYC

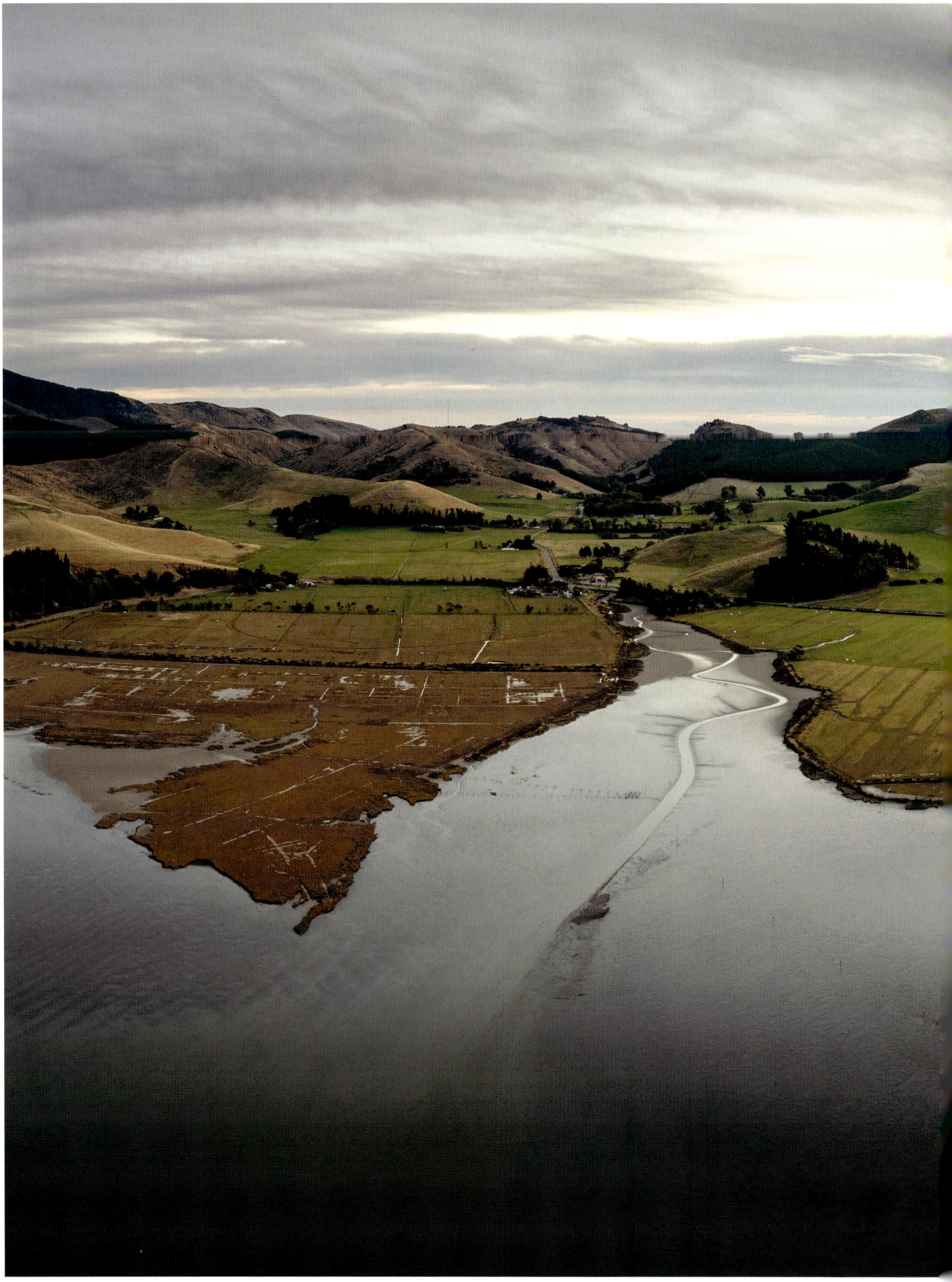

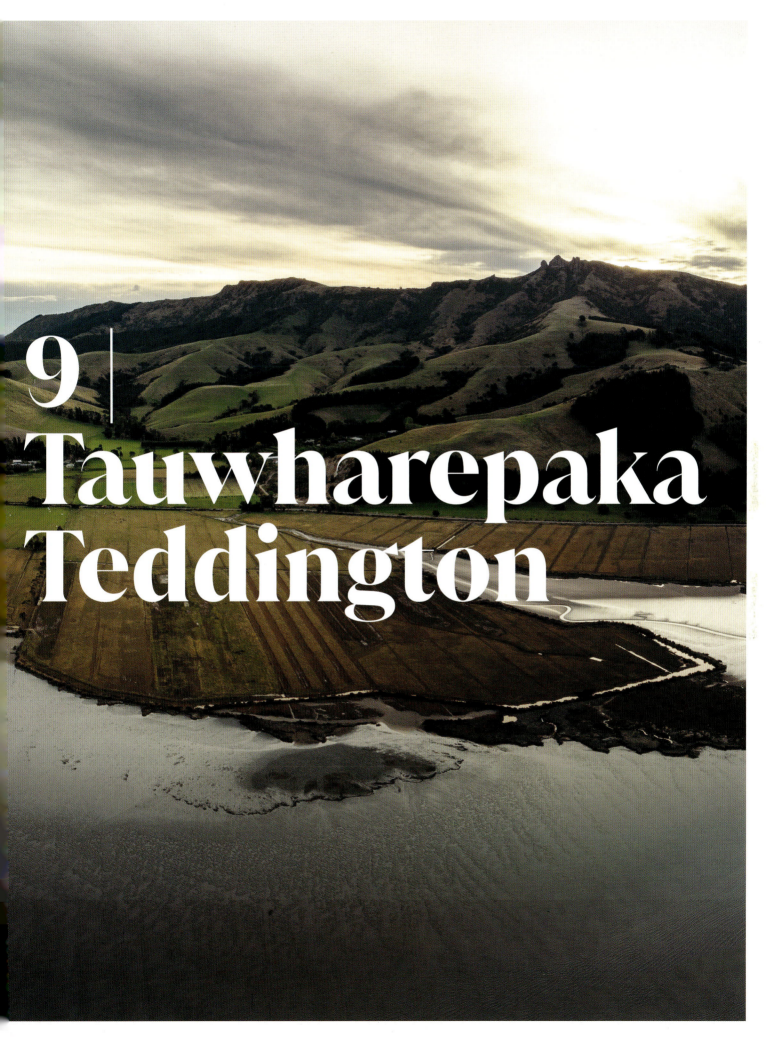

9 | Tauwharepaka Teddington

The distinguishing feature of the head of Whakaraupō, stretching from Teddington through Allandale, Ōhinetahi, Governors Bay and Sandy Bay, is its extensive tidal mudflats and saltmarsh vegetation which, though degraded, still support many indigenous plant and bird species. 'Whaka' is the Ngāi Tahu dialectical form of 'whanga', meaning 'harbour' or 'bay'. Thus Whakaraupō means 'harbour or bay of the raupō reed'. Originally the name applied only to the head of the harbour, where the reeds grew in a swamp, not to the whole harbour as it does today.[1]

❊

The saltmarsh and mudflats were well understood and utilised by Māori, but created all sorts of problems for European settlers dependent on sea transport. Over time, at least eight jetties serviced the head of the harbour, evidence of its economic and recreational significance. Of some jetties, almost nothing is known. For others there is more documentary evidence available. Today one sad jetty remains in Governors Bay, neglected, earthquake-damaged and marooned at mid- to low tide — but about to be reborn as a recreational asset and a marker of the once vital relationship between land and sea. The next three chapters look at the bays that constitute the 'head of the harbour', beginning with Head of the Bay or Tauwharepaka Teddington.

Teddington, so the story goes, was originally 'tide-end town': the village on the River Thames, west of London, was the point beyond which the tide no longer reached. The name made its way to Lyttelton Harbour when schoolteacher William Flower Blatchford acquired a farm below the slopes of Mount Bradley and named it 'Teddington' after his old London home.[2] Just as in the English Teddington, the tide once came right up to the gate of the Blatchford farm. The name Teddington came to apply to the area surrounding the junction of the Teddington–Charteris Bay road and Gebbies Pass road. To complicate matters, for the first 40 years of European settlement the area was commonly known as 'Head of the Bay' or 'Gebbies Flat'. Current topographical maps still carry the label 'Head of the Bay'. Locals just referred to 'the salt flats'.

Māori gave the name Moepuku to the headland separating Te Wharau Charteris Bay from Teddington. It looked, they said, like a sleeping taniwha. The headland between Teddington and what we now know as Allandale was named Kaitangata by Māori, and later Mansons Peninsula by European settlers.[3] Two main streams drain the Teddington area. Waiake, meaning 'water from up high', drains the hill country below Mount Bradley, Kaituna Pass and McQueens Pass. Te Rapu, meaning 'to search for', drains the central area of Teddington. At the mouth of one of the streams was a place known as Tauwharepaka, home to a small building where the season's fishing catch was prepared and dried.[4] Māori used waka to travel the harbour and navigate the tidal mudflats and the channels gouged by Waiake and Te Rapu. This was an area rich in kaimoana. There were frequent trips over Tara o Te Rangi Hikaia Gebbies Pass to trap tuna (eels) at Te Waihora Lake Ellesmere and Wairewa Lake Forsyth. The tuna, together with rig from the harbour, were dried for later consumption and for trade. Pārera grey duck, kukupako black teal, tatā brown duck and pāteke brown teal were hunted all around the shores of Te Waihora. The slopes around Waiake and Te Rapu were also a great source of harakeke.

In 1842 Captain William Mein Smith, surveyor general to the New Zealand Company, was directed to map the harbours on the South Island's east coast. He visited Whakaraupō, then known as Port Cooper, but was doubtful about the head of the harbour as a site for development. If a commercial harbour were to be located there, it would require reclamation, dredging, expensive sea walls and long jetties out to deeper water.[5] The prevailing easterly wind produced an unwelcome swell, and only at Rāpaki was there wood near the shore. Mein Smith preferred Akaroa Harbour for possible settlement. Two years later, tasked with finding a site for the proposed Scottish settlement of New Edinburgh, surveyor Frederick Tuckett visited Port Cooper and considered the head of the harbour to be a good site for a town, with fertile land and easy access over the hills (Gebbies Pass) to the plains. The mudflats remained a problem, however, and Tuckett selected Otago Harbour instead.

Meanwhile, on the Canterbury Plains, Scotsmen John and William Deans had established a farm at Riccarton in 1843 with the contracted help of fellow countrymen John Gebbie and Samuel Manson. Two years later, having worked out their time with the Deans brothers, John and Samuel, with their wives, Mary and Jean, arranged to lease land from local Māori. Samuel leased 2000 acres of bush-covered hill country stretching from near Governors Bay to Charteris Bay, while John took up adjacent land running back from Teddington to Te Waihora Lake Ellesmere.

For the two families, including their then total of eight children, the sea journey to the head of the harbour in May 1845 began badly. By the time they reached the notorious Sumner Bar, the wind was very strong and the sea rough. The women and children were landed, and had no choice but to spend the night in a cave, hungry and cold. At the other end of the perilous trip they had to navigate the winding channel carved by the stream through the mudflats. Starting from scratch, the families built homes and established thriving dairy farms.

This pioneering enterprise was disrupted by yet another plan to establish a settlement at the head of Port Cooper. In December 1848 Captain Joseph Thomas arrived in Lyttelton with instructions to select, survey and prepare a site for the chief town of the Canterbury Association's intended Church of England

An aerial view of Teddington cradled by Moepuku on the left and Kaitangata Mansons Peninsula on the right, 1978. Te Waihora Lake Ellesmere is visible in the distance.
V. C. BROWNE & SON, 16644/16669

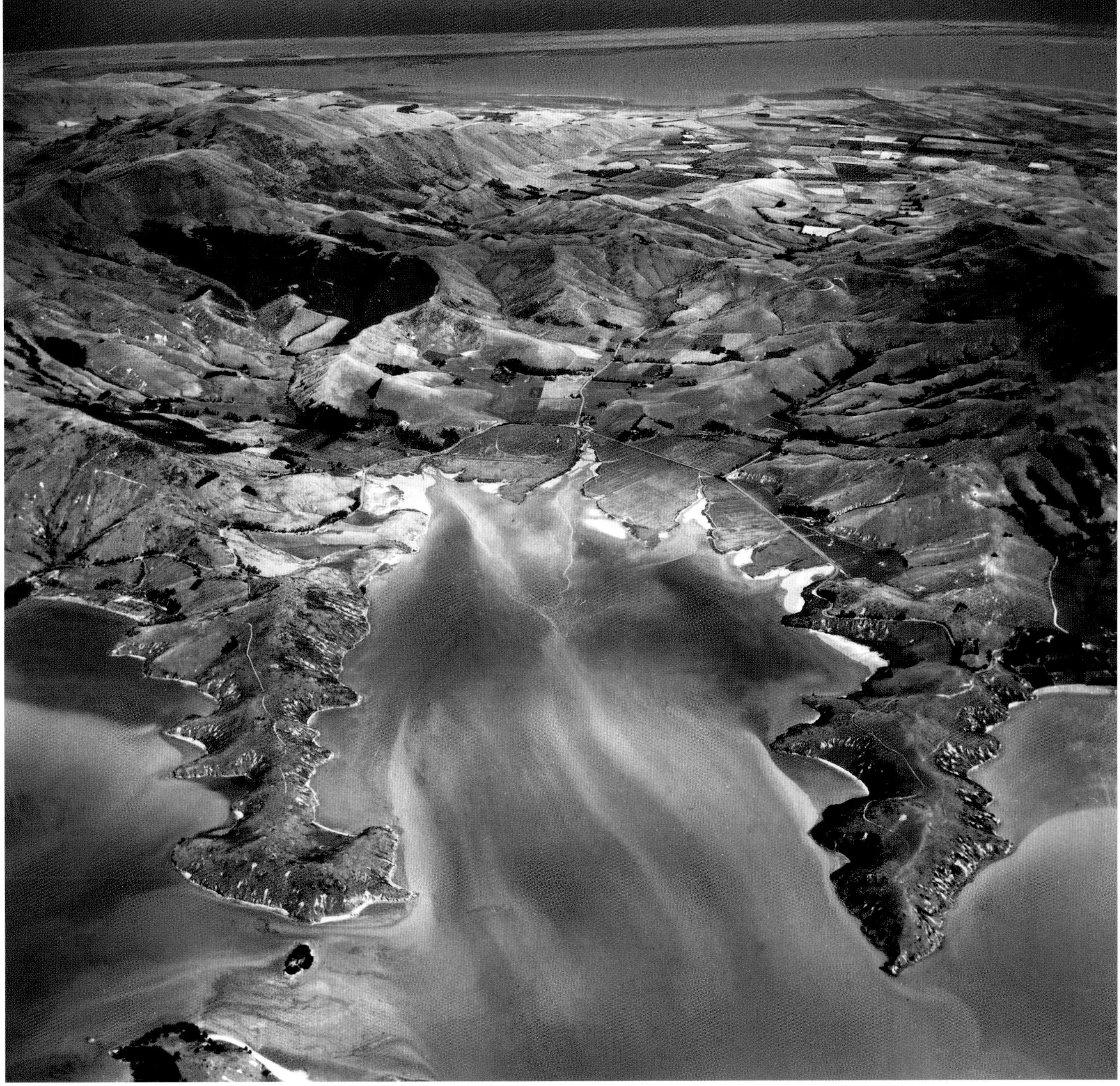

settlement. Thomas thought the area known as Head of the Bay might be suitable if the mudflats were reclaimed, using local stone to build an embankment from what was briefly termed Gleigs Island (Ōtamahua Quail Island) to the mainland. The new settlement would be centred on what is now Teddington, with botanical gardens at Charteris Bay, the government domain located in present-day Governors Bay and the port at Rāpaki. At this formative stage the name Governors Bay (or Government Bay) was used to describe the whole area at the head of the harbour.

All Māori leases in Port Cooper were invalidated on 10 August 1849, leaving the way clear for the Canterbury Association to develop the land at the head of Port Cooper. However, attractive as the location was, it lacked flat land and sufficiently deep water for a port. Surveyor Charles Torlesse reported that he got 'stuck in the mud flats on the way to Gibies [Gebbies] farm and had a wet walk'.[6] So, 18 months before the arrival of the first sizeable group of Canterbury Association immigrants, the site of the future city of Christchurch was shifted from the head of the harbour to the Canterbury Plains, and the port from Rāpaki, which had been designated a native reserve, to its present location of Lyttelton. The Manson and Gebbie families were granted new licences by the Canterbury Association and were later able to purchase land in their own right. At the same time, parcels of sea-front land became available to Canterbury Association immigrants.

For the first 10 years of the Gebbie and Manson families' lives at Head of the Bay, there was no road around the harbour to the port town of Lyttelton. In 1856 a narrow bridle path was made from Lyttelton as far as 'Gibbie's Flat', but by 1863 even this had been allowed to 'fall into decay', according to the local press.[7] So passage by sea was vital, albeit challenging. Seventeen-year-old Susannah Chaney arrived at Lyttelton aboard *Randolph* in 1850 and was promptly engaged by Samuel Manson as a domestic servant. In later life, Susannah recalled being taken to Head of the Bay in a whaleboat. 'The tide was out and there was a big expanse of mudflats. I was taken ashore on a sledge drawn by two bullocks. There was a tub lashed to the sledge, and on to this a seat was fixed.'[8] It was the first farm Susannah had ever seen.

Jane Deans, wife of John Deans, who had supported the Scottish families in their new enterprise, also enjoyed Gebbie and Manson hospitality. In 1855 she travelled to Lyttelton and then took the boat to Head of the Bay, arriving in the evening. Arrival and departure were determined by the tides, since 'a boat getting stuck in that [the mudflats] might have to remain there with its freight, living or dead, till the tide rose again to float it off. It might be twelve hours.'[9]

The difficulty of constructing roads around the harbour and over the Port Hills to the Canterbury Plains prompted *Lyttelton Times* correspondent Robert Greaves to suggest in 1855 that the fledgling settlements of Christchurch and

The Manson family at Kains Hill, Head of the Bay, c.1864–65.
CANTERBURY MUSEUM, HAY FAMILY COLLECTION, 1915.35.177

Lyttelton make better use of sea access. He proposed the building of a sea wall across the entrance of 'Gibbe and Manson's Bay' (present-day Teddington), using stone from Aua King Billy Island. A canal 30 feet broad and 8 feet deep could then be constructed in a line to the high-water spring tide mark at Head of the Bay. At the top of the canal a float or dock of 2–3 acres with a half-tide gate could be built. The drained land would be available for agricultural development, with the addition perhaps of a tidal mill. A road should then be constructed 'up the northern face of the low range of hills' (Gebbies Pass) and down to the plains. This plan would 'decrease the expenses and risks attendant upon the transport and shipment of wool and other exports'.[10] Nothing came of the proposal.

Of all the settlements in the harbour, Teddington remains the most puzzling in terms of its jetties. In February 1867 the chairman of the Port Victoria Road Board, Thomas Potts, invited tenders for the 'erection of a wooden tramway and jetty at the Head of the Bay'.[11] Two days after the tsunami of 15 August 1868, the *Lyttelton Times* reported that 'the jetty, 300 feet long, at the head of the bay has been carried away and that Mr Manson's paddocks have been flooded'.[12] Sheep were drowned, and the beach paddocks were so salty they were unusable for several years. Seawater travelled 500 metres inland almost to the point where St Peter's Church now stands. Early the following year, the Road Board invited tenders for the repair of the jetty, and in February 1872 it sought bids for forming the 'Jetty Road, Head of the Bay', with specifications available from Mr D. Gebbie.[13]

Exactly what happened to this jetty — if it was indeed built — is not clear. As the port of Lyttelton and the town of Christchurch grew, Teddington increasingly

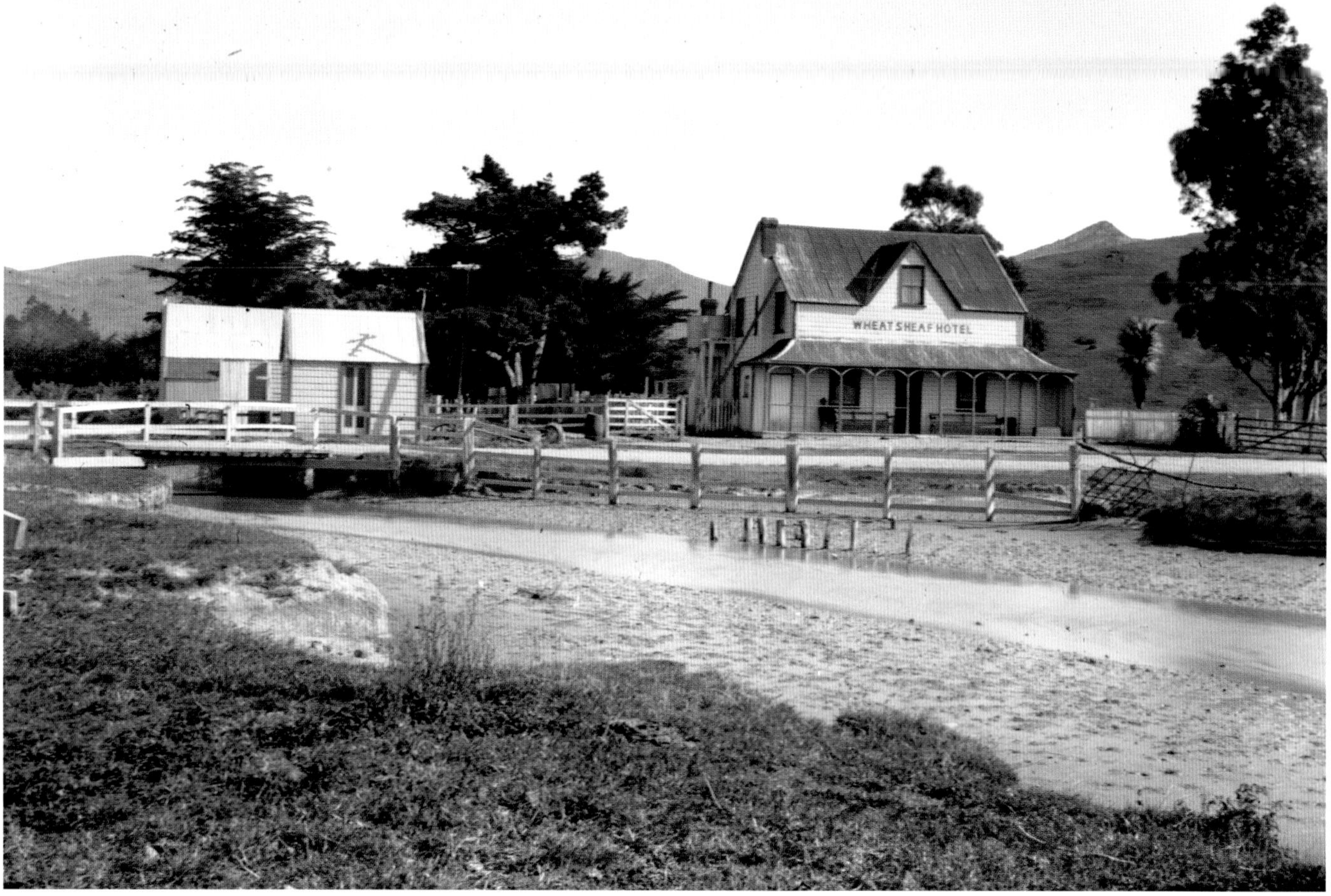
WHEATSHEAF HOTEL

became a hub for the transport of farm produce from its hinterland. At the same time, silting of Te Rapu channel may have caused the repaired jetty to become unusable except at high tide. Instead, cutters bringing stores to families at Head of the Bay and Gebbies Valley, and taking out produce to Lyttelton on the return trip, would run up the flats as far as they could, unload their cargo onto drays, load up again with the return cargo and wait until high tide. Cutter owners over time included Cameron Broths, Bill Hughes, Bill Hayders, Agar and Roberts, Agar and Thomas, Andy Briggs and Bert Deane.

In April 1909 the clerk of the Mount Herbert County Council wrote to the Lyttelton Harbour Board requesting a meeting regarding 'a proposed small wharf at Teddington for the purpose of landing small goods'.[14] At the meeting a local deputation explained that many residents were using motor launches to take their produce to Lyttelton and that a wharf would greatly facilitate loading. The distance by road was 11 miles, they explained, and cost 18s per ton, while carriage by sea cost only 7s 6d per ton.

The harbour board's engineer, Cyrus Williams, went up the harbour in an oil launch to survey the situation. His report of 15 November noted that oil launches and small craft up to 3-foot draft could, at half tide, reach the site of an 'old wharf' near Teddington. At this site the channel was 340 feet from the shore, had about 5 feet at high water and drained almost dry at low tide. Since the original jetty was 300 feet long, this indicates a fair increase in sedimentation and/or a shift in the path of the channel itself. Williams noted that the channel was very narrow and tortuous but was roughly marked with stakes, and that short boats could ascend the channel some distance above the old wharf site.

Some members of the delegation suggested that the wharf be located further up the channel, thereby reducing its proposed length by 100 feet and the cost by about £100. The local community would then use scoops to dig out the channel at low tide. Williams thought this was quite practicable but potentially difficult to maintain. He advised putting a jetty at the site of the old wharf, at a cost of about £250, to handle about 250 tons of cargo annually.

At this point the story of a jetty at Teddington becomes embroiled in politics, patch protection and intransigence. Following Williams' advice the Harbour Improvement Committee recommended such a jetty on condition that the harbour board acquire the site and that the Mount Herbert County Council contribute £10 a year towards the interest on the cost of construction. In reply, the council pointed out that wharf dues were already collected in Lyttelton, that such a tax was not levied on wharves in Governors Bay, Church Bay and Charteris Bay, that 'goods put over the jetty at Teddington is far more than the other three put together', and that this was likely to increase further as 'the farmers in the immediate vicinity are going in for grain growing'.[15] The council 'strongly opposed' paying

The Port Victoria Road Board Office on the left and the Wheatsheaf Hotel on the right at Teddington. Te Rapu stream, flowing down from Gebbies Pass, formed a channel which gave access for small boats right up to the hotel junction.
CANTERBURY MUSEUM, LOVELL SMITH COLLECTION, 19XX.2.3633

the proposed charge. The harbour board then moved to apply the £10 per annum to all the outlying jetties under its jurisdiction, and, in retaliation for the council's attitude, it also 'refused to contribute to the upkeep of the Governors Bay wharf the following year'.[16]

By September 1912 the harbour board was reporting that a channel to Teddington had been marked and a launch taken up the channel. The erection of 40 small beacons to mark out the channel was approved in December. Just what happened then is unclear, because in September 1913 a letter from launch skipper J. Sinclair to the harbour board outlined a problem.

> I write to ask if your Board could do anything to assist us in any way as we are at a loss to know how to get the goods from Teddington. As you know we had to go alongside the bank at the Channel to get it. Now the owner of the property has stoped [sic] the approach on the West side. The proper road is on the East side so all trade is stoped. There is more produce brought from this bay than any bay in the harbour. And yet there is no [illegible] of any sort. We have been trading there the past 4 years and have been a great saving to the Farmers as we are able to carry the goods at half the cost they had to pay before.[17]

Cyrus Williams reminded the harbour board that he had already reported on this issue in 1909. He noted the altered conditions: the channel had been marked with beacons at a cost of £20 9s 3d; the board was now collecting wharfage on all its outlying jetties; and the owner of the land where the flax was shipped appeared to have cut off the access to the water. Until the foreshore at the old wharf, with access to the public road, was vested in the harbour board, no new jetty could be built. A frustrated Williams concluded: 'I remain rather surprised that those who are interested in the trade do not use their influence in their governing body to assist this Board in providing facilities, instead of throwing obstacles in the way.'[18]

At this point documentary evidence dries up. There is no reference to the actual construction or subsequent use of another jetty either in the newspapers of the time or in the harbour board archives. Rex Gebbie recalls his father talking of barges coming right up the channel at high tide to load wool and wheat by the old bridge outside the Wheatsheaf Hotel. Similarly, wool from the Loudon farm was sent out by barge from just below the hotel, using the channel markers to get out to deeper water. Ra Blatchford could recall flax being brought down from the hillsides by horse and sledge as late as 1914–15; it was transferred to horse and dray and taken to a landing on the channel downstream from the Wheatsheaf.[19]

There exists an undated set of harbour board plans for a 'proposed' Teddington Jetty. On the ground there is physical evidence of the remains of two jetties:

Remnants of a long jetty on the east bank of the Te Rapu channel. Channel markers are to the left of the jetty and the remains of a rabbit-proof fence to the right. From the early years of the twentieth century locals had been lobbying for a jetty and/or dredging of the channel at Teddington. It seems likely that this jetty was constructed just before or just after the First World War.
JANE ROBERTSON

one, seemingly short, on the western bank of the channel closer to the original Manson farmstead, and the other, the remnants of which are more intact and run parallel to the rabbit-proof fence, on the eastern bank. The route to this latter jetty is visible in the deeply incised ruts flanking the channel. Whatever happened at Teddington in the two decades after 1912–13, the need for access by sea diminished — at first gradually, and then rapidly — as the quality of local roads improved and local trucking businesses became viable.

Schemes for reclaiming what were regarded as unproductive mudflats at the head of the harbour were regularly aired. One such scheme, proposed as the First World War drew to a close, envisaged the reclamation of Charteris Bay and Head of the Bay (Teddington), construction of a new 'inner harbour' at Church Bay, and the connecting of this 'new Lyttelton' by rail line over Gebbies Pass to Motukarara. This would enable produce from the Ellesmere district, Rolleston, Lincoln, Rakaia, Ashburton and Methven to be discharged straight to the port at Church Bay and would reduce congestion in the Christchurch–Lyttelton railway tunnel. The reclamation would involve building a retaining mole at the end of the spur between Head of the Bay and Governors Bay to the nearest point on Quail

Island and further connecting the island with the point north of Church Bay. This would afford 2650 acres of new pasture.[20]

A variation on this plan was resurrected in 1929 when local farmers proposed reclaiming the area of mudflats between Andersons Point and Mansons Point. The spoil from dredging the main harbour channel, instead of being deposited in Little Port Cooper, Camp Bay and Gollans Bay, could be used to reclaim some 1500 acres of mudflat at Teddington. This would provide additional flat grazing land and would also offset the harbour board's dredging costs. Other head of the harbour sites lent themselves to similar treatment.[21] It is worth remembering that this proposal came not so very long after the completion of the reclamation at Naval Point, near the port (see chapter 16).

The harbour board's response was scathing. The scheme was both 'impracticable and undesirable', and 'there is no need for us to spend more than five minutes over this report . . . [The board] condemns the whole proposition from beginning to end.'[22] According to the harbour board engineer, filling the area between Andersons Point and Mansons Point to an average level of 4 feet above high water would require about 30 million tons of dredgings — about 30 years' work. Also, the water at the head of the harbour was too shallow to float the dredge. And, 'The filling up of this bay would result . . . in a considerable reduction in the volume of the most useful part of the "tidal compartment" of the harbour and this would certainly have an adverse effect on the tidal scour in the entrance channel.'[23] Moreover, the dredged material would retain a very high percentage of salt for many years, meaning its production value would be limited. The total cost of the rejected proposal was estimated by the harbour board to be £184,000.

Nevertheless, what sea-adjacent, low-lying land that could possibly be farmed *was* farmed, flat land being at a premium in the harbour and saltmarsh being broadly regarded as unproductive wasteland. According to Bruce Gebbie, the northernmost parcel of land on the seaward side of the main Governors Bay–Teddington road is mainly 'saltweed' and unlikely ever to have been intensively farmed, although it was stopbanked, drained and grazed periodically. Bruce has childhood memories of this area being completely submerged during spring tides. The adjacent area, between the Teddington quarry and the Wheatsheaf Hotel, is presumably a little higher and was grazed by the Manson family in the later part of the nineteenth century. It was probably in this area that sheep were drowned in the 1868 tsunami.

Later, this second parcel of land was acquired by the Foley family. In the early 1950s Maurice Foley raised stopbanks to prevent the intrusion of an occasional king tide, and put drains through the paddocks. He worked the ground and left it open to allow the rain to wash the salt through, then reseeded most of the area. Sadly this work did not prevent sheep from again being drowned in the 1960 tsunami. Some years ago, soil was carted in to build up some low-lying parts for the present owners. The third parcel of land, to the east of Te Rapu Channel, is slightly higher and without any remedial treatment was fertile enough to have been cropped for wheat in the late nineteenth century. A fourth, smaller area, known as 'Crab Bay', was built up in the 1970s by Dick and Julia Hall.

In December 1933, a new 3YA radio transmitting station was opened near the summit of Gebbies Pass. Five years later, a receiving station was built on the Teddington flats near the jetty landing; this handled transmissions from national stations and overseas shortwave stations, work which had until then been carried out at the 3YA transmitter. A technician was stationed at the small receiving base, which was described, rather bleakly, as being 'near the sea coast on a salty marsh, about two feet above sea level'.[24]

Low-lying land and structures were exposed not only to king tides, but also to tsunami. The largest tsunami to reach New Zealand since that of 1868 rolled up Lyttelton Harbour over 23 and 24 May 1960. In Teddington, about midnight, David Gebbie heard a rumble like an approaching earthquake, went outside and found water lapping around his house. Daybreak revealed the extent of the damage. Waves had travelled as far inland as St Peter's Church. The ground floor of the Wheatsheaf Hotel was covered in 3 feet of water and empty beer barrels had floated away from the outhouse. The road from the bottom of the Allandale hill to the Wheatsheaf was a quagmire, with receding water still running across it in places and dead and exhausted sheep lying along its length. Maurice Foley lost about 200 sheep from paddocks on both sides of the road: the force of the wave carried the animals out of their paddocks and into a nearby property owned by the Witte family. Fences were destroyed and ditches blocked. Flounder, conger eels and red cod lay in the paddocks. Dogs chained to their kennels were drowned. As the *Press* reported, Mary Packer 'managed to keep up a supply of beer which was welcomed by locals as they strove to clean up the mess', though their efforts tended to be thwarted by fresh tidal surges coming through.[25]

In the early 1960s the sea-level road along the Teddington straight was built up about a metre before being sealed. Prior to this, spring tides flooded the road several times a year, leaving a bonus supply of fish trapped behind the stopbank protecting the Gebbie farm. The raising of the road meant no repeats of the disappointment experienced on at least one occasion by the Governors Bay School children, whose annual cricket match against Diamond Harbour School had to be called off because the road was flooded with the tides and no one had remembered to check.[26]

Local residents had their favourite fishing spots. Bruce Gebbie's first fishing experience was dragnetting with his employer Lloyd Blatchford in the early 1960s. 'We used to drive down farm tracks on Anderson's Point, clamber down the cliffs

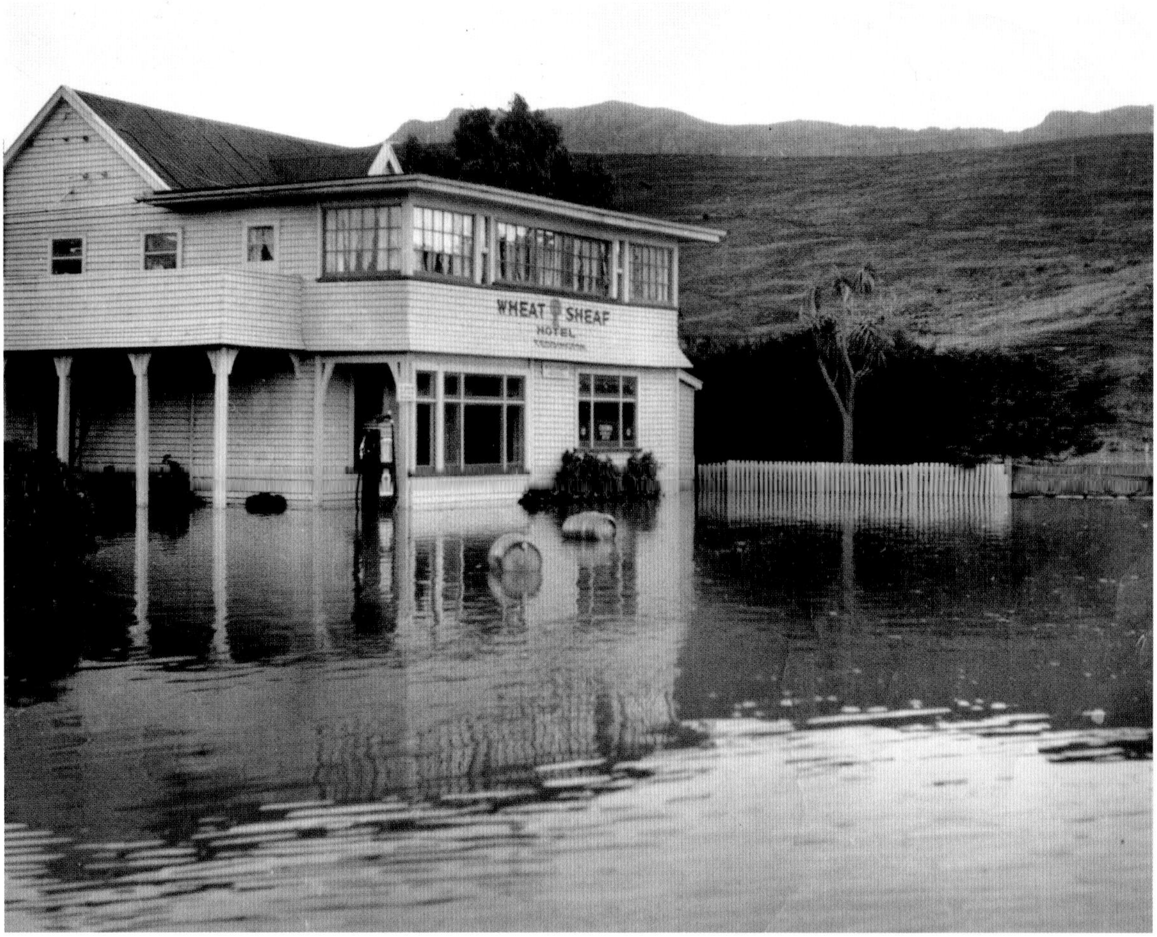
WHEAT SHEAF
HOTEL

ABOVE The Wheatsheaf Hotel in Teddington following the tidal wave of May 1960. The ground floor of the hotel was covered in a metre of water and empty beer barrels (centre) floated.
CHRISTCHURCH *STAR*, COURTESY OF BETTY SCULL

RIGHT Bruce Gebbie featured in the Christchurch *Press*, 25 May 1960. The caption read: 'Fruits of the flood — Bruce Gebbie holds a large eel which was trapped at the front of his parents' farmhouse at Teddington yesterday during one of the freak tides [1960 tsunami].'
COURTESY OF BRUCE GEBBIE

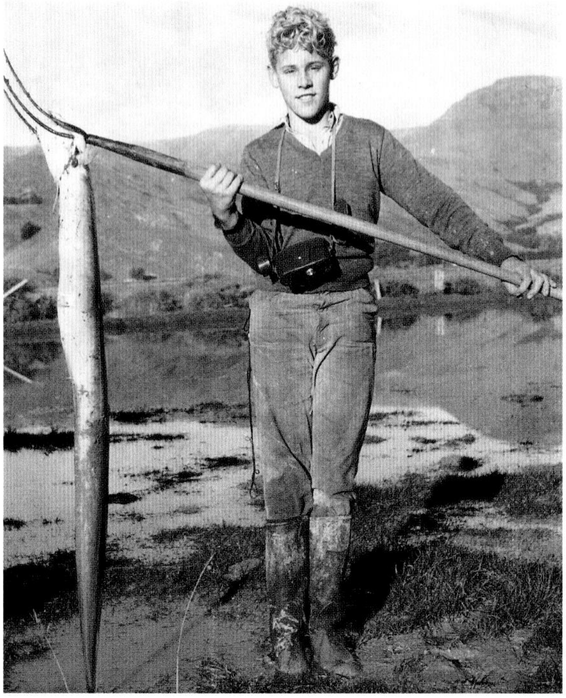

at the north end and drag the hole between the point and King Billy Island at low tide.'[27] They caught a respectable 40 flounder in two drags. Later, Bruce would team up with friends Charlie Gaunson, Dave Turner and John Allan to drag for flatfish off Māori Gardens, Windy Point, a small beach between the shipwrecks and nearby Walkers Beach on Quail Island, and a beach near the tip of Mansons Point. Diamond Harbour jetty was a good place to fish for red cod and piper (also known as garfish or ihe), while blowfish or 'puffers' could be caught in the hundreds.

In a rerun of the original Canterbury Association plan to locate Christchurch at the head of the harbour, the possibility was aired in Parliament in 1962 of a satellite city on the warm slopes of the southern side of the harbour. Fortunately for the harbour environment this never eventuated. Fortunate, because the saltmarsh there has been designated in the Christchurch District Plan as a Site of Ecological Significance for its distinctive and diverse vegetation communities. It is a nationally significant bird habitat, used by at least 10,000 waterbirds of over 30 species every year. Many of the bird species that feed on the mudflats and in the channels use the areas of saltmarsh for high-tide roosting.[28] The Whaka-Ora Healthy Harbour initiative regards raupō as the kaitiaki of the saltmarsh and mudflats, and has plans to re-establish this once-prolific plant. Someday, conceivably, the reclaimed land on the margins of the current saltmarsh will once again become part of the head of the harbour's natural ecology.

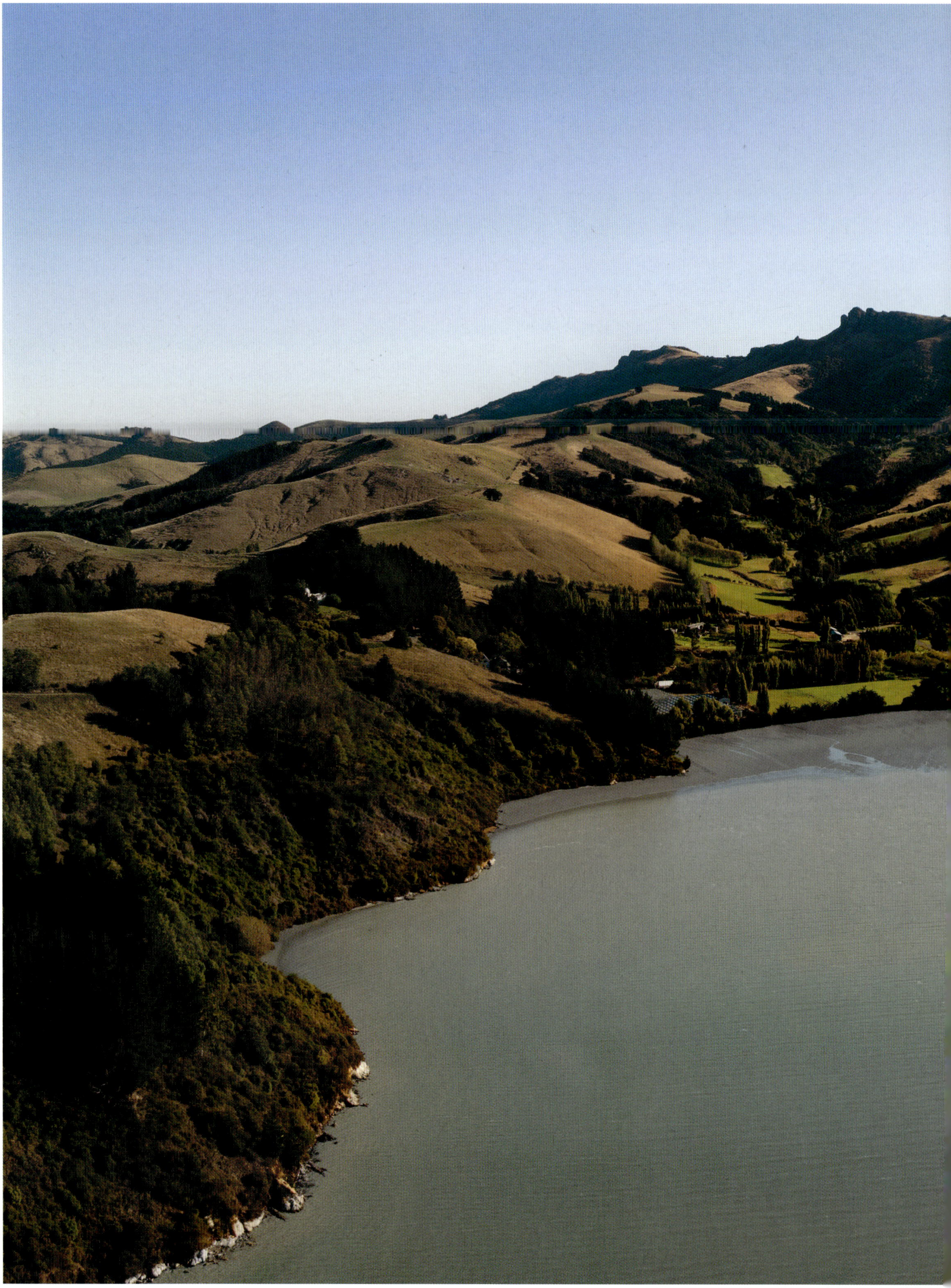

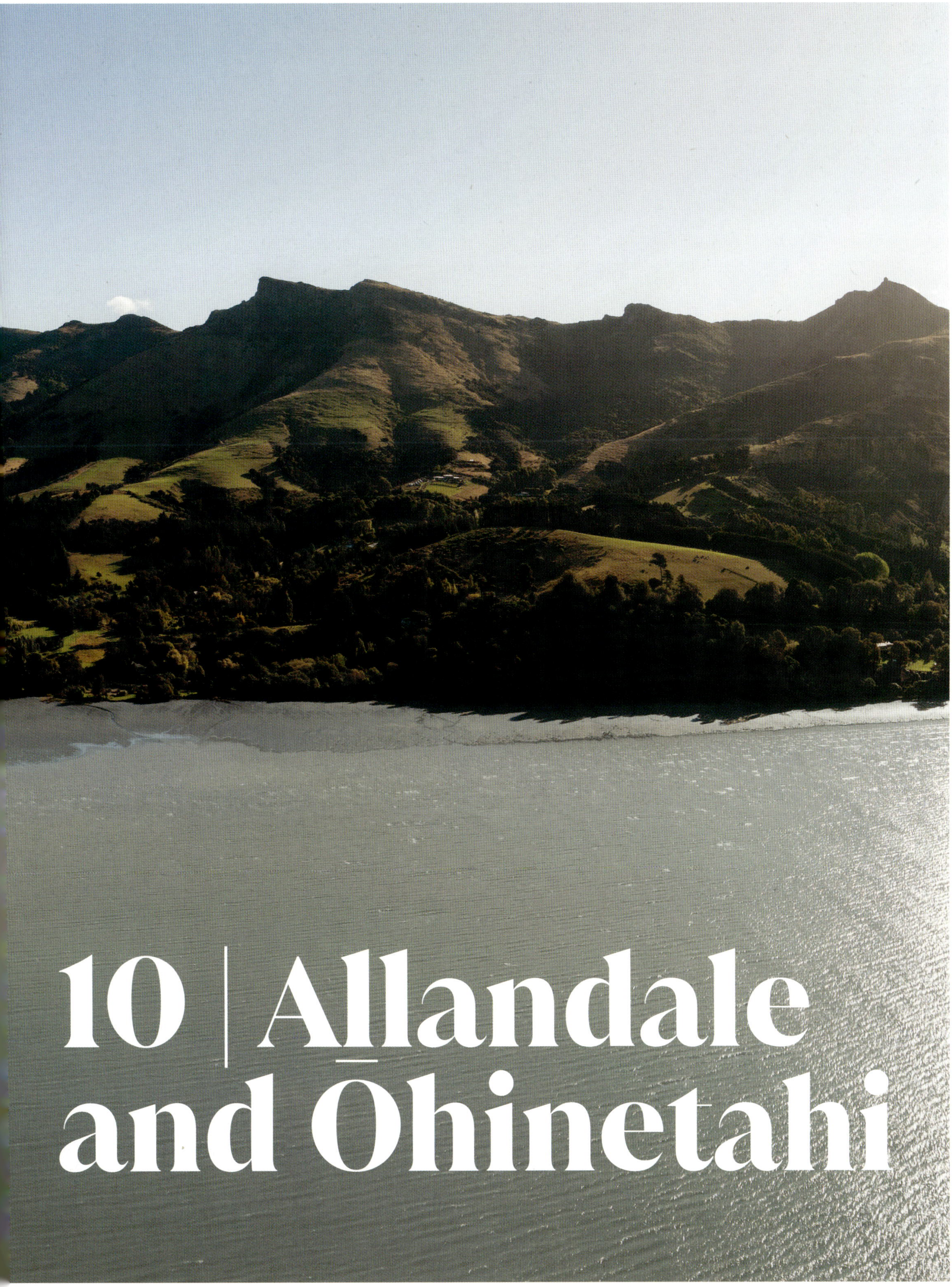

10 | Allandale and Ōhinetahi

In the cradling arm of Kaitangata Mansons Peninsula lie the sheltered little settlements of Allandale (also once known as Hodgsons Bay and then Bloors Bay) and Ōhinetahi. Waitaha came to this area in the fifteenth century, settling there in kāinga. In the late sixteenth century Ngāti Māmoe established kāinga at Ōhinetahi and Allandale, among other sites in Whakaraupō.

✸

Despite the vagaries of the peninsula's weather, Māori harvested a range of vegetables. The microclimate at Allandale and Ōhinetahi supports early and rapid growth; kūmara, taro and hue (gourds) could be grown, and aruhe (the root of the bracken fern) was prized and grown in quantity. It was roasted and pounded into a tough dough. Karaka (despite the toxicity of the kernel), hīnau and pikiraki berries were used, and starch and sugar were obtained from tī kōuka cabbage trees. The head of the raupō, when it was still green, served to make a kind of porridge.

In addition to the food resources, the plentiful native bush surrounding the harbour, including long-gone tōtara, rimu, kahikatea, miro and mataī, provided building materials, fuel and medicinal supplies. Kawakawa, prolific around the foreshore, was valued for its medicinal properties. Soft harakeke, abundant on the flats and hillsides, was used to make kete, while a stiffer harakeke was used for making rain capes and sandals. Hōanga (sandstone) from Aua King Billy Island was used to grind pounamu and other stone tools. Arcs of cockle banks at the mouth of Teddington, near Aua, were accessible at low tide and can still be seen occasionally today.

Life was disrupted as Ngāi Tahu began a southwards migration from the North Island east coast. Accounts of what happened next, from Cowan (1923), Taylor (1952), Couch (1974) and Gilles (1997), differ in detail if not in substance.[1] According to Cowan, Ngāti Māmoe constructed a pā, fortified with a palisade of split tree trunks, a ditch and parapet, near the shore at the head of Governors Bay, probably in the vicinity of present-day Ōhinetahi.[2] Having overcome Ngāti Māmoe at the village of Ōhinehou (Lyttelton), Ngāi Tahu chief Te Rakiwhakaputa made his claim to Whakaraupō at Rāpaki. Ngāi Tahu then defeated the Ngāti Māmoe pā at the head of the harbour. Te Rakiwhakaputa left his son Manuwhiri to establish ahi kaa (title to land through occupation) in the area. Manuwhiri demolished the vanquished Ngāti Māmoe pā and built a new pā further up the hill, naming it Te Pā Whakatakataka.[3] According to Cowan, Chief Manuwhiri, who had many sons but only one daughter, named the adjacent area Ōhinetahi ('place of the one daughter'). At that time the name was not confined, as today, to the single valley but encompassed the area from Allandale to just south of

Te Rāpaki-o-Te Rakiwhakaputa.[4] At some point, maybe during the Kaihuānga feud in the later 1820s, the pā and kāinga at Ōhinetahi were abandoned.

One of the earliest European settlers at Allandale was 27-year-old Paul Nixon Hodgson from Carlisle in Cumberland, who arrived in Lyttelton with his mother Grace on *Labuan* in August 1851.[5] Hodgson owned all the land on the sea front at Allandale. According to his daughter, Mary Hodgson, many years later you could 'still see [at Allandale] the remains of an old stone jetty he built. He used to row to Lyttelton with produce, and was caught in the tidal wave which emptied the harbour in 1868.'[6]

Paul Hodgson's farm was known as Burnside. He also operated the nearby Burnside Quarry, from which he extracted a pale sandstone, much in demand for building in Lyttelton and Christchurch for 'interior work'. Transportation of this stone by sea would have been necessary, given the poor conditions of the bridle path to Lyttelton. Hodgson and the proprietor of the Travellers Rest in Governors Bay, William Forster, lobbied unsuccessfully at a local meeting held in 1874 to determine the location of a new jetty in the area. In the meantime, sailing craft or lighters could come in at high water to within 100 yards of the beach and load up with stone. This was then taken via Sumner to the Heathcote River and on into Christchurch. After the completion of the rail tunnel linking Lyttelton with Christchurch in 1867, the stone could go through to the town by rail, eliminating the need to cross the dangerous Sumner Bar.

In 1911 Hollis and Brown of Lyttelton built a house for newlyweds James and Hilda Allan just above the foreshore at Allandale. Materials for the house were brought from Lyttelton by barge, landed on the small beach adjacent to the foreshore water trough and hitching post, and transported to the building site by horse and dray.

In July 1919, following hard on the heels of the Teddington jetty controversies, the Lyttelton Harbour Board received a letter from J. B. Beckett, of the firm Stewart, Beckett & Co., asking if a small wharf could be built at Allandale so that fruit and produce for which the area was well known could be shipped directly to Lyttelton (presumably instead of having to go out via jetties at Teddington or Governors Bay). The owners of other orchards in the area were willing to contribute to the cost of an annual charge. There is no record of any response from the harbour board and no jetty was built.

The shallow water at the head of the harbour that posed such problems for working jetties was also responsible for some vivid, sometimes alarming, childhood memories, as Gladys Robertson recalled:

> One hot day my fathers [sic] sisters Elizabeth, Sara and Jane with some of the Allan girls were bathing at Manson's Point. Elizabeth said Oh, this mud here is lovely and slippery — come and try. With that a big Sting Ray which she had her foot on, put his barb right through her leg and started to drag her out to sea, but her sisters and friends hung on, and at last the barb came out. They got a sledge and horse to take her home. The wound poisoned and they had a job to save her life, and she could not eat fish again all her life or she would be very ill.[7]

Stingrays still frequent the shallow waters at Allandale. They do not bother humans unless bothered by humans.

Jessie Scott remembered another startling event. On her way to school in March 1912 she saw a whale stranded in what was then known as Bloors Bay in Allandale. The whale was lashing its tail in an attempt to move to deeper water. On their way home from school about a dozen local children paddled out to have a closer look at the by then dead creature. 'Some children climbed onto the whale's back but I was not among them.'[8] At high tide the whale was hitched to a launch and towed to Lyttelton, where it attracted large crowds at the wharf. Experts identified it as a female strap-toothed beaked whale, 18 feet 3 inches in length and weighing 1 ton 16 hundredweight.

The shallowness of the water at Teddington, Allandale and Governors Bay led to the popularity of a 'sport' that today would be inconceivable. In the summer of 1931, the *Press* gave an account of a party of young men staying in the area who, having spotted a shoal of dogfish in the shallows, armed themselves with a sabre, pitchfork, bayonet attached to a pole, cricket bat, spear and sickle and amused themselves by slaughtering all the fish they could, not for food but just for the thrill. Over a hundred large dogfish were left to the gulls.[9]

Fish were plentiful and fishing popular, and there are legendary stories of rig, which returned to shallow water to give birth to their live young. For example:

> They used to come in their thousands through the heads of Lyttelton Harbour . . . Those fish used to follow [a trail] and it came right through up to the flats in the Allandale area and the flats of the Teddington area. The local people knew when it was happening . . . they could tell by the number of seabirds that were clouding the sky above the approaching shoal of rig. There were so many thousands of them coming up that they pushed the ones in the front right up onto the shoreline and that's when all the locals . . . rushed down with clubs and anything that could hit the fish on the heads with and kill them . . .[10]

Looking down into Allandale, with the community hall on the left and Mansons Peninsula stretching toward Lyttelton. Ōtamahua Quail Island is in the centre distance.
V. C. BROWNE & SON, COURTESY OF DAVID BUNDY

The number of dead fish piled on the beach meant using the 'one and only telephone' at postmistress Jessie Allan's 'to ring through to the one and only at Rāpaki and the Māori people immediately came round with horses and carts and they would fill up the carts with the rig because the rig bypassed the Rapaki Bay'.[11]

Delicate-fleshed frostfish are known to strand themselves on gently sloping beaches on calm, frosty nights. David Bundy's grandfather, William Harris, would scout around the foreshore at Allandale after a heavy frost and bring home frostfish, draped over his shoulder, which would then be cooked for breakfast. Hector's dolphin is today classed as nationally vulnerable, but in the 1950s and 1960s strandings occurred not infrequently at Governors Bay and Allandale. Usually the dolphins had sustained cut injuries from nets (there were no netting restrictions at the time) or propellers.

In the 1950s two boats were moored off the Allandale Reserve. One was *Hinemoa*, a big old double-ended clinker lifeboat that owners Jody Harris and Alfred Small would row out to their favourite fishing ground off Moepuku and drag for flounder. The two would leave their nets in a cave on the west side of Mansons Peninsula. The second — a flat-bottomed, home-built boat — was owned by Peter Dunbier and used for recreational rowing and fishing.

The Radcliffe brothers showed the local lads how to make things in their workshop. One winter, the boys built a group of 14-foot canoes in the fruit-packing shed at Allandale. They would put the boats in at Potts Point or Sandy Bay and head out to Quail Island. David Bundy remembered paddling into the wreck of the big clipper ship *Darra*. 'At full tide you'd go in the hold inside, paddle along inside. Our canoes were only made of canvas. I don't know how we didn't rip the bottom out of them.'[12]

Where the Allandale Hall and Domain now stand was once an intertidal zone. When the minister of lands approved the creation of a public reserve there in the mid-1890s, locals levelled the land, threw up a berm at the seaward end using horse-drawn scoops, and planted a shelterbelt of macrocarpa trees. The hall was built in 1896 and quickly became a focal point for the community, hosting a wide variety of local entertainments. Volunteers rolled up their sleeves again after the 1960 tsunami flooded the Allandale Hall and covered the floor in silt; the nearby Turner orchard lost about 150 newly planted apricot trees, and flounder had to be picked off the tomato plants. On a positive note, local residents collected bags of flounder from the paddocks and shallow pools of water.[13]

The foreshore between Allandale and Governors Bay has suffered from neglect and downright abuse over the decades. In the late 1940s a roadside dump was opened on the mudflats at the site of the present-day Allandale Reserve. Contractors dumped clay there, but some farmers and other residents also used it to get rid of all manner of rubbish over the years. Later, a reclamation grant from the Marine Department enabled an adjacent area to be infilled as a site for domestic refuse, attracting huge numbers of rats. Prior to infill, this upper littoral area had been home to the best remaining example of raupō in the harbour basin. In 1994, after many complaints from locals, the dump was finally closed, but little was done to rehabilitate the area and there are fears today that rising seas may cause the site to disgorge its buried detritus into the upper harbour waters.

The sea is meanwhile nibbling away at the historic stone walls, built in 1857 by prisoners from the Lyttelton Gaol. These walls shored up what was once the main transport route from Governors Bay to Allandale, known as Beach Road or the Old Coach Road, now commonly called the foreshore road (more accurately, track). At the Allandale end of the road the original road surface remains, each tip dray load of hand-knapped stone still visible.[14]

The walls had already been damaged by the transit of heavy machinery during the construction of the Governors Bay sewerage scheme in 1989. The city council is working with members of the local community to bolster the walls and improve the track surface so that the foreshore road and the rebuilt Governors Bay jetty can take their place as significant historical and recreational features in the emerging Head-to-Head Walkway. At the same time, the council has also begun to focus on coastal hazards adaptation planning in anticipation of rising sea levels. Parts of the foreshore road, despite current remediation, will

conceivably be under water at high tide by the end of this century, if not before.

In other positive initiatives, the owners of Kaitangata Mansons Peninsula, Penny Mahy and Rob Stowell, are planting the erosion-prone peninsula in native vegetation. The Living Springs Allandale Stream Restoration Project is retiring substantial amounts of land from grazing and planting natives alongside the Waimawete Stream and its tributaries to stem the flow of sediment and toxic nutrients into the harbour. These, along with other projects supported by the Whaka-Ora Healthy Harbour initiative, will ultimately advantage upper harbour marine and bird life. Currently the foreshore walk between Governors Bay and Allandale is an excellent place from which to view the many seabirds and waders that gather on the mudflats. Oystercatchers, stilts, herons, godwits, kingfishers, terns, gulls, ducks and spoonbills can be seen most days.

Continue on the road north-west from Allandale and you pass through lovely, wooded Ōhinetahi, home to St Cuthbert's Church — rebuilt after the Christchurch earthquakes — and the reconstructed Ōhinetahi homestead, with its renowned garden developed by architect Sir Miles Warren, his artist sister, Pauline Trengrove, and her architect husband, John.

One of the earliest European settlers in Ōhinetahi Valley was Londoner Robert Harris, who with his wife, Mary Elizabeth, and nine children, arrived in Lyttelton on *Steadfast* in June 1851. An uncorroborated local story suggests that their first home was a hole cut out of the hill near the Sage Reserve, to the north of Church Lane, with bullock skins covering the entrance.[15] Robert was listed on the electoral role as a brickmaker and Robert Jnr as a bricklayer. It seems that the men had a brickmaking business on the foreshore at the intersection of Beach Road and Church Lane.

Another early settler in Ōhinetahi was lawyer Christopher Alderson Calvert. Calvert had a cottage prefabricated in Lyttelton to a design by architect Benjamin Mountfort and transported across the harbour by local Māori. The land and cottage then changed hands several times in rapid succession. Owners of Rosemary Cottage, as it was known, included William Thomson, who ran a dairy farm and also sold firewood to Lyttelton. An 1853 advertisement in the *Lyttelton Times* sought contracts for 'the Conveyance of Firewood from the upper end of Governor's Bay to Lyttelton, at the rate of 60 cords a month for twelve months'. The contract was to include the building of a punt 'capable of carrying from 12 to 15 cords each trip and of draught sufficiently light for the navigation of Governor's Bay'.[16] In 1855 Thomson sold his farm to politician and soon-to-be second superintendent of the Canterbury province, William Sefton Moorhouse.

A sea lion on the Allandale foreshore. The two men are most likely Allandale residents Charles Edward Radcliffe (left) and Jody Harris.
COURTESY OF MURRAY RADCLIFFE

ABOVE Christopher Alderson Calvert commissioned young architect Benjamin Mountfort to design a cottage. The cottage was prefabricated in Lyttelton and transported by sea to the head of the harbour by local Māori. Originally known as Hemmingford Cottage, then as Rosemary Cottage, the building was subsequently substantially altered to become the Potts' family homestead Ōhinetahi.
CANTERBURY MUSEUM, MOUNTFORT ARCHITECTURAL PLAN: HEMMINGFORD COTTAGE, GOVERNORS BAY, 1852. 280

BELOW The homestead at Ōhinetahi built by Thomas Potts in the mid-1860s. The stone for the central portion was quarried on Quail Island and the nearby peninsulas and brought to Ōhinetahi by boat.
CANTERBURY MUSEUM, W. A. TAYLOR COLLECTION, 1968.213.2727

Meanwhile, having inherited a large sum of money from his father's gun-making business, Thomas Henry Potts, with his wife, Emma, and their first three (of an eventual 13) children, arrived in Lyttelton in April 1854. Potts may have been trained as a gunsmith, but his real interests lay in the natural world of birds and plants. He established a successful cattle station on the eastern side of the Upper Rangitata River, and then looked for property closer to Christchurch. In February 1858 Potts bought the Moorhouse house and land in Governors Bay, eventually increasing his holding to about 600 acres. To house his ever-expanding family, in 1863–64 he set about remodelling Rosemary Cottage, which Moorhouse had already extended. In March 1866 keen diarist Joseph Munnings recorded that Potts had 'pulled down the centre of the House and is now building a nice stone one, the stone from quarries on Quail Island and one at the back of his house'.[17] By 1867 there stood a substantial three-storeyed building of locally quarried rhyolite with sandstone detailing, flanked by Moorhouse's timber wings and with a surrounding verandah.[18]

Transporting the stone from Quail Island was a challenge, given the extent of the upper-harbour mudflats and the weight — 700 kilograms plus — of some of the blocks. Thomas Potts's diary for 1865 sheds light on the process. On 15 February, 'Bonnington, whose craft brought some dressed stone for Waterworth [the stonemason], threw the stone overboard in spite of warning, where no team can find footing.'[19] This suggests that offloading the stone by dropping it into the sea in a retrievable place was a possibility, albeit an unlikely one. Potts makes a number of references to his men 'drawing up stone from the beach' for the verandah foundations. In April, he and Emma took the boat to meet the stonemason at the site of a proposed quarry on the peninsula. Potts agreed to find Waterworth tools, a boat and, if possible, a punt also. During May, men from Ōhinetahi were landing timber sent by 'Michelson's craft'. On 6 June a boat arrived with about 1000 feet of timber, and on 20 June *Antelope* arrived with more timber, 2 tons of flour and ten bags of bran. Given the logistical challenges, it is hardly surprising that when riding home from a holiday in Christchurch Potts came face-to-face with his entire gang of workmen, who had downed tools and were setting out for the newly discovered Otago goldfields.

What we don't know is whether, at this stage, there was a jetty at Ōhinetahi. In an undated photo of the homestead taken from the foreshore road, a jetty structure is visible just below the house, although it appears already to be neglected. It may have been built by Potts to land stone blocks, but it does not seem a substantial structure, and Potts makes no reference to a jetty at Ōhinetahi in his 1865 diary. He does mention using 'Hodgson's boat', suggesting that he did use the stone jetty built a little further around the foreshore by Paul Nixon Hodgson.

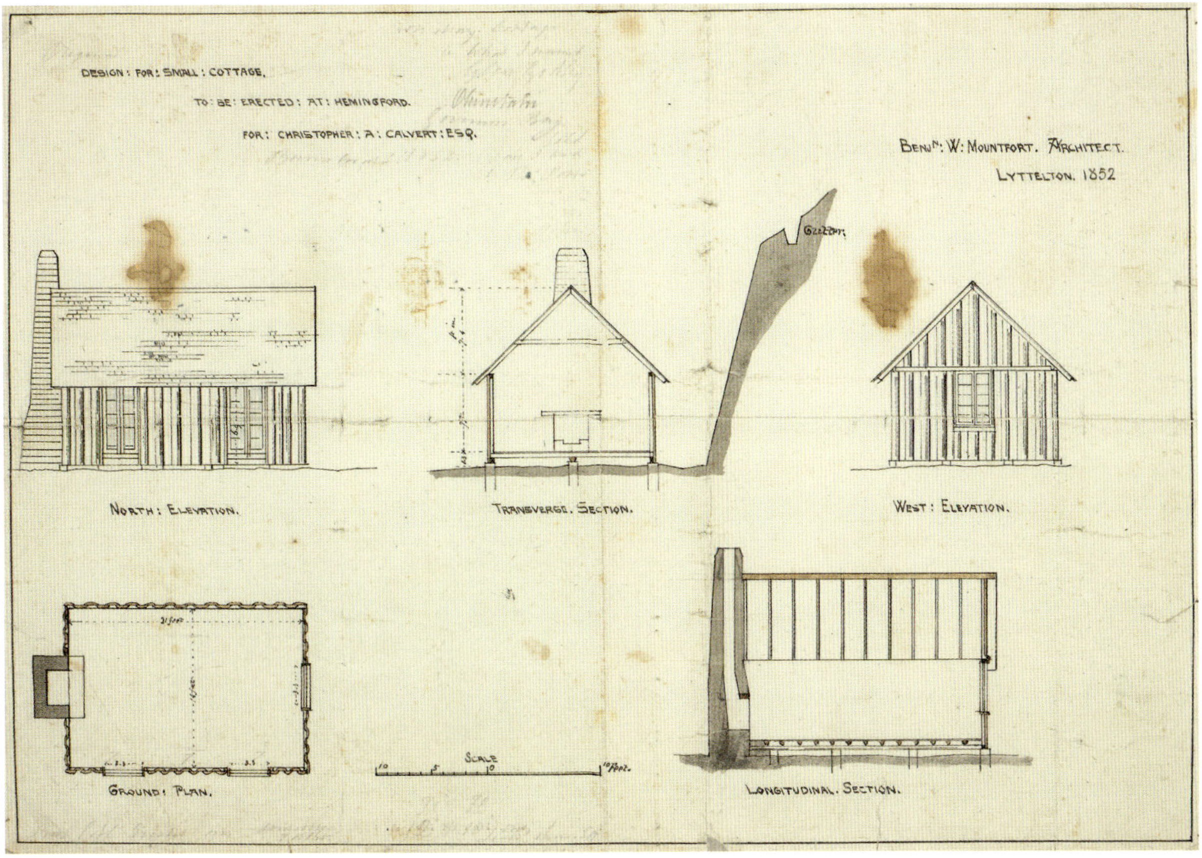
DESIGN: FOR: SMALL: COTTAGE.
TO: BE: ERECTED: AT: HEMINGFORD.
FOR: CHRISTOPHER: A: CALVERT: ESQ.
BENJN: W: MOUNTFORT. ARCHITECT.
LYTTELTON. 1852
NORTH: ELEVATION.
TRANSVERSE. SECTION.
WEST: ELEVATION.
GROUND: PLAN.
SCALE
LONGITUDINAL. SECTION.

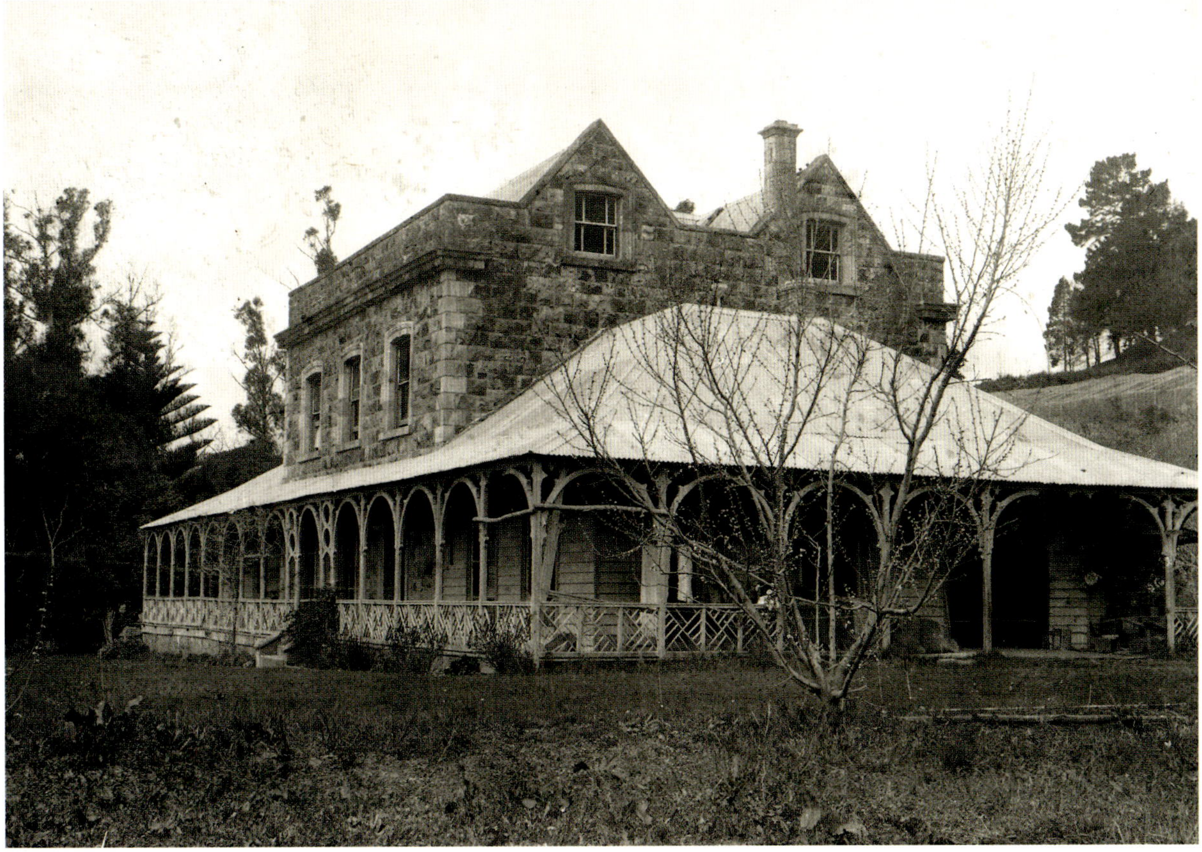

At the very least, the family would have needed a convenient landing point for their many local boat trips. During the school holidays, for instance, the family enjoyed spending time on the harbour. One night, Potts and his boys went fishing by torchlight and caught 20 fine pātiki. In January 1865 they went boating with the Hodgsons, calling in at Diamond Harbour to see the Stoddart family. A party of 11, including Thomas, Emma and several of the children, spent the day on Quail Island, which Potts was farming, having purchased the island from friend Mark Stoddart in 1862. The children enjoyed watching the sheep, and the fishermen drawing in their nets. On another trip to the island the family brought home lots of pipi. On 15 January 1865 Thomas Potts and sons Donald and Ambrose went across to Quail Island in the afternoon for a good view of the arrival of Governor Sir George Grey at Lyttelton, although unfortunately the Governor's visit was cancelled. When the August 1868 tsunami reached New Zealand, the Potts boys were naturally keen to walk across to Quail Island on the exposed seabed when the water left the harbour, but their father warned them of the danger of the returning surge and refused to let them go out.

At the end of the school holidays, reluctant Potts children had to return to boarding school in Christchurch. On 30 January they were 'all up early ready for the five elder ones to start for school. EP [Emma Potts] with Walter and the victims to Port in the boat.' And after the Easter break, 'all up early as it is "Black Monday" with the children. All of them with EP and Trounce to assist by Hodgson's boat. They had to wait some time with the tide.'[20]

Potts's men used their employer's boat for taking produce to market, picking up supplies and servicing the stock on Quail Island. There were concerns about the boat's condition, as Potts recalled: 'Trounce says the boat leaks very much. He wants me to buy another boat, but I don't seem to see it — we have not had enough work out of this.'[21] In March, Emma and Edith went servant hunting in Christchurch, taking Hodgson's boat to the port. In April, Emma, her parents, her brother and his wife and a new nurse arrived in Hodgson's boat. The party returned to port in early May, finding that with the nor'east wind and the tide against them, the trip took more than three hours. In a nice domestic touch, Emma and George went to port in the Potts boat to buy a stove.

An exceptionally community-minded man, Potts knew how heavily the local farmers relied on transporting produce by sea, and he played a crucial role in securing the first public jetty in Governors Bay (see chapter 11). Potts was vocal, too, about the loss of habitat for birds of the Port Hills and championed the retention of native bush as well as the planting of magnificent exotic species. In his best-known publication, *Out in the Open* (1882), Potts reflected on life in Governors Bay and the environmental damage that had already occurred in the area:

The homestead at Ōhinetahi with a somewhat neglected jetty just below the house. The difficulty of accessing the bay by sea is evident.
BRYONY MACMILLAN

> Living close to the beach in a sheltered nook in Port Cooper, at no great distance from the extensive area of Lake Ellesmere, it may be that I have been more than usually attentive to these wandering voices [of seabirds], since few woodland birds now frequent the slopes of our picturesque hills, like many other districts once clothed with stately trees and bright-leaved shrubs. Shade and shelter gone, bare stems with whitened tops remain, and point to the work of the ruthless bushman.[22]

There were, however, still birds to be seen: 'on the mud flats at the head of the harbour, patched here and there with a dwarf growth of zostera, and banks of time-bleached shells, as the tide ebbs, flocks of godwits (*Limosa Novae Zealandia*e) arrive and probe the yielding surface with their long bills . . .'[23]

The foreshore at Ōhinetahi was further exploited when, after Potts's time, a sizeable quarry at Potts Point pushed the land seawards and hollowed out the cliff face bordering Beach Road. Wharf piles were once visible at Potts Point, suggesting that some sort of landing place, in an area of deeper water, might have enabled the loading of stone from the quarry. As with so much shoreline human activity, the physical evidence has long disappeared along with the memories. In the later 1950s the Mount Herbert County Council let a contract to Isaac Construction to rebuild and seal the road from Governors Bay to Teddington. Isaacs reopened the old county quarry at Potts Point and installed a crushing plant, which supplied aggregate for the new road; trucking this around the foreshore was hard on the historic road and culverts.

Adjacent to the quarry, the Radcliffe brothers constructed a concrete slipway (which is still visible), where a wharf may once have stood. They used the slip to launch their X Class clinker sailing dinghy, used mainly for fishing. Herbert Ensor moored a Seamew yacht, *Glynt*, halfway between Church Lane and Potts Point. The Ensor children, with their cousins and friends, had a great time paddling canoes, sailing *Glynt* and generally growing up at ease in the marine environment. When a dead elephant seal came into the bay and 'threatened to stink us all out', Herbert Ensor 'hooked the corpse behind the *Glynt* and towed it around to the other side of Mansons Peninsula where we kids would go and see the progress of its decomposition on a beach there'.[24]

If it can be well maintained, the Allandale–Ōhinetahi–Governors Bay Foreshore Track offers a walk suitable for all ages and abilities at a most historical and ecologically sensitive intersection of land and sea in Whakaraupō. The tide appears to be turning against human exploitation of this vulnerable environment.

ABOVE Herbert and Ruth Ensor bought Ōhinetahi homestead in 1952 and raised their family there. Here the Ensor children and their cousins have fun on the water at the head of the harbour in the 1950s.
COURTESY OF PAUL ENSOR

BELOW Winstone Hinchey, Janet Meares, Richard Ensor, Peter Meares and Paul Ensor show off their head-of-the-harbour rig catches.
COURTESY OF PAUL ENSOR

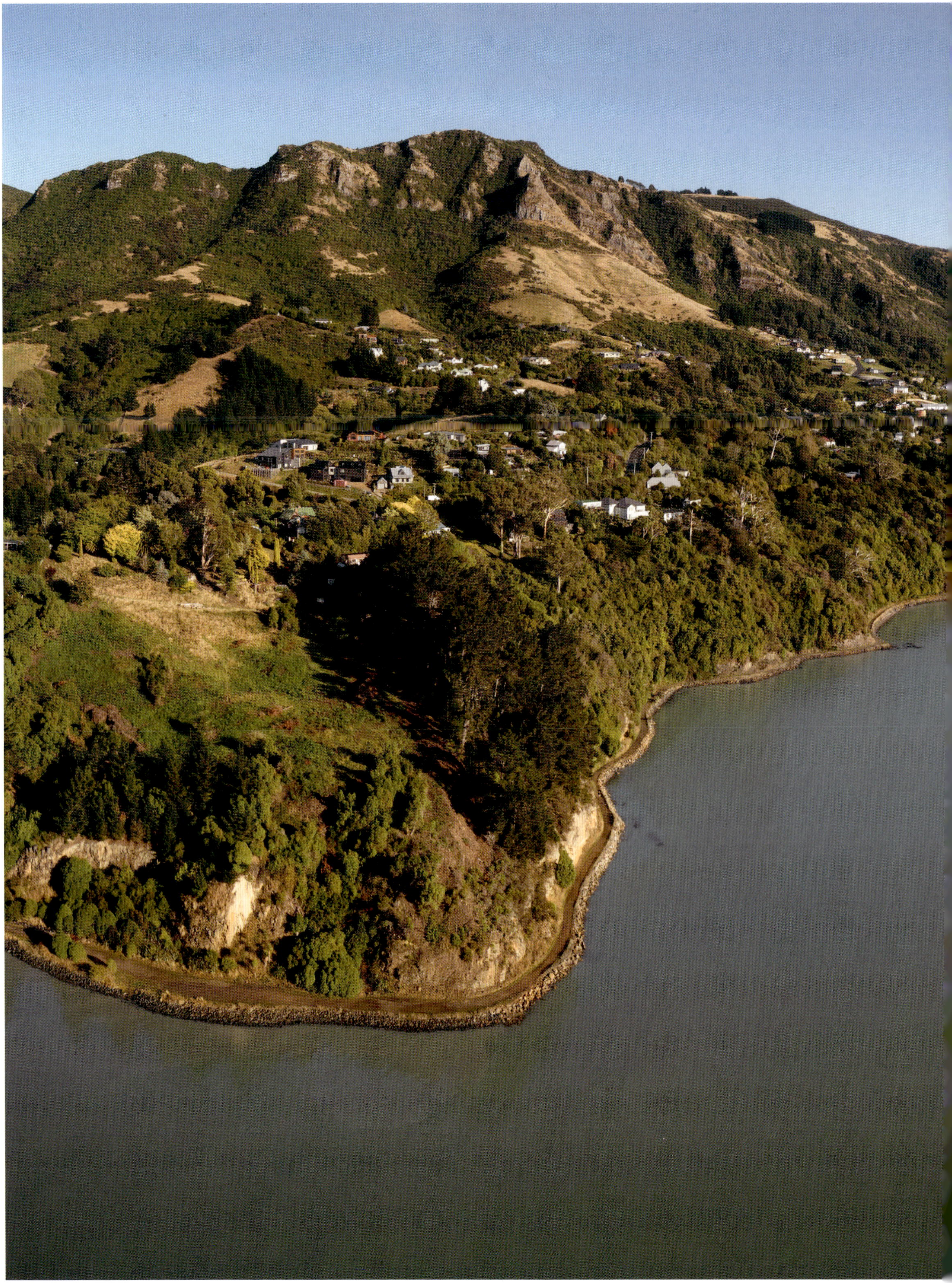

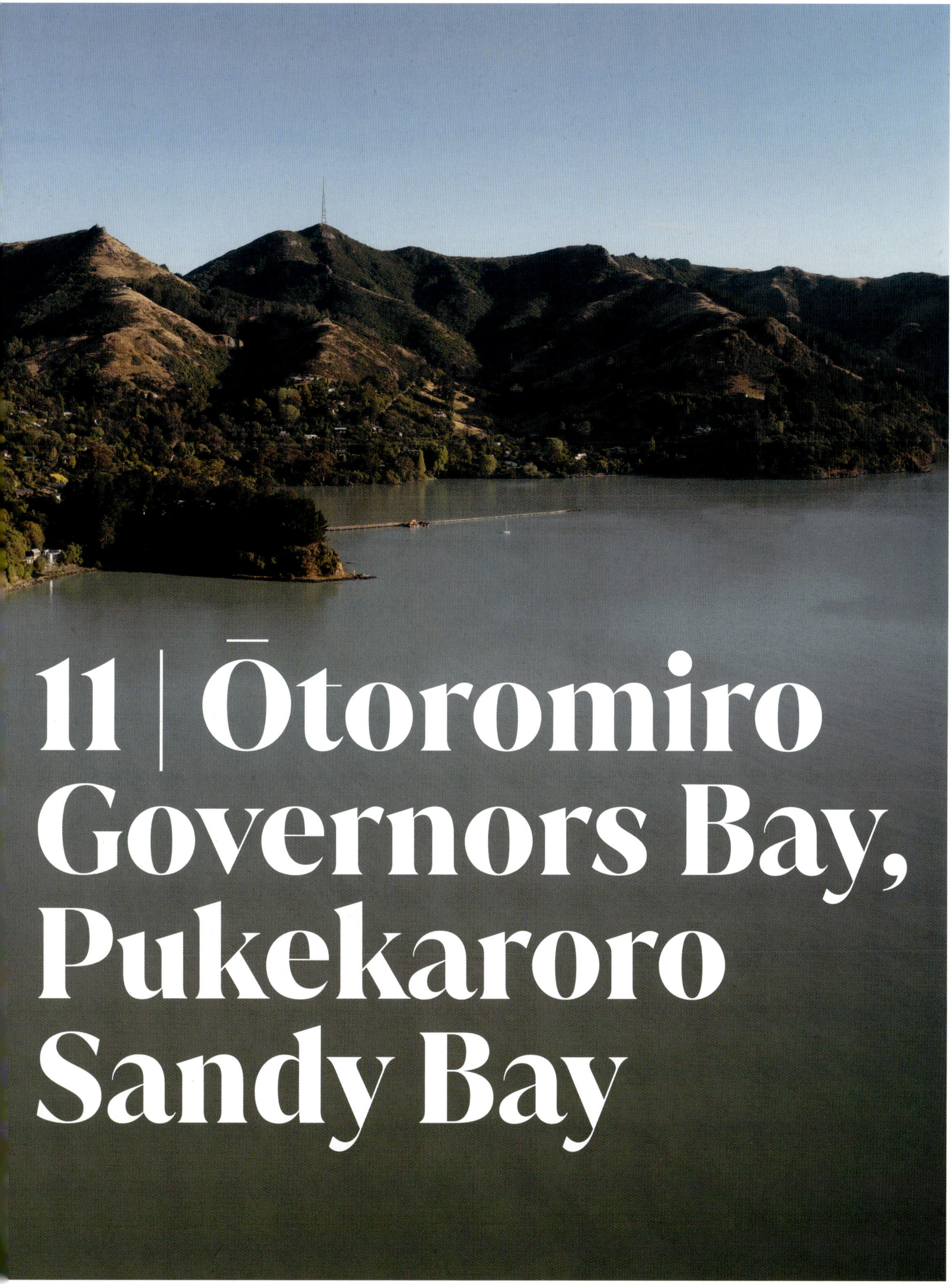

11 | Ōtoromiro Governors Bay, Pukekaroro Sandy Bay

According to current topographical maps, 'Governors Bay' refers to that large scoop which extends from Sandy Bay Point to the tip of Mansons Peninsula and includes Ōhinetahi and Allandale. However, with Ōhinetahi and Allandale included in the previous chapter, this chapter focuses on the smaller area extending from Sandy Bay Point to Potts Point — originally known as Dyers Bay.

Although this is a small stretch of coastline it has, at various stages over the past 160 years, been home to four different jetties. The one damaged and decaying jetty remaining, remarkable for its 296-metre length, is being rebuilt. Its continued presence is a physical reminder of the battle with the harbour mudflats and the determination of Governors Bay residents to retain sea access to their settlement at all costs.

Governors Bay was a favoured place for Waitaha, and later Ngāti Māmoe and Ngāi Tahu. Names for the waterfront within Dyers Bay tell us much about the particular resources valued by Māori. Around the long Governors Bay jetty was Ōtoromiro ('the place where miro was cut and shaped with an adze'). Further north, present-day Sandy Bay was known as Pukekaroro ('the gathering place of seabirds'). The valley running down from Dyers Pass towards the harbour was Parakiraki ('the very dry place'). Sadly, miro no longer grows in Ōtoromiro.

By the time the first Canterbury Association settlers arrived in Lyttelton in 1850, there were no longer any Māori kāinga in Governors Bay. Our first description of the bay comes from Henry Sewell, who was in the province to sort out the affairs of the Canterbury Association. On 16 February 1853 Sewell had arranged to go to the head of the harbour to follow up on rumours of coal in the vicinity. A boatman had been hired for an 8.30 a.m. departure from Lyttelton on the high tide, but he failed to turn up. Sewell and his wife, Elizabeth, and Captain Simeon with his wife and children, along with Bishop-designate Thomas Jackson's secretary, Christopher Calvert, decided to make the day one of 'pleasure' instead and visit another, more accessible part of the head of the harbour.

As Sewell recalls, they 'landed on a little sandy and shelly beach near a cottage and a holding of a Mr Dyer and his sister . . . the two with a young man of the name of Parsons constitute the settlement'.[1] John Dyer and his sister, Mary Ann, had arrived in Lyttelton in June 1851 and, together with Charles Parsons, built a small cottage at the foot of what is now Dyers Pass Road. The three had come out on *Canterbury* with Captain Simeon, who was a member of the management committee of the Canterbury Association and had taken up John Godley's vacated position as resident magistrate.

Sewell was an astute observer of early colonial settlement. He noted that the young men had built a neat wooden one-roomed cottage with a loft above. A small shed behind served as a kitchen and dairy, and a tent served as a cheese room. Here John, Mary Ann and Charles made between two and three pounds' worth of cheese a week and butter for the Lyttelton market. They also had calves, pigs and poultry. Mary Ann ran a small school. The greatest need, Sewell considered, was for a road or at least a horsepath to Lyttelton.

By the end of the decade, Joseph Munnings was working for Dyer and Parsons. In a diary entry for 14 November 1859 Munnings recorded that he was 'up early and helped to load the boat with potatoes, wood and peas etc. and started about nine for port in the whale boat and rowing the punt behind us with oars'.[2] By 21 December he was carrying new and old potatoes, peas, black and red currants, raspberries and strawberries to Lyttelton. Given that sea access from the beach would be possible only at or near high tide, it was clear that a jetty would be a big advantage. At some point, John Dyer and/or Charles Parsons built a private stone and wood jetty on the foreshore below the cottage. In January 1875 the *Lyttelton Times* reported that the ballast lighter *Annie* had 'parted her chain' during a heavy easterly sea and drifted up to the head of the bay 'to within a chain of Mr Parson's wharf'.[3] Parson's jetty features clearly in an undated photo, which also records the first public jetty in the bay.

With its sheltered microclimate, Governors Bay attracted a number of early settlers wanting to take advantage of the burgeoning populations in Lyttelton and Christchurch by establishing farms, orchards and market gardens. They then sought to transport their produce out of the bay with more ease than the poorly maintained bridle path, completed in 1856 and linking Teddington and Lyttelton, allowed. In December 1858 Thomas Potts and provincial engineer Edward Dobson inspected the Dyers Bay waterfront to determine the site for a public jetty. They settled on 'that portion of the beach almost contiguous to Mr Perceval's [sic] garden' — what we now know as Sandy Bay beach. The following

In this 1877 view of Lyttelton Harbour from Governors Bay, the government jetty at Sandy Bay is just visible on the left. The road to Lyttelton climbs the hill behind.
ALEXANDER TURNBULL LIBRARY, PUBL-0016

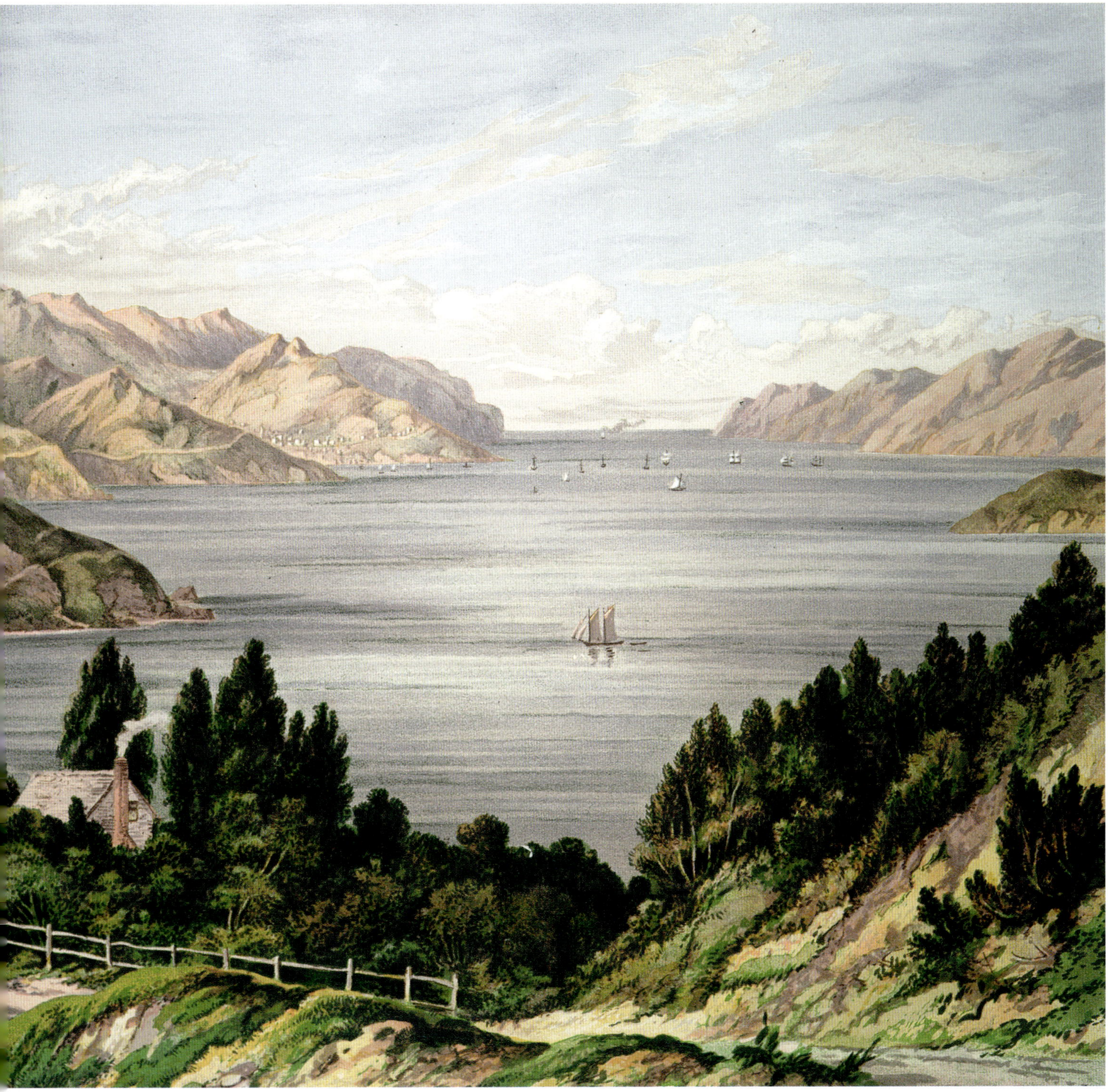

year, the Canterbury Provincial Council voted £100 for the construction of what became known as the 'government jetty', and spent a further £100 during 1862 to secure road access.

Seeing a commercial opportunity, Westby Percival, well known as a somewhat litigious character, put 23 acres of adjacent land on the market at £10 an acre cash, even before the jetty was built. The land was freehold 'with a frontage to the Beach and Governor's Bay Roads of more than half a mile and adjoining the jetty at Dyer's Bay lately erected'.[4] Percival considered that the situation of his land, with the additional benefit of the proposed jetty, and the advantages of bathing, fishing and boating, would lend itself to the 'lucrative establishment of a first class Boarding House and Sanatorium'[5].

The Small family, newly arrived in Dyers Bay, would have welcomed the presence of a jetty. Fleeing Australia and an abusive marriage, Mary Small (who assumed the surname Phipps to lessen the chances of being followed by her husband) leased a cob cottage near the foreshore. There she made a new life for her children, William, John (Jack), Archibald, James and Emma. Oldest daughter Mary Ann joined the family sometime later. The soil was good, there was a stream nearby and there was a ready market for the vegetables and fruit carried around the bridle path to the port by the boys. The family traded eggs and fowls with Māori at Rāpaki, grazed cattle on the tussock slopes, and bought a boat to transport their wares. At the jetty they could sell direct to visitors arriving off the steam launches. Later, Jack Small worked as a boatman for some years and at one time had the contract for running stores to the leper colony at Quail Island.

However, the government jetty soon proved unsatisfactory. Thomas Potts pointed out in 1863 that a small sum of money spent on the jetty could prevent its destruction from high tides. At low tide, boats could be stuck in the mudflats. There was much local lobbying for a better-sited jetty since requests that the existing jetty be repaired and lengthened fell on deaf ears. A determining factor was depth of water — but self-interest meant that vocal locals also agitated for a jetty near *their* property. At a meeting in March 1874, three sites were considered: the location of the present-day long jetty; on the beach in Sandy Bay, location of the government jetty; and where the remains of the Sandy Bay Point jetty can still be seen.

William Forster, proprietor of the Travellers Rest Hotel at the junction of the old Dyers Pass Road and the present road to Lyttelton, proposed two jetties: one at the present location, and the other at Sandy Bay Point (also known as Percivals Point) or at Hodgson's Bay (present-day Allandale). He claimed that there was a mine of undeveloped wealth in the stone quarries on Hodgson's property, but that this resource could be exploited only if the stone could be transported by sea. Hodgson agreed, and also argued that the farmers at that end of the bay could not compete because the cost of transit by road negated any profit margin. Charles Parsons spoke in favour of Dyers Point, the site of the current long jetty, which, he claimed, had the greatest depth of water (not so) and had already been surveyed. The meeting concluded with a decision to locate the jetty at Dyers Point.[6]

Tenders were called for construction of the jetty, and in April the *Press* reported that when the jetty was finished a steamer would run daily between the bay and Lyttelton. By November the paper was advertising land for sale 'situated close to the New Jetty'.[7] The new jetty was convenient in terms of its central location. For example, it brought visitors to within easy reach of the Whitecliffs Hotel, the local store and the Ocean View Hotel. When the Ocean View was up for sale (again) in 1875, the auctioneer stressed that it was 'opposite the new jetty'.[8] In 1876, the new proprietor of Whitecliffs Hotel advertised comfortable board and residence to which access could be gained via a steam launch running daily from Lyttelton following the arrival of the 9.30 a.m. and 4.30 p.m. trains. In January 1877 Agar and Roberts were advertising a twice-daily steam launch run between Lyttelton and Governors Bay at a fare of 4s return. Construction of the jetty prompted the metalling of the foreshore road.

The jetties on the beach at Sandy Bay and at the foot of John Dyer and Charles Parson's property are clearly visible. The jetty at Percival's Point/Sandy Bay Point has not yet been built, meaning that the photo pre-dates 1883.
DONATED TO THE GOVERNORS BAY HERITAGE TRUST BY GAVIN BAIN

ABOVE The short jetty, Governors Bay, c.1885–1910. The well-formed road in the foreground continued on around the foreshore to Allandale.
AUCKLAND ART GALLERY TOI O TĀMAKI, 2008/19/113

BELOW Governors Bay. Visitors to the bay walked up the hill, having arrived by launch from Lyttelton. Given that those pictured have no picnic baskets, their destination is probably the Ocean View Hotel.
CANTERBURY MUSEUM, 19XX.2.4422

Even before the construction of the second public jetty, Governors Bay was a popular location and destination for fund-raising bazaars. When the newly built St Cuthbert's Church required a parsonage, the community swung into action. At the end of December 1865 a large marquee was set up in a paddock belonging to Charles Parsons. Stalls sold crafts and refreshments. Approximately 300 visitors arrived via Dyers Pass in the new Cobb & Co. coach and from Lyttelton in the steamer *Betsy Douglas*, which berthed at the government jetty in Sandy Bay. The scale of fund-raising events and the amounts they raised increased over the years. In December 1873 the steamers *Halcyon* and *Mullogh* made three trips each from Lyttelton, and many visitors came over Dyers Pass to enjoy a bazaar and picnic fund-raiser for St Cuthbert's and St Peter's. Six hundred people enjoyed George Oram's sit-down dinner.

Despite the construction of the jetty at Dyers Point, access at low tide remained a challenge for the steam launches that plied the harbour, and locals asked for a channel to be dredged. Lyttelton Harbour Board engineer C. Napier-Bell reported that for 2000 feet from the pier the water shoaled from 16 inches to 3 feet at low-water spring tides. The dredge would therefore be stranded except at the top of high water, and the harbour board dredge simply could not undertake the work. Only five years after its construction, Napier-Bell could say that the jetty was just very badly sited as far as access to deep water was concerned.[9] As if to reinforce the point, on a beautiful summer's day in February 1880, 90 Christchurch Hotel employees left port on the steam launch *Lyttelton* bound for a picnic in Governors Bay. The tide was out when the launch arrived at the head of the harbour and the passengers had to clamber ashore on rocks — about a mile from the jetty and an hour's slipping and rock-clambering from the Ocean View Hotel.[10]

Napier-Bell proposed a jetty at what he named Raupaki Point, otherwise known as Percivals Point, the site considered — and rejected — at the 1874 residents' meetings. Here a depth of 3 feet at low-water spring tides could be reached 150 feet from the rocks, sufficient depth for the steam launch presently in use. A road would need to be cut for about 30 chains around the rocks and a connection made with the main road. So in March 1883 the Lyttelton Harbour Board invited tenders for the construction of an alternative jetty, this time at Percivals Point, Governors Bay.

The new structure was commonly known as Smalls jetty. Percivals Point later came to be known as Sandy Bay Point. The narrow track that now runs from Sandy Bay round to the remaining jetty piles was once a busy official road providing access to the bay for cargo and visitors. When the house originally built for Mary Small by her family (now known as Rowan House) became home to the Gilpin family in 1914, they turned it into a tearoom and guesthouse. Visitors arriving by launch at Sandy Bay Point would walk up the path from the

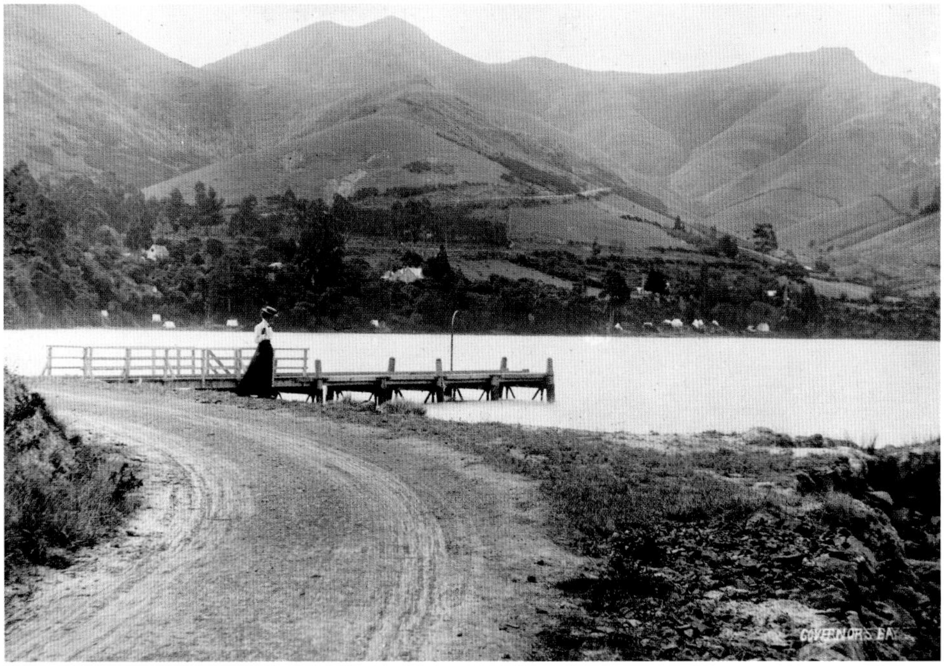
GOVERNORS BA

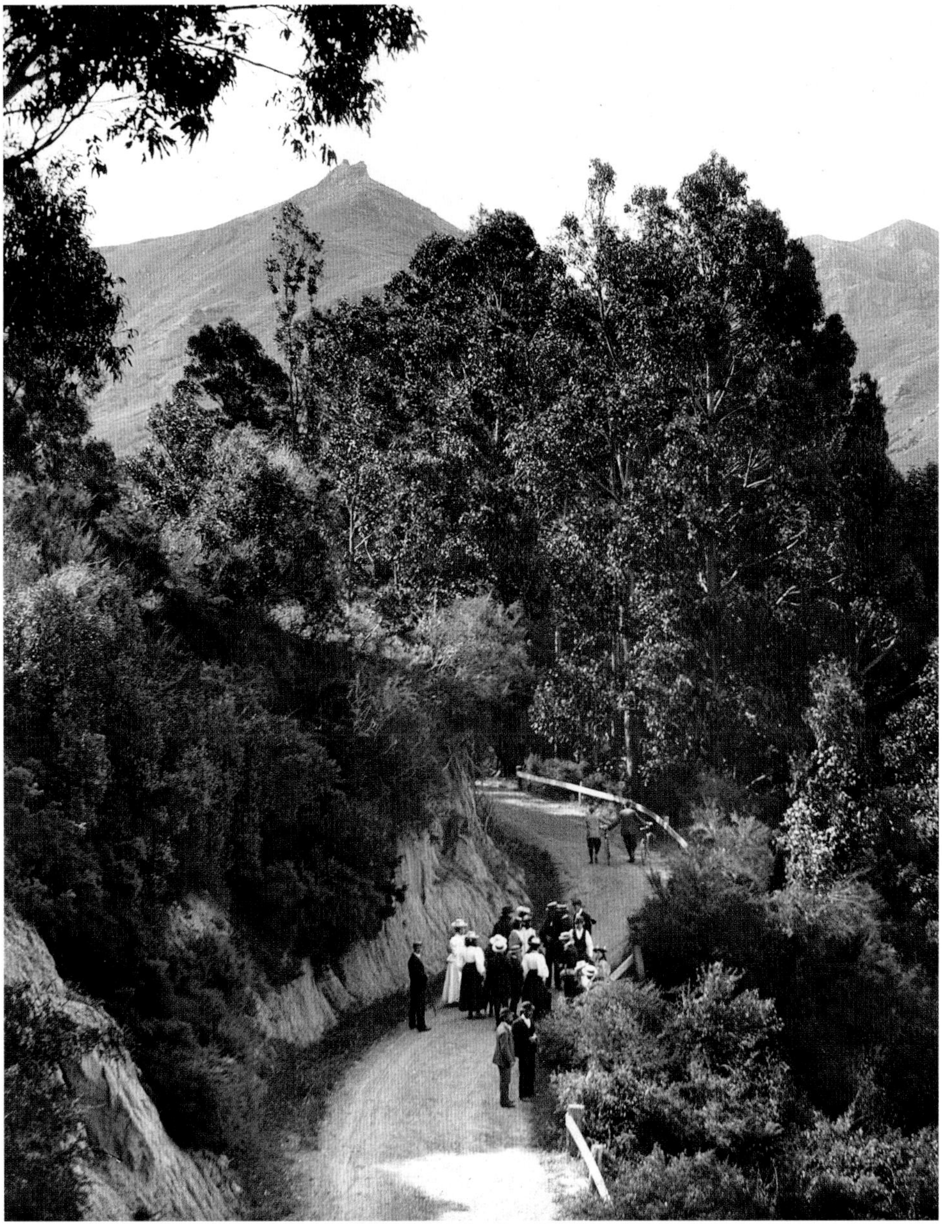

beach, under the arched whale bones at the entrance to the garden, and enjoy scones, meatloaf, sandwiches and soft drinks.

Regular jetty access to the head of the harbour directly boosted trade for boarding houses. One such in the heart of Governors Bay, Ellerslie, was described as 'within but a few miles of Lyttelton with which it is in regular communication by coach and steamer . . . an ideal spot for tourists, and for city residents desiring a quiet rest in the bracing atmosphere of the sea coast'.[11] Some families supplemented their income by offering a room or two in their homes to holidaymakers. Some visitors simply pitched their tents along the foreshore between the two main jetties. This popularity caused problems. In 1909 the Mount Herbert county clerk asked for a constable to be stationed at Governors Bay:

> I would point out that during the last few years, Governors Bay has become a favourite resort for holiday makers and campers. On holiday occasions the Lyttelton launches take up as many as 1000 to 1500 people while quite a large number walk or cycle over the hill from Christchurch, and it must be admitted that among such a large crowd there are always some who are ready to despoil the property of others . . .[12]

In the 1920s Stanley Radcliffe would put his bike on the train at Heathcote, transfer it onto *John Anderson* at Lyttelton, disembark at the Sandy Bay jetty and bike around to see his Harris relatives in Allandale.[13] For school picnics in the 1930s John Allan and his fellow Governors Bay pupils caught a boat to Quail Island from the Sandy Bay jetty. 'You'd get in there when you couldn't get into the big one [Governors Bay jetty].'[14]

The two jetties were popular fishing spots. Frank Brown and Bill Hall favoured the smaller jetty on the point at Sandy Bay where the water was deeper and they could go garfishing. 'The tide would have to be right too, anywhere from a little before high tide, to half way out.'[15] Sometimes, 'when the fish were running and the tide was not right until after midnight', the boys would 'rise at perhaps 1am, load up and go off down to the jetty. On one occasion we took a frying pan down with us, caught our fish, and at daybreak lit a fire and fried them. We wouldn't have exchanged this breakfast for the grandest meal in Christchurch.'[16]

In November 1935 two lads — James McFaul and James Kevin — walked over the hill from Christchurch to Governors Bay. They fished from the long jetty, and then tried their luck at the deeper water off the Sandy Bay jetty. McFaul was walking backwards, unwinding his lines, when he fell off the edge of the jetty. Kevin threw a lifebuoy and then jumped in to try to save his friend, who was struggling in the rough sea. Despite all efforts, including help from local resident Angus Small, McFaul died, the coroner returning a verdict of accidental drowning. McFaul's family attempted to sue the Lyttelton Harbour Board because the jetty had been constructed without railings at the end so that cargo could be loaded. As a result of this accident the Sandy Bay jetty was dismantled in 1938. Only the piles remain today.

Meanwhile, silting up continued to hamper access to the 'upper jetty'. In February 1908 Lyttelton Harbour Board engineer Cyrus Williams prepared a memorandum on the dredging of a channel 'from the lower to the upper wharf in Governors Bay'. He concluded that making a channel 50 feet wide, with side slopes of 6 to 1 and a depth of 5 feet at low water, would mean dredging 17,306 cubic yards of material. The harbour board's Priestman dredge could do the job with the help of a small tugboat and two barges to carry away the spoil. However, he noted, 'by the time the work was finished at one end the other end would require to be gone over again. It seems to me that the cost would be out of all proportion to the benefits.'[17]

Tui camp, Governors Bay, 1890s. The end of the 'upper jetty' can be seen on the left and, just discernible, on the Sandy Bay foreshore to the right of the yacht is the jetty built by Dyer and Parsons.
HOCKEN COLLECTIONS, UARE TAOKA O HĀKENA, 1345_01_002A

ABOVE Governors Bay jetty, c.1905. The jetty was built in 1874 and extended to its present length in 1913. Note the absence of rails at the seaward end to enable loading of farm produce.
CANTERBURY MUSEUM, 19XX.2.5232

BELOW This jetty, built in 1883 to provide better access to deep water, was demolished in 1938 following a fatal accident. The jetty was known variously as Percivals Point jetty, Smalls jetty and Sandy Bay jetty. Its remnant piles are still visibale at the point beyond Sandy Bay.
CANTERBURY MUSEUM, CHARLES BEKEN COLLECTION, 1955.81.713

Shortly after that, a petition signed by most bay residents argued that the upper wharf's accessibility by road made it much handier for visitors and less expensive for commerce than the 'lower [Sandy Bay] jetty'. The petitioners sought an extension to their upper jetty, the dredging of a channel, clearing of the foreshore and improved bathing facilities. A deputation of residents met with representatives of the Lyttelton Harbour Board. They pointed to the increase in produce coming out of the head of the harbour, in particular flax and wool. Several spoke in favour of closing the lower jetty. Costs could be covered by a toll levied on visitors using the upper jetty.

The deputation was asked to calculate the quantity of goods, number of passengers and 'probable amount of contributions toward the work by settlers in the district' and come back to the harbour board with 'something definite'. In a speedy response, Governors Bay resident Dr Pairman indicated that there would be wharfage on anything between 800 and 1000 tons and that the number of visitors to the bay annually was around 30,000. With the jetty extended and a channel dredged, farmers could dispatch all their wool in a single day rather than over a week or more; more grain would be grown in the district, given the current prohibitive cost of cartage; and a great stimulus would be given to fruit and vegetable growing, dairying, poultry and egg farming, beekeeping, and other industries suitable for smallholdings. The levying of a small charge on the many visitors each year would defray costs and provide a sinking fund for ongoing maintenance.[18]

Despite such energetic soliciting, the Harbour Improvement Committee advised the harbour board not to consider extending the jetty or dredging a channel. Repair of the short, upper jetty could be undertaken at a cost of £250 as long as the Mount Herbert County Council would agree to pay 6 per cent per annum for 20 years on the cost of the repairs. The council must have been reluctant, as in 1910 the harbour board decided to close the 'upper wharf' at Governors Bay as an economy measure.[19] It was declared unsafe for traffic of any kind.

Towards the end of 1911, interesting reports appeared in local papers suggesting that the upper jetty might be extended to connect with the lower jetty at a cost of £6000. A year later, the improvement committee changed its mind and recommended that the upper jetty be extended so that launches could use it in any tide, at an estimated cost of £1500–£2000. Construction began, using Australian hardwood timber, but progressed haltingly. A visitor to Governors Bay complained to the *Press* in March 1913 that work on the jetty was at a standstill.[20] Finally, by August that year the jetty had been completed to its full 950-foot length. At the time of the extension, Eddie Radcliffe was going to school in Governors Bay. After class the children would rush down to the jetty, where there was a trolley on railway lines that transported materials to the construction end. The workmen would allow the children to get into the trolley and push themselves up and down.[21]

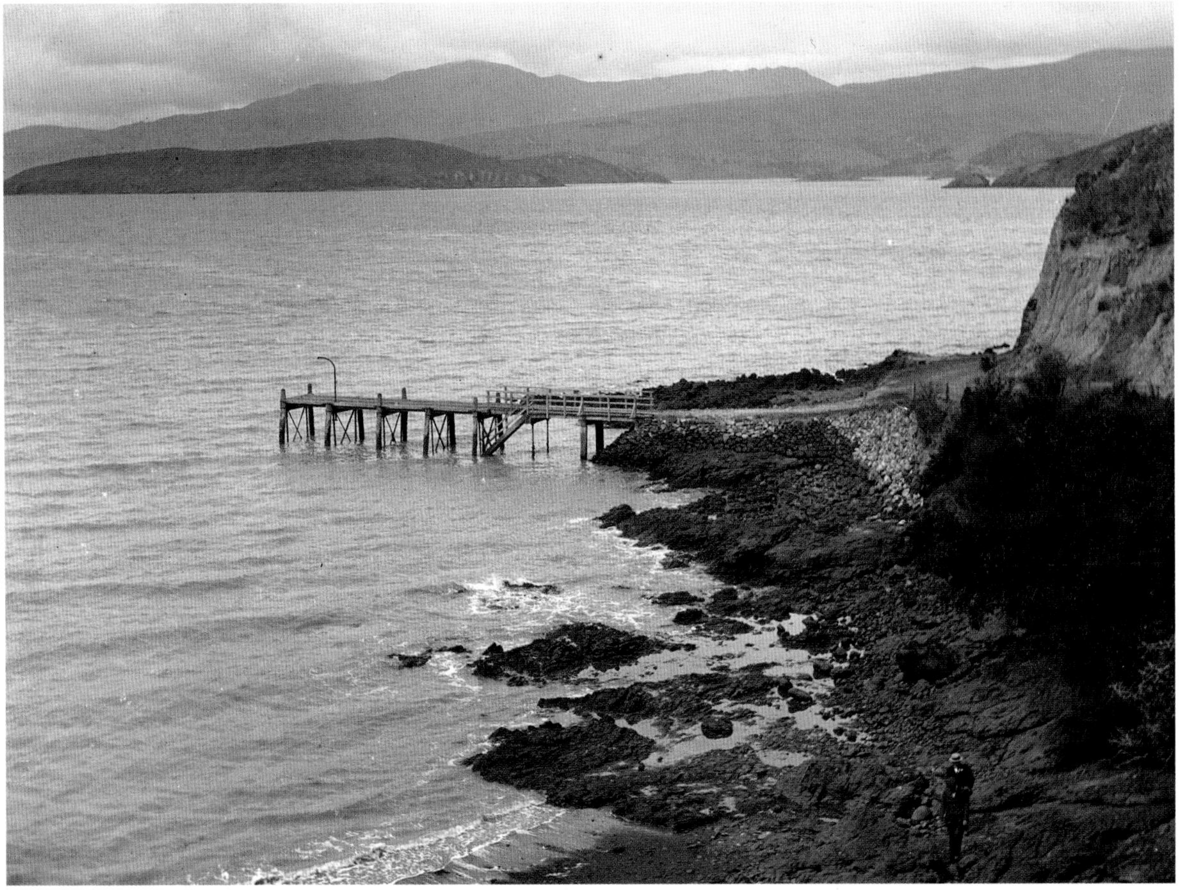

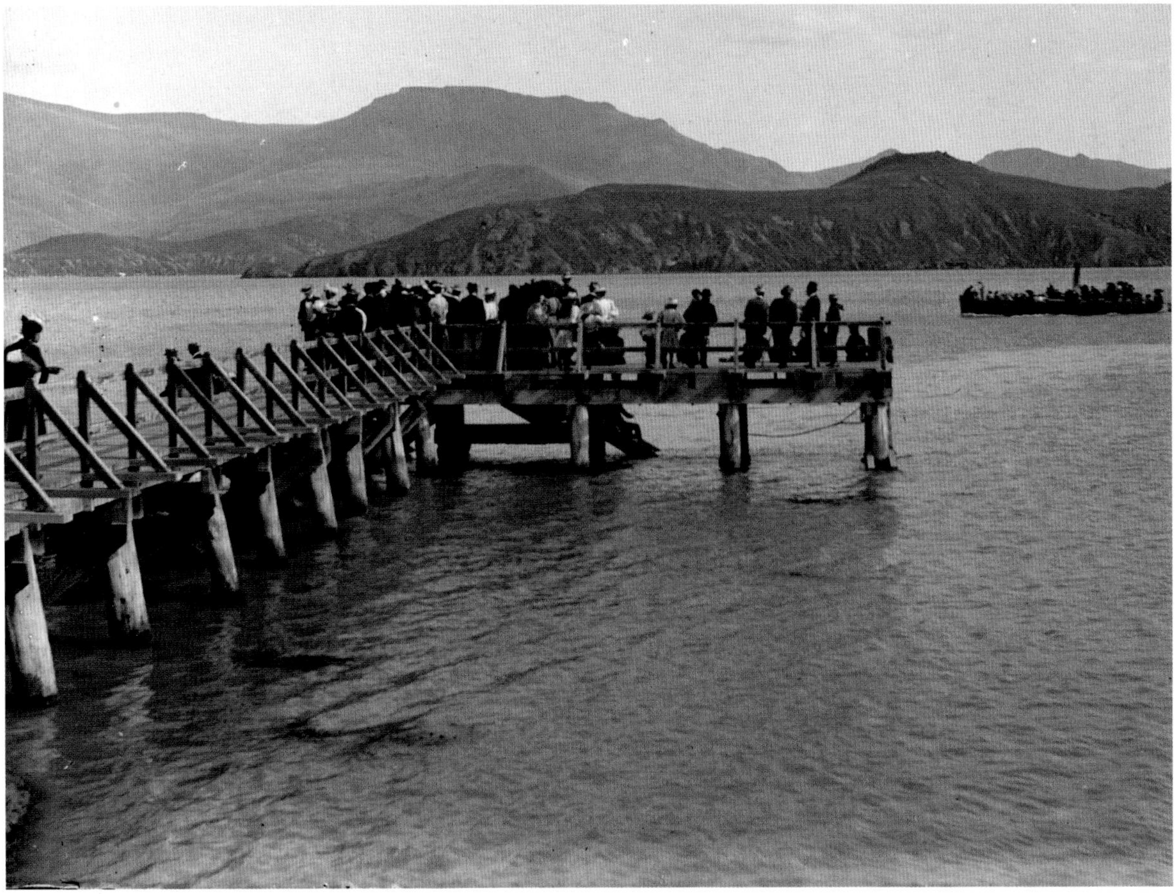

Not everyone was happy with the 1913 extension. A disgruntled reader wrote to the *Press*, just before the official opening of the Rāpaki jetty along the coast, to point out that the newly extended Governors Bay wharf had never been graced by an official visit. It was, however,

> extremely unlikely that they [officials] would be able to get down by water, as it is only at high tide that anything beyond small motor boats can approach it, and at low water it stands out high and dry in the mud. I feel sure, however, that the chairman [of the harbour board] would place his motor-car at the service of the members and drive them over, and if low water, they would have the opportunity of walking it and viewing the most shameful waste of public money that it has ever been my lot to witness.[22]

When a Christchurch resident took a walk over the hill to Governors Bay in June 1918, 'one of the first things that came into my view (completely spoiling the beauty of the bay) was a hideous, snake-like structure, standing out in the mud'. Later in the day he strolled down to the wharf and watched as *Purau* steamed up and 'gracefully settled in the mud some two chains from the wharf, and there she stuck for about two hours, the passengers subsequently being taken on board in the dinghy'.[23]

The idea of connecting the two jetties resurfaced. In September 1913 the Christchurch *Star* reported that 'the eighteen-hundred-foot jetty which it is intended to run out at Governors Bay will be the longest in Canterbury and one of the longest in New Zealand'.[24] The extension, 'which will end quite close to the old jetty', would allow 4-foot depth at low water. The use of old timber would mean a cost of £800 as against £2500 with new timber. This proposed extension to the extension seems to have sunk without trace.

Despite being by far the longest jetty or wharf structure in the harbour, the upper Governors Bay jetty was still inadequate at and around low tide. In 1927 residents again petitioned the Lyttelton Harbour Board to provide better water access, primarily by dredging a channel. The board remained reluctant. Acting engineer Percy Fryer pointed out that a depth of 3 feet 9 inches at ordinary low water seemed reasonable to him, especially given that there was a regular motor service by road and a very small amount of water-borne traffic. Ex-resident John Hadfield, following a visit to Governors Bay in 1930, wrote to the *Press* that 'the jetty would appear to be of more use now as a promenade than for the purpose for which it was built'.[25]

Regardless of the tidal difficulties, access by sea continued to be hugely popular with visitors. A regular steamer service ran from Lyttelton to Governors Bay on Sundays and public holidays, carrying picnickers and visitors to the Pleasure

Gardens at the Ocean View Hotel. Vessels on the run included *Canterbury*, *Waiwera*, *John Anderson*, *Purau* and *Monica*. The 35-ton steel *John Anderson*, built in Lyttelton and launched in November 1891, was registered to take 250 passengers on harbour excursions. *Purau* and *Monica* were still carrying passengers to the bay in the 1920s, but only at high tide.

For local children the foreshore was an enormous playground. Angus Small remembered picnics at Smalls beach, swimming, hut building, flying kites, tussock sledging and a precious model yacht. His son Graeme remembered 'whizzing down' on foot from the old Governors Bay School to Sandy Bay to go swimming, juniors at one end of the beach, seniors at the other, with a changing shed for the girls. Every Guy Fawkes, the Scouts organised a bonfire on the beach at Sandy Bay. People came from all around the head of the harbour to enjoy the fire, a 'couple of big dixies of savs' and a sing-along with Angus Small playing the accordion.[26]

When the nor'westers funnelled down the valley from the Sign of the Kiwi, the wind would hit the water in a line between the remaining piles of the Sandy Bay jetty and the long jetty. The children made trimarans about 2 feet long out of flax stalks, with a flax-stalk mast tied back with string and a lug sail. These were serious racing vessels. 'When put in the water the strong wind caught it, and it would just rocket across the harbour to Manson's Point.'[27] Simon Agar remembered childhood holidays at Sandy Bay: 'At low tide, my brother and I used to mud slide on our bellies half way to the main jetty on small sheets of plywood. After we were done, we would climb the private track up to Rowan House totally covered in mud head to foot.'[28]

At Cholmondeley Children's Home in the 1940s, Neil Withell recalled:

> We were allowed to play on the rocky beach below [Cholmondeley] but we were told to stay together and not wander away. Under no circumstances we were [sic] to venture onto the jetty unaccompanied.
>
> We were then told that, at an earlier 'camp', a little boy had walked out onto it and a BIG OCTOPUS came up over the side and dragged him into the sea. After some time on the beach, we all formed a line and walked down the centre of the jetty to the very end and back, petrified at every step.[29]

Local residents built a den for the Sea Scouts on the foreshore between the long jetty and Sandy Bay. In December 1960 more than 100 Sea Scouts gathered to

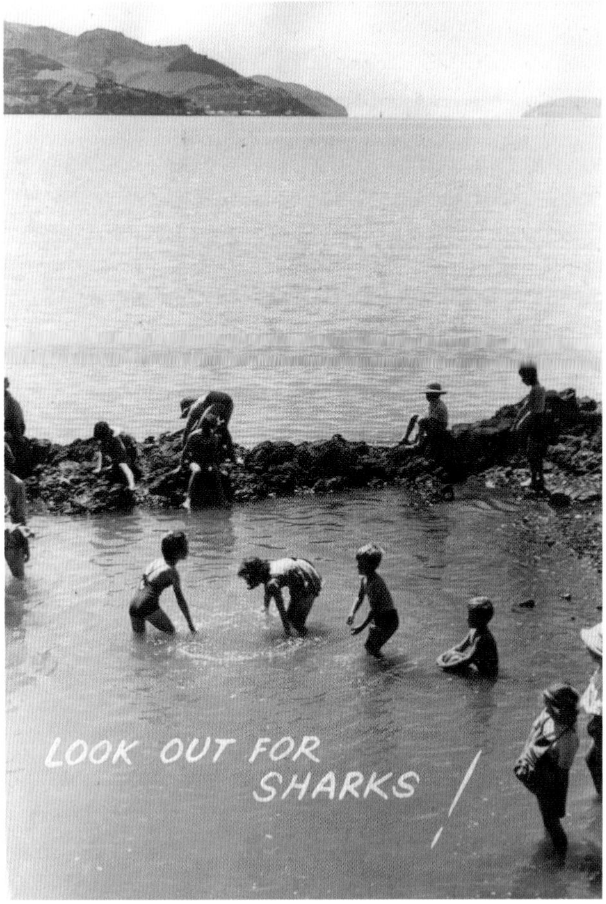
LOOK OUT FOR
SHARKS !

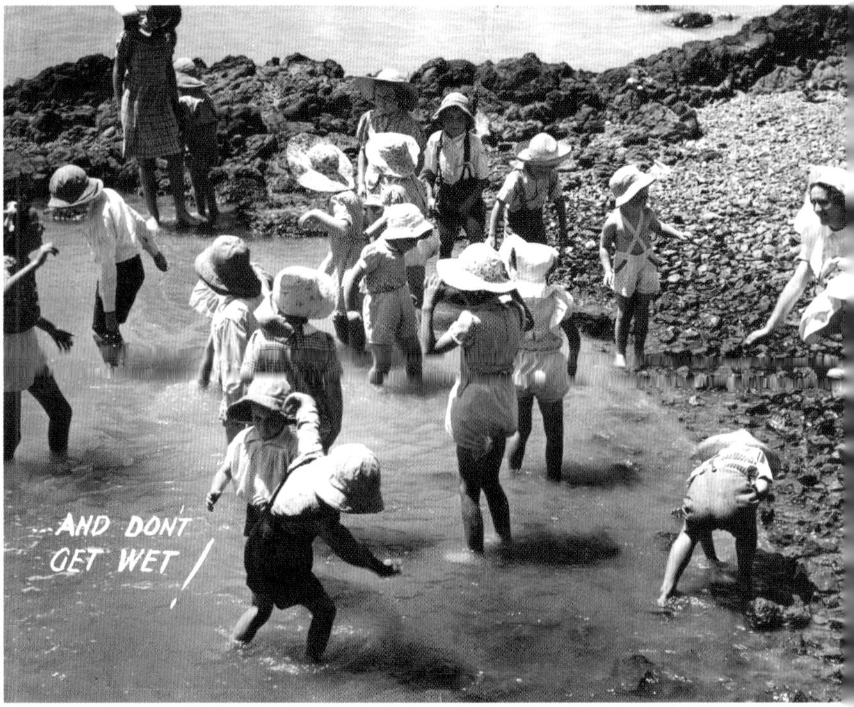
AND DON'T
GET WET !

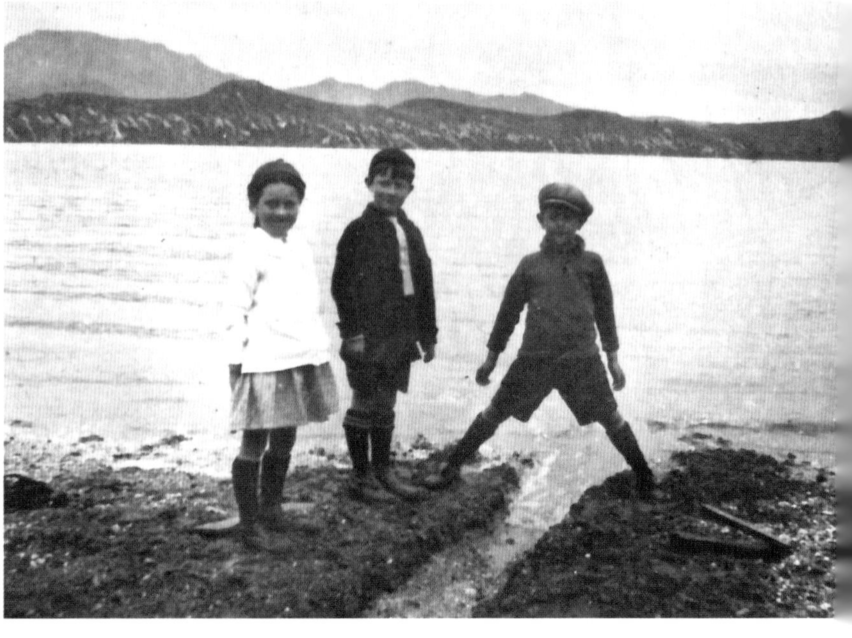

ABOVE AND ABOVE RIGHT Youngsters from Cholmondeley Children's Home on the foreshore by the long jetty.
CHOLMONDELEY CHILDREN'S CENTRE ARCHIVE

RIGHT Having fun on the beach at Sandy Bay.
COURTESY OF GRAEME SMALL

celebrate the launching of their new training boat and the opening of the new den. The 18-foot *Vigilant*, which had a centreboard for sailing, was built in the bay by Lionel Jefcoate. At the launching ceremony the six-member Governors Bay junior crew manned the boat with lofted oars, then rowed to the site of the new den.

In the mid-1950s Mount Herbert County Council and the Lyttelton Harbour Board discussed the possibility of dredging a large basin to accommodate moored boats on the Sandy Bay side of the Governors Bay jetty, with a dredged channel leading out to deeper water. The harbour board wanted the moored boats out of its inner harbour at Lyttelton Port. The council agreed to upgrade Jetty Road, replace the timber bridge and form a large parking area down near the base of the jetty. In the end the project was stymied by the estimated cost (approximately £2000 annually) of constantly having to keep the access channel open.[30]

In the meantime, boatbuilder Lionel Jefcoate approached the council chairman in 1958 about setting up a boatbuilding shed and slipway by the long jetty. Jefcoate had already been building boats entirely without power tools on a little flat promontory to the north of the jetty. Go-ahead was signalled with a handshake — no consents and no surveying fee. The rental to the council was £10 per annum, as was the slipway fee to the Lyttelton Harbour Board. Lionel built a 40-foot by 30-foot boatshed and a slipway just to the east of the jetty. The boatshed was extended a further 50 feet by 40 feet and a second slipway built in 1962. From there Lionel singlehandedly built a range of yachts, launches, fishing boats and cabin cruisers. He also overhauled and maintained boats in the harbour area. It was a big event in the bay whenever a boat was launched.

Launching the 32-foot cutter *Calypso* from Lionel Jefcoate's boatbuilding shed in Governors Bay, 1960. When the 18-horsepower auxiliary motor was started just after the launch, it backfired and petrol ignited under the cockpit. The fire was rapidly extinguished.
COURTESY OF GRAEME SMALL

Māori Gardens

On the rocky, cliff-backed foreshore between Pukekaroro Sandy Bay and Rāpaki, there is a small sandy beach where Māori, harvesting the abundant kaimoana from the adjacent reef, likely beached their waka.[31]

Today there are four (once five) baches tucked in between the sea and the cliff face and accessed either by sea or by a steep track from the Lyttelton–Governors Bay road. These small holiday homes were built in the early 1930s by yachties who wanted a place to bunk down in the harbour rather than pack up and go home after a day's sailing. The settlement was known locally as Harkess Bay or, more commonly now, Māori Gardens. Why 'Māori Gardens' is speculative. Possibly because it was adjacent to the abandoned settlement of Taukahara or 'Little Rāpaki', where Māori had once grown wheat and potatoes. Or perhaps because it was a popular place for locals from Rāpaki to gather kaimoana.

Back in England when the Canterbury Association drew up plans for a settlement based at the head of Lyttelton Harbour, its members assumed there would be road access at sea level in the upper harbour. As a result, the foreshore around the head of the harbour, including the stretch between Rāpaki and Sandy Bay, was impossibly designated 'road reserve'. So the baches at Māori Gardens were unwittingly built on a road reserve. Over the decades, the bach owners have always paid rates to the Mount Herbert County Council and subsequently the Christchurch City Council.

A Coastal Reserves Investigation carried out by the Department of Lands and Survey in 1982 recommended that the baches be removed to avoid giving the impression that this was a privately owned beach. Removal of the cottages would, the investigation claimed, encourage more use of the beach by people arriving by boat. In submissions to the Banks Peninsula District Council in 1990, bach owners, including one whose association with the bay went back to 1935, opposed the removal of the cottages, pointing out that it was not unusual over the summer for up to 50 visitors to be on the beach at one time. Tramping clubs lunched and swam there before returning to their cars at the Sign of the Takahe. It was a particularly popular bathing and picnic spot for Governors Bay residents, including the children from Cholmondeley Children's Home.[32] The bach occupants also provided a valuable custodial service, helping boats caught on the reef, giving first aid, cleaning up rubbish and tending the native bush.

Today, despite landslips, earthquakes and bureaucratic fiats, the baches remain, in part because the levying of rates by successive councils has given tacit approval of their existence. Owners are only allowed to do necessary maintenance, not to make additions or carry out significant alterations. No new building can occur on the road reserve. The cottages survive as an important part of the cultural landscape, telling yet another story of the relationship between land and sea in Whakaraupō Lyttelton Harbour.

From left: Graeme Small, Neil Crosby and another keen paddler on the beach at Māori Gardens, c.2005, having kayaked around Quail Island on a still winter morning.
MAX GRANT

With his business right on the foreshore, Jefcoate was more exposed than most harbour dwellers to an unpredictable ocean. In 1960 he experienced the full force of the tsunami rolling across the Pacific. In his words:

> An unexpected drama unfolded as the first wave swept through the boatshed about 11.20 p.m. to a depth of five feet, bursting the slipway doors aside and taking everything buoyant out into the harbour — timber, paint etc. Some was salvageable later from the beach. Electric motors were ruined by mud and salt water. A fishing boat on the slip floated away and returned almost to the same spot two tides later! A new yacht building needed a section of bottom planking removed to prevent her from also floating away![33]

At Sandy Bay Graeme Small saw the harbour empty out.

> I was about 11 or 12 . . . I looked out — hmmm, it's a low tide, there's no water. And it was right out as far as the end of Quail Island. Quail Island was high and dry . . . I rushed inside and said, 'Oh, there's no water.' 'What d'you mean?' I said, 'There's no water in the harbour, it's all gone.' They said, 'Rubbish.' They came out and, 'Oh, where's it gone?'. . . Woooof, back up it came. I took the day off school — I bunked it. My parents didn't know until late in the day. I took a sugar bag . . . down to Māori Gardens. There were fish stranded on the beach. I took the sugar bag and got flounders and sole . . .[34]

Eventually, in January 1988, Lionel launched his fiftieth, and final, boat at the slipway. As the *Bay News* reported, 'The day was chosen because it was one of the few tides high enough during the year to launch on — a far cry from the days [in the 1950s] when Lionel could see almost 1.75 metres of water outside his shed at high water.'[35] A drop in demand for wooden boats, a government tax and the arrival of the sewage treatment plant not far around the corner from the boatshed encouraged him to sell the shed to marine broker Steve Cunard and move to Havelock in the Marlborough Sounds. A 'spectacular blaze' destroyed the Cunard boatbuilding business on 4 May 2000 and removed a landmark from the foreshore.[36] Steve Cunard was subsequently charged with arson and later made bankrupt.

In June 1988 the Governors Bay Community Association wrote to the Lyttelton Harbour Board expressing concern about the state of the jetty. The change in the use of the jetty was evident in the association's argument for its retention. The association pointed out that the jetty was of key importance as a recreational facility in the upper harbour. 'A walk to the end of the jetty is a very popular activity

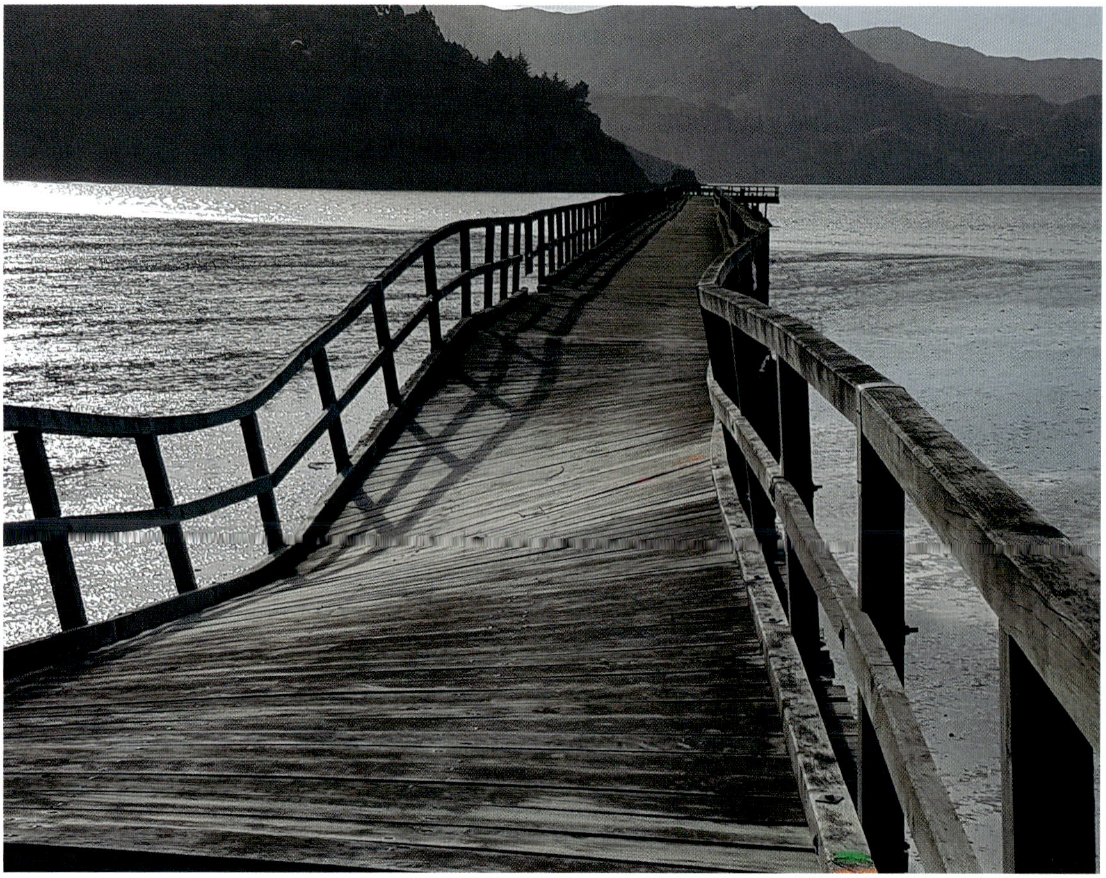

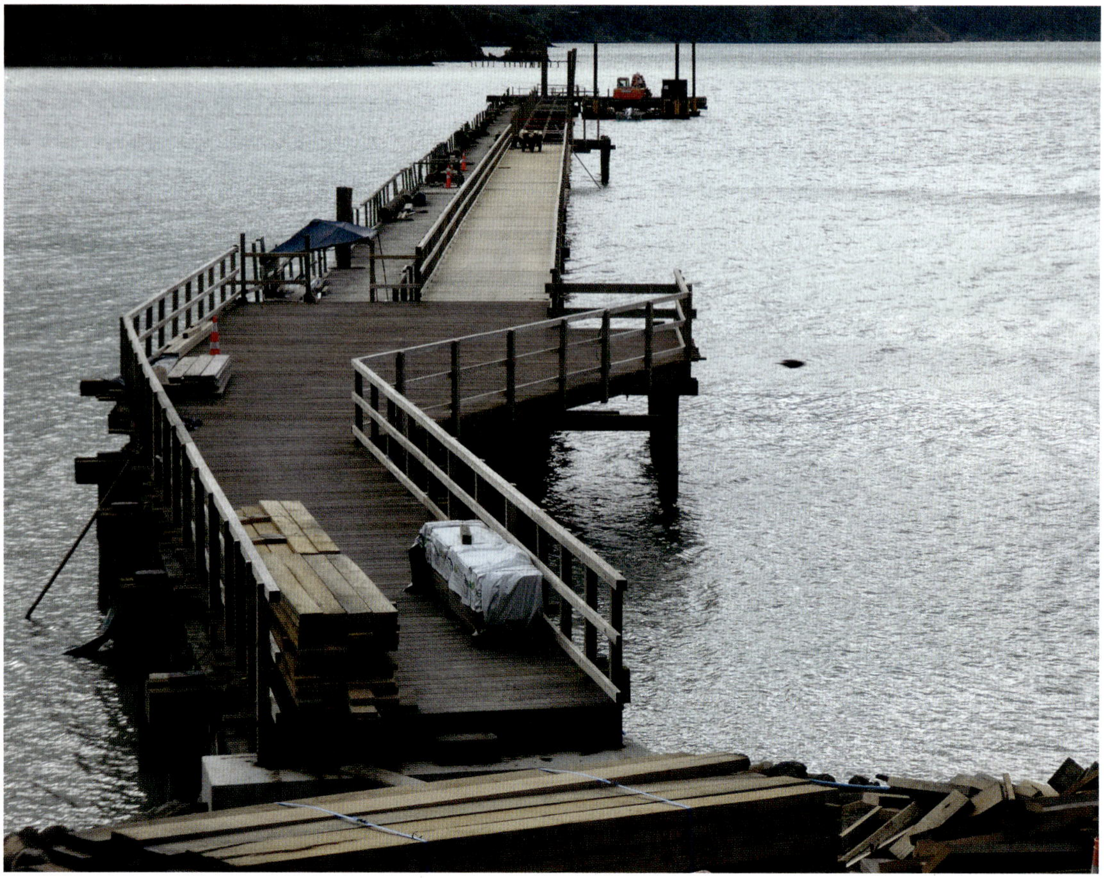

for visitors and allows non boaties to experience the harbour from out in the bay.'[37] The association also pointed to the historical significance of the jetty — the last of its type in the area.

The harbour board commissioned a report on the jetty, which indicated that around $15,000 would be needed in the next year to carry out necessary repairs, and that such expenditure would have to be repeated at regular intervals. The board therefore offered the Mount Herbert County Council the 'opportunity' to accept the future responsibility for the jetty. Should the council decline, the board would have to consider restricting public access or demolishing the jetty completely since it was no longer used for commercial purposes but was essentially a public recreation facility.

Inspections in 1993 and 1994 confirmed community concern about the condition of the long jetty. Twenty new piles were driven under the jetty in 1997, the pile-driver being mounted on a flat barge made from mussel buoys. At the sea end of the jetty the 10-metre-long piles went 4 metres into the silt. Typically, about a third of the work was done by local volunteers in order to keep costs down. By May 1999 a total of $68,814 had been spent to bring the jetty up to scratch.[38]

Despite this work, the Governors Bay jetty was closed in 2011 when a post-earthquake inspection declared it unsafe. By June 2014, 63 piles were found to need replacing. The following year, after the Christchurch City Council announced it had no plans to repair the jetty, the local community formed a 'save the jetty' committee, and five months later the Governors Bay Jetty Restoration Trust registered as a charity. The city council agreed to support the community initiative and in September 2016 approved transfer of the ownership of the jetty to the trust for $1. Since then the trust has worked tirelessly to secure concept drawings, cost estimates, funding, resource consent and, importantly, ongoing community support through the efforts of volunteers. At the time of writing, the jetty rebuild is scheduled for completion in April 2023.

In a recent development, the jetty restoration trust has also secured an historic Lyttelton building that will complement the new jetty. In 1923 the Canterbury Yacht and Motor Boat Club built a new clubhouse on land made available by the Lyttelton Harbour Board in Dampiers Bay (now Te Ana Marina). With the construction of a new club facility at Erskine Point in 1957, the original clubhouse was sold to the Lyttelton Sea Scouts, who used it as their den from the late 1960s until the 1990s. In the early 2000s four local supporters purchased the building, thereby ensuring its survival. The Governors Bay Jetty Restoration Trust saw an opportunity to relocate the old clubhouse to Governors Bay and position it on the foreshore, where Lionel Jefcoate's boatshed once stood, for use as a community facility. Planning is under way to secure this new future for the small blue boathouse.

ABOVE The Governors Bay jetty in 2019, awaiting its rebuild. The deck of the new jetty will be 70 centimetres higher than that of its predecessor to accommodate sea level rise.
GOVERNORS BAY RESTORATION TRUST, LOUISA EADES

BELOW The new Governors Bay jetty under construction in 2023. The remains of the old jetty, visible on the left, will be demolished once construction is complete.
RUSSELL HARRIS

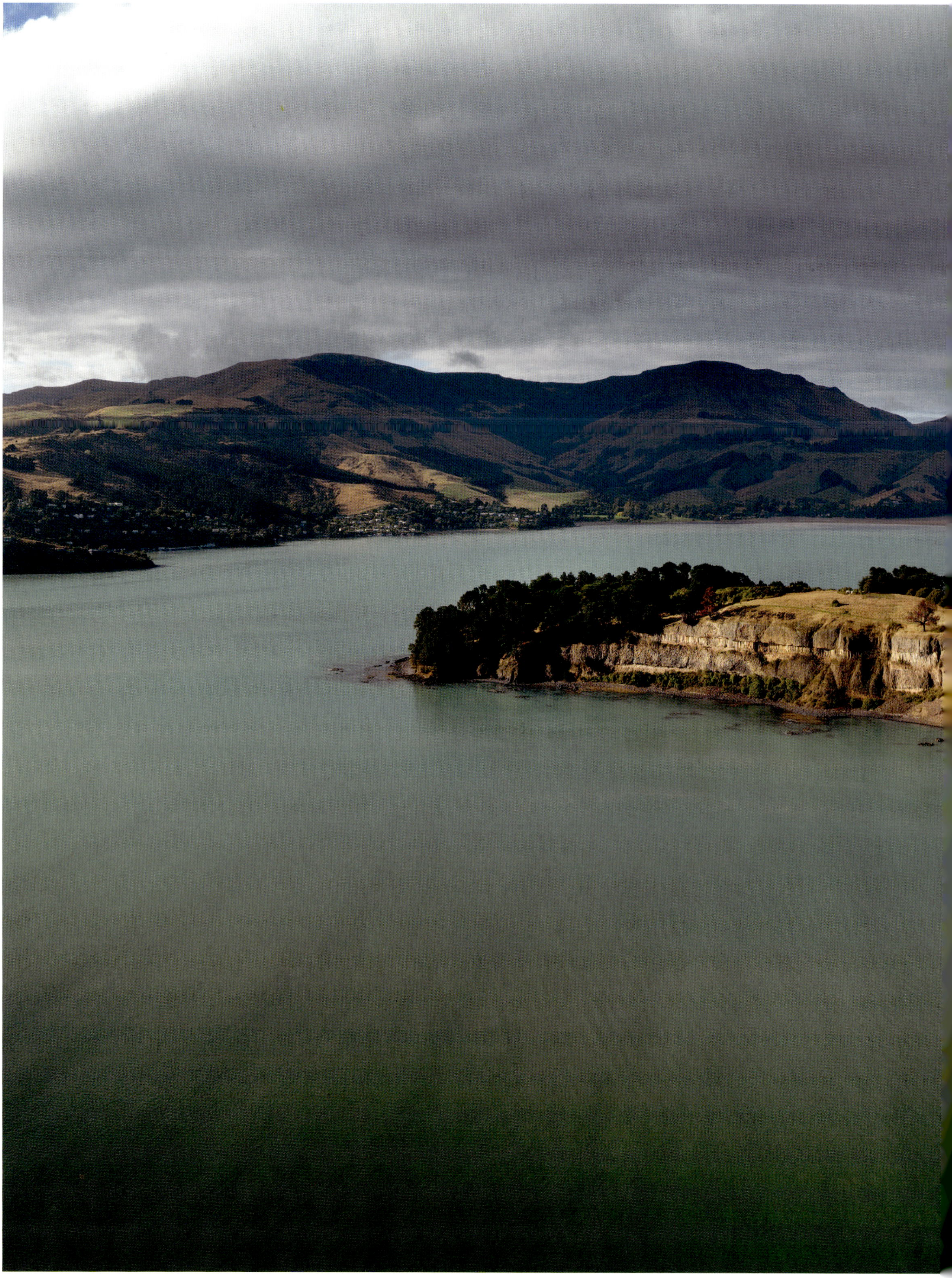

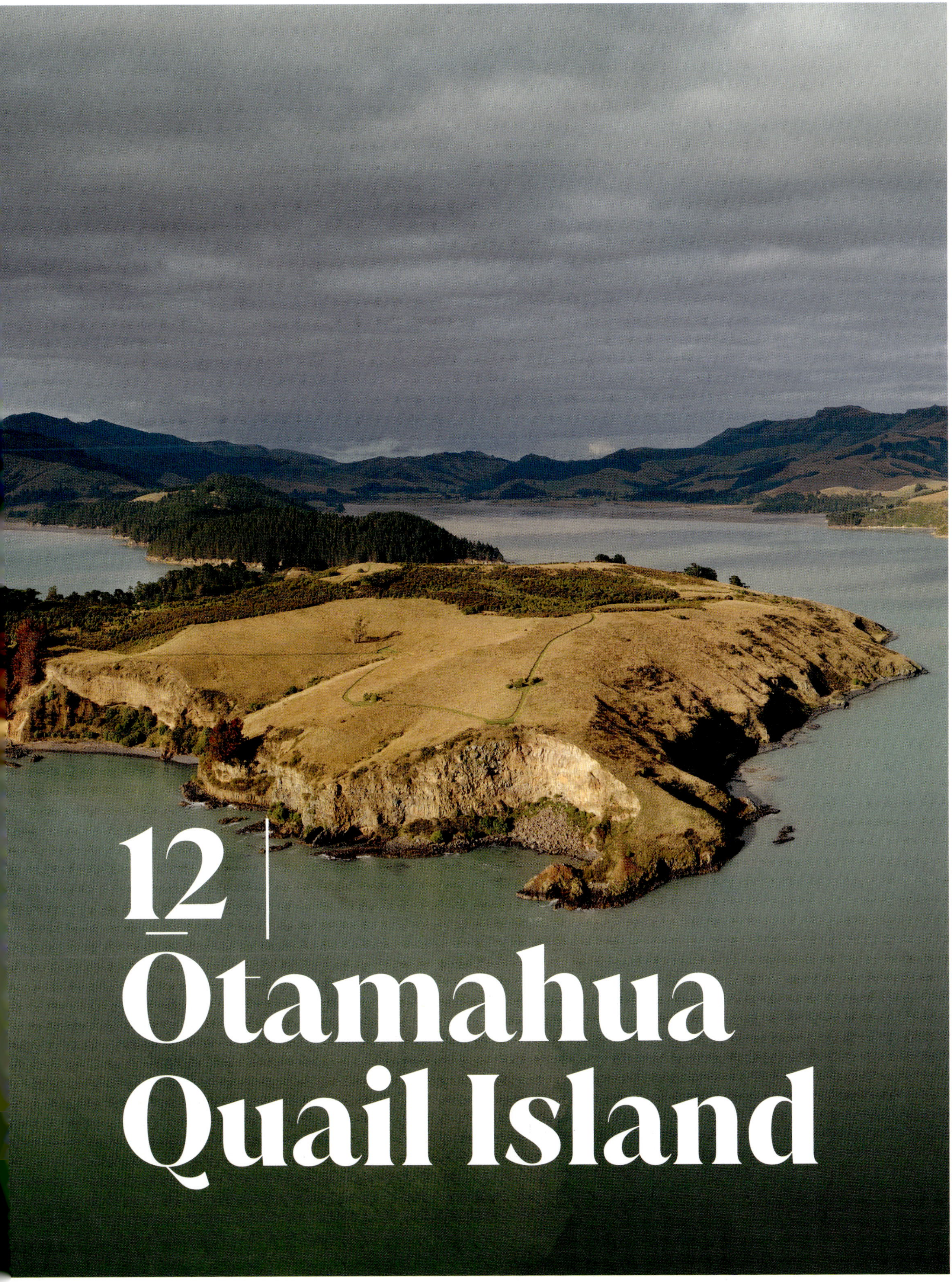

12 | Ōtamahua Quail Island

Live on an island and you have no choice but to confront the sea on a regular basis. In a harbour rich with stories, Ōtamahua Quail Island boasts more than its fair share. Covering just over 80 hectares, it has been a place of sustenance and of sadness, and has reinvented itself many times over the past 170 years.

While it does not appear that Māori had a permanent settlement on Quail Island, the names Ōtamahua ('the place where children collect seabird eggs') and Te Kawakawa ('the pepper tree', valued for its medicinal uses) tell us much about the island's pre-European resources. It is ironic that this large island in the upper reaches of Whakaraupō should have been named by European settlers after a native New Zealand bird (the koreke) that was declared extinct in 1875 and then, briefly, after The Reverend George Robert Gleig, member of the Canterbury Association Committee, who never set foot in Aotearoa New Zealand. Today, Te Hapū o Ngāti Wheke (Rāpaki) hold mana whenua over the island.

Māori from Rāpaki and other settlements in Whakaraupō had no need of jetties. Their waka could be beached on any convenient sandy shore. Ōtamahua, with its sheltered sandy beaches on the southern side, and shelly beach to the south-west facing Aua King Billy, was an important mahinga kai, in particular kaimoana and birds. Huge kupenga (fishing nets) made of harakeke were used for catching pātiki, pioke, kōiro and Quail Island groper. An early sea captain reported a net stretching from Rāpaki to Ōtamahua. Several umu sites have been discovered on Ōtamahua, and a whare for shelter stood on the island at the time of the first European settlers.

The Port Cooper District purchase of August 1849 extinguished Māori title to all land in the Port Cooper area (with the exception of two small reserves). This included Ōtamahua, although Māori did challenge its inclusion in the purchase. Arriving on *Charlotte Jane*, brothers Edward, Henry and Hamilton Ward, from Killinchy in the north of Ireland, won the ballot for the island and decided to farm there. The oldest brother, Edward (24 when he arrived, with brothers aged 19 and 15), explored the island by boat on 1 February 1851. He was impressed with the 'fine rich grass, soil, abundant springs of water' and thought light of any inconveniences arising from isolation. Quail Island's advantages were 'a pretty site, closeness to the port market, besides good grass run for cows, without the trouble of fences or fear of straying far away; pleasant too in being on the sea and a likely place for fishing and shooting'.[1]

The brothers needed a boat. Edward Ward oversaw the building of *Lass of Erin*, a 1-ton, 24-foot yawl, launched on 13 March 1851. Five days later, Edward

Edward Ward, who arrived on the *Charlotte Jane* with his brothers Henry and Hamilton and won the ballot for Ōtamahua Quail Island, 1849. They built a house and established their farm before Edward and Henry were drowned on the harbour in June 1851.
CANTERBURY MUSEUM, 5962

OPPOSITE ABOVE View from the terrace in front of Mr Fitzgerald's house at Lyttelton, 15 November 1852. The small white speck on Ōtamahua Quail Island (centre left) is the Ward brothers' house. Two dwellings can be seen in Governors Bay to the left of Kaitangata Mansons Peninsula.
CANTERBURY MUSEUM, J. E. FITZGERALD, 1938.238.33

OPPOSITE BELOW The Ward brothers' newly built house with the view towards the port of Lyttelton and the Lyttelton Harbour heads, 1851.
CANTERBURY MUSEUM, WILLIAM HOLMES, SCULP. H. ADLARD, WHH.5

and Hamilton took six goats over to the island on the yawl. Building materials for the house under construction on the island came over the same way. Since there is no indication in Edward Ward's journal that they built any sort of jetty on the island, they presumably ran the yawl up on the southern beach (where visitors now swim) at high tide. This is confirmed in the journal:

> At twelve o'clock took cargo of piles and house frame in the yawl to the Island, putting ashore at the inner bay . . . We returned with but one tack, holding our wind well across, though it was blowing right into the harbour; but it was an ebb tide. It is of no use to attempt it from the point of the Island if the tide is flowing.[2]

Building material accumulated on the beach until the Ward brothers constructed a road up the hill to the house site. On 31 March, noted Edward, 'I . . . had the satisfaction of seeing before I left the Island, the bullock, "Big Thomas", take his first load of "house" up the new road.'[3] Things did not always go so smoothly, however. In April, Edward and a companion tried taking a load, which included the shingler who had been working on the house, across the mud to the 'outer point' where they had left the boat. Unfortunately, Big Thomas got badly bogged.

Firewood for the new house and for a lime kiln was gathered further up towards the head of the harbour since Ōtamahua had already been denuded of bush. They would load the yawl with as much wood as could be carried (about 1½ cords) back to the island. But they soon found Lyttelton Harbour can be unforgiving: a calm surface may be transformed in seconds by southerly, nor'westerly or easterly gales. On 23 June Edward and Henry set off to gather more firewood. The following day the alarm was raised in Lyttelton and the *Lass of Erin* was found upturned on a beach, with firewood drifting about the bay. The next day, the dog that had accompanied the brothers returned to the island, having run around the end of the bay. Both brothers were drowned. It was two months before Henry Ward's body was discovered. According to Charlotte Godley,

> There were boats out searching, for two or three days, in vain; but on the Friday we got word that the body of the eldest was washed on shore, at the head of the harbour, and a boat started to fetch it; but such a fearful storm came on, and lasted all Saturday, that the boat could get no further than the Island, and we, in the port, were half afraid that this boatful was lost too.[4]

The youngest brother, Hamilton, remained in Lyttelton, and when another Ward brother, Crosbie, arrived from Ireland, the brothers arranged for the farm to be

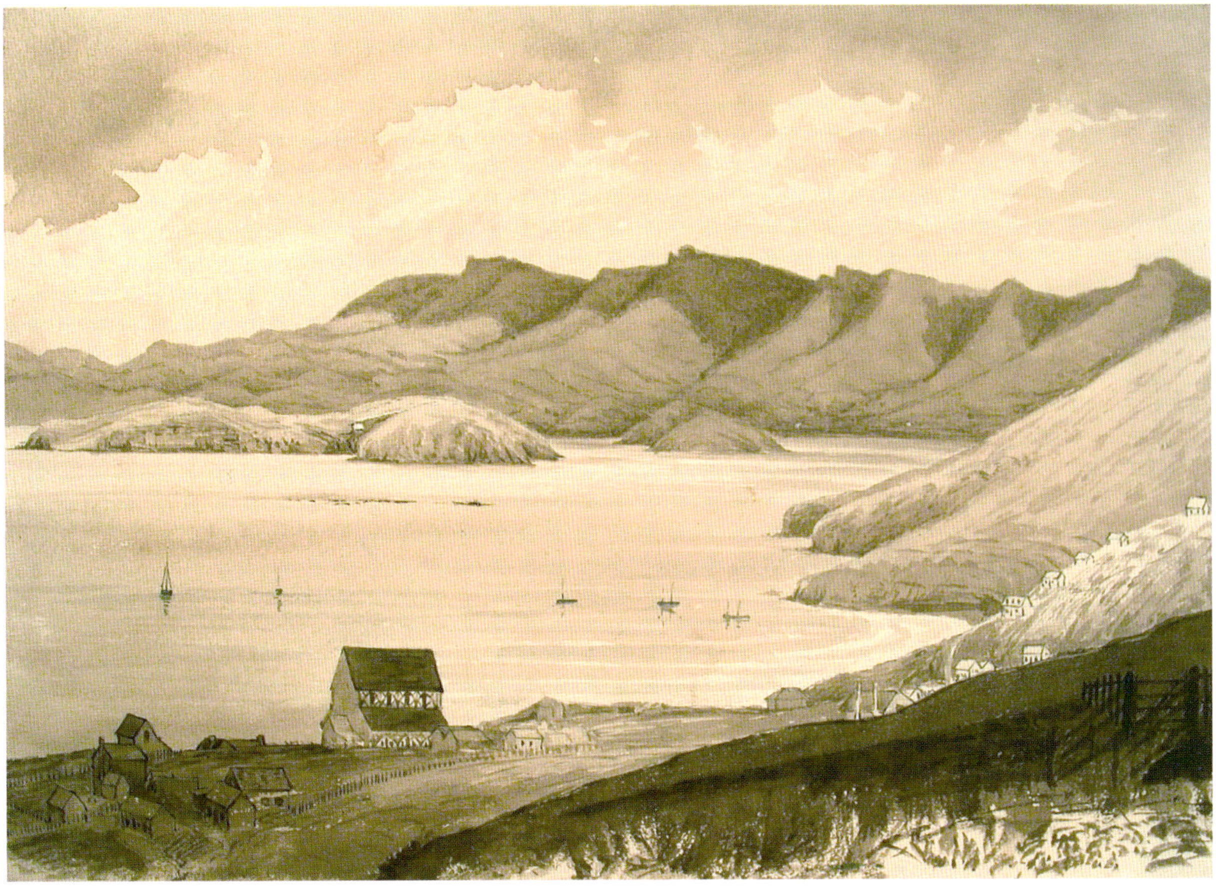

Plate 1

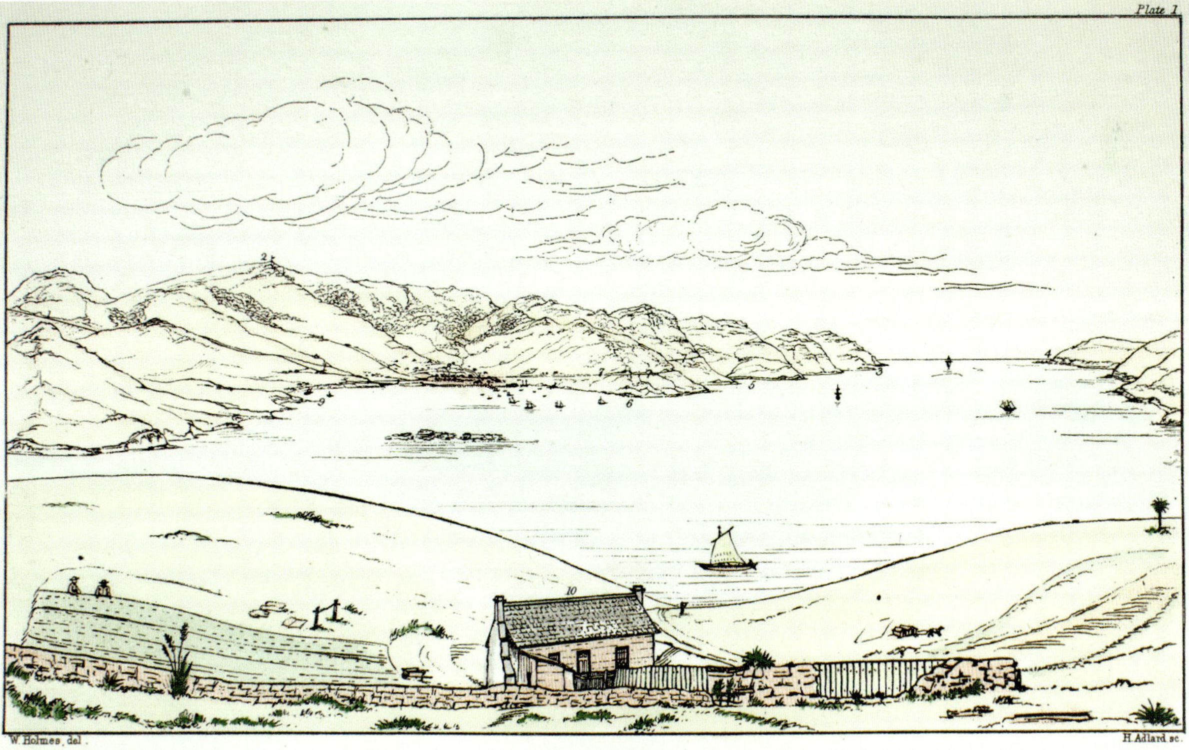

W. Holmes, del. H. Adlard sc.

Lyttelton Port Victoria, and Harbour.

leased to Dr Moore of Charteris Bay. When Moore sold up his Charteris Bay farm in 1858, Mark Stoddart of Diamond Harbour purchased Quail Island, King Billy Island and the adjacent peninsula. Stoddart advertised free occupation of the (Wards') house for 'an industrious family man who will undertake to look after the place and see that any stock . . . are undisturbed by persons landing'.[5] The tenant could make a good income by working the free stone for contractors or by fishing for the Lyttelton market.

Ownership of the land on Quail Island may have been more trouble than it was worth. Despite Edward Ward's comment about abundant springs, a serious lack of fresh water meant that fire was a constant danger. Stoddart repeatedly advertised in the *Lyttelton Times* in 1860 cautioning people landing on the island against setting fire to the grass. He also offered a £5 reward for information leading to the conviction of whoever stripped the house on Quail Island of 'carpeting, glass, grate etc.'[6] In February 1863 Stoddart, likely with some relief, sold the property to his friend Thomas Potts of Ōhinetahi, Governors Bay. Potts ran sheep on the island and took advantage of the desirable straw-coloured sandstone available for quarrying. Alex Shepherd and James Haigh must have leased a quarry from Potts, since in 1864 they were advertising delivery of 'first-class freestone in any quantity from the Quail Island quarry'.[7]

From the early 1850s until around 1874, columnar basaltic rock was worked from two ballast quarries on the north-west side of Quail Island. The remains of these quarries, along with their loading platforms and the mooring bolts used to secure ballast craft to the shore, are still visible. Ballasting was a hazardous occupation. In 1859 the coasting schooner *Sea Bird* capsized in a nor'west squall while ballasting off the point of the island. The three crewmen made it ashore in a dinghy.[8] In 1873 James Payne's cutter *Christina* was returning from Quail Island with a cargo of stone when a squall caught it. It heeled over and sank in 10 fathoms of water.[9]

Most of the stone walls built on Quail Island — on the hillside behind the quarantine station and leper colony buildings, and along the foreshore of sandy Whakamaru Beach — were constructed in the 1880s by prisoners from the Lyttelton Gaol, using stone they cut from a rhyolite quarry overlooking Walkers Beach. The 'Hard Labour Gang' was brought over each morning by launch at 8.30 a.m. and returned at 3.00 p.m. In the 1980s the northernmost ballast quarry was reopened, and a cableway constructed, to extract rock for rebuilding the sea walls at the current ferry wharf and for repairs around Whakamaru Beach.

In March 1874 Thomas Potts offered the minister of health the use of Quail Island for human quarantine purposes, the facilities on Rīpapa Island having

Quarry on the north-west face of Quail Island. The columnar basaltic rock seen in this photo was in demand for ships' ballast.
JANE ROBERTSON

been overwhelmed at times with large numbers of quarantined immigrants. The provincial government wasted no time. The plan was to use Quail Island as a 'spillover' site for those unfortunate new arrivals whose ships carried an infectious disease. By early July single men's quarters had been completed, and in September the superintendent, William Rolleston, purchased 100 acres from Thomas Potts. Single men from *Rakaia* (in quarantine on account of outbreaks of mumps, measles and scarlet fever) were transferred to the new quarters just as the whole island was proclaimed a quarantine station on 11 February 1875.

When completed, the quarantine complex included two large hospital wards, a kitchen and a day room, barracks and a caretaker's cottage, designed to accommodate a total of 200 people. All the materials had to be brought to the island by boat, and since the jetty closest to the building sites was not constructed until 1881, the point of landing and departure appears to have been the gently sloping, sandy beach adjacent to the complex. There was another jetty, at the site of the present-day wharf and commonly known as the 'outer jetty'. This jetty could be used at all tides but was more exposed to the prevailing easterlies. It was also further away from the main building site. The exact date of this jetty's construction is unclear — the earliest extant reference is to 1889, but it is likely to have been built before that.

In fact, after all that work, Quail Island was little used for immigrant quarantine purposes, but served more for those suffering from infectious diseases *within* New Zealand. For example, in December 1879, following an outbreak of diphtheria, all 102 children from the Lyttelton Orphanage were quarantined on the island. They returned to the orphanage in late January, having, hopefully, enjoyed some of the summer's pleasures of the beach and sea. The island was also used as a convalescent sanatorium during the Spanish influenza epidemic of 1918–19 despite the by then dilapidated condition of the quarantine buildings.

The keeper of the quarantine station, Charles Henry Hancock, was returning to Quail Island from Lyttelton in November 1878 when his boat capsized. Mrs Hancock, who saw the incident, ran down to the beach. Her husband signalled her twice before going down with the boat. Mrs Hancock lit a fire on the hill to attract the attention of ballast men nearby. They searched for Hancock without success and then made for Lyttelton to raise the alarm. A steam launch came over to the island to take Mrs Hancock and her three children back to port. The following day the boat was found about 200 yards from the beach in 8 feet of water — further evidence of the fickleness of Lyttelton Harbour seas.

In November 1881 5 acres on Quail Island were set aside as a quarantine ground, this time for cattle. Later the area was extended to accommodate sheep, horses, pigs and dogs. Tenders were called for the building of a stock jetty to land the quarantined animals. The spot selected was relatively sheltered and had a depth of 6 feet at low tide.[10] J. Stinson won the contract, and on 8 August 1881 the *Star* reported that the almost finished jetty was 'a most substantial piece of work'. It consisted of a 60-foot-long stone embankment joined by a wooden jetty of a further 48 feet, which enabled vessels to use the jetty in any tide. A fine rock sea wall, built by the Lyttelton Gaol prisoners, abutted the road from the jetty to the quarantine buildings.

In early 1906 the stock wharf (also known as the southern jetty or inner jetty) was widened by 4 feet, the landing stage increased to double the original size, and the hand-cranked, double-winch crane raised. Landing steps were also added. The largest crates and boxes containing sheep or cattle could now be landed or taken off with ease.[11] A short railway with hardwood rails, running from the top of the T-junction to the shore, facilitated the landing of quarantined animals in boxes as well as supplies.

Over the years, both jetties fell into disrepair. In 1939 the 'outer jetty' was fenced off for public safety reasons and with a view to eventual dismantling. Ten years later, nothing further had happened. The stock wharf was still used by visiting launches and by the resident farmer, who took advantage of the crane for loading his wool clip. According to a February 1953 letter from the Lyttelton Harbour Board to the secretary for marine, both jetties had deteriorated still further. 'Launches and passengers should be forbidden the use of the jetties until such time as the Lands and Survey Department [who by then had jurisdiction over the island] put them in a proper state of repair.'[12]

Sometime between 1953 and the 1970s the 'outer jetty' was taken down, and in 1981 a new jetty was built on the same site. It seems that something similar

ABOVE The single men's quarters and cookhouse on Ōtamahua Quail Island, c.1890. Note the stock jetty in the distance and the stone wall built by prisoners from Lyttelton Gaol.
ALEXANDER TURNBULL LIBRARY, PA7-53-19

BELOW Inspection of the stock jetty in 1953. It seems there may have been plans in the mid-1970s to rebuild this jetty, but if so, they came to nothing.
ARCHIVES NEW ZEALAND, CALW CH167 BOX 17, C.2759

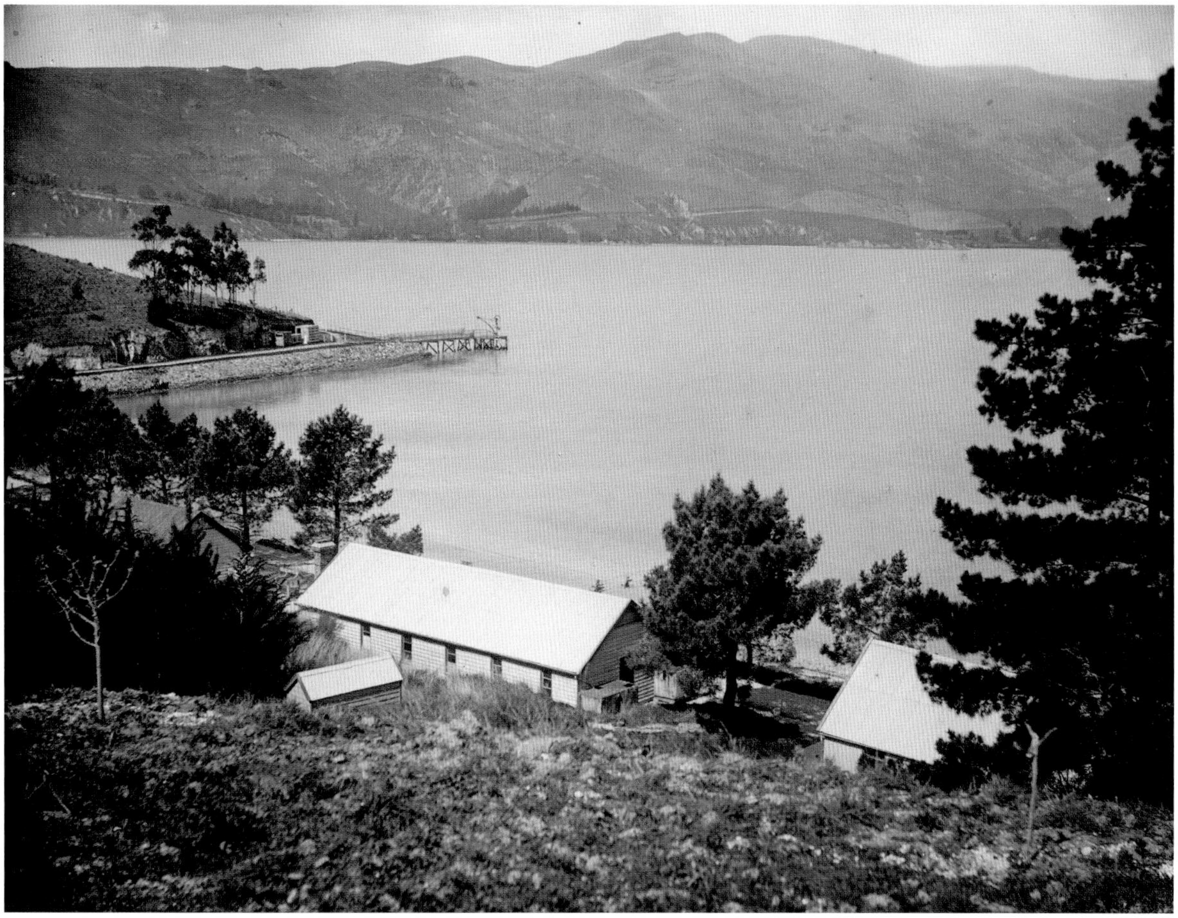

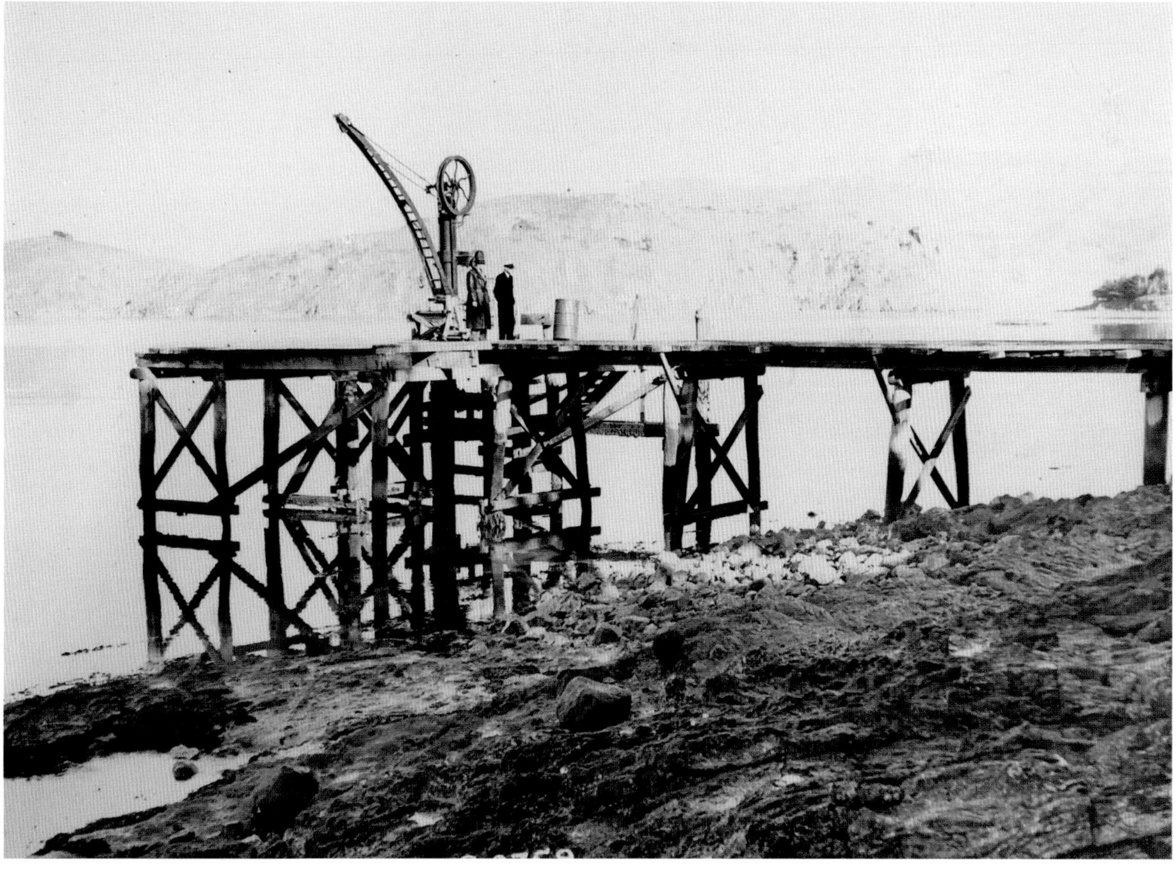

The east or outer (deeper water) jetty in 1953. This jetty had been fenced off for public safety reasons since 1939. In 1981 a new jetty was built on the site.
ARCHIVES NEW ZEALAND, CALW CH167 BOX 17, C.2756

was intended for the stock jetty. In the mid-1970s Lyttelton Harbour Board pilot Euan Crawford agreed, on a strictly extra-curricular basis, to take a barge-load of material across to Quail Island for use in the rebuild of the stock jetty. Part way across to the island the Lyttelton fire siren sounded, an event that required the attendance of the pilots in port. Euan tied the barge up to the old pile beacon and sped back in the ferry to change somewhat guiltily into his pilot's garb.[13]

Any plans there might have been to rebuild the stock jetty faltered. Further neglect led to the final dismantling of the nearly 140-year-old structure in 2018, despite its role in historic events of the early twentieth century, including four successive expeditions to the South Pole.

In 1901, Robert Falcon Scott's British Antarctic Expedition used Lyttelton as its base. Scott's 23 Siberian huskies were quarantined on Quail Island prior to departure south on the expedition ship *Discovery*. The dogs had travelled from Siberia to London, London to Melbourne, and then on to Lyttelton via Port Chalmers. From the port they were barged to Quail Island. How happy they must have been to be let loose on Quail Island and get fit again after their long confinement. Sadly, none would survive the expedition. Scott's Aberdeen terrier Scamp, who made the trip out on board *Discovery*, was kept on Quail Island until his master's return.

When Ernest Shackleton mounted an expedition to the South Pole in 1907–9, Quail Island became a temporary home for 15 untamed, feisty Manchurian ponies. Shipped from Shanghai to Sydney and then to Lyttelton, they were transported from Shackleton's ship *Nimrod* to the island by lighter, to be 'broken in' and trained for work in the Antarctic. Nine dogs were also brought up from Rakiura Stewart Island. On 31 December, two weeks after landing on Quail Island, 10 of the ponies were loaded at the stock jetty onto lighters and carried in very rough seas to *Nimrod* in Lyttelton in preparation for departure to the ice. An unprecedented 50,000-strong crowd covered every available vantage point in the harbour to farewell *Nimrod*. Remarkable archived film footage of the departure survived. Which is more than can be said for the ponies.

Scott returned to Lyttelton in 1910 with the ship *Terra Nova*. Six weeks before his arrival, in mid-September, 19 Siberian ponies and 31 Siberian huskies, plus two 'Eskimo dogs', were landed at Lyttelton having spent around 50 days at sea en route from Manchuria. The ponies and dogs were loaded onto a lighter, which was towed by the launch *Canterbury* to the stock wharf at Quail Island. The ponies were then hoisted in individual boxes, by hand crane, onto the wharf. A reporter from the *Lyttelton Times* noted that the ponies were, unsurprisingly, 'very weak in the knees' after their long sea voyage and the dogs 'gloomy'.[14] On a return visit six weeks later, the same reporter found them much recovered and in fine form. A Siberian trainer, Demitri Gerof, was responsible for the dogs.

> A small sledge, running partly on two wheels, has been made for exercising the dogs. Five dogs comprise a team for this little vehicle, the animals being harnessed in pairs with the indispensable leader making up the odd number. Armed with a heavy pole, shod with iron and a stout spike at one end [used principally as a brake], Demetri [*sic*] seats himself on the sledge and immediately he gives an order in some unintelligible monosyllable the dogs dash off at full speed.[15]

The dogs were often exercised in this way on the road running up from the jetty, but at low tide dogs and ponies could use the stretch of sandy beach below. At the end of October, Scott inspected the animals and declared himself 'exceedingly pleased with both the horses and the dogs'.[16] Unfortunately, the ponies were in fact of poor quality and ill suited to prolonged Antarctic work. By 9 December 1911, only two ponies on the ice were still alive and they were shot shortly thereafter. None of the men who reached the South Pole survived the return journey.

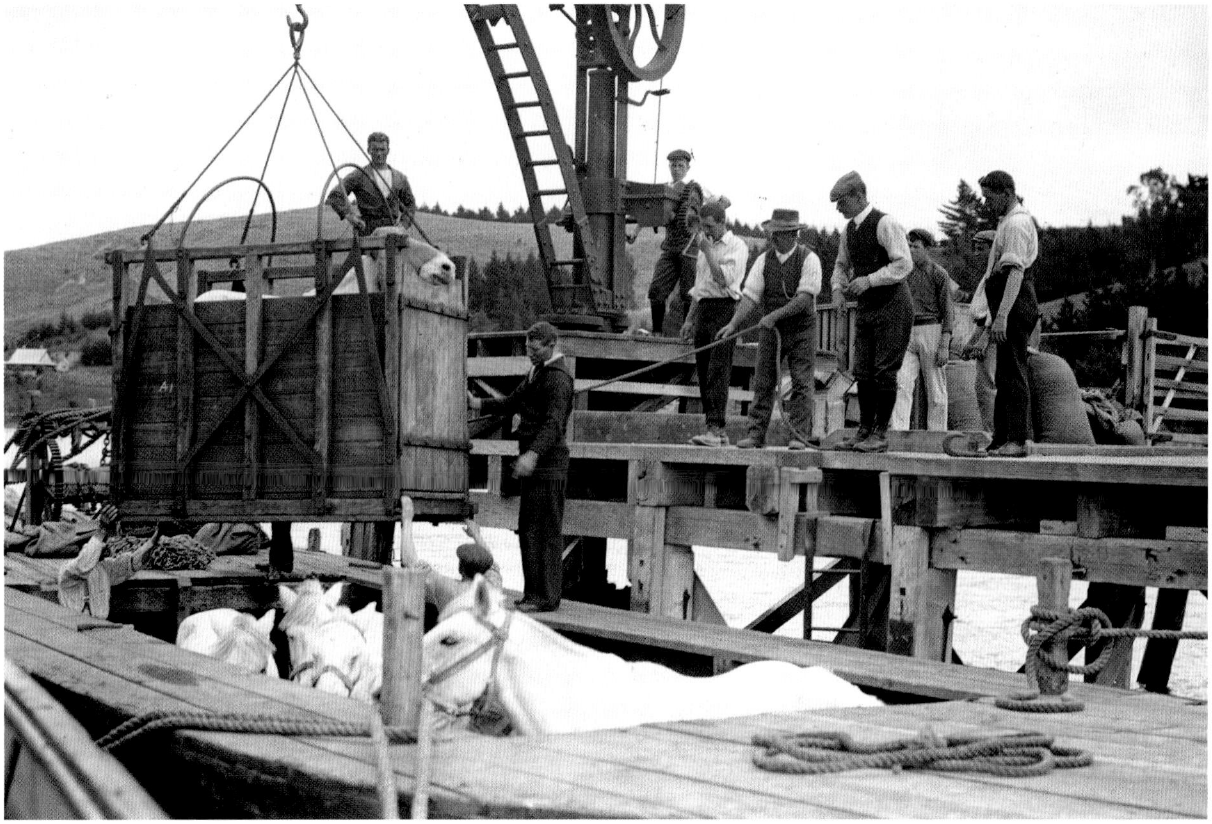

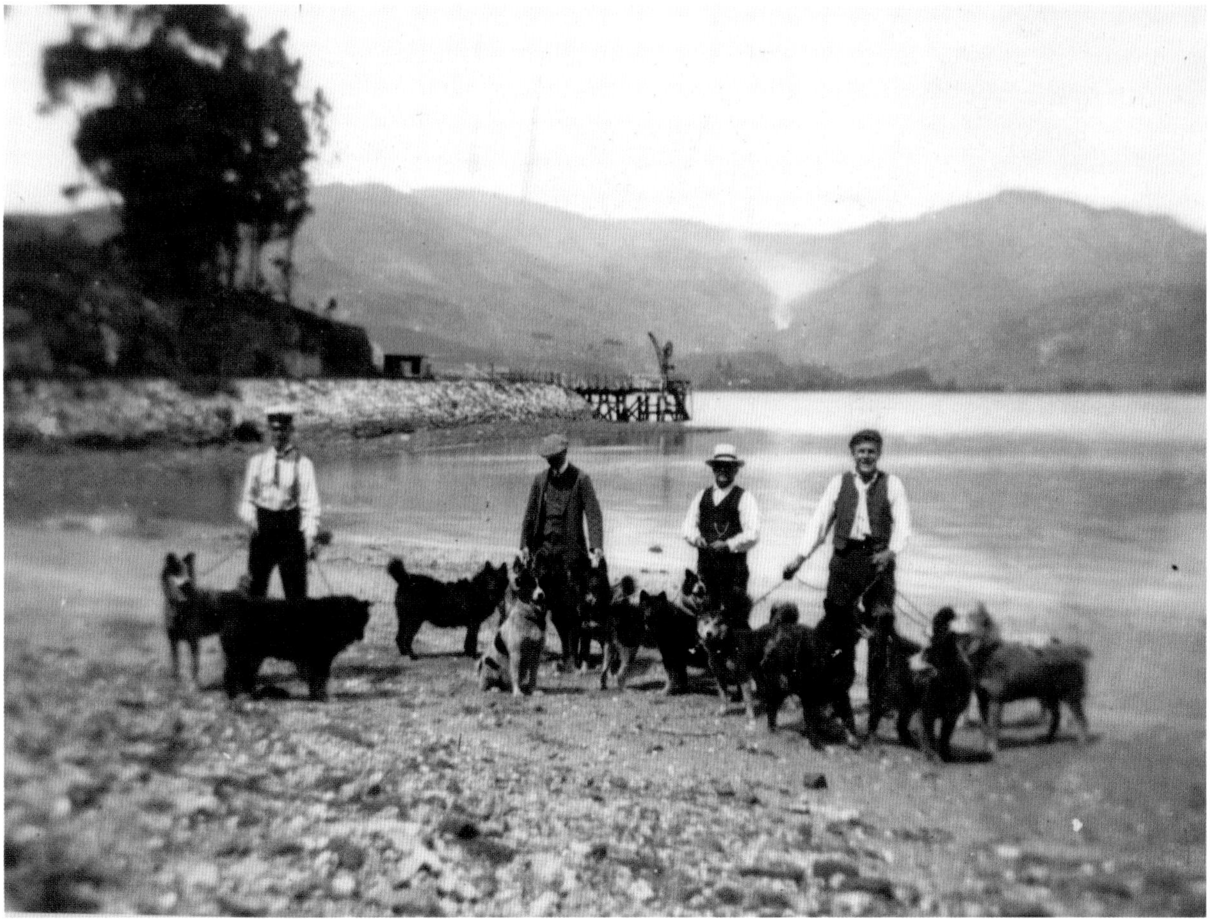

Meanwhile, back in Lyttelton, seven Himalayan mules arrived from Calcutta (Kolkata) in September 1911. Described as 'scarcely bigger than large dogs, shaggy-coated, long-eared, with hard sinewy legs',[17] the mules were housed on Quail Island in conditions of great secrecy until *Terra Nova* returned to the Antarctic in December. In the event, the mules proved instrumental in the search and recovery of the bodies of Scott, Wilson and Evans, after which the animals were taken back to Scott Base and shot.

The last dogs to be interned on Quail Island were 15 Yukon huskies intended for Richard E. Byrd's first Antarctic expedition (1928–30). The dogs were exercised daily when weather permitted, either in double harness with six or more dogs or with five dogs in single harness. They were then transported to Aoraki Mount Cook to be hardened off for their work on the ice. The expedition was a success, with all those involved returning safely.

ABOVE Unloading ponies for quarantine on Quail Island prior to travelling to Antarctica with Robert Falcon Scott's *Terra Nova* expedition, 1910.
CANTERBURY MUSEUM, LESLIE HINGE PHOTOGRAPH, 19XX.2.4180

BELOW Lieutenant H. Pennell (left) and J. Thomas with Siberian dogs training to join Robert Falcon Scott's expedition to Antarctica, 1911. The stock jetty is visible in the distance.
LYTTELTON MUSEUM, 11670.1

As well as hosting animals bound for the Antarctic, the island also became a base for the Burnham Industrial School's annual camps. The school was set up in 1874 for the care and reformation of children whose backgrounds were often troubled, and its camps were designed as an incentive for good conduct. The first camp was held in 1904. The boys caught the train to Lyttelton and marched through the streets headed by their brass band. 'The appearance of the lads, with their blue jerseys and caps and brown haversacks, was decidedly smart.'[18] The total party of 70 was then taken to Quail Island in the Defence steam launch *Ellen Ballance*.

For some camps, over 100 boys were divided into two big squads. In earlier years the boys were quartered in one of the old quarantine buildings. Later, they camped in tents on the beach adjacent to the wharf. Their days consisted of swimming (after rising at 6.00 a.m.), prayers and breakfast, domestic work, physical and military drill, fishing and boating, more domestic work and drill, recreation, rifle shooting, and lights out at 8.30 p.m. In February 1909, following the annual inspection of the cadets, a boat race was held between a crew of senior Burnham boys, who manned the Defence boat *Flying Fish*, and a crew of junior boys trained by the son of the caretaker of Quail Island, who manned *Dolphin*. After a very spirited race, the junior boys won by several lengths.[19]

Ellen Ballance was in demand for another civilian purpose, one that highlights the difficulty of providing education for children living in the remoter communities of Lyttelton Harbour. In 1903 the Quail Island caretaker William Thomas wrote to the Lyttelton member of Parliament, George Laurenson, asking if the launch could call at the island daily to take his children to school in Lyttelton. Laurenson, in requesting help from the defence minister, added that Thomas was

Boys from the Burnham Industrial School carrying out military drills on the beach at Quail Island as part of their annual summer camp.
CANTERBURY MUSEUM, 21931/2

OPPOSITE ABOVE The Quail Island leper colony. The building on the right in the main photograph is the caretaker's residence and the two-storeyed structure is the quarantine hospital. On the left, among the trees, are three huts that were occupied by leper patients (later the numbers increased). The inset image shows a Māori patient and his companion, a cockatoo.
CHRISTCHURCH CITY LIBRARIES, IMG0090, PHOTOCD 2

OPPOSITE BELOW Patients from the leper colony with a nurse and her assistant (possibly Matron Carston and Miss Beattie) on the verandah of a Quail Island bungalow, c.1922–23. Note the pet cockatoo in the cage.
LYTTELTON MUSEUM, NOLA MUIR COLLECTION, 7981.1

a very respectable man with a large family. The service was offered for two years and then discontinued. In 1909 Laurenson wrote again asking if the replacement launch for *Ellen Ballance* could provide the same service: pick up the children on the way across from Rīpapa Island in the morning and drop them off in the afternoon as the launch returned to Fort Jervois. The Hay family of Charteris Bay also wrote to Laurenson asking if their two children — Catherine, age seven, and Robert, six — could be picked up similarly. The children were, of necessity, boarding during the week in Lyttelton, but Mrs Hay was keen to have them closer to home. The Defence Department resurrected the service for a four-month trial and then discontinued it on the grounds of cost.

At the same time that Quail Island was associated with the high-profile drama of Antarctic exploration, it was quietly hosting another group of detainees. There are times when, instead of representing access and adventure, jetties must simply mock those who cannot use them. Quail and Rīpapa Islands were both used to quarantine and imprison, in some cases with little hope of ever regaining freedom.

So it was between 1906 and 1925, when Quail Island was home to men suffering from leprosy. There was great public fear of this contagious, long-term disease. The *Press*, sometime after the first patient was isolated, described it as 'a living

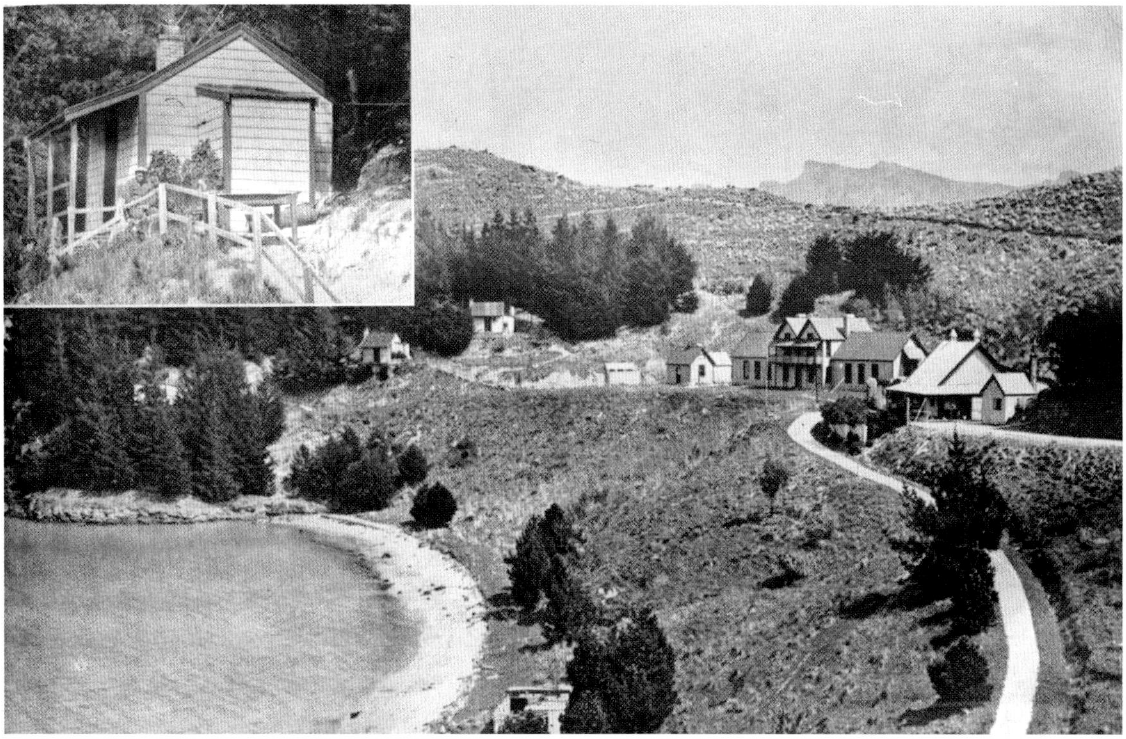

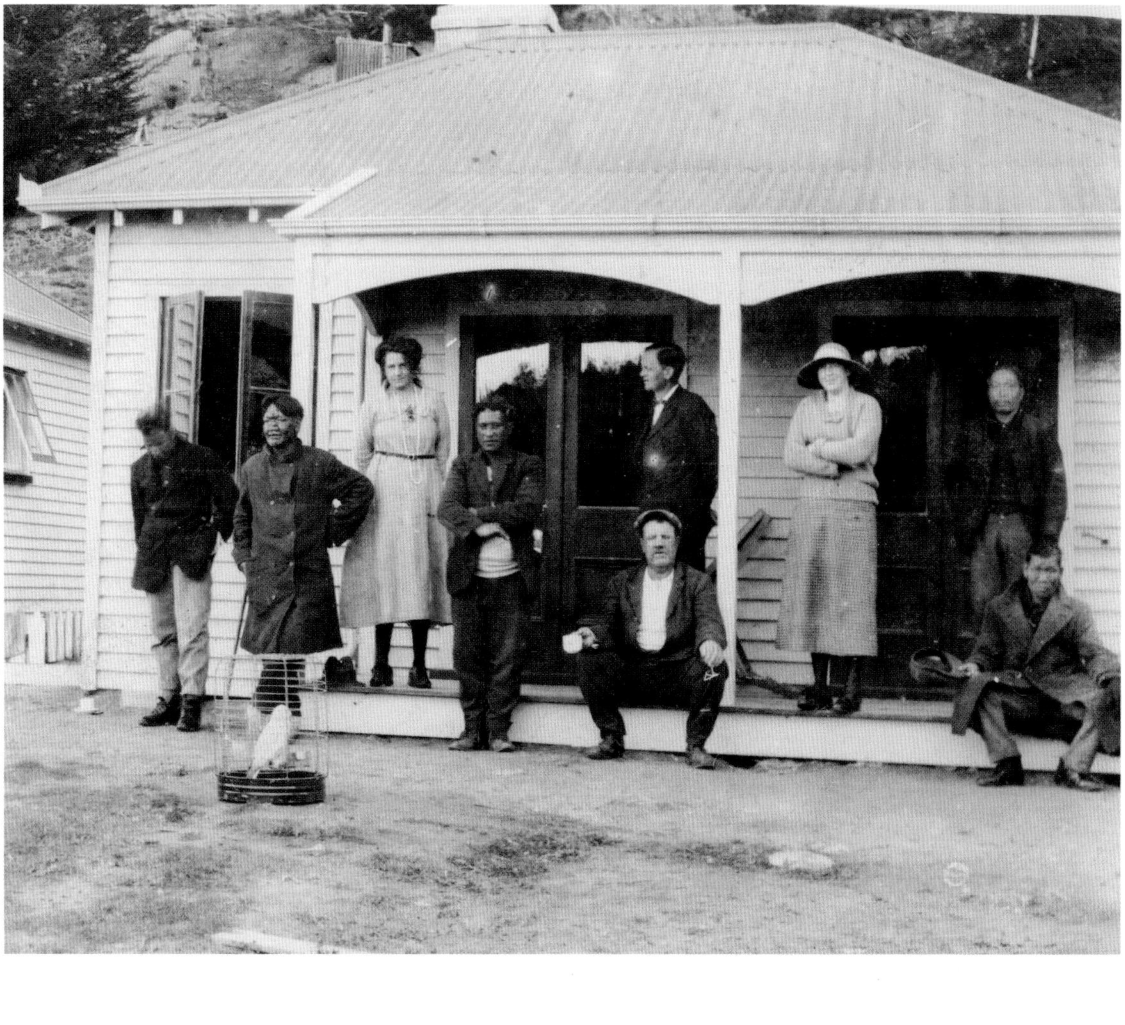

death'.²⁰ To complicate matters, the island was under dual control: the Health Department had charge of the leprosy station while the Agricultural Department controlled the stock quarantine station. Local MP George Laurenson voiced three main objections to the establishment of a leprosy colony on Quail Island: the island's proximity to the 'closely populated' town of Lyttelton; the potential to disrupt animal quarantine operations (some opponents of the leper station argued that prize stock were in danger of contracting leprosy); and the consequent disruption of plans to build a prison on the island. To these arguments was added the fact that the pupils of Burnham Industrial School would no longer be able to have their annual camp on Quail Island. There was also concern that patients might simply walk off the island, since 'it is as easy to walk away from the island at low tide as it is to cross Cathedral Square'.²¹

The first leprosy patient, Will Vallance, was isolated in an empty quarantine building on the island in 1906 in what was only ever intended as a temporary measure. A doctor's visit once a month and occasional visits from relatives were all the human contact he had, apart from the island caretaker, who fed and provided for him. To make matters worse, he was lodged in the big, empty hospital building — formidable accommodation for a man alone. The following year the Health Department built a hut for Will, and in November 1908 he acquired his first company in the form of Timothy Kokiri, the second leprosy patient on the island.²² Tim Kokiri was declared cured in 1909 and discharged. However, having apparently been rejected by his family in Tauranga, he chose to return to Quail Island to care for the ageing and increasingly blind Vallance.

Regardless of opposition, the colony grew because no other suitable location could be agreed on. As more patients arrived, further small huts were built to accommodate them. At one point nine men were contained in the 'leper village' on the hillside above the second swimming beach. They were not permitted off the island or to roam far from the area immediately adjacent to the hospital and leper cottages.

Tensions on the island increased after J. H. T. MacKenzie was appointed caretaker of the leprosy colony in 1912 and Robert Henderson was appointed the Agriculture Department's new caretaker in the summer of 1915–16. Henderson was uncomfortable about the contact he was required to have with, as he saw it, the leprosy-contaminated MacKenzie. The two clashed often. One of Henderson's jobs involved carting coal, firewood and other supplies up from the wharf. He refused to have any contact with MacKenzie, who was not allowed to touch the crane trolley on the jetty or use the shelter there. On one occasion at the jetty, MacKenzie was handed three parcels by the launch captain. The middle parcel was for Henderson, who became very angry and aggressive at its having been handled by MacKenzie.

As Benjamin Kingsbury observes, 'the wharf was a landmark in the island's geography of stigma. It was where Quail Island met the mainland and where MacKenzie most often met Henderson.'[23] MacKenzie dreaded going to the jetty because of the unpredictable nature of Henderson, who publicly labelled MacKenzie a 'leper-contact'.

The stigma manifested itself in other ways. Growing up at the head of the harbour, William Gebbie never learned to swim because, he claimed, he and his sibling were not allowed to explore or play on the mudflats in case they picked up any driftwood or discards from the island that might harbour leprosy bugs. Launchman Andrew Anderson found that picnic parties were reluctant to call in at Quail Island. Lyttelton grocers threatened to boycott the island, given the perceived risk of infection.

While the establishment of a leper colony on the island is not directly connected with the two jetties, which were constructed in an earlier period, it is worth reflecting on what the stock jetty, in particular, might have meant to the leprosy patients. Every day the men would have seen arrivals and departures. They would have watched the comings and goings of the Antarctic expedition

Health officials gathered outside the huts and bungalows on Quail Island. Dr Charles Upham, port health officer (in Panama hat), and Jack Annan, assistant health officer and the Health Department's Lyttelton disinfecting officer, with his wife, Annie.
CHRISTCHURCH CITY LIBRARIES, WALKLIN COLLECTION

animals and men. They saw the world passing by, knowing that such freedom was denied them. For many years they were not even able to walk down to the jetty, so close to their small village.

There were visitors. The Lyttelton doctor Charles Upham came across regularly, sometimes with other health officials. From time to time local parishioners gathered on the island for a church service. On one occasion a party of singers shipped a piano over to the island in the launch *John Anderson*. They landed at the stock jetty and lugged the piano up the hill to the quarantine station buildings, where they sang a variety of sacred and popular songs. In April 1925 a three-valve wireless set with a loudspeaker was installed. To mark the occasion 60 people travelled across to the island on *John Anderson* for a 'wireless concert'. Māori concert parties from Rāpaki would also entertain the men. However, with the exception of the medical staff, all visitors were required to keep a 'safe' distance.

Shortly before the leper colony was officially disestablished, two events occurred which were designed to improve the quality of life for the men. One was the arrival of a new recreation hall. This was an ex-Defence Department guard house which had stood on a wharf at Lyttelton since the early years of the First World War. The contractor, instead of dismantling and re-erecting the 9-ton building, chose to transport it in one piece on a pile-driving pontoon along with a crane which was used to unload the building, not at the jetty but directly onto the beach at Quail Island. From there it was winched 50 chains to its final location. The second event involved the director general of the Health Department, Thomas Valintine, recommending that a rowing boat be provided for the men. This was purchased by public subscription and moored off Lepers Beach (now known as Skiers Beach). A small jetty was built adjacent to the boatshed that housed the craft. The leper colony matron, Margaret Carston, saw it as providing the patients with healthy exercise and affording them a 'slightly wider outlook'.[24]

Perhaps too wide an outlook. Despite the improvements, one patient was unwilling to remain on the island any longer. George Wilson Phillips may have contracted leprosy when he was a soldier on active service in the New Zealand Expeditionary Force Advance Party in Sāmoa in 1916. He had a mild form of the disease and, having spent nine years on Quail Island, decided to leave in January 1925. One account has Phillips arriving at Orton Bradley's homestead in Charteris Bay at 11.00 p.m. one night, dressed as a clergyman. There he rang for a taxi and headed for Christchurch — which was the last anyone saw of him.[25] This begs the question as to how Phillips got from the island to the mainland. The indication seems to be on foot at low tide, although this would have involved swimming the narrow channel between King Billy Island and Moepuku. Perhaps the newly acquired rowboat came in handy.

On the morning of 19 August 1925 the steamer *Hinemoa* left Lyttelton and anchored near Quail Island. Eight patients — Jim Lord, Will Vallance, Pakira Matawai, Ah Pat, Ah Yip, Ipirini Apa Apa, Te Ono Parao and George Pocock — were taken from the jetty to the steamer by lighter to be transported to the much larger leper colony on Makogai Island in Fiji. Most of the patients never saw New Zealand again. The leper colony on Quail Island was then officially closed. The link with the Antarctic ended when Byrd's huskies were transferred from the island in 1929. That year also marked the last use of the island as an animal quarantine station, although the quarantine grounds were not officially abolished until 1954. It might seem that the island was all but abandoned from then on. But not so.

Tucked away on the south-west side of Quail Island, adjacent to the ships' graveyard — resting place of up to 13 scuttled vessels — is a long, shelly beach known as Walkers Beach. In the early years of European settlement, shell was freely removed from beaches around Whakaraupō to supply ballast for boats. The practice was curtailed when local landowners complained about the erosion of the foreshore in certain bays, though trying to police the ban proved difficult for the Lyttelton Harbour Board and the Mount Herbert County Council. In the 1920s R. W. Walker saw an opening to supply shell grit to returned servicemen who were being encouraged to take up poultry farming. After some years of taking shell and facing multiple prosecutions, Walker approached the Department of Agriculture in 1929 and secured the sole permit to take shells from a south-west–facing beach on Quail Island. The proviso was that the shells removed should only be those cast up by the tide — not those that constituted the permanent deposit. Later, the Department of Lands and Survey leased a designated area to Walker, which meant the permanent shell deposit could be exploited.

In 1932, at the age of 19, Walker's son Bernard took over the business (known as 'Ovo Grit') after his father died of tuberculosis. The shell gathering was hard, physically demanding work, as Bernard later recalled:

> The beach we used was approachable only at half tide because mudflats appeared at low water about 100 yards offshore. In the early days we'd get there on one tide, stay the night in a kind of wigwam made from an old sail and load up the next day, rowing three tons (60 sacks) out to the launch as soon as it lifted on the tide, in half ton loads in a big flat-keeled dinghy. Later we did get a small outboard, and finally a barge . . . This barge or lighter could carry seven tons and the drill was to float it onto the mudflats, just at the lower end of the

sloping beach. Then the bagged shell was wheeled aboard, two sacks at a time along a plank walkway . . . The lighter would then be floated off the beach at high tide (not always as easy as it sounds) and towed back to Lyttelton.[26]

Bernard Walker used the launch *Foam*, which had started life as a powered whale-chaser, for about 25 years. Half a ton of shell would be piled around the bow deck and cabin, and two and a half tons on the after-deck and in the hold. The fierce southerlies that could blow up so suddenly on the harbour were always a challenge, and after some years Walker cut out the after-deck and put in a long hatchway with four removable hatches. This put the weight down inside the hull and made *Foam* more stable and seaworthy. Nevertheless, with a full load she sat perilously low in the sea.

When he decided to do away with the barge, Bernard Walker had a purpose-built boat made by Miller and Son at Lyttelton. She was christened *Otamahua* and launched in 1957. *Otamahua* was designed to be suitable for use as a Lyttelton Harbour ferry should the shell-gathering concession ever be removed. As it was, she continued in the shell business right up until 1970, when Walker cancelled his licence.

ABOVE Bernard Walker screening shell on Walkers Beach. The shell was then bagged and loaded on the beached barge. Bernard's father started the business in the 1920s supplying shell grit to returned servicemen who were being encouraged to take up poultry farming.
COURTESY OF EVAN WALKER AND IAN MCLENNAN

BELOW A jetty-like structure at the east end of Whakamaru Beach adjacent to the Sea Cadet boatshed and likely associated with cadet activities. This structure appeared sometime in the mid- to late 1940s and was gone again by the late 1950s.
CANTERBURY MUSEUM, W. A. TAYLOR COLLECTION, 19XX.2.3277

Once Quail Island was no longer used for human quarantine purposes, various groups took advantage of its relative isolation within easy reach of Christchurch. This was not always without drama. In August 1938 a group of 10 boys (members of the Secondary School Christian Union) and four adults were camping on the island. At 2.00 p.m. on 29 August they were waiting at the jetty, as arranged, to be taken off the island by *Awhina Nui*.[27] Very heavy seas meant the launch, which was based in Port Levy, could not make it to Lyttelton. One boy was unwell with suspected measles, and since there was no longer any telephone communication with the mainland some of the group worked their way over to the Lyttelton side of the island and lit a signal fire on the beach. They also sent SOS torch messages. Finally, the harbour master got the message and sent the harbour board launch *Ruahine* to pick up the lads, but not until well after dark.[28]

From 1943 until 1950, the Navy League Sea Cadet Corps leased an acre and a half on the island for training purposes. The lease was extended to the whole island in 1950. The tenancy included the use of, and responsibility for, the old quarantine barracks on Whakamaru Beach and the old stables.[29] The first combined Sea Cadet camp in New Zealand was held in January 1943, with cadets coming from Christchurch, Dunedin and Wellington. The Navy League's camps

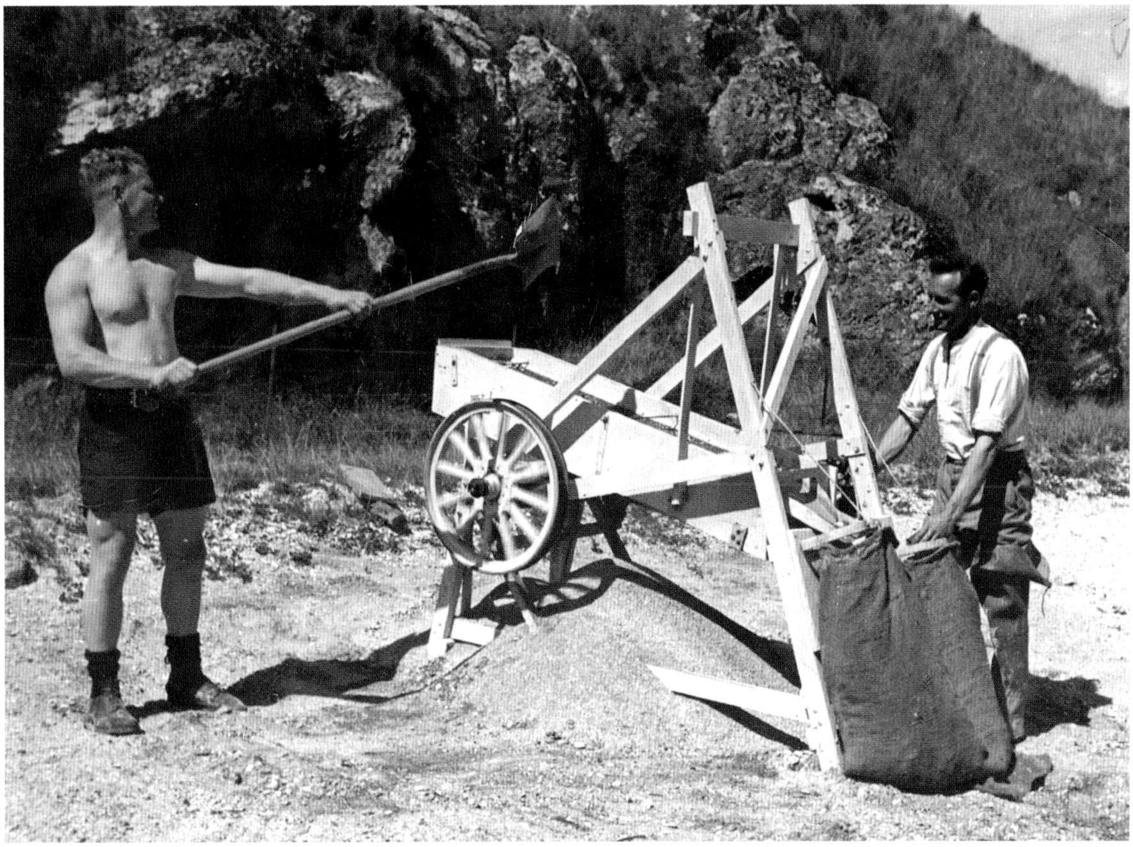

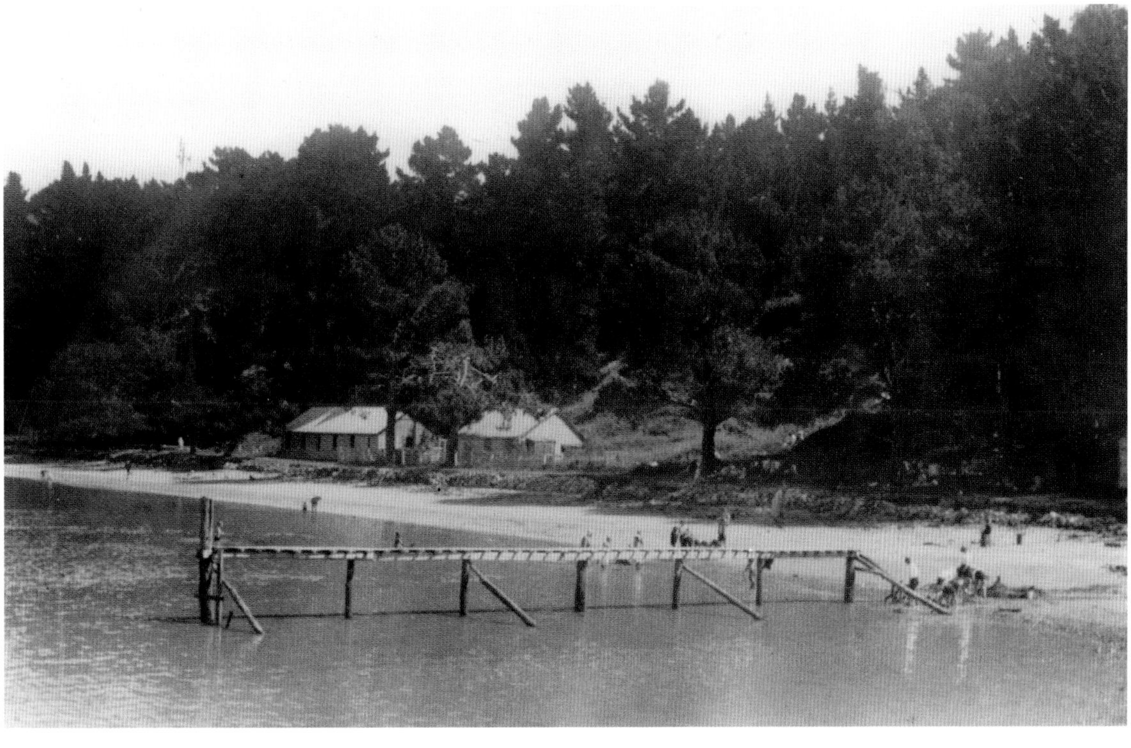

on Quail Island were so successful that it was given official recognition as the national headquarters for Sea Cadets.

Later in 1943 the quarantine barracks were remodelled to better accommodate the large numbers of cadets. A *Press* report on the January 1944 camp detailed the cadets' daily activities. These included rifle drill, squad drill, shooting, practical seamanship, knots and splices, wire and hemp splicing, blocks and tackle, signalling in semaphore, Morse and the international code of flags, heaving the lead, boatwork — including sailing in the two 25-foot whalers and three skiffs — and swimming.[30] Such training fitted Sea Cadets for entry to the Royal New Zealand Navy.

It is not clear which jetty was used to disembark cadets, officers and supplies for the large numbers of personnel involved, since both the inner (stock) and outer jetties were in poor condition, with the outer jetty already fenced off to the public. Probably it was the stock jetty since that was closer to the centre of operations. There was also another, much more flimsy structure which may well have been connected with the Navy League Sea Cadet Corps sailing activities on Quail Island. The Sea Cadet whaleboats were housed in a nearby boatshed. By the late 1950s the only evidence of this structure were pile stumps, which farmer David Halliwell finally pulled out with his Massey-Ferguson tractor as they became a danger to boats using the bay.[31] Despite its success with the camps, the Navy League could not sustain the rental and maintenance of the facilities and surrendered its lease in 1951 in favour of Rīpapa Island.

With the quarantine barracks on Whakamaru Beach once again abandoned, some families were able to enjoy the ready-made shelter, as Pete Dawson remembers:

> My family used to holiday on Quail Island each year for a month from New Year's Day in the late '50s and through to the end of the '60s. We stayed in the barracks. My brother Dave and I learnt to sail there. There was only one barrack building then. The steel beams that spanned the main hall of the barracks were still there and were used for slinging hammocks. Dad, Dave and I always slept in hammocks throughout the whole time that we stayed although sometimes I used to sleep on our yacht, particularly if there was a heavy sou'wester blowing so that we had an anchor watch if the anchors started to drag the yacht ashore.[32]

Following the deaths of the Ward brothers in 1851, farming mostly languished on Quail Island until December 1931, when the animal quarantine station closed and the island was leased by the Department of Lands and Survey. Between 1958 and 1975 David Halliwell grew between 5 and 6 acres of Arran Banner potatoes each year and produced wool from 300–400 Romney ewes. The potatoes, grown on the island's frost-free north-east side, were the first to reach the Lyttelton market. David used his 19-foot launch *Rawene* to transport his wool clip and early potatoes. The harvested potatoes would be stored in boxes which were then taken by tractor to the stock jetty, carried down the steps onto the foredeck of *Rawene* and, depending on the tides, transported across to the now-disused jetty at Charteris Bay — from where they would be collected by Governors Bay Transport, a trucking firm, en route to the Christchurch produce markets. On one occasion David had loaded a day's digging of potatoes, in their 40-pound boxes, onto his launch at low tide, gone off to do something else and come back to find that the launch had drifted, wedged itself under the jetty with the incoming tide, and gone down with its cargo.[33] The crane on the dilapidated stock jetty was used for loading the wool clip and for landing timber for repairs to gates and buildings.

In addition to farming, David also ran the picnic ground, mowed the lawns, let out buildings on Whakamaru Beach to holidaymakers and kept the beaches clear of rocks. Visitors to the island travelled on *Ngātiki*, one of the Diamond Harbour ferries, and were landed at either jetty. David then transported their belongings to Whakamaru Beach with his tractor. The water at the southern jetty was too shallow for *Ngātiki* to use except at full tide.[34] Other visitors simply ran their boats up onto the sandy beaches on the south side, much as Māori did in centuries past, and picnicked, swam and fished. The beaches and mudflats off Quail Island were a favourite place to trawl for sole and flounder. Derek Jones summed up the boyhood pleasures of a harbour holiday on Quail Island. 'Sleep in tents, row out every morning, lift the nets — no fish, no breakfast — dinghies, P-Class yachts, water skiing, best holidays of my life.'[35]

The most recent — and arguably the most exciting — chapter in the story of Quail Island began in 1987 when the management of the island was transferred to the Department of Conservation. The following year saw the launch of an ambitious ecological restoration project, spearheaded by the Ōtamahua Quail Island Ecological Restoration Trust in partnership with DOC and Ngāti Wheke of Rāpaki. The trust aimed to restore indigenous vegetation and fauna, and provide refuge for locally extinct or rare and endangered species of the Banks Peninsula region. It also wished to recognise the island's historical and cultural significance and encourage public engagement.

Today, over 30 years on, the revegetation of the island is visible from all around the harbour. By 2018 over 9500 native trees had been planted on Ōtamahua. Intensive pest eradication, combined with the growth of the new plantings, has

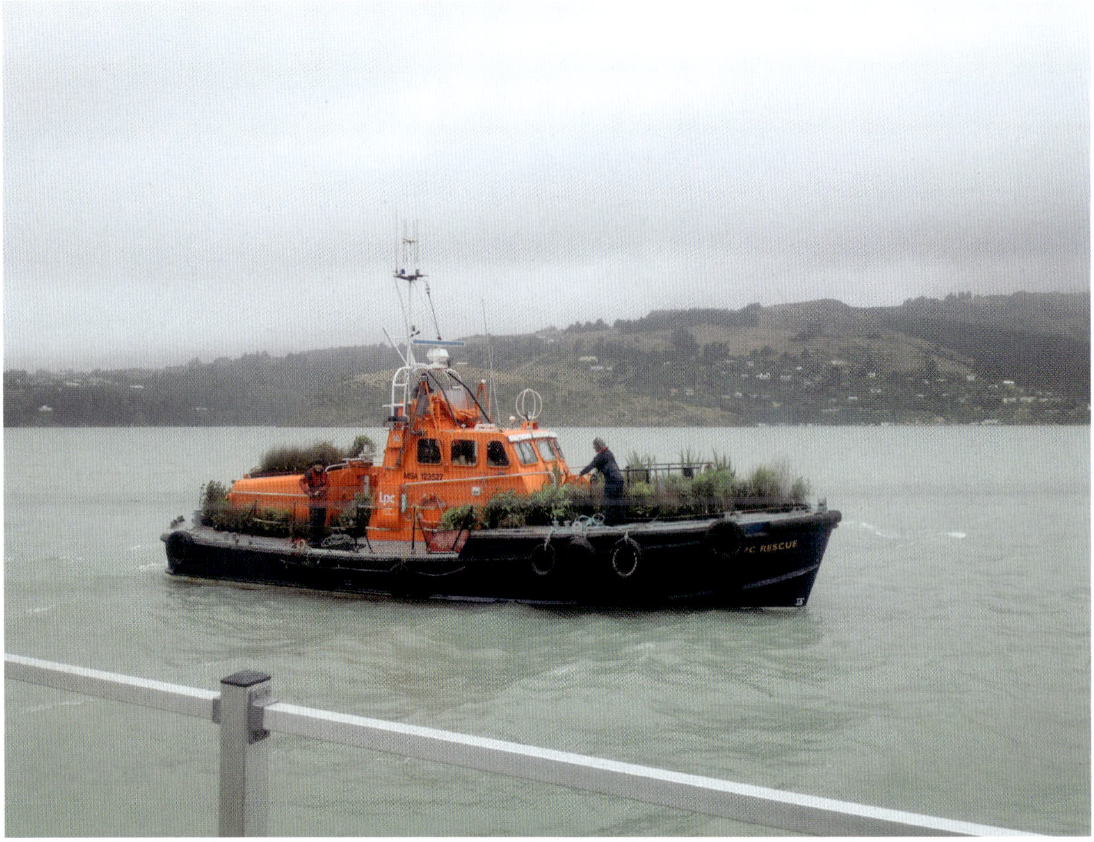
MSA 123527
lpc
RESCUE

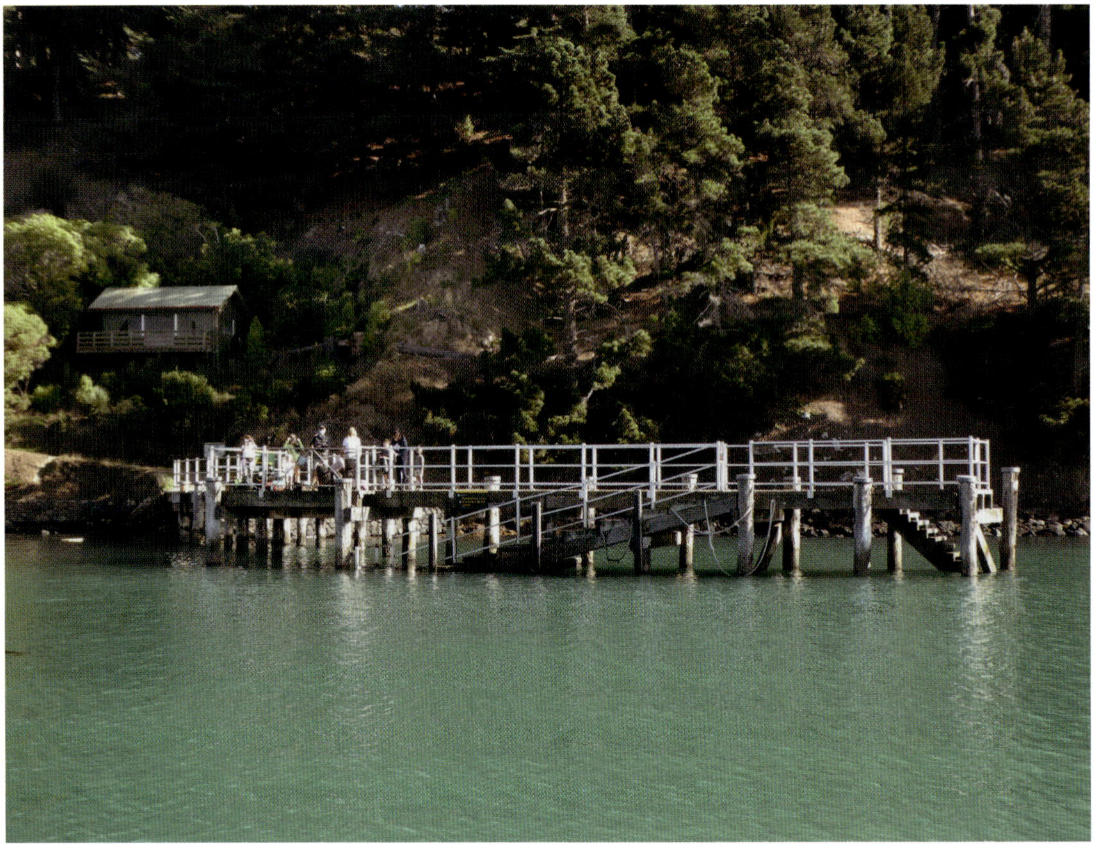

encouraged the presence and/or return of kererū, korimako, pīpīwharauroa, kororā, riroriro, kōtare, pīwakawaka and tauhou, as well as a number of invertebrates. The most recent developments have been the transformation of the historic caretaker's cottage into a 12-bunk tramping hut (evidence of the island's finally welcoming visitors) and the installation of a 9-metre-tall pouwhenua named Te Hamo o Tū Te Rakiwhānoa.

The ecological restoration work could not have happened without the rebuilding of the long-condemned and finally dismantled outer jetty. In May 1980 approval was sought from the Marine Division of the Ministry of Transport for the construction of a new 'all tides' jetty. Costing $29,482, the new jetty (designed and built by the Lyttelton Harbour Board), together with a 4.5-kilometre walkway, was opened on 6 December 1981. From 1982 there has, once again, been a regular ferry service from Lyttelton and Te Waipapa Diamond Harbour to Ōtamahua. The jetty and ferry have enabled the annual transport of thousands of native plants and hundreds of volunteers to the island. They have also made the unique history of Ōtamahua available to all those who wish to visit.

Pouwhenua Te Hamo o Tū Te Rakiwhānoa on Ōtamahua.
JANE ROBERTSON

OPPOSITE ABOVE The Lyttelton Port Company supports the Ōtamahua Quail Island Ecological Restoration Trust by donating the services of staff and a Port Company pilot boat to transport plants to Ōtamahua for the annual planting programme.
LYTTELTON PORT COMPANY

OPPOSITE BELOW In 1981 a new 'all-tides' jetty, designed by the Lyttelton Harbour Board, and built on the site of the old 'outer jetty', became the arrival and departure point for all visitors to Ōtamahua Quail Island. Black Cat Cruises operate a ferry service to and from the island.
JANE ROBERTSON

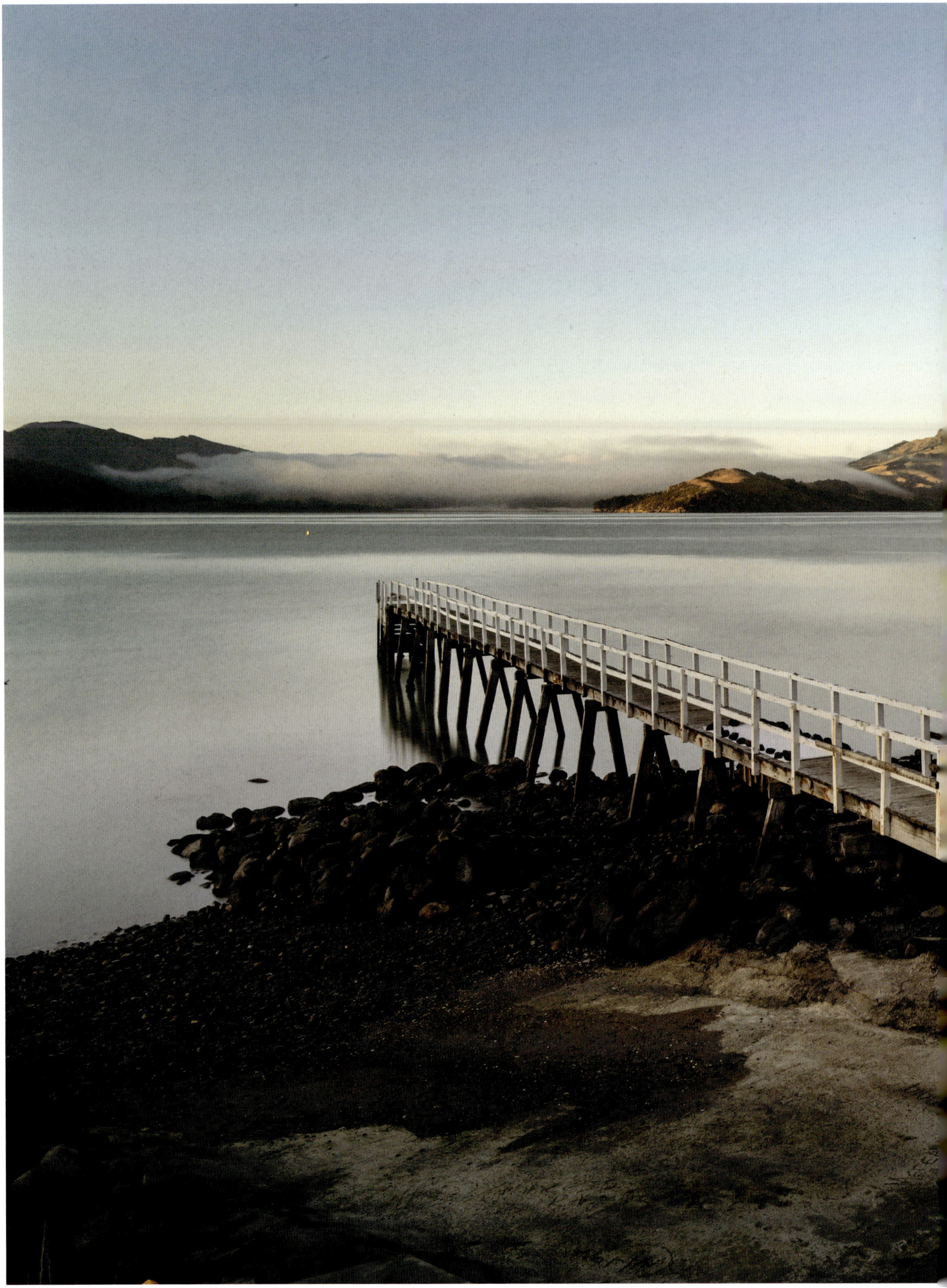

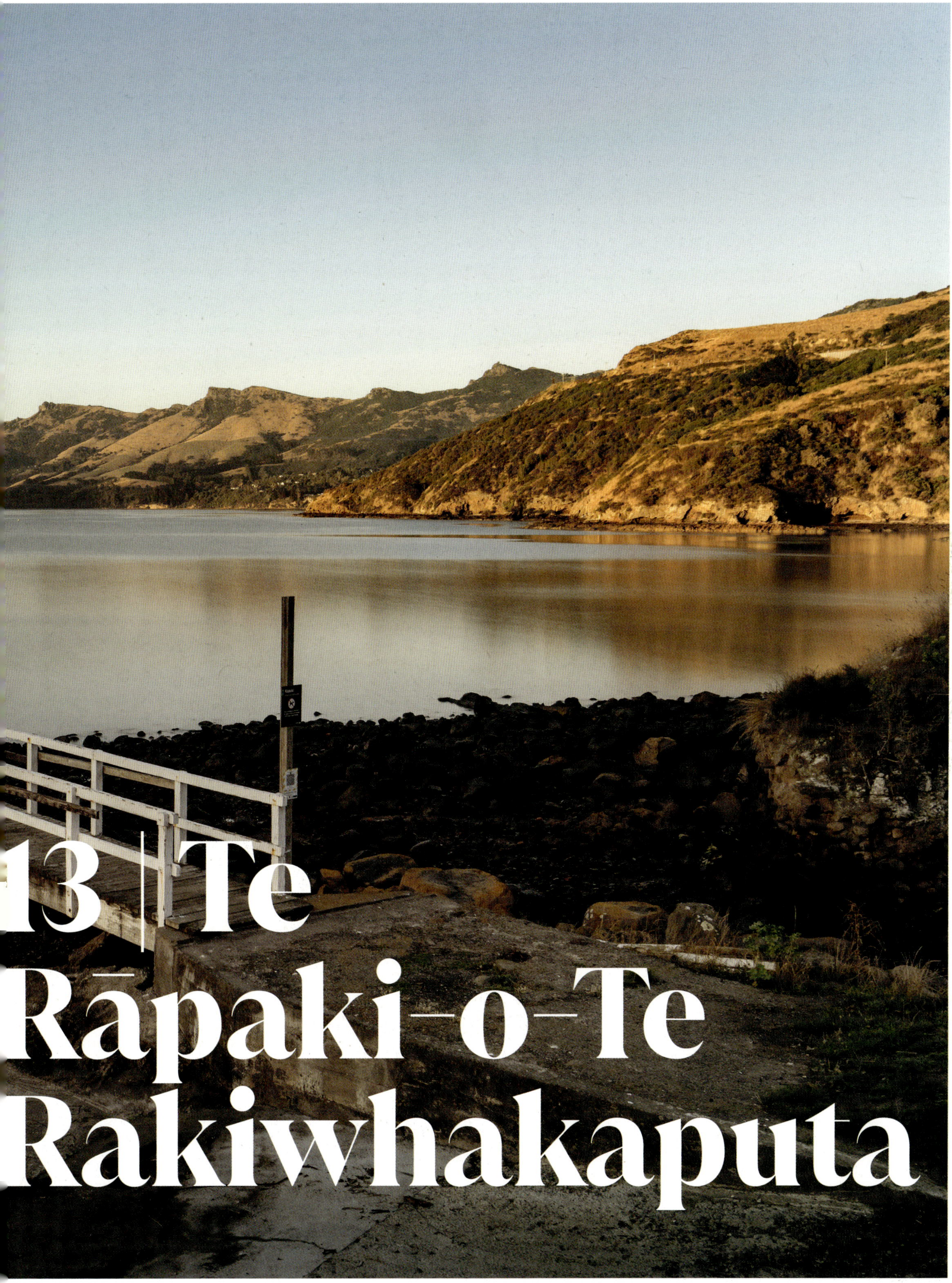

13 | Te Rāpaki-o-Te Rakiwhakaputa

Set in a beautiful, sheltered bay with a lovely swimming beach, on the northern shore of Whakaraupō Lyttelton Harbour, the Māori settlement of Te Rāpaki-o-Te Rakiwhakaputa[1] is home to Te Hapū o Ngāti Wheke, one of four Ngāi Tahu papatipu rūnanga (traditionally owned, marae-based communities) situated on Te Pātaka-o-Rākaihautū Banks Peninsula. It has a distinctive, well-maintained and much photographed jetty. How and why has this jetty survived in a harbour where so many others have been neglected or lost?

✽

The community of Rāpaki lies in the shadow and shelter of the imposing Te Poho o Tamatea ('the breast of Tamatea'), named after Tamatea Pōkai Whenua ('Tamatea the seeker of lands'), descendant of Tamatea Ariki Nui, who commanded the *Tākitimu* from Hawaiki to Aotearoa. At some point Tamatea Pōkai Whenua set out to explore the southern island of Aotearoa. On a coastline largely devoid of sheltered inlets, the unexpected bulbous peninsula of volcanic rock with its many sheltered bays would have been a surprising and welcome find. Tamatea must have explored the big inlet on the peninsula's eastern side (what we now call Lyttelton Harbour) by sea or by viewing it from high on the surrounding hills, since he named it Whakaraupō after the great quantities of raupō growing at the head of the harbour.

On their return trip overland from Southland, Tamatea and his men were caught in a southerly storm on the hills above Rāpaki. Without their fire sticks they could not survive the cold. So Tamatea appealed to his atua for help, and ahi tipua (volcanic fires) from the North Island mountains Tongariro and Ngāuruhoe came in response. The fires travelled down the islands, touching the ground at various points before landing near Te Upoko o Kurī (named after Te Rakiwhakaputa's grandfather Kurī, and renamed Witch Hill by European settlers). Tamatea and his men were saved by the warmth, and they named the huge wall of rock on the flanks of the hill Te Ahi a Tamatea ('the fire of Tamatea', later named the Giant's Causeway and now known, especially to climbers, as Rāpaki Rock). The fire continued down the hill, into the sea and across to Ōtamahua Quail Island, where it burnt the cliff black. The fire then travelled across the harbour to create Ōtarahaka (two trachyte dykes, known as the Remarkable Dykes) at the head of Waiake Stream, Teddington. This legend is also recalled in the Māori name for the Port Hills, Ngā Kohatu Whakarekareka o Tamatea Pōkai Whenua ('the smouldering boulders of Tamatea Pōkai Whenua').

Commuters on the road between Lyttelton and Governors Bay may notice a damp area on an intertidal section of the beach at Rāpaki, even at low tide. These thermal springs discharging through the beach sand, their waters averaging 33°C, are linked to the alpine fault and traverse the Canterbury Plains under the water table. While we now know that the springs are unrelated to the volcanic origins

ABOVE Approaching Te Rāpaki-o-Te Rakiwhakaputa from the east. Te Poho o Tamatea (the breast of Tamatea) is directly ahead keeping watch over the kāinga. The road continues on to Governors Bay.
HOCKEN COLLECTIONS UARE TAOKA O HĀKENA, 26127, C/NE3334/98, 2400_01_003A

BELOW Residents of Rāpaki thrived on kaimoana, the bounty of the sea. Here an unnamed woman and child gather shellfish into a woven kete on the beach at low tide.
CANTERBURY MUSEUM, W. A. TAYLOR COLLECTION, 19682133208

of Banks Peninsula,[2] for the residents of Rāpaki they must have provided further evidence of the fires that warmed Tamatea. Altogether there are five warm springs within a 15-kilometre radius of Rāpaki.

From the fourteenth century onwards, Whakaraupō attracted Waitaha, Ngāti Māmoe and finally Ngāi Tahu. With the bountiful food resources of Whakaraupō in his sights, Ngāi Tahu warrior chief Te Rakiwhakaputa landed his waka on a sheltered beach, took off his rāpaki (waist mat), and laid it on the ground as his claim to the area, which thereafter was known as Te Rāpaki-o-Te Rakiwhakaputa. When the chief moved on to claim other land, he left his son, Wheke, to establish and defend the fledgling kāinga of Rāpaki. Hence the name of Rāpaki Marae — Wheke.

Foot trails connected Rāpaki Māori with settlements at Pūrau, Koukourārata Wairewa, Takapūneke, Taumutu, Kaiapoi and further afield over the length and breadth of Te Waipounamu the South Island. But travel about the harbour and peninsula by waka, so easily drawn up to shore, must have been favoured.

The main attraction of Whakaraupō must have been the plentiful kaimoana and bird life. The beaches were a reliable source of pipi and tuaki (cockles) gathered by women and children. Rocky outcrops hosted mussels and pāua. Fish were caught in rock fish traps where they were left exposed by the receding tide. Huge nets were worked by men in waka, catching shoals of fish with the flood tides. James Cowan described vividly the hapū cooperation required to manage such large nets, working from the beach at Rāpaki:

> [G]reat flax nets fully quarter of a mile long used to be made for the catching of shark . . . These immensely long seines were fully six or eight feet deep and were worked by canoes, which would take one end out into mid-harbour, the other being made fast, and sweep the great kupenga around the shoals of fish making their way up the harbour with the flood tide. Huge quantities of sharks and other fish were caught in this manner, a fishing fashion which was only possible under the old tribal system when the whole strength of the hapu was available for such tasks.[3]

Such catches would include aua (yellow-eyed mullet), which gave the Māori name to what is commonly known as Aua King Billy Island. Arthur Te Rangihiwinui Couch recalled, as a boy in the early twentieth century, gathering pioke on the mudflats at Governors Bay while fending off stingrays. The rig was brought back to Rāpaki, 'the centre bones removed, the fish cut down the middle to within an inch of their tail ends, salted and peppered to combat flies and thrown over a wire fence to dry for winter food'.[4]

The rocky cliffs of Ōtamahua Quail Island were covered with seagull and other

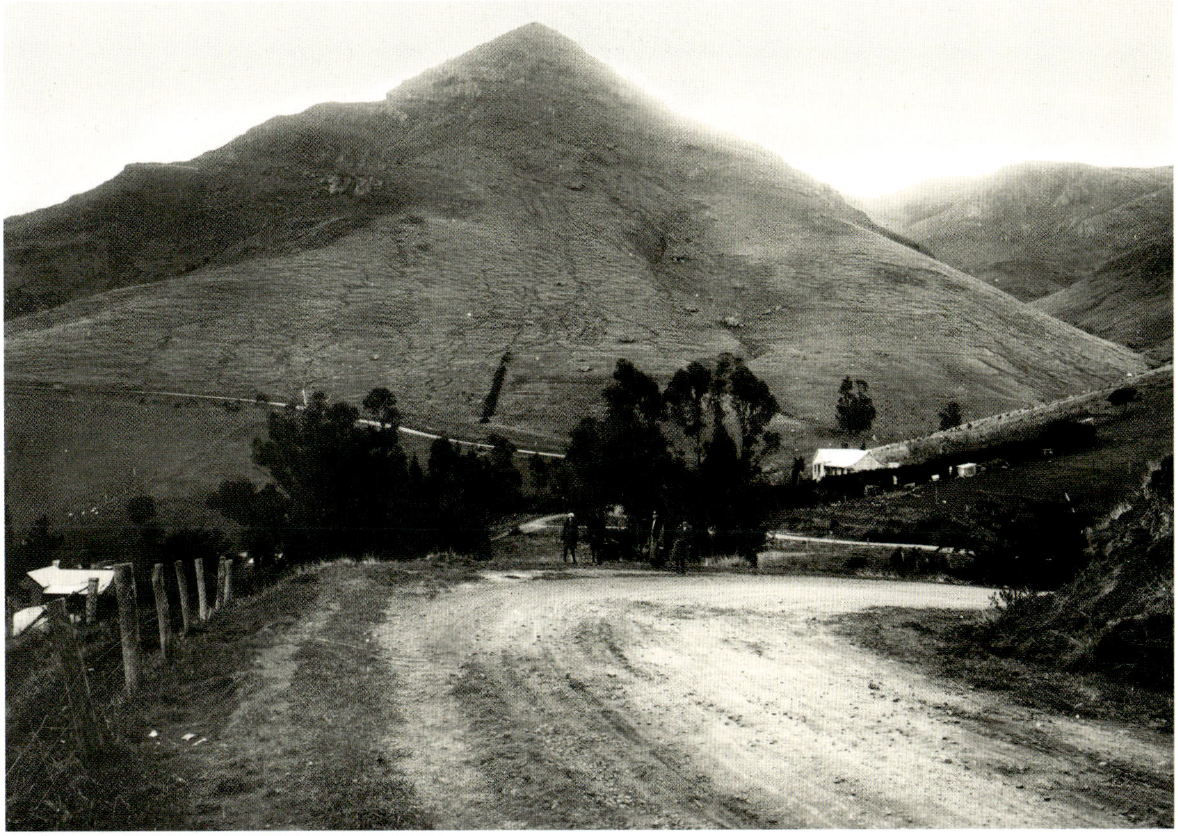

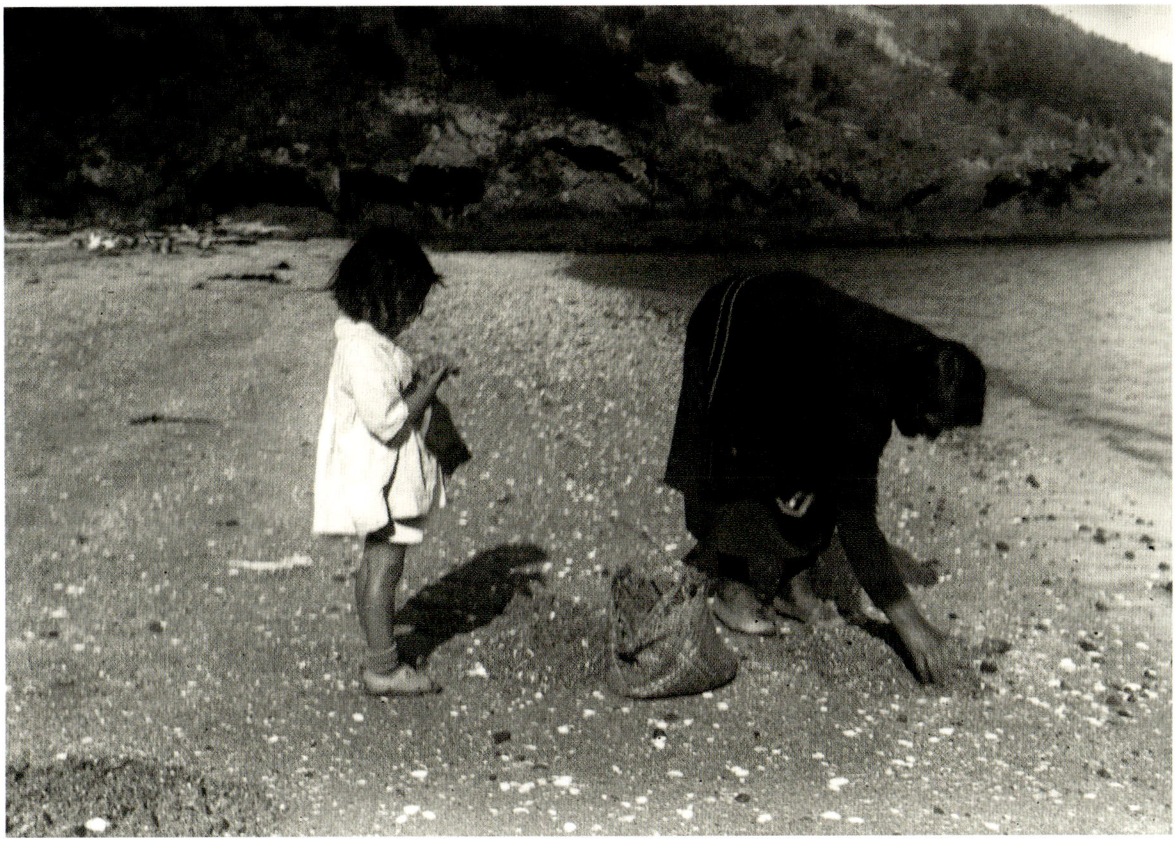

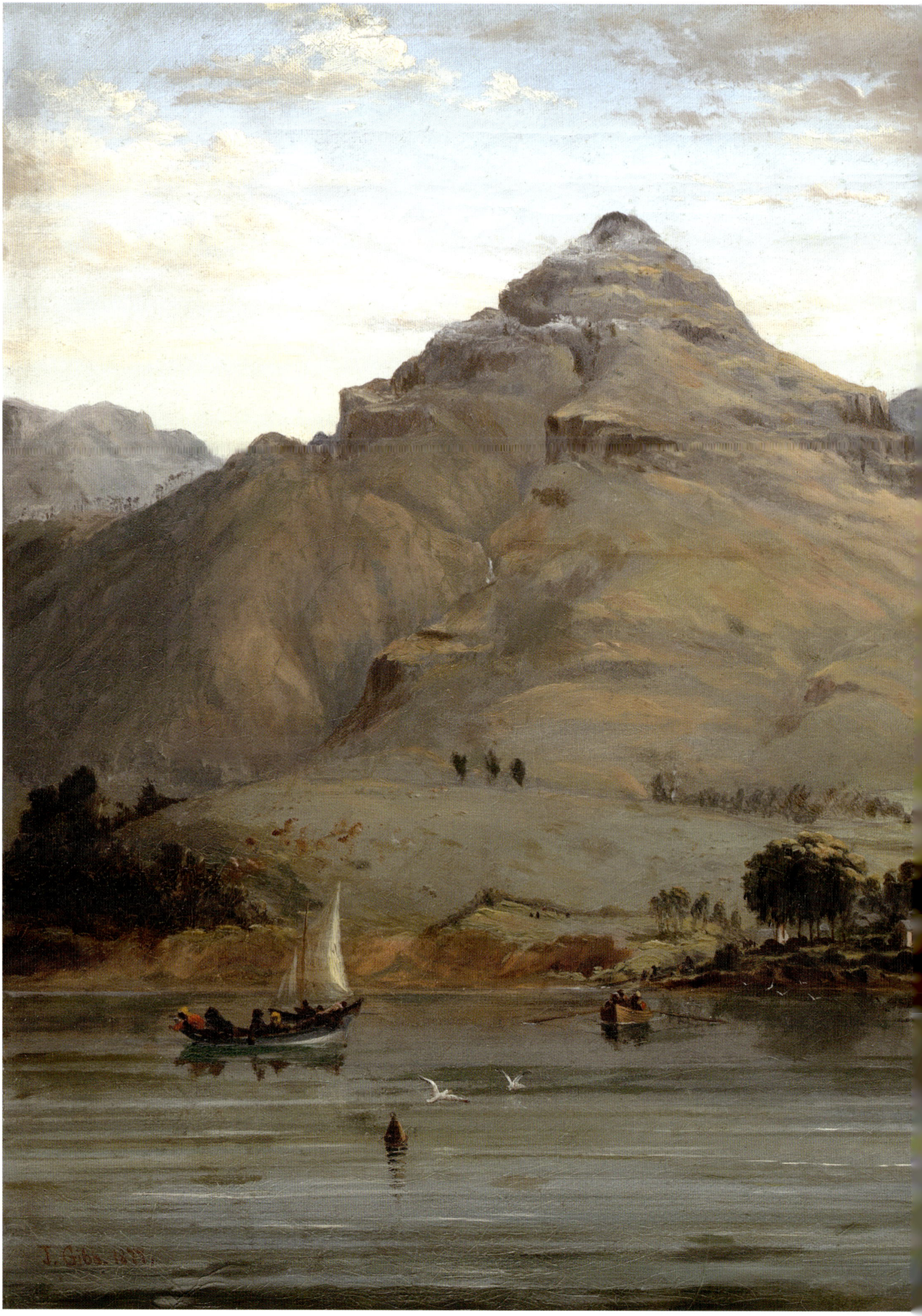

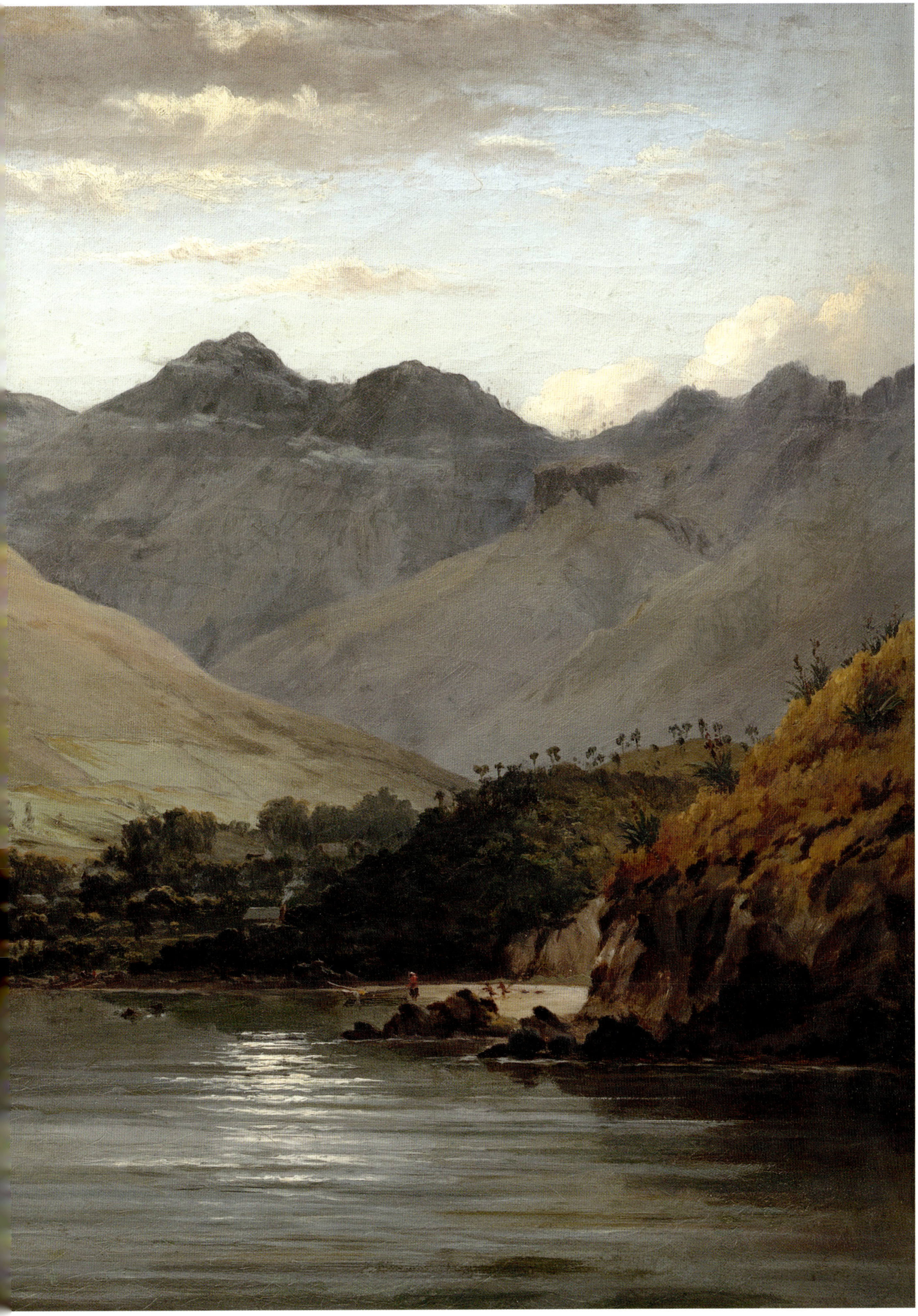

PREVIOUS PAGES Rāpaki, Lyttelton Harbour, 1877. This painting by J. M. Gibb was made after the building of the school and the protestant church, but well before the building of Wheke Hall or the Gallipoli jetty. As well as the boats on the water, another is visible being launched or hauled in on the beach at the right.
CANTERBURY MUSEUM, 1964.56.1

seabird nests and were also home to tītī muttonbirds. An earlier name for the island was Kawakawa, acknowledging the culinary and medicinal native shrub that grew there. Pūtakitaki paradise shelduck were hunted during their moulting period when flight was impossible. Kererū, kākā, tūī and weka were abundant. Birds cooked and preserved in their own fat and tied up in sea-kelp baskets were a large part of the winter food supply.

So the kāinga at Rāpaki thrived. As the pressure on resources increased, Ngāi Tahu at the head of Whakaraupō of necessity became well-seasoned travellers and traders. There were frequent trips over Te Tara o Te Rakihikaia Gebbies Pass to trap tuna (eels) at Te Waihora and Wairewa. Produce flowed to and from southern areas, up the coast, down to Raekura Redcliffs, across Ihutai Avon Heathcote Estuary and up the coast again to the pā at Kaiapoi. There were seasonal expeditions using the well-used trails to Te Manahuna Mackenzie Country for the annual weka hunt, to Rakiura Stewart Island for tītī, or to Te Tai Poutini Westland for pounamu to trade. On these long trails, Māori used water bags or pōhā made of bull kelp harvested from Whakaraupō. Aua, sandwiched between Ōtamahua and Moepuku, was a source of fine sandstone used for grinding and polishing pounamu.

This well-established way of life was shattered by a perfect storm of negative events. The intertribal Kaihuānga feud, triggered initially by a breach of protocol around 1825, escalated to the point where all Ngāi Tahu on Te Pātaka o Rākaihautū were involved in fighting. This was followed by the devastating raids of the Kāpiti-based Ngāti Toa chief Te Rauparaha. Depleted in numbers and demoralised, Ngāi Tahu were in no condition to withstand Te Rauparaha, who, having sacked the mighty pā at Kaiapoi, pursued escapees to Whakaraupō. Ngāti Toa warriors attacked the settlements at Rāpaki and Rīpapa (the latter they found deserted) before moving on to Akaroa and the slaughter at Ōnawe. Twice raided, the inhabitants of Rāpaki either fled south or made their way in canoes to Pūrau, where they found refuge in the Motuhikarehu bush in the lee of Te Ahu Pātiki.

Later, the introduction of European diseases — influenza, whooping cough, mumps, tuberculosis, venereal disease and particularly a measles epidemic in 1848–49 — to which Māori had no immunity, coincided with this intense period of instability and further ravaged Ngāi Tahu on the peninsula, leaving them vulnerable to the predation of land-hungry European settlers.

Signing of the Port Cooper Deed took place at Ōketeupoko, as Lyttelton was then known, in August 1849 (see chapter five).[5] A reserve of 850 acres was established at Rāpaki and another of 10 acres at Pūrau. Control of and access to traditional mahinga kai was lost. Harry Evison refers to the Port Cooper Purchase as a 'cynical sham', 'imposed on the unwilling Ngāi Tahu by duress'.[6] Pūrau survivors eventually moved, some to Koukourārata, which became a place of refuge for many Māori, and the rest to Rāpaki. Families at Taukahara, just west of Rāpaki, were the last to abandon their papakāinga and relocate to Rāpaki.

Rāpaki itself was almost lost. Captain Joseph Thomas had initially favoured Rāpaki as the location for the new port of Lyttelton. It would have been handy to the proposed settlement at the head of the harbour (today's Teddington) and, even when the site for Christchurch town was shifted to the swampy plains, the moderate gradient over the hills behind Rāpaki (what we now know as Rāpaki Track) would have provided an accessible route to the plains. News of the Māori Reserve designation prompted a change of plan, however, and Ōhinehou Cavendish Bay became the site for the township and port of Lyttelton.

Over a period of 25 years te ao Māori in Whakaraupō was turned upside down. Yet in the midst of such turbulence Ngāi Tahu demonstrated great fortitude and ability to adapt. The arrival of European sealers, whalers and flax traders from the 1830s onwards opened up opportunities for trade, for the acquisition of European technology (especially whaling longboats), for employment on whaleboats and at shore stations, and for the growing of new food sources such as mutton, pork and potatoes. Gardens were planted and extended. Firewood and flax fibre were in demand. Māori at Rāpaki traded with whalers at Waitata Little Port Cooper and Koukourārata Port Levy. In talking with James Cowan early in the twentieth century, Ngāi Tahu kaumātua Hone Taare Tikao spoke of three long whaleboats hauled up on the sand at Rāpaki and used to take produce to Lyttelton.[7]

With the arrival of European immigrants from 1850 onwards, Māori at Rāpaki grew wheat and potatoes and raised pigs, cattle and horses for sale at the new port town. The men gained employment in the flurry of construction accompanying the new settlement. This included work on the challenging Lyttelton–Sumner road over Tapuwaeharuru Evans Pass and the bridle path to the head of the harbour, as well as construction of the Christchurch–Lyttelton rail tunnel and on the wharves.

In January 1860, Māori from Kaiapoi, Rāpaki, Pūrau, Koukourārata, Akaroa, Wairewa and Taumutu gathered in Ōhinehou to address Governor Thomas Gore Browne. They sought land in the port for a market place. 'We are like unto a cormorant sitting on a rock. The tide rises, it flows over the rock, and the bird is compelled to fly. Do thou provide a dry resting place that we may prosper.'[8] The petitioners sought 'a landing for our boats' and a place where they could sell firewood, potatoes, wheat, pigs, fish and other items. As requested, a rood of land was purchased by the Crown in June 1863. In relation to travel between Ōhinehou and Rāpaki, Charles Torlesse noted in his journal in August 1849 that colleague Octavius Carrington had found a skin of ice across the bay.[9]

Māori who travelled regularly to Te Waihora for tuna would call in to see the Manson and Gebbie families, who settled at Teddington in 1845. They also had a

ABOVE This little wooden church at Rāpaki, built in 1869, was lovingly restored in time for the 150th anniversary celebrations in 2019. In this photo from the 1920s–1930s (judging by the dress) the church bell hangs from the mānatu (ribbonwood) tree.
CANTERBURY MUSEUM, W. A. TAYLOR COLLECTION, 1968.213.4012

BELOW Wheke, the Māori meeting house at Rāpaki, on opening day, 30 December 1901. The Minister for Education W. C. Walker, the Mayor of Lyttelton and several local members of Parliament were present, along with Māori from Kaiapoi, Wairewa Little River, Taumutu, Temuka and Wairarapa.
CHRISTCHURCH CITY LIBRARIES, PHOTOCD 5, IMG0041

very good relationship with Mary Phipps (Small) and her family in Dyers Bay.[10] Rāpaki residents participated enthusiastically in fêtes at Governors Bay, sporting activities at Teddington and boat racing on the harbour. At the Queen's Birthday Lyttelton regatta in 1851 the first race involved five five-oared whaleboats, four of which were manned by Māori steersmen and crews. Māori won. Presumably to avoid such a total settler rout at the next regatta, Māori were allocated their own race. Residents at the head of the harbour alerted their neighbours at Rāpaki when the shoals of rig gathered in the shallow waters to give birth to their live young, generally in early January.

The village prospered. A Protestant whare karakia (church) was opened in 1869, and a Roman Catholic whare karakia in 1874. The latter has long since disappeared, but the Protestant church remains, surrounded by its urupā, overlooking the beach and jetty, well tended and loved. A restoration project, driven by the hapū, ensured the church was in fine condition for its 150th anniversary in 2019.[11] A school, opened in November 1878, still stands in the bay, though long since closed. The rūnanga hall, built by Rāpaki whānau at a cost of £260 and named after Wheke, the son of Te Rakiwhakaputa, was opened in 1901. (In 2010 a beautiful new whare whakairo replaced the ageing hall, and a wharekai was added in 2018.)

Transport into and out of Rāpaki was by foot, canoe or, later, horse and trap, though road access was poor and subject to slips. In January 1902 a letter to the Lyttelton Harbour Board, signed by the Rāpaki residents, asked, '[C]an you erect a Jetty at our Pah?' The petitioners explained that they had recently had a big gathering of visitors at Rāpaki and anticipated more such events in which people would arrive by boat. 'At our gathering on Monday the Steam Launch brought many visitors & the trouble to land there was regrettable, especially the ladies and children. The natives waded into the water up to their waists and had to carry the majority ashore.'[12]

The harbour board stalled. The harbour master, asked by the board about the likely usage of such a jetty, replied: 'I may safely say that I do not think it would be used once a year. As all the natives have their horses and traps to drive in and out.' He also observed that the presence of a wharf might induce ships' boats to call in at Rāpaki, thereby 'causing friction with the natives'.[13] A costing was nevertheless done for a 96-foot by 8-foot jetty and a 120-foot 'approach', which would enable 5 feet of water at the steps at low tide. With the total cost estimated at £211, the Harbour Improvement Committee declined approval.

Undaunted, the community at Rāpaki petitioned again the following year. This time they pointed out that for many years they had been paying charges on goods to the harbour board 'without having any advantage therefrom'.[14] They wanted the steamers that regularly plied the harbour to be able to land goods and passengers.

One of the sticking points for the harbour board at this time was the fact that the foreshore was not vested in the board and that, consequently, the board could not recoup costs by charging for the use of jetties. The response to this second petition was that 'the question [would] stand over pending the vesting of the foreshore in the Harbour Board'. Unaccountably, the cost of building a jetty had risen to £305 in the intervening 18 months. The harbour board's engineer, Cyrus Williams, reaffirmed that a jetty was unlikely to be much used. The vesting of the foreshore in the harbour board occurred in 1905 (hence a flurry of harbour jetty-building shortly thereafter), but there was no apparent further follow-up with Rāpaki.

A different tack was taken in 1906 when Rāpaki schoolteacher C. A. Lyon wrote to the Lyttelton Harbour Board pointing out the urgent necessity for a boat slip at Rāpaki beach. Boats arriving at the bay had to be hauled up over the rough stones, a task requiring five or six people, especially at low tide. A slip with a windlass would enable fishing boats to be brought ashore and would advantage the picnic parties that favoured Rāpaki as a summer resort. Lyon pointed out that while he was sure that the Rāpaki residents would support his application, he had not told them that he was writing 'in case it might prove that I was awakening in them hopes that were only doomed to be disappointed'.[15]

Lyon was right. Rāpaki watched as new jetties went up at Little Port Cooper, Church Bay and Charteris Bay, and existing jetties were majorly overhauled or almost entirely rebuilt in Diamond Harbour, Charteris Bay and Governors Bay. The undoubtedly frustrated, but persistently polite Rāpaki residents petitioned the harbour board for a third time in August 1915. Their letter carried over 50 signatures. They referred to 'the inconvenience, hardships and loss we undergo through having no wharf accommodation at our settlement'.[16] Use of the road to Lyttelton entailed a costly cartage charge of 10 shillings a ton.

This time the response was more positive. Board engineer Percy Fryer submitted a plan and cost estimate. The jetty would be 5 feet wide and have a total length of 171 feet from high water mark, of which 50 feet would be built of stones from the beach, and the remaining 121 feet of timber. A landing stage 12 feet by 6 feet with steps 3 feet wide would be provided at the outer end. This would allow for 3 feet of water at low tide. Total cost would be about £130, the reduction on previous quotations achieved by budgeting for the use of good second-hand timber from Lyttelton rather than new.

Asked to indicate projected usage of a jetty, Paani McKenzie, a Rāpaki resident who signed his letter 'For the Maoris of Rāpaki', suggested about 26 tons of coal, 25 cords of wood, 12 tons of chaff and 120 bags of grass seed, plus passengers. The community numbered about 85, he said, and there had been a considerable increase in the number of hui and tangi which meant that sea access would be advantageous.

The board could expect to make £10 or £12 per annum wharfage. A year later and the jetty build was under way, using ironbark for the piles, girders, planking and steps, and jarrah for handrails. There would be sufficient depth of water at high tide to admit any of the harbour steamers, including the tug *Lyttelton*.

The women at Rāpaki had been ambivalent about the idea of a jetty, afraid that youngsters using it might drown. Opinion changed after an incident involving Andrew Anderson's launch, *Matariki*. Typically passengers jumped ashore while the boat was held firm against a flat-topped rock. One night, when a concert party was returning from performing in Lyttelton, a sou-wester blew up suddenly. Anderson couldn't risk *Matariki* near the rocks and returned to Corsair Bay, where he could land the group safely. They then had to walk to Rāpaki in the cold and driving rain. The women's support was promptly secured.[17]

The Rāpaki jetty was opened on 23 September 1916. It was named the 'Gallipoli Jetty' in honour of the eight local men who served overseas in the First World War, four of whom fought on Gallipoli.[18] One of these, Waitere Manihera, of the 1st Maori Contingent A Company, was killed in action. It was quite possibly the service of these men, such a large number from a very small settlement, that changed the harbour board's mind regarding a jetty at Rāpaki. That plus the reduced cost of construction. Rewi Couch points out that the jetty must have been one of the first

Rāpaki village. The schoolhouse is clearly visible just above the jetty. The hall at centre right is Wheke, and below is the church and urupā. The Lyttelton–Governors Bay road cuts across the hillside at the top.
CANTERBURY MUSEUM, W. A. TAYLOR COLLECTION, 1968.213.6327

memorials to the Gallipoli campaign built in Aotearoa.[19] Visitors to the opening — including members of the harbour board, the board's engineer and secretary, the harbour master, and the mayors of Woolston and Lyttelton — arrived from Lyttelton in the launch *Purau* and presumably disembarked at the new jetty.

The Rāpaki jetty was in the news in November 1916 when Lieutenant J. C. Tikao returned on furlough from the front. Visitors arriving from Tuahiwi and beyond were met in Lyttelton by the oil launch *Matariki* and taken up harbour to the new jetty. At the settlement they were treated to an excellent dinner followed by speeches, singing and a dance.

On 21 January 1929 the chairman of the Rāpaki rūnanga, Eruera Manihera, wrote to the Lyttelton Harbour Board about the former wooden steamer *Wootton*, owned by shipwright G. Whitford of Lyttelton. *Wootton* had for some time been anchored off the Rāpaki beach. The rūnanga had already protested about its presence, pointing out that the beach was the private bathing and fishing place of the inhabitants of Rāpaki, but the harbour board claimed it was powerless to remove the hulk. In the latest development, *Wootton* had been washed up onto the rocks at the east end of the bay and badly holed. Whitford's intention was to shore up the hulk and use her as a houseboat, and to that end *Wootton* was towed to Lyttelton by the steamer *John Anderson* and placed on the patent slip for repair. Manihera concluded in his letter: 'I am legally informed that the control of the foreshore is invested in your board and I wish to enter a most emphatic protest against his [Whitford] being allowed to do so as her presence there is most objectionable for more than one reason.'[20]

Despite the protest, by mid-February *Wootton* was back at Rāpaki being used by the Royal Naval Volunteer Reserve as part of a training exercise. About forty men and eight officers were instructed in practical seamanship, including handling small boats under oars and sails, signalling and lead line work. Thereafter it was used as a houseboat. Rāpaki residents' fears were realised in the winter of 1931 when, in a sou'west gale, *Wootton* began to drag its moorings. *John Anderson* was sent to the rescue, but by then the vessel was driving onto the rocks.[21] In the process of grounding, *Wootton* caused significant damage to the Gallipoli Jetty. Despite this, the boat remained at Rāpaki for a long time, as evidenced by a 1949 aerial photo.

Children naturally gravitated to the foreshore. Playing on the beach, fishing and exploring around the rocks were popular pastimes. Herewini Banks grew up at Rāpaki in the 1940s. She recalls: 'On Sundays we'd come running up from the beach in our bathing suits, and straight into church. You didn't have to get dressed up.'[22] Rewi Couch remembered how easy it was to gather kaimoana:

Living off the foreshore was an important part of feeding the family when I was growing up, and collecting pipi and cockles was a normal part of activity. There used to be kelp on racks and pāua in the rock pools and you could go round here, never leave the reserve, and get a couple of bags of mussels and a bag of pāua.[23]

For Tasman Gillies a favourite memory was going crab hunting on the rocks with his pōua (grandfather). 'A lot of my whānau and extended whānau are drawn to the sea. They have spent a lot of time working on fishing boats or container ships — as a whānau we have a real affinity to the sea.'[24]

June Swindells regarded the beach as 'the centre of our universe'. In summer, with jobs completed at home, the Rāpaki children would spend all day on the

Aerial photo of Rāpaki in 1949, with the houseboat *Wootton* against the jetty.
V. C. BROWNE & SON, LT1-14

Te Upoko o Kurī Witch Hill monument

High up on the crest of Te Upoko o Kurī there is a memorial to the soldiers of St Martins, Opawa and Rāpaki who lost their lives in the First World War. The memorial was the initiative of Mr and Mrs A. Anderson, built in memory of their son, Frederick, who died during the Battle of Messines. The plans to build the memorial were approved by the Summit Road Scenic Reserves Board in October 1917, just four months after Frederick Anderson died. The seat, made of unfaced basalt quarried nearby, included two bronze plaques inscribed with the names of the fallen soldiers (including eight-times Wimbledon tennis champion Anthony Wilding) and a third plaque featuring the Rupert Brooke poem 'The Dead'. The plaque facing towards Rāpaki and Whakaraupō bore the following inscription:

He whakamaharatanga tenei mo tangata toa o te iwi Maori o Rapaki i tuku atu nei i a ratou ki te mate mo te Kingi me te Iwi i te Whawhai Nui
[In memory of the Rāpaki boys who gave their lives in the great war for king and empire]
Waitere Manihera
Fell at Gallipoli 6 August 1915
Tamateraki Tene
Died at Auckland 27 April 1916

The memorial was destroyed in the Christchurch earthquakes of 2010 and 2011 and the plaques were stolen or lost. It has since been restored and was a poignant site of commemoration marking the Armistice Day centenary on 11 November 2018.

fore-shore. A circle of rocks covered with corrugated iron served to cook the cockles and pipis collected on the beach at low tide. The biggest cockles could be found underwater in the mud. There were huge rock oysters at the jetty, and sea beetroot beneath it. Rig hung over the jetty to dry provided chewing gum. The children gathered fruit and berries from local gardens to complete their foraging. Such kai was free, and freely available. 'We were poor but never poor,' notes June, who regrets that her mokopuna cannot now enjoy such a carefree lifestyle in a harbour whose health has been neglected over the decades.

By the middle decades of the twentieth century, as roads improved and car ownership became more common, travel by sea declined and the maintenance of jetties languished. In August 1957 the secretary-manager of the Lyttelton Harbour Board pointed out to the secretary for marine that the board's request of 1952 to demolish the Gallipoli Jetty at Rāpaki had received no reply. The Marine Department advised the harbour board that it had 'overlooked' the request and that it raised no objection to demolition provided no hazards remained which could cause damage to small craft. Once again, nothing happened.

In February 1971 Wera Couch wrote on behalf of the Rāpaki rūnanga to the Lyttelton Harbour Board. He pointed out that for some time the people of Rāpaki had been worried about the safety of their small children playing on the jetty. The decking had many gaps and most of the side rails had fallen away. At a meeting on 7 February, he wrote, Rāpaki residents had passed a resolution requesting that efforts be made to restore the wharf to its original condition, thus making it safe and fit for use. Couch further pointed out that when the jetty was opened on 23 September 1916, 'it was dedicated as a Memorial to the young men of Rapaki who served in the Great War and fought on Gallipoli, one of whom was killed there in that battle'.[25] He reminded the harbour board that the wharf was named 'Gallipoli' and was opened by Mrs M. J. Miller, wife of the then chairman of the board and mayor of Lyttelton. Finally, Couch reminded the board that Rāpaki beach was popular among picnickers, and that the restoration of the jetty would be of great benefit to boat users.

The harbour board's chief engineer, J. B. Bushell, inspected the jetty and reported that almost all the decking and hand-railing would need to be replaced, as well as some of the piles. The approach to the inshore end of the jetty was in poor condition, with the original boulder breakwater having been washed down. In an early example of cooperation between community and harbour board, it was agreed that the Rāpaki community would undertake the repair work, with the board staff doing the pile-driving plus 'such other specialised work as would impose unreasonable difficulties if not carried out by the Board's staff and equipment'.[26] The cost was estimated at £2500.

In March 1975 restoration was finally declared complete. Since then, there

The Witch Hill memorial in February 2018, awaiting new plaques.
JANE ROBERTSON

have been ongoing discussions regarding ownership and maintenance of the jetty involving Rāpaki, the Māori Land Court, Banks Peninsula District Council and Christchurch City Council.[27] Te Hapū o Ngāti Wheke holds mana whenua and mana moana over Whakaraupō and its catchment. In May 1998 the Ministry of Fisheries received an application from Wiremu Gillies, on behalf of Te Hapu o Ngāti Wheke Rūnanga ki Rāpaki, for the creation of a mātaitai reserve at Rāpaki. Such reserves are part of the Fisheries (South Island Customary Fishing) Regulations and are identified as traditional fishing grounds. The regulations allow tangata tiaki/kaitiaki (area managers) to use bylaws to administer and manage customary food-gathering with the aim of protecting and fostering mahinga kai species. On 18 December 1998 Rāpaki Bay became New Zealand's first mātaitai reserve.[28]

In 2017 the area of protection was extended with the establishment of a Lyttelton Harbour Whakaraupō Mātaitai Reserve covering the inner two-thirds of the harbour. Surveys had already suggested that the recreational bag limits had been set too high, and an update of the bylaws to ensure sustainability and enhance stocks was put out for consultation in December 2019 and approved in 2020. The update included setting reduced recreational daily limits for a number of fish and shellfish species; prohibiting the taking of shellfish other than pāua, tuaki, pipi, kūtai, pāpaka or tio; prohibiting the taking of seaweed except karengo and wakame; and closing two areas to taking tuaki in order to allow for the enhancement of those tuaki beds.[29] At the time of writing, Te Hapū o Ngāti Wheke (Rāpaki) Rūnanga has applied to extend the Lyttelton Harbour Whakaraupō Mātaitai Reserve to the harbour heads.

The rūnanga is one of the prime movers in the Whaka-Ora Healthy Harbour plan designed to restore the cultural and ecological health of Whakaraupō as mahinga kai. Five partner organisations — Environment Canterbury, Te Hapū o Ngāti Wheke, Te Rūnanga o Ngāi Tahu, Christchurch City Council and Lyttelton Port Company — in collaboration with the Whakaraupō Lyttelton Harbour community, have developed a holistic catchment management plan for Lyttelton Harbour: ki uta ki tai, from the mountains to the sea. For Te Hapū o Ngāti Wheke this includes the elimination of wastewater discharges, reducing sedimentation and achieving a water quality standard consistent with Whakaraupō as mahinga kai. In advocating for close monitoring of the kaimoana harvest, Te Hapū o Ngāti Wheke is guided by the principle 'Mō tātou, ā, mō kā uri ā muri ake nei' ('For us and our children after us').

ABOVE Men and boys stringing up eels to dry as part of a gathering at Rāpaki to celebrate the 120th anniversary of the signing of the Treaty of Waitangi in 1960.
CHRISTCHURCH CITY LIBRARIES, CCL-DW-8255

BELOW Wi Tauwhare (left) with Pat Hutana, Rāpaki Jetty, c.1956.
COURTESY OF DONALD COUCH

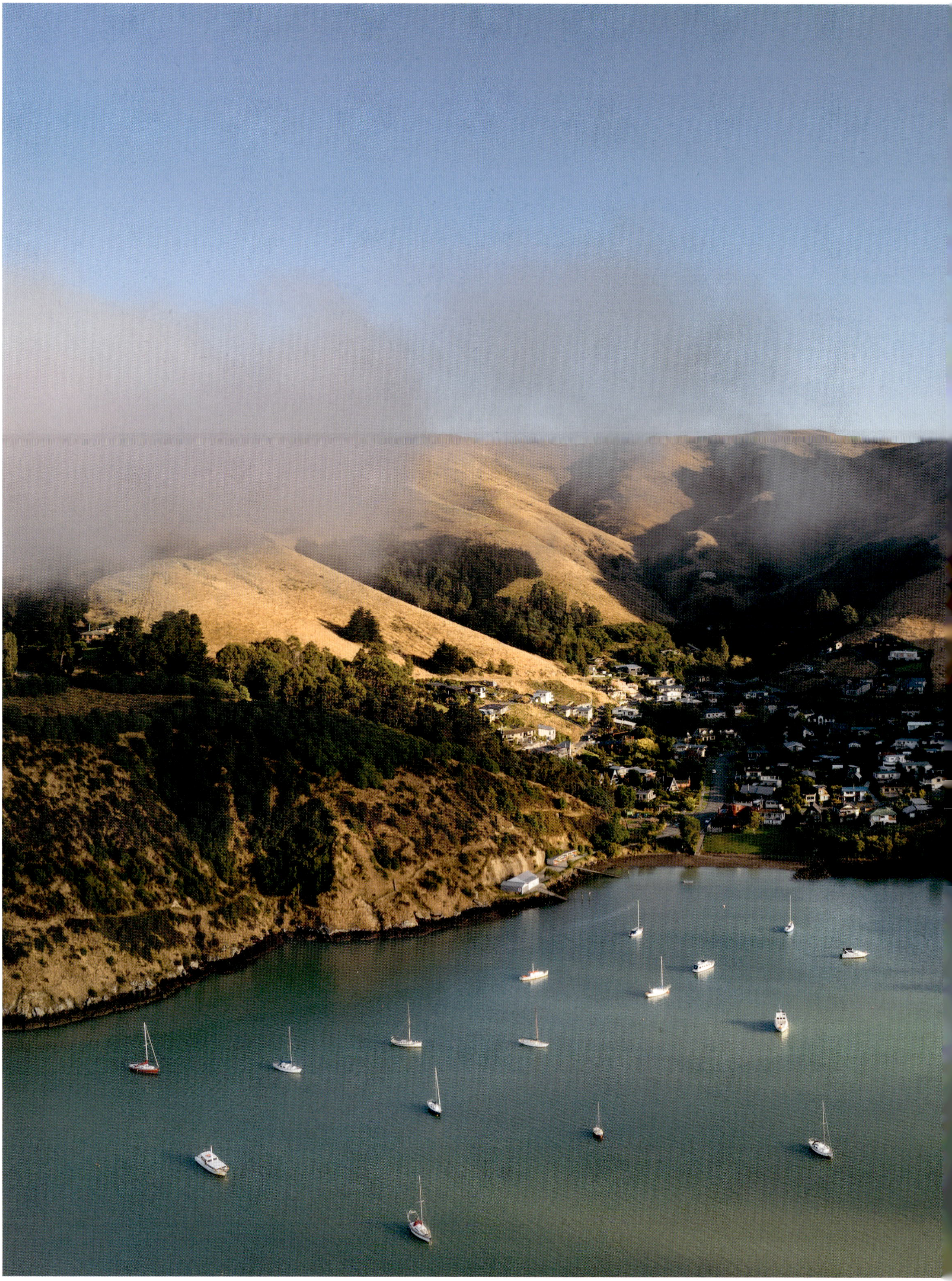

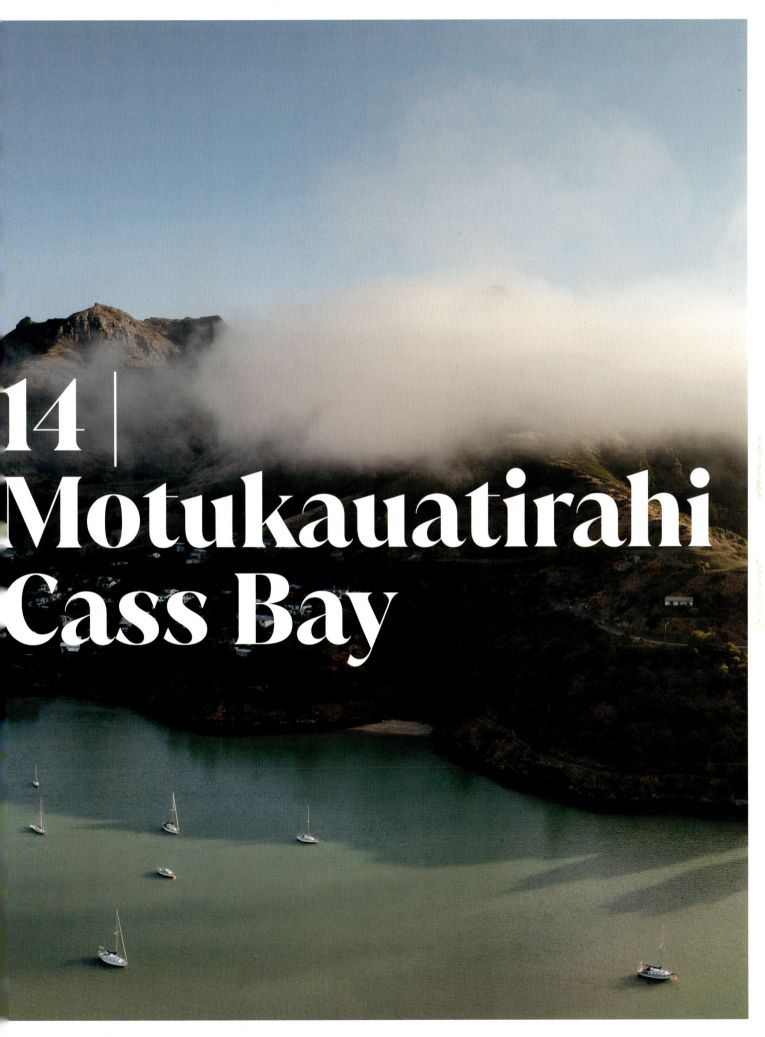

14 | Motukauatirahi Cass Bay

Today we know Motukauatirahi Cass Bay as a popular and attractive residential suburb with a safe swimming beach, a dinghy storage area and slipway, and a large number of swing moorings available to yachties. Unlike all the other settlements around Lyttelton Harbour, it seems never to have had a jetty as such. For much of its recorded history Cass Bay was farmed, but otherwise remained relatively undeveloped, its potential popularity stymied by waste discharge from the slaughterhouse high on the hill above the bay.

✽

Later, as the site of a Royal New Zealand Navy munitions depot, it became a place of mystery, with low-lying brick and concrete magazines snaking their way up the hill surrounded by a high concrete and wire fence. The magazines are still there, though no longer functional and much less easily seen in the whole fabric of the bay.

Cass Bay was known to Māori as Motukauatirahi — 'great fire-making tree grove'. Like Corsair Bay — Motukauatiiti, or 'little fire-making tree grove' — the bay was home to many kaikōmako trees that were used for fire making. According to Māori legend, Māui was curious to know where fire came from. So he extinguished all the fires and then approached Mahuika, the goddess of fire and his grandmother, in her cave in a burning mountain. Mahuika gave Māui fire in the form of one of her burning fingernails, but when Māui extinguished fingernail after fingernail Mahuika became angry. With her last fingernail she set fire to both land and sea, trapping her errant grandson. Māui appealed to Tāwhirimātea, god of weather, and Whaitiri-matakataka, goddess of thunder, who extinguished the raging fires. But the seeds of fire remained in the māhoe and kaikōmako trees. Māui brought back dry sticks of these trees and showed his people how to rub them together and make fire.[1]

Above Cass Bay and Corsair Bay is a group of rocky peaks which curve inward into a huge half-cup, open to the south. Down the sides of this cup are the remains of an old lava stream which ran out into the harbour at Cass Bay in the form of a black reef. Māori named the flanks of this cup Te Moenga o Wheke ('Wheke's sleeping place').[2] Just as at Rāpaki, there are warm volcanic springs at Motukauatirahi which would have been familiar to local Māori. In 1883 geologist R. M. Laing reported two springs on the western side of the bay. The location has since been much modified by road formation and the construction of recreation facilities, but a pool of warm, sulphurous water still remains.[3] The presence of kaikōmako and warm springs must have been a further expression of the bounty of Whakaraupō for early Māori settlers.

Yorkshireman Thomas Cass first came to New Zealand in December 1841 when he was 24, as a surveyor for the New Zealand Company. He returned to England and was then hired as an assistant to Captain Joseph Thomas, chief surveyor for the intended Canterbury Association settlement. As noted earlier, Cass arrived in Lyttelton Harbour in December 1848 and set up camp at what seems to have been known briefly as Port Lincoln (and also, jokingly, as Rogues Bay) but would soon become known as Cass Bay. It was there that he was joined by Charles Torlesse and Henry Cridland (the other 'rogues', perhaps?); in July 1849 all three moved to Cavendish Bay (Lyttelton), and in 1851 Cass became chief surveyor for the Canterbury Association.

The surveyors were busy preparing for a new town whose exact location was yet to be determined. They made use of the existing settlements in Whakaraupō — in particular at Pūrau, Head of the Bay and Rāpaki — as points of contact, and seem to have criss-crossed the harbour regularly. For example, on 22 January 1849 Torlesse left the Deans brothers' farm at Riccarton and travelled over to Rāpaki, where he had great difficulty in getting a canoe. 'At last with the inducement of 5/- prevailed upon Billy and two women to push me across — heavy head wind and flood tide. Arrived at Puru [sic] at 5½ pm.'[4] There he picked up two new arrivals and returned to Rāpaki in another boat, arriving back in Riccarton at 9.15 p.m. On 31 January Torlesse was again over the harbour to Pūrau, this time with Cass. On 1 February Captain Thomas and Torlesse went to the head of the harbour in John Gebbie's boat, landing at Rāpaki with a party bound for Motunau, up the coast. In early July Torlesse had lunch with Donald Gollan at Gollans Bay and then returned to Cass Bay, with Captain Thomas, in a whaleboat. Torlesse wrote to Edward Stafford in Nelson that Cass had made an excellent survey of the harbour. What is striking is how the young surveyors and early settlers in Whakaraupō used the harbour as a highway. The services of boatbuilders and boat owners were in high demand.

In 1851, 50 acres of freehold land, with or without 500 acres of adjoining pasturage, was advertised for sale in Cass Bay. The landowner was The Reverend Edward Puckle of the Heathcote Parsonage, who had pre-purchased his land in England and arrived as officiating minister on *Randolph* in December 1850 with his wife, six children and (expecting commodious accommodation) 70 tons of furniture, which was unfortunately washed out on the tide. It is unlikely that the Puckle family ever resided in Cass Bay. Many early settler clerics engaged in a form of what we might now call 'land banking'.

Puckle's land does not seem to have sold immediately. Cass Bay was used to graze cattle, sheep and horses and, since the provincial government had made no provision for abattoir facilities near Lyttelton, it became the go-to place for the town's butchers to get animals slaughtered. Butcher George Hunt was listed as working at Cass Bay as early as October 1851. John Parkinson, who later set himself up in the business of landing large numbers of sheep, cattle and horses at Gollans Bay (see chapter 17), had sheep grazing at Cass Bay. He was charged 2s 6d per dozen on a weekly basis and the sheep had 1500 acres to run over. By

ABOVE Cass Bay abattoir on the hill by the stand of pine trees. The dark shed near the foreshore, most likely a boat shed, has a slipway running down to the sea.
CANTERBURY MUSEUM, W. A. TAYLOR COLLECTION, 1968.213.407

BELOW The brick and concrete Cass Bay abattoir, rebuilt in 1902 to a state-of-the-art design with ventilation and lighting built into the roof.
CANTERBURY MUSEUM, RICHARD WOLFE COLLECTION, 65071/4

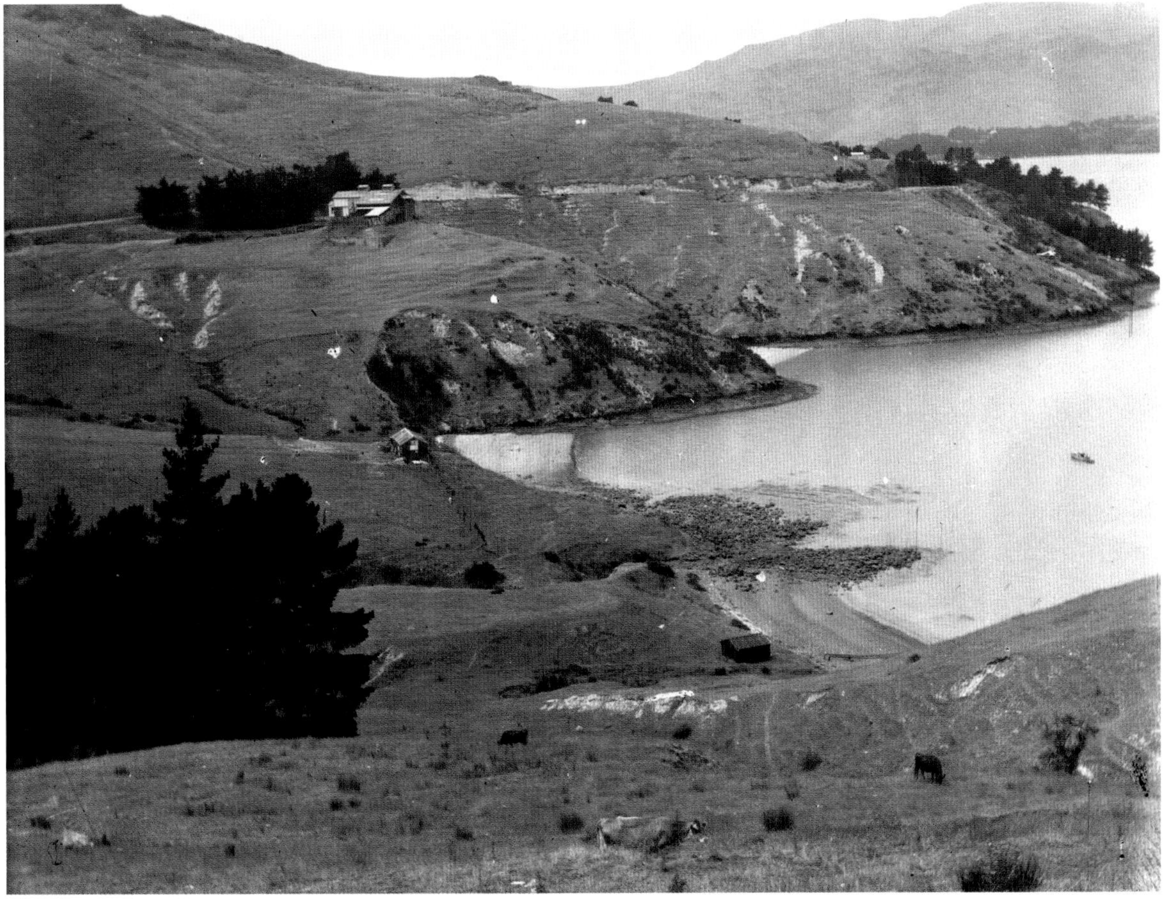

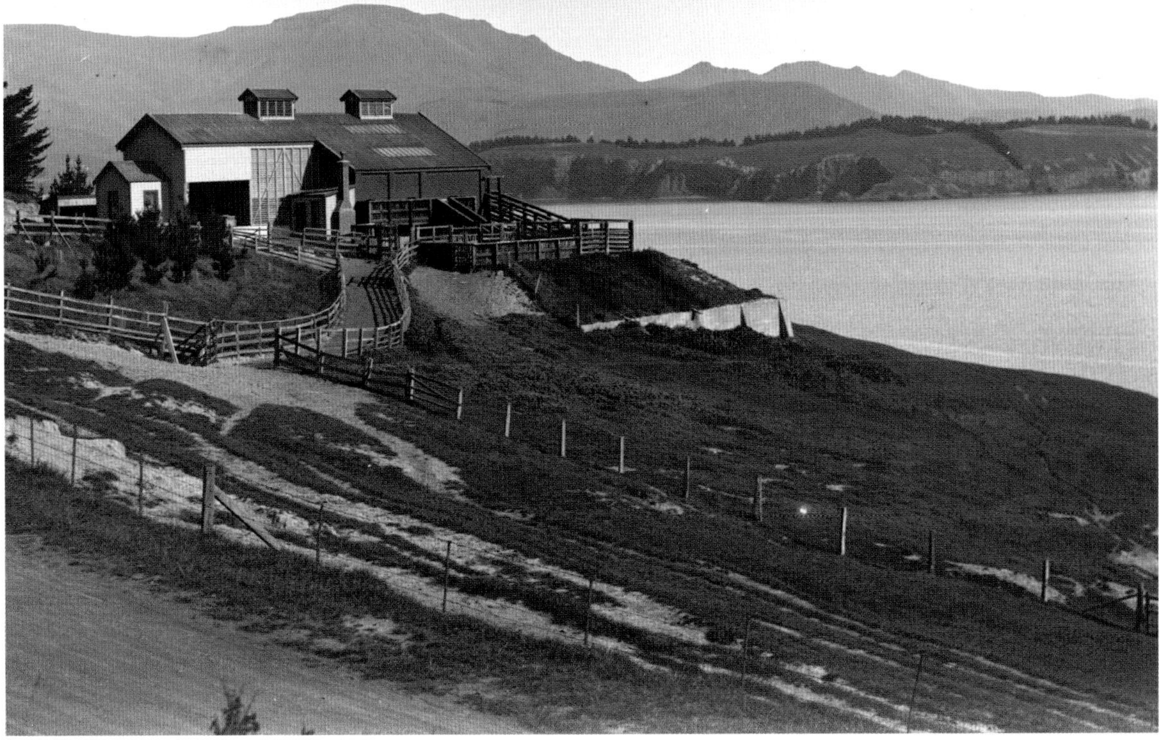

1856 Eli Salt of 'Cass's Bay Run' was advertising pasturage for cows at £1 per head and calves at 12 shillings. Salt also owned a retail warehouse in Lyttelton where, among other things, he sold lime and bricks made at his brickworks in Salts Gully (now Hawkhurst Road).

By 1863 Charles Baker, who was dairy farming at Magazine Bay (then known as Bakers Bay), seems to have extended his farm boundaries eastwards (controversially) and westwards as far as Cass Bay.[5] John Webb ran a dairy farm at Cass Bay between 1870 and 1878 before moving to Lyttelton, where he purchased a grocery business. In March 1889 Roderick Gallagher's dairy farm and house in the bay was threatened by a major bush and grass fire that began on the Cashmere hills and spread rapidly in the nor'west wind to Rāpaki, Cass Bay, and on to Corsair and Dampiers Bays.

It is highly likely that the produce from these farms went out to Lyttelton via sea, since land transport, even over the short distance between Cass Bay and Lyttelton, was difficult and expensive. As early as 1856 the hills behind Cass Bay were being considered as the possible route for a road over the Port Hills to Christchurch. The idea was abandoned, given that the cost would be nearly equal to that of the financially fraught Evans Pass route. The idea surfaced again in 1913 with a proposal to build a road from Murray Aynsley Hill over the Rāpaki Track and into Lyttelton via Cass Bay, This would have provided a more direct route to Christchurch than the circuitous Evans Pass–Sumner–Redcliffs–Ferrymead route. Construction on the city side of the Port Hills would be relatively simple, but the deep gullies and steep, rocky volcanic bluffs on the harbour side above Rāpaki and Cass Bay made such a project uneconomic and the idea was once again abandoned.

Beside farming, Cass Bay was used for a variety of purposes. Given that it offered the only relatively flat land on the north side of the harbour (Rāpaki excepted), the Lyttelton Football Club practised there. In 1884 the Christ's College annual swimming races were held in the bay. The students were transported from Lyttelton by steam launch, 'which had its passenger carrying capacity tested to the utmost'.[6] In case of emergency 'or the unfriendly visit of a voracious sea-fish', a couple of boats were provided for the safety of the boys during the races. The Lyttelton-based Martini-Henry Rifle Club opened a rifle range in Cass Bay in February 1892 on land belonging to R. M. Morten. Morten, who owned a lot of land on the Port Hills, offered the land free of charge on the understanding that no dogs would be allowed on the range to worry the sheep. In 1898 the Lyttelton Borough Council considered acquiring land in Cass Bay for a public cemetery.

In October 1884 the council gave permission to Garforth and Lee to erect a slaughterhouse in Cass Bay. Previously they had run a similar operation in Corsair Bay from mid-1875, but moved it around to Cass Bay after shipwright Malcolm

Miller complained to the Lyttelton Borough Council about the nuisance caused by the slaughterhouse.

By 1893 the slaughterhouse licence was held by Owen and Dyer. However, there was concern about the regulation of abattoirs, which were multiplying to meet the needs of the growing Lyttelton and Christchurch populations. Hygiene was an issue, with residents and authorities on high alert following the spread of bubonic plague from eastern Asia to port cities around the world. Lyttelton lads engaged in rat-catching extended their operations as far as Cass Bay. On 1 May 1900 it was reported that 'sixty-six rats were brought from that locality, which, as the site of a slaughterhouse, is much affected by the vermin'.[7]

In May 1901 the Lyttelton Borough Council purchased the site and surrounding land (55 acres) from Morten for £25 per acre and began a rebuild of the facilities to a design by J. C. Maddison. Contractor W. Scott built the slaughterhouse, sheep pens, a draughting yard for cattle and another for sheep and pigs. The slaughterhouse itself, 38 feet by 32 feet, was built of brick on a concrete foundation. A bathroom was constructed nearby for the workers, and Lyttelton Borough water mains were extended to the site. In July 1902 the borough abattoir was officially opened, the first public abattoir in the district. 'The drainage is excellent, refuse being carried away by a pipe about a foot in diameter, which discharges into the harbour about 150 yards from the works.'[8] Charges for killing were 2s 6d per head for bullocks and 4d each for sheep.

Lyttelton locals still recall the abattoir, and the small bay below has been known variously as Abattoir Bay, Blood Bay, Flea Bay, Lady Bay and Sandy Bay. Butchers working towards the end of the abattoir's operation included Jones (nicknamed Bones), Mac MacDonald and Charlie Wells. Children used to visit the abattoir to watch the killing. 'Blood and guts flowing down to the red sea'[9] and 'sharks feeding at the bay below'[10] are a common shared memory, although Peter Chinnery, who lived in the bay and swam there frequently, encountered no sharks.

> I used to spend a lot of time at the old abattoir when I was a kid too. Collecting sheep ear tags to put on my belt. Mac Mcdonald, Charlie Wells and another guy we all called bones but never knew his real name. I used to clean and salt down sheep intestines used for sausage skins among other things and put them in barrels. I used to get sheep's brains for Dad too otherwise they would've gone for fertilizer I think. Good times though.[11]

> . . . The abattoir had a pet sheep that used to lead the others into the slaughter house but it would go straight through back out to the

paddock. Bones used to bring us free meat for our pets and he would take us round there to watch a beast killed.¹²

Allen Curnow wrote a poem based on his primary school days in Lyttelton in 1922–23, in which he recalled a sneaky visit to the abattoir with friend Bob Crawford. He remembered the slaughterhouse being 'as cool as a church inside' and the outfall of the killing 'discharging over the rock-face misting all the way to the green bay water . . . where the round stain dilates'.¹³ Around the small headland, holidaymakers swam happily in Corsair Bay. The Cass Bay abattoir, with its ocean discharge, operated until 1964.

In addition to the cavalier treatment of the harbour waters, one of the themes running through all early accounts of life on the harbour is a lack of compassion for any form of marine life. In February 1915 a 10-foot-long bottlenose whale entered Pūrau Bay. Shot at a couple of times, the whale retreated towards Fort Jervois, where the gunners finally captured it. The whale was then towed by a launch to Cass Bay and cut up, its blubber being sold to a Christchurch firm.

Aerial view of Cass Bay, 1962, with the ammunition stores clearly visible snaking up the hill and the abattoir still operating on the headland to the right. The farmhouse where the Chinnery family lived between 1940 and 1950 is in the centre of the bay below the road.
V. C. BROWNE & SON, 6808-6823

By the mid-1930s, with a shortage of state houses in Lyttelton, the Lyttelton Borough Council was looking for land to expand. The council owned 55 acres of land in Cass Bay, used to graze stock for the abattoir. Cass Bay could potentially be transformed into a 'model suburb' of Lyttelton township. At the very least the abattoir could be removed, freeing up sites for 'weekend cottages'.¹⁴ Also, the increase in the fleet of yachts, launches and other pleasure craft meant that a number of boat owners could not secure moorings in the inner Lyttelton harbour. An additional boat harbour might be constructed at Cass Bay, which was considered to be more naturally protected than Magazine Bay (also the possible site for a boat harbour), with a sufficient depth of water and a more generous hinterland for sheds and slipways. As always, yachties and other interested parties disputed the suitability of various boat harbour locations and voiced their own preferences. Pūrau, Church Bay, Governors Bay and Port Levy all had their advocates and detractors.

The Chinnery family farmed in Cass Bay in the 1940s. The milk and cream from their 35–50 cows went to Lyttelton and Rāpaki. The family also made hay from 4 acres of lucerne, grew potatoes for the Christchurch market, tended two pine plantations and raised calves and pigs. As a lad, Peter Chinnery walked daily from Cass Bay to West Lyttelton School, bringing home cows from the family's Corsair Bay farm on his return.

The outbreak of war in 1939 put any housing or boat harbour development

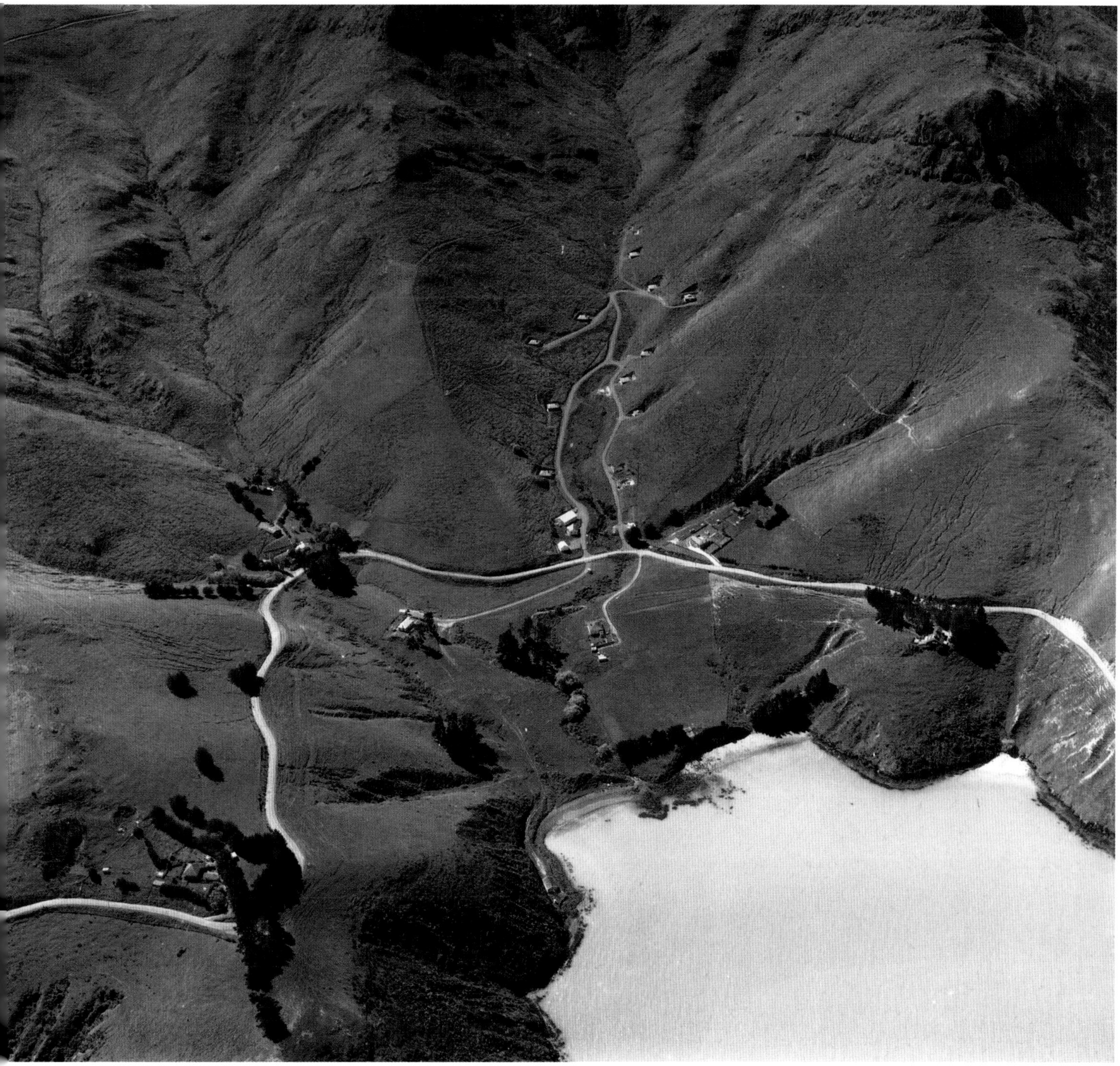

plans on hold. Lyttelton became the second major Royal New Zealand Navy base in the country, from 1942 to 1945. To meet the demands of wartime munitions supply, the navy constructed new depots, one of which was at Cass Bay — selected because it was largely uninhabited, was not visible from the Lyttelton Harbour heads and could be accessed by sea. Cass Bay was, in fact, a default location after a facility built at Tikao Bay, Akaroa Harbour during 1942–43 turned out to be a white elephant. The magazine site was too far by road or sea from the port of Lyttelton, which it was designed to serve, and the magazines, as planned, would be only 200 or 300 yards away from the mining depot, with no natural feature to protect the one in the event of an explosion in the other.

Land in Cass Bay was requisitioned from local farmers. Ten brick and concrete magazines, an ammunition-processing building, camp/administration buildings, a four-man hut, guardhouse, flag station and extensive fencing were built in 1943. Farmer Charles Chinnery hauled the concrete posts that carried the fence surrounding the compound up the steep hill. On occasions when the navy was blasting, rocks would fall on the farmhouse front lawn, one just missing Peter Chinnery's younger brother. The magazines had spark-proof floors, damp-proof construction and a constant inside temperature. A navy gun was mounted adjacent to the Lyttelton–Governors Bay road and passing traffic had to await a naval escort through the bay. This gun was later given to the Dunedin Sea Cadet Corps.

It appears that the navy's original intention was to barge the munitions from Cass Bay to warships in the inner harbour. They reclaimed land in the bay, constructed a building on it, developed a landing 'hard' for the barges, and built steps. In the event, the bay was found to be too shallow for laden barges and the navy resorted to transporting the munitions by road.[15]

After the war the Department of Scientific and Industrial Research used the Cass Bay site for an ionosphere station, where it conducted experimental testing of radio frequencies. The armament depot was officially closed down in 1962. Noeline Allan's father grazed land at the top of the military enclosure, and she remembers, following the closure, truckloads of ammunition being removed. The lovely gardens to the front of the complex languished, the white stones their only reminder.

(In January 1980 Cass Bay residents got a nasty surprise when a spectacular blast gutted one of the magazines. The orange and purple flames that shot through the roof were visible from the Christchurch side of the Port Hills. This was not ammunition remaining from the Second World War, which had been completely removed by 1967, but gelignite that had been recently and unofficially stored in the disused magazine. Residents were woken the following morning by another loud explosion; this time it was the army carrying out legitimate manoeuvres in the form of a mock assault on Quail Island.)

One of the Cass Bay ammunition stores. Despite the 2010/11 earthquakes, the brickwork is in perfect condition.
JANE ROBERTSON

In October 1965 the Navy League Sea Cadet Corps was given the go-ahead by the DSIR to use some of the buildings at Cass Bay for the Sea Cadet Unit TS (Training Ship) *Steadfast*. The unit was 'a training and leadership group for young people between 13–18 who were interested in maritime and life skills'.[16] The first Sea Cadet unit in New Zealand, TS *Steadfast* was formed in 1929 in Christchurch as the Canterbury Division of the Navy League Sea Cadets. Units followed in Dunedin in 1938, Wellington (Petone) in 1941, and then Auckland in 1943. In 1958, a second Christchurch unit, TS *Cornwell*, was formed at Sumner and Redcliffs. As a result of the Christchurch earthquakes TS *Steadfast* and *Cornwell* merged to form TS *Godley*.

Six old concrete ammunition stores, an old wooden house, a large store and a garage were made available to the Sea Cadets. The ammunition stores were used for classrooms, clothing storage, recreation space and sleeping accommodation for weekend camps. The coastal location did much enhance the unit's scope for training.

A large boatshed and a slipway were built on the north-west shore of Cass Bay on land that had been reclaimed for military purposes in the Second World War. Lieutenant Commander Victor Fifield remembered 'a windlass and a nice slipway and plenty of storage space and a few buoys laid out there so they could put their boats out'.[17] Not long after, the method of launching and hauling up the Navy League boats was deemed unsatisfactory, so the shed was extended and the door widened by 10 feet. A new concrete slipway for two 27-foot whalers and a boat slip for a 16-foot cutter were built. A cradle for the whaler and two light cradles for the skiffs were also ordered.[18] A patent slip enabled a yacht to be brought in

at high tide and left high and dry when the tide receded. The craft's hull could be scrubbed, the residue washed off in the next high tide and a new coat of antifouling applied at the second low tide before relaunching.[19]

After the war, the long-delayed Cass Bay subdivision plan resurfaced. In December 1945 the *Press* reported that authority would be sought from the government to subdivide council land into residential sections 'on modern town-planning lines'.[20] Even so, it took another 20 years, and the completion of the road tunnel connecting Christchurch and Lyttelton in 1964, before the first 76 sections appeared on the market, ranging in price from £650 to £1400. This could be the beginning, according to the *Press*, of 'major seaside housing development around the harbour'.[21]

In a controversial move, swing moorings were installed in the late 1960s, despite the concerns of many boat owners that in the absence of a wave barrier the site was too exposed to the south-west. The Banks Peninsula Cruising Club criticised the Lyttelton Harbour Board's 'apathy and lack of interest in pleasure craft'.[22]

In 1970 plans were drawn up for a dinghy shelter and launching ramp at the land end of the navy boatshed and local sewage tank. Dinghies were required to access the increasing number of yachts moored in the bay. These developments signalled a transition from industrial to recreational use of Cass Bay, now a popular residential area, swimming spot, kayaking base and boat mooring location. As part of the Head-to-Head Walkway the bay has an impressive walking track connecting it to Corsair Bay and Ōtūherekio Pony Point Reserve.

In the 1990s the former Armament Depot land was purchased by the Banks Peninsula District Council, following consultation with the Cass Bay community. The intention was to create a recreational reserve for the community with walking tracks, including one to the Summit Road. TS *Steadfast* was to remain on site 'but not at the expense of the development of the area for general recreation as was intended in the original purchase'.[23] The area was transferred to Christchurch City Council at the time of amalgamation in 2006, and the gates were locked to the public. The land has been managed by Port Hills rangers as part of the regional park network. The grounds around the built facilities are managed and maintained by Sea Cadet unit TS *Steadfast* and the Royal New Zealand Navy Volunteer Reserve.

Over the past 30 years the Cass Bay community has planted native trees and developed tracks on local reserves. 'Since 2020, as part of the Whaka-Ora Healthy Harbour initiative, the community has planted thousands of native trees along the stream margins to reduce sedimentation in Lyttelton Harbour and restore local biodiversity.'[24] In 2021 Christchurch City Council consultation on a draft landscape plan to open up the ex-Armament Depot land to the public, develop walking tracks and continue regenerative planting received widespread support. At the time of writing the reserve has just been opened to the public.

ABOVE A publicity shot for the Cass Bay development, 1976.
ARCHIVES NEW ZEALAND, R. COAD, 6539, R24811575

BELOW Two yachts beached at Cass Bay following overnight storms, 29 January 1988.
CHRISTCHURCH *STAR*, CCL-DW-69981

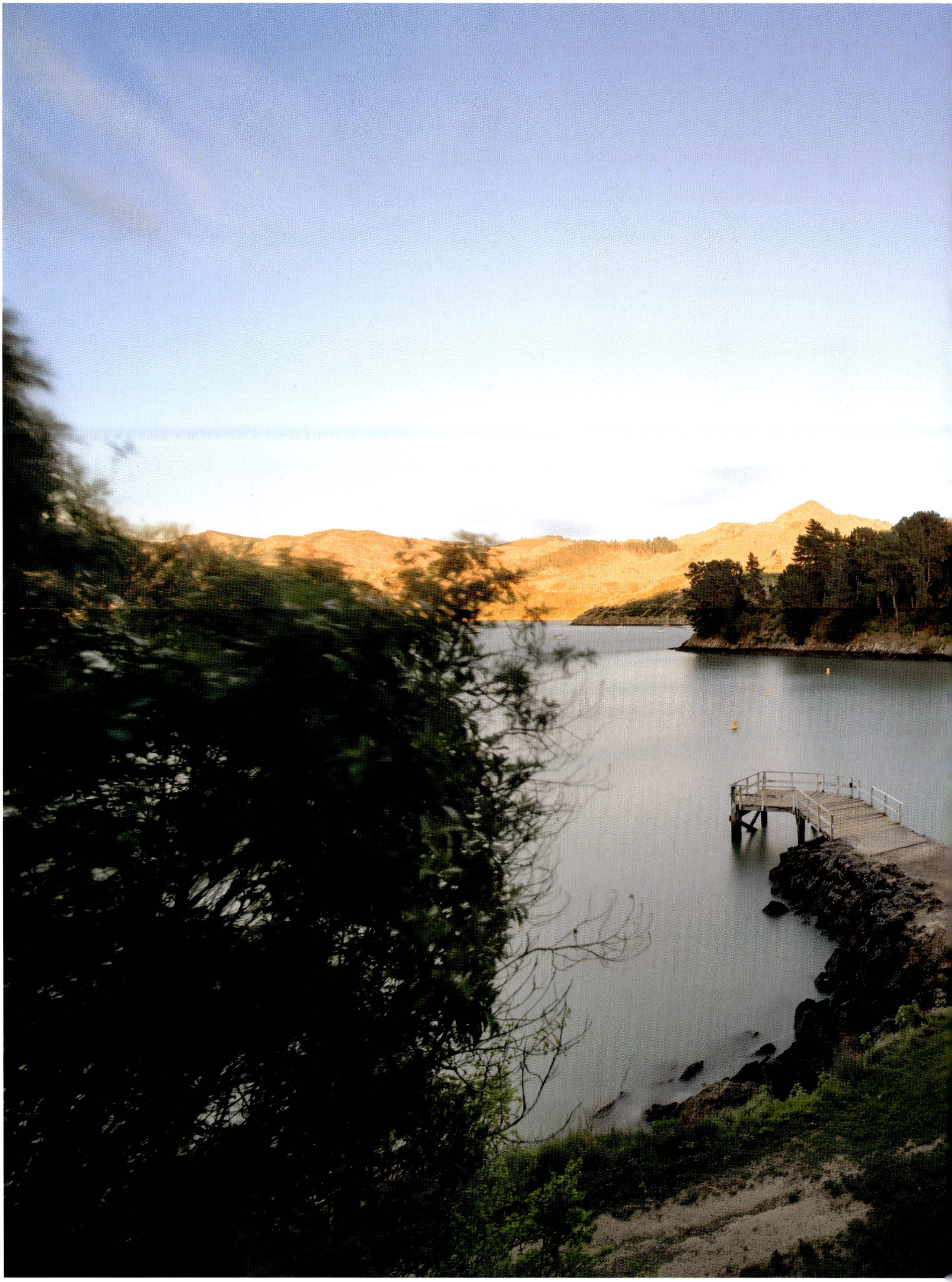

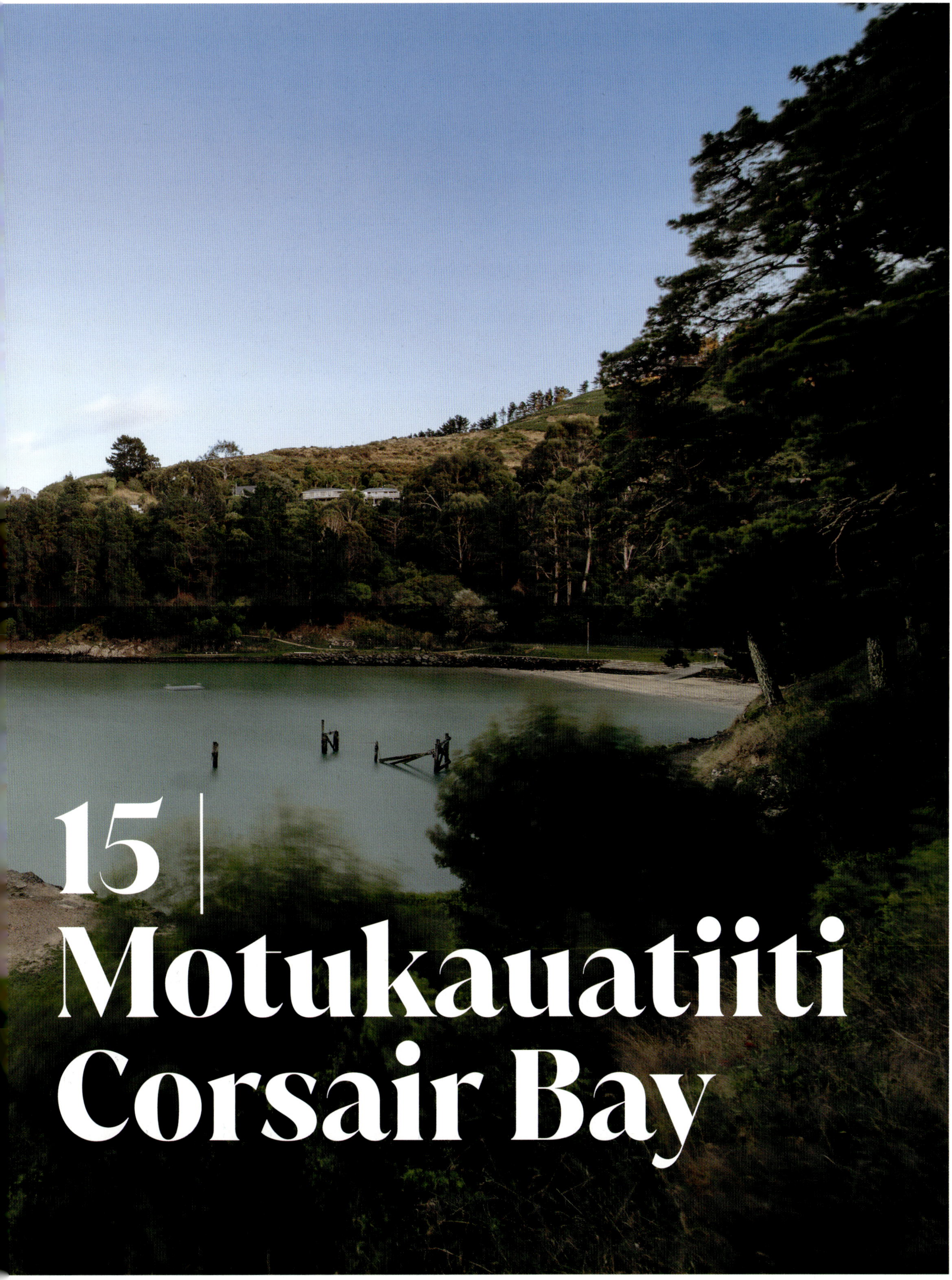

15 | Motukauatiiti Corsair Bay

Today, Corsair Bay is one of the most accessible and popular swimming spots in Whakaraupō. Its golden era, however, was the early twentieth century, when it was regarded as the jewel in the crown of Canterbury swimming resorts and billed as 'the playground of the plains'. In January 1924 the *Press* reported that 'the beach and hillsides were covered with picnic parties and the water was literally black with hundreds of bathers. Thousands of holiday makers arrived by the morning trains.'[1] This chapter tells the story of Corsair Bay's spectacular seaside popularity.

✹

The Māori name Motukauatiiti, meaning 'little fire-making tree grove', was supplanted early in the second decade of the Canterbury Association settlement. In April 1861 the Melbourne-based steamship *Omeo*, which traded between Australia and New Zealand, dragged her anchors in a strong sou'west gale. The anchors then tangled with the cables of Captain Thomas Gay's whaling brigantine, *Corsair*, anchored in Erskine Bay (today Lyttelton's inner harbour). *Corsair*'s cables snapped. The harbour master put men on board *Corsair* and they managed to land it a little beyond Grubb and Allen's shipbuilding yard, where it held fast on a low rocky shelf. The following day, it was discovered that *Corsair*'s hull had been badly damaged and holed. It was condemned and sold, but then lay for six years before salvage and repair.

In the 1850s and 1860s Corsair Bay would have seemed well removed from Lyttelton township and a suitable place for industrial enterprises. Initially the bay was used for boatbuilding, repairs and launching. Ten to twelve men worked on the construction of the steamer *Avon* in 1859. The 69-ton steamer *Moa* was put together (from materials sent out from England) on the slip at Corsair Bay and launched there in 1864 to quite a fanfare: the steamer *Gazelle* brought a large party of the owner's friends, who joined an already large group of onlookers, all cheering as the *Moa* was christened and launched.

In 1874 Malcolm Miller, with sons Archie and Jack, built a slipway in Corsair Bay able to take coastal vessels of up to 70 tons, and this secured plenty of work for his shipyard. In August 1881, however, fire took hold of a £100 ketch awaiting repairs on the Miller slip. The fire quickly spread to the boatbuilding shed and destroyed everything. The shed was uninsured — a £150–200 loss.[2] In 1907 Miller moved his business to the port.

Businessman William Langdown built a number of brick kilns in Christchurch and the wider Canterbury area, including one at Corsair Bay. Langdown owned a fleet of vessels which he used, amongst other things, to bring lime in from Kaikōura or Motunau for his Corsair Bay and Heathcote kilns. The kiln was still operating in 1906 when it was offered for sale by Prisk and Williams. It is possible that the Corsair Bay jetty, built in 1906–7, was constructed using stone from the demolished lime kiln. There is no sign of the kiln in early photos of the jetty.

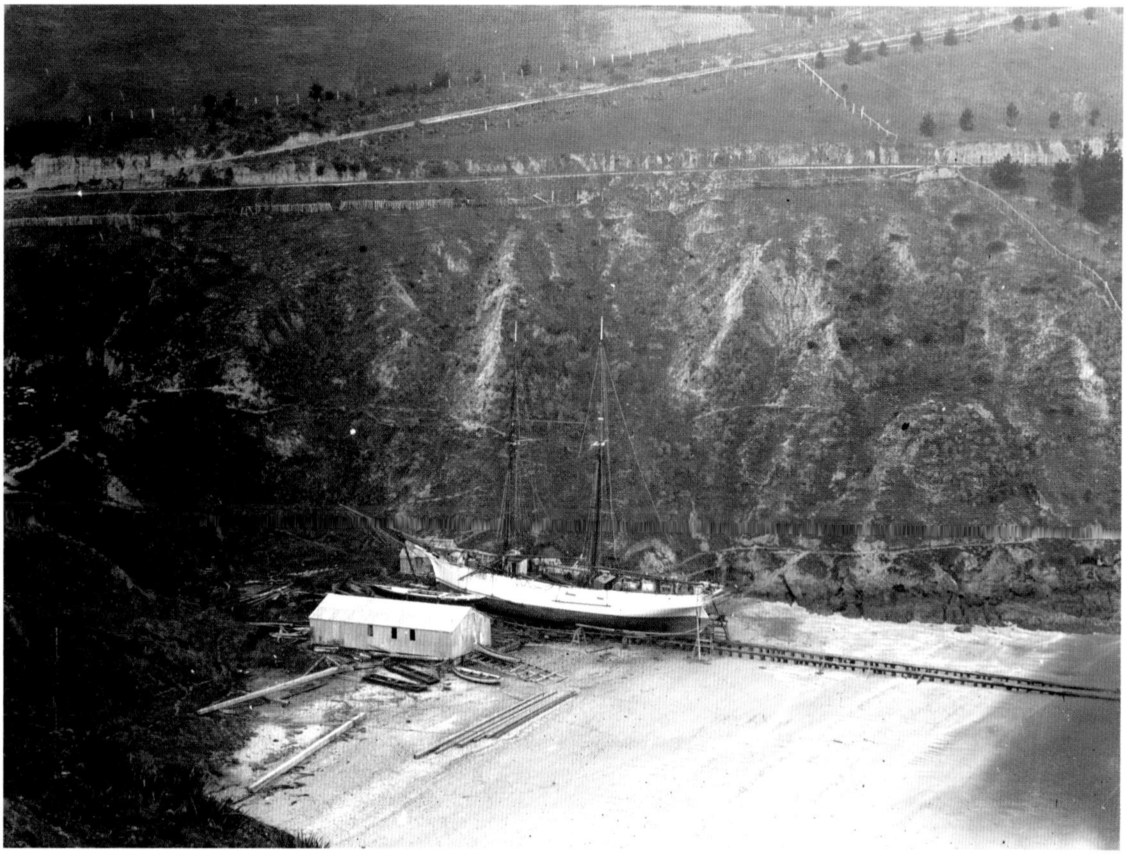

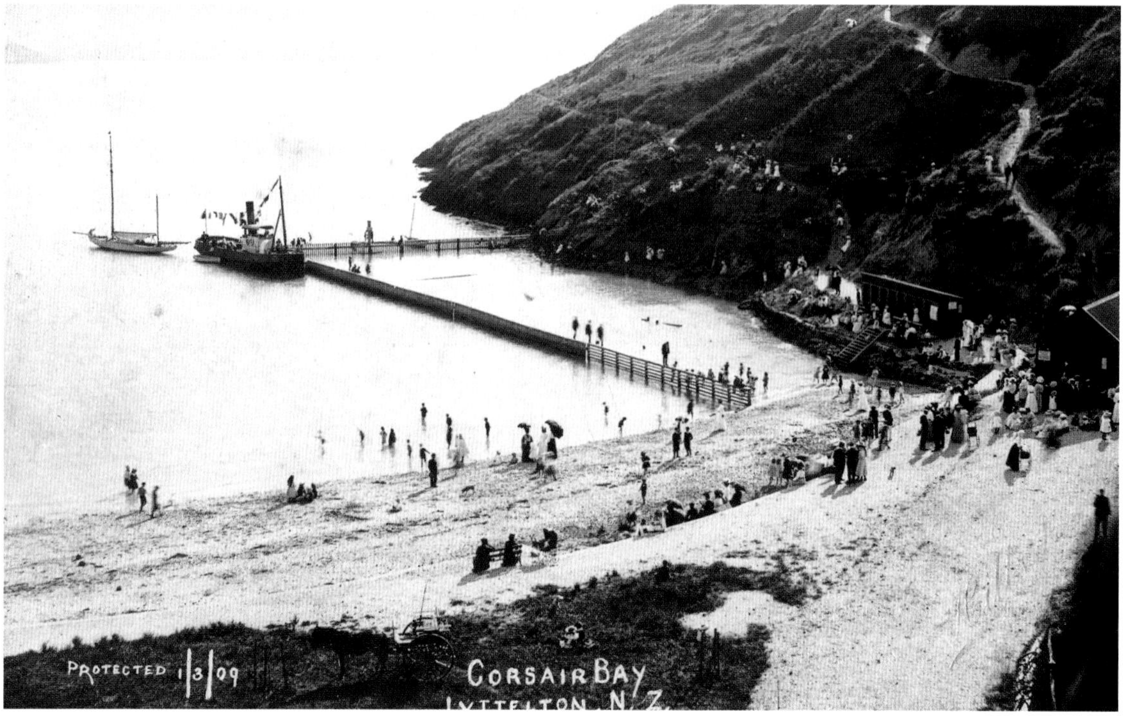
PROTECTED 1/3/09
CORSAIR BAY
LYTTELTON. N.Z.

Such small industries were a feature of the early years of European settlement in Lyttelton Harbour. In most cases the evidence of their existence has long disappeared, overlayed by changing circumstances and the material needs of later generations.

In the late 1860s and early 1870s prisoners from the Lyttelton Gaol worked to improve the Governors Bay road. With the opening of the railway tunnel in 1867, Christchurch residents could take the train to Lyttelton and walk around the road to Corsair Bay. With its clear water and sandy bottom, the bay was a popular venue for school picnics. From 1886 Christ's College and Boy's High swimming sports were held there. The Lyttelton Rifle Club shifted from Cass Bay to Corsair Bay and opened its new range in October 1893 with a picnic on the sandy beach.

Largely thanks to the initiative of Thomas Henry Potts of Governors Bay, trees were planted to create a seaside domain extending from the back of the graving dock in Lyttelton across three spurs of hills to Corsair Bay. This provided recreational shelter for a town largely without significant stands of trees. In 1891 the Domain Board came under the control of the Lyttelton Borough Council, who took responsibility for its upkeep. The board decided to improve the track to the beach, and to extend the water supply to the beach 'for the large number of residents who visit the bay during the summer months'.[3] Sadly, although a good walking track still connects Corsair Bay with adjacent Magazine Bay, the domain itself has long been neglected, its purpose perhaps largely forgotten.

A suspected outbreak of bubonic plague in 1902 saw the erection of a temporary infectious diseases hospital close to the seashore in Corsair Bay. This included a 12-foot by 15-foot canvas-over-wood 'tent' for the first patient, as well as tents for nurses and doctors, for dressing and for food preparation. There was panic in Christchurch and rather a lot of finger-pointing in the direction of Lyttelton, which was regarded by some as an unsanitary town. Concerns included old, dilapidated buildings, damp cellars and, worst of all, fowl houses.

The *Lyttelton Times* reported that despite the borough council having raised the bounty for rats to 6d per head, 'it will be almost impossible to adequately fight the vast armies of the rodents, who swarm off the vessels to the wharves, and from the wharves to the residences'.[4] Within a week the temporary structures adjacent to the beach had been removed, reports of the 'plague' seemingly more alarmist than factual. There was also concern about the proximity of patients to two dairy farms, abattoirs, Miller's slip and the increasing numbers of swimmers and picnickers.

In November 1903, perhaps in response to increasing local agitation for better facilities at Corsair Bay, the borough council accepted Hollis and Brown's tender of £50 for constructing a shelter shed. To do more than this would require legislation. So, in 1905, it presented a bill to Parliament 'to vest the Foreshore of Corsair

ABOVE Shipbuilding and repair in Corsair Bay. This is probably Malcolm Miller's business, which operated between 1874 and 1907. The slipway could take coastal vessels of up to 70 tons.
CANTERBURY MUSEUM, J. J. KINSEY COLLECTION, 1940.193.220

BELOW The swimming enclosure and ladies' bathing sheds (far right), shortly after their construction at Corsair Bay in 1907. Although the enclosure was not intended for use as a jetty, there is a steam launch alongside.
CANTERBURY MUSEUM, CANTERBURY HISTORICAL ASSOCIATION COLLECTION, 2000.198.624

Bay, Lyttelton Harbour, in the Mayor, Councillors and Burgesses of the Borough of Lyttelton absolutely, and to place the control of the aforesaid foreshore in the said Mayor, Councillors and Burgesses, as a pleasure resort for the public of Canterbury'.[5] The creation of the Corsair Bay Recreation Reserve marks the true beginning of what was to become the bay's huge popularity with the Canterbury public.

The following year the borough council put a stop to the removal of shell from Corsair Bay beach for lining pathways or for use as poultry grit. Then, during 1906–7, between 30 and 40 prisoners from the Lyttelton Gaol worked on turning Corsair Bay into just such a pleasure resort. They removed Miller's boat slip and repair sheds, then built a substantial sea wall of about eight chains across the beach above high-water mark. A flight of wide concrete steps gave access to the beach. The space above the sea wall was levelled for use as a playground, and the shore was cleared of rocks and debris. The prisoners then constructed a roadway on the east side of the bay, at the end of which Corsair Bay's first jetty was built. A depth of 6 feet at low tide enabled launches to come alongside at any time. The road to the jetty was connected by a track to the roadway through the domain, and seats were placed at various points around the bay. A shelter house provided further seating. Corsair Bay was about 20 minutes' walk from Lyttelton through the domain, or 10 minutes by steam launch.

Although work was still in progress, the Lyttelton Borough Council decided to hold an 'official opening' for the Corsair Bay pleasure resort in November 1906. Lured by the promise of toys, fruit and sweets, children turned out in force with their mothers. The mayor, Mr S. R. Webb, in speaking to the large crowd, said that 'the first duty of municipal corporation was to look after the convenience and comfort of the people. The second was to provide for their recreation and enjoyment.'[6] He hoped that the Corsair Bay development fulfilled the latter.

A ladies' room was added to the shelter house, and by December 1907 enclosed salt-water baths with a changing shed and freshwater shower had been constructed at the western end of the bay. None of the contemporary newspaper reports mention that a key reason for the enclosure was probably the presence of the abattoir around the point in Cass Bay. Since the abattoir discharged directly into the sea below, it must have attracted sharks.[7]

The new pleasure resort was beset by problems. In June 1907 heavy sou'west winds had almost completely torn away the rubble approach to the new jetty. Newly built paths in the bay began to subside on account of the heavy rain. Immediately after the completion of the salt-water baths, men dominated their use to the virtual exclusion of women and children. There was talk of building another bath just for women in the little cove next to Corsair Bay. Instead, the council decided to reserve the hours between 9.00 a.m. and 5.00 p.m. for the exclusive use of women and children, meaning that if men wanted to swim in an enclosed, shark-proof area they had to do so in the early morning or evening. Letters to the editor expressed disappointment at the unfair treatment. One Lyttelton resident called it a 'gross injustice'. 'The women don't use the baths much . . . but they have the entire day set aside for them.'[8] A number of men had 'a conscientious objection to going into deep waters to which the rare but predatory shark has access'. They looked forward to 'a proper adjustment of the regulations, and to the safeguarding of their water-rights'.[9] A petition signed by a 'large number' of Lyttelton residents requested extra accommodation and facilities for male bathers at Corsair Bay. The hours for women and children were changed and changed again.

In 1908 the borough council passed a bylaw to provide for the 'decent and orderly control of Corsair Bay as a pleasure resort'.[10] Following reports of men entering the women's enclosure, and even getting into the bathing sheds, changing facilities for men were built on the east side of the bay. The enclosure, however, was to be reserved 'entirely' for the use of women and children since, according to one councillor, 'the bay outside the enclosure was perfectly safe . . . there was no danger from sharks'.[11] One 'Lady Bather' expressed her disdain for the men's request. 'Why are the men in such a flurry over the baths? . . . The baths were built for women and children but now the poor men want them. I say let them have the bath. We can do as we have done before, bathe in the open.'[12] There

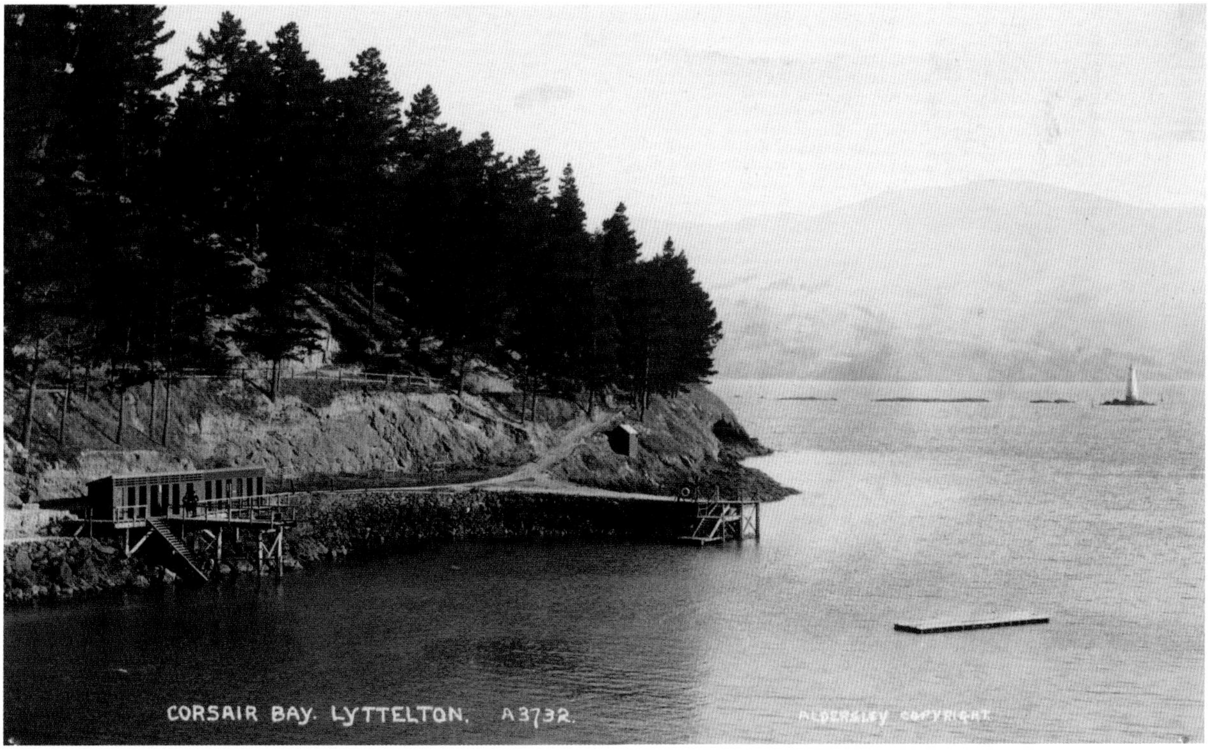
CORSAIR BAY. LYTTELTON. A3732.
ALDERSLEY COPYRIGHT

The new jetty and men's bathing sheds with a raft for swimmers. The bulk of the jetty is formed from rock rubble, which was vulnerable to wash-out.
CANTERBURY MUSEUM, ALDERSLEY PUBLICATION, SOUTHLAND MUSEUM COLLECTION, 01714

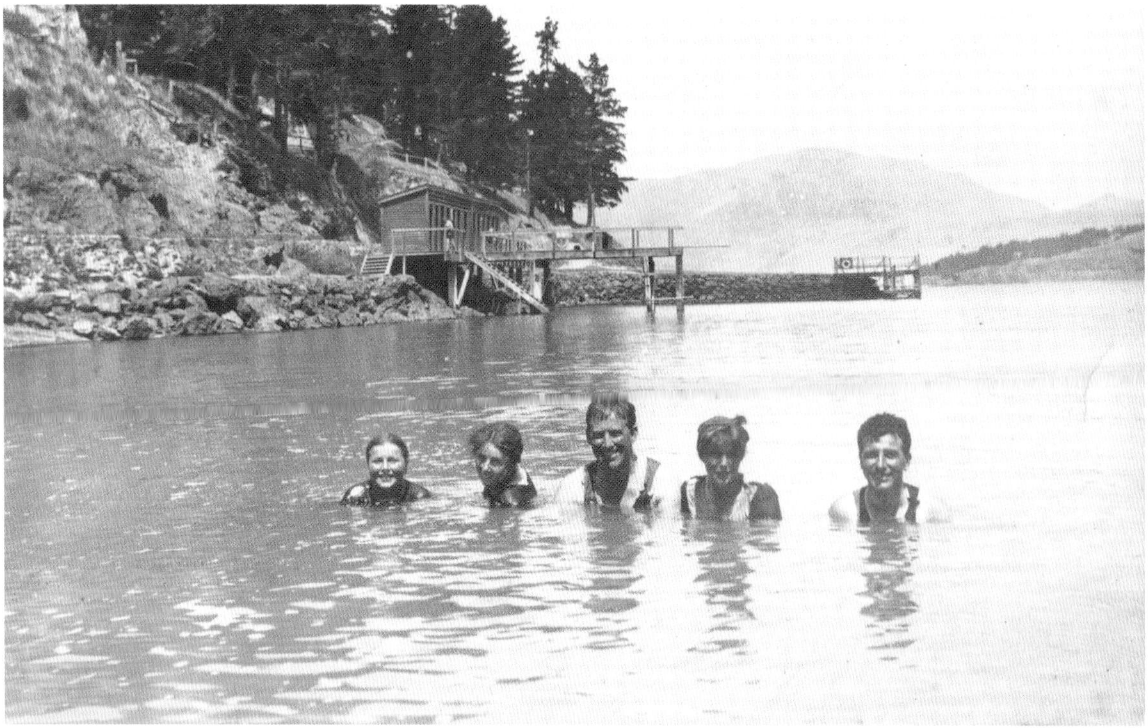

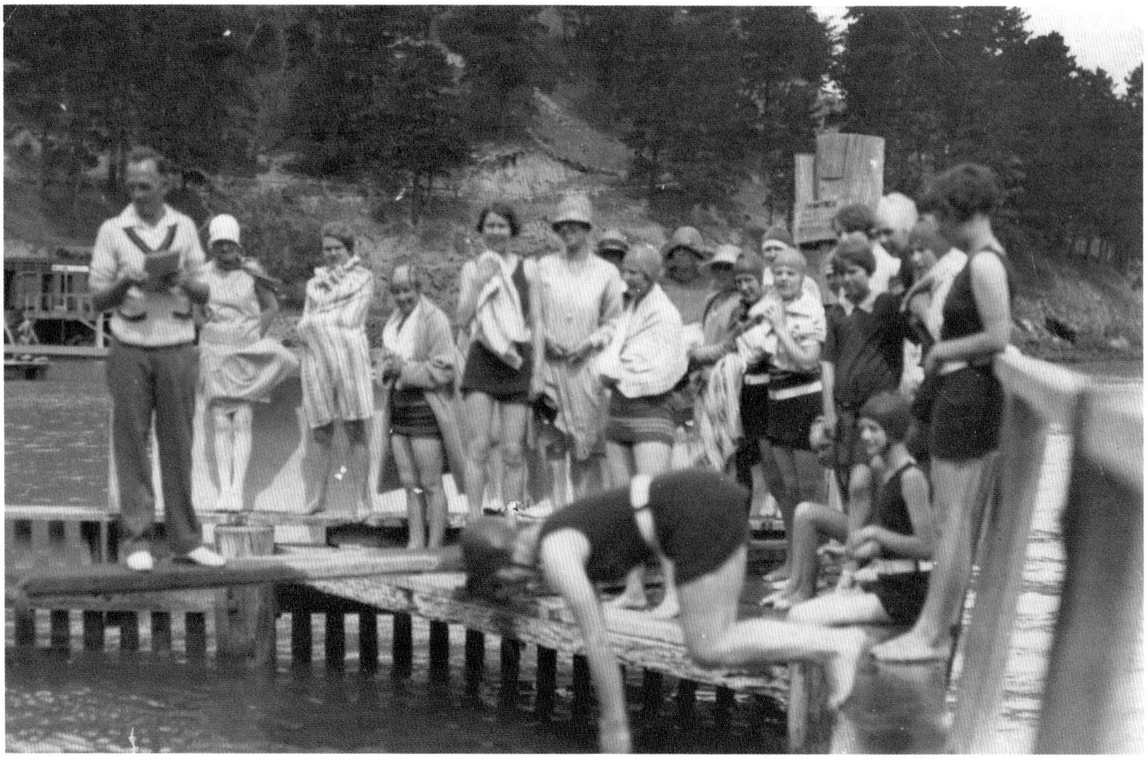

was a suggestion in 1909 that the whole of Corsair Bay be enclosed for swimming, but fishermen complained that they would not be able to land their nets.

No sooner had the men's sheds been built than there were complaints about graffiti and 'foul language'. The walls of the men's dressing shed were covered in 'pencilled filth'. Boys and young men were in the habit of bathing without proper dress at Corsair Bay. The bay was described as a 'hotbed of vice'. Increased vigilance ensured that women and children were largely protected from such behaviour. The only mixed bathing occurred on selected days when a male instructor gave swimming lessons to a number of 'ladies' who 'are clad, if perhaps not all gracefully, at least sufficiently and decently'.[13]

The Lyttelton Ladies' Swimming Club wrote to the borough council requesting shelves in the bathing sheds to accommodate ladies' hats. One councillor remarked that 'very few of the hats now worn would lie on an ordinary shelf'.[14] The council agreed to place a number of hooks in the sheds.

Despite the gender war, the new facilities were extremely popular. The mayor of Lyttelton considered the possibility of running a special 'bath train' from Christchurch. The opening of the swimming season in November was celebrated with a carnival involving swimming races, afternoon tea, and music from the Lyttelton Marine Band playing on board the steamer *Purau*. On behalf of the Christ's College boys and masters, A. E. Flower wrote a letter of thanks for the use of Corsair Bay for the school swimming sports. He compared the bay more than favourably with several English and Australian bathing resorts. *Purau* began a regular launch service to the bay in 1909. In December 1913 the Christchurch *Star* reported that 'of late the traffic has grown to such an extent that motor launches and ferry steamers maintain a fairly constant service'.[15] There was talk of building a new jetty for the steamers. Corsair Bay hosted the Christchurch Rowing Regatta, school swimming sports, an inter-schools boat race, a ladies' swimming club, the Lyttelton Sports Club and many other fixtures.

The bay required constant maintenance to keep it clean of detritus from the sea and humans. One letter to the editor described it as 'the dirtiest-looking and most vile-smelling beach ever I wish to frequent'.[16] In 1918 James Loader was appointed caretaker for the bay, and he supplied visitors with hot water and milk. The following year a raft was secured in the centre of the bay for swimmers. Improvements to the boat landing were proposed, and Orton Bradley donated 100 trees for planting at Corsair Bay and Charteris Bay.

The shark threat surfaced from time to time. A handrail was built along the swimming baths barricade in 1909 to better protect women and children from 'the ravages of the predatory shark'.[17] In December 1912 a shark estimated to be 6–7 feet long was reported in the bathing enclosure. In January the following year the alleged shark was trapped and found to be a 4-foot rig, toothless and

ABOVE Corsair Bay bathers, pre-1930. The three women, from left, are Reta Bundy, Ethel Bundy and Ivy Bundy. The men's changing shed and diving platform are behind, and the jetty is in the distance.
COURTESY OF DAVID BUNDY

BELOW Girls' swimming race at Corsair Bay. The girls may be participating in a school race or may be members of the Lyttelton Ladies' Swimming Club. To help date the image, Una Sinclair (third girl from the left) was born in 1904.
COURTESY OF STEPHEN MCKELVEY

malnourished. One newspaper correspondent suggested that the practice of trawling for flatfish from the Corsair Bay beach and leaving dead fish on the foreshore following a trawl was likely responsible for the presence of the rig. It seemed more likely that someone had placed the fish in the baths as a joke.

By 1920 the *Lyttelton Times* could report that no more delightful spot could be found near Christchurch than Corsair Bay. However, its very popularity was a problem, as the *Press* reported:

> Corsair Bay was crowded, the number there being estimated at 2500, the crowd travelling by launch and on foot to that favourite watering place. The bathing and sanitary accommodation there proved utterly inadequate to meet the requirements of the vast crowd. The heat of the day drove the majority of the holidaymakers into the water, and the bay was black with bathers, many of the younger generation undressing in any available corner.[18]

In a single week in March 1926 Corsair Bay was the destination on consecutive days for 320 pupils from Christ's College, 550 from Boys' High, 600 from Girls' High and 500 from the Technical College for Girls. Schools from outlying areas of Canterbury travelled to picnic at the bay, including Southbridge School, whose 650 pupils arrived in Lyttelton by special train. The fact that the train fare to Lyttelton had not increased, while tram fares to other Christchurch seaside resorts had, further encouraged visits to the harbour.

In 1922 the start of a motor bus service between Lyttelton and Corsair Bay marked the beginning of the end for the ferries. On Sundays the bus would meet the train from Christchurch, making an easy transition at the port for visitors. The following year, changing sheds for boys and girls were added to those for men and women. The Corsair Bay Swimming and Life Saving Club was also formed, and its members were involved in a surprising number of rescues over the years. Children falling into deep water from the swimming bath barricade was a recurring problem. Bernard Demicheli, a launchman employed by Lyttelton Ferry Launches Ltd, dived into the water fully clothed to rescue a schoolboy who had fallen from the Corsair Bay jetty.

Behaviour in the bay continued to be a hot topic. There was debate about the presence of campers and their rowdy and poor behaviour, including young men having women in their tents. The Lyttelton Borough Council struggled to maintain and update facilities. In January 1929 heavy seas caused the collapse of part of a retaining wall and the concrete steps leading down to the beach. Wooden seats were also washed away. Four years later, southerly gales tore decking and railing from the launch jetty. Once again, part of the approach to the jetty was washed out by the sea, and fresh deposits of sand and shingle formed banks nearby. The following year the raft was torn from its moorings and stranded on the beach.

There were problems, too, with men diving from the platform at the men's bathing sheds at low tide when the water was shallower than it appeared. In 1922 a 15-year-old lad dived from the low springboard (about 6 feet in height) into about 2½ feet of water. He was taken from the water unconscious with a serious neck injury. In summer 1930, a young man dived off at low tide and broke his neck. He later died in hospital. A decision was made to extend the platform 30 feet into deeper water by building a ramp and a low-level platform for diving. However, the new springboard broke just after it had been installed when a swimmer 'of rather above the average weight' was making a running dive.[19] Despite signs warning of the danger of diving at low tide, swimmers continued to do just that and sustain spinal injuries as a result.

The southerly storms, to which the bays on the north side of the harbour were exposed, tended to arrive suddenly and with speed. Malcolm Miller's multi-race-winning keel-yacht *Pastime* was anchored in Corsair Bay when a

A busy Corsair Bay in the 1940s. Several yachts are tied up to the men's diving platform.
LYTTELTON MUSEUM, 8003.1

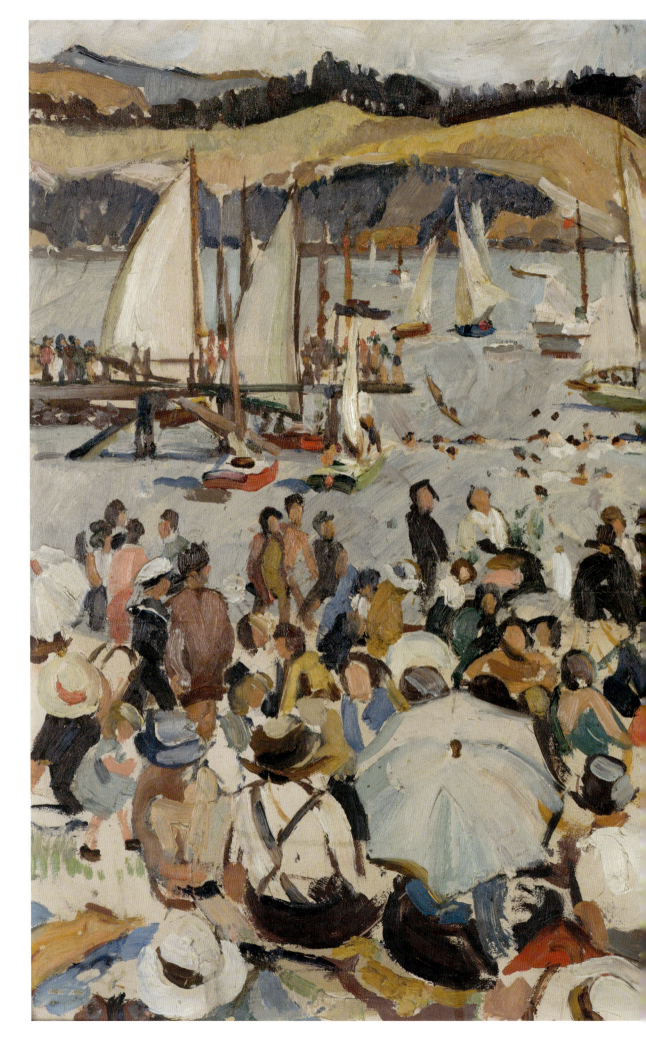

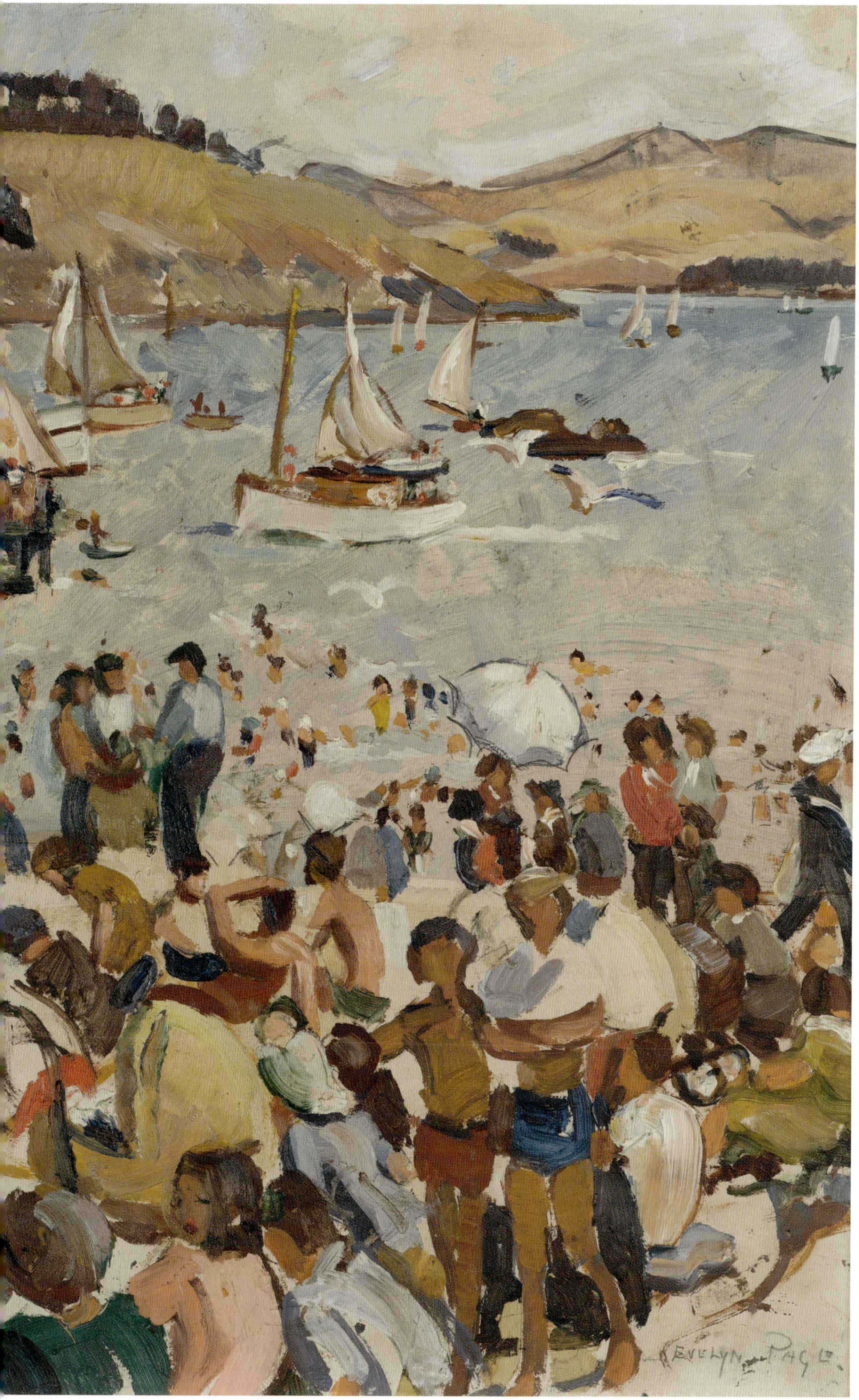
EVELYN PAGE

PREVIOUS PAGES Evelyn Page captured perfectly the popularity of Corsair Bay in this early 1940s painting, *New Year holiday (Corsair Bay)*.
HOCKEN COLLECTIONS, UARE TAOKA O HĀKENA, 73/200

sou'west gale came 'screaming' across the harbour. *Pastime* began to drag its anchor. The crew got it under a small jib and reefed mainsail to take it out of the bay, but it started to drift ashore. After grazing the raft and ripping a plank off it, *Pastime* eventually rammed the stone wall twice with its bowsprit before it could be made fast to the jetty. This was November 1931 and the second race in the Sanders Cup was under way. One yacht was blown ashore, its crew jumping out in time to keep it off the rocks. Another race yacht capsized near the reef, and the crew clung precariously to the upturned boat until rescued by George Andrew's cutter *Mandalay*.[20]

Rivalry between the waning launch services was fierce. In January 1933 competition was so keen that fares were halved, and in at least two instances passengers were carried free. An attempt at 'touting' for passengers from the trains on the railway crossing and in the railway yard was quickly stopped by the Railway Department. This rivalry could have unfortunate consequences. On one occasion two launches were moored at the Corsair Bay jetty. A third launch arrived and requested the others to move and allow him to moor. They refused. To alight, the passengers had to climb over other boats, and in the process one woman slipped and injured her ankle. The incident ended up in court.

Corsair Bay retained its popularity through the years of the Second World War. New piles were driven in the swimming enclosure, and a platform erected on the outside from which to start short-distance swimming races. Two piles were driven further out in the bay for distance swimming races. Obstructions in the water near the raft, responsible for many minor injuries to swimmers, were lifted out using the Harbour Board's pile-driving pontoon. The main obstruction proved to be a large piece of iron plating with several pieces of iron chain attached. This had acted as a mooring many years previously when the bay was used for careening small vessels for cleaning and painting. The Lyttelton Borough Council discussed the possibility of getting assistance from other local bodies for the upkeep of Corsair Bay since it was a facility that belonged to and was used by the whole city. Asking the Christchurch City Council for a grant, which would likely be referred to the Domains Board, would be like trying to get blood out of a stone, according to one borough councillor.

By 1944 the Corsair Bay jetty had been declared unsafe and the Lyttelton Harbour Board decided to demolish and rebuild it at a cost of about £479. The borough council agreed to contribute £50, plus black pine decking and railing from the old Colonists' Hall in Lyttelton. Demolition began in July 1945. It was suggested that the shark-proof enclosure around the 'baths' at the bay be removed, as children sometimes fell from the planking into the sea and the custodian frequently had to prevent boats from mooring at the structure. However, removal was considered to be difficult and costly, requiring the use of a pile-driver. When the Cass Bay abattoir finally closed in 1964, the shark-proof enclosure was removed by Teddington quarry owner Ra Blatchford.

Stephen Estall recalled his first trip to Corsair Bay around 1953:

> The whole day was really exciting for a Christchurch boy, doing things I'd never done before. The first bit of excitement was the train through the tunnel and the sighting of the ships on the other side. A special feeling I still get incidentally, even 65 years later, when I come out of the tunnel and 'hit' Lyttelton. Then, in the early days, there was a launch to Corsair Bay and lots of family fun until the end of the day when the launch took our sunburnt bodies back to Lyttelton. My grandmother loved swimming at Corsair Bay and I think of Nana often on my walks there and the sight of the gently ebbing water.[21]

Today, when recreation options are so much more diverse and widespread, Corsair Bay is a shadow of its former self. The bathing sheds and swimming enclosure are gone, as are most of the picnicking facilities. The domain linking Lyttelton with Corsair Bay has effectively ceased to exist, although a track still winds through the aged pine trees. Passenger ferries have long since ceased calling. But the beautiful sandy beach remains a popular summer attraction and a jetty of sorts is still there, used by families fishing and by walkers on the coastal track.

Corsair Bay Jetty in 2019, with what remains of the men's bathing shed platform centre foreground.
JANE ROBERTSON

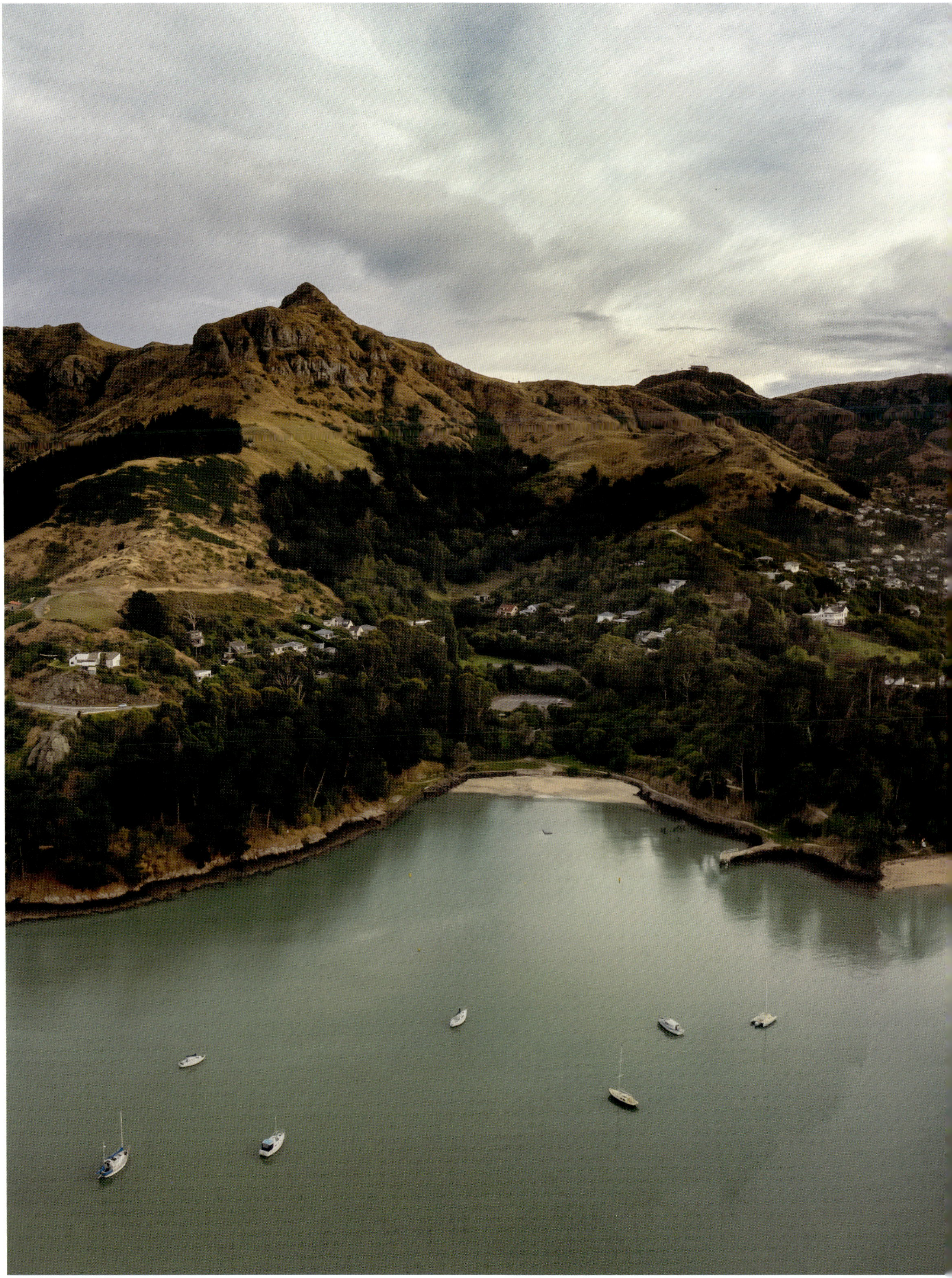

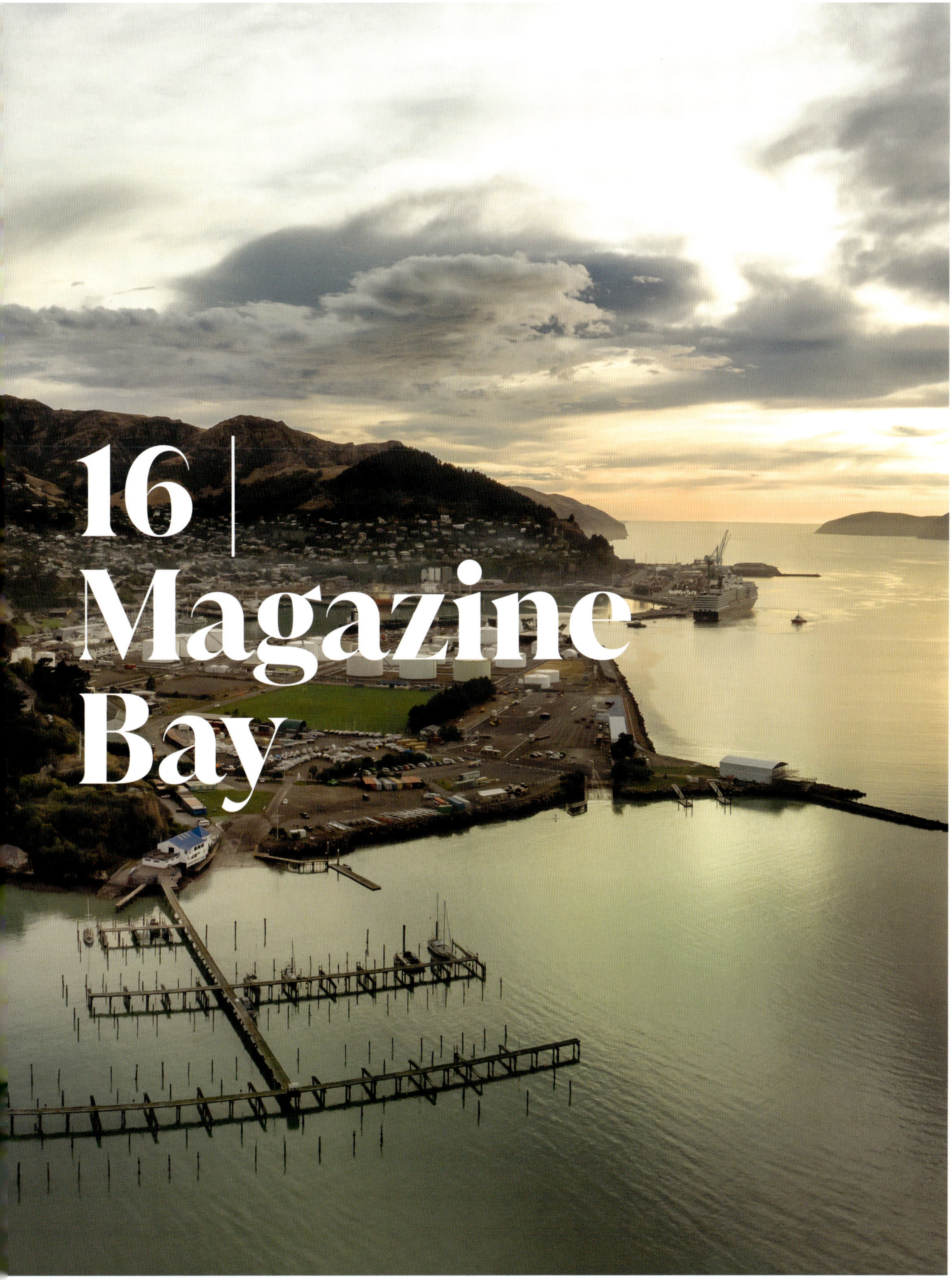

16 | Magazine Bay

Wedged between Motukauatiiti Corsair Bay and much-modified Dampiers Bay on the outskirts of Lyttelton port and township, tiny Magazine Bay is all but invisible from the road, yet punches well above its weight historically. For a good 60 years it was known as Bakers Bay after Charles Baker, who arrived in Lyttelton with his family in 1851 on *Duke of Bronte* and ran sheep and a dairy farm in the bay, supplying milk to the Lyttelton township.

✳

The name Magazine Bay appears only in the first decade of the twentieth century, despite the fact that the powder magazine from which it takes its name was there as early as 1874. The magazine housed explosives for port and road construction and was accessed by means of a stone jetty. At high tide, vessels arriving with large quantities of gunpowder were legally required to land the powder on the jetty and transport it 40 yards to the magazine. A cottage was built on site in 1875 for the magazine caretaker.

Bakers Bay was also used to offload livestock. Whether the presence of the stone jetty encouraged this (or whether it was even permitted to unload animals at a jetty intended for the transport of gunpowder) is unclear. Certainly, before the jetty was built for the magazine, unloading was fairly primitive. In February 1867, seven years before the jetty was built, the SS *Airedale* anchored off Bakers Bay, hauled her cargo of horses up from the hold and put them over the side to swim ashore unassisted. Over 60 horses from some of the best studs in the North Island were landed within a few hours.[1]

In 1874 a letter from the chairman of the Port Victoria Road Board, Thomas Henry Potts, encouraged the Lyttelton Borough Council to extend the 'orphanage Road' out of Lyttelton towards Cass Bay. Given the almost inaccessible steepness of this road, Lyttelton's southern boundary had, for years, been fixed at about Dampiers Bay. A better road, argued Potts, would enable shipwrights to set up businesses in Bakers Bay or Corsair Bay. Houses would follow industry, and the local slaughter yards could be moved to a more distant site. Potts urged the council to consider Bakers Bay as the site for an infirmary, 'where fever-stricken convalescents from the plains would soon drink in health from the pure sea breezes that visit that spot'.[2] He encouraged the development of a recreation ground at Bakers Point, attractively planted in trees and offering access to an excellent bathing place. The infirmary did not go ahead in Bakers Bay, but a recreational domain on the point did.

The bay was one of several sites used by Lyttelton resident John Grubb for his shipbuilding business. Early photos show a boatshed, slipways and boatbuilding activity. In January 1878 the Lyttelton Harbour Board discussed strengthening Grubb's slip at Bakers Bay so that it could take the harbour dredge for repair work. This prompted the chairman of the harbour board to suggest that it was time to build a graving dock. Grubb's tender of £130 for putting the dredge on his slip was accepted. Even getting a boat from Grubb's slip back to the port could be challenging in the unpredictable harbour seas. At one point the schooner *Zior* was being towed by a steam launch following repair work at Bakers Bay. Once out of the bay, *Zior* caught the full force of the southerly wind and sea and was driven towards the rocks, beyond the control of the launch. The tug *Lyttelton* came to the rescue.

Among other government responses to a perceived Russian threat in the Pacific in the 1880s, four second-class spar torpedo boats were ordered from Chiswick-based J. I. Thornycroft & Co. at the considerable cost of £3150 each. In May 1884 *Defender* (for Lyttelton's defence) and *Taiaroa* (for Port Chalmers') arrived in Port Chalmers. Eight months later *Defender* was towed to Lyttelton by the government steamship *Stella*. However, in a portent of things to come, there were no facilities to house the boat.

The following year a 5-acre military reserve was gazetted at Bakers Bay. A corrugated-iron-clad shed and an iron-rail slipway with a wheeled iron cradle were built for *Defender* (plus the two other torpedo boats whose arrival in Lyttelton was anticipated). Lieutenant Colonel Alexander Lean, commander of the Canterbury

This photo from the mid-1920s shows the 1874 magazine with its jetty and, above and to the left, the caretaker's house and garden. The Erskine Point Battery was sited at the end of the ridge above the buildings. Charles Moir, who was the caretaker for many years, was an excellent gardener.
CHRISTCHURCH CITY LIBRARIES, 2632

Crowded and busy Bakers Bay (now Magazine Bay) in 1897. The *Croydon Lass* is shown on John Grubb's slipway. Centre foreground is Grubb's workshop.
CHRISTCHURCH CITY LIBRARIES, PHOTOCD10, IMG0039

Volunteer District, then asked John Grubb to remove his boatbuilding workshop and slip. The Lyttelton Harbour Board rallied behind Grubb, arguing that he should be compensated for any move but that, in fact, it was the torpedo boat that really belonged in a different berth inside the harbour moles, especially given that it could not be launched from Bakers Bay for days at a time on account of the weather. Grubb's business remained in the bay for some time to come, in later years run by son James.

A visit to tiny Magazine Bay today reveals a hidden jewel of a swimming beach. Despite activity just around the corner at the Naval Point Club, the bay is very quiet and it is difficult to imagine that it once housed, simultaneously, the magazine and attached jetty, Grubb's boatbuilding shed and slipway and the torpedo boat shed with its slipway.

In 1885, at the height of the Russian scare, a 6-inch breech-loading gun was established on Erskine Point (known to Māori as Tapoa) above the magazine building, and the magazine was taken over by the military to store ammunition for the gun. This was to be a practice gun for the Armed Constabulary, commanding the entrance to the port between the breakwaters. Targets were set up on the nearby reef, 850 yards distant, and on Quail Island, 2500 yards from the battery. Prisoners from the Lyttelton Gaol upgraded the battery in 1891 when a 7-inch muzzle-loader was installed and a gunner's cottage added. There was also a house for a caretaker, occupied for many years by Charles Moir and his family. Joy Thompson, Moir's granddaughter, remembers visiting her grandfather at Magazine Bay. Soldiers were stationed at the white gates on the Lyttelton–Governors Bay road, and the family had to give a password before they could be escorted through the gate and down to the house. According to Joy, her grandfather always carried a bunch of keys with him and wore a whistle as a precaution against possible interference.

A group of five men from the Torpedo Corps, formed in 1886 and trained in the use of mines, was responsible for maintaining the torpedo boat and associated facilities and for training volunteer recruits. The New Zealand Maritime Record notes *Defender* as

> something of a curiosity. With a length of 63 feet, she was only 7ft 6in in the beam and her displacement was twelve tons. Steam power was provided by a locomotive boiler to a single engine of 173 horsepower. She had two funnels side by side and a conning tower with quarter inch bulletproof plating to protect the coxswain. *Defender* was originally capable of steaming at 17½ knots over a measured mile; a high speed for those days. The boat was equipped with a 36-foot spar tipped with a gun cotton charge, which projected over the bow of the vessel and would be exploded on the side of a ship below the water line. A Nordenfelt gun was also fitted.[3]

Curiosity aside, the story of the torpedo boat is really one of indecision, mismanagement, incompetence and neglect.[4] The shed and slip, as designed, were almost completed when, according to the *Star* newspaper, a bungle occurred in the plans and the sea-end of the slip was found to be high and dry. The slip, which was 'so steep it imperilled the vessel's launch in anything less than calm seas',[5] had to be extended by an additional 90 feet.[6] *Defender* ended up spending most of

Torpedo boat *Defender* being taken through its paces in Lyttelton Harbour, c.1890s, with Ōtamahua Quail Island in the background. *Defender* was purchased as part of New Zealand's defence against a perceived Russian threat to the Pacific.
CANTERBURY MUSEUM, J. J. KINSEY COLLECTION, 1940.193.2

its service career moored in the inner harbour near the dry dock.

In March 1886 Rear Admiral R. A. E. Scott, honorary commodore of the Naval Artillery Volunteers, arrived to inspect the Lyttelton Naval Volunteers and was taken out on the harbour in *Defender*. According to the *Lyttelton Times* reporter the boat's engines were so rusty that she could only muster 12 knots. 'The boat is only brought out once in three months, or thereabouts, and consequently a valuable piece of machinery is not in gear when wanted. The engines were in no order whatever . . .'[7] The reporter also commented on the design and placement of the slip: 'The Admiral's inspection was to have been made on Saturday, but there was a slight swell, and the boat could not therefore leave the slip.'

In an even more scathing article two days later, the author suggested inviting tenders for a gigantic placard to be painted on Godley Head announcing: 'To Russians and all others whom it may concern. Hostile parties wishing to shell the Port of Lyttelton are requested to time their visit for fine weather, otherwise they cannot be fittingly received by the local authorities.'[8]

The following year *Defender* collided with a Lyttelton wharf, damaging its stern-post, stern hull plates, woodwork and propeller shaft. The propeller itself was lost. The complete unsuitability of the torpedo boat location was confirmed in April 1895 when a severe easterly gale washed away 40 feet of John Grubb's slipway in Bakers Bay and caused the torpedo boat slip to twist and work in the heavy run 'like a huge sea serpent'.[9]

Defender was never much more than an expensive showpiece, impressing locals in Lyttelton's 1885 regatta by, when the opportunity allowed, tearing through the water at about 18 knots. There is no evidence the vessel was ever armed, and the Naval Volunteers much preferred working with the artillery. Outmoded and neglected, the torpedo boat was decommissioned in 1896. Later, Lyttelton steam launch proprietor Mark Thomas bought the boat and salvaged its engines, boilers, machinery and military hardware, dumping the remaining hulk on Pūrau beach. There the boat remained, a curiosity and a plaything for children, until 1959, when the remains were apparently broken up and bulldozed into a number of shallow pits by the Mount Herbert County Council.

In 1996 Allandale resident and local historian David Bundy was tasked by the community-based charitable trust Project Port Lyttelton with recovering the remains of *Defender*. Using a 1958 aerial photograph of Pūrau beach, Bundy was assisted by a team of New Zealand Army mine-detecting specialists. In 1998 the remains were found scattered over a 10 by 30 metre area, and then taken to Lyttelton. Today the restored *Defender* can be viewed, complete with a spar torpedo, in the Thornycroft Torpedo Boat Museum, on the site of the former magazine.[10] The museum, open on Sunday afternoons, is well worth a visit.

The battery was abandoned after 1905, when the gun was declared obsolete.

RIGHT Ten-year-old Clive Goodenough sitting on the conning tower of *Defender*'s discarded hulk, Pūrau Beach, c.1950.
THORNYCROFT TORPEDO BOAT MUSEUM, LYTTELTON

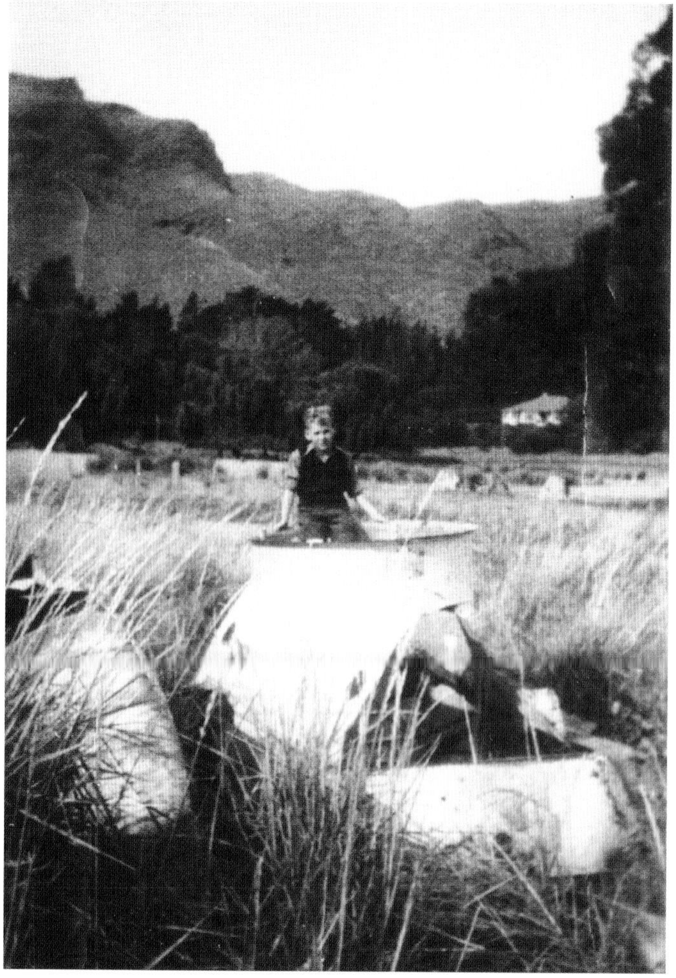

BELOW An aerial view of Lyttelton Port and the nearly completed Naval Point reclamation, 1923. The reclamation significantly altered the relationship of Magazine Bay and the shoreline to its immediate west. Between Ōtamahua Quail Island and the reclaimed area is the reef known to Māori as Kamautaurua.
ARCHIVES NEW ZEALAND, ARC/831

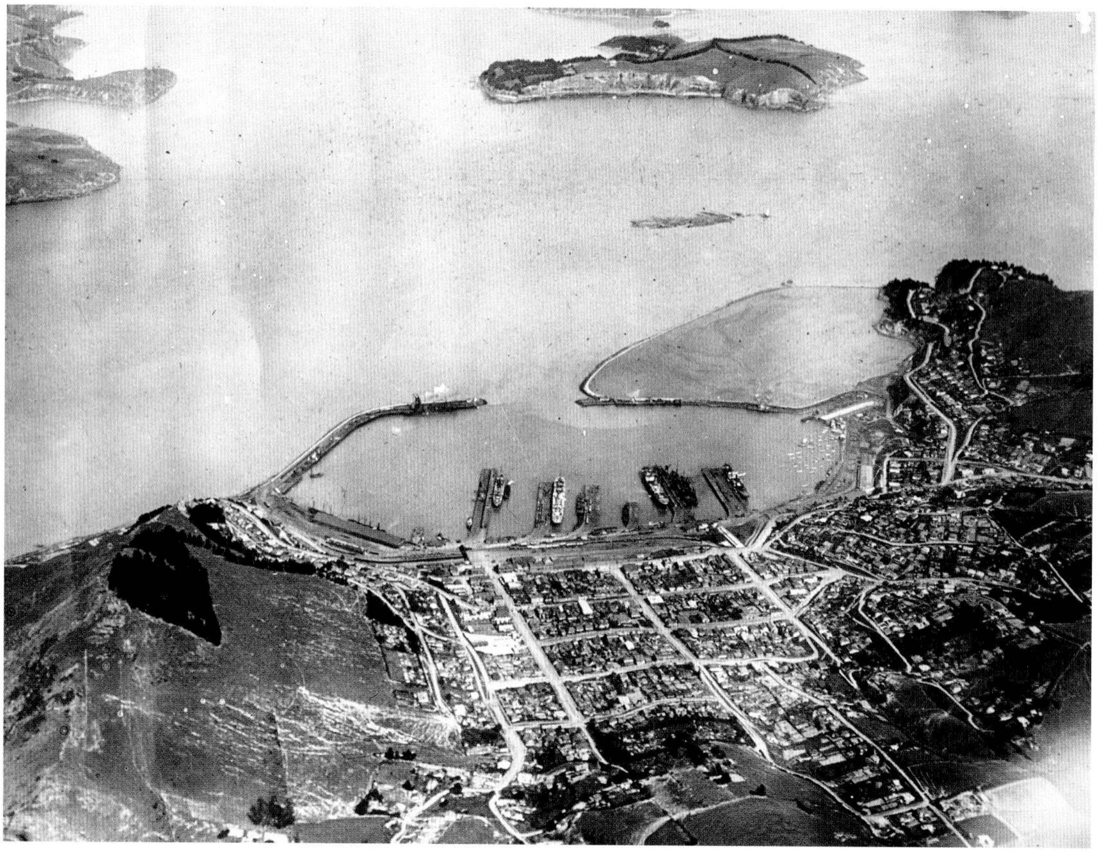

In 1934 it was cut up for scrap, and the barrel was tipped over the cliff; later it was rescued and rejuvenated, to be housed at TS *Cornwall* in Redcliffs before finally moving to the Ashburton RSA in 2016. The military reserve reverted to local council control in 1984 and is known as the Magazine Bay Recreation Reserve.

By the first decade of the twentieth century the port of Lyttelton had most definitely outgrown the confines of Erskine Bay. Christchurch businessmen complained about the high rail charges to the port and the increase in wharfage charges to pay for the new dredging programme. The idea of a port at Heathcote and a canal into Christchurch had been gaining favour since the 1880s. In the end, cost, and the problems associated with a river as opposed to a deep-water port, scuppered the proposed plans. Also rejected was Lyttelton MP George Laurenson's idea of reclaiming the area between Quail Island and Head of the Bay (Teddington), using spoil from harbour dredging, to create almost 2000 acres of flat land for expansion. The idea of further reclamation on either side of Erskine Bay was taken up instead, but not before a letter to the *Press* made the somewhat audacious suggestion of removing the portion of the Port Hills between Heathcote Valley and Lyttelton and using the excavated material for reclamation works in the harbour and estuary.

The 72-acre reclamation at Naval Point began in 1909 with the building of a protective embankment from the western end of the mole. The work, expected to take five years, was eventually completed in eight. Suitable stone was hard to come by and, once in place, suffered from subsidence (up to 40 feet at one point) and from the battering of southerly storms. No sooner had breakwater work begun than, in December 1909, a southerly gale washed away weeks of accumulated stone and rubble. The pathway around the cliffs to the Lyttelton Domain was interrupted by the quarrying operations that provided stone for the breakwater. Walkers still struggled around the quarry face on what was left of the path, in danger of falling rock loosened by the blasting above. In 1919 the harbour board agreed to reimburse the Lyttelton Borough Council for the cost of reinstating the pathway.

The Lyttelton waterfront was changing. An early swimming beach at Dampiers Bay had already been lost to reclamation in the early 1880s. Swimming facilities were then built at Sandy Bay in 1885, including a bathing shed with eight compartments and a freshwater shower, a breakwater and shark-proof enclosure, an access path and a caretaker's cottage. The beach was popular with Lyttelton locals. In 1913, however, the suction dredge *Canterbury* began dumping spoil behind the newly created embankment, and the beach at Sandy Bay was lost. Industrial gains came instead

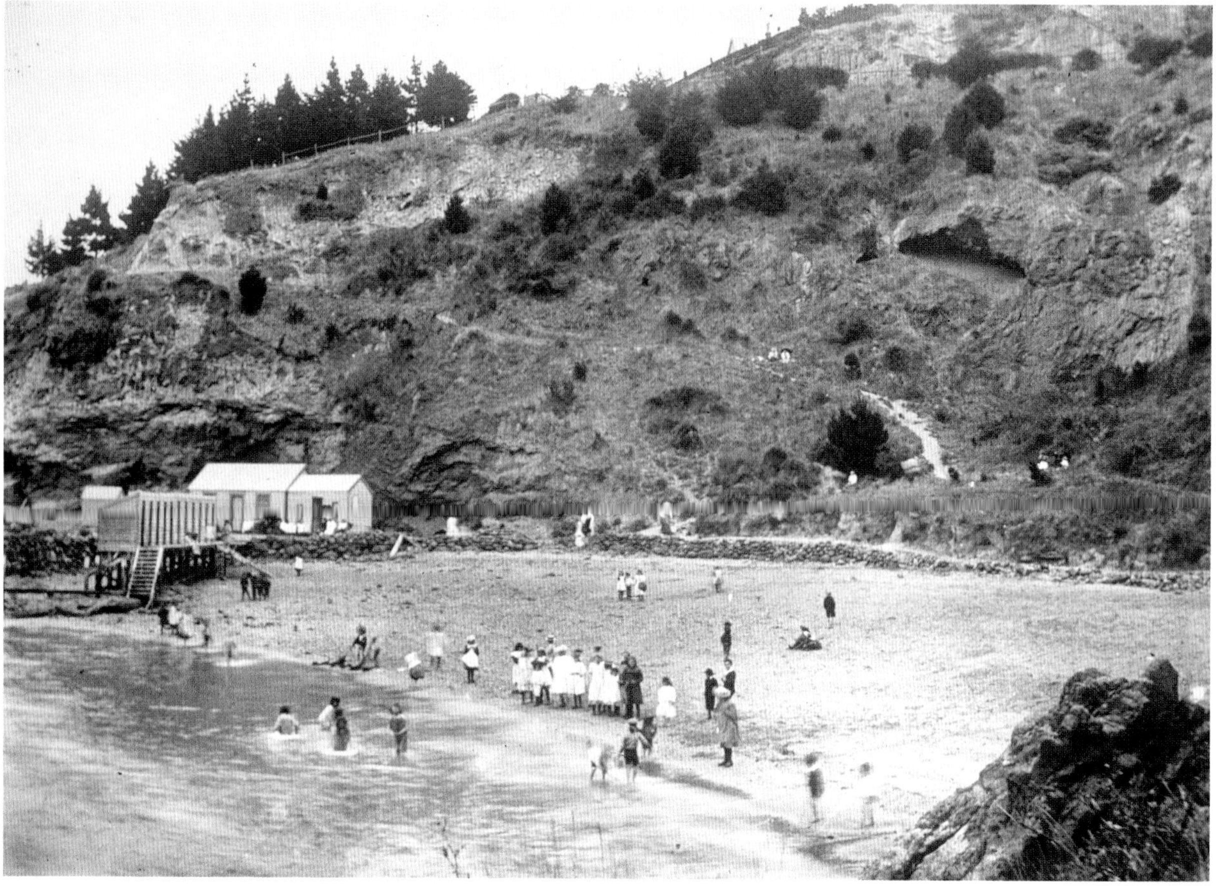

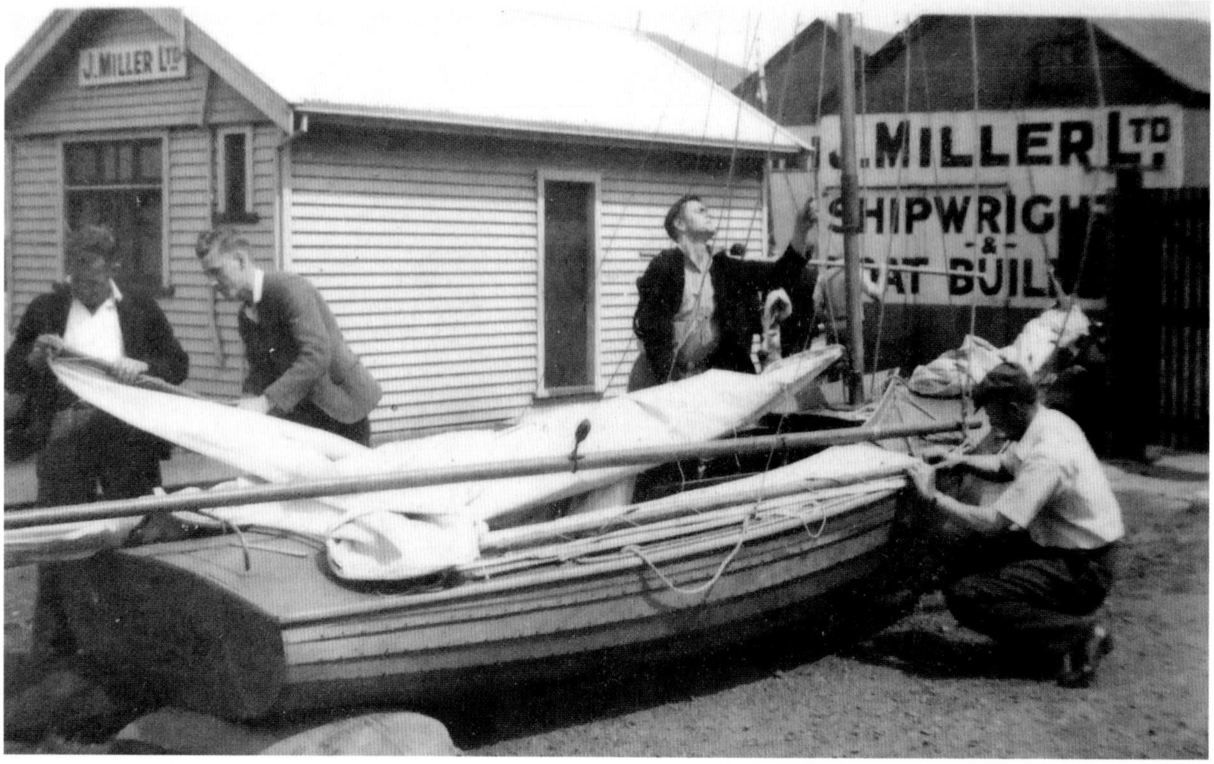
J. MILLER LTD
J. MILLER LTD
SHIPWRIGH
&

in the form of roads, railway sidings, and steel storage tanks for oil companies Vacuum Oil and British Imperial Oil. The relationship of Bakers/Magazine Bay to the town and port of Lyttelton was significantly changed as a result.

The notion of a boat harbour was raised at various times from about 1919 onwards. The Lyttelton Harbour Board was anxious about the room taken up in the inner harbour by yacht and motor-boat moorings. 'Probably never since the old days when the cutters, ketches and schooners used to race, has sailing been so popular in Lyttelton as it is now,'[11] observed the *Press*. Boatbuilding was flourishing, with the Miller and Whitford sheds occupying the waterfront adjacent to the graving dock. The Canterbury Yacht and Motor Boat Club (CYMBC), re-formed in 1921 after a hiatus during the First World War, built a clubhouse over the shore adjacent to the Miller boatsheds. A slipway with two trolleys on rails, built by the Lyttelton Harbour Board in 1928, led steeply to the water at the west end of the clubhouse. Once boats were landed, they had to be carried across the railway lines and stored clear of the tracks. Room for expansion was very limited.

The beginning of George Brasell's yachting career coincided with the re-formation of the CYMBC. As a 14-year-old schoolboy, George took on young sailors from Auckland and Dunedin in the first National Youth Contest, held in Dunedin in 1926. Sailing 12-foot Takapunas, and much to everyone's surprise, George Brasell and Hubie Norris took out the Cornwall Cup for Lyttelton. As George later recalled:

> Looking back, it is hard to realise how primitive our yachting was. We had no resin-bonded plywood or stainless steel. Our yachts were built out of solid kauri and fittings were mostly hand made. Sails were made from cotton material and usually had the flow in the leech instead of the luff.[12]

ABOVE Sandy Bay (c.1890s in this photo) was a popular bathing beach for Lytteltonians prior to its incorporation in the Naval Point reclamation. Bakers Bay/Magazine Bay was just round the corner to the left.
ARCHIVES NEW ZEALAND, ARC/815

BELOW Sanders Cup winner George Brasell with *Venus* outside Miller's boatbuilding shed, Lyttelton, 1930s.
NAVAL POINT CLUB ARCHIVES

Without international competitions, the hotly contested Sanders Cup was the premier contest for New Zealand sailors, drawing spectators from all around the country. (Today, it remains the country's oldest sailing trophy.)

In 1931 Lyttelton Harbour Board engineer Percy Fryer reported that there were only two sites in the harbour that could realistically be considered for a boat harbour: Diamond Harbour and Magazine Bay. The latter, with a breakwater extending 1900 feet out from the reclamation mole and 700 feet out from the western point of the bay, was Fryer's preferred option. The harbour board rejected the proposal on the basis of cost. The pressure continued, no doubt compounded by the establishment of the Banks Peninsula Cruising Club (BPCC) in 1932. The new club needed a base in the inner harbour, at the very least to provide for a dinghy shelter, lockers, storage, wash room and committee room. Coincidentally the Lyttelton Rowing Club went into recess, and the BPCC bought and adapted their building, which had its own floating ramp, thus solving the dinghy-launching problem. In 1937 the harbour master reported that 'every available mooring at Dampiers Bay, on the western side of the inner harbour, is occupied and there is a waiting list'.[13]

The question of a boat harbour was discussed at a special general meeting of the BPCC in March 1938. An area of 6 to 10 acres dredged out of the reclaimed land was proposed and rejected by the Lyttelton Harbour Board as unsuitable and impractical. Pūrau, as suggested by the harbour board, was considered by many club members to be an impossible place to moor in a nor'westerly.[14] Meanwhile, the CYMBC gradually migrated southwards across the reclaimed area. In 1956 the area where the Naval Point Club now stands was leased from the Lyttelton Borough Council. A large rocky point was levelled, a clubhouse built in 1957 and a slipway into Magazine Bay constructed by club volunteers. In 1960 the harbour board built a jetty for the club. This is one of the few coastal sites in Christchurch where boats can be launched in all tides.

Two years later, the Lyttelton Harbour Board presented to Parliament the Loan and Empowering Bill 1962, which, among other things, provided for a small craft (fishing fleet and pleasure craft) harbour at Magazine Bay. The cost would be around £400,000. Perhaps the cost was regarded as prohibitive because in 1964 the harbour board proposed to lay 270 yacht moorings in Pūrau. Governors Bay and Cass Bay were also considered, but the former would require extensive and expensive dredging and reclamation, and the latter could not accommodate club buildings and facilities because it was zoned residential.

In 1972 the BPCC, through a slow accumulation of funds and thousands of hours of voluntary labour, finally got the clubhouse it had longed for. The Peter Bevan-designed building, which received a New Zealand Institute of Architects award and was listed as a notable building by the Banks Peninsula District Council, stood out on the waterfront, adjacent to Miller's boatbuilding in what is now Te Ana Marina. In November 1999 the Lyttelton Port Company summarily demolished the building, without notice or compensation, to free up more flat land in the western inner harbour. This move was much criticised by local residents.

It wasn't until 1981 that the long-discussed Magazine Bay Marina finally took shape. The marina took the Lyttelton Harbour Board 12 months to construct at a cost of $750,000. The design, developed in the United States, featured a 300-metre-long floating breakwater made from 33,000 old tyres filled with polyurethane foam and chained together in pods. The initial provision was for 74 berths, with allowance to increase the facility to a maximum of 345 berths.[15] Many prospective boat owners refused to purchase a mooring because of what they considered to be

Launching from the Canterbury Yacht and Motor Boat Club slipway built in 1952 on land leased from the Lyttelton Harbour Board.
NAVAL POINT CLUB ARCHIVES

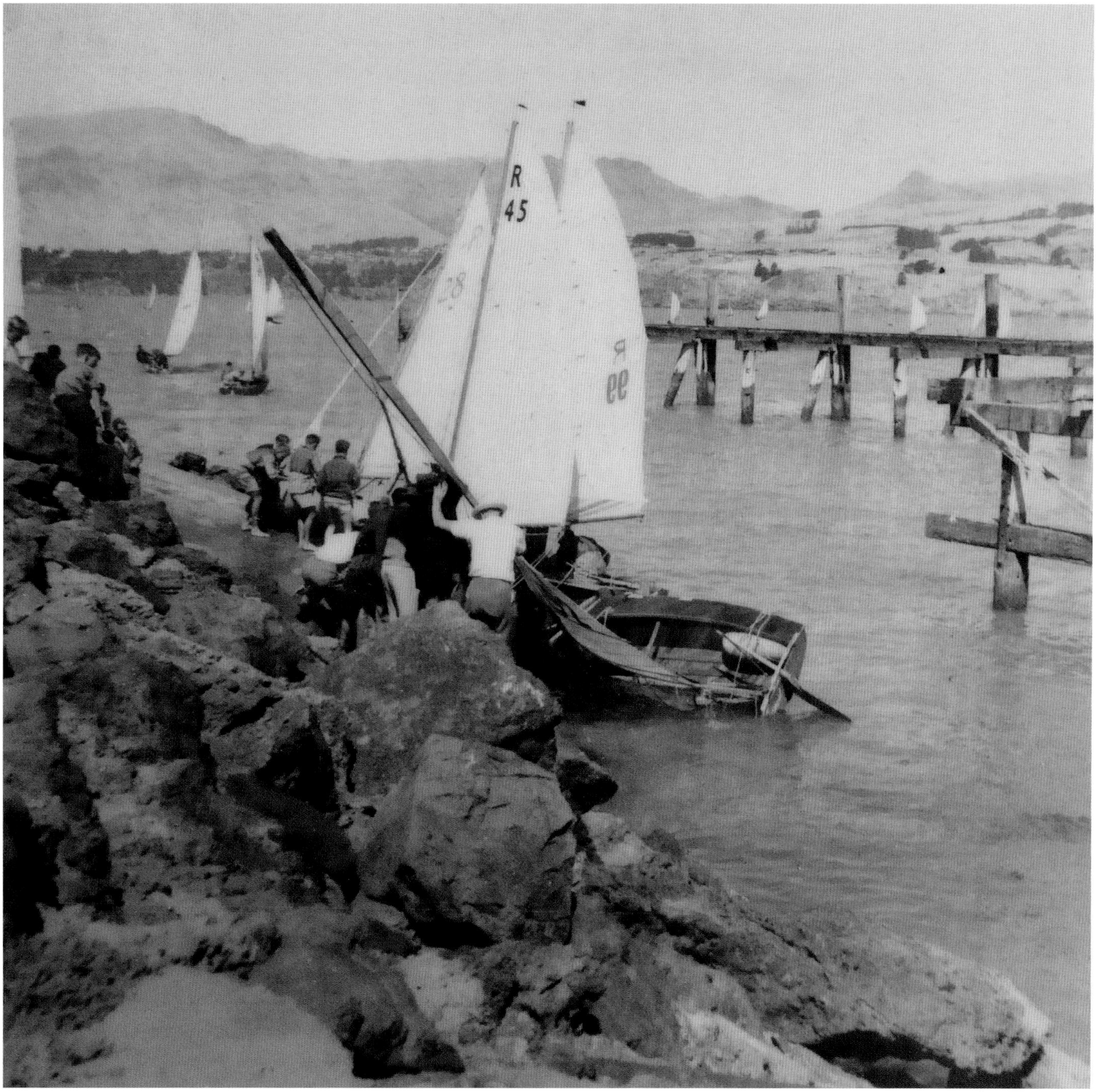
R
45
28
R
99

the exorbitant cost for an unnecessarily fancy development. Others warned of the danger from southerly storms and argued for an inner harbour marina — which the Port Company was resisting because it was under pressure to develop cool-store facilities for the fishing industry. The new marina opened in 1982. Although it worked reasonably well, the floating breakwater did not offer sufficient protection from southerly gales or extreme events.

In 1987 the Port Companies Act required harbour boards around the country to relinquish all non-commercial activities, and jurisdiction over the Magazine Bay Marina passed to the Banks Peninsula District Council. Ten years later the council approved a rebuild, and in June 1999 the floating tyre breakwater was removed and a new concrete and polystyrene structure, designed to accommodate 238 berths, was assembled at much greater expense. On 10 October 2000 the Lyttelton Yacht Marina was sold to a local syndicate for $3.3 million.

Two days later, a fierce southerly storm wrecked the new breakwater and created havoc in the marina. The floating breakwaters of polystyrene coated in concrete disintegrated, littering the harbour. Walkways buckled and broke up. Yachts were torn from moorings and dashed against marina structures and each other. Thirty-two vessels sank. These, noted the *Press*, included '*Argo*, which was scuttled by firemen to prevent it damaging other vessels; *Alchemy*, which was pummelled to bits between a floating jetty and a walkway; the classic cruiser *Waikiri* and Banks Peninsula Cruising Club commodore Brian Weenink's $130,000 vessel *Simply Irresistible*'.[16] Another vicious storm in 2010 sank two more vessels. Wind gusts of up to 111 km/h caused waves described by one young eyewitness as 'humungous'.

Years of litigation and inaction followed. Many yacht owners chose to take their boats out of the harbour for safer mooring in other bays or other regions. There was, lamented the *Press*, a disenchantment with boating 'for the young and old, the well-heeled and poor, who'd poured love into stone and steel and wood, and dreamt of going to the islands or teaching their kids to sail or pottering around in boats'.[17]

The Canterbury Yacht and Motor Boat Club and Banks Peninsula Cruising Club amalgamated in 2001 to form the Naval Point Club. Following the Canterbury earthquakes, and the decision to further extend the port eastwards beyond Cashin Quay and into Te Awaparahi Bay, the Lyttelton Port Company initiated the development of a new floating-berth, inner-harbour marina. Te Hapū o Ngāti Wheke gifted the name Te Ana to the former Dampiers Bay area, reflecting the significance of Te Ana o Huikai, a bay just beyond the dry dock. The bay had been a sheltered rest area for journeying waka, with a plentiful supply of fish and shellfish, much used by chief Huikai on his journeys to and from Koukourārata Port Levy. The new marina's three piers rest on 226 steel piles embedded at a depth of between 9 and 15 metres. All the berths are supplied with power and water, making life much easier for those who live permanently on their boats.

The promenade at Te Ana Marina means the public can once again access the waterfront in the inner harbour. Stylised paving patterns reflect te aramoana ('the pathway of the sea'), and patterns of stylised zig-zag waves echo those on the wharenui Wheke at Rāpaki Marae, with a chevron pattern representing the reef shark. A public gathering and play area represents a landing beach and coastal edge near where the historic coastal edge used to be.[18] Whakairo by Caine Tauwhare from the Whakaraupō Carving Centre acknowledge the history and values associated with Te Ana o Huikai and Whakaraupō.

Also reflecting Māori heritage, waka ama (outrigger canoes) are used frequently on the harbour, for general recreation and in training for competition. Te Waka Pounamu Outrigger Canoe Club is based at Naval Point. Waka taua (war canoes)

In October 2000 a fierce southerly storm wrecked the new breakwater at Magazine Bay and 32 boats in the marina sank.
NAVAL POINT CLUB ARCHIVES

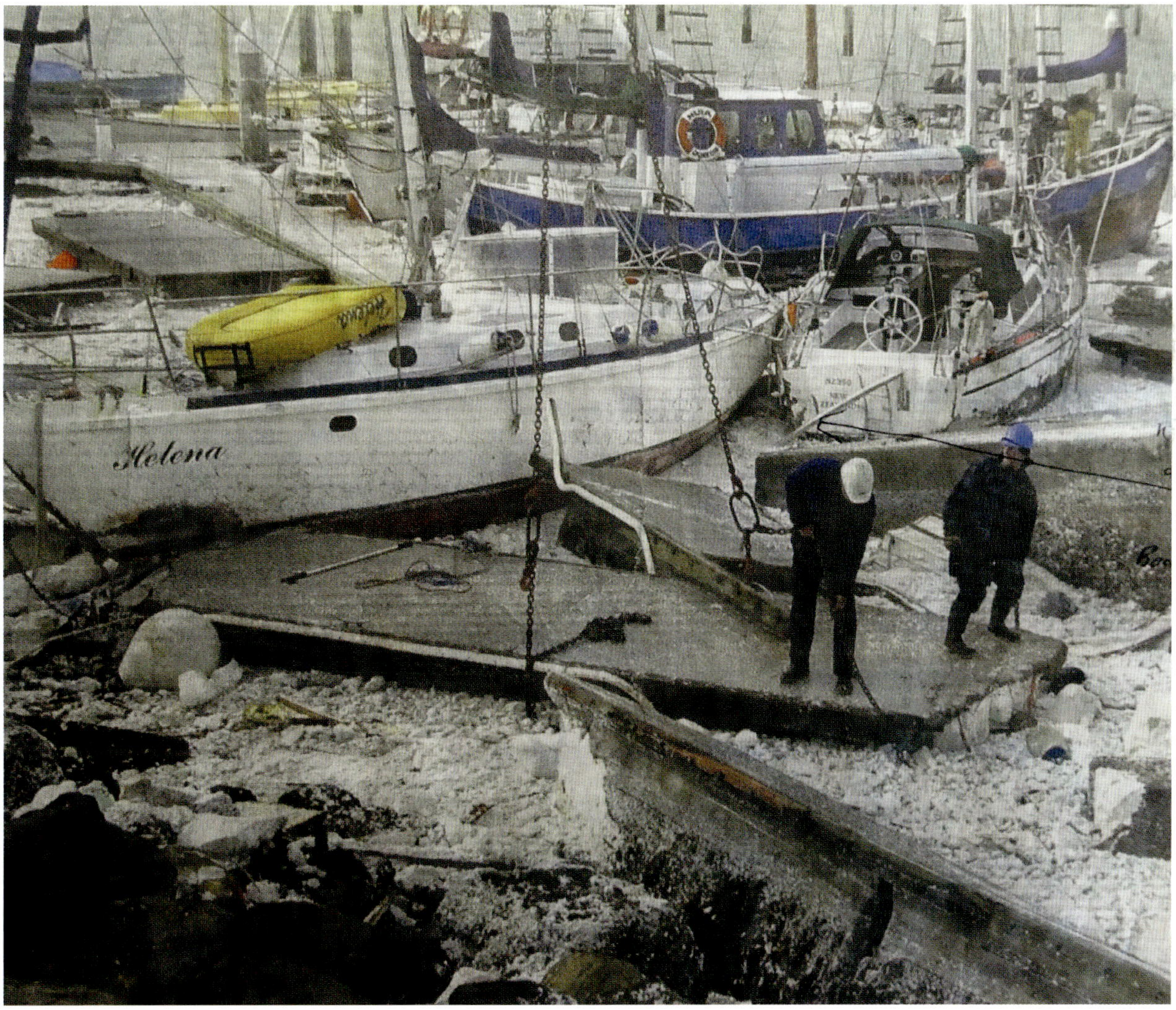
Helena

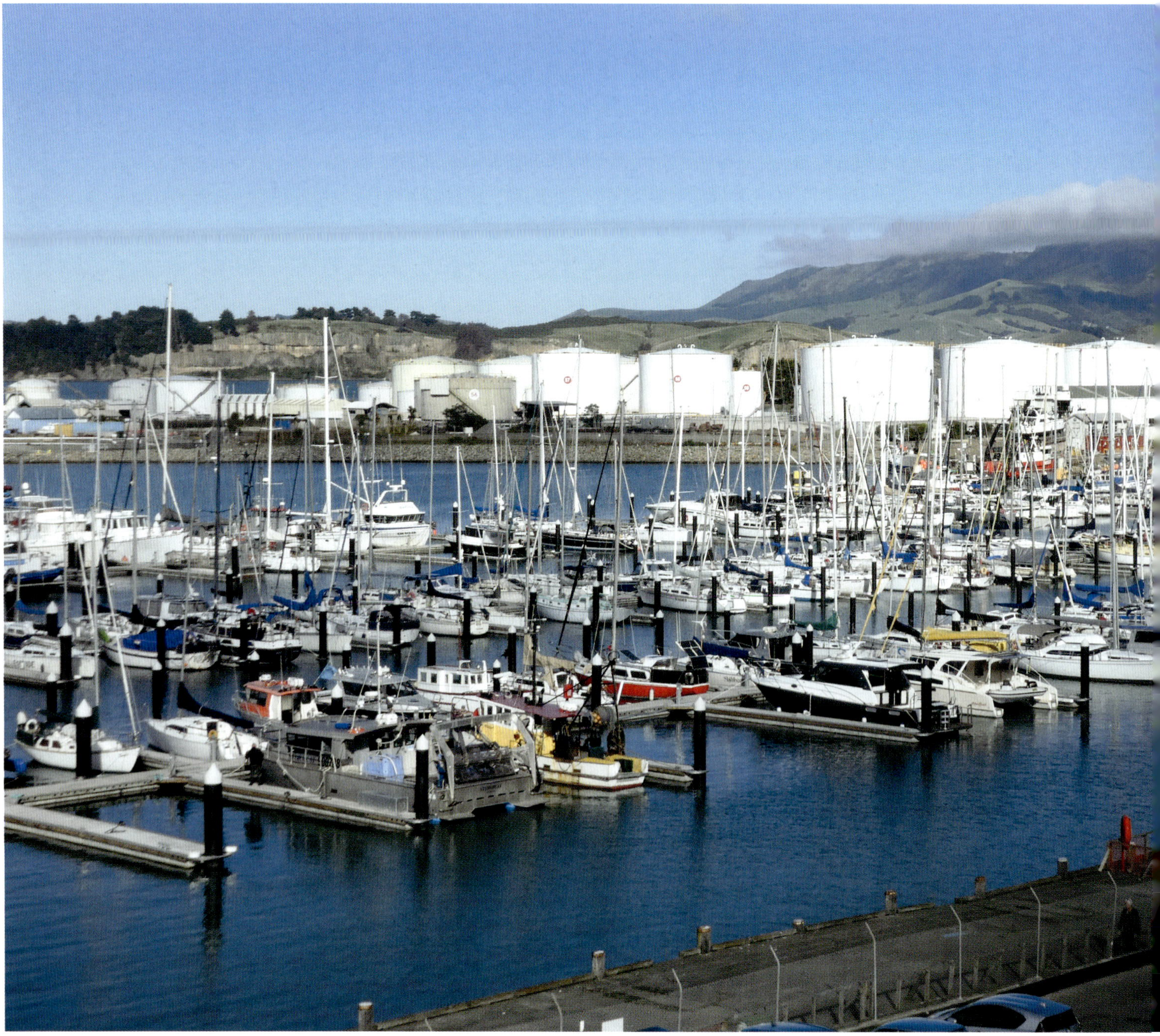

and waka unua (sailing canoes) may become more frequent sights with the ongoing revitalisation of waka culture around the Pacific, in Aotearoa and in Te Waipounamu.

Most recently, and as a precursor to the redevelopment of the foreshore area at Te Nukutai o Tapoa Naval Point,[19] the Christchurch City Council, with help from the Lyttelton Port Company, removed 52 concrete piles that had remained in place after the damage to the marina in 2000. The removal opened up the space leading to the Naval Point Club boat ramps, making the area safer for boaties. The city council has set aside $10.6 million for redevelopment work and sought public input into its plans.

Magazine Bay is yet another reminder that our best endeavours, and most advanced technology, can be thwarted by the forces of nature. As residents of the harbour have come to understand over the centuries, the relationship between land and sea in Whakaraupō is both productive and destructive.

Following storm damage to the Lyttelton Yacht Marina in October 2000 and the Canterbury earthquakes of 2010/11, the Lyttelton Port Company developed a new floating-berth inner-harbour marina. Te Ana Marina is set between two traditional sites, Ōhinehou and Te Ana o Huikai, in what was once known as Dampier Bay.
JANE ROBERTSON

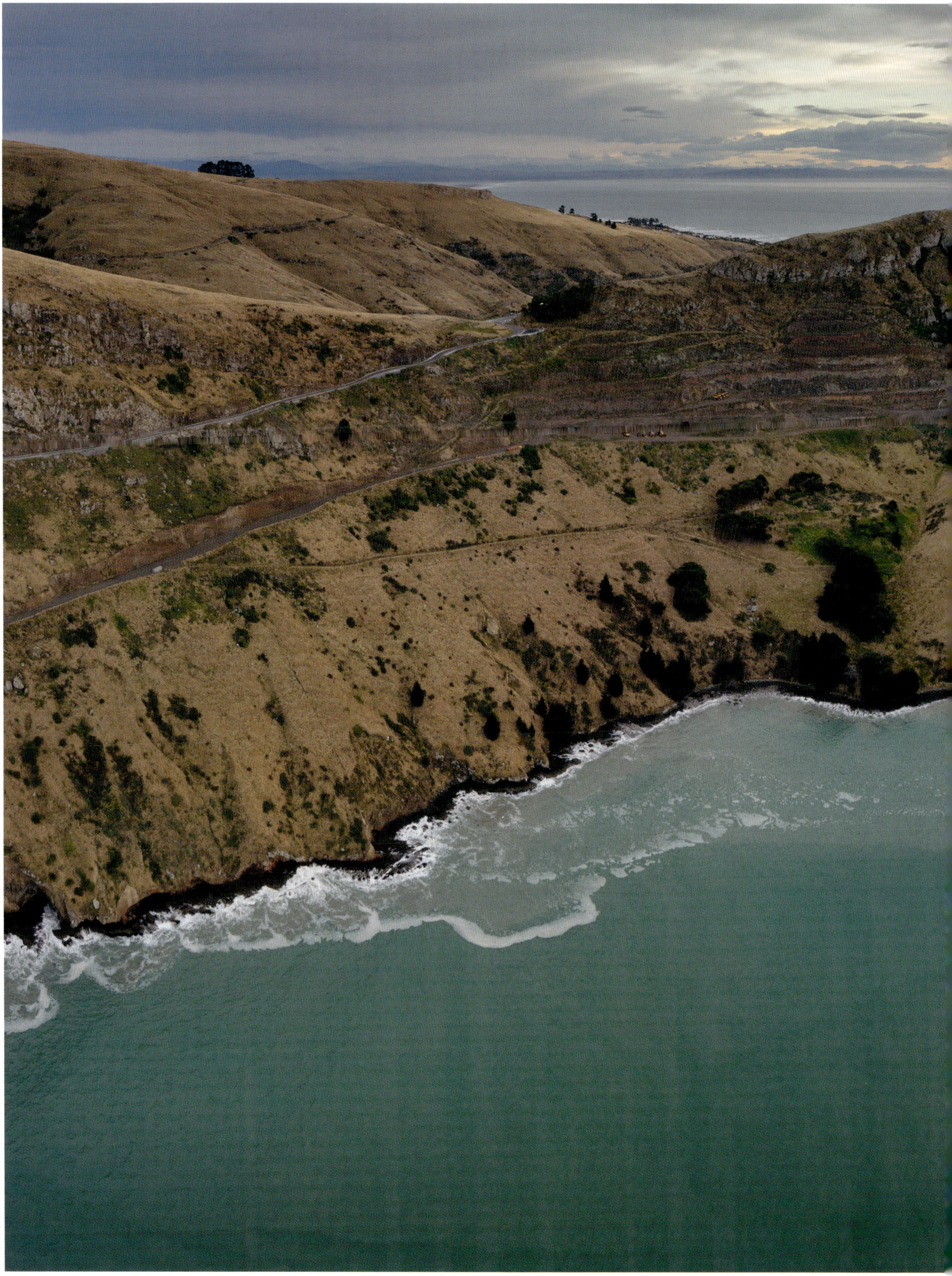

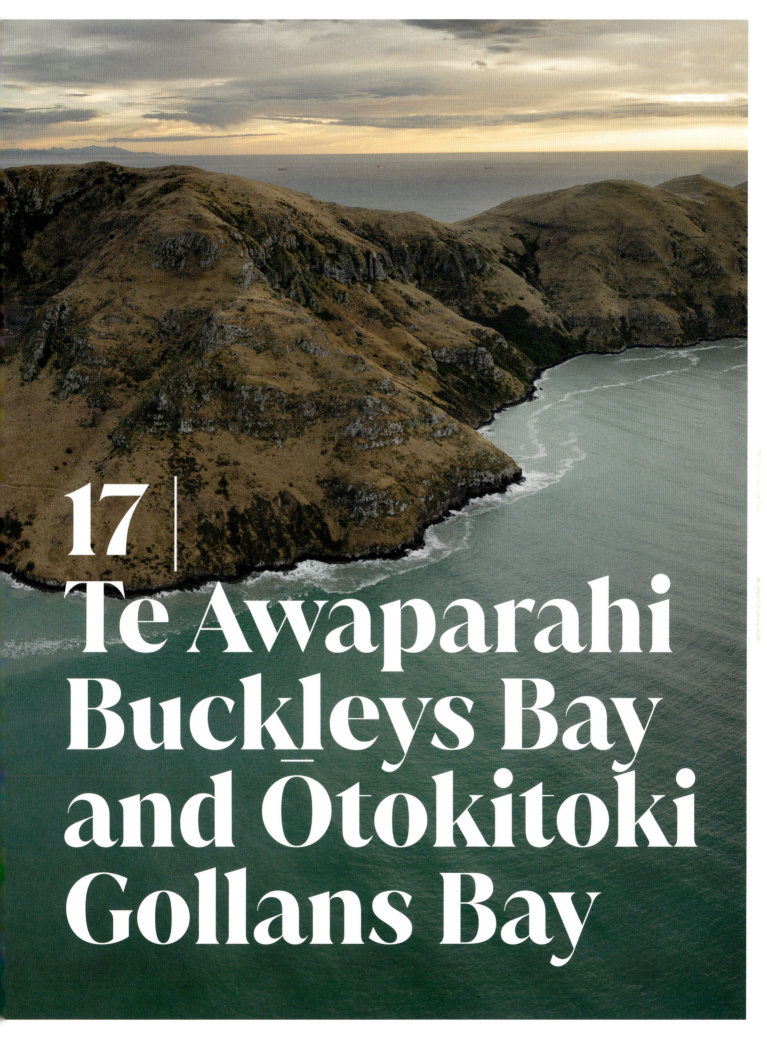

17 | Te Awaparahi Buckleys Bay and Ōtokitoki Gollans Bay

Between Erskine Bay, where the port of Lyttelton was established, and Awaroa Godley Head, at the easternmost end of the harbour, are several largely unknown bays. Unknown, because they have disappeared completely or because they remain largely inaccessible. Baden Norris called them the 'forgotten bays' of Lyttelton.[1] Heading eastwards from the inner harbour they are: Te Awaparahi Buckleys Bay (previously known by European settlers as Comptons Bay, then Polhills Bay); Ōtokitoki Gollans Bay; Livingstone Bay (also known as White Lady Bay); Breeze Bay (one-time Nor-West Bay and Fern Bay); and Mechanics Bay (also known as Lighthouse Bay and Cable Bay).

*

The range of hills extending from Godley Head to Tapuwaeharuru Evans Pass was known as Mahoenui, a name also used by some of the residents of Gollans Bay.

In Canon J. W. Stack's 1894 sketch map detailing Māori place names of Lyttelton Harbour, the site of an 'old pa' is marked on the slope to the east of Gollans Bay and overlooking Fern Bay.[2] According to W. A. Taylor, this was the location of a Ngāi Tahu pā called Ōtokitoki ('place of the axes') from where could be seen 'the whole of Pegasus Bay to the north and the coastline south towards Long Look Point (Panau)'.[3] A spring close by provided fresh water. However, Taylor describes other Māori pā structures in the area which have since been identified as sites relating to farming or European military activities. So whether there was in fact a pā in this highly strategic location remains unconfirmed.

Two of the bays between Lyttelton and Godley Head had interesting histories of European settlement and use prior to their erasure or disfigurement in the interests of Lyttelton Harbour Board/Port Company expansion. Buckleys Bay had a jetty. Gollans Bay might have had six 1200-foot and four 800-foot jetties had city and harbour development taken a different turn. Breeze Bay makes a brief appearance at the end of the chapter for its one claim to fame. Mechanics Bay, with its jetty, features in stories of Godley Head (see chapter 18).

The coastline stretching east from Lyttelton was dry, precipitous and generally not conducive to settlement. In April 1851 Elizabeth Hart purchased 50 acres of land in Buckleys Bay, between Windy Point and Battery Point, but never lived there.[4] The early names Comptons Bay and Polhills Bay are linked to the construction of the road running above the bay which was to connect Lyttelton with Sumner. George Compton arrived in Lyttelton in June 1849 with his wife, Elizabeth, and young family, to take up a position as the construction superintendent for No. 1 Road Party. He clashed with chief surveyor Captain Joseph Thomas and was replaced. He went on to establish the Mitre Hotel, where he acted as host until his death by suicide on January 1859.

Taking over from Thomas in November 1849, Baker Polhill lived in the bay below the newly forming road; hence, for a short time, Polhills Bay. In May 1855 the *Lyttelton Times* was making reference to 'Polhill's Bush', from where locals gathered firewood. Baker Polhill was later employed by the Lyttelton Customs Department as a 'tide waiter' or customs officer.

In January 1859 Henry Buckley, his wife, Eliza, and children Mary, Eliza Ann, James, John and baby Rose arrived from Plymouth in the United Kingdom aboard *Clontarf*. Henry had sold his dyeing business in order to bring his family to New Zealand. To begin with the family lived at Gollans Bay, and then Henry purchased 4 acres in Polhills Bay with grazing rights to a much more extensive area. He imported dairy cows from Australia, landing them in the sea with the help of cork lifebelts. The family also raised goats. They delivered milk to Lyttelton by boat in fine weather and by land, with the use of bullocks, in bad weather. For additional income, Henry worked as a fisherman.

Henry built a two-storey house for the family, at what gradually became known as Buckleys Bay, in 1865. After Eliza's death, he married Louisa Mobley in September 1867. Louisa and Henry had 13 children together, only three of whom survived birth to grow up at Buckleys Bay. When Henry died in 1898, Louisa married Robert Garnett and continued to live in the bay until her death in 1925. The farm was taken over by Henry Buckley's son-in-law William Taylor. William and his wife, Sarah, lived there with their six children until 1930, when William Richard Norris converted the dairy farm to a piggery. Scraps were collected from Lyttelton hotels and sledged down from the road to feed the pigs.

Norris sold out to his brother-in-law Captain Albert Anderson in 1932. The old two-storey home was demolished in 1937 and a modern house built higher up the slope, closer to the Sumner road. Anderson made a track down to the beach through the farm and did more than any past resident to encourage visitors. A small shop was built close to the picnic ground, where Anderson's youngest daughter, Dorothy, sold refreshments. Dawn Dawson remembers her Aunty Ivy running the little shop but making no allowance for family members in terms of a free orange juice. The Christchurch *Press* described Buckleys Bay as having 'a small and attractive but little known bathing beach' to which access could only be gained through private property.[5] The bay, with its slipways, wharf platform, fine sandy beach and baches, became a favourite picnicking, swimming and fishing spot for Lyttelton people. Swimmers had to be wary, however — large sharks were occasionally reported in the bay.

A gunpowder magazine, a rifle range and a blacksmith's shop were constructed in the bay when it was still being referred to as Polhills Bay. The Lyttelton Volunteer Artillery regularly used the rifle range for practice and competition. We know there was a boatshed and a slipway at Buckleys Bay, and according to a *Press* report there was also a jetty. In April 1921, the Lyttelton Sea Scouts and the North Linwood Troop of Boy Scouts held their Easter camp at Buckleys Bay. One day some of the boys were standing on a rocky point when they sighted a

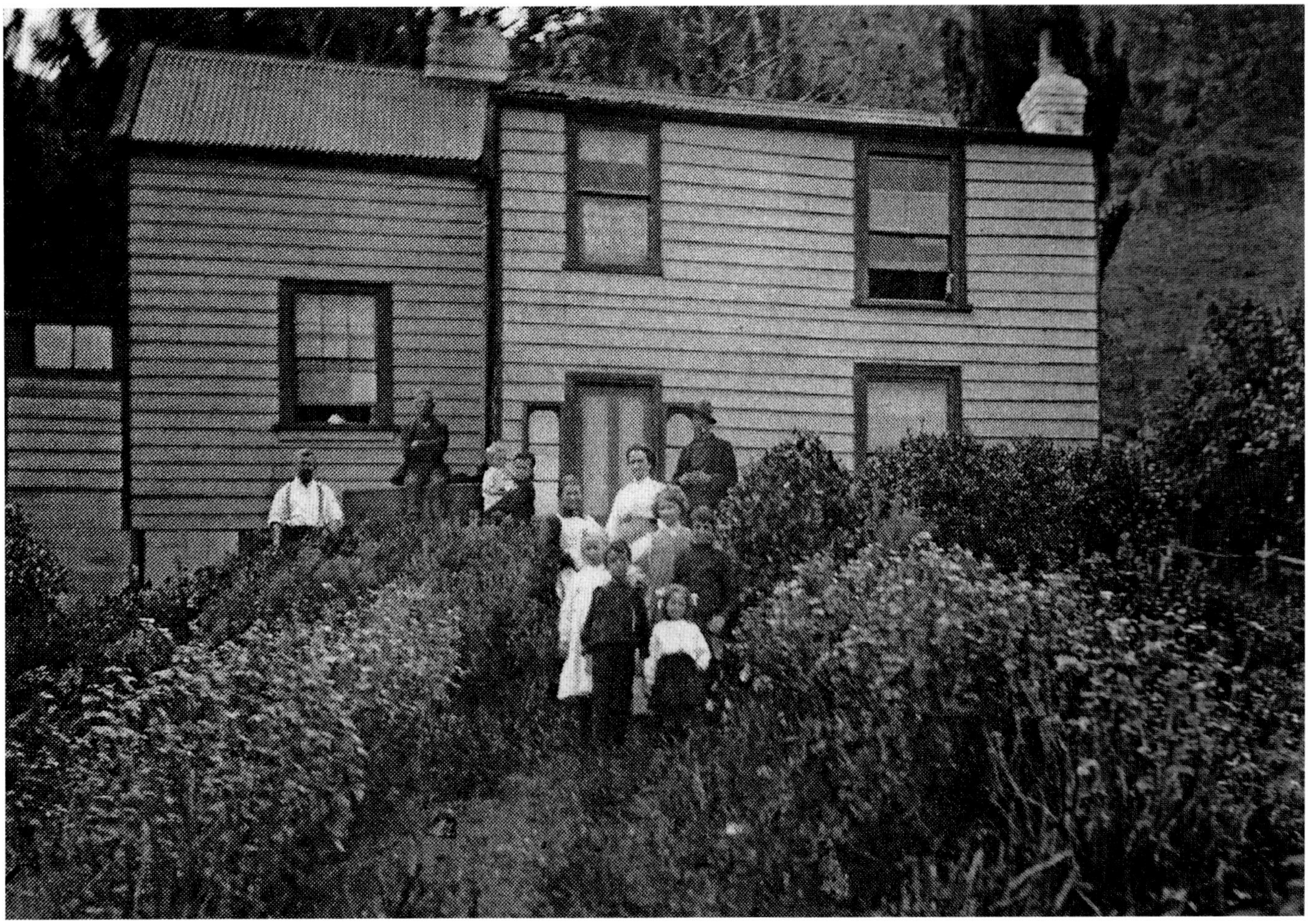

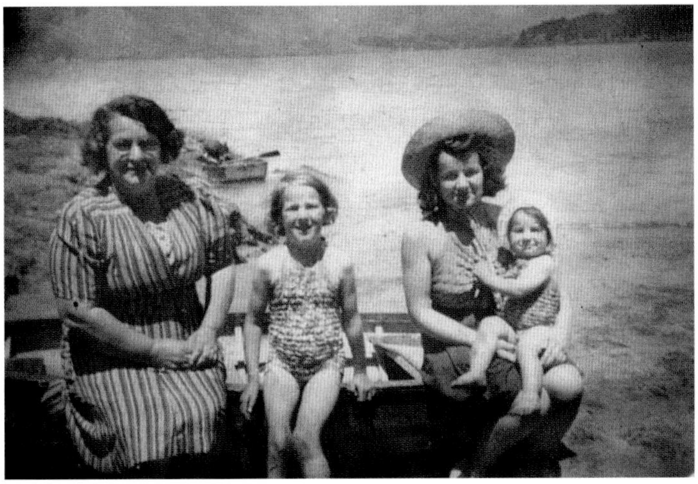

ABOVE The original homestead at Buckleys Bay, with Henry Buckley (on right, wearing hat) and his family in the front garden, c.1890. The Buckleys farmed dairy cows and goats, delivering milk to Lyttelton by sea (in fine weather) and land. For extra income Henry also worked as a fisherman.
LYTTELTON MUSEUM, 12182.1

LEFT Pearl, Yvonne, Audrey and Dawn Norris on the beach at Buckleys Bay.
COURTESY OF DAWN DAWSON

motor launch beating up against a heavy sea and a sou'west wind. The launch, which appeared to be half-awash, then broke down just off Buckleys Bay. The Scouts signalled those aboard to bring the launch into the bay. Using the paddles on board, the crew were just able to make the jetty. Overnight, a pounding against the jetty damaged the boat, but the Scouts were able to row it to Lyttelton the following day and hand it over to the owner.[6]

Gollans Bay, which lies directly below Tapuwaeharuru Evans Pass, was used early on by whaling ships. It is clearly marked on the 1838 chart of Lyttelton Harbour drawn by J. M. Fournier of the French warship *Heroine*, which was in the area to protect French whaling interests. Fournier labelled the bay Anse Radou ('Repair Bay'). Its deep water enabled ships to moor close to the shelter of the harbour cliffs. Surveyor Charles Torlesse referred to it in his journal as 'Old Jim's Bay'. According to New Zealand Company surveyor Alfred Wills, who called it 'Old Tem's Bay', 'it was the best place on the north side of the harbour for large vessels to offload stock destined for the plains'.[7]

Donald Gollan, who gave the bay its lasting European name, was born in Culloden, Scotland, and trained as a civil engineer and surveyor. He had already worked on the River Clyde, and on the construction of the Leith pier and artificial harbour on the Firth of Forth, when he came to New Zealand in 1841 to work for the New Zealand Company. In 1849 Gollan was appointed public works overseer for the Canterbury Association. He used Old Tem's/Jim's Bay as his base while taking his turn supervising the challenging construction of the Sumner road, and it was thereafter known as Gollans Bay. The extreme terrain behind and above Gollans Bay required the No. 2 Road Party to land equipment in the bay and haul it up the steep cliffs to the work site.

The bay offered a temporary, basic home to a number of early settlers. About the same time Donald Gollan was based there, George Day, his wife, Ann, and their children also lived there in a tent while George worked as a labourer on the Sumner road. In 1850 Isaac and Mary Philpot with their (then) four children arrived on *Randolph* and based themselves in a whare (shelter) in Gollans Bay before moving on to Riccarton. Any children in the bay would have been excited by the stranding and capture of a young 19-foot sperm whale just offshore in June 1852.

By 1851 Lyttelton merchants Longden and Le Cren had purchased 50 acres in Gollans Bay and were promising stock importers that they would erect stockyards and improve the landing place in the bay. Le Cren built himself a house there. The pair seem to have moved on about 1853 in favour of enterprising Londoner

John Parkinson, who was already operating in the bay and who, having survived a broken thigh and severe bruising when his horse reared and fell back on him, went on to become the driving force behind the import of large numbers of sheep, cattle and horses. The animals would be forced overboard and swum ashore from ships anchored close by in the bay's deep waters. Prospective buyers could view the stock on site.

Parkinson grazed sheep high on the Godley Head promontory. Later, Lyttelton butcher William Cook leased land for a slaughterhouse and yards. Gollans Bay must have been quite a hub of activity given the numbers of animals pastured there at times. In October 1851 Parkinson was advertising the expected arrival of 1500 fine-woolled ewes from Sydney, along with 200 heifers and steers plus a number of draught and saddle horses and mules. In March 1854 the *Lyttelton Times* reported that 'three of the five cattle ships advertised for this port arrived this week bringing the total of 600 sheep, 34 horses and 440 head of cattle'.[8] The collector of customs noted that vessels landing sheep and cattle at Gollans Bay were able to avoid the waterside officer and the customs duties he collected.

Various families dairy-farmed in Gollans Bay, although it was a struggle to make a decent living. The children of the last family to farm there — the Forwards — walked to the Lyttelton District High School each day, winter and summer, in bare feet. (Much later, Gollans Bay would be used as an informal dump, eventually becoming the municipal landfill for Lyttelton. The dump closed in 1992.)

The relative ease with which stock could be landed at Gollans Bay suggested to some businessmen that the port of Lyttelton had been wrongly sited in the much shallower Cavendish Bay. Felix Wakefield (surveyor and brother of Edward Gibbon Wakefield) championed Gollans Bay for its deep water with good holding ground and its proximity to Sumner valley. Lyttelton, on the other hand, was a 'miserable place . . . exposed to furious winds, without wood, water or gardens, or space for exercise'.[9] Vessels of over 500 tons had to anchor offshore while their cargoes unloaded into lighters which could then access the port jetty. This double handling was costly. A proposal that attracted a lot of attention and press coverage through the 1850s involved a deep-water jetty at Gollans Bay, linked by a low-level railway tunnel under Evans Pass and through to Sumner. Another tunnel would pass through the overhanging sea cliffs at Sumner and enable the railway to continue on to Heathcote and thence into Christchurch. Gollans Bay and Lyttelton would be linked by tram road.

Today this may seem a surprising route by which to connect Lyttelton and Christchurch. But at the time Sumner, with its access over the Sumner Bar to the estuary and Heathcote River, was an important link between the port and the town on the plains. Vested interests — and as influential a figure as the provincial engineer Edward Dobson — championed the Sumner tunnel from Gollans Bay, while Lyttelton residents and businessmen resisted any possibility that the port might be relocated wholly or partially to Gollans Bay. The suitability of Gollans Bay as a potential deep-water port was fiercely debated in the *Lyttelton Times*: some correspondents claimed it was too open to damaging swells from the heads, while others asserted there was no swell at all from the north-east.

A neutral engineering opinion was sought from G. R. Stephenson, nephew of the famous railway-man George Stephenson. He dismissed the Sumner route in favour of a direct Lyttelton–Christchurch tunnel. By 1858–59 opinion had largely shifted in favour of a railway line through the Port Hills from Lyttelton to Heathcote. The unsuitability of Gollans Bay was confirmed by W. B. Bray, chairman of the Lyttelton Wharf Commission, who reported that the commissioners could find 'no argument in its favour which is not more than counter-balanced by the many disadvantages of its exposed position, and by the cost of the stupendous works which must be constructed there to resist the great force of the ocean'.[10]

ABOVE In the 1880s the threat of war with Russia prompted the fortification of what came to be known as Battery Point, complementing the construction of Fort Jervois across the harbour. This photo from 1958 shows a gun from the 1880s at a quarry in Gollans Bay.
CHRISTCHURCH CITY LIBRARIES, DW-110611

BELOW Battery Point is the only site in Canterbury where coastal defence structures were set up to protect the country against three different threats of invasion: the 1880s Russian scare, the First World War and the Second World War.
ALEXANDER TURNBULL LIBRARY, PACOLL-4161-01-040-9

Meanwhile, the steep promontory separating Gollans Bay and Buckleys Bay was in demand for a different reason. Between 1865 and 1875 the Canterbury Artillery Volunteers used a 12-pounder Armstrong gun battery here for gunnery practice. In the 1880s, the threat of war with Russia prompted the mounting of two 7-inch, 7-ton rifled muzzle-loading guns on what was known as Battery Point. This complemented the fortification of Fort Jervois on Ripapa Island directly across the harbour. The first gun on the promontory was located 17 metres above sea level with a searchlight below. The second gun was 60 metres up the steep hillside, with a battery observation post and magazine/store shed nearby. Accommodation for 15 men was constructed near the lower gun emplacement, with a barracks block for 60 men higher up the hillside. The battery was maintained until 1910, when the guns were declared obsolete and sold.

Battery Point was reactivated as a coast artillery searchlight station from 1914 to 1918. Two Nordenfelt QF guns relocated from Fort Jervois were mounted there, but not until 1919, after the end of the war. In 1925 the facilities were removed and the land leased by the Defence Department for grazing. However, coastal defence plans in advance of the Second World War involved placing two 4-inch breech-loading Mk. VII guns at Battery Point and upgrading the whole site. The contractor first had to build a winch and trolleyway down the 92-metre drop from the road to get the guns into position. A magazine, engine room and war shelter were built, and during the course of the war additional firepower and searchlights were added. The searchlight emplacements were built into the cliff face of the rocky, inaccessible coastline.

Battery Point was manned by Special Reservists, mostly young men under 21 years of age who had received three months' full-time instruction and subsequent training. It operated as an examination battery, checking vessels entering the harbour and requiring correct identification procedures. On 12 October 1939 a local fishing boat, *Dolphin*, was returning from a trip beyond the heads. The men aboard were skipper and owner Frederick James Brasell and his partner, William Henry Willman. According to the lieutenant commander in charge of the battery, *Dolphin* refused to stop at the request of the battery duty officer, as the regulations required. Heading straight at the battery without permission was a major infringement of the rules, and the battery frantically signalled Brasell to stop, using flags and Morse lamp. Brasell was unfamiliar with Morse and so ignored the signal. The battery was left with no option but to fire a 'heave-to' warning shot, which, instead of missing the fishing boat, hit the engine room. *Dolphin* sank rapidly and Brasell drowned.

Two days later, Willman gave his account of the incident. He believed Brasell was fully conversant with the emergency regulations, having been in and out of the harbour regularly since the outbreak of war. Willman claimed that the examination vessel *John Anderson* was not at her usual station and Brasell decided to take *Dolphin* closer to the battery to obtain permission to enter the harbour. At that point the warning shot struck *Dolphin* on the starboard bow and the engine exploded violently. Brasell was seriously wounded in both legs and, despite Willman's attempts to rescue him, was dragged under by the inrush of water in the wheelhouse as *Dolphin* went down. Williams climbed the rigging and, when that submerged, swam to a lifebuoy, from where he was eventually picked up by *John Anderson* when it arrived on the scene.[11] The trawler was raised several days later and Brasell's body was recovered from the wheelhouse. A court of inquiry established no culpable negligence on the part of the men manning Battery Point. Who made a change in the deflection of the gun, causing it to strike the trawler, was never disclosed. Mrs Brasell was given a compassionate grant of £2000 plus the uninsured value of the boat and gear.

In November 1940 the Lyttelton Harbour Board launch *Ruahine* was returning from Little Port Cooper when a burst of machine-gun fire from Battery Point caused the skipper to turn about smartly and head down the harbour again. At much the same time, gunners at the battery were accused (possibly maliciously) of consuming 80 bottles of beer in one afternoon.

Despite the tragedy of *Dolphin*'s sinking and the possible lack of discipline among the young men of the 18th Heavy Battery, relations between the military and residents of Buckleys and Gollans Bays were generally very cordial. The troops often borrowed boats to go fishing. By September 1941, 151 people were stationed at Battery Point, including 49 WAACs (Women's Army Auxiliary Corps). The area is now designated as the Battery Point Historic Reserve — the only site

ABOVE The 'N' Battery, Garrison Artillery in camp at Battery Point Barracks, Lyttelton, 1899.
LYTTELTON MUSEUM, 14985.67

BELOW In October 1939, just after the outbreak of the Second World War, a warning shot fired from Battery Point struck and sank the *Dolphin* and killed its skipper, Frederick James Brasell. This photo shows *Dolphin* following its salvage by Lyttelton Harbour Board staff. The shell hole is visible below the porthole.
LYTTELTON MUSEUM, 10719.1

in Canterbury where coastal defence structures were set up to protect the country against three different threats of invasion: during the 1880s Russian scare, the First World War and the Second World War.[12]

The Lyttelton Harbour Board had long been considering Buckleys Bay as a location for expansion of the port. In 1956 the harbour board took over Buckleys Bay and Gollans Bay. The Anderson house was moved to serve as a project administration office, and 48 acres of Buckleys Bay were infilled for the Cashin Quay development.

The expansion of the port eastwards, the building of Cashin Quay and the construction of a tunnel road were all designed to address problems that had dogged the port since its inception 100 years previously. There had long been interest in the idea of a river or canal port as an alternative or addition to Lyttelton. The idea resurfaced in the first decade of the twentieth century largely because businessmen and farmers were fed up with the bottlenecks at Lyttelton and the hefty charges (deemed 'a scandal' by one Lyttelton Harbour Board member) for rail freight.[13] Harbour board engineer Cyrus Williams was asked to explore extended or alternative berthages for the port. His report, presented in 1905, discussed four possibilities. One involved an extension eastwards between the breakwater and Sticking Point; a small basin could be protected by new moles. Another involved the construction of jetties at Gollans Bay and a rail connection to Lyttelton. The third and fourth options involved the construction of a completely new port on the Christchurch side of the Port Hills, with a canal from Sumner leading to dock sites at Heathcote and/or Opawa Linwood.[14]

An outside opinion was sought from the English firm of consulting engineers Coode, Son and Matthews. They recommended that the port remain at Lyttelton, with additional berthage created to the east of the current port. The plan was to reclaim 36 acres at Buckleys Bay and build two moles enclosing 260 acres of Gollans Bay. Six jetties, each 1200 feet long, with provision for four others of 800 feet, would be constructed. The cost of this option was very significantly less than that of creating a canal port. By 1912 the idea of an alternative port was all but dead in the water, much to the dismay of those who had speculated on land in Heathcote. Because the tonnage of shipping at Lyttelton did not increase greatly after 1909, the need for an extension diminished, in the short term anyway.

The possibility of a road tunnel connecting Christchurch and Lyttelton resurfaced in the late 1940s and, with it, the need for port expansion. In 1948 the Lyttelton Harbour Board advertised throughout the Commonwealth for an engineer-in-chief. The successful applicant was James A. Cashin, senior assistant engineer at the port of Liverpool, a highly qualified man of wide experience.

Cashin arrived in March 1949. He was sceptical about the need for expansion, but acknowledged that during any inner harbour modernisation additional berthage would be needed. Cashin read previous engineering reports, looked at wave patterns in Lyttelton Harbour and concluded, much to everyone's surprise, that a short, straight breakwater at Sticking Point would be sufficient to protect large ships berthed at a wharf running parallel to the shore. A large eastern reclamation between the breakwater and Gladstone Pier would provide space for cargo handling by road and rail and for large transit sheds.

Based on the positive outcomes of modelling carried out at Cashin's request at the Wallingford Hydraulic Research Station in Berkshire, and local investigations carried out by J. B. Bushell, a recent graduate of the University of Canterbury School of Engineering, the Lyttelton Harbour Board made the decision to proceed with port expansion as recommended by the engineer-in-chief. Investigations into the rock cliffs backing Buckleys Bay indicated that it would be suitable for quarrying stone for the breakwater and reclamation. The land in Buckleys Bay, belonging to the Defence Department and two local farmers, was secured by voluntary sale and Buckleys Bay was duly swallowed up in the Cashin Quay development. Gollans Bay was also affected when an additional quarry was opened there in 1958 to service the expansion. At the height of operations, 5000 cubic yards of rock were removed from the quarry each day. Over five years later, 4 million cubic yards of rock and spoil had been removed. On 28 November 1964 Cashin Quay was officially opened. The opening of the road tunnel between Heathcote and Lyttelton just nine months previously meant that goods arriving at, and departing from, Cashin Quay could be serviced by road as well as rail transport.

Lyttelton port and township were badly damaged in the Canterbury earthquakes, and the quarry at Gollans Bay was closed. Earthquake recovery minister Gerry Brownlee, using emergency powers, directed Environment Canterbury and the port to produce the draft of a Lyttelton Port Recovery Plan by July 2015. The published plan identified current port infrastructure in need of major repair and outlined how capacity might be increased to accommodate future international freight demand.[15]

Amongst other things, the recovery plan provided for the reclamation of up to 24 hectares of land for a new container terminal within Te Awaparahi Bay adjacent to the existing, already consented 10-hectare reclamation for port operational land. The aim was to gradually move the operations of the port eastwards, away from Lyttelton township and the old 'inner harbour'. In order to accommodate larger ships, the Lyttelton Port Company also wished to deepen and widen the main navigational channel and to create and deepen ship-turning basins adjacent to Te Awaparahi and Cashin Quay reclamations.

Gollans Bay quarry was reopened following repair work and an extension

Cashin Quay reclamation, c.1963, swallowing up Buckleys Bay. James Cashin was appointed engineer-in-chief in 1949. Following extensive research, he concluded that a short, straight breakwater at Sticking Point would be sufficient to protect large ships berthed at a new wharf running parallel to the shore.
CHRISTCHURCH CITY LIBRARIES, PHOTOCD 11, IMG0057

to the quarry haul road. It provided most of the fill for the new reclamation, supplemented by rubble from post-earthquake demolitions in Christchurch city. Ironically the long talked-about and historically contentious expansion of Lyttelton Port to the east has been in part enabled by the tragedy of the Canterbury earthquakes. The shape of the harbour east of Lyttelton continues to change dramatically.

Beyond Gollans Bay lie relatively untouched and little-visited Livingstone Bay, Breeze Bay (formerly Nor-West Bay) and Mechanics Bay. Here the cliffs plunge down steeply to the rocky shoreline. In April 1915 Nor-West Bay was the site of a tragic accident. Mary Killeck and her husband and son had gone for a walk from Te Onepoto Taylors Mistake. Somehow they got to the relatively inaccessible Nor-West Bay, where they gathered wood on the beach. To get out of the bay they had to climb a steep bluff. Mary managed well for a time, but then felt she could go no further. Her husband turned back to help her, but at that moment she collapsed, lost her footing and fell two or three hundred feet to the rocks below. She survived the fall, but died before a rescue party from the Godley Head Lighthouse, or the Defence Department launch from Lyttelton, could reach her.[16]

Sixteen years later, a drama unfolded near the Lyttelton Harbour heads that was to give Breeze Bay its name. In December 1931 the Canterbury Steam

OPPOSITE Blasting at Gollans Bay quarry to provide additional stone for the Cashin Quay breakwater and reclamation, 27 June 1960.
CHRISTCHURCH CITY LIBRARIES, CHRISTCHURCH *STAR*, DW-109321

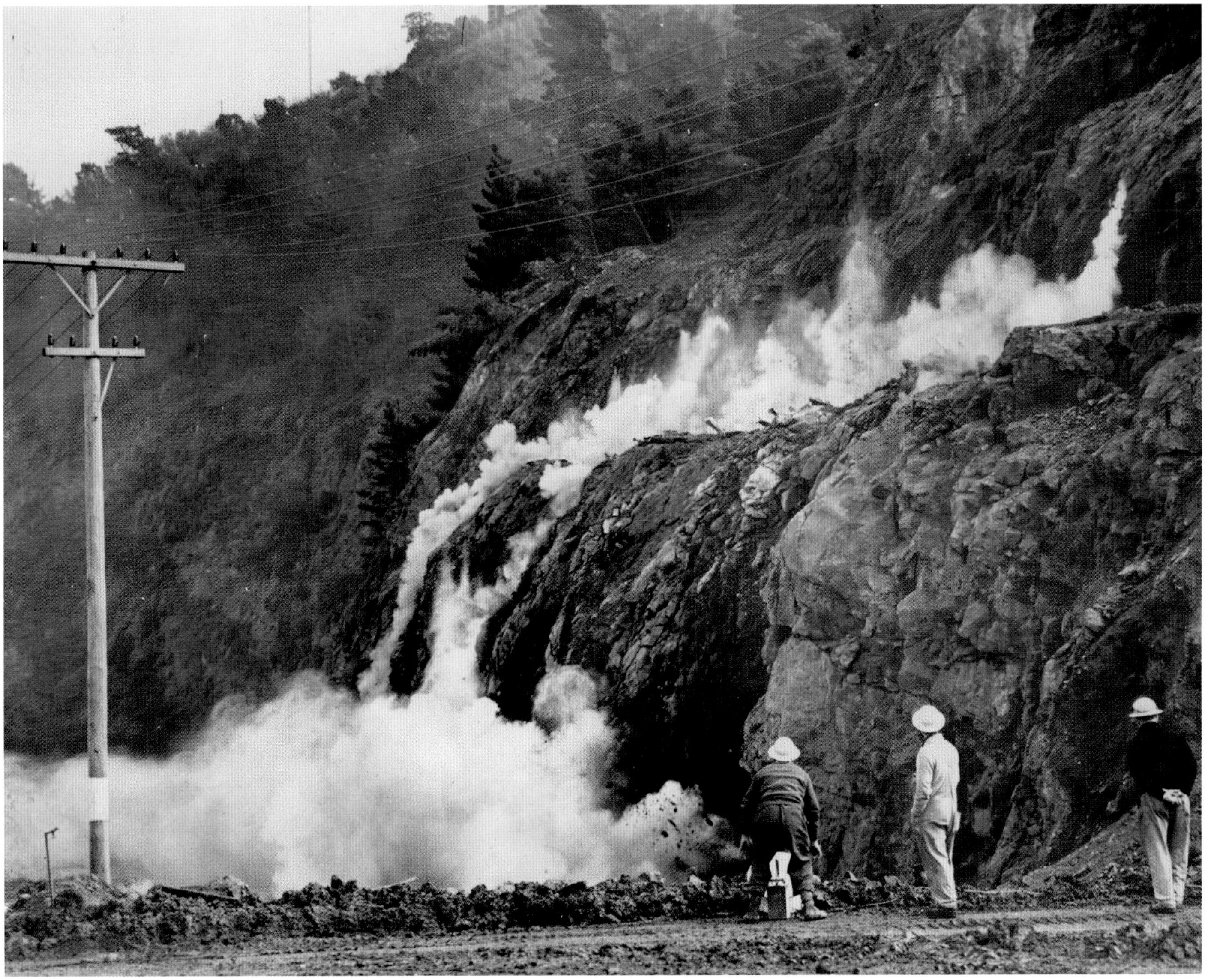

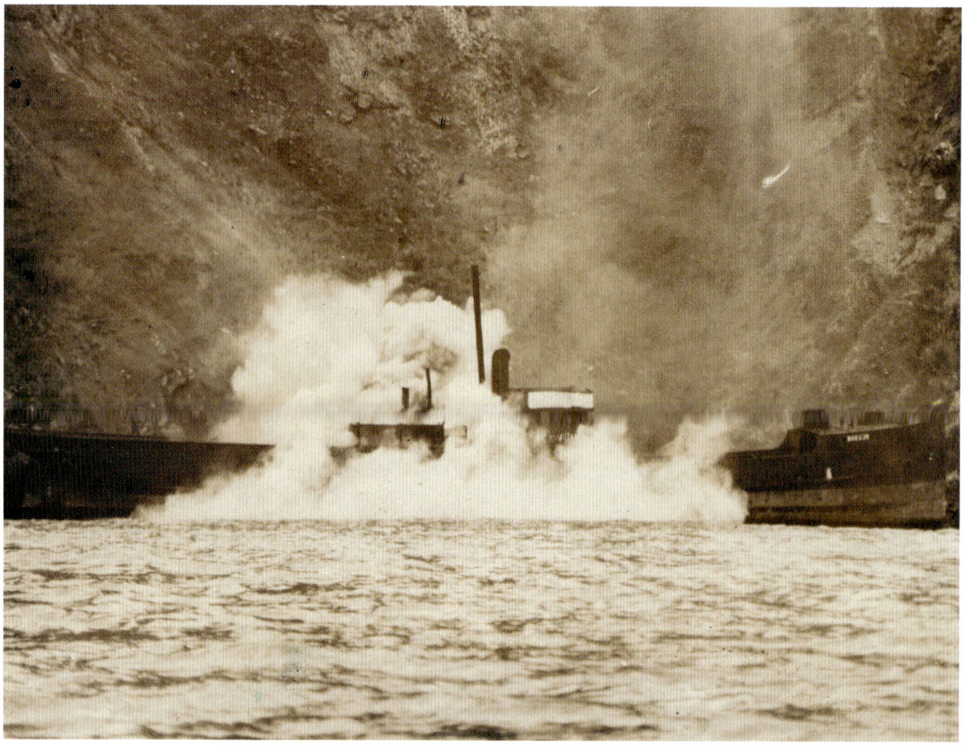

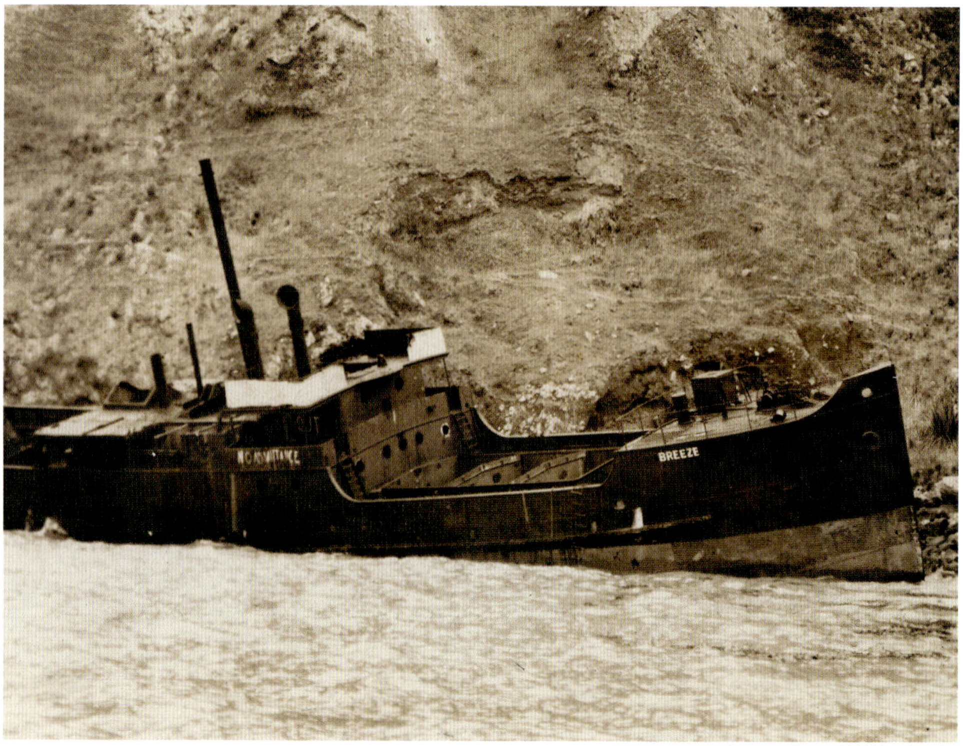
BREEZE

Company coaster *Breeze* was en route from Wellington to Lyttelton when it ran aground in thick fog at Port Robinson. *Breeze* was refloated, and reached Lyttelton by the end of the day. However, an examination revealed that repairs would cost more than the 286-ton steamer was worth, and its owners offered the vessel to the Navy Department for target practice.

The plan was for the sloops *Veronica* and *Laburnum* to fire 20 rounds from each of their two guns. Six rounds from each gun were to be high-explosive shell. If this failed to sink *Breeze*, an explosive charge would be placed on board and it would be blown up. On 11 February 1932 the official visitors who were to watch the target practice boarded *Veronica*. The mine-sweeper *Wakakura* took *Breeze* in tow and, after a couple of minor mishaps with the towline, proceeded down the harbour, escorted by *Laburnum* and followed by a chartered launch full of newspaper representatives. A very heavy south-easterly sea was running, with *Wakakura* and *Breeze* 'climbing up one side of the big rollers and plunging down the others'.[17] The strain on the towing hawser was too great and the line parted. *Breeze* pulled away from *Wakakura*, drifted towards Nor-West Bay and ran aground.

It was decided to blow up the stranded vessel. A naval party boarded it and laid explosives attached to a seven-minute fuse. The harbour board tug, the cutter *Deveron* and several launches watched at a respectable distance until a cloud of smoke shot up followed by a dull reverberation, and *Breeze* slowly settled down and heeled over towards the harbour. One of the nearby launches had on board a party of children and adults from the Russell's Flat School picnic being held at Corsair Bay, and they witnessed the demise of the stranded steamer.

The story of the final, isolated bay before Godley Head — previously Lighthouse Bay, now known as Mechanics Bay — is reserved for the next chapter.

In 1932 the damaged Canterbury Steam Company coaster SS *Breeze* ran aground on a rock ledge in Nor-West Bay during an abortive attempt to use it for target practice. It was blown up and Nor-West Bay subsequently became known as Breeze Bay.
LYTTELTON MUSEUM, 12148.1; 12152.1

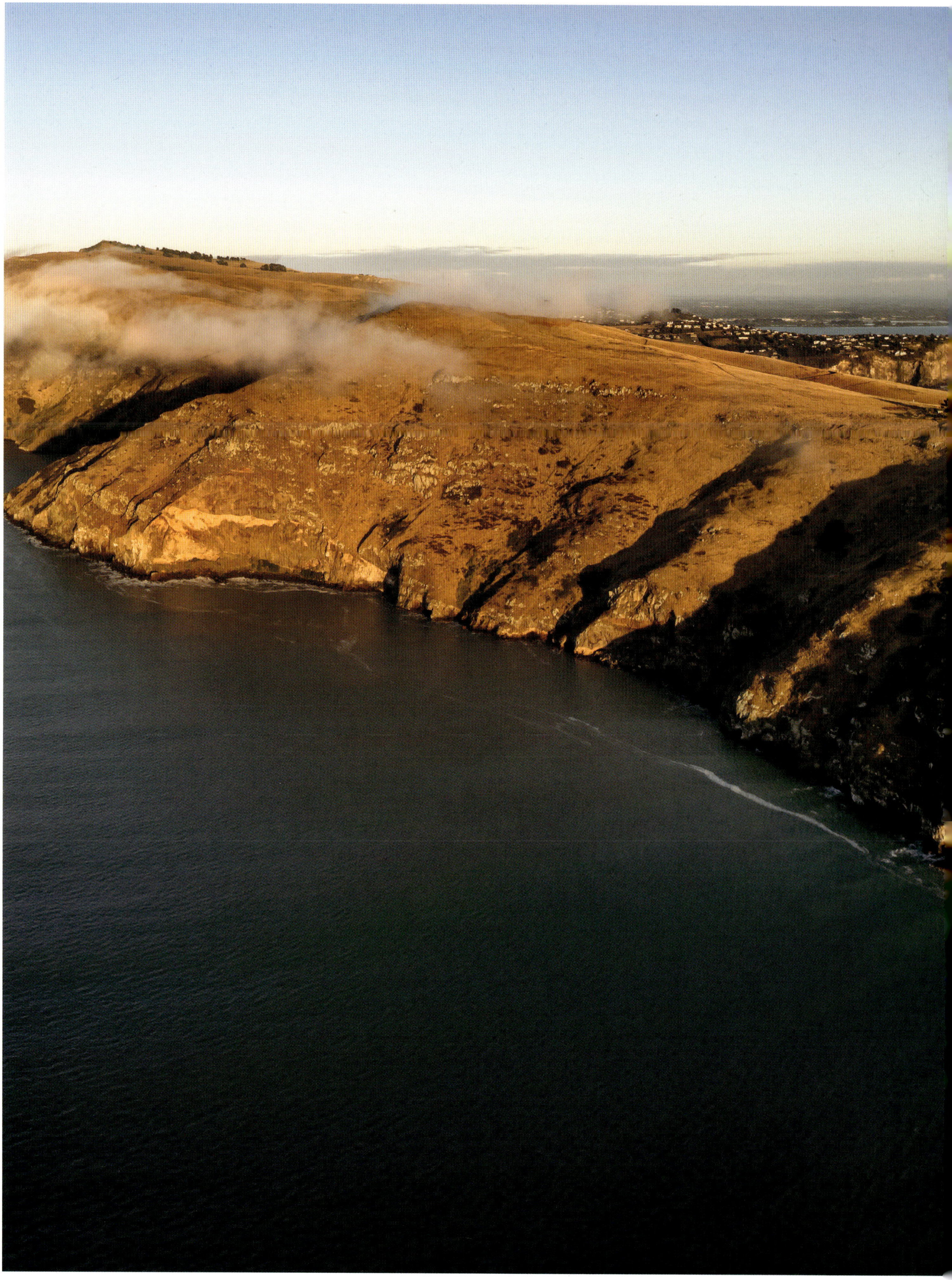

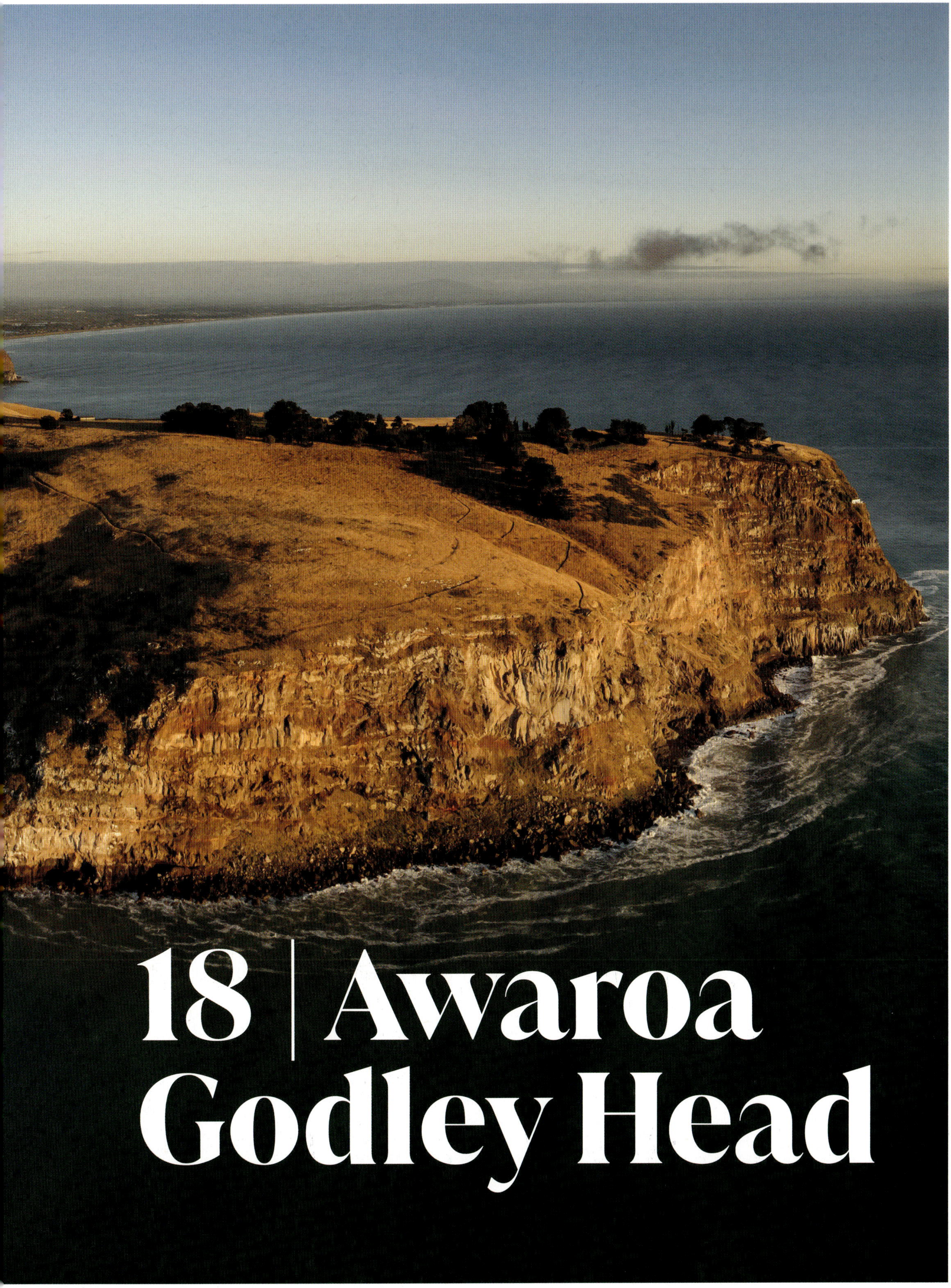

18 | Awaroa Godley Head

Two Māori names are associated with the bulky headland that separates Whakaraupō from Te Onepoto Taylors Mistake. One is Awaroa or 'long water'. The other is Ōtokitoki — 'the place of axes'. From the dry, windswept headland, towering cliffs drop vertically to the sea. It is a formidable, unforgiving spot.

✱

In 1838, having purchased what he thought to be the whole of Banks Peninsula and formed the French government–backed Nanto-Bordelaise Company, Captain Jean-François Langlois in his whaler *Cachalot* was 'well-nigh dashed to pieces there' on a 'pile of rocks'.[1] For some years thereafter, in a reminder of the peninsula's whaling industry, the point was known as Cape Cachalot (cachalot being an alternative term for the sperm whale). The present name, after John Robert Godley, co-founder of the Canterbury settlement, dates from 1851.

Once Erskine Bay had been determined as the location for the new Canterbury Association port and port town of Lyttelton, there was an urgent need to signal the entrance to the long, narrow harbour, then known as Port Cooper. As early as 1849, chief surveyor Captain Joseph Thomas reported that Cape Cachalot would be an ideal site for a lighthouse. Clearly the prominent headland could also serve a strategic purpose, and in 1851 Godley Head was declared a defence reserve. A decade later and there was still no lighthouse. According to the Lyttelton Wharf Commission Inquiry of 1863,

> seamen all assert that some *leading landmark*, by which they could run on for port boldly and confidently, is absolutely and immediately required. All the headlands near the entrance of Port Lyttelton, when capped by fog, or in thick weather, or when the light is very dim, become so much alike in outline, colour, and general appearance, that even the oldest of our local coasting sailors cannot distinguish Godley or Adderley Head from any other.[2]

The inquiry would have drawn on evidence such as that of David McKenzie, who chartered the schooner *Augustus* from Te Hoiere Pelorus Sound. *Augustus* arrived off the Lyttelton heads on 30 June 1859. There was no mark, flag or beacon to indicate the harbour entrance, and the wind was building towards gale force. To avoid being wrecked on Godley Head, the skipper of *Augustus* was forced to remain in open water beyond the heads until four o'clock the next afternoon. McKenzie called for 'some proper distinguishing mark' at the heads.[3] Similarly, in

April 1863 Captain Boyd, skippering *Geelong*, arrived at Godley Head in dense fog and had to feel his way with the lead very slowly around the head.

In March 1863 the Marine Board determined that Godley Head would indeed be the site for a lighthouse. Securing the funding took time, however, and it was not until 31 March 1865 that a lighthouse and two lighthouse keepers' cottages were completed and the much-anticipated beacon was illuminated for the first time. Sixty hectares of the defence reserve were re-gazetted as a lighthouse reserve. Eleven yards back from the edge of the headland and over 400 feet above sea level, the lighthouse consisted of a 32-foot, locally quarried stone tower topped with a fixed dioptric (refracting) white light, designed and built in England. The light, powered by rape or colza oil and transmitted by mirrors and glasses, was visible for 34 miles in clear conditions. Powering the light required one of the keepers to work the plunger of the hand pump 1200 times each morning to force oil up to the lantern.

The cottages housing the keepers and their families were substantial, double-stone, semi-detached dwellings with slate roofs, built by contractor John McCosker. Each house had four good-sized rooms with a storeroom and other

Whakaraupō Lyttelton Harbour to the left, Awaroa Godley Head centre and Te Onepoto Taylors Mistake to the right, 1977. The vertical cliffs at the easterly end of Awaroa are evident. Transporting building materials to the end of the headland, for the lighthouse keeper's cottages, was particularly challenging.
V. C. BROWNE & SON, 16327-16328

outbuildings, including a dairy and a fowl house. The principal keeper lived in the northern building, his assistant in the southern one. The cottages were supplied with iron rainwater tanks capable of storing 3000 gallons, vital for survival on the waterless headland. The whole small settlement was enclosed by a stone wall about 5 feet high, which provided some shelter from the fierce winds and perhaps enabled a garden to be grown.[4]

The total cost of the build was £4706.[5] Some of the stone was quarried locally, but all other materials were brought by boat from Ferrymead to Taylors Mistake, from where a tram-road, constructed by the provincial government and the contractor, ran to the lighthouse complex. The *Lyttelton Times* commented that the builder completed the work 'under very great disadvantage'.[6] The sea was unforgiving. In particular the Sumner Bar, only 3 miles from Godley Head, lived up to its notorious reputation. The lighter *Hannah*, carrying sand, lime and timber for the lighthouse construction, came to grief on the bar and broke up within half an hour. In February 1865 three men involved in the build were rowing a load of fresh water from Sumner to Godley Head when their boat capsized, again on the bar. Two of the men, Charles Massey and William Eadie, were picked up by the lifeboat crew, but the third went down before rescuers could reach him, leaving a widow and large family.

Although remote, the lighthouse attracted visitors, evidenced by the remarkable photos of people posing around and inside the structure. Only a few days after it went into operation, Lyttelton folk were enjoying 'a pleasant ride or a good walk' to view the new structure and the magnificent views from the headland, breathtaking on a clear day. The head keeper's wife offered all visitors a cup of tea and a slice of fruitcake. As visitor numbers increased, a charge of sixpence was requested.

Children were born and raised at the lighthouse. In June 1868 Mrs Chapman, wife of the head lighthouse keeper, gave birth to a daughter in Lyttelton. John F. Ericson, a Swede, lived with his family at Godley Head from the end of 1880 to 1883, when he moved on to Waipapa Point. Ericson and his wife, Charlotte, had six children when they came to Godley Head, and another two girls were born there. How these lighthouse children were schooled is unclear. The next lighthouse keeper, John Frederick Rayner, who spent 10 years at Godley Head, wrote to the Board of Education in August 1891 seeking assistance in the education of children living at the lighthouse. The board agreed to recognise an appropriately qualified person as the teacher of an 'aided school' and make an allowance of £5 per head of attendance. Given that there were two families living on the headland, schooling the children 'in situ' was really the only option.

The lighthouse was some 4 to 5 miles from Lyttelton and could be accessed in two ways: via a packhorse track for about 2 miles along the rocky ridge from the

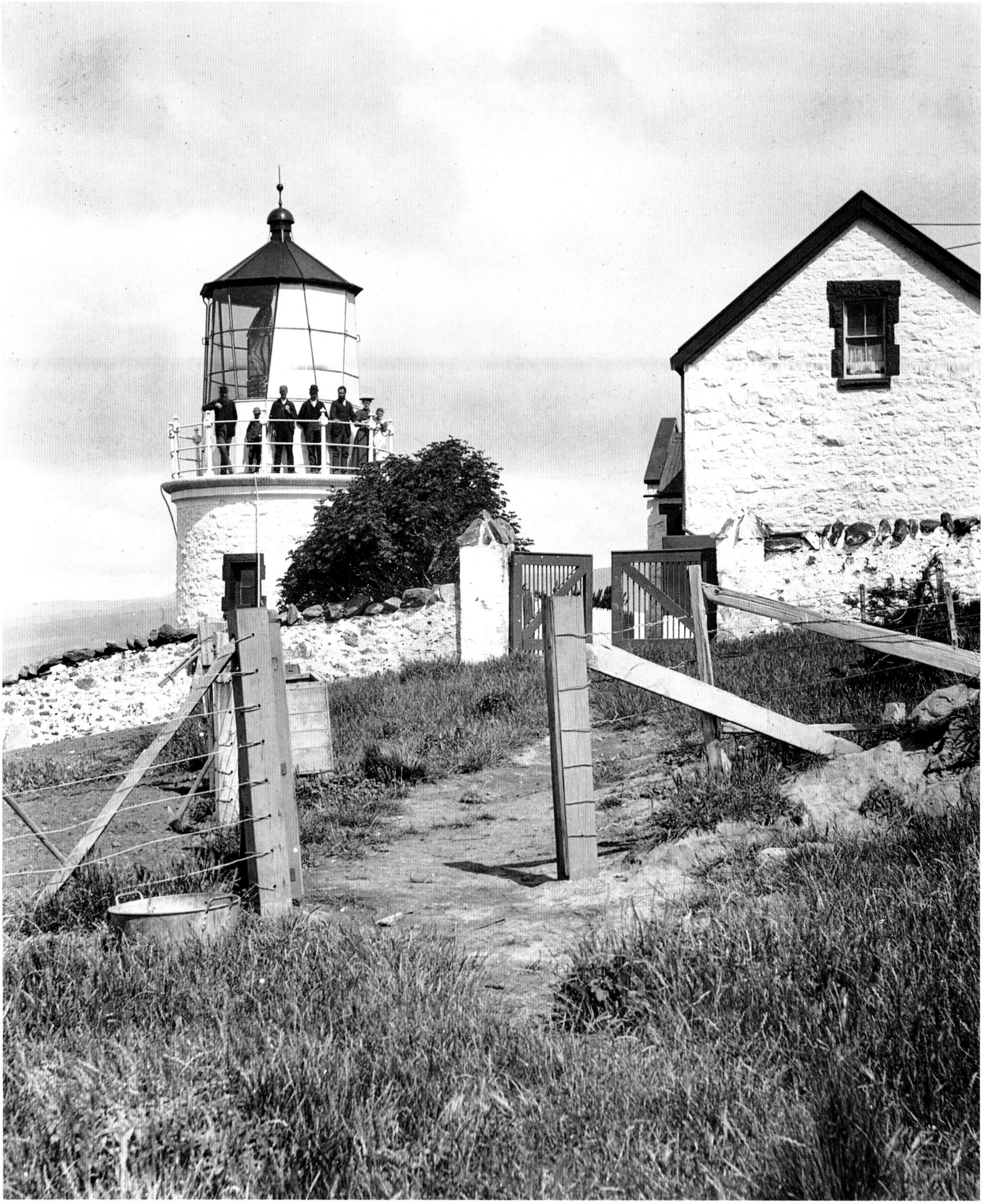

The lighthouse at Godley Head and the lighthouse keeper's family, perhaps, c.1882–85. The stone wall encircling the cottages provided some shelter from the fierce winds.
CHRISTCHURCH CITY LIBRARIES, CHRISTCHURCH *STAR*, 14458

zig-zag at Evans Pass; or by boat to a small stone and wood landing stage, built in 1867 by William Graham of Lyttelton, at the eastern head of Mechanics Bay (also known earlier as Lighthouse Bay). The beach in the bay was covered with huge boulders and subject to an almost constant heavy swell, so landing stores for the families and oil for the light was precarious and difficult. From the beach, goods had to be carried by a long-suffering packhorse via a zigzag path up the steep 150-metre cliff to the lighthouse on its patch of flat headland.

Unfortunately, heavy gales in February 1868 demolished the landing stage. The force of the swell, which 'ran white' all across the harbour, moved large stones of nearly 2 tons in weight. The gales also tore slates off the lighthouse keepers' cottages. Landslips damaged the zigzag track. The Christchurch architect Benjamin Mountfort was asked to design improvements to the buildings and the jetty. The *Lyttelton Times* described the sterling job he did in securing the houses:

> The roofs of the keepers' houses and store were stripped, strengthened, braced and covered with corrugated galvanized iron, laid with very deep top and side laps screwed down and secured to the roof, and further protected by iron bars outside at the top and bottom

OPPOSITE The lighthouse was a popular destination for visitors, who all received a cup of tea and a slice of fruitcake.
ARCHIVES NEW ZEALAND, ARC/862

of each row of sheets, bolted at intervals of two feet through the iron,
battens, boards and purlines, thus making it impossible for one sheet
to blow off, unless the whole roof goes. The roof is also bolted from
the principles to the floor of the bedrooms, so that the advantage of
all the weight of the floor is brought to bear as a counterpoise against
the force of the wind.[7]

Mountfort decided the jetty needed to be relocated westwards to a more relatively sheltered part of Mechanics Bay. About three chains of beach road and sea wall were blasted through the rough, heavy boulders. Three large rocks were used as the basis for a landing place, and a small storehouse was built on the shore to house oil and other stores prior to communication with the lighthouse. In 1894 the Marine Department undertook to build an all-weather landing stage and put up a crane. Despite all these improvements, those arriving at the jetty always had to jump smartly from their vessel onto the concrete wharf and risk a drenching as they walked around the track with the sea dashing spray high in the air. Government steamers, amongst them *Stella*, *Hinemoa* and *Matai*, would call in with supplies once every three months.

The jetty on the foreshore in Mechanics Bay was joined in 1880 by another structure. The Lyttelton Harbour Board set up a system of 'telephonic communication' between Lyttelton and the port's outlying stations at Godley and Adderley Heads. Wires were carried on ordinary poles along the pack track towards the Godley Head lighthouse. About a quarter of a mile short of the lighthouse the line of poles snaked down the steep hillside to a cable house on the narrow foreshore. A 3512-yard length of old Cook Strait cable then carried the wires under the sea to another cable house at Little Port Cooper, from where the wires were poled up to the signal station high on Adderley Head.

In 1926 the Public Works Department had 41 unemployed men working on the rough pack track between Evans Pass and Godley Head. By September, the new shingle road was sufficiently completed to allow a large lorry to deliver a load of cement and shingle to the lighthouse. In April 1928, however, the borough council was forced to close the road indefinitely to the public on account of its 'disgraceful condition'.[8] Those who continued to use it did so at their own risk. The road did enable access for the lighthouse keepers and their families, allowing supplies to be trucked in and the lighthouse children to go to school in Lyttelton. But even for those familiar with the route it could be challenging. Only when the network of defences was built on Godley Head during the Second World War did the road receive the full attention it required. Even then, fog could reduce visibility to the point where the crew of the Lyttelton St John Ambulance, called to evacuate a seriously ill soldier, were forced at times to walk ahead of the ambulance to guide the driver. It took the ambulance 75 minutes to cover 8 miles.[9]

The next major development came in 1908 when a Slaughter's Cotton Powder fog-signal station was built on a short, precipitous peninsula immediately south of the lighthouse. A rough, steep pathway from the lighthouse to the small iron hut was cut into the cliff by five men from the Public Works Department, using pick axes and gelignite.

> The track looks down into the sea all the way, and is handrailed, of necessity; above it the cliffs rise perpendicularly, where they do not overhang. At one point, where a dyke of hard, time-defying rock juts like a huge buttress from the cliff, the path enters a little tunnel. From the steep slopes and numerous angles of the track one comes at last to the little natural platform where the signalling device stands, ugly and alone. Two yards from the hut the platform ends abruptly, a vertical drop forming one wall of a remarkable cut in the rocky mass.[10]

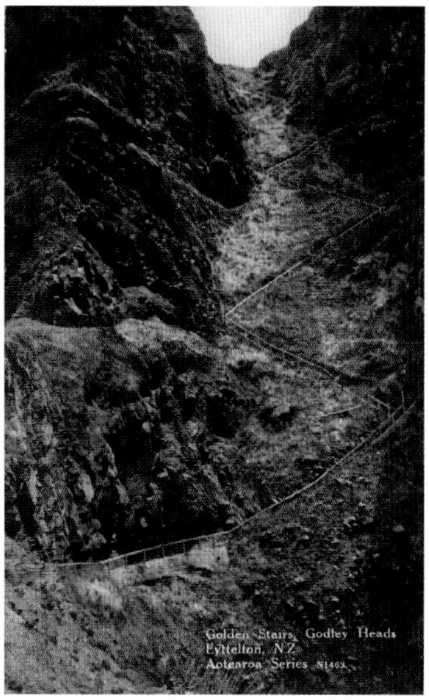
Golden Stairs, Godley Heads
Lyttelton, NZ
Aotearoa Series

In 1908 a fog horn was mounted on Godley Head on a short, precipitous peninsula immediately south of the lighthouse. The fog-signal station was accessed by zig-zag wooden stairs cut into the cliff using pick axes and gelignite. The keeper often descended the stairs in the dark and in heavy fog to load up the Slaughter's Cotton Powder firing mechanism.
GODLEY HEAD HERITAGE TRUST

The handrailed track was nicknamed the 'Golden Stairs'. The keeper descended the stairs, often in the dark and always in heavy fog, collected charges from the magazine and loaded up the Slaughter. He wound up the alarm's counterweight and set it in action. An endless belt carried the charges to the top, ignited the fuse and flung the charge into the air at a predetermined interval. The loud explosion reverberated in the hollowed rock cliffs behind the fog signal station (bringing down loose bits of rock with every shot) and could be heard up to 8 or 9 miles away — although strong winds reduced its effectiveness. The signalmen and their families at Little Port Cooper were unable to sleep while the apparatus was blasting its warning. Frustratingly for mariners, it was out of action for some time in 1920 following a landslide. The fog signal was operated by the lighthouse keeper until 1927, when it was replaced by a compressed-air warning system nearer the lighthouse.

If the fog signal proved disruptive, so, too, did the misfiring of shells from artillery practice on Rīpapa Island. In December 1907 the principal lighthouse keeper picked up exploded shell fragments, one nearly 4 pounds in weight, some 70–80 yards from the keepers' houses. The lighthouse keeper wrote to the Marine Department warning of the potentially dangerous practice.

Another aid to mariners was installed in 1914 midway between Godley and Adderley Heads. The lighted whistling buoy was a large, circular structure topped by a 16-foot iron tower supporting a powerful Aga flashlight worked by compressed acetylene gas. As the buoy rolled on the swell, compressed air was forced out through the 10-inch horn, creating not so much a whistle as a sound akin

The caption for this 1971 Christchurch *Star* photo refers to the building as the lighthouse keeper's cottage, Godley Head. However, this was never the keeper's cottage, which was rebuilt on flat land at the top of Godley Head (out of range of the guns) when the lighthouse was moved down the cliff. This was the 'fog room', which replaced the Slaughter signal in 1927.
CHRISTCHURCH CITY LIBRARIES, CHRISTCHURCH *STAR*, CCL-STARP-02269A

to 'the bellow of a cow in great pain', according to the *Star*.[11] It was nicknamed 'Moaning Minnie'. When the Godley Head lighthouse, 450 feet above sea level, was obscured by banks of fog, the light from the whistling buoy in the clear air below was visible to ships seeking entrance to the harbour. On quiet, still nights, the 'familiar, comforting sound' could be heard as far away as Governors Bay and in Christchurch's eastern suburbs.[12]

The lighthouse keeper could play a critical role in sea rescues. In May 1934 four fishermen in two open boats were caught off Godley Head when a gale-force nor'westerly backed suddenly to the south. Keeper T. B. Smith saw the boats in trouble and phoned through to Sumner. The Sumner lifeboat put out and confronted the full force of the storm around Whitewash Head. Using their powerful searchlight, the lifeboat crew located and rescued all four fishermen, but had to abandon the boats.

Because of the shortage of water at Godley Head, fire was an ever-present threat. In January 1936 a lighted match or a cigarette butt dropped by two young men and a boy out rabbit shooting started a major grass fire. Lighthouse keeper

Smith organised a party of men from the small settlement to fight the fire and called the Sumner Volunteer Fire Brigade. About 30 men tackled the blaze. The cable station and shed down at the jetty were surrounded by flames. To save the fog-signal station, the firefighters lowered a man on a rope; he beat back the fire, but suffered burns to his face and arms. Later that afternoon the wind changed, sending the fire away from the lighthouse towards Evans Pass.

In 1938 the threat of war in Europe prompted the New Zealand government to reconsider its coastal defence system, which had long since fallen into disuse. A decision was made to build a long-range counter-bombardment battery at Godley Head to deal with hostile vessels. The army asked for the existing road from Evans Pass to Godley Head to be widened for heavy traffic. While this work was under way, a lorry laden with stores for the lighthouse rolled twice on a newly formed section and went down a steep bank.

By the time war was declared in September 1939, the only parts of the battery completed were the road widening and a 122-metre access tunnel for searchlights. Thereafter, work accelerated. In early 1942 the rapid advance of Japanese forces revealed New Zealand's vulnerability to invasion. The entire peninsula from St Andrews Hill/Lyttelton Port to Godley Head was declared a Fortress Area and placed under martial law. Following the installation of the temporary Taylor Battery, a comprehensive system of infantry and anti-tank defences was constructed to protect the Godley Head 80th Coast Battery. Two 6-inch Mk XXIV guns with a range of 25,000 yards were installed by December 1941 (a third was added, but not until the war was over). As historian Gordon Ogilvie notes,

> In addition to the guns there were three battery observation posts, two searchlight emplacements, an access tunnel, underground magazines, a battery plotting room, underground bomb shelters, pill boxes, engine room, miniature rifle range and accommodation for over 400 military personnel, including 80 to 90 members of the Women's Army Auxiliary Corps who served in the observation posts and plotting room.[13]

At the height of the Japanese invasion scare, a total of 128 officers and 2893 other personnel were stationed within the fortress area. On a dry, windswept, precipitous headland, the logistics of feeding, watering and transporting this number of personnel (to say nothing of waste disposal) would have been challenging.

The lighthouse keeper must have been less than happy with the upheaval. For a start, the contractor building up the earthworks of the defence magazine managed to dump a load or two over the edge down onto the already precarious fog-signal track, damaging the steps, handrails and ramps. Then, since the lighthouse and keeper's cottage conflicted with the sighting of the guns, creating a dead water lane out to 16,000 metres, it was decided to relocate both. In late 1941 the lighthouse and keepers' cottages, built in 1865, were demolished. The light mechanism was moved down the cliff face to where the fog signal stood and mounted on a new tower. A new weatherboard keeper's house was built inland 100 metres to the west, behind the battery. An assistant keeper's house was constructed 60 metres west of the battery.[14]

The re-siting of the keeper's house was a protracted affair. The district engineer suggested that in the interim the keeper might be accommodated and fed with the troops stationed at the Godley Head battery. However, as he explained to the Public Works Department in Wellington (revealing in the process the prejudices of the military),

> the matter of shifting the lighthouse keeper at Godley Head appears to have reached an impasse — the defence authorities will not have him within the present defence area. They are not willing to provide him with accommodation or meals in the camp. Confidentially, I may add that Lieut. Colonel Lyon who is in charge of the camp states that the lighthouse keeper is not a desirable person to have mixing with the troops.[15]

Of all the military installations, the two searchlight emplacements had the most intimate relationship with the turbulent ocean. Installed by May 1940, they were mounted at sea level on the harbour side of Godley Head, in Mechanics Bay. Like almost all the defence structures on Godley Head they were built of reinforced concrete. Their semicircular bay window front was fitted with sliding steel shutters to protect the lights when not in use. The roofs were strengthened against rock fall from the cliff face above. In the early stages of the war, each light was manned through the hours of darkness. Given the spartan nature of the emplacements it must have been a cold and tedious watch.

The inner searchlight emplacement, known as the 'sentry light', remained stationary throughout the night, forming a barrier of light through which any unknown vessel entering the harbour had to pass. The outer light, known as the 'sweep', ranged back and forth across the harbour entrance. 'When a known vessel entered the harbour, both lights were dipped so as not to illuminate it for an enemy submarine. The ship was then trailed into the harbour by the sweep light to ensure no enemy vessel used it as a cover to enter the harbour.'[16] As a bonus, seagulls learned that they could use the searchlight beam to hunt fish at night.

Those on watch accessed the searchlights via a steep, switchback footpath.

From left, military buildings, lighthouse keeper's house, the Godley Head 80th Coast Battery and, down the cliff, the fog-horn house and relocated lighthouse. Taylors Mistake is centre background.
V. C. BROWNE & SON, 10494/10519, 1967

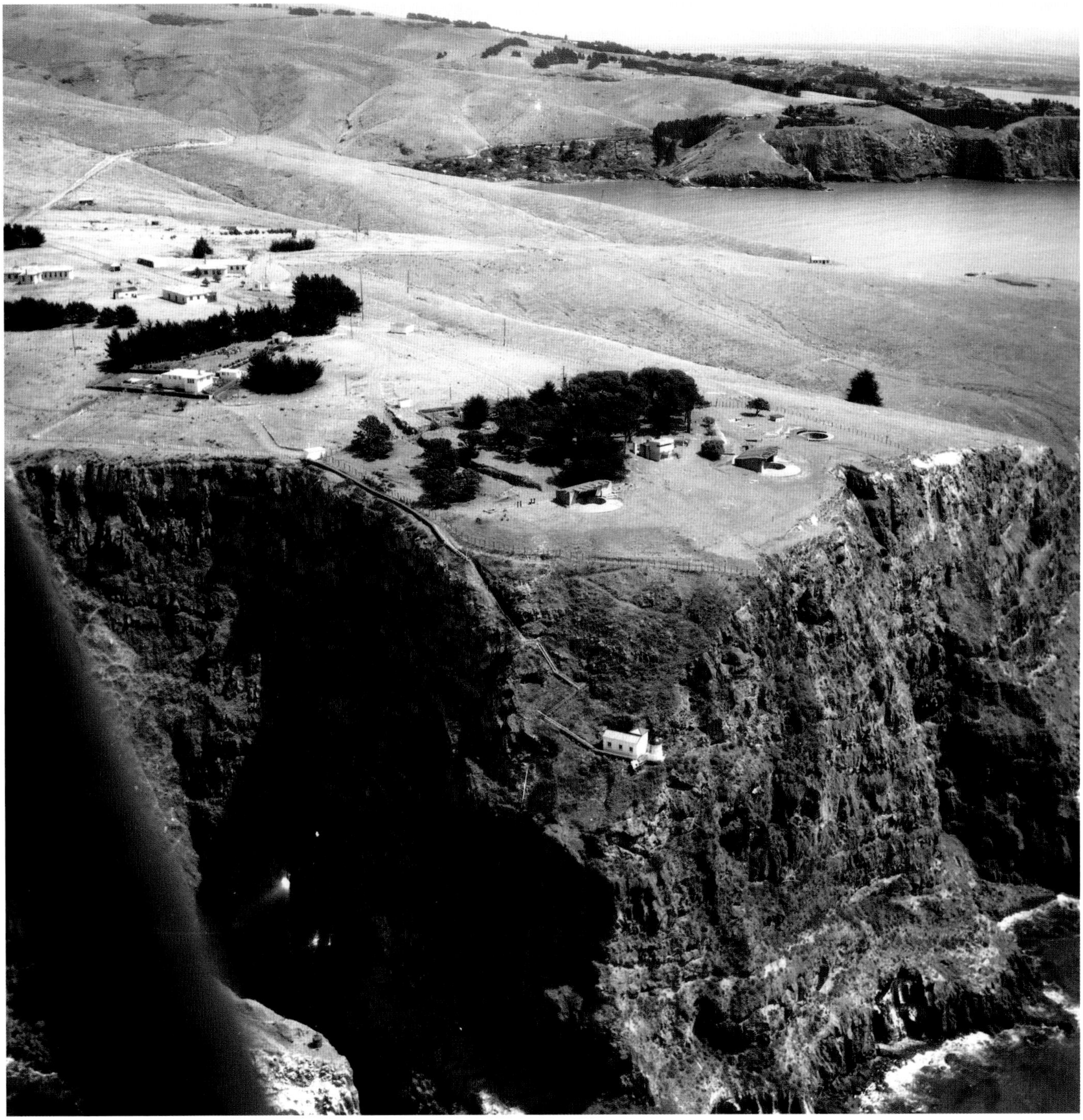

This track was metalled in 1942 by battery personnel, who wheeled the gravel down in barrow-loads. The last section of the track could not be cut on account of an obstructive bluff, so a team of West Coast miners drove a 122-metre tunnel through the bluff. The tunnel exit was a short distance from the searchlight emplacements. In the Christchurch earthquakes of 2011, the path from the sea end of the tunnel to the emplacements was obliterated and one emplacement seriously damaged.

The challenge of defending New Zealand's extended coastline was fully revealed only after the war when it was discovered that the Norwegian whaler *Adjutant*, acting as an auxiliary for the German armed merchant raider *Komet*, laid 10 magnetic mines in deep water just outside the Lyttelton heads. Fortunately, the mines were never detonated; but nor were they found.

After the war, operations were steadily run down until, in 1948, the Compulsory Military Training Act was passed and Godley Head was designated as a corps training camp. In 1958 the coastal artillery was disestablished within the army, the guns were scrapped and all removable buildings taken from the camp site. Despite this, the Godley Head Battery and associated camp remain one of the country's 'most intact and extensive examples of coastal defences' from the Second World War era.[17] The headland is now owned and operated by the Department of Conservation. In partnership with the Godley Head Heritage Trust, DOC continues to restore many of the buildings and structures around the headland. A spectacular campsite, nestled amongst the defence buildings, was opened in 2016.

The Godley Head light was connected to mains electricity in 1946 and was automated in 1976 when it was handed over to the Lyttelton Harbour Board. The Christchurch earthquake of February 2011 damaged the approach path down the cliff face, but left the light and the compressor building largely untouched. However, the large aftershock in June 2011 sheared off much of the cliff face to the immediate south of the lighthouse, leaving the structure clinging to the cliff by its 'toenails'. The lighthouse was decommissioned, and the buildings and tower were gifted to DOC for possible removal. In July 2013 professional abseilers removed the copper dome and outer glass housing from the teetering lighthouse and, after several unsuccessful attempts, a helicopter transported the light in sections to the DOC compound nearby for storage. It had been decided that there was no need to replace the lighthouse. However, the persistence of a group of experienced mariners resulted in the installation of a new light, which began operating in December 2015.[18]

ABOVE The eastern searchlight at Godley Head, April 2003. Both searchlights are now gone except for a scattering of concrete.
GODLEY HEAD HERITAGE TRUST

BELOW An abseiler working on the cliff above the lighthouse in preparation for its removal, post-earthquake, 2013. The large aftershock in June 2011 left the lighthouse clinging to the cliff face by its 'toenails'.
STUFF LIMITED

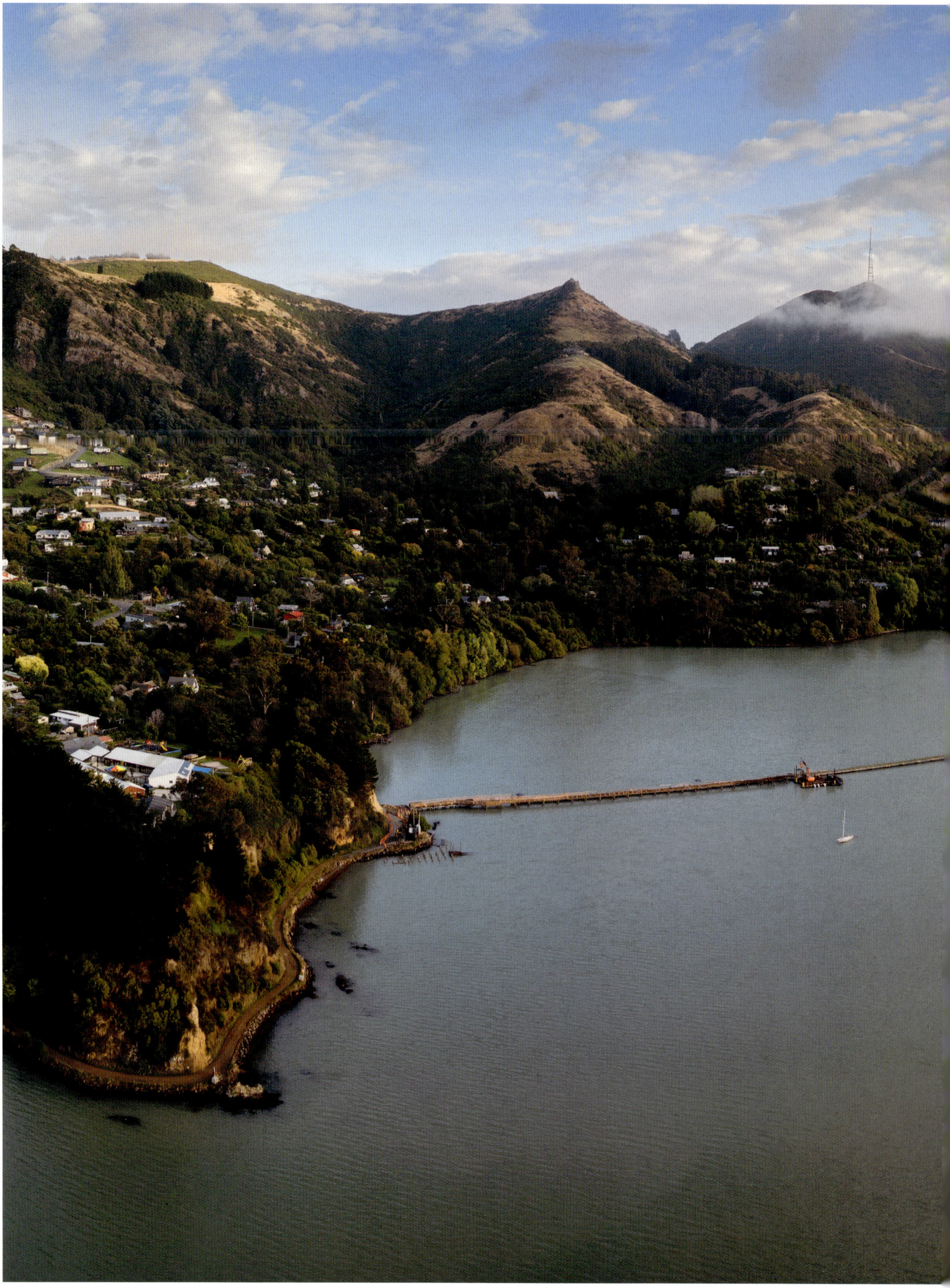

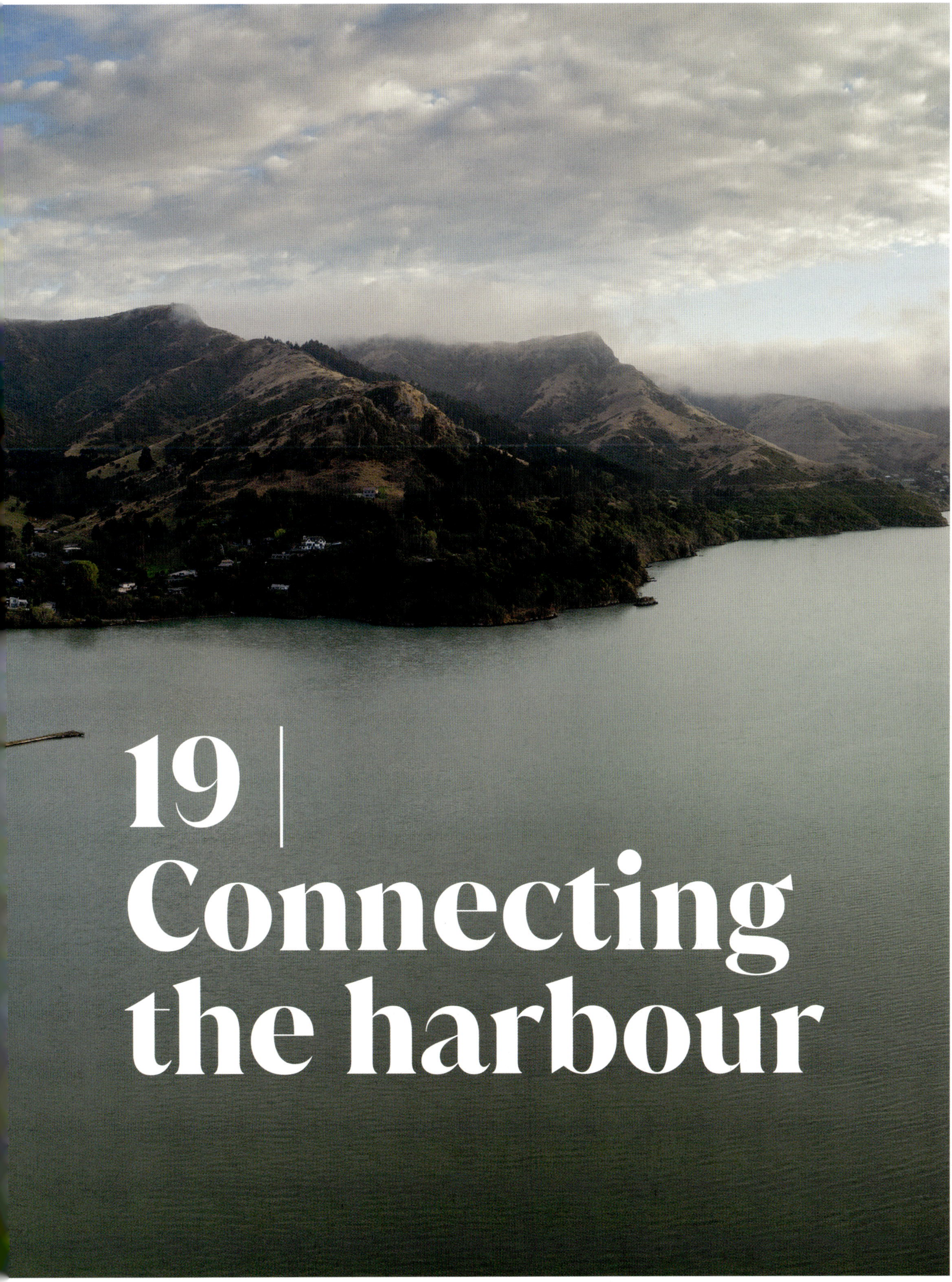

19 | Connecting the harbour

The small boats — dinghies, yachts, steam and later motor launches — that once connected the edges of Whakaraupō Lyttelton Harbour are largely unheralded. Yet they provided a lifeline for early European settlers. These small, multifunctional boats braved all weathers and upper harbour mudflats, carrying produce, supplies, animals and people. They rescued other vessels in distress and, in turn, sometimes required rescuing. Recklessly overloaded by today's standards, they carried parties of excited picnickers to harbour 'resorts'. Their skippers had intimate knowledge of the fickle peninsula weather, and lived in the communities they served.

❉

This chapter draws on a small selection of the many possible boats to write about; it tells their stories to give a 'feel' for the important role they played and the affection in which they were often held.

One of the best-loved and longest-serving steam launches to ply the waters of Lyttelton Harbour and Banks Peninsula was the SS *John Anderson*. Built at J. Anderson and Sons' yards in Lyttelton (the engine was made at the firm's Christchurch workshop) and named after the original founder of the Christchurch engineering firm, it was the first steel launch to be constructed in Canterbury. Displacing 35 tons, at 90 feet long with a beam of 14 feet and a depth of 7 feet, *John Anderson* could carry 80 tons of cargo on a draft of 5 feet and could accommodate 250 passengers. At 80 horsepower it made around 12 knots on a moderate consumption of coal. The *Press* reported that 'it was first intended to build her as a launch but . . . [s]he is decked all over and will be fitted with masts and rigged as a steamer'.[1]

John Anderson was launched with much fanfare in December 1891, just in time for the summer day trippers. On Boxing Day it took somewhere between 500 and 600 'excursionists' to Diamond Harbour (this is well before Diamond Harbour was developed as a settlement; there would have been very scant facilities for so many people). It regularly visited Pūrau, Governors Bay, Port Levy, Pigeon Bay, Little Akaloa and Okains Bay and, according to Bert Witte, was able to navigate the shallow waters up to the Teddington jetty, as well as the lower tides around Lyttelton Harbour, and large groups made much use of its capacity. When picnicking parties exceeded its 250 limit, *John Anderson* would tow an additional two vessels.

As always on the harbour, there were accidents. In March 1894 the Bradleys of Charteris Bay were sailing a vessel away from the wharf and *John Anderson* was steaming out from the opposite side of the same jetty. Neither noticed the other until too late, and they collided. The Bradley boat was forced over and started to take in water, but *John Anderson* was brought to a halt before too much damage occurred.

John Anderson, packed to the gunwales, in the inner harbour at Lyttelton. Built at J. Anderson and Sons' yards in Lyttelton and launched in December 1891, it was the first steel launch to be constructed in Canterbury.
LYTTELTON MUSEUM, 6239.1

The steamer fulfilled all sorts of tasks. Every so often it was used for a burial at sea. There was a profitable sideline in taking people outside the heads for a day's deep-sea fishing. In May 1899 *John Anderson* plus three accompanying boats returned to port with 3½ tons of fish including cod, hāpuku, ling, skate and even a conger eel. Once in port, the fishers abandoned most of the catch. More questionably, *John Anderson*'s engineer Thomas Griffiths was once accused of smuggling tobacco and cigars on which duty had not been paid. During the Lyttelton Regattas *John Anderson* was the focus of a spectacular fireworks display.

Gladys Robertson (née Bamford), who grew up in Governors Bay, had a story to tell about *John Anderson* and launch rivalry.

> One Sunday, my sisters Margaret & Jessie & I had visited my grandparents in Lyttelton. We were coming home at 4PM. Margaret wanted to come home on Purau but I loved John Anderson and insisted on going on her. I think the Captains must have had an argument on who's boat could go the fastest. Well we got out the moles, with Purau hot on our stern. John took a straight line for the short wharf and we expected Purau to go to the long wharf, but she got up a great speed and took off for Quail Island. We sat on the seat

and watched and when she swung round and faced us her bow was right out of the water with speed, she came straight at us, but poor kids we thought she would turn off, but a deck hand rushed along & pitched us along to the cabin & told us to go in the cabin quickly and stay there. With that there was a splintering crash & poor old John lay on her side with Purau half over us. She slid back into the sea & backed off & set off happily for her destination. Our engines were not damaged & we crawled in to the short wharf w[h]ere we were hurried off. As far as I know John went back to Lyttelton under her own steam but still on her side. I think Purau only had to pay to fix her up.[2]

In 1921 George Wood purchased *John Anderson*, continuing to run it in Lyttelton Harbour and to the Banks Peninsula bays. At the outbreak of war in 1939, the government requisitioned the steamer and used it as an examination boat for vessels entering the Lyttelton Heads. There were incidents. It was while *John Anderson* was not at its usual station that the fishing boat *Dolphin* was mistakenly sunk by a warning shot from Battery Point, with the loss of the vessel and her skipper (see chapter 17). The following year, the examination steamer collided with a fishing launch off the heads. The two men in the fishing boat, ironically named *Why Worry*, leapt onto the deck of *John Anderson* as their boat sank beneath them.

Following its long working life in Lyttelton Harbour and around the peninsula bays, *John Anderson* was relocated to Picton. It met a watery fate when a gale blew it from the landing stage out into Kura Te Au Tory Channel, where it sank.

George Agar started out as a Lyttelton waterman in the company of others such as Johnny Roberts, George Messiter, Tom Ockford, Tom Wyman, Jimmie O'Neil, Davy Strickland, Tom Smeaton, Jack Durham, George Brown, Jack Walsh and George Plummer. These men used 15- to 18-foot whaleboats, known as lighters, to load, unload and generally service the larger ships that sat out in the harbour, sometimes for months, as they waited for their cargoes. George Agar's first lighter was charmingly called *Bluetailed Fly*.

As the town and port grew, George and partner Johnny Roberts decided to try their fortunes in steam. In 1875 they ordered a steam launch to be constructed in London at a cost of £1350. The launch was shipped out to Lyttelton on board *Desdemona*, fitted out on Millar's slip in Corsair Bay, and named *Lyttelton* at its launch in June 1876. *Lyttelton* was made of iron, 50 feet long with an 11-foot beam, and driven by twin 9-horsepower engines. It drew only 2 feet 9 inches, and could accommodate 60 passengers.

Agar and Thomas's annual picnic at Governors Bay. George Agar is the older man with full grey beard in the centre with fob watch in view. Quite likely it is Mark Thomas standing next to him, again with fob watch.
COURTESY OF SIMON AGAR

On its maiden voyage the *Lyttelton* took a group of old port identities up the harbour to Governors Bay. The trip took 26 minutes, with the launch hitting its promised maximum of 9 knots. The value of *Lyttelton*'s shallow draft was almost immediately evident. In October a large party of men, women and children associated with the Loyal Rangiora Lodge of Oddfellows left port on an excursion to Rhodes Bay (Pūrau). The women and children boarded the tug *Titan* while the men travelled across in the lighter *Novelty*. Arriving in at low tide, the passengers were unable to disembark from the tug until *Lyttelton* came to the rescue and landed the entire party safely.

Lyttelton was engaged in a variety of tasks. From 1877 onwards it became a favourite regular on the Governors Bay Sunday run, which provided a good return for its owners. Sometimes a band entertained excursionists as they steamed up the harbour. George Agar and Johnny Roberts were joined by Mark Thomas, and on Roberts's death the firm was renamed Agar and Thomas. The two skippers did not take any risks. On one occasion children from the Catholic School in Lyttelton were returned from Governors Bay to Lyttelton by land as Captain Agar considered it too dangerous to put out in a strengthening sou'wester. On Good Friday in 1877, so many visitors wanted to board *Lyttelton* for a cruise on the harbour that Agar and Thomas arranged for the launch to tow additional boats.

Early in 1877 *Cardigan Castle* arrived from London and was ordered into quarantine. *Lyttelton* towed the ship's boats to Quail Island, where the single men were landed, and to Rīpapa Island, where married couples and single women were to be confined. This process was repeated in October 1878 when *Waitangi* was ordered into quarantine due to an outbreak of scarlet fever. When the men from Parihaka were imprisoned on Rīpapa Island in 1880, *Lyttelton* ran excursion trips down the harbour to view the Māori prisoners' quarters from the water.

One of *Lyttelton*'s last tasks was towing a lighter containing 15 Manchurian ponies to Quail Island for their quarantine before joining Shackleton's south polar expedition. In 1907 *Lyttelton* was beached at the ships' graveyard on the western end of Quail Island.

In April 1883 George Agar travelled back to Britain to order another, larger launch, *Lyttelton* proving too small for the rapidly increasing passenger traffic to Governors Bay and elsewhere. Built by the Millwall shipwrights Yarrow and Co. (who had also built *Lyttelton*), this all-steel craft was 60 feet long and 12 feet in the beam, with a top speed of 10–11 knots and capacity for 100 passengers on deck.

Shipped to Lyttelton aboard the SS *Iconic* in December 1883, the vessel was assembled by McKay and Stevenson of the Victoria Boiler Works in Lichfield

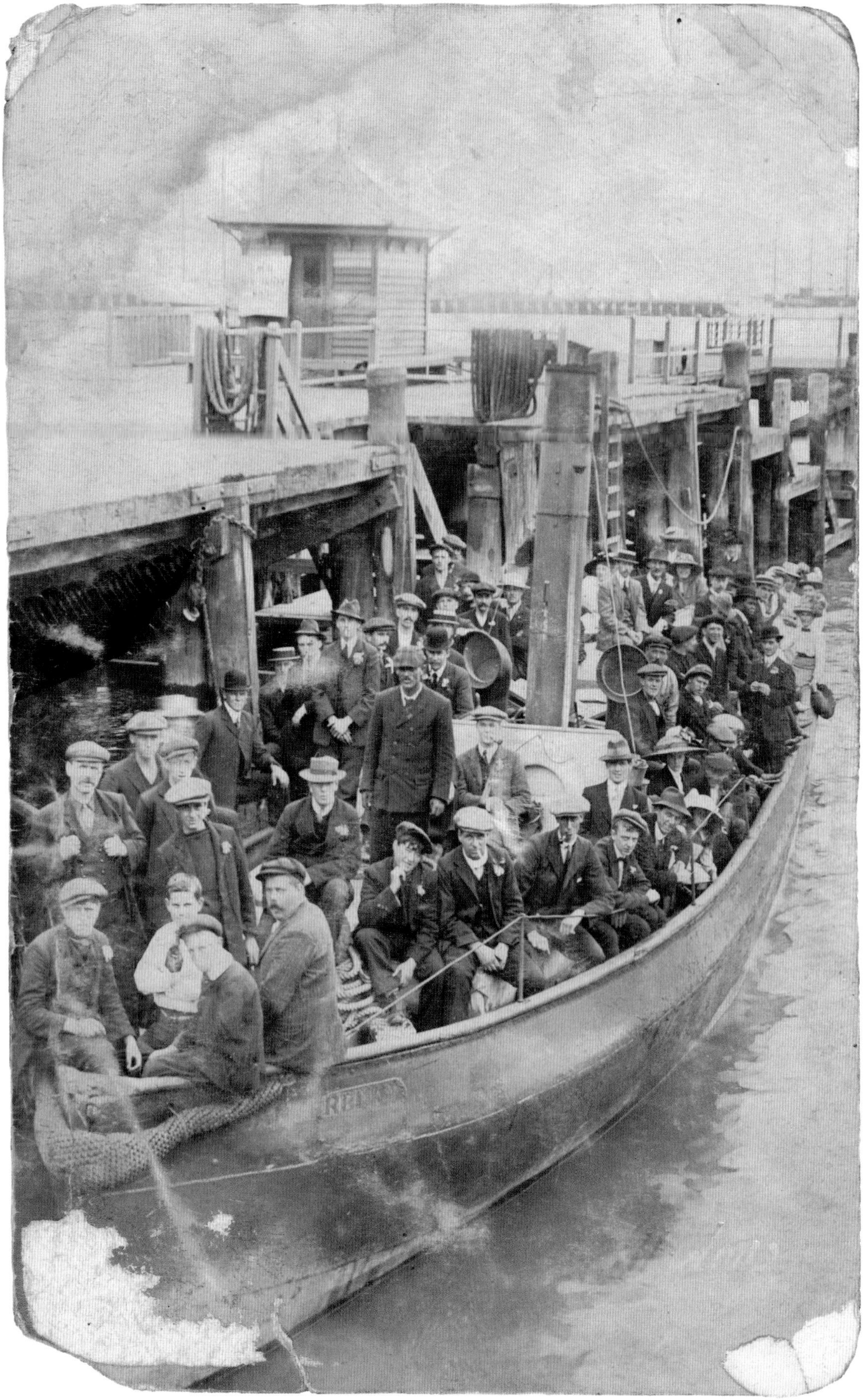

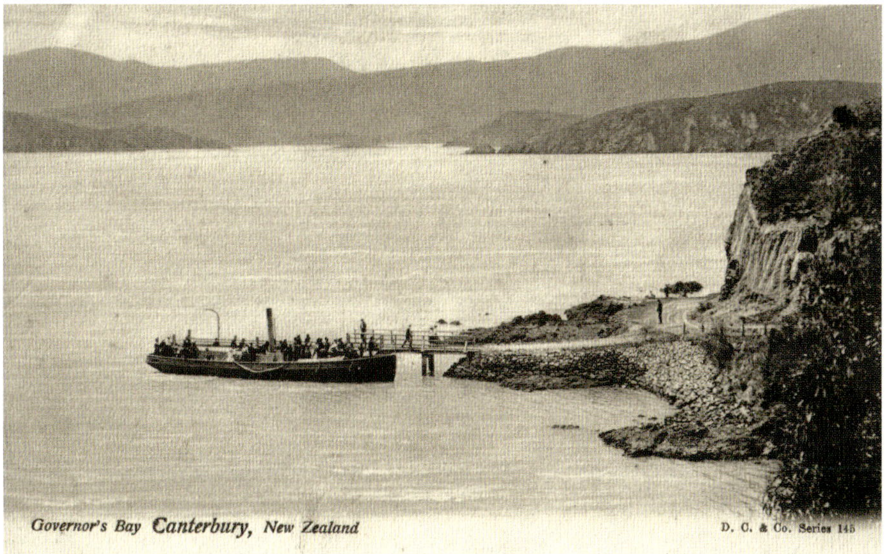
Governor's Bay Canterbury, New Zealand
D. C. & Co. Series 145

LEFT The steamer *Canterbury*, built for George Agar by Yarrow and Co., Millwall, London, was launched in Lyttelton in December 1883. This postcard shows the *Canterbury* at the Governors Bay jetty.
COURTESY OF CORAL ATKINSON

OPPOSITE Steamer *Canterbury* packed with Lyttelton watersiders on their annual picnic, c.1900. It could accommodate 100 passengers on deck.
LYTTELTON MUSEUM, 9039.1

Street. Christened *Canterbury* at its launch on 22 December, it was immediately in demand with the busy Christmas and New Year holiday traffic on the harbour, particularly on the Governors Bay run. Its owners would generously transport certain school groups, destined for camp in Governors Bay, free of charge. George Agar, in particular, was much loved for his geniality and generosity.[3]

In the later 1880s Agar and Roberts ran moonlight fishing excursions just outside the harbour heads, returning to port early morning. For Queen Victoria's Golden Jubilee in June 1887, a day of celebration at Lyttelton was rounded off in the evening with a procession of six boats towed by *Canterbury* around the inner harbour. The boats were all illuminated with coloured lights, and fireworks were set off as they moved slowly along.

Two years later George Agar reported seeing three large whales playing in the harbour as he piloted *Canterbury* from Rhodes Bay to the port. To the great delight of Lyttelton's children, in the winter of 1891 *Canterbury* took in tow, just off the heads, an 'immense' dead whale, which it brought up the harbour to Rhodes Bay. The whale was reported as being nearly 100 feet long and 40 feet broad. *Canterbury*'s skipper then capitalised on the event by running trips to the bay to view the carcass. In an activity that would certainly never be condoned today, *Canterbury* took out a group on a very successful shag cull. The launch lay in Double Bay on the east side of Port Levy, and 'in about two hours and a half [they] killed over six hundred fish-destroying birds'.[4]

As with all the launches working out of Lyttelton, *Canterbury* was always on call informally to attend accidents at sea. When a sudden westerly squall struck and capsized the yacht *Queen Mab* just outside the moles in May 1898, *Canterbury* went to the assistance of the three young crewmen, one of whom was 'much exhausted'. 'The wind was rapidly increasing in violence, and was lifting the seas like smoke across the western breakwater.'⁵ The steam launch took a dinghy containing two of the crew in tow, but a huge sea swamped the dinghy. All three were finally rescued, while the tug *Lyttelton* and *John Anderson* assisted in towing in the sunken yacht.

Well into the twentieth century many of the harbour dwellers depended on the lifeline offered by the launch services and were grateful for them. In September 1908 residents of Pūrau gathered on the jetty and made a presentation to T. Hempstalk and F. Lawfield, master and engineer of *Canterbury*, 'in recognition of their courtesy and attention to the patrons of the launch in the trade between Purau and Lyttelton'.⁶

Following the subdivision of the Diamond Harbour estate, the Lyttelton Borough Council sought tenders for the running of a ferry between Lyttelton and Diamond Harbour for an initial six months. The tender submitted by Agar and Thomas was accepted, and *Canterbury* went in for a thorough overhaul prior to commencing the service in December 1913. In June 1914, however, *Canterbury* was withdrawn from the Diamond Harbour run and replaced by the oil launch *Te Rino* prior to the purchase of a larger, more up-to-date vessel.

The demand for launch services on the harbour grew in the first decade of the twentieth century. In December 1908 Charteris Bay resident Andrew Anderson took possession of a new motor launch, built to order by Charles Bailey of Auckland. Built of kauri with a double-skinned hull, *Matariki* measured 33 feet in length and had a draught of 2 feet. With its 10-horsepower 'Frisco' Standard oil engine, it could reach 9 knots. On a trial run from Governors Bay to Lyttelton and return, *Matariki* covered the distance in 50 minutes. The *Press* reported that 'the launch is beautifully finished, and being a very roomy and comfortable boat, should prove a great boon to her owner and the residents of Charteris Bay, when travelling across the ofttimes choppy seas of Lyttelton Harbour'.⁷ In 1915 the Lyttelton Borough Council refitted *Matariki* to increase its carrying capacity on the Lyttelton–Diamond Harbour route.

The year after its launch, Anderson was just departing Lyttelton for Charteris Bay when leaked petrol caught fire on board *Matariki*. Although the fire was extinguished before any major damage to the launch, Anderson badly burnt both hands, losing nearly all the skin on the right hand.⁸ Several years later, the skipper was crossing the harbour in *Matariki* when, close to the moles, it struck a submerged object. The jolt threw Anderson against the cabin door, causing a gash that required five stitches. An incident of a different sort was reported in 1921.

Matariki was approaching the Charteris Bay jetty late at night when the engine cut out suddenly and could not be restarted. Lamplight revealed a live 8-foot-long shark jammed between the propeller and the skeg. It took an hour to remove the shark, which a museum curator helpfully identified as a female combtooth.[9]

As with all the harbour ferries, the tasks required of *Matariki* were varied. In February 1910 Christchurch was abuzz in anticipation of a visit from the British commander in chief, Field Marshal Viscount Kitchener, who was to inspect the Lyttelton Harbour defences. *Matariki* was secured as a guard boat while the steamer *Purau* was requisitioned for use as an examination boat. On the morning of the inspection, the steamers *Monica*, *Purau*, *Canterbury* and *Matariki*, as well as the defence launch *Te Whaka*, busily transported men of the Permanent Artillery and the Garrison Artillery Volunteers across to Fort Jervois on Rīpapa Island. Lord Kitchener was taken down the harbour in the tug *Canterbury* to view Godley and Adderley Heads, and from there to Rīpapa Island, where a guard was drawn up on either side of the landing stage. The tug came as close as the tide permitted. Lord Kitchener was then transhipped to *Te Whaka* in order to access the Fort Jervois jetty. Once he had very briefly inspected the assembled men and the fort itself (which he declared 'obsolete'), he was whisked back to Lyttelton. *Matariki* and the other harbour steamers were then left to transport all the soldiers, who were only at the fort for show, back across the harbour.

The area just inside and outside the harbour moles was a tricky space for launch proprietors in good weather or bad. One June morning in 1930, *Matariki* left the launch jetty for Church Bay and just outside the moles it ran into the small steamer *Orewa*, coming out from the cattle jetty. Andrew Anderson was found to be responsible for the collision. He had not kept a proper lookout and his vessel had not given way as it should.

A couple of years later, the *Press* reported 'huge seas breaking on the rocks on the far side of the harbour, with clouds of spray nearly 100 feet high at times'.[10] At low tide there was a continuous line of breakers across the entrance to Charteris Bay. In the late afternoon *Matariki* tried to leave Church Bay but was prevented by the heavy surf. Later it tried again, this time successfully, heading out towards Quail Island and then towards the harbour moles.

Matariki was put up for sale in January 1938 and joined the fleet belonging to Toy's Motors. Toy's ran a service between Diamond Harbour and Lyttelton using the motor launches *Awhina Nui* and *Matariki* in conjunction with a 'motor bus' at the Diamond Harbour end. This put Toy's in competition with *Owaka*, *Onawe*, *Tui* and *Reremoana* — launches operated by W. C. Cleary & Co. From the outbreak of war, no more is known about *Matariki*.

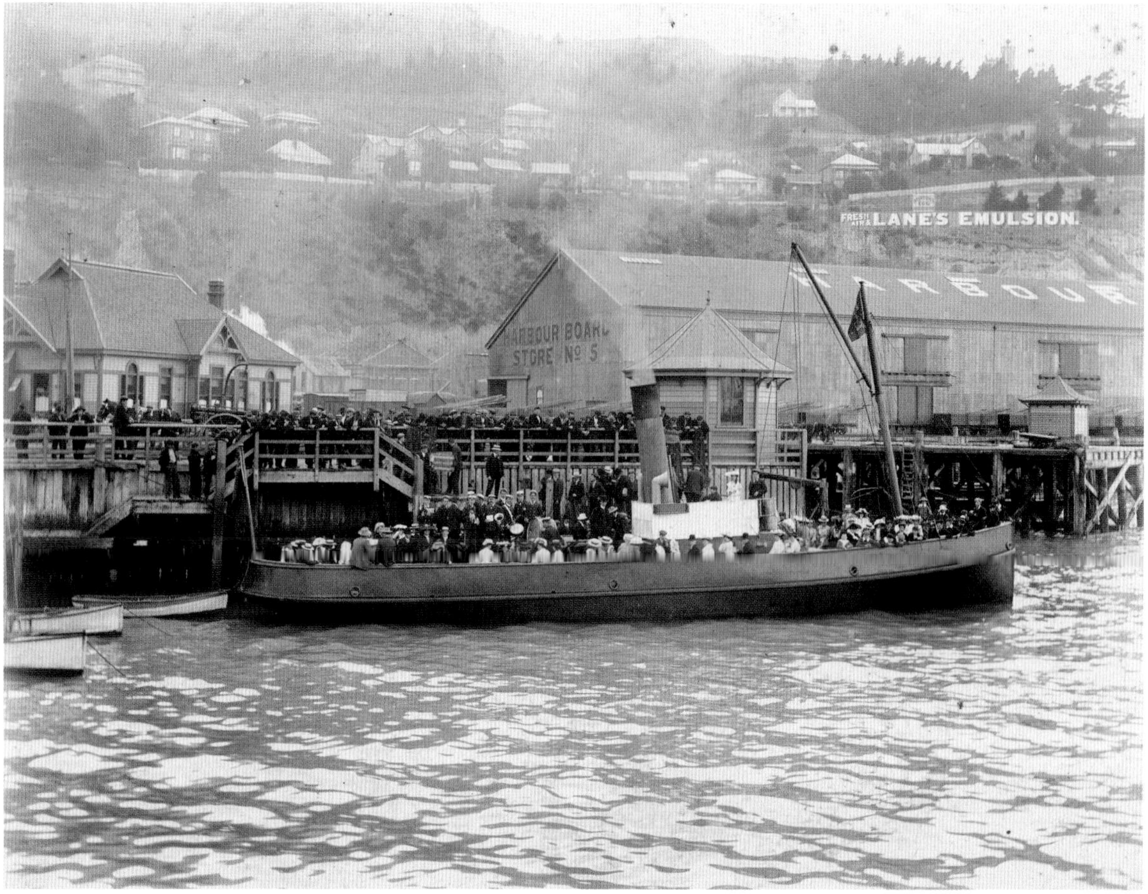
LANE'S EMULSION.
STORE No 5

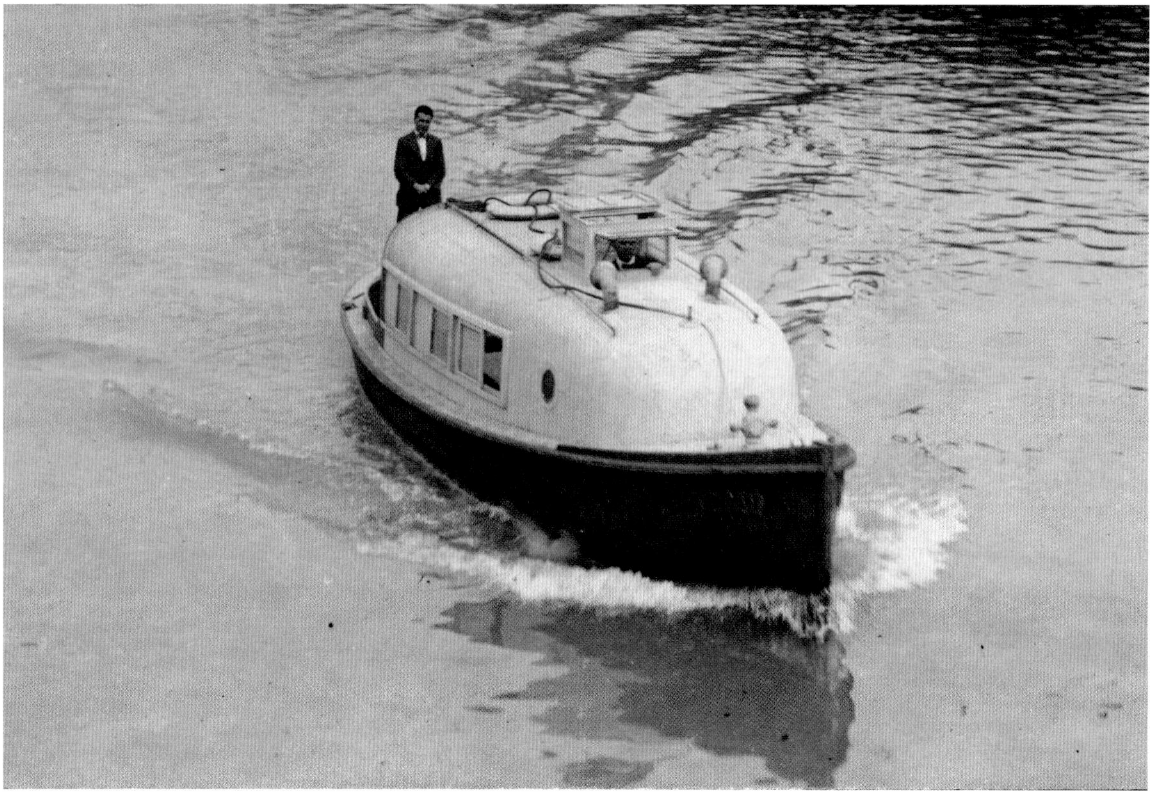

When the Lyttelton Borough Council purchased the 350-acre Diamond Harbour estate for subdivision in 1913, it undertook to provide a ferry service for those intending to live across the harbour, most of whom were expected to be working in Lyttelton. *Canterbury*, as noted above, covered the first six months, after which the council purchased the oil launch *Ruahine*. The 35-foot *Ruahine*, which could take 45 passengers, was described as 'speedy and comfortable'. Its engine was moved forward in 1915–16 to increase passenger accommodation. Over summers *Ruahine* made six return trips daily, reducing to four during the mid-winter months. The cost of the return trip was 6d — or 4d for Diamond Harbour property owners.

However, the council charged private ferry operators for conveying passengers (3d per head) and freight to Diamond Harbour and elsewhere, but made no charge for *Ruahine*, which was also allowed to compete with other launches on other runs. Angry private ferry operators felt disadvantaged. So from 1916 the council proscribed *Ruahine* from carrying passengers or goods other than to the municipal seaside resorts of Corsair Bay and Diamond Harbour at any time when a privately owned boat was available.

In 1918 Bert Rhind won the contract for the Diamond Harbour ferry service. Rhind augmented his fleet — consisting of *Reo Moana* (fitted with a new Kelvin four-cylinder engine specially imported from England in 1929) and *Moturata* — by purchasing *Ruahine* from the council. He could then use the most appropriately sized launch to meet passenger demand. In February 1922 Rhind's Motor Launches was registered with subscribers H. A. Rhind, W. C. Cleary, B. T. Demicheli, B. A. Arnesen, J. Gerrard, J. D. Bundy, T. M. Hunter and C. A. Henderson. *Onawe* was added to the fleet in the same year. In 1927 the 47-foot, 40-horsepower launch *Owaka*, built by Collings and Bell of Auckland, joined the Lyttelton Harbour launch fleet. She could accommodate 140–150 passengers, 60 of them seated in the 'well ventilated' cabin. The addition of *Owaka* meant that Lyttelton Ferry Launches — as Rhind's business was renamed — could handle well over 400 passengers at any one time. W. C. Cleary operated as the agent for Rhind's.

Ruahine was temporarily put out of action in 1933 when the Lyttelton–Wellington ferry *Rangatira* lost control and ran into the floating crane-ship *Rapaki*, which in turn ran into the breastwork of the wharf and crushed the little oil launch against the wharf. *Ruahine*'s cabin and top-hamper was stripped off and thrown into the sea, and her hull was also extensively damaged.

The economic and social climate was changing. In 1931 the Lyttelton Borough Council received no tenders on its specifications for the Diamond Harbour ferry service. The current contractors, Lyttelton Ferry Launches, offered to run the service for a subsidy of £175 a year. Councillor McDonald argued that the launch company had the council over a barrel and the council should consider running its

ABOVE SS *Purau*, purchased by George Agar on his last trip to England in 1898. *Purau* was a steel vessel, 75 feet long and drawing 4 feet 6 inches, built by Yarrow and Co. on the Thames River and put together in Lyttelton by J. and A. Anderson Ltd. It could accommodate up to 220 passengers.
LYTTELTON MUSEUM, 11391.1

BELOW The Lyttelton Borough Council purchased the 35-foot oil launch *Ruahine* around 1914 to provide a ferry service for the new subdivision at Diamond Harbour. In 1918 Bert Rhind won the contract for the ferry service, purchased *Ruahine* from the council and added *Reo Moana* and *Moturata* to the fleet.
LYTTELTON MUSEUM, 10134.1

own service. Councillor Comer thought the request for an increase was justified. The company had lost the government subsidy for Fort Jervois, as well as most of the cargo trade, which went to Diamond Harbour by lorry. A penny a head could be levied on all passengers landed at Diamond Harbour by outside steamers and launches. Councillor Gower pointed out that the new road to Diamond Harbour would kill off transport through Lyttelton.

Lyttelton Ferry Launches went into voluntary liquidation in 1943. Launches *Owaka*, *Onawe* and *Reo Moana* were purchased by J. D. Bundy, B. I. Demicheli and J. Jeffries, who formed a new company to continue the service. W. W. Toy also began a Lyttelton–Diamond Harbour launch service in the 1940s, running the ferries *Awhina Nui* and *Tarawai*. Sutton Brothers took over this service in 1944. During the Second World War, when shortages of fuel and tyres restricted road transport on Banks Peninsula, the launch fleet also ran to some of the peninsula bays, picking up cheese, bales of wool and general farm produce, as Betty Agar recalled:

> The launches ran whatever the weather. I'd make a bolt for the front of the boat if it was raining: there was precious little shelter on any of the ferries. I hated the *Reo Moana* — it rolled like anything. Shut inside the little hatch she had, I'd be afraid that she'd turn over in bad weather . . . I remember Ray Sutton with a grin from ear to ear as the boat thrashed into rough seas . . .[11]

When Sutton Brothers folded in the mid-1950s and no one else seemed willing to take over, the borough council stepped into the breach, purchasing *Onawe* and *Ngatiki*. And when revenue from the cross-harbour trade faltered, the council diversified into the tourist trade, taking on charter work, fishing trips and moonlight cruises. Still the ferries struggled to break even. The sealing of the road to Christchurch smoothed out the corrugations that had deterred residents of the south bays from driving to Lyttelton and the city. A school bus service started up.

In 1989 the newly formed Banks Peninsula District Council took control of the launch services. Lyttelton Harbour Cruises was set up in 1991 as a local authority trading enterprise, and in 1999 the Black Cat Group, already successful in Akaroa Harbour, took over the running of the Lyttelton–Diamond Harbour ferry service. From May 2001 the purpose-built, high-speed catamaran *Black Diamond* replaced the historic *Onawe*. Faster and more frequent crossings, greater comfort and better coordination with bus services in Lyttelton meant that patronage of the ferries increased. In 2020 Black Cat extended its ferry service contract for a further 12 years. It also runs trips to Ōtamahua Quail Island and Rīpapa Island. Replacing the now ageing ferry with a low-emission launch is currently under consideration.

Launch skippers ran a vital and much appreciated service. At times they did indeed live 'on the edge' as rapid weather changes and fierce seas challenged their small boats.

The launch *Toi Toi* joined the Lyttelton Harbour fleet in 1916 to replace *Stanley* on the Lyttelton–Port Levy run. The 32-foot *Toi Toi* was powered by an 18-horsepower, three-cylinder automatic engine and carried 45 passengers. On 26 May 1924 *Toi Toi* set out on its regular run from Port Levy. On board were owner and skipper Harry Grennell (remembered as 'one of the best launch men in the area'),[12] his brother Dick and a 15-year-old Christchurch lad, Clarence Barter, who was returning from a baching holiday in Port Levy. At Adderley Head the launch ran headfirst into a 'terrible sea' stirred up by a northerly gale. As *Toi Toi* rounded the head, the heavy sea wrenched off the for'ard hatch cover and waves poured in. As the launch began to sink, the Grennell brothers lashed a lifebuoy around Clarence Barter and the three tried to swim to shore. But the group found themselves being dragged further out, and Barter, exhausted in the breaking seas, was washed away. The undertow beneath the main cliff made landing there impossible, and Harry and Dick Grennell struggled for over half a mile to the Little Port Cooper Point where, after a terrible pounding in the surf, they were washed up on the rocky beach at the foot of the cliff. Bleeding badly, they dragged their way up the cliff to alert the men in the signal station.

About noon, signalman Ernest Bumstead, climbing up from the Little Port Cooper settlement to the Adderley Head Signal Station, heard what he thought was a cry from down the hill. He could see nothing but, having taken over the watch from his colleague, went out to check again and spotted a figure stumbling over the brow of the hill. It was Dick Grennell, bloodied and in the final stages of exhaustion. The signalman took off much of his own clothing to cover Grennell, who had lost most of his in the pounding seas, and set off down the hill where he found Harry Grennell, in an even worse condition. Once in the shelter of the signal station, Bumstead phoned the chief signalman to bring up warm clothing and first aid gear from the settlement below. He also alerted Lyttelton to the disaster. Chief signalman Jack Burns and some of the women went to look, unsuccessfully, for the missing boy.

John Anderson also experienced the same gale-force conditions, skipper Captain Thomas Hempstalk describing it as 'the most treacherous sea I have ever experienced and I have been sailing out of Lyttelton for the past twenty years'.[13] Hempstalk described the 'fearsome sight' at Adderley Head, with 'spray being flung fifty or sixty feet up the cliffs'. He spotted *Toi Toi*, sticking up nearly straight with its bow down and stern in the air. The Lyttelton tug set out for Little Port Cooper early afternoon with Dr Gilmour on board. The tug searched up and down the Adderley head shoreline without success. Meanwhile, some of

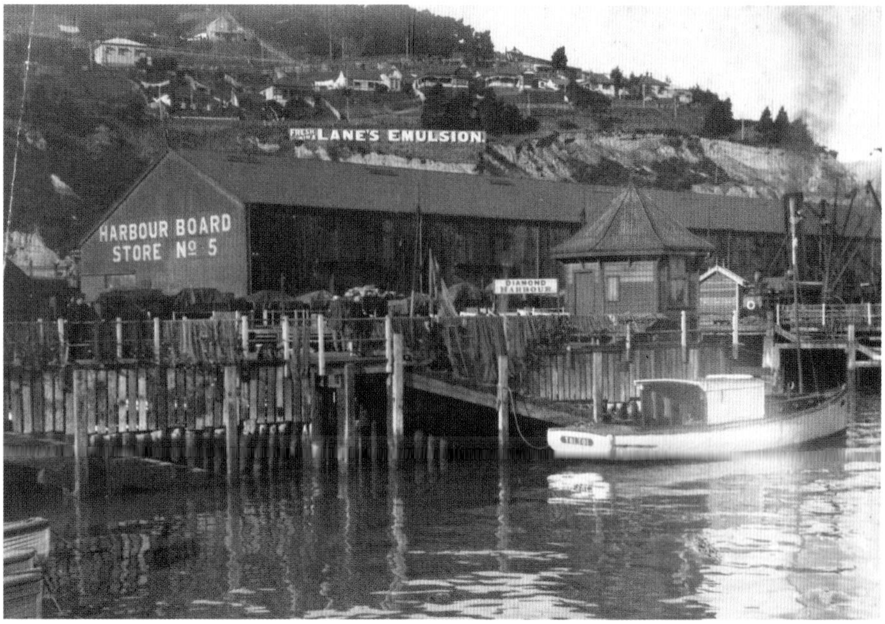
LANE'S EMULSION
HARBOUR BOARD
STORE No 5
DIAMOND
HARBOUR

Launch *Toi Toi* at the Diamond Harbour jetty in Lyttelton. In 1924 *Toi Toi* went down in a storm off Adderley Head. Harry and Dick Grennell just made it to shore but 15-year-old Clarence Barter drowned.
LYTTELTON MUSEUM, 14985.85

the wreckage from *Toi Toi* started to wash into Little Port Cooper.

The loss of a launch and a boy's life prompted questions about the control of small launches plying the bays. Some thought the harbour master should decide whether it was safe for vessels to put to sea. Others considered it was up to the master of each vessel to make the call. If the harbour master were to give the go-ahead for a boat which was then swamped, there would be an action against the Lyttelton Harbour Board. In the meantime, until a new launch commissioned by Harry Grennell arrived, *Onawe*, followed by the Akaroa launch *Orari*, covered the much-needed tri-weekly service to Port Levy.

Built in 1915 by Bailey and Lowe in Auckland, the 40-foot *Onawe* could make 9½ knots on its 25–35 horsepower engine. It carried 54 passengers and was fitted with electric light. In December 1919 *Onawe* was purchased by Captain G. Nelson from Basil Henning (who operated as a launch proprietor on Akaroa Harbour) to replace *Purau* on the Lyttelton Harbour and bays trade. The launch became a regular on the Governors Bay weekend visitor run, leaving Lyttelton on Saturdays at 10.00 a.m. and 2.00 p.m., returning at 4.35 p.m. and 6.15 p.m. Sundays were busier still, with four return trips through the day. The launch also took fishing parties outside the harbour heads.

In 1922 Rhind's Motor Launches Ltd. purchased the 'fine' passenger launch *Onawe* from Captain Nelson to augment his existing fleet. The launches, 'which are four of the best in Lyttelton Harbour', were to be used to run ferry services between Lyttelton and Governors Bay, Corsair Bay, Pūrau and Charteris Bay.[14] *Onawe* was temporarily assigned to the tri-weekly Lyttelton–Port Levy run when *Toi Toi* sank off Adderley Head in 1924. In the Lyttelton Regatta of the same year, *Onawe* won the motor-boat race on handicap, taking it out from the Port Levy-owned *Seabird*, which had been used in Auckland in the chase of Count Felix von Luckner.

Over the years *Onawe*, like all the harbour launches, was involved in numerous rescues. In December 1933 a whaleboat skippered by two officers and three ratings of the Royal Naval Volunteer Reserve capsized in a nor'west squall off Gollans Bay. The men climbed onto the upturned hull and were eventually rescued by the sailing boat *Boojum*, after which *Onawe* arrived to tow the whaleboat back to Lyttelton. Another nor'west gale in February 1939 caused the pontoon alongside the steamer *Kent* to be blown out through the moles into a very choppy outer harbour, taking with it two seamen who had been painting *Kent*. *Onawe* rescued the men and towed the pontoon back.

The launch was re-engined in 1936 and again in 1941. About 1944 it was refitted by Millers to provide more passenger accommodation. Unfortunately, in attempting to rescue a small yacht caught in a sudden southerly squall, *Onawe* was thrown up on the rocks and badly holed. It was salvaged, repaired and returned to service. Coming into the Rīpapa Island jetty on one occasion, *Onawe* straightened up and refused to steer. The rudder had fallen off. The launch *Ngatiki* towed it back to port. In a fine example of the collegiality that prevailed in the port, launch operator Fred Sutton arranged for a crane to lift *Onawe*'s stern out of the water. Sinclair and Melbourne cobbled together a steel shaft and rudder, and the launch was back in the water within a couple of hours.

A safe and dependable vessel, *Onawe* was the only launch tasked with taking stores out to fishing vessels at the heads. As one boatie recalled, 'I heard many stories about her towing small fishing boats back into the harbour . . .'[15] Lyttelton and Diamond Harbour residents still remember being on *Onawe* when it was caught in the big storm of October 2000. It took 45 minutes to get from Lyttelton to Diamond Harbour and four hours to get back, the launch forced to shelter in the lee of Quail Island. The same storm destroyed the marina at Magazine Bay.

Long-time locals still have vivid, happy memories of *Onawe* with its beautiful bow wave. As one recalled, 'Once they put the Volvo Penta engine in *Onawe* after the refurbish, she could hit her boot straps. I used to love in rough weather when she'd pitch so much you could sometimes see water at the window . . .'[16] Youngsters lent a willing hand. 'Hands up who didn't steer her as the skippers did tickets? . . . Yip and I think I would have been 10–14 years old.'[17] 'The 7.30 a.m. trip was the freight trip and you got a free ride for helping load and unload the freight.'[18] On one occasion, *Onawe* overheated just after leaving the Diamond Harbour wharf. 'I had to scoop up seawater from over the side to put into the cooling water system so we could carry on our merry way to Lyttelton.'[19] Another highlight was the party cruises: 'Out the Heads, rope holding the wheel & the entire crew & party dancing around a keg in the stern!'[20]

Onawe was eventually sold and transported to Putiki Bay on Waiheke Island to be used as a family cruiser.

In August 1954 a new harbour ferry replaced *Awhina Nui*. *Ngatiki*, commissioned by Sutton Brothers, was built in Lyttelton by Millers. It was made from kauri timber salvaged from the Elmwood homestead in Heaton Street, and the deck was teak. *Ngatiki* was 48 feet long with an 83-horsepower engine and could carry 90 passengers. Dogs rode on top. John Fox regularly crossed from Diamond Harbour to Lyttelton, where he caught the bus to Cashmere High School. He remembers the launch being referred to as 'the floating oven' in hot weather because of its lack of ventilation.[21] Another nickname was the 'waterbus' on account of *Ngatiki*'s bus-like design. Peter de Burgh-Thomas remembers the diesel and old painted wood smell of *Ngatiki* and being up front with his dad, who piloted the ferries for a time.

Ngatiki had more than its fair share of misfortune. It was stolen from its Lyttelton berth one evening and beached on Rīpapa Island, from where it had to be towed off and back to Lyttelton. More worryingly, in an often-crowded inner harbour there was a long history of minor collisions and near-misses involving passenger launches and other vessels. One of the worst occurred on Friday, 6 March 1998, when *Ngatiki*, carrying eight passengers at the time, collided with the harbour tug *Purau* in the port of Lyttelton. According to Christopher Moore, 'the ferry just imploded . . . there was safety glass everywhere, and people were badly cut'.[22] The launch was badly damaged on the starboard side, just aft of amidships. Bruce Ansley has written of his wife Sally's experience as a passenger that morning:

> The boat had almost reached its berth in Lyttelton port when one of the harbour tugs came pounding out from the wharf, rode up onto the ferry's cabin and all but crushed it in half, 'like', said Chris, 'a bomb going off.' The passengers had seen it coming. They lined up in the stern mesmerized by approaching disaster. Sally dove over the side and struck out in the icy green water. The tug's black hull

swept past her, crashed into the ferry, slid back. Sally felt herself being sucked under. Exhausted by fright and cold she fought to the surface, certain she was going to die until she looked up into the face of an Asian seaman leaning over the rail of a freighter. He dropped a lifebuoy beside her. . . She swam for its light, kicked back towards the ferry, still afloat amidst the wreckage. A woman grabbed her hand and hauled her onto the boarding platform at the back of the boat.[23]

The marine enquiry that followed controversially found the ferry master to blame for failing to keep a proper lookout and for going too fast in the inner harbour. He was fined $2000.

Ngatiki was bought by boatbuilders Stark Brothers, who repaired and refurbished it as a charter vessel. It had been back in service only a few months when it was caught in the violent southerly storm of 12 October 2000 that destroyed the Magazine Bay Marina. *Ngatiki* was the last vessel to sink in the marina. A concrete pontoon crashed through its starboard side and wedged there, and it was towed to an inner harbour mooring 'like a submarine', then left by the insurers to gather mould. Along came Canterbury Coastguard chief Del Hurley. He bought *Ngatiki* from the insurance company, repaired and refurbished it and turned it into a family cruise boat. 'She's a happy little ship. She reminds me of Thomas the Tank Engine, with that "just let me get to work" attitude. She has a lovely, gentle roll, as if happy to be back in the water.'[24]

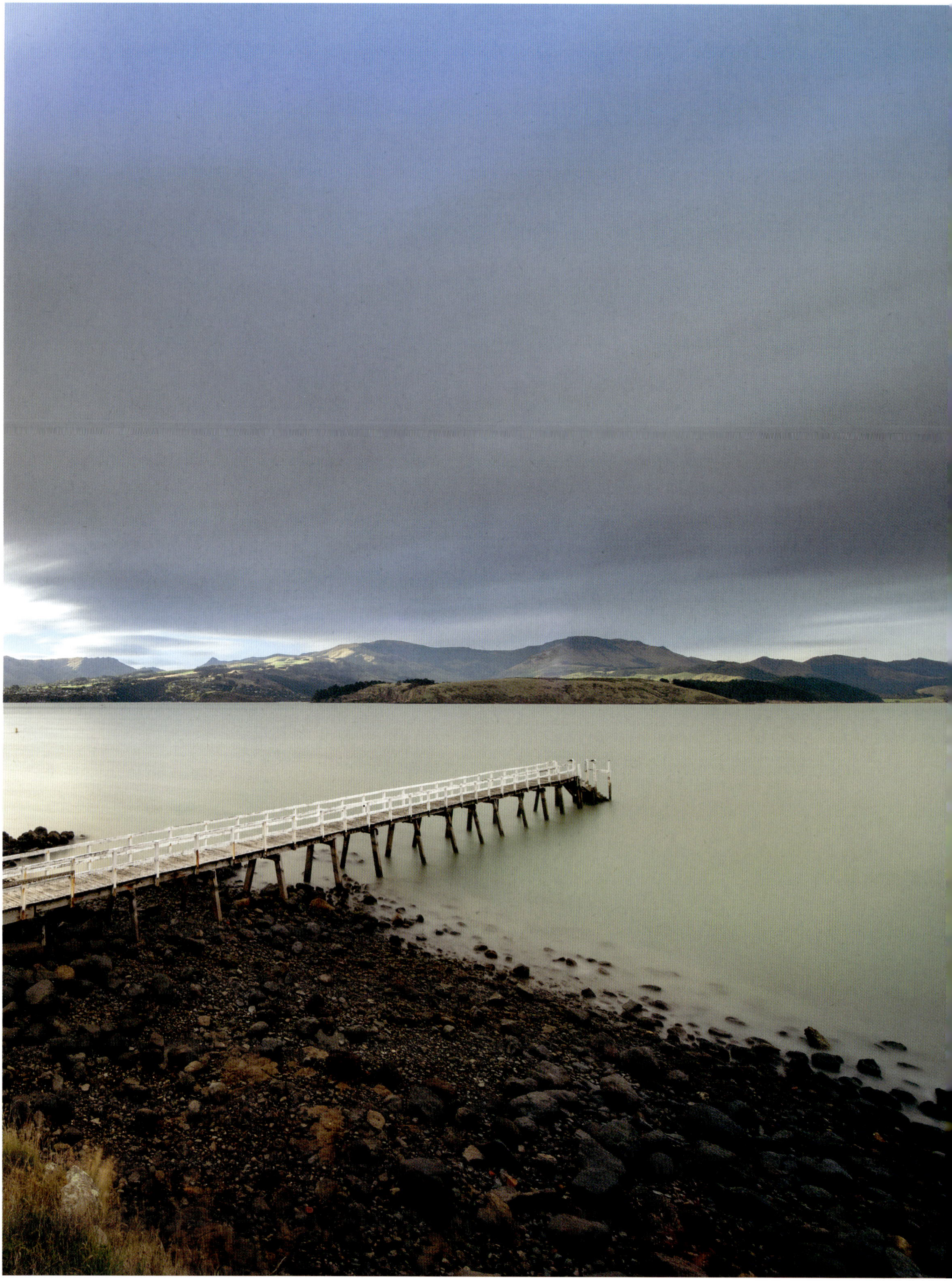

Afterword

From our house on the edge of an eroding cliff at the head of the harbour, I can watch the relentless ebb and flow of the tide, calming soliton-like waves, rolling easterly whitecaps, violent southerly storms. Mostly it is a quiet part of Whakaraupō, the preserve of the gulls, herons, oystercatchers, stilts, terns, shags, godwits, spoonbills and other birds that thrive in the shallows and on the mudflats.

Now, as I reflect on over five years of living with what I still call 'the jetty book', it occurs to me that this is really a story of resourceful human adaptation to a rugged land and seascape created through violent volcanic eruption. Historically, dwellers in Whakaraupō, be they Waitaha, Ngāti Māmoe, Ngāi Tahu or Pākehā, have lived in narrow spaces between a mountainous landscape and a sometimes treacherous sea. For a long time, criss-crossing the harbour by sea, dangerously life-claiming as it could be, was swifter and more economical than passage by land. Hence the tauranga waka or traditional canoe landing places, and, later, the jetties built by European settlers.

The resources of the harbour have been well used — one might say plundered. The sea floor has been raked for shellfish and dredged to create channels for shipping. Enormous quantities of mud have been uplifted and dumped in the bays. Everywhere the cliff faces have been quarried for ballast, building, road maintenance and reclamation.

There have been multiple plans to tame the harbour, including a settlement (eventually a city) at Tauwharepaka Teddington and a port at Rāpaki; the reclamation of Te Wharau Charteris Bay; and a new inner harbour at Kaioruru Church Bay and deep-water port at Ōtokitoki Gollans Bay. None of these eventuated. The greatest actual transformations have taken place at Ōhinehou Lyttelton, where a port was built and the foreshore reclaimed, and there have been further large reclamation projects at Naval Point, at Cashin Quay and now at Te Awaparahi Bay.

The harbour itself is changing. Stand on Summit Road above Ōtoromiro and look down the harbour towards the headlands of Awaroa and Te Piaka, and you can see the latest port reclamation at Te Awaparahi Bay extending to the east and the south, a large, square block in an undulating seascape. At the head of the harbour the noticeable recession of mud from the shoreline may be a result of land uplift at Governors Bay and Allandale following the Canterbury earthquake sequence. Locals joke that the mud is migrating to fill up the newly dredged navigation channel.

The mountains and hills of Whakaraupō, once forested and then stripped almost bare, are slowly greening again, thanks to groups such as the Summit Road Society, the Ōtamahua Quail Island Ecological Restoration Trust, the Rod Donald Trust, and Te Hapū o Ngāti Wheke partnered with Living Springs, along with many individuals and families on privately owned land. Such initiatives are gradually advancing the Whaka-Ora Healthy Harbour vision of restoring the ecological and cultural health of Whakaraupō Lyttelton Harbour as mahinga kai, for generations to come.

Our use of the harbour has changed. For those of us who live on the edges of Whakaraupō the sea is no longer our primary mode of transport (unless we commute from Diamond Harbour). Nor, mostly, do we rely on it for sustenance. Rather it is a recreational space — a 'nice to' rather than a 'need to'. We swim, sail and fish. We share Whakaraupō with fish, shellfish and native birds, and in working to protect our own environment we enhance theirs. We also care enough about our built heritage to rescue and rebuild, as community projects, some of the much-valued and originally hard-fought-for structures that connect the land and the sea in this ancient volcanic crater.

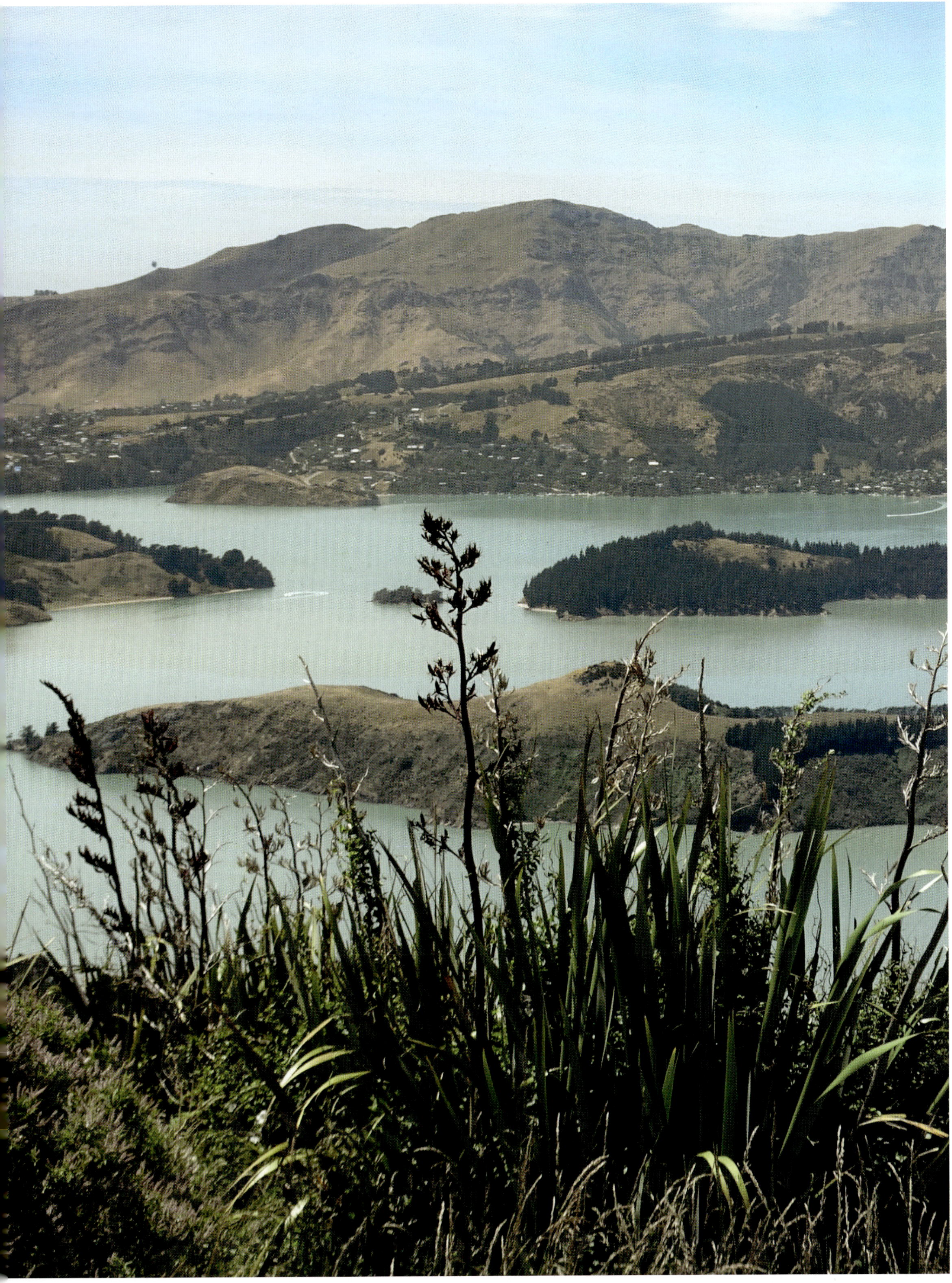

Notes

Introduction

1. Jacky Bowring, Nancy Vance and Mick Abbott, 'Between Seascape and Landscape: Experiencing the Liminal Zone of the Coast', in Mike Brown and Kimberley Peters (eds), *Living with the Sea: Knowledge, Awareness and Action* (London: Routledge, 2018), p. 9.

Chapter 1. Living on the edge

1. Deidre Hart, *Sedimentation in the Upper Lyttelton Harbour*, report to Environment Canterbury, January 2004, p. 5.
2. Dyanna Jolly (Dyanna Jolly Consulting) and Ngā Papatipu Rūnanga Working Group, *Mahaanui Iwi Management Plan* (Ngāi Tūāhuriri Rūnanga, Te Hapū o Ngāti Wheke [Rāpaki,] Te Rūnanga o Koukourārata, Ōnuku Rūnanga, Wairewa Rūnanga, Te Taumutu Rūnanga, 2013).
3. Harry C. Evison, *The Long Dispute: Maori Land Rights and European Colonisation in Southern New Zealand* (Christchurch: Canterbury University Press, 1997), p. 130.
4. Charlotte Godley, *Letters from Early New Zealand 1850–1853* (Christchurch: Whitcombe & Tombs, 1951), p. 27.
5. Port Cooper was renamed Port Victoria in 1848, and changed again to Port Lyttelton in 1857.
6. Captain William Mein Smith, Report, November 1842, in Edward Jerningham Wakefield, *The Handbook for New Zealand* (London: John W. Parker, 1848), pp. 328–9.
7. Louise Beaumont, Matthew Carter and John Wilson, *Banks Peninsula Contextual Historical Overview and Thematic Framework*, report prepared for Christchurch City Council, June 2014.
8. Lyttelton Wharf Commission Report, *Lyttelton Times*, 25 July 1863.
9. Ibid.
10. *Lyttelton Times*, 2 January 1902.
11. The cup was won by Lyttelton boat *Betty* in 1926–28 and by *Avenger* in 1932–33. George Brasell won for Canterbury in 1931, while Eliot Sinclair further retained the cup for Lyttelton, sailing *Irene* in 1934 and 1935 and *Avenger* in 1936. Lyttelton boatbuilder Fred Dobby built no fewer than nine Sanders Cup defenders.
12. New Zealand Historic Bills, Lyttelton Harbour Board Land Bill 1905, www.nzlii.org/nz/legis/hist_bill/lhblb1905661341/, accessed 20 September 2019.
13. Papers re Sites used as Jetties and Wharves, Lyttelton Harbour Board, CH518, RC89C-0148-007; R24981701, ANZCRO.
14. Ibid.
15. *Lyttelton Times*, 19 March 1912.
16. Papers re Sites used as Jetties and Wharves, October 1912. Lyttelton Harbour Board, CH518, RC89C-0148-007; R24981701, ANZCRO.
17. *Press*, 4 November 1920.
18. *Star*, 6 May 1914.
19. Mark Trainor, *A History of the Mount Herbert County Council 1902–1980*, Mount Herbert County Council, 1984.
20. *Lyttelton Times*, 8 March 1897.
21. Bruce Gebbie, email to Jane Robertson, 14 September 2020.
22. *Press*, 14 June 1930.
23. Opinions Market Research Ltd, *Anecdotal Evidence of Changes to the Natural Environment of Lyttelton Harbour / Whakaraupō Prior to 2000*, report prepared for Lyttelton Harbour/Whakaraupo Issues Group, June 2013, www.healthyharbour.org.nz/wp-content/uploads/2019/05/Opinions-Market-Research-Ltd-2013-Anecdotal-evidence.pdf, accessed 12 December 2020.
24. Bruce Gebbie, email to Jane Robertson, 14 September 2020.
25. David Bundy, personal communication, various dates 2020.
26. Neil McLennan, email to Jane Robertson, 31 March 2020.
27. Christchurch City Council, *Harbours and Marine Structures Activity Management Plan: Long Term Plan 2015–2025*. 16 December 2014, www.ccc.govt.nz/assets/Documents/The-Council/Plans-Strategies-Policies-Bylaws/Plans/Long-Term-Plan/ActivityManagementPlanHarboursAndMarineStructures.pdf, accessed 29 August 2019.

Chapter 2. Waitata Little Port Cooper

1. This according to William Anderson Taylor, *Lore and History of the South Island Maori* (Christchurch: Bascands, 1952), p. 62, http://nzetc.victoria.ac.nz/tm/scholarly/tei-TayLore-t1-body1-d6.html, accessed 24 July 2019.
2. Félix Maynard, *The Whalers*, ed. Alexandre Dumas (London: Hutchinson, 1937), p. 174.
3. *Star*, 19 May 1919.
4. Gordon Ogilvie, *Banks Peninsula: Cradle of Canterbury* (Wellington: GP Publications, 1990).
5. An Old Colonist [William Pratt], *Colonial Experiences; or, Incidents and Reminiscences of Thirty-Four years in New Zealand* (London: Chapman & Hall, 1877).
6. Department of Conservation, History of Adderley Head Signal Station. www.doc.govt.nz/parks-and-recreation/places-to-go/canterbury/places/banks-peninsula-area/adderley-head-signal-station, accessed 30 November 2017.
7. Lyttelton Harbour Board, Signal Station Little Port Cooper, XBAH-A002-1817, ANZCRO.
8. *Star*, 16 February 1880.
9. Chief Harbour Master F.D. Gibson to the Secretary for Public Works, 20 May 1873. CAAR, CH287, CP257/, R8420114, ANZCRO.
10. *Star*, 21 October 1880.
11. *Lyttelton Times*, 10 March 1874.
12. *Lyttelton Times*, 26 February, 1880. The 'broad pathway' has now eroded away and access is pretty much limited to rock scrambling. The contractor had difficulty completing work on the boat slip and breakwater because there were too few sufficiently low tides over the period of the contract. He was threatened with having to pay for the lost time.
13. *Star*, 1 May 1883.
14. Ibid.
15. *Lyttelton Times*, 8 January 1859.
16. One family, displaying symptoms of smallpox, was landed at Gravesend and came out to Lyttelton the following year. RootsChat, Newton Family, www.rootschat.com/forum/index.php?topic=1266.9, accessed 3 March 2018.
17. *Lyttelton Times*, 13 October 1860.
18. Paul Ensor, personal communication, December 2021.
19. *Press*, 6 May 1908. The P. Nolan mentioned in the *Press* report is likely to have been Oliver Archibald Nolan, who worked as a signalman between 1904 and 1910.
20. *The Nolan. The Newsletter of the O'Nolan Clan Family Association*, March 2009, Issue 19, http://nolanfamilies.org/archives/newsletter/TheNolan-19.pdf, accessed 12 March 2018.
21. *Star*, 1 May 1883.
22. From 1876 until 1886, the spoil dredged to keep the Lyttelton Harbour channels sufficiently deep was dumped in Little Port Cooper and Camp Bay. Then there was a respite until 1925, when the practice resumed. In those first 10 years, 14,346 barge-loads of spoil, totalling some 3.66 million metric tonnes, were deposited in the Camp Bay area. In theory, outgoing currents near the harbour heads took the mud out to sea, but without doubt much of it stayed in the bays. The harbour board took regular soundings not only of the main channel depth but also to monitor what was happening in Camp Bay and Little Port Cooper. Plentiful newspaper correspondence from the time indicates that the dumping of spoil was a contentious issue then, as it is now.
23. Harbour Improvement Committee minutes 1879–1920, Lyttelton Harbour Board, XBAA CH519, //298, R25041261, ANZCRO.
24. *Press*, 6 August 1908.
25. *Press*, 1 November 1927.
26. Comment made on *Between Land and Sea: Living on the Edge in Whakaraupō Lyttelton Harbour* blog, April 2018, by Jill Ineson, Helen's daughter. Helen was married to Jack Condon, who was stationed at Little Port Cooper after the First World War.
27. Comment made on *Between Land and Sea: Living on the Edge in Whakaraupō Lyttelton Harbour* blog, April 2018, by Enid Keenan, daughter of Jim Welsh, who relieved at Little Port Cooper in 1939.

28   *Press*, 12 May 1924.
29   *Press*, 7 February 1999.

Chapter 3. Te Pōhue Camp Bay

1   Gordon Ogilvie, *Place Names of Banks Peninsula and the Port Hills* (Christchurch: Canterbury University Press, 2017), p. 45.
2   *Lyttelton Times*, 29 April 1863.
3   *Lyttelton Times*, 12 August 1863.
4   *Lyttelton Times*, 5 September 1863. The assumption seems to be that this necessity for living under canvas prompted the name 'Camp Bay'. However, the name dates back to 1852 at least (and maybe earlier). More likely the bay was used by the Pūrau-based Greenwood or Rhodes farm staff as a convenient campsite for shepherding and mustering.
5   *Press*, 6 February 1864.
6   *Lyttelton Times*, 17 October 1863.
7   *Press*, 29 December 1863.
8   Ibid.
9   *Press*, 11 December 1863.
10   *Lyttelton Times*, 5 January 1864.
11   Camp Bay Quarantine Barracks, CAAR CH287, CP232/, R8418486, ANZCRO.
12   R. Armstrong to Provincial Secretary, Inspection of buildings at Camp Bay, 29/1/1864, CAAR CH287 19936 Box CP 49, Archives NZ.
13   Lazaret: A hospital for the treatment of contagious diseases; a place of detention for people in quarantine. [It. *lazzaretto*, fr. *lazzaro*, a leper].
14   Mary Stapylton-Smith (comp.), *Adderley to Bradley: A History of the Southern Bays of Lyttelton Harbour* (Diamond Harbour: Friends of Diamond Harbour Library, 2009), p. 22.
15   *Press*, 7 July 1865.
16   *Lyttelton Times*, 20 November 1865.
17   *Lyttelton Times*, 28 November 1865.
18   Grant Hughes, Quarantine, in Kete Christchurch, CCL, http://ketechristchurch.peoplesnetworknz.info/site/documents/show/244-quarantine#.WjFk6iN7FhE, accessed 6 August 2019.
19   John Galbraith, Immigration Officer, Report on Quarantine Barracks, 1 August 1871, CAAR CH287, CP252, R8419779, ANZCRO.
20   *Star*, 16 September 1933.
21   Great Grandma's Wicker Basket, Camp Bay Cemetery Records, Banks Peninsula, http://greatgrandmaswickerbasket.blogspot.com/2014/02/camp-bay-cemetery-records-banks.html, accessed 6 May 2018.
22   *Press*, 15 February 1916.
23   *Star*, 4 September 1918. No mention of the dismal circumstances and official neglect associated with the 'historic spot'.
24   *Press*, 3 March 1919.
25   Ogilvie, *Place Names of Banks Peninsula*, p. 46.
26   Stapylton-Smith, *Adderley to Bradley*, p. 27.
27   Camp Bay jetty damage 1954, Lyttelton Harbour Board, XBAA, CH518 668/A002-402, R25017215, ANZCRO.
28   Paul Rogers, *Memories of Camp Bay*, private typescript, courtesy of Noel Rogers.
29   Ibid.

Chapter 4. Ripapa Island

1   Barry Brailsford, *The Tattooed Land: The Southern Frontiers of the Pa Maori* (Wellington: A. H. & A. W. Reed, 1981), p. 160.
2   Ngāi Tahu Claims Settlement Act 1998, Schedule 88, Tōpuni for Ripapa Island, Lyttelton Harbour, www.legislation.govt.nz/act/public/1998/0097/latest/DLM431323.html, accessed 12 August 2019. 'The concept of Tōpuni derives from the traditional Ngāi Tahu custom of rangatira (chiefs) extending their mana (power and authority) over areas or people by placing their cloaks over them. Tōpuni status therefore confirms the overlay of Ngāi Tahu values on these public conservation areas. The Tōpuni does not override or alter the existing status of the land, but ensures that Ngāi Tahu values are recognised, acknowledged, and provided for.' DOC, Māori, Tōpuni, www.doc.govt.nz/about-us/our-partners/maori/, accessed 12 August 2019.
3   *Press*, 6 June 1873.
4   *Press*, 5 May 1873.
5   Report on the state of Police Depot Christchurch and Quarantine buildings, Ripa Island, by F. Strouts, 3 June 1874, CAAR CH287, 20410, Box CP658/a, R21994752, ANZCRO.
6   Ibid.; *Lyttelton Times*, 3 April 1873.
7   *Lyttelton Times*, 25 September 1873.
8   *Lyttelton Times*, 28 July 1880. Other newspaper reports were much more disparaging.
9   Ibid.
10   A *Press* article from 6 August 1888 gives a detailed description of the operation of the 'disappearing' guns. Peter Wilkins points out that 'the disappearing guns were initially developed in England as a cheap and effective protection for gun crews from naval fire. Once high angle or plunging fire and aerial bombardment were developed the advantage of disappearing guns was lost and emplacements of the en barbette variety became more practical.' Email correspondence, Peter Wilkins to the author, 15 August 2022.
11   Jonathan Roberts, *The Diary of Jonathan Roberts: Bank Clerk, Athlete, Convict and Escapee*, facsimile edition (Christchurch: Lyttelton Times Company, 1977). bankspeninsulageopark@gmail.
12   The drawbridge was still capable of being raised and lowered when the army decided to demolish the fort in 1954. The Lyttelton Harbour Board intervened and obtained a stay of orders.
13   David Gee, *The Devil's Own Brigade: A History of the Lyttelton Gaol 1860–1920* (Millwood Press, Wellington, 1975).
14   Heritage NZ Fort Jervois, www.heritage.org.nz/the-list/details/5306, accessed 4 June 2018. For a detailed description of the site, click on 'additional information'.
15   Kevin Clements, *Back from the Brink: The Creation of a Nuclear-Free New Zealand* (Wellington: Bridget Williams Books, 1988 and 2015 [e-book]).
16   *Lyttelton Times*, 20 April 1889.
17   *Lyttelton Times*, 23 February 1910.
18   *Lyttelton Times*, 29 November 1893.
19   Wikipedia, Compulsory Military Training in New Zealand, https://en.wikipedia.org/wiki/Compulsory_military_training_in_New_Zealand, accessed 9 June 2018.
20   Samuel Veale Bracher, *Ripa Island: A Lesson for Conscriptionists* (London: Friends' Peace Committee, 1914), p. 9, http://heritage.christchurchcitylibraries.com/Publications/1910s/RipaIsland/PDF/CCL-73787.pdf, accessed 9 June 2018.
21   Ibid. The First World War was just around the corner.
22   *Press*, 12 January 1918.
23   *Press*, 21 February 1918.
24   The location of the hut was identified by the Sea Cadets. It was destroyed in the *Wahine* storm, 1968. Email communication, Peter Wilkins to Jane Robertson, 15 August 2022.
25   Ibid., 4 March 1918. Von Luckner and Kirscheiss may not have considered the late winter/early spring sea temperatures luxurious.
26   Lynley Galbraith, *Gardiner Memories*, Jackson family archive, p. 10.
27   *Press*, 14 September 1937.
28   *Press*, 14 April 1938. There is a suggestion that permission to visit the island was withheld because the trip was funded by the German Nazi government.
29   For this material on Pile Bay I have drawn extensively on Baden Norris's chapter in Mary Stapylton-Smith (comp.), *Adderley to Bradley: A History of the Southern Bays of Lyttelton Harbour* (Diamond Harbour: Friends of Diamond Harbour Library, 2009), pp. 33–36.
30   *Press*, 28 January 1937.
31   *Press*, 12 December 1932.

Chapter 5. Pūrau

1   Donald Couch, *Pūrau Māori History: A Ngāi Tahu View*, paper in progress, 2018. The presence of a fortified Ngāti Māmoe pā on Te Ahu Pātiki Mount Herbert, long promulgated by European historians, is not supported by contemporary Ngāi Tahu scholars.
2   Gordon Ogilvie, *Place Names of Banks Peninsula and the Port Hills* (Christchurch: Canterbury University Press, 2017), p. 50.
3   Joseph Hugh Greenwood, *Diary*, Ref: MS-0878. Alexander Turnbull Library, Wellington, /records/22893178.
4   Quoted in Harry Evison, *The Long Dispute: Maori Land Rights and European Colonisation in Southern New Zealand* (Christchurch: Canterbury University Press, 1997), p. 136.
5   Elisabeth Ogilvie, *Purau* (Christchurch: Caxton Press, 1970), p. 31.
6   Greenwood, *Diary*.
7   Ogilvie, *Purau*, pp. 33–35. Ogilvie, *Place Names of Banks Peninsula*, p. 51. I have found no record of where they were sent.
8   Elisabeth Ogilvie. *Elisabeth with an 's'. A Childhood Memoir*, p. 45, Jackson family archive.

9. Harry C. Evison, *Te Wai Pounamu: The Greenstone Island* (Wellington & Christchurch: Aoraki Press, 1993), pp. 214, 221–222. Couch, *Pūrau Māori History*.
10. Pūrau NR 876 was the only reserve where a single individual, Wikitoria Nohomutu, was named as recipient of the award. This land was bequeathed to Rahera Muriwai Uru in 1913 and on-sold to Mrs Christina Gardiner the following year for £360. Thus in 1914 Ngāi Tahu land rights in Pūrau were extinguished. (Couch, *Pūrau Māori History*, pp. 6–7).
11. J. Hight & C. R. Straubel, *A History of Canterbury* (Christchurch: Whitcombe & Tombs, 1957), p. 117.
12. Charles Obin Torlesse, *The Torlesse Papers: The Journals and Letters of Charles Obins Torlesse Concerning the Foundation of the Canterbury Settlement in New Zealand 1848–51*, ed. Peter Bromley Maling (Christchurch: Pegasus Press, 1958), p. 40.
13. Edward Ward, *The Journal of Edward Ward 1850–51* (Christchurch: Pegasus Press, 1951), p. 13.
14. Ibid, pp. 91–92.
15. *Lyttelton Times*, 31 July 1882.
16. Charles Perry Cox, *Personal Notes and Reminiscences of an Early Canterbury Settler* (Christchurch: Canterbury Publishing Company, 1915), p. 21.
17. 'Recollections of an old pioneer. As recounted by Mr James Ashworth in 1918.' *Akaroa Mail and Banks Peninsula Advertiser*, 21 September 1926.
18. Frances Cresswell, *Old Homes of Lyttelton Harbour* (Christchurch: Pegasus Press, 1974), p. 3.
19. 'Recollections of an old pioneer.'
20. Extract from Letters from Edward Dobson to A. E. Woodhouse, 1934, quoted in Ogilvie, *Purau*, p. 45.
21. *Lyttelton Times*, 11 January 1862.
22. Ogilvie, *Purau*, p. 47.
23. *Star*, 20 January 1872.
24. Ogilvie, *Purau*.
25. *Press*, 27 August 1919.
26. Lynley Galbraith, *Gardiner Memories*, Jackson family archive, p. 10.
27. Eleanor Isherwood, *A School Marm in New Zealand*, Jackson family archive.
28. Frank Jackson, *My Memories of Purau*, Jackson family archive.
29. Ogilvie, *Elisabeth with an 's'*, p. 13.
30. *Lyttelton Times*, 1 April 1893.
31. *Lyttelton Times*, 16 April 1892.
32. Much more detail about the families living in Pūrau can be accessed in Ogilvie, *Place Names of Banks Peninsula*; Ogilvie, *Purau*; and Mary Stapylton-Smith (comp.), *Adderley to Bradley: A History of the Southern Bays of Lyttelton Harbour* (Diamond Harbour: Friends of Diamond Harbour Library, 2009).
33. Galbraith, *Gardiner Memories*.
34. Memo from the Engineer's Office, Lyttelton Harbour Board, 17 January 1916, XBAA, CH518, 668/A002-401, R25017214, ANZCRO/ECan. As an example, the day after approaching the harbour board, Harold Gardiner was due to ship out 600 sheep.
35. Harbour Master's Report 23 October 1952, XBAA, CH518, 668/A002-402, R25017215, ANZCRO/ECan.
36. Letter from Alan Jackson of Glenrowan, Pūrau to Lyttelton Harbour Board, 9 November 1952, ibid.
37. Letter to the Mount Herbert County Council from the Secretary for Marine, 19 February 1953, ibid.
38. Lyttelton Harbour Board, Memorandum for Resident Engineer A. J. Charman, 16 January 1962, ibid.

Chapter 6. Te Waipapa Diamond Harbour

1. Dr Matthew Morris, *Diary* (unpublished), Cotter Medical History Trust, quoted in Mary Stapylton-Smith (comp.), *Adderley to Bradley: A History of the Southern Bays of Lyttelton Harbour* (Diamond Harbour: Friends of Diamond Harbour Library, 2009), p. 72.
2. Letter from Stoddart and Sprot to Superintendent on the signal service at Diamond Harbour, 14 May 1862, CAAR, CH287, CP29/, R22190346, ANZCRO.
3. *Lyttelton Times*, 9 March 1861.
4. Louise Beaumont Heritage Landscape Consultant, Stoddart Point Reserve Landscape History and Conservation Report Prepared for Christchurch City Council, June 2016, www.ccc.govt.nz/assets/Documents/The-Council/Plans-Strategies-Policies-Bylaws/Plans/Park-management-plans/16-657353-Stoddart-Point-Reserve-Conservation-Report-FINAL-2016-06-07-Copy.compressed.pdf, accessed 5 September 2019.
5. *Lyttelton Times*, 12 March 1866.
6. *Lyttelton Times*, 9 January 1861.
7. *Press*, 30 April 1869.
8. *Star*, 31 July 1879.
9. *Star*, 6 August 1879.
10. Oliver Hunter, *The Magnostic Philosopher of Church Bay: The Life and Works of Oliver Hunter, 1882–1979* (Christchurch: Friends of the Diamond Harbour Library, 2006).
11. *Star*, 2 January 1875.
12. Quoted in Ewan Henderson, *Henderson of Zetland* (Ewan Henderson, 2014), p. 206.
13. *Press*, 20 April 1874.
14. Ibid.
15. *Press*, 28 October 1880.
16. *Press*, 29 October 1881.
17. *Lyttelton Times*, 31 December 1891.
18. *Press*, 24 June 1899.
19. Papers re Sites used as Jetties and Wharves, Lyttelton Harbour Board, XBAA CH518, RC89C – 0148/7, R24981701, ANZCRO.
20. Lyttelton Borough Extension Act, 1911, No. 36, 7b, www.nzlii.org/nz/legis/hist_act/lbea19112gv1911n36460/, accessed 4 June 2019.
21. 16 March 1912, *Diary of E. R. Chudleigh 1866–1921*, quoted in Julie King, *Flowers into Landscape: Margaret Stoddart 1865–1934* (Christchurch: Robert McDougall Art Gallery & Hazard Press, 1997), p. 85.
22. *Star*, 6 February 1913.
23. *Press*, 22 April 1918.
24. *Press*, 23 January 1915.
25. *Star*, 6 August 1915.
26. *Press*, 18 January 1916.
27. *Lyttelton Times*, 16 October 1915.
28. Quoted in Stapylton-Smith, *Adderley to Bradley*, p. 166.
29. Maurie (Maurice) Agar, *Autobiographical Notes*, email, Simon Agar to Jane Robertson, 22 September 2020.
30. The drowning reference is to the death of a young boy who fell from the Sandy Bay/Percivals Point jetty at the head of the harbour in 1938. Lyttelton Harbour Board correspondence, outlying jetties, 1913–1945, XBAA, CH518, 668/A002-401, R25017214, ANZCRO/ECan.
31. Proposed new jetty at Diamond Harbour 1946, MA50C/1/453, Lyttelton Harbour Board, Archives NZ/ECan.
32. *Press*, 5 September 1944.
33. Lyttelton Harbour Board correspondence, outlying jetties, 1946–1966, 27 January 1965, XBAA, CH518, 668/A002-402, R25017215, ANZCRO/ECan.
34. Letter from C. Paine to the Diamond Harbour Burgesses Association, 12 February 1966, ibid.
35. Lyttelton Borough councillor and harbour board pilot Euan Crawford drove the ferry to keep the service going (an activity he described as 'very extra-curricular'), and the appointment of Peter van den Berg to manage the service rescued it from total collapse.
36. Tony Ussher and Katharine Watson, *Diamond Harbour Wharf: Conservation Report* (Christchurch City Council, 2020).

Chapter 7. Kaioruru Church Bay

1. *An Early Conservationist: The Life of Oliver Hunter*, unpublished manuscript, Hunter archive.
2. *Lyttelton Times*, 4 June 1867.
3. *Star*, 8 August 1898.
4. *Press*, 18 July 1873.
5. *Star*, 2 August 1873.
6. Oliver Hunter, *The Magnostic Philosopher of Church Bay: The Life and Works of Oliver Hunter, 1882–1979* (Christchurch: Friends of Diamond Harbour Library, 2006), p. 31.
7. Colin Amodeo with Bill Huntley, *The Mosquito Fleet of Canterbury* (Christchurch: Caxton Press, 2005), p. 237.
8. *Lyttelton Times*, 16 November 1859.
9. Support for application to erect a jetty at Church Bay, CAAR CH287, 19946, Box CP229 ICPW 130/1870, Archives NZ.
10. *Press*, 22 December 1879.
11. *Press*, 22 September 1973.
12. Hunter, *Magnostic Philosopher*, p. 7. It was not until 1907 that a public jetty was built in the bay.
13. Ibid, p. 8.
14. Ibid.
15. *Press*, 3 November 1913. Late morning, the picketers did allow the produce to be landed and stores loaded.
16. Mary Harrison, email to Jane Robertson, 21 May 2020.

17 Department of Conservation, Loader Cup winners, www.doc.govt.nz/news/events/awards/loder-cup-award/all-winners-from-1929, accessed 12 April 2019.
18 *Press*, 9 February 1907.
19 Mary Stapylton-Smith (comp.), *Adderley to Bradley: A History of the Southern Bays of Lyttelton Harbour* (Diamond Harbour: Friends of Diamond Harbour Library, 2009), p. 264.
20 Ibid, p. 263. This is after the closure of the Charteris Bay School (which Oliver Hunter, his brothers and sisters and the Henderson children attended) and well before the opening of the Diamond Harbour School.
21 The races and cricket must have taken place on the beach, there being virtually no other flat land.
22 Elsie Locke, *The Kauri and the Willow* (Wellington: P. D. Hasselberg, Government Printer, 1984).
23 Sir Miles Warren, *Ohinetahi* (Sir Miles Warren, 2014), p. 19.
24 Marion Coxon, email to Jane Robertson, 14 September 2020.
25 Ibid.
26 Nick Tolerton, Wayne Nolan and Mandy Nelson, *Sailing in a Volcano: 100 Years of Club Sailing from Lyttelton* (Christchurch: Naval Point Club, Lyttelton, 2021), p. 125.

Chapter 8. Te Wharau Charteris Bay

1 Moore's cherished cattle included Brother Phil, Cranberry, His Honor, General Wolfe (bulls); Flash, Duchess, Creamy, Dunny (cows). *Akaroa Mail and Banks Peninsula Advertiser*, 22 April 1890.
2 Karen Gregory-Hunt, *Orton Bradley Park, Charteris Bay — A History* (Christchurch: Lands and Survey, 1986).
3 *Star*, 12 April 1901. The water wheel also powered a saw bench, drive lathes, a drill and a grindstone for blade shearers.
4 Gregory-Hunt, *Orton Bradley Park*, p. 29.
5 *Press*, 4 April 1927.
6 *Star*, 2 September 1886.
7 Mary Stapylton-Smith (comp.), *Adderley to Bradley: A History of the Southern Bays of Lyttelton Harbour* (Diamond Harbour: Friends of Diamond Harbour Library, 2009).
8 Ibid., p. 17.
9 R. O. Bradley, *A Sort of Diary* (Diamond Harbour: Friends of Diamond Harbour Library, 2009), p. 32.
10 Ibid., p. 66.
11 Oliver Hunter, *Diary 1907–1909*, entry for Tuesday, 18 February 1908. Hunter Archive.
12 Ibid., Saturday, 14 March 1908.
13 *Lyttelton Times*, 26 September 1889.
14 Maurice Leech archive, courtesy of Max Manson.
15 *Press*, 25 October 1922.
16 *Press*, 14 March 1914.
17 *Lyttelton Times*, 3 April 1919.
18 *Press*, 12 April 1934.
19 *Press*, 30 June 1936.
20 Carolyn and Brendon Leech, email to Jane Robertson, 15 September 2020.
21 Sarah Leech, email to Jane Robertson, 16 September 2020.
22 James Hay's obituary also mentions two daughters. *Star*, 25 September 1914.
23 *Press*, 4 November 1904.
24 *Press*, 16 May 1905.
25 *Press*, 5 July 1906.
26 *Press*, 3 August 1935.
27 *Star*, 25 June 1915.
28 *Press*, 9 August 1921.
29 Wellington Classic Yacht Trust, www.wcyt.org.nz, accessed 20 September 2020.
30 Mary Mackey, *Aquatic Sports in Lyttelton, 1920–1971*, Christchurch Teachers College Research Report, 1971, p. 19. Courtesy of the author.
31 Ibid., p. 25.
32 Paul Pritchett's chapter on the Charteris Bay Yacht Club in Stapylton-Smith, *Adderley to Bradley*, p. 271.
33 Ibid., p. 273.

Chapter 9. Tauwharepaka Teddington

1 According to Ngāi Tahu leader, scholar and politician Teone Taare Tikao. Herries Beattie, *Tikao Talks: Ka Taoka Tapu o Te Ao Kohatu – Treasures from the Ancient World of the Maori* (Auckland: Penguin Books, 1990), p. 105.
2 Edith Paine, *The Southern Bays of Lyttelton Harbour* (Christchurch: Pegasus Press, 1970), p. 9. Colin Amodeo with Ron Chapman, *Forgotten Forty-Niners: Being an Account of the Men & Women who Paved the Way in 1849 for the Canterbury Pilgrims in 1850* (Christchurch: Caxton Press, 2003), p. 14.
3 Made familiar again through Margaret Mahy's novel and subsequent television series *Kaitangata Twitch*.
4 Paula Smith and Sue Grimwood, *Banks Peninsula Community Mapping*, Christchurch City Council, 2018, www.ccc.govt.nz/assets/Documents/The-Council/Community-Boards/Banks-Peninsula-community-board/Banks-Peninsula-Community-Mapping.pdf, accessed 15 July 2020.
5 Amodeo, *Forgotten Forty-Niners*, p. 69.
6 Charles Obin Torlesse, *The Torlesse Papers: The Journals and Letters of Charles Obins Torlesse, Concerning the Foundation of the Canterbury Settlement in New Zealand 1848–1851*, ed. Peter Bromley Maling (Christchurch: Caxton Press, 2003), p. 55. The name Gebbie was spelled in a variety of ways.
7 *Lyttelton Times*, 4 April 1863.
8 Janet O'Loughlin, *Mindful of My Origin: The Mansons of Kains Hill* (Christchurch: Caxton Press, 2009), p. 54.
9 Jane Deans, *Letters to my Grandchildren* (Christchurch: Cadsonbury Publications, 1995), pp. 31–32.
10 *Lyttelton Times*, 27 January 1855.
11 *Lyttelton Times*, 7 February 1867.
12 *Lyttelton Times*, 17 August 1868.
13 *Lyttelton Times*, 5 February 1872.
14 Papers re Sites used as Jetties and Wharves, XBAA, CH518, RC89C-0148/7, R24981701, ANZCRO.
15 Mount Herbert County Council Minute Book, 1903, p. 402. Courtesy of Murray Radcliffe.
16 Luke Trainor, *History of the Mount Herbert County Council* (Lyttelton: Mount Herbert County Council, 1984), p. 18.
17 Papers re Sites used as Jetties and Wharves, XBAA, CH518, RC89C-0148/7, R24981701, ANZCRO.
18 Ibid.
19 Lachie Griffen, *Bay News*, vol. 54 [no date], p. 18.
20 *Lyttelton Times*, 12 November 1918.
21 *Akaroa Mail and Banks Peninsula Advertiser*, 18 June 1929.
22 *Press*, 5 September 1929.
23 Ibid.
24 *Press*, 26 August 1938.
25 *Press*, 25 May 1960.
26 Graeme Small, interviewed by Jane Robertson, 2 December 2014.
27 Bruce Gebbie, email to Jane Robertson, 14 September 2020.
28 Christchurch District Plan: Site of Ecological Significance Statement, https://districtplan.ccc.govt.nz/Images/DistrictPlanImages/Site%20of%20Ecological%20Significance/SES%20H%2012.pdf, accessed 11 July 2020.

Chapter 10. Allandale and Ōhinetahi

1 Atholl Anderson, *Report on Māori Archeological Sites in Whakaraupō and Adjacent Areas*, Ngāi Tahu Research Centre, University of Canterbury, 2019.
2 James Cowan, *Maori Folk-Tales of the Port Hills, Canterbury New Zealand* (Christchurch: Whitcombe & Tombs, 1923).
3 Donald Couch (2017), cited in Anderson, *Report on Māori Archeological Sites*, p. 21.
4 R. Hampton, Ōhinetahi: The Place of One Daughter, essay, Canterbury Museum, DRC Folder 1111 ARC1993.2.
5 Hodgson Family, Carlisle, UK, http://genforum.genealogy.com/hodgson/messages/930.html, accessed 23 September 2013.
6 Newspaper article, 'Pioneer Home Demolished' (no attribution). Scrapbook belonging to Diana Thomson 1965–69, courtesy of David Bundy.
7 Gladys Robertson (née Bamford), handwritten notes, Hussey archive.
8 Jessie Scott, handwritten notes, Hussey archive.
9 *Press*, 20 January 1931.
10 Coyla Radcliffe-Olliver, interviewed by Lyn Wright, 2 June 2001. GBHT archive.
11 Ibid.
12 David Bundy, interviewed by Jane Robertson, 23 August 2011.
13 *Star*, 24 May 1960.
14 David Bundy, personal communication, August 2022.
15 F. R. Inwood, *Governors Bay: Reminiscences of past and present days* (1935), p. 1, http://christchurchcitylibraries.com/DigitalCollection/Archives/Archive17/Reminiscences/Pages/Archive17-001.asp, accessed 14 March 2012.
16 *Lyttelton Times*, 2 July 1853.
17 Joseph Munnings, *Diaries*, 8 May 1862–30 May 1864, p. 57. Box 1, Folder 2, Canterbury Museum.

18 The sandstone is reported to have been quarried variously from Quail Island (Te Ara – The Encyclopedia of New Zealand, www.teara.govt.nz/en/biographies/2p27/1, accessed 8 May 2012); the point opposite Quail Island (GBHT archived notes); and Potts' Peninsula (F. Cresswell, 1974).
19 *The Diary of T. H. Potts 1865*, transcribed by Paul Star, May 2018, p. 7.
20 Ibid., p. 5.
21 Ibid., p. 6.
22 Thomas Henry Potts, *Out in the Open* (Christchurch: Capper Press, 1976), p. 226.
23 Ibid., p. 228.
24 David Bundy, email communication, 20 April 2015.

Chapter 11. Ōtoromiro Governors Bay, Pukekaroro Sandy Bay

1 W. David McIntyre (ed.), *The Journal of Henry Sewell 1853–7: Vol. 1* (Christchurch: Whitcoulls, 1980), p. 147.
2 Joseph Munnings, *Diaries*, Box 1, Folder 1, 23 July 1859–3 May, 1862, p. 20, Canterbury Museum.
3 *Lyttelton Times*, 15 January 1875.
4 *Lyttelton Times*, 2 April 1862.
5 *Lyttelton Times*, 22 January 1859.
6 Governors Bay jetty, CAAD, CH287, CB 207/, R8420806, ANZCRO.
7 *Press*, 21 November 1874.
8 *Lyttelton Times*, 17 June 1875.
9 *Lyttelton Times*, 3 September 1879.
10 *Lyttelton Times*, 14 February 1880.
11 The Cyclopedia of New Zealand [Canterbury Provincial District], 1903, NZETC, http://nzetc.victoria.ac.nz/tm/scholarly/tei-Cyc03Cycl-t1-body1-d5-d17.html, accessed 22 March 2020.
12 Letter from County Clerk, Mr Field, Mount Herbert County Council Letter Book, 1909, p. 336. Courtesy of Murray Radcliffe.
13 Coyla Radcliffe-Oliver, interviewed by Lyn Wright, 2 June 2001, GBHT archives.
14 John Allan, interviewed by Jane Robertson, 8 August 2011.
15 *Bay News*, June 1993, pp. 4–5.
16 Ibid., quoting from 17 January 1937 diary entry.
17 Memorandum, Cyrus Williams to Chairman of Lyttelton Harbour Board, 3 February 1908, XBAA, CH518, RC89C-0148/7, R24981701, ANZCRO/ECan.
18 Letter, T. W. Pairman to Lyttelton Harbour Board, 27 March 1908, ibid.
19 *Press*, 9 November 1910.
20 *Press*, 12 March 1913.
21 Murray Radcliffe, interviewed by Jane Robertson, 14 August 2014.
22 *Press*, 21 September 1916.
23 *Press*, 8 June 1918.
24 *Star*, 13 September 1913.
25 *Press*, 14 June 1930.
26 Graeme Small, interviewed by Jane Robertson, 22 January 2015.
27 Graeme Small, quoted in Katharina Small. *The Smalls of Governors Bay: The Descendants of Stephen and Mary Elizabeth Small* (Christchurch, 2018).
28 Simon Agar, personal communication, 25 August 2020.
29 Neil Withell, resident at Cholmondeley in the 1940s, quoted in Colin Amodeo, *A Beautiful Haven: Celebrating 80 years of Cholmondeley Children's Home 1925–2005* (Christchurch: Cholmondeley Children's Home Inc., 2005), p. 65.
30 Murray Radcliffe, personal communication, 19 February 2018.
31 My thanks to Janette Park and Graeme Small for sharing material relating to Māori Gardens.
32 Letter to Banks Peninsula District Council from A. J. Riley, 12 March 1990. Courtesy of Janette Park.
33 Lionel Jefcoate, *57 Boats later . . .* (Havelock: Lionel Jefcoate, 2013), p. 111.
34 Graeme Small, interviewed by Jane Robertson, 2 December 2014.
35 'Yachting Notes', *Bay News*, vol. 46 (1998), p. 39. The *Bay News* piece has Lionel seeing '1.75 metres of water outside his shed at low water' — surely an error. I have taken the liberty of emending.
36 *Press*, 5 May 2000.
37 Lyttelton Harbour Board, General Correspondence 1989, Governors Bay and Corsair Bay, XBAA, CH518, 669/A002-409, R25017220, ANZCRO/ECan.
38 J. Nicol, *Harbour Link*, issue 20 (May 1999).

Chapter 12. Ōtamahua Quail Island

1 Edward Ward, *The Journal of Edward Ward 1850–51* (Christchurch: Pegasus Press, 1951), p. 119.
2 Ibid., pp. 155–56.
3 Ibid., p. 160.
4 Charlotte Godley, *Letters from Early New Zealand 1850–1853* (Christchurch: Whitcombe & Tombs, 1951), p. 214.
5 *Lyttelton Times*, 4 May 1859.
6 *Lyttelton Times*, 4 April 1860.
7 *Lyttelton Times*, 25 August 1864.
8 *Lyttelton Times*, 12 February 1859.
9 *Press*, 22 December 1873.
10 *Star*, 28 April 1881. Despite this figure, the stock jetty was not the preferred low-tide landing point.
11 *Press*, 2 February 1906.
12 Lyttelton Harbour Board, XBAA, CH518, 669/A002-406, R25017217, ANZCRO/ECan.
13 Interview with Euan Crawford, 7 December 2020.
14 *Lyttelton Times*, 16 September 1910.
15 *Lyttelton Times*, 26 October 1910.
16 *Lyttelton Times*, 1 November 1910.
17 *Lyttelton Times*, 2 September 1911.
18 *Press*, 25 January 1904.
19 *Star*, 9 February 1909.
20 *Press*, 12 October 1907.
21 *Press*, 16 June 1911. Not quite that easy.
22 Timothy Kokiri was variously known as Tim or Tom Kokere, Jimmy Kokere, James Kokiri and Hemi Kokiri. Lindsay J. Daniel, *Companion to Otamahua — Quail Island — A Link with the Past: Additional Notes on the Human History of the Island* (Christchurch: Otamahua-Quail Island Restoration Trust, 2017), available as an e-book from the Restoration Trust, www.quailisland.org.nz/index.php/shop
23 Benjamin Kingsbury, *The Dark Island: Leprosy in New Zealand and the Quail Island Colony* (Wellington: Bridget Williams Books, 2019), p. 82.
24 *Press*, 6 September 1922.
25 Peter Jackson, *Otamatua — Quail Island: A Link with the Past* (Christchurch: Department of Conservation, 1990 and 2006 [revised]), p. 42.
26 Bernard Walker, *True Grit: Bernard Walker's Recollections of an Unusual Occupation* (Evan Walker and Otamahua–Quail Island Ecological Restoration Trust), p. 5.
27 Not clear which of the two jetties.
28 *Press*, 30 August 1938.
29 Heritage New Zealand Pouhere Taonga, Ōtamahua/Quail Island Historic Area, www.heritage.org.nz/the-list/details/9552, accessed 10 April 2019.
30 *Press*, 20 January 1944.
31 Pete Dawson, Facebook comment, Lyttelton, 5 May 2019.
32 Ibid.
33 Murray Radcliffe, Facebook comment, 26 March 2019.
34 Daniel, *Companion to Otamahua — Quail Island*.
35 Derek Jones, 'Lyttelton Ain't No Place I'd Rather Be', Facebook comment, 7 June 2020.

Chapter 13. Te Rāpaki-o-Te Rakiwhakaputa

1 Hereafter I shorten Te Rāpaki-o-Te Rakiwhakaputa to Rāpaki.
2 Sammy Griffin, Travis W. Horton and Christopher Oze, Origin of Warm Springs in Banks Peninsula, NZ, *Applied Geochemistry* 86 (2017): pp. 1–12.
3 *New Zealand* (Christchurch: Whitcombe & Tombs, 1954), p. 42.
4 Arthur (Hiwi) Couch, *Rapaki Remembered: History and Reminiscence* (Christchurch: Te Waihora Press & Canterbury Maori Studies Association, 1987), p. 19.
5 Ōketepoko ('basket of heads') was the name of a craggy peak towering above Cavendish Bay. Ōhinehou, the Māori name used for an area further west around Salt's Gully, eventually prevailed as the name for the whole Lyttelton township.
6 Harry Evison, *The Ngai Tahu Deeds: A Window on New Zealand History* (Christchurch: Canterbury University Press, 2007), p. 128.
7 James Cowan, *Maori Folk-Tales of the Port Hills, Canterbury New Zealand* (Christchurch: Whitcombe & Tombes, 1923), p. 50.
8 *Lyttelton Times*, 7 January 1860.
9 Charles Obin Torlesse, *The Torlesse Papers: The Journals and Letters of Charles Obins Torlesse Concerning the Foundation of the Canterbury Settlement in New Zealand 1848–51*, ed. Peter Bromley Maling (Christchurch: Pegasus Press, 1958).
10 It is interesting that the settlers who developed good relationships with Māori tended to be the Scots, who were not always well accepted in the English colony, and a woman like Mary Small, who had fled persecution and singlehandedly made a new life for her family.

11 Donald Couch, *Rāpaki Church Sesquicentinnial, 1869–2019* (Lyttelton: Te Hapū o Ngāti Wheke Publishing, 2019).
12 Lyttelton Harbour Board, general correspondence, Rāpaki jetty, XBAA, CH518, 798/A002-1036, R25017782, ANZCRO/ECan.
13 Ibid.
14 Ibid.
15 Ibid.
16 Ibid.
17 Couch, *Rapaki Remembered*, p. 64.
18 The four Rāpaki men who fought on Gallipoli were Waitere Manihera, Anatipa Manihera, Henare Paipeta and John Charles Tikao. The total Rāpaki population at this time was 64. The discrepancy between the figure of 85 given by Paani McKenzie and this number probably reflects a fluctuating population caused by the war and by the ongoing movement of whānau between peninsula settlements.
19 *Press*, 14 January 2012.
20 Lyttelton Harbour Board, general correspondence, Rāpaki jetty, XBAA, CH518, 798/A002-1036, R25017782, ANZCRO/ECan.
21 *Press*, 25 June 1931.
22 Helen Brown, 150 Years Young, *Te Karaka*, issue 82 (June 2019).
23 Rewi Couch, A Taste for Pūtakitaki, *Te Karaka*, issue 62 (July 2014).
24 Kaituhi Morgan Lee, A Third Generation Tangata Tiaki, *Te Karaka*, issue 68 (December 2015).
25 Lyttelton Harbour Board, general correspondence, Rāpaki jetty, XBAA, CH518, 798/A002-1036, R25017782, ANZCRO/ECan.
26 Ibid.
27 Donald Couch, personal communication, 4 April 2022.
28 Ministry of Fisheries, Rāpaki Mātaitai Reserve, June 2002, https://healthyharbour.org.nz/wp-content/uploads/2019/05/Ministry-of-Fisheries-2002-Rapaki-Mataitai-1.pdf, accessed 9 April 2022.
29 Fisheries New Zealand, Lyttelton Harbour/Whakaraupō Mātaitai Reserve Proposed bylaws, www.fisheries.govt.nz/news-and-resources/consultations/bylaws-for-the-lyttelton-harbourwhakaraupo-mataitai, accessed 15 April 2000.

Chapter 14. Motukauatirahi Cass Bay

1 Wiremu Grace, How Māui Brought Fire to the World, *Te Kete Ipurangi*, Te Tāhuhu o te Mātauranga, 2016, https://eng.matauranagamaori.tki.org.nz/Support-materials/Te-Reo-Maori/Maori-Myths-Legends-and-Contemporary-Stories/How-Maui-brought-fire-to-the-world, accessed 12 November 2019.
2 James Cowan, *Maori Folk-Tales of the Port Hills, Canterbury, New Zealand* (Christchurch: Whitcombe & Tombs, 1954), p. 11.
3 David R. Given, *Warm Springs at Cass Bay, Banks Peninsula, Canterbury* (Auckland: Botany Division, DSIR, 1983).
4 Charles Obin Torlesse, *The Torlesse Papers: The Journals and Letters of Charles Obins Torlesse Concerning the Foundation of the Canterbury Settlement in New Zealand 1848–51*, ed. Peter Bromley Maling (Christchurch: Pegasus Press, 1958), p. 49.
5 *Lyttelton Times*, 11 March 1863.
6 *Star*, 29 February 1884.
7 *Lyttelton Times*, 1 May 1900.
8 *Lyttelton Times*, 3 June 1902.
9 Robin Dungey, 'Lyttelton Ain't No Place I'd Rather Be', Facebook page, January 2019.
10 Toni Robertson, ibid.
11 Peter Butterworth, ibid, June 2019.
12 Lawson Rowe, ibid, January 2019.
13 Allen Curnow, 'The Unclosed Door', in Elizabeth Caffin and Terry Sturm (eds), *Allen Curnow: Collected Poems* (Auckland: Auckland University Press, 2017), pp. 293–94.
14 *Press*, 3 July 1935. The *Press* headline read: 'Removal of abattoir at Lyttelton. It is expected that the Lyttelton Borough Council will shortly consider a proposal to remove the municipal abattoir from its present site at Cass Bay.'
15 Brian Downey, email to Jane Robertson, 20 August 2020. Brian obtained this information from the late Tom Hay of Corsair Bay, who was a soldier on guard duty at HMS *Steadfast* during the Second World War.
16 *Lyttelton Review*, issue 255 (May 2020), p. 6.
17 RNZN Communicators Association, interview with Lieutenant Commander Victor Fifield, April 1996, https://rnzncomms.org/memories/fifield, accessed 8 October 2019.
18 Navy Department files, Cass Bay Depot buildings and services, CAXP, CH150, 530/, R18988958, ANZCRO.
19 Guy Ditfort, email to Jane Robertson, 21 November 2019.
20 *Press*, 29 December 1945.
21 *Press*, 10 November 1965.
22 BPCC minutes (12 July 1961) 1959–1966, Z Arch 70, CCL.
23 Noeline Allan on the Cass Bay Residents Association Information Page, Facebook, 11 April 2020.
24 Jenny Healey, Cass Bay Residents' Association Chairperson and Reserves Management Committee Chairperson. Personal message, 26 October 2022.

Chapter 15. Motukauatiiti Corsair Bay

1 *Press*, 2 January 1924.
2 *Star*, 13 August 1881.
3 *Lyttelton Times*, 6 February 1895.
4 *Lyttelton Times*, 15 May 1902.
5 *Lyttelton Times*, 3 July 1905.
6 *Lyttelton Times*, 23 November 1906.
7 Locals remember the sea running red with blood. Facebook discussion, 'Lyttelton — Ain't No Place I'd Rather Be', September 2018.
8 *Lyttelton Times*, 26 December 1907.
9 *Lyttelton Times*, 15 September 1910.
10 *Lyttelton Times*, 22 January 1908.
11 *Press*, 28 January 1908.
12 *Lyttelton Times*, 29 January 1908.
13 *Lyttelton Times*, 2 March 1910.
14 *Lyttelton Times*, 1 November 1910.
15 *Star*, 31 December 1913.
16 *Press*, 3 March 1914.
17 *Lyttelton Times*, 19 October 1909.
18 *Lyttelton Times*, 27 December 1921.
19 *Press*, 11 January 1933.
20 *Press*, 23 November 1931.
21 Stephen Estall, comment on 'Lyttelton — Ain't No Place I'd Rather Be', 2 September 2018.

Chapter 16. Magazine Bay

1 *Lyttelton Times*, 27 February 1867.
2 *Press*, 12 August 1874.
3 New Zealand Maritime Record, NZ National Maritime Museum, *Defender*, www.nzmaritime.co.nz/thornycroft.htm, accessed 23 November 2018.
4 James W. Hunter III, The Archeology of Military Mismanagement: An Example from New Zealand's Colonial Torpedo Boat Defences, 1884–1900, *Bulletin of the Australasian Institute for Maritime Archaeology*, no. 33 (2009): pp. 1–10.
5 *Lyttelton Times*, 30 March 1886.
6 *Star*, 27 April 1885.
7 *Lyttelton Times*, 30 March 1886.
8 *Lyttelton Times*, 2 April 1886.
9 *Star*, 16 April 1895.
10 Christchurch City Libraries blog, https://cclblog.wordpress.com/tag/lyttelton-harbour/, accessed 10 July 2019.
11 *Press*, 29 December 1923.
12 George Brasell Remembers His Sailing Days, in Nick Tolerton, Wayne Nolan and Mandy Nelson, *Sailing in a Volcano: 100 Years of Club Sailing from Lyttelton* (Christchurch: Naval Point Club Lyttelton, 2021), p. 25.
13 *Press*, 7 December 1937.
14 BPCC minutes, 1937–1948, Z Arch 70, CCL.
15 Lyttelton Harbour Board, XBAA, CH518, 781/A002-941, R25017694, ANZCRO.
16 *Press*, 13 October 2000.
17 *Stuff*, Lyttelton's Bad Friday, 9 October 2010, www.stuff.co.nz/the-press/christchurch-life/4214523/Lyttelton's-bad-Friday, accessed 1 December 2018.
18 *Architecture Now*, Inspired by the Past: Te Ana Marina, https://architecturenow.co.nz/articles/inspired-by-the-past-te-ana-marina, accessed 8 May 2020.
19 Te Nukutai o Tapoa, a name gifted recently by Te Hapū o Ngāti Wheke, refers to the former headland of Erskine Point, material from which contributed to the reclamation of Naval Point in the early twentieth century.

Chapter 17. Te Awaparahi Buckleys Bay and Ōtokitoki Gollans Bay

1 Baden Norris, *Forgotten Bays of Lyttelton*, 2006. I am indebted to this account — the only one I have found to document something of the early settlement of these bays.
2 J. W. Stack, W. A. Taylor, W. H. S. Roberts and W. Deans, Maori Placenames of Banks Peninsula, map, 1894, 993.84 MAO, CCL.
3 W. A. Taylor, Lore and History of the South Island Maori: Port Cooper or Whakaraupo (Bay of the Raupo Reeds), http://nzetc.victoria.ac.nz/tm/scholarly/tei-TayLore-t1-body1-d6.html, p. 57, accessed 30 June 2022.

4. *Lyttelton Times*, 26 April 1851.
5. *Press*, 8 January 1932.
6. *Press*, 9 April 1921.
7. Gordon Ogilvie, *Place Names of Banks Peninsula and the Port Hills* (Christchurch: Canterbury University Press, 2017), p. 87.
8. *Lyttelton Times*, 16 March 1854.
9. Quoted in Colin Amodeo with Ron Chapman, *Forgotten Forty-Niners: Being an Account of the Men & Women who Paved the Way in 1849 for the Canterbury Pilgrims in 1850* (Christchurch: Caxton Press, 2003), p. 110.
10. *Press*, 25 July 1863.
11. Report on sinking of trawler *Dolphin*. www.flickr.com/photos/archivesnz/10044887175, accessed 18 May 2020.
12. Heritage New Zealand Pouhere Taonga, *Battery Point Historic Area*, www.heritage.org.nz/the-list/details/7553, accessed 15 January 2019.
13. W. H. Scotter, *A History of Port Lyttelton* (Christchurch: Lyttelton Harbour Board, 1968).
14. Ibid.
15. Canterbury Earthquake Recovery Authority, Lyttelton Port Recovery Plan, Christchurch, 2015, www.lpc.co.nz/wp-content/uploads/2015/09/Lyttelton-Port-Recovery-Plan.pdf, accessed 6 February 2019.
16. *Press*, 5 April 1915.
17. *Press*, 12 February 1932.

Chapter 18. Awaroa Godley Head

1. Félix Maynard, *The Whalers*, ed. Alexandre Dumas (London: Hutchinson, 1937), p. 173.
2. Lyttelton Wharf Commission Inquiry, *Lyttelton Times*, 25 July 1863.
3. *Lyttelton Times*, 6 July 1859.
4. *Lyttelton Times*, 13 April 1865.
5. Godley Head Heritage Trust, The Lighthouse, www.godleyhead.org.nz/the-lighthouse.html, accessed 4 July 2019.
6. *Lyttelton Times*, 25 June 1868.
7. *Lyttelton Times*, 25 June 1868.
8. *Press*, 17 April 1928.
9. *Press*, 14 August 1940.
10. *Lyttelton Times*, 26 September 1908.
11. *Star*, 25 July 1914.
12. Paul Ensor, personal communication, January 2022.
13. Gordon Ogilvie, *Place Names of Banks Peninsula and the Port Hills* (Christchurch: Canterbury University Press, 2018), p. 86.
14. Godley Head Heritage Trust, The Lighthouse.
15. Godley Head: Lighthouse and Fog Signal, 1936–1948, Archives NZ, CAXP CH150 2954 Box 176.
16. Godley Head Heritage Trust. The Searchlights, www.godleyhead.org.nz/searchlights.html, accessed 26 May 2020.
17. Heritage New Zealand Pouhere Taonga, www.heritage.org.nz/the-list/details/7554, accessed 7 December 2019.
18. Sensor Systems NZ Ltd, www.sensorsystems.co.nz/news/sabik-led-350h-replaces-damaged-lighthouse-at-godley-head-lyttelton-harbour-canterbury-nz, accessed 11 July 2019.

Chapter 19. Connecting the harbour

1. *Press*, 21 November 1891.
2. Access to Gladys's handwritten account courtesy of the Hussey family.
3. Sadly, George Agar died while on a visit to London in 1898 to order yet another launch (*Purau*).
4. *Lyttelton Times*, 20 January 1900.
5. *Lyttelton Times*, 25 May 1898.
6. *Lyttelton Times*, 11 September 1908.
7. *Press*, 27 August 1908.
8. *Lyttelton Times*, 22 March 1909.
9. *Stratford Evening Post*, 8 November 1921.
10. *Press*, 16 January 1932.
11. Quoted in Mary Stapylton-Smith (comp.), *Adderley to Bradley: A History of the Southern Bays of Lyttelton Harbour* (Diamond Harbour: Friends of Diamond Harbour Library, 2009), p. 166.
12. Interview with Euan Crawford, 7 December 2020.
13. *Press*, 27 May 1924.
14. *Press*, 7 October 1921. It is just possible that *Onawe* had another owner around this time. Master mariner Captain Robert Hatchwell arrived in Lyttelton in 1883 and worked for the New Zealand Shipping Company for 37 years. With his two daughters, Winifred and Margery, Captain Hatchwell ran the Devonia Navigation School for officers and naval cadets for more than 40 years from his home in Lyttelton, teaching on weeknights. Hatchwell was also first commodore of the Canterbury Yacht and Motor Boat Club and the family were keen supporters of the Lyttelton Seamen's Institute. *Onawe* was the family launch. Captain Hatchwell entered *Onawe* in the 1916 Lyttelton Regatta's motor-boat handicap race, and it came fifth out of 19 boats. Whether it was the same *Onawe* that went on to ply the Diamond Harbour run is unclear.
15. Comment from 'Troy', Classic Yacht Association of New Zealand, https://classicyacht.org.nz/cyaforum/topic/ex-lyttelton-ferry-onawe, accessed 15 August 2020.
16. Adrian Te Patu, Diamond Harbour Facebook page, 8 August 2020.
17. Adrian Te Patu and Jono Welsh, ibid.
18. Roland Sommer, ibid.
19. Michael O'Neill, ibid.
20. John Luney, Lyttelton, ibid.
21. *Diamond Harbour Herald*, No. 167 (May 2013), https://diamondharbour.info/diamond-harbour-herald, accessed November 2020.
22. Stayplton-Smith, *Adderley to Bradley*, p. 168.
23. Bruce Ansley, *A Long Slow Affair of the Heart* (Dunedin: Longacre Press, 2008), p. 51.
24. Del Hurley, interviewed in the *Press*, 25 April 2002.

Bibliography

Books

Amodeo, Colin. *A Beautiful Haven: Celebrating 80 years of Cholmondeley Children's Home 1925–2005*. Christchurch: Cholmondeley Children's Home Inc., 2005.

———, with Ron Chapman. *Forgotten Forty-Niners: Being an Account of the Men & Women who Paved the Way in 1849 for the Canterbury Pilgrims in 1850*. Christchurch: Caxton Press, 2003.

———, with Bill Huntley. *The Mosquito Fleet of Canterbury*. Christchurch: Caxton Press, 2005.

Anderson, Atholl. *Report on Māori Archeological Sites in Whakaraupō and Adjacent Areas*. Ngāi Tahu Research Centre, University of Canterbury, 2019.

———. *The Welcome of Strangers: An Ethnohistory of Southern Māori A.D. 1650–1850*. Dunedin: University of Otago Press in association with Dunedin City Council, 1998.

——— and Te Maire Tau (eds). *Ngāi Tahu: A Migration Story*. Wellington: Bridget William Books, 2008.

Ansley, Bruce. *A Long Slow Affair of the Heart*. Dunedin: Longacre Press, 2008.

Beattie, Herries. *Tikao Talks: Ka Taoka Tapu o Te Ao Kohatu — Treasures from the Ancient World of the Maori*. Auckland: Penguin Books, 1990.

Bradley, Reginald. *Orton: A Sort of Diary*. Christchurch: Friends of Diamond Harbour Library, 2009.

Brailsford, Barry. *The Tattooed Land: The Southern Frontiers of the Pa Maori*. Wellington: A. H. & A. W. Reed, 1981.

Brown, Mike, and Kimberley Peters (eds). *Living with the Sea: Knowledge, Awareness and Action*. London: Routledge, 2018.

Carson, Rachel. *The Edge of the Sea*. London: Panther Books, 1965.

Clements, Kevin. *Back from the Brink: The Creation of a Nuclear-Free New Zealand*. Wellington: Bridget Williams Books, 1988 & 2015 (e-book).

Couch, Arthur (Hiwi). *Rapaki Remembered: History and Reminiscence*. Christchurch: Te Waihora Press & Canterbury Maori Studies Association, 1987.

Couch, Donald. *Rāpaki Church Sesquicentinnial, 1869–2019*. Lyttelton: Te Hapū o Ngāti Wheke Publishing, 2019.

Cowan, James. *Maori Folk-Tales of the Port Hills, Canterbury New Zealand*. Christchurch: Whitcombe & Tombs, 1923.

Cox, Charles Perry. *Personal Notes and Reminiscences of an Early Canterbury Settler*. Christchurch: Canterbury Publishing Company, 1915.

Cresswell, Frances. *Old Homes of Lyttelton Harbour*. Christchurch: Pegasus Press, 1974.

Daniel, Lindsay J. *Companion to Ōtamahua — Quail Island — A Link with the Past: Additional Notes on the Human History of the Island*. Christchurch: Ōtamahua-Quail Island Restoration Trust, 2017 (e-book).

Deans, Jane. *Letters to my Grandchildren*. Christchurch: Cadsonbury Publications, 1995.

Deans, John. *Pioneers of Canterbury. Deans Letters 1840–1854*. Wellington: A. H. and A. W. Reed, 1937.

Durie, Mason. *Ngā Tai Matatū: Tides of Māori Endurance*. Auckland: Oxford University Press, 2005.

Evison, Harry C. *The Ngai Tahu Deeds: A Window on New Zealand History*. Christchurch: Canterbury University Press, 2007, p. 128.

———. *The Long Dispute: Maori Land Rights and European Colonisation in Southern New Zealand*. Christchurch: Canterbury University Press, 1997.

———. *Te Wai Pounamu — The Greenstone Island: A History of the Southern Maori During the European Colonization of New Zealand*. Wellington & Christchurch: Aoraki Press, 1993.

Gee, David. *The Devil's Own Brigade: A History of the Lyttelton Gaol 1860–1920*. Wellington: Millwood Press, 1975.

Godley, Charlotte. *Letters from Early New Zealand 1850–1853*. Christchurch: Whitcombe & Tombs, 1951.

Henderson, Ewan. *Henderson of Zetland*. Ewan Henderson, 2014.

Hight, J., and C. R. Straubel, *A History of Canterbury*. Christchurch: Whitcombe & Tombs, 1957.

Hunter, Oliver, and Mary Stapylton-Smith. *The Magnostic Philosopher of Church Bay: The Life and Works of Oliver Hunter, 1882–1979*. Christchurch: Friends of the Diamond Harbour Library, 2006.

Jackson, Peter. *Otamatua — Quail Island: A Link with the Past*. Christchurch: Department of Conservation, 1990 and 2006 (revised).

Jefcoate, Lionel. *57 Boats later . . .* Havelock: Lionel Jefcoate, 2013.

King, Julie. *Flowers into Landscape: Margaret Stoddart 1865–1934*. Christchurch: Robert McDougall Art Gallery & Hazard Press, 1997.

Kingsbury, Benjamin. *The Dark Island: Leprosy in New Zealand and the Quail Island Colony*. Wellington: Bridget Williams Books, 2019.

Locke, Elsie. *The Kauri and the Willow*. Wellington: P. D. Hasselberg, Government Printer, 1984.

McIntyre, W. David (ed.). *The Journal of Henry Sewell 1853–7: Vol. 1*. Christchurch: Whitcoulls, 1980.

Maynard, Félix. *The Whalers*, ed. Alexandre Dumas. London: Hutchinson, 1937.

Ogilvie, Elisabeth. *Purau*. Christchurch: Caxton Press, 1970.

Ogilvie, Gordon. *Place Names of Banks Peninsula and the Port Hills*. Christchurch: Canterbury University Press, 2018.

———. *Banks Peninsula: Cradle of Canterbury*. Wellington: GP Publications, 1990

O'Loughlin, Janet M. *Mindful of My Origin: The Mansons of Kains Hill*. Christchurch: Caxton Press, 2009.

Paine, Edith. *The Southern Bays of Lyttelton Harbour*. Christchurch: Pegasus Press, 1970.

Potts, Thomas Henry. *Out in the Open*. Christchurch: Capper Press, 1976.

Pratt, William (An Old Colonist). *Colonial Experiences; or, Incidents and Reminiscences of Thirty-Four Years in New Zealand*. London: Chapman & Hall, 1877.

Roberts, Jonathan. *The Diary of Jonathan Roberts: Bank Clerk, Athlete, Convict and Escapee*, facsimile edition. Christchurch: Lyttelton Times Company, 1977.

Robertson, Jane. *Head of the Harbour: A History of Governors Bay, Ōhinetahi, Allandale and Teddington*. Christchurch: Philip King Publisher for the Governors Bay Heritage Trust, 2016.

Scotter, W. H. *A History of Port Lyttelton*. Christchurch: Lyttelton Harbour Board, 1968.
Small, Katharina. *The Smalls of Governors Bay: The Descendants of Stephen and Mary Elizabeth Small*. Christchurch, 2018.
Stapylton-Smith, Mary. *Diamond Harbour: Portrait of a Community*. Diamond Harbour: Diamond Harbour Community Association, 1993.
———. *The Other End of the Harbour*. Christchurch: Hazard Press, 1990.
——— (comp.). *Adderley to Bradley: A History of the Southern Bays of Lyttelton Harbour*. Diamond Harbour: Friends of Diamond Harbour Library, 2009.
Taylor, W. A. *Lore and History of the South Island Maori*. Christchurch: Bascands, 1952. Available at http://nzetc.victoria.ac.nz/tm/scholarly/tei-TayLore-t1-body1-d6.html
Tolerton, Nick, Wayne Nolan and Mandy Nelson. *Sailing in a Volcano: 100 Years of Club Sailing from Lyttelton*. Christchurch: Naval Point Club Lyttelton, 2021.
Torlesse, Charles Obin, *The Torlesse Papers: The Journals and Letters of Charles Obins Torlesse Concerning the Foundation of the Canterbury Settlement in New Zealand 1848–51*, ed. Peter Bromley Maling. Christchurch: Pegasus Press, 1958.
Trainor, Luke. *History of the Mount Herbert County Council*. Lyttelton: Mount Herbert County Council, 1984.
Vyse, Jerry. *Time to Go: A Journey from Old Deal to New Zealand*. Jerry Vyse, 2009.
Wakefield, E. J. *The Handbook for New Zealand*. London: John W. Parker, 1848.
Ward, Edward. *The Journal of Edward Ward 1850–51*. Christchurch: Pegasus Press, 1951.
Warren, Sir Miles. *Ōhinetahi*. Sir Miles Warren, 2014.

Unpublished documents

Couch, Donald. *Pūrau Māori History: A Ngāi Tahu View*. Paper in progress, 2018.
Galbraith, Lynley. *Gardiner Memories*. Jackson family archive.
Gillies, Bill. Pre-European History for Governors Bay and the Recent and On-going History of Original Tangata Whenua of Whakaraupō. Notes from Lyttelton Recreational Centre, 24 July 1997.
Greenwood, Joseph Hugh. *Diary*. MS-0878. Alexander Turnbull Library, Wellington. Available online.
Hampton, R. *Ōhinetahi: The Place of One Daughter*. Essay. Canterbury Museum.
Hunter, Mabel. *An Early Conservationist: The Life of Oliver Hunter*. Hunter archive.
Hunter, Oliver. *The Buried Marine Meadow in Charteris Bay*. Typed manuscript. Hunter archive.
———. *Diaries*, Hunter archive.
Isherwood, Eleanor. *A School Marm in New Zealand*. Jackson family archive.
Mackey, Mary. *Aquatic Sports in Lyttelton, 1920–1971*. Teachers College Research Report, 1971. Accessed from the author, Mary Harrison.
Mount Herbert County Council Minute Book, 1903. Murray Radcliffe.
Munnings, Joseph. *Diaries*. Canterbury Museum.
Norris, Baden. *Forgotten Bays of Lyttelton*, 2006.
Ogilvie, Elisabeth. *Elisabeth with an "s". A Childhood Memoir*. Jackson family archive.
Potts, Thomas Henry. *The Diary of T. H. Potts 1865*, transcribed by Paul Star.
Rogers, Paul. *Memories of Camp Bay*. Private document.
Walker, Bernard. *True Grit: Bernard Walker's Recollections of an Unusual Occupation*. Evan Walker and Ōtamahua–Quail Island Ecological Restoration Trust.

Articles, reports and theses

Beaumont, Louise. *Stoddart Point Reserve Landscape History and Conservation Report*. Prepared for Christchurch City Council, June 2016.
———, Matthew Carter and John Wilson. *Banks Peninsula Contextual Historical Overview and Thematic Framework*. Report prepared for Christchurch City Council, June 2014.
Christchurch City Council. *Harbours and Marine Structures Activity Management Plan: Long Term Plan 2015–2025*. Christchurch City Council, 16 December 2014.
Given, David R. *Warm Springs at Cass Bay, Banks Peninsula, Canterbury*. Botany Division, DSIR, 1983.
Gregory-Hunt, Karen. *Orton Bradley Park, Charteris Bay — A History*, ed. John Wilson. Christchurch: Department of Lands and Survey, 1986.
Griffin, Sammy, Travis W. Horton and Christopher Oze. 'Origin of warm springs in Banks Peninsula, NZ'. *Applied Geochemistry* 86, 2017.
Hart, Deidre. *Sedimentation in the Upper Lyttelton Harbour*. Report to Environment Canterbury, January 2004.
Hunter, James William. 'Throwaway Navies: Naval Transition, Abandonment Processes, and the Archaeology of Australasia's Torpedo Boat Defences, 1884–1924'. PhD thesis, School of Humanities and Creative Arts, Flinders University, 2012.
———. The Archeology of Military Mismanagement: An Example from New Zealand's Colonial Torpedo Boat Defences, 1884–1900. *Bulletin of the Australasian Institute for Maritime Archaeology*, 2009: 33.
Report prepared for Lyttelton Harbour/Whakaraupo Issues Group, June 2013.
Smith, Paula, and Sue Grimwood. *Banks Peninsula Community Mapping*. Christchurch City Council, 2018.
Ussher, T., and K. Watson. *Diamond Harbour Wharf: Conservation Report*. Christchurch City Council, 2020.

Websites

Architecture Now. Inspired by the Past: Te Ana Marina. https://architecturenow.co.nz/articles/inspired-by-the-past-te-ana-marina
Bracher, Samuel Veale. *Ripa Island: A Lesson for Conscriptionists*. London: Friends' Peace Committee, 1914. https://heritage.christchurchcitylibraries.com/Publications/1910s/RipaIsland/PDF/CCL-73787.pdf
Christchurch City Libraries Blog. https://cclblog.wordpress.com/tag/lyttelton-harbour
Christchurch City Council. Christchurch District Plan: Site of Ecological Significance Statement. https://districtplan.ccc.govt.nz/Images/DistrictPlanImages/Site%20of%20Ecological%20Significance/SES%20H%2012.pdf
Classic Yacht Association of New Zealand. https://classicyacht.org.nz/cyaforum/topic/ex-lyttelton-ferry-onawe

Cyclopedia of New Zealand [Canterbury Provincial District], Governors Bay, 1903. NZETC. http://nzetc.victoria.ac.nz/tm/scholarly/tei-Cyc03Cycl-t1-body1-d5-d17.html

Department of Conservation, History of Adderley Head Signal Station. www.doc.govt.nz/parks-and-recreation/places-to-go/canterbury/places/banks-peninsula-area/adderley-head-signal-station

Department of Conservation. Loader Cup winners. www.doc.govt.nz/news/events/awards/loder-cup-award/all-winners-from-1929/

Department of Conservation. Māori. Tōpuni. www.doc.govt.nz/about-us/our-partners/maori

Fisheries New Zealand, Bylaws for the Rāpaki *Mātaitai*, New Zealand Gazette, 7 December 2000. https://gazette.govt.nz/notice/id/2000-go9052

Fisheries New Zealand, Lyttelton Harbour/Whakaraupō Mātaitai Reserve Proposed bylaws, 29 April 2020. www.fisheries.govt.nz/news-and-resources/consultations/bylaws-for-the-lyttelton-harbourwhakaraupo-mataitai

Geanology.com. Hodgson Family Carlisle UK. http://genforum.genealogy.com/hodgson/messages/930.html

Godley Head Heritage Trust. The lighthouse. www.godleyhead.org.nz/the-lighthouse.html

———. The searchlights. www.godleyhead.org.nz/searchlights.html

Grace, Wiremu (2016). 'How Māui brought fire to the world'. *Te Kete Ipurangi*. Te Tāhuhu o te Mātauranga. https://eng.matarangamaori.tki.org.nz/Support-materials/Te-Reo-Maori/Maori-Myths-Legends-and-Contemporary-Stories/How-Maui-brought-fire-to-the-world

Great Grandma's Wicker Basket. Camp Bay Cemetery records. http://greatgrandmaswickerbasket.blogspot.com/2014/02/camp-bay-cemetery-records-banks.html

Heritage New Zealand Pouhere Taonga. Fort Jervois. www.heritage.org.nz/the-list/details/5306

———. *Battery Point Historic Area*. Report for The New Zealand Heritage List Rārangi Kōrero. www.heritage.org.nz/the-list/details/7553

———. Ōtamahua/Quail Island Historic Area. www.heritage.org.nz/the-list/details/9552

Hughes, Grant. *Quarantine*. Kete Christchurch, Christchurch City Libraries. http://ketechristchurch.peoplesnetworknz.info/site/documents/show/244-quarantine#.X3ITuS1L2Uk

Lyttelton Borough Extension Act, 1911, No. 36, 7b. www.nzlii.org/nz/legis/hist_act/lbea19112gv1911n36460/

Lyttelton Harbour Board Land Bill, 1905. www.nzlii.org/nz/legis/hist_bill/lhblb1905661341

New Zealand Maritime Record, NZ National Maritime Museum. *Defender*. www.nzmaritime.co.nz/thornycroft.htm

Ngāi Tahu Claims Settlement Act 1998. Schedule 88, Tōpuni for Rīpapa Island, Lyttelton Harbour. www.legislation.govt.nz/act/public/1998/0097/latest/DLM431323.html

RootsChat, Newton Family. www.rootschat.com/forum/index.php?topic=1266.9

RNZN Communicators Association. Interview with Lieutenant Commander Victor Fifield, April 1996. https://rnzn-comms.org/memories/fifield

Sensor Systems NZ Ltd. www.sensorsystems.co.nz/news/sabik-led-350h-replaces-damaged-lighthouse-at-godley-head-lyttelton-harbour-canterbury-nz

Star, Paul. Potts, Thomas Henry. Te Ara Encyclopedia of New Zealand. https://teara.govt.nz/en/biographies/2p27/potts-thomas-henry

Stuff. Lyttelton's Bad Friday, 9 October 2010. www.stuff.co.nz/the-press/christchurch-life/4214523/Lyttelton's-bad-Friday

The New Zealand Maritime Record, NZ National Maritime Museum. www.nzmaritime.co.nz/thornycroft.htm

The Nolan. The Newsletter of the O'Nolan Clan Family Association, March 2009, Issue 19. http://nolanfamilies.org/archives/newsletter/TheNolan-19.pdf

Voices against War: Courage, conviction and conscientious objection in WW1 Canterbury. http://voicesagainstwar.nz

Waitangi Tribunal, *The Ngai Tahu Report 1991*, section 9 Banks Peninsula. www.justice.govt.nz/tribunals/waitangi-tribunal/Reports/wai0027%201991%20Report

Wellington Classic Yacht Trust. www.wcyt.org.nz

Wikipedia. Compulsory Military Training in New Zealand. https://en.wikipedia.org/wiki/Compulsory_military_training_in_New_Zealand

Newspapers

Akaroa Mail and Banks Peninsula Advertiser
Harbour Link
Lyttelton Times
Press (Christchurch)
Star (Christchurch)
Stratford Evening Post

Glossary

Te reo Māori

ara moana sea route
aua yellow-eyed mullet
hapū kinship group or subtribe
harakeke flax
hoka red cod
kaikōmako Pennantia corymbosa, native plant
kaimoana seafood
kāinga village
kererū native pigeon
koiro conger eel
koreke native New Zealand quail
kōwhai Sophora microphylla, S. tetraptera, native tree
kupenga fishing nets
kūtai mussels
mahinga kai food-gathering place or resource
mana whenua customary rights
manu bird
manuhiri visitor
manuhuahua bird cooked and preserved in its own fat and tied up in a sea-kelp basket
mānuka tea tree, Leptospermum scoparium
mararī butterfish
mokopuna grandchild
nohoanga temporary settlement
pā fortified village
pāpaka crab
papakāinga ancestral village
pāua abalone
pōhā kelp water bag
pōhuehue maidenhair vine, Muehlenbeckia complexa
pātiki flounder
pioke dogfish, rig
pūtakitaki paradise shelduck
rāwaru blue cod
rimurimu seaweed
tangata whenua people of the land, indigenous people of Aotearoa New Zealand
tauranga waka traditional canoe landing point
tio oyster
tītī muttonbird
tuaki cockle
tuna eel
umu earth oven
urupā burial ground
waka canoe
whai repo stingray
whānau extended family
whare house, building
wharekai dining hall
whare karakia church
whare whakairo carved meeting house

Place names

Aua King Billy Island
Awaroa Godley Head
Horomaka Banks Peninsula (also known as Te Pataka o Rakaihautū)
Ihutai Avon Heathcote Estuary
Inainatu Pile Bay
Kaioruru Church Bay
Kā Pākihi Whakatekateka o Waitaha Canterbury Plains
Kaitangata Mansons Peninsula
Koukourārata Port Levy
Mahoenui range of hills extending from Awaroa Godley Head to Evans Pass
Motukauatiiti Corsair Bay
Motukauatirahi Cass Bay
Ngā Kohatu Whakarekareka o Tamatea Pōkai Whenua Port Hills
Ōhinehou Lyttelton
Ōhinetahi
Ōtamahua Quail Island
Ōtokitoki/Mahoenui Gollans Bay
Ōtoromiro Governors Bay
Papa Koiro cave on the east side of Waitata Little Port Cooper
Pukekaroro Sandy Bay
Pūrau
Pūtaringamotu Riccarton
Raekura Redcliffs
Rīpapa
Tapuwaeharuru Evans Pass
Tara o Te Rangi Hikaia Gebbies Pass
Tauwharepaka Head of the Bay/Teddington
Te Ahi a Tamatea Rāpaki Rock
Te Ahu Pātiki Mount Herbert
Te Ana Ngati Mamoe cave on the west side of Waitata Little Port Cooper
Te Ara Whānui o Makawhiua Port Levy Harbour
Te Awaparahi Buckleys Bay
Te Onepoto Taylors Mistake
Te Pātaka o Rākaihautū Banks Peninsula
Te Piaka Adderley Head
Te Pōhue Camp Bay
Te Pōhue The Monument/Camp Bay
Te Rāpaki-o-Te Rakiwhakaputa
Te Rapu stream at Teddington
Te Tara o Te Rakihikaia Gebbies Pass
Te Upoko o Kurī Witch Hill
Te Waihora Lake Ellesmere
Te Waipounamu South Island
Te Waipapa Diamond Harbour
Te Wharau Charteris Bay
Upoko o Kurī Stoddart Point
Wairewa Lake Forsyth
Waitata Little Port Cooper
Wakaroa Pigeon Bay
Whakaepa Pā
Whakaraupō Lyttelton Harbour

Image credits

Page 1: Te Wharau Charteris Bay; pages 2–3: Awaroa Godley Head; page 29: Ōtamahua Quail Island; pages 30–31: Waitata Little Port Cooper; pages 44–45: Te Pōhue Camp Bay; pages 62–63: Rīpapa Island; pages 80–81: Pūrau; pages 104–5: Te Waipapa Diamond Harbour; pages 126–27: Kaioruru Church Bay; pages 144–45: Te Wharau Charteris Bay; pages 164–65: Tauwharepaka Teddington; pages 180–81: Allandale and Ōhinetahi; pages 196–97: Ōtoromiro Governors Bay; pages 218–19: Ōtamahua Quail Island; pages 244–45: Te Rāpaki-o-Te Rakiwhakaputa jetty; pages 264–65: Motukauatirahi Cass Bay; pages 278–79: Motukauatiiti Corsair Bay; pages 294–95: Motukauatiiti Corsair Bay and Magazine Bay; pages 312–13: Ōtokitoki Gollans Bay; pages 330–31: Awaroa Godley Head; pages 346–47: Ōtoromiro Governors Bay; page 366: Te Rāpaki-o-Te Rakiwhakaputa jetty; page 392: Awaroa Godley Head all © John Doogan

Pages 12–13: Map designed by Andrew Douglas-Clifford, The Map Kiwi

Pages 14–15: Tauwharepaka Teddington mudflats; page 369: Lyttelton Harbour both © Jane Robertson

Endpapers: Environment Canterbury, Corsair Bay jetty, 1944, MA50C/1/451

Abbreviations used in image credits

ANZCRO Archives New Zealand Te Rua Mahara o te Kāwanatanga Christchurch Regional Office
BPCC Banks Peninsula Cruising Club
CBYC Charteris Bay Yacht Club
CCL Christchurch City Libraries
DHHA Diamond Harbour Historical Association
GBHT Governors Bay Heritage Trust
NZETC New Zealand Electronic Text Collection

Acknowledgements

My thanks to the residents, ex-residents of, and those associated with, Whakaraupō Lyttelton Harbour who have generously shared memories, family archives, images and time. Mary Harrison and Marion Coxon gave me unstinted access to the Hunter archives. Anne Ogilvie and Jane Taylor went to great lengths to make available Gardiner/Jackson family material. Simon Agar and Bruce Gebbie shared excellent material through sustained email conversations. Paul Ensor and David Bundy gave me valuable feedback on a draft manuscript. Paul Wilkins provided specialist knowledge of the harbour light and fog horn on Godley Head and of military matters relating to Fort Jervois, Rīpapa Island. Others whose contributions I have sought or drawn on include Noeline Allan, Dick and Lesley Barnett, Peter Chinnery, Euan Crawford, Sue Currie, Dawn Dawson, Guy Ditfort, Brian Downey, Philippa Drayton, Louisa Eades, Stephen Estall, Laurel France, Lindsay Gough, Jenny Healey, Mick Horgan, Helen Halliwell, Carolyn and Brendon Leech, Sarah Leech, Stephen McKelvey, Ian McLennan, Neil McLennan, Max Manson, Tracey Ower, Janette Park, Paul Pritchett, Murray Radcliffe, Ivan and Paul Rogers, Marton Sinclair, Graeme and Katharina Small, Paula Smith, Paul Star, Bill Studholme, June Swindells, Jane Taylor, Joy Thompson, Evan Walker, Sam Yeatman and Peter May, Nancy Vance.

Thank you to Frances Husband for generous access to the Diamond Harbour and Districts Historical Association archives, and to Lizzie Meek and Murray McGuigan, who went well beyond the call of duty in providing me with access to the Te Ūaka Lyttelton Museum photographic archive. Staff at the Naval Point Club, Lyttelton, enabled and encouraged me to draw on their extensive library records. I am very grateful to Nicolas Boigelot of Canterbury Museum, whose support with sourcing historic images has been immense. My thanks also to the staff at Christchurch City Libraries and Archives New Zealand (Christchurch Branch) for their excellent support.

The images that introduce each chapter were taken by photographer John Doogan, while the map of Whakaraupō is the work of cartographer Andrew Douglas-Clifford. Thank you both for work that significantly enhances this publication.

My sincere thanks to Donald Couch (Ngāi Tahu), of Te Hapū o Ngāti Wheke (Rāpaki), for responding patiently to my enquiries, providing feedback on work-in-progress and generously sharing his knowledge of the Māori history of Whakaraupō. Ngā mihi nui ki a koe. Also to Andrew Scott, general manager at Te Hapū o Ngāti Wheke (Rāpaki), for assistance and advice.

It is a special privilege to have one's work, created in isolation, transformed by others, and to be involved in that process in such a smooth and inclusive manner. My publishing team at Massey University Press has been a delight to work with. Special thanks to Matt Turner for his meticulous and empathetic editing, to Sarah Elworthy whose design work has captured so well the spirit of the harbour, and to Emily Goldthorpe for patiently steering me through the many pre-publication tasks. Tracey Borgfeldt has overseen the entire publication project. Thank you, Tracey, for always engaging me in the process and sustaining my confidence. You have been such a pleasure to work with.

Publishing local history with a limited audience and commercial return is challenging. Ultimately this book would not exist without generous financial assistance from the Lyttelton Port Company, the Rod Donald Banks Peninsula Trust, the Governors Bay Heritage Trust, the Christchurch City Council and the Canterbury History Foundation.

My thanks are due, above all, to my partner, Russ, who has walked with this project (literally) — listening, soothing, offering me valuable critical insights and unconditional support. Arohanui.

Index

Page numbers in **bold** refer to images.

A

A. Rhind and Co. 121
Acheron Bay *see* Pūrau
Acheron (survey ship) 89
Acland, Colin 58
Adderley, Charles 32
Adderley Head 32, 33, **35**, 37, 57, 333, 338
Adderley Head Reserve 94, 99
Adderley Head Signal Station 26, 34, 36, 37, 39, **40**, 73, 107, 361
    fiftieth anniversary of closing 43
Addington saleyards, Christchurch 57
Agar and Roberts 173, 203, 351, 352, 355
Agar and Thomas 173, 352, 356
    annual picnic, Governors Bay **353**
Agar, Betty 122–23, 360
Agar, George 153, 351, 355
Agar, Keith Trevor **123**
Agar, Maurie 123
Agar, Simon 211
Akaroa 17, 33, 83, 84, 86, 92, 143, 168, 252
Allan, James and Hilda 184
Allan, Jessie 186
Allan, John 179, 206
Allan, Noeline 274
Allandale Hall 187
Allandale (Hodgsons Bay, Bloors Bay) 27, 167, **180–81**, 182, 183–89, **186**, **188**, 202, 206, 368
Allandale–Ōhinetahi–Governors Bay Foreshore Track 195
Allen, James 109
Ames, James 34
Anderson, Albert 316
Anderson, Andrew Alexander 149
Anderson, Andrew William 94–95, 137, 152, 154–55, 157, 235, 257, 356–57
Anderson, Dorothy 316
Anderson, Emma (née Metcalf) 152
Anderson, Frederick 160
Anderson, Grant 160
Anderson, Kate Bowery (née Bradley) 149
Anderson, Kate (née Bradley) 152
Anderson, Len 78
Anderson, Robert 26, 137, 150, 152
Anderson, William 150
Andersons jetty 160
Andrews, George 292
Annan, Jack and Annie **235**
Ansley, Sally 364–65
Antarctic expeditions 228–29, **230**, 231, 235–36
Arnesen, B. A. 359
Ashworth family 147
Ashworth, James 57, 93
Ashworth, Robert 93
Aua King Billy Island 27, 86, 107, 171, 179, 183, 221, 236, 248
Awaroa Godley Head 301, 319, **330–31**, 332, 333–34, **334**
    'fog room' 339, **340**, **342**
    fog signal station and 'Golden Stairs' track 339, **339**, 341–42
    jetty (*see under* Mechanics Bay (Lighthouse Bay, Cable Bay))
    lighthouse 11, 73, 326, 333–35, **336**, **337**, 337–38, 340,
    'Moaning Minnie' lighted whistling buoy 339–40
    Second World War defences **243**, 341–42, **344**, 345

B

Baker, Charles 270, 296
Baker, Owen 159
Bakers Bay *see* Magazine Bay (Bakers Bay)
Bakers Point jetty (Golf Jetty, Half-Way Jetty, Bakers jetty) 158, 159
ballast industry 110, 131–32, 137, 152, 224, 237
Banks, Herewini 258
Banks Peninsula *see* Te Pātaka o Rākaihautū Banks Peninsula
Banks Peninsula and Canterbury Plains New Zealand: birds-eye view **18**
Banks Peninsula Cruising Club 77, **77**, 78, 79, 277, 305–6, 308
Banks Peninsula District Council 27, 263, 306, 308, 360
barges 71, 140, 163, 174, 184, 207, 217, 228, 237–38, 274
Barter, Clarence 361
Battery Point 70, 315, 320, **321**, **323**, 323–24, 351
Beckett, J. B. 184
Bee (brig) 19, 33, 34
Black Cat catamarans 28, 122, 125, 243, 360
Black Point 128, 129, 132, 146
Blatchford, Lloyd 177, 179
Blatchford, Ra 174, 293
Blatchford, William Flower 167
Blue Jacket (immigrant ship) 53–54
Bluecap Gang 86
boatbuilding 163, 213, **213**, 215, 217, 281, **282**, 284, 297–99, **299**, 301, **304**, 305
boats 11, 348, 367
    see also barges; dinghies; ferry services; launches; lifeboats; lighters; moorings; sea transport; storms and rough seas; yachts and yachting
    ballast craft 110, 112, 131–32, 134, 137
    fishing boats 131, 138, 213, 215, 256, 259, 306, 323, 351, 363
    whaling and sealing boats 19, 33, 34, 84, 253, 318
Boddam, Lieutenant Colonel 70
Bowater, Barry **22**
Bradley, Alice (née Shailer) 149, **151**
Bradley, Frances 147, 149
Bradley, Louis 149
Bradley, Orton 147, 149, 150, 153, 154, 158, 160, 236
Bradley, Robert Reginald 147, 149, 150
Bradley family 6, 20, 149, 150, 152, 153, 156, 349
    homestead **148**
Bradley jetty 158, 159
Brasell, Frederick James 323
Brasell, George **304**, 305
Bray, W. B. 320
Breeze (Canterbury Steam Company coaster) 326, **328**, 329
Breeze Bay (Nor-West Bay; Fern Bay) 314, 315, 326, 329
brickworks 270, 281, 283
Briggs, Andy 173
Briton (troopship) 56
Brothers' Pride (immigrant ship) 51, 54, 152, 157
Broths, Cameron 171, 173
Brown, Frank 206
bubonic plague 283
Buckley, Henry 316, **317**
Buckley, Louisa (née Mobley, later Garnett) 316
Buckley family 316, **317**
Buckleys Bay *see* Te Awaparahi Buckleys Bay
Bumstead, Ernest 361
Bundy, David 186, 187, 301
Bundy, J. B. 359, 360
Bundy, Reta, Ethel and Ivy **266**
Burgess, John 134
Burnham Industrial School annual camp 231, **232**, 234

383

Burns, Jack 361
Burns family 42–43
Burnside Quarry 184
bus services 288, 357, 360, 364
Bushell, J. B. 261, 325
Byrd, Richard E. 231

C

Calvert, Christopher 199
Calvert, Christopher Alderson 189
Cameron brothers' ballast quarry and jetty 110, **111**, 112, 113, 124, 134
Camp Bay *see* Te Pōhue Camp Bay
Candy, Marjorie (née Pearson) 57
Candy, Richard (Dick) 56, 57–58, 78
Canterbury Artillery Volunteers 320
Canterbury Association 20, 32, 47, 89–90, 107, 129, 146, 170, 199, 214, 221, 268, 281, 318
Canterbury (immigrant ship) 92, 199
Canterbury (steam launch) 10, 55, 94, 96, 119, 121, 211, 352, 354, 355, **355**, 357
Canterbury (tug and dredge) 41, 42, 73, 303
Canterbury Yacht and Motor Boat Club (CYMBC) 78, 160, 217, 305, 308
Cape Cachalot 333
car travel 9, 125, 138, 156, 261
Carrington, Octavius 253
Carston, Margaret 236
Carter, Tommy 37, **38**, 41
Cashin, James A. 324–25
Cashin Quay 11, 27, 324–26, **326**
Cass, Thomas 20, 89–90, 267–68
Cass Bay *see* Motukauatirahi Cass Bay
Chalmers, Adam 153
Chaney, Susannah 170
Charlotte Jane (immigrant ship) 90, 147, 221
Charteris Bay *see* Te Wharau Charteris Bay
Charteris Bay Golf Course 26, 158–59
Charteris Bay Yacht Club 142, 143, 157, 159, 160, **162**, 163
  rescue launch *Te Wharau* **161**, 163
Charteris, Francis Richard 146
Childs, Archie **161**
Chinnery, Charles 274
Chinnery, Peter 271–72
Chinnery family 272
Cholmondeley, Hugh Hebert 154
Cholmondeley Children's Home 211, **212**, 214
Christchurch City Council 27, 214, 263, 277, 292, 311
Christchurch Rowing Regatta 287
Chudleigh, Edward 119
Church Bay *see* Kaioruru Church Bay
Church Bay Gully 129, 131, **133**, 136
Cleary, Tom 122
Cleary, W. C. 359
Clibborn, Mr 24
Cobb & Co coaches 204
Collins, Don **139**
Compton, George and Elizabeth 315
Condon, Helen 42
Cook, William 319
Cooper, Daniel 33
Coppersmith, J. 74
Cornwell (Navy League training ship) 79
Correspondence School 57, 99
Corsair Bay *see* Motukauatiiti Corsair Bay
Corsair Bay Recreation Reserve 283–84
Corsair Bay Swimming and Lifesaving Club 288
Couch, Arthur Te Rangihiwinui 248
Couch, Rewi 257–58, 259
Couch, Wera 261
Cowan, James 248, 253
Cox, Charles Perry 92
Crawford, Bob 272
Crawford, Euan 228
Cridland, Henry 20, 268

Crosby, Neil **214**
Cunard, Steve 215
Curnow, Alan 272
Curnow, T. M. 99
Currie, Edgar 154
Cyclone Giselle (1968) 58, 74

D

Dampiers Bay 217, 270, 296, 297, 303, 306
  see also Te Ana Marina
Dawson, Dawn 316
Dawson, Pete 240
Day, George, Ann and family 318
Daymond, James and Mary 53
de Burgh-Thomas, Peter 364
Deal boatmen 38
Dean, Bert 173
Dean, George 92–93, 96
Dean, Hannah (née Rathbone) 92
Dean, Mark 99
Dean, Mary Ann 92
Deans, Jane 170
Deans, John 168, 170
Deans, William 168
Deans family 20, 84, 268
Deep Sea Fishing Company **130**, 131, 132
Defender (torpedo boat) 298–99, **300**, 300–301, **302**
Demicheli, Bernard 288, 359, 360
Department of Conservation (DOC) 11, 28, 76, 79, 241, 345
Dermott, Fitzherbert 51
Deveron (RNVR training cutter) 76, 329
Diamond Habour *see* Te Waipapa Diamond Harbour
Diamond Harbour Park 118
dinghies 11, 21, 36, 41, 43, **102**, 103, 122, 123, 125, 157, 159, 210, 224, 237, 241, 266, 277, 305, 306, 356
Dobson, Edward 93, 200, 319
Dolphin (fishing boat) **322**, 323, 351
Donald, Dr 48
Drayton, Philippa 159
dredging 26, 41, 42, 204, 207–8, 210, 213, 298, 303, 306, 367
Drewitt, Bink **161**
Drewitt, James 156, 160
Dudley, Charles 163
Dunbier, Peter 186
Dyer, John 199, 200, 203
Dyer, Mary Ann 199, 200
Dyers Bay 198, 199, 253
  see also Māori Gardens; Ōtoromiro Governors Bay; Pukekaroro Sandy Bay (Percivals Point)
Dyers Pass 57, 204

E

Eadie, William 335
Eagle, Elsie 43
Eaglesome, Mr 109
earthquakes 2010/11 11, 27, 28, 76, 79, 114, 125, 143, 147, 153, 154, 167, 189, 217, 260, 308, 325–26, 345, 368
education
  see also Correspondence School; and names of individual schools
  Godley Head lighthouse children 335, 338
  transport to school 137, 138, 231–32
Edwards, Ted 74
Edwin Fox (immigrant ship) 68
electric power 57, 58, 149
Ellen Ballance (Defence Department steam launch) 231–32
Ellerslie boarding house 206
Empress (balloon) 37
Ensor, Herbert 195
Ensor, Paul **194**
Ensor, Richard **194**
Ensor family **194**, 195
Ericson, John F., Charlotte and family 335
Erskine Point Battery 298, 299, 301, 303
Estall, Stephen 293

F

Farr, Samuel 90
Fern Glen, Pūrau 76, 95, 99
ferry services 363
    Charteris Bay to Lyttelton 149, 154, 158, 363
    Church Bay to Lyttelton 140, 154, 158
    Corsair Bay to Lyttelton 287, 288, 292, 293, 363
    daily whaleboat service, Pūrau to Lyttelton 92–93
    Diamond Harbour to Lyttelton 28, 106, 113, 114, 119, 121, 122–23, **123**, 125, 141, 356, 357, 359–60, 363, 368
    Governors Bay to Lyttelton 154, 203, 204, 206, 210–11, 362, 363
    Port Levy to Lyttelton 361, 362, 363
    Pūrau to Lyttelton 94–95, 100, 154, 356, 363
    Quail Island to Diamond Harbour and Lyttelton 28, 243
    vehicular ferry proposal 124–25
Fifield, Victor 275
fires 55, 57, 93–94, 224, 270, 340–41
legends 247, 248, 267
Fisher, C. 112
Fisheries (South Island Customary Fishing) Regulations 263
fishing and shellfish gathering
    see also kaimoana
    commercial fishing 38, 131, 136, 224, 259, 287, 308, 316, 363, 367
    domestic fishing and shellfish gathering 61, 113, 168, 177, 179, 185–86, 193, **194**, 195, 206–7, 215, 221, 248, **249**, 254, 258, 259, 261, **262**, 263, 293
    mātaitai reserves 263
    recreational fishing 186, 202, 231, 241, 316, 323, 350, 355, 360, 362
Fitzgerald, James Edward 38
Fleming, R. J. 24
Flower, A. E. 287
Foley, Maurice 176–77
Fooks, C. E. 90
Forster, William 184, 202
Fort Jervois *see under* Rīpapa Island
Forward family 319
Fournier, J. M. 318
Fox, John 364
Fox, William 90
Fryer, Percy 26, 210, 256, 305

G

Galbraith, John 36, 54
Galbraith, Lynley (née Jackson) 76, **95**, 96, 100
Gallagher, Roderick 270
Gallagher, W. G. 26
Gallipoli Jetty *see under* Te Rāpaki-o-Te Rakiwhakaputa
Gardiner, Harold 94, 99
Gardiner, Henry Dent 55, 94, 99
Gardiner, Linton 94, 99
Gardiner, Mary Ann 94
Gardiner family 78, 86, 94, 95, 96, 99
Garforth and Lee 270–71
Garnett, Robert 316
Gatehouse, Jack **59**
Gaunson, Charlie 179
Gebbie, Bruce 26, 176, 177, **178**, 179
Gebbie, David 177
Gebbie, John 147, 168, 268
Gebbie, Mary 168
Gebbie, Rex 174
Gebbie, William 235
Gebbie family 20, 84, 90, 170, 253
Gebbies Pass *see* Te Tara o Te Rakihikaia Gebbies Pass
Genie (yacht) **22**
Gerrard, J. 359
Gillies, Tasman 259
Gillies, Wiremu 263
Gilmour, Dr 138, 361
Gilpin family 204
Ginders, Ric and Aileen 103
Gleig, George Robert 221

Godfrey, R. W. 137–38
Godley, Charlotte 19, 222
Godley, John Robert 32, 114, 199, 333
Godley Head *see* Awaroa Godley Head
Godley Head Heritage Trust 345
Godley House 114, **115**, 118, 121, 122, 125
Gollan, Donald 268, 318
Gollans Bay *see* Ōtokitoki Gollans Bay
Goodenough, Clive **302**
Governors Bay *see* Ōtoromiro Governors Bay
Governors Bay Community Association 215, 217
Governors Bay Jetty Restoration Trust 28, 217
Governors Bay Progress League 124–25
Governors Bay Transport trucks **25**, 241
Graham, William 337
Greaves, Robert 170–71
Greenwood brothers 20, 47, 83–84, 86
    house built by Samuel Manson 84, **91**, 92
    use of, and lease of Māori land 47, 83–84, 86, 107
Grennell, Dick 361
Grennell, Harry 361, 362
Grey, Sir George 193
Griffiths, Thomas 350
Grubb, James 299
Grubb, John 107, 297–98, 299, 301
Guthard, Henry 74

H

Hadfield, John 26, 210
Haigh, James 224
Hall, Bill 206
Halliwell, David 240–41
Hamilton, Fitzroy George 73
Hancock, Charles Henry 226
Hannam, Edward 74
Harris, Jack 96
Harris, Jody 186, **188**
Harris, Mary Elizabeth 189
Harris, Robert 189
Harris, William 186
Hart, Elizabeth 315
Hawkins, Harvey 114, 118
Hay, Catherine 232
Hay Cottage **141**
Hay, Gilbert 157, 158
Hay, James (Hays Bay) 157, 158, 159
Hay, James (Pigeon Bay) 33, **130**, 131, 132, 150
Hay, Jean **130**, 131
Hay, John (Hays Bay) 158
Hay, John (Pigeon Bay) 137, 138, 142
Hay, Robert 232
Hay, William 150, 153
Hay family (Hays Bay) 157, 232
Hay family (Pigeon Bay) 20, 84, 152
Hayden, Jim 132
Hayders, Bill 173
Haydon, John 132, 134
Haydon and Payne 132, 134
Hays Bay 157–58, **159**
Head of the Bay 17, 20, 39, 84, 92, 167, 170, 171, 173, 175, 268
    see also Tauwharepaka Teddington
Head-to-Head walkway 28, 187, 277
Heathcote 23, 206, 281, 303, 319, 320, 324, 325
Hempelman, George 19, 33–34
Hempstalk, Thomas 361
Henderson, Barbara 112–13, 140
Henderson, C. A. 359
Henderson, Christina (née Tait) 112
Henderson, Gideon **112**, 112–13, 138, 140, 153
Henderson, John 113
Henderson, Robert 234–35
Henderson, Ted **98**
Henderson family 112–13
    cottage, Diamond Harbour 112, **113**
    Pleasant View cottage, Diamond Harbour 112, **113**, 140
Hendry, Keith **161**

Historic Places Trust (Heritage New Zealand Pouhere
    Taonga) 79
Hodgson, Grace 184
Hodgson, Mary 184
Hodgson, Paul Nixon 184, 190
Hodgson family 193
Holder, Thomas 132
Hollis and Brown 149, 152, 184
Hooper, Walter 74
Horomaka see Te Pātaka o Rākaihautū Banks Peninsula
horse travel and transport 39, 57, 76, 89, 92, 94, 99, 109, 123,
    138, 150, 153, 174, 184, 185, 186, 187, 254, 337
Hughes, Bill 173
Hunt, George 268
Hunter, Arthur 134, **135**, 136, 150, 153
Hunter, Eliza 112, 134, **135**, 136, 141
Hunter, John 99
Hunter, Mabel 136
Hunter, Marion 136
Hunter, Oliver 55, 129, 132, 134, 136–37, **137**, 138, 140,
    141, 142, 155, **161**
Hunter, Phyllis **137**, 138, 140
Hunter, Robert 138, 153
Hunter, Robinson 150
Hunter, T. M. 359
Hunter, Violet **137**, 138, 140
Hunter family 113, 137, 138, 152, 153
Hunter House 134, **135**, 136, **141**
Hurley, Del 365
Hutana, Pat **262**

I

Inainatu Pile Bay 78, **78**
Irwin, Des **161**
Isaac Construction 195
Isherwood, Eleanor 95, **95**, **98**, 99

J

Jackson, Alan 100
Jackson, Frank 95–96
Jackson, Harry and Henrietta 99, 100
Jackson, Lynley see Galbraith, Lynley (née Jackson)
Jackson, Thomas 199
Jackson family 86, 99
Jane Douglas (steam launch) 55, 96
Jefcoate, Lionel 163, 213, 215
Jeffries, J. 360
Jervois, Sir William 70
jetties 7, 8, 9, **10**, 11, 20, 21, 23–26, 27, 137, 200, 261
    see also names of individual jetties
    community involvement in management 27–28, 261, 263
    equipped with cranes 25, 57, **120**, 154, 226, 241, 338
    harbour board charges 23–24, 25–26, 118–19, 173–74,
        256, 257
John Anderson (steamer) 11, 21, 24, 94, 95, 96, **97**, 99, **120**, 206,
    211, 236, 258, 323, 349–51, **350**, 356
John Anderson Launch Company 118–19
Jones, Derek 241
Jones, Malcolm 27

K

Kaiapoi 65, 67, 252, 253
Kaihuānga feud 65, 67, 184, 252
The Kaik, Pūrau 95, 99
kaimoana 47, 90, 107, 109, 113, 129, 146, 147, 168, 214, 248,
    249, **259**
see also mahinga kai
Kaioruru Church Bay 26, **85**, 110, **126–27**, 128, **132–33**, **139**,
    140, **141**, **150**, 154, 160, 175, 272, 357, 367
    early European settlement 129–32, 134–36
    holiday homes 140–41, 143
    jetty 11, 23, 27, 28, 132, 137–38, **139**, **142**, 143, 158, 159, 173
    land subdivisions 140, 143
    map of quarries **130**
    picnics and visitors 138, 140

Kaitangata Mansons Peninsula 167, **169**, 182, 185, 186, **186**, 189,
    195, 211
Keenan, Enid 42
Keir, Wendy and Alex 58
Keirangi Farm, Camp Bay 43
Kevin, James 206–7
Killeck, Mary 326
King Billy Island see Aua King Billy Island
Kingdon, George 147
Kitchener, Herbert, 1st Earl Kitchener 73, 357
Kokiri, Timothy 234
Koskella family 55
Koukourārata Port Ashley 20
Koukourārata Port Levy 20, 23, 33, 37, 41, 57, 65, 84, 93, 94, 99,
    113, 248, 252–53, 272, 308
    jetty 103, 125

L

land transport see bus services; cars; horse travel and
    transport; rail transport; roads and road transport; trucking
    services
Langdown, William 281
Langlois, Jean-François 333
launches 21, 123, 173
    charges for use of jetties 24, 25–26, 118–19
    passenger traffic 21, 25–26, 118–19, 138, 154, 203, 204, 206,
        210–11, 270, 287, 292, 349, **350**, 352, **354**, 355, **355**
    (see also ferry services)
Laurence, John 134
Laurenson, George 231–32, 234, 303
Le Cren, John 38, 318
Lean, Alexander 298–99
Lee brothers 47
Leech, Brendon 156
Leech, Carolyn (née Smart) 156
Leech, Sarah 156
Leeming, Major 76
lifeboats 37, **38**, 186, 335, 340
lighters 20, 24, 55, 110, 184, 200, 229, 237–38, 319, 335, 351, 352
Linwood High School 141–42
Little Port Cooper see Waitata Little Port Cooper
Living Springs Stream Restoration Project 189, 368
Livingstone Bay (White Lady Bay) 314, 326
Long Point (Cabbage Tree Point) 34, **35**, 36
Longden and Le Cren 318
Lorraine, Charles (David Mahoney) 37
Luttrell, Alfred 94
Lyon, C. A. 256
Lyttelton see Ōhinehou Lyttelton
Lyttelton (steam launch) 149, 204, 352, **354**, **355**, 355–56
Lyttelton (tug) 43, 55, 99, 122, 257, 298, 356
Lyttelton Borough Council 119, 121, 123–24, 155, 270, 271, 283,
    284, 285, 288, 292, 297, 303, 359–60
Lyttelton Borough Extension Act 1911 119
Lyttelton Boxing and Sports Club 78
Lyttelton Fanciers' Club 78
Lyttelton Ferry Launches 359–60
Lyttelton Fire Brigade picnic, Pūrau **97**
Lyttelton Football Club 270
Lyttelton Gaol prisoners' construction work 70–71, 187, 224,
    226, 283, 284, 299
Lyttelton Golf Club 154
Lyttelton Harbour Board 36, 58, 79, 258, 345
    see also Lyttelton Port Company
    costs and charges 23–26, 118–19, 124, 173–74, 208, 256, 257
    dredging 155, 204, 208, 213, 298
    jetties 9, 11, 23–26, 41–42, 56–57, 58, 118–19, 123–24, 137, 154,
        155, 158, 160, 163, 204, 207, 208, 215, 217, 226, 228, 243,
        254, 256–57, 261, 292
    marina 305, 306, 308
    pleasure craft facilities 277
    port expansion 324–26, **326**
    shell removal 237
    silting 11
Lyttelton Harbour Board Land Act 1905 23

Lyttelton Harbour Cruises 360
Lyttelton Harbour Improvement Committee 24, 41, 154, 173, 208, 254
Lyttelton Harbour Whakaraupō Mātaitai Reserve 263
Lyttelton Ladies' Swimming Club 287
Lyttelton Naval Volunteers 301
Lyttelton Port Company 11, 27, 43, 76, 79, 243, 263, 306, 308, 311, 315
    see also Lyttelton Harbour Board
Lyttelton Port Recovery Plan 325–26
Lyttelton Regatta 21, 112, 160, **161**, 254, 301
Lyttelton Rifle Club 283
Lyttelton Rowing Club 306
Lyttelton Sunday School 93
Lyttelton Volunteer Artillery 316
Lyttelton Wharf Commission 320
Lyttelton Wharf Commission Inquiry (1863) 333
Lyttelton Yacht Marina 308

M

MacDonald, Mac 271
Mackenzie, J. H. T. 234–35
Mackey, David 141
Mackey, Fred 103, 142, 160, **161**, 163
Mackey, Hazel (née Hunter) **137**, 140, 141, 142, **161**
Mackey, Ian 141
Mackey, Marion 103, 141, 142
Mackey, Mary 103, 141
Maddison, J. C. 271
Magazine Bay (Bakers Bay) 21, 272, 283, **294–95**, 296, 297, **298**, 305, 311
    boatbuilding and repair 297–99, **299**, 301
    Canterbury Yacht and Motor Boat Club slipway 306, **307**
    jetty 297, **298**, 306
    military reserve, shed and slipway 298–301, 303
Magazine Bay Marina 305–6, 308, **309**, 363, 365
Magazine Bay Recreation Reserve 297, 303
mahinga kai 19, 33, 89, 113, 183, 221, 252, 263, 368
    see also kaimoana
Mahy, Penny 189
Manihera, Eruera 258
Manihera, Waitere 257
Mannix, Constable 138
Manson, Jean 168
Manson, Samuel 84, 147, 168, 170
Manson family 20, 84, 92, 170, **171**, 176, 253
Mantell, Walter 89
Manuwhiri 183
Māori 8, 84, 89, 93, 247–48, 252–53
    see also Te Rāpaki-o-Te Rakiwhakaputa; and under names of other bays and settlements
    trading 19, 33, 34, 92, 93, 252, 253
Māori Gardens 179, **196–97**, 214, **214**, 215
Māori land 47, 83–84, 107, 168
    'extinguishment' of title by purchase 84, 89, 170, 221, 252
    invalidation of leases 170
    reserves **88**, 89, 221, 252
    'unoccupied' land 89
March, John Edwin 68
Marten, R. M. 270
Martini-Henry Rifle Club 270
Massey, Charles 335
Massey, William 74
Matariki (steam launch) 24, 94, 95, 99, 136, 137, 138, 140, 154–55, **155**, 159, 257, 258, 356–57
Matawai, Pakira 237
May, Peter 58
May Queen (iron barque) 55–56
Maynard, Félix 33, 34
McCosker, John 334
McCready, Douglas 58
McFaul, James 206–7
McKenzie, David 333
McKenzie, James 73
McKenzie, Paani 256–57

McLennan, Neil 27
McTaggart, Bob and Jack 74
Meares, Janet and Peter **194**
Mechanics Bay (Lighthouse Bay; Cable Bay) 314, 315, 337, 342
    jetty 11, 315, 338
Medley, Mary Catherine 68
Millar, M. J. 119
Miller, Malcolm 270–71, 281, 289, 292
Miller, Mrs M. J. 261
Miller and Maughan 132
Miller boatbuilding sheds **304**, 305, 306
Ministering Children's League 154
Moepuku peninsula 107, 146, 167, **169**, 186, 236
Moir, Charles 298, 299–300
Monica (steam launch) 94, 119, 211, 357
Moore, Christopher 364
Moore, Thomas Richard 147, 224
    house **148**
Moore family 147, 152
Moorhouse, William Sefton 189, 190
moorings 103, **104**, 266, 272, 277, 292, 305, 306
Morefield, Dick **161**
Morris, Matthew 107
motor boats see launches
Motukauatiiti Corsair Bay 9, 21, 270–71, 272, 277, **278–79**, 280, 359
    boatbuilding and repair 281, **282**, 284, 297
    early European settlement 281, 283
    jetties 23, **279**, 281, 284, **285**, 288–89, **289**, 292, 293
    picnics and visitors 280, 283–84, 285, 287, 288, **289**, **290–91**, 292, 293, **293**, 329
    swimming 280, **282**, 283, 284–85, **285**, **286**, 287–88, 289, 292–93
Motukauatirahi Cass Bay 26, **264–65**, 266, 267, 270, **273**, **276**, 277
    abbatoir 266, 268, **269**, 270–72, **273**, 284, 293
    ammunition stores 272, **273**, 274, 275, **275**, 277
    early European settlement 267–68, 270
    subdivision **276**, 277
Motunau 86
Mount Bradley 146, 167
Mount Evans 58, 67, 84, 89
Mount Herbert see Te Ahu Pātiki Mount Herbert
Mount Herbert County Council 9, 23, 24–25, 58, 100, 103, 124–25, 137, 173–74, 195, 206, 208, 213, 214, 217, 237, 301
Mountfort, Benjamin 189, 337–38
Mullogh (steamer) 68, 110, 204
Munnings, Joseph 190, 200
Mystery (ballast boat) 132

N

Napier-Bell, C. 204
Naval Point see Te Nukutai o Tapoa Naval Point
Naval Point Club 306, 308, 311
Navy League Sea Cadets 79, **79**, 238, 240, 275, 277
Neilsen, Soren 69
Nelson, G. 362
New Brighton 23
New Zealand Company 19–20, 89, 168, 267, 318
New Zealand Garrison Artillery **72**, 73, **322**, 323, 357
Newell, Dr 138
Ngāi Tahu 8, 19, 33, 65, 67, 83, 89, 146, 147, 183, 199, 246, 248, 252, 253, 315
Ngāti Māmoe 8, 19, 33, 65, 83, 182, 183, 199, 248
Ngāti Toa 252
Ngatiki (passenger launch) 141, 241, 360, 363, 364–65
Nohomutu, Tiemi 83, 86, 89
Nolan, Elizabeth Mary (née Pascoe) 41
Nolan, Oliver Archibald 41
Nolan, Paddy 41
Norris, Baden **78**
Norris, Hubie 305
Norris, Pearl, Yvonne, Audrey and Dawn **317**
Norris, William Richard 316
Norris family 78

Novelty (lighter) 110, 352
Nuttall, James 74–75
Nuttall, Tom 74

O

Oakley, Mary Jean (née Hunter) 138
Ocean View Hotel 203, 204, 210–11
Officers Point 39
    Timeball Station 34
Ogilvie, Gordon 34
Ōhinehou Lyttelton 17, 34, 57, 110, 136, 137, 138, 170–71, 173, 183, 252, 253, 274, 303, 305, 319, 333
    port **346–47**
    port location and expansion **302**, 303, 319–20, 324–26, **326**, 367–68
Ōhinetahi **180–81**, 182, 183–84, 189–90, 193, 195
    homestead 189, 190, **191, 192**
    jetty 190, **192**, 193, 195
Okains Bay 109, 136
Old Mac's Hut **141**
Onawe (passenger launch) 24, 58, 122, 125, 141, 357, 359, 360, 362–64
Oram, George 204
Orton Bradley Park 147, 149, 150
Ōtamahua Quail Island 20, 86, 147, 152, **155**, 170, 175–76, **186**, 187, 193, **218–19**, 220, **223**, **247**, 248, 252, 274, 299, 360
    Department of Conservation reserve 28
    jetties 11, 225, 226, **227**, 228, **228**, 235–36, **239**, 240, **242, 243**
    leper colony 138, 154, 202, 224, 232, **233**, 234–37, **235**
    picnics and visitors 106, 206, 235, 238, 240, 243
    pouwhenua Te Hamo o Tū Te Rakiwhānoa 243, **243**
    quarantine station 69, 70, 224–26, **227**, 228, 232, 234, 240, 352
    quarantining and training of Antarctic expedition animals 228–29, **230**, 231, 235–36, 352
    quarries 190, 224, **225**
    revegetation project 28, 241, **242**, 243
Ōtamahua Quail Island Ecological Restoration Trust 241, 243, 368
Otamahua (shell-gathering boat) 238
Ōtokitoki Gollans Bay 86, **312–13**, 314, 315, 316, 318–20, 323, 324, 325–26, **327**, 332, 363, 367
Ōtoromiro Governors Bay 17, 23, 26, 27, 57, 92, 154, 170, 175, 183, 185, 186, 187, **196–97**, 198, 254, 272, 368
    early European settlement 199–206
    environmental damage 193, 195
    Lionel Jefcoate's boatbuilding shed 163, 213, **213**, 215, 217
    local children's activities 211, **212**, 213
    picnics and visitors 9, 204, **205**, 206, 208, **209**, 210–11, 352, **353**, 355, **355**, 362
    school 177, 206, 211
Ōtoromiro Governors Bay jetties 20, 23, 26, 173, 174, 184, 200, **200**, 202–3, **203**, 204, **205**, 206, **207**, 207–8, **209**, 210, **355**
    accidental drowning 124, 206–7
    earthquake damage and repairs 27, 28, 143, 167, 199
    long jetty **10**, 11, 20, 26, 199, 203, 206, 210, 211, 213, 215, **216**, 217
Outlying Jetties By-law 1912 24
Owen and Dyer 271
oyster farming 129

P

Packer, Mary 177
Page, Evelyn, *New Year holiday (Corsair Bay)* **290–91**
Paine, Clarence 125
Pairman, Dr 208
Papa Kōiro 33
Paradise Bay jetties 154, 156, **157**
Parihaka 69–70, 352
Parkinson, John 268, 318–19
Parsons, Charles 199, 200, 203

Pascoe, Elizabeth Jane 41
passive resisters (conscientious objectors) 74–75
Pastime (keel-yacht) 289, 292
Pauaohinekotau Point 128, 129
Paul, Robert Bateman 107
Payne, Christina 112
Payne, James 110, 112, 131, 132, 134, 224
Payne's quarry 123, 131–32, 158
Percival, Westby 202
pest eradication 43, 241
Philip, Prince, Duke of Edinburgh 156
Phillips, George William 236
Philpot, Isaac, Mary and family 318
Pigeon Bay 36
Pile Bay 78, **78**, **85**
Pine Grove *see* Upoko o Kurī Stoddart Point
Plasted, Charles 112
Pleasant View cottage, Diamond Harbour 112, **113**, 140
Plimmer, George 68
Polhill, Baker 315–16
Port Companies Act 1987 308
Port Cooper 19, 20, 33, 47, 84, 86, 89, 90, 107, 168, 170, 333
    see also Whakaraupō Lyttelton Harbour
Port Cooper Deed, 1849 83, 89, 221, 252–53
Port Hills **18**, 32, 84, 86, 193, 247
Port Levy Harbour
    see also Koukourārata Port Levy; Te Ara Whānui o Makawhiua
Port Levy Road Board 119
Port Victoria Road Board 171, **172**, 297
Potts, Ambrose 193
Potts, Donald 193
Potts, Edith 193
Potts, Emma 190, 193
Potts, George 193
Potts, Thomas 94, 107, 109, 119, 171, 190, 193, 200, 202, 224, 225, 283, 297
    Out in the Open (1882) 193, 195
Potts Point quarry 195
Pratt, William 34
Pritchett, Paul 158, 160, 163
Project Port Lyttelton 301
Puckle, Edward 268
Pukekaroro Sandy Bay (Percivals Point) 20, 23, 27, **196–97**, 199, 211, **212**, 215, 303, **304**
    jetties 200, **200**, 202, **203**, 204, 206–7, **207**, 208, **209**
Punjaub (immigrant ship) 54, 68–69
Pūrau 19, 20, 21, 23, 27, 41, 47, 50, 51, 57, 65, **80–81**, 82, **85**, 141, 150, 154, 272, 301, 306, 356
    army manoevres 96, 99
    boat service to Lyttelton 92–93, 94–96, **95**
    dances in the woolshed 94–95
    early European settlement 83–94, 268
    Māori residence and impact of European settlement 83–84, **86–87**, 89, 107, 248, 252–53
    picnics and visitors 93, 95, 96, **97**, 99, 100, 103, 352
    plan of Native Reserve No. 1, Pūrau (also named as Acheron Bay), 1849 **88**
    schools 92, **98**, 99
    urupā 83, 86, 89
Pūrau Homestead 90, **91**, 93–94, 95, 100
Pūrau jetty 23, 25, **80**, 90, 92, 94, 95, **97**, 100, **101**, 103, 113, 137, 356
    dinghy facilities **102**, 103, 125
Purau Motor Camp 103
Purau (steam launch) 94, 95, 119, 210, 211, 258, 287, 350–51, 357, **358**, 362
Purau (tug) 364

Q

Quail Island *see* Ōtamahua Quail Island
quarantine stations *see under* Ōtamahua Quail Island; Rīpapa Island; Te Pōhue Camp Bay
quarrying 110, 112, 113, 124, **130**, 131–32, 134, 136, 152, 153, 184, 190, 195, 202–3, 224, 303, 367
    Gollans Bay 324–25, **327**

R

Radcliffe, Charles Edward **188**
Radcliffe, Eddie 208
Radcliffe, Stanley 206
Radcliffe brothers 186–87, 195
radio 177, 274
rail transport 141, 175, 184, 203, 226, 253, 283, 288, 292, 293, 303, 319, 320, 324
Rākaihautū 17
Randolph (immigrant ship) 36, 170, 268, 318
Rāpaki *see* Te Rāpaki-o-Te Rakiwhakaputa
Rayner, John Frederick 335
Red Head 55
rescues 11, 42–43, 55, 93, 121, 134, 138, 157, **161**, 163, 258, 288, 292, 298, 323, 326, 335, 340, 348, 352, 355–56, 361–62, 363
Rhind, Bert 359
Rhind and Co. shipping company 76
Rhind's Motor Launches 359, 362–63
Rhodes, George 47, 86, 89, 90, 92, 93, 129, 147
Rhodes, Robert Heaton 47, 86, 89, 90, 92, 93, 128, 129, 131, 147
Rhodes, Sophia (née Latter) 89, 90, 93
Rhodes, William Barnard 47, 86, 89, 90, 92, 129, 147
Rhodes family 20, 47
Rich, Stan 156
Riley, Fred 156
Rīpapa Island 39, **62–63**, 64, 79, 240, 360, 364
    bridge to the mainland 73–74
    Fort Jervois 65, 70, **71**, 72–76, **75**, 79, 96, 320, 339, 357
    fortified pā 65, **66**, 67, 78
    jetty 11, 28, 65, 67–68, 76, **77**, 79, 357, 363
    magazine 76, 79
    Parihaka Māori imprisonment 69–70, 352
    picnics and visitors 76, 79
    prison 74–76, 232
    quarantine station 48, 54, 55, 65, 67, **68**, 68–69, 70, 224–25, 232, 352
roads and road transport 9, 21, 25, **25**, 46, 170, 173, 174, 175, 177, 261, 270
    bridle paths 170, 184, 200, **200**, 202, 253
    Camp Bay to Pūrau **49**, 57, 58, **78**, 100
    Diamond Harbour to Christchurch 125, 360
    Dyers Pass road 199, 202, 204
    Governors Bay to Allandale (Beach Road, Old Coach Road) 187, 195, **205**
    Governors Bay to Lyttelton 200, **200–1**, 214, 247, **249**, 256, 274, 283, 299
    Lyttelton to Sumner 253, 315, 318
    pack track between Evans Pass and Godley Head 338–39, 341
    Pūrau to Diamond Harbour and Charteris Bay 100, **101**, 119, 122, 134, 140
    Pūrau to Port Levy 94
    road to Stoddart jetty 109
    road tunnel, Lyttelton to Christchurch 277, 324, 325, 360
Roberts, Johnny (of Agar and Roberts) 351
Roberts, Jonathan (prison escapee) 71
Robertson, Gladys (née Bamford) 184–85, 350
Robin Hood Hotel 110
Robinson, Police Magistrate 83, 86
Robinsons Bay jetty 143
Robson, Bill 74
Rod Donald Trust 368
Rogers, Paul 58, **59**, 60
Rogers, Trevor and Noel 58, **59**, 60
Rokohouia 17
Rolleston, William 132, 225
Rosemary Cottage, Ōhinetahi 189, 190, **191**
Rowan House 204, 206, 211
Rowe, George Herbert 147
rowing regattas 158, 159, **159**
Royal Naval Volunteer Reserve 258, 277, 363
Royal New Zealand Navy base, Lyttelton 274
Ruahine (oil launch) 56, 121, 238, 323, **358**, 359
Russian invasion scare, 1880s 70–73, 298–301, 320, 324
Ryan, Elizabeth 39
Rye, Maria 50

S

Salt, Eli 270
Sandford, John 67
Sandy Bay *see* Pukekaroro Sandy Bay (Percivals Point)
Scott, Jessie 185
Scott, R. A. E. 301
Scott, Robert Falcon 228–29, 231
Scott, W. 271
Scratchley, Peter 70
sea level rise 11, 187, 189
Sea Scouts 211, 213, 217, 316
sea transport 19, 20, 21, 23, 58, 94, 99, 100, 118, 136, 152, 154, 157–58, 170, 175, 184, 348, 367
    see also boats; ferry services; launches; storms and rough seas; waka; whaleboats
    animals 100, 221–22, 226, 229, **230**, 268, 297, 319
    building materials 94, 140–41, 154, 184, 190, 222, 225, 228, 335
    firewood 189, 222
    household and farm supplies 9, 41, 57, 84, 136, 154, 173
    produce 9, 84, 92–93, 94, 99, 109, 112–13, 136, 152–53, 154, 173, 184, 193, 200, 202, 208, 241, 253, 316, 360
    to school 137, 138, 231–32
    stone from quarries 184, 190, 202–3, 224
sedimentation 9, 11, 17, 19, 26–27, 155, 173, 189, 207, 263, 277
Sewell, Elizabeth 199
Sewell, Henry 199–200
Shackleton, Ernest 229
shell removal 237–38, **239**, 283
Shelly Bay (now Traffic Cops' Bay) 153
Shepherd, Alex 224
Shetland Islanders 112, 131, 134, 152, 157
Shortland, Edward 19, 83–84
Simeon, Captain 199
Simpson, Mary-Ann 152, **152**
Simpson, Thomas 'Seal' 150, 152, **152**
Simpson family 152, **152**
Sinclair, Eliot **22**, 142–43
Sinclair, Harold 140
Sinclair, J. 174
Sinclair, Una **139**
Sinclair family 20, 84, 143
Slaughter's Cotton Powder fog-signal station, Godley Head 339
Small, Alfred 186
Small, Angus 207, 211
Small, Graeme 211, **214**, 215
Small, Jack 202
Small, Mary (Phipps) 202, 204, 254
Small family 202
Smalls jetty 204, 206, **209**
Smart, Barry 156
Smart, Harold 156
Smarts jetty 154, 156, **157**
Smith, Grace (née Gardiner) 57
Smith (later Stapylton-Smith), Cedric 56, 57, 58
Smith, T. B. 340–41
Smith, William Mein 20, 168
Society of Canterbury Colonists 90

Sprot, Mark 107–8, 109
St Cuthbert's Church, Ōhinetahi 189, 204
Stafford, Edward 268
Stapylton-Smith, Mary 58
   Adderley to Bradley 58
   The Other End of the Harbour 58
Stapylton-Smith, Pamela 57
Stapylton-Smith, Paul 58
Stephenson, G. R. 320
Stewart, Roland 121
Stinson, John 132, 134, 226
stock route, Charteris Bay to Pūrau 134, **135**, 136
Stoddart, Agnes 109, 118
Stoddart, Anna Barbara (née Schjott) 109, **111**, 118, 119
Stoddart, Frances 109, **111**
Stoddart, James 109, **111**
Stoddart, Margaret **108**, 109, **111**, 118
   painting of old Diamond Harbour jetty **116–17**
Stoddart, Mark Pringle 9, 20, 107–8, 109, 110, **111**, 114, 129, 132, 140, 193, 224
   subdivision of property 114
Stoddart, Mary 109, 118, 119
Stoddart Cottage 109, 112, 118
Stoddart family 109, 114, 119, 193
Stoddart jetty **9**, 20, 107, 109, 114, 119
   see also Te Waipapa Diamond Harbour jetty
Stoddart Point *see* Upoko o Kurī Stoddart Point
storms and rough seas 20–21, 39, 55–56, 58, 78, 103, 141–42, 153, 168, 289, 292, 298, 303, 333, 337–38, 340, 357
   capsized boats 36, 150, 157, 224, 226, 355–56
   drownings 38, 73, 150, 222, 226, 361–62
   southerly storm 12 October 2000 308, 363, 365
   Toi Toi sinking 61–62
Stowell, Rob 189
Stringer, Ian **161**
Strouts, Frederick 67
Stuart-Wortley, James 90
Summit Road Society 368
Sumner 23, 34, 118, 184, 275, 319, 324, 340, 341
   tunnel proposal 319, 320
Sumner Bar 168, 184, 335
'Sunbeams' club 140
Sunnyside Asylum 37
Sutton Brothers 360, 364
Sutton, Fred 363
Swift, Captain 34
Swindells, June 261

T

Taiaroa 67
Tait, Samuel 113
Tamatea Pōkai Whenua 19, 247
Tarewai (steamer) 123, **123**
Taununu 65, 66, 67, 78
Tauwhare, Caine 309
Tauwhare, Wi **262**
Tauwharepaka Teddington **164–65**, 167–68, **169**, 185, 200, 253, 254, 367
   see also Head of the Bay
   jetties 11, 20, 23, 26, 167, 171, 173–75, **175**, 184, 349
   saltmarsh and mudflats 166, 167, 168, 170, 175–77, 179
   school 150
Taylor, William and Sarah (Buckleys Bay) 316
Taylor, William (drowned in Charteris Bay) 150
Taylors Mistake *see* Te Onepoto Taylors Mistake
Taylor's Private Family Hotel and Pleasure Gardens, Diamond Harbour 118
Te Ahu Pātiki Mount Herbert 86, 92, 93, 110, **133**, **156**
Te Ana Marina 306, 308–9, **310–11**
   see also Dampiers Bay
Te Ana Ngāti Māmoe 33
Te Ara Whānui o Makawhiua 33
   see also Port Levy Harbour
Te Awaparahi Bay reclamation 325–26, 367–68
Te Awaparahi Buckleys Bay (Comptons Bay; Polhills Bay) **312–13**, 314, 315–16, 323, 324, 325, **326**
   boatshed, slipway and jetty 11, 315, 316, 318
Te Hapū o Ngāti Wheke 11, 67, 221, 246, 263, 308, 368
Te Nukutai o Tapoa Naval Point
   reclamation 176, **302**, 303, 305
   redevelopment of foreshore area 311
Te Onepoto Taylors Mistake 326, 332, **334**, 335, **341**
Te Pātaka o Rākaihautū Banks Peninsula 17, 19, 33, 67, 89, 246, 252
   birds-eye view **18**
   French 'purchase', 1840 83
Te Piaka 32, 33
Te Poho o Tamatea 247, **249**
Te Pōhue Camp Bay 19, 41, **44–45**, 47, **48–49**, **56**, 67, 113
   education reserve 55, 56
   farms for returned servicemen 56
   graveyard 54, 55
   jetty 23, 25, 43, **50**, 53, **56**, 56–57, 58, **59**
   quarantine station 48, **50**, 50–51, **52**, 53–55, 67, 94
   'Wee Ona' cottage 58, **59**, 60
Te Pōhue The Monument **132**
Te Rakiwhakaputa 183
Te Rāpaki-o-Te Rakiwhakaputa 67, 168, 214, **244–45**, 246, **250–51**, **257**, **259**, 268, 367
   children's activities 258–59, 261, **262**
   churches 254, **255**
   impact of European settlement 252–54
   jetty (Gallipoli Jetty) 11, 23, 28, 210, **244–45**, 246, 254, 256–58, **257**, 261, **262**, 263
   Māori residence and land 19, 33, 83, 84, 89, 93, 163, 170, 186, 202, 221, 236, 247–48, **249**, 252–53
   mātaitai reserve 263
   visitors 254, 256
   Wheke, wharenui 254, **255**, 309
Te Rauparaha 67, 252
Te Rūnanga o Ngāi Tahu 263
Te Tara o Te Rakihikaia Gebbies Pass 167, 168, 171, 173, 175, 177, 252
Te Upoku o Kurī Witch Hill monument 260, **260**
Te Waihora Lake Ellesmere 168, **169**, 253
Te Waipapa Diamond Harbour 9, 21, 23, 28, 41, 51, **85**, **104–5**, 107, 110, 122, 150, 154
   see also Upoko o Kurī Stoddart Point
   Diamond Harbour estate subdivision 114, 118, 119, 121, 122, 155, 356
   early European settlement 107–13
   ferry services 106, 113, 114, 119, 121, 122–23, 124–25
   picnics and visitors 118, 119, 121–22, 349
   school 57, 99, 123, 177
   subdivision of Diamond Harbour estate 114, 118, 119, 121, 122, 155, 359
Te Waipapa Diamond Harbour jetty 9, 20, 23, 100, **104**, 106, 107, 109, 114, **116–17**, 118–19, **120**, 121, 123–24, **124**, 179, **362**
   see also Cameron brothers' ballast quarry and jetty; Stoddart jetty
   parking and dinghy facilities 125
   proposed additional jetty 124
Te Waipounamu South Island 17, 19
Te Waka Pounamu Outrigger Canoe Club 309, 311
Te Whaka (defence launch) 73, 357
Te Whakarukeruke 67
Te Whakataupuka 65, 67
Te Wharau Charteris Bay 17, 21, 23, 27, 57, 129, 138, **144–45**, **151**, 160, 170, 175, 356, 367
   early European settlement 147–53
   holiday houses 156, 158
   jetty **6**, 11, 20, 23, 25, 26, 27, 137, **144**, 152–53, 154, 155, 173, 241, 357
   school 113, 150, **151**
   subdivision 158
   visitors 149, 150, 156, 157, 158
Te Whiti o Rongomai 69, 70

Teddington *see* Tauwharepaka Teddington
telephone communication 34, 37, 57, 58, 59, 186, 238, 338
Thackwell, H. W. 74
thermal springs, Rāpaki 247–48
Thomas, Joseph 89–90, 168, 170, 253, 267–68, 315, 333
Thomas, Mark 301, 352
Thompson, Joy 299–300
Thomson, William 189, 231–32
Thornton, G. 50, 53
tidal zone (takutai moana) 7, 17, 166, 167, 168, 187
Tikao, Hone Taare 253
Tikao, J. C. 258
Timaru 38, 89
Titan (paddle tug) 37, 110, 352
Tohu Kākahi 69, 70
Toi Toi 24, 361–62, **362**, 363
Toomey, Balfour 37, **38**, 39
Toomey, John 37
Torlesse, Charles 20, 89–90, 170, 253, 268, 318
Toy, Wal 123, 360
Toy's Ferry Launches 123, 357
Travellers Rest Hotel 202
Trengrove, John 189
Trengrove, Pauline 189
trucking services 9, 25, **25**, 57, 100, 175, 241
tsunami
    1868 20, 92, 171, 176, 184, 193
    1960 142, 163, 176–77, **178**, 187, 215
Tuckett, Frederick 168
Tuna Tuoro 83
Turner, Dave 179
Turner, Emily **137**

U

Upham, Charles **235**, 236
Upoko o Kurī Stoddart Point 103, 107, 109, 114, 121–22, 122, 127
    cottage built for Mark Stoddart and Mark Sprot
        (Waterman's Cottage) 107, **108**, 108–9
    Patriotic Carnival 1915 121–22
    signal staff 107–8
    Stoddart Cottage 109, 112, 118

V

Valintine, Thomas 236
Vallance, Will 234, 237
von Luckner, Felix 75, **75**, 363

W

W. Cleary & Co, 357
Waitaha 8, 17, 19, 182, 199, 248
Waitata Little Port Cooper **30–31**, 33–34, 36–37, **42**, 55, 253
    closing of signal station and settlement 43, 57–58
    communications with Lyttelton 34, 37, 338
    Deal boatmen 38
    houses 36, 37, 39, **40**
    jetty 11, 23, 26, 41–42, **42**
    pilot station 34, **35**, 36, 37, 39, 339
    school 36, 37, 39, **40**, 43
    sea rescues and attempts 42–43, 361–62
    women's lives 36, 41, 42
Waiwera (steam launch) 55, 94, 96, 114, 211
waka 19, 248, 308, 311, 367
Wakaroa Pigeon Bay 20
Wakefield, Felix 319
Walker, Bernard 237–38, **239**
Walker, R. W. 237
Walkers Beach, Quail Island 27, 179, 224, 237, **239**
Walter, Charlie 92, 94
Ward, Crosbie 222, 224
Ward, Edward 90, 221–22, **222**
Ward, Hamilton 221, 222, 224
Ward, Henry 221
Ward family 20, 240

Warren, Sir Miles 140–41, 189
weather *see* storms and rough seas
Webb, John 270
Webb, S. R. 284
Weenink, Brian 308
'Wee-Ona' cottage, Camp Bay 58, **59**, 60
Wells, Charlie 271
Whaka-Ora Healthy Harbour Initiative 189, 263, 277, 368
Whakaraupō Carving Centre 309
Whakaraupō Lyttelton Harbour 18, 19, 32, 33, 39, 41, 84, **222**, **346–47**
    see also boats; Port Cooper; sea transport; storms and rough
        seas; and names of individual bays and settlements
    early Māori residents 8, 247–48, 252–53
    map **12–13**
    naming by Tamatea Pōkai Whenua 19, 247
whaleboats 19, 21, 33, 34, 37, 84, 86, 92–93, 147, 170, 240, 253, 254, 268, 318, 351, 363
whaling station, Waitata 33–34
Wharf Labourers' and Lumpers' Association 99
wharves *see* jetties
Wheatsheaf Hotel, Teddington **172**, 174, 176, 177, **178**
White, Ian 156
White, J. A. **161**
Whitecliffs Hotel 203
Whitelaw, John 51
Williams, Cyrus 23–24, 173, 207, 324
Williams, Reg 74
Williman, William Henry 323
Wills, Alfred 318
Withell, Neil 211
Witte, Bert 349
Wood, George 351
Wood, Mary Jane 93
Woods, Thomas 51, 92
Woods' Purau Accommodation House 92, 112
Wootton (wooden steamer hulk) 258, **259**, 262
Worrall, James 74
Wreck Bay 103
Wyman, Tom 108–9, 114

Y

yachts and yachting 21, 103, 142–43, 156, 160–63, **163**, 305, 306, **307**, 308
    Ferguson-Rich Trophy 160, 163
    Lyttelton Regatta 21, 112, 160, **161**, 254, 301
    Sanders Memorial Cup 21, 23, 143, 292, 305
Yeatman, Sam 58
Young Men's Christian Association 78

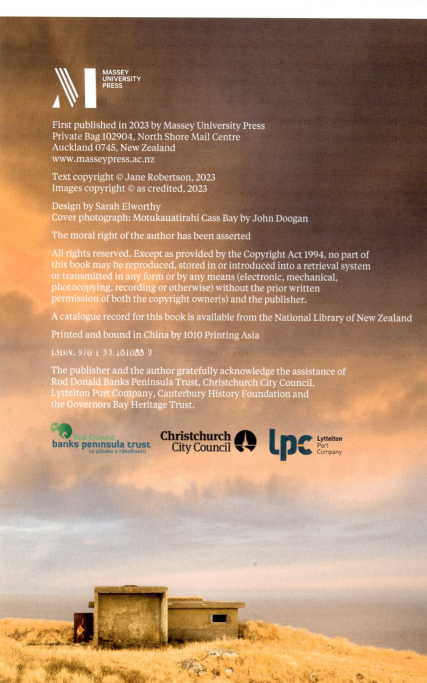

First published in 2023 by Massey University Press
Private Bag 102904, North Shore Mail Centre
Auckland 0745, New Zealand
www.masseypress.ac.nz

Text copyright © Jane Robertson, 2023
Images copyright © as credited, 2023

Design by Sarah Elworthy
Cover photograph: Motukauatirahi Cass Bay by John Doogan

The moral right of the author has been asserted

All rights reserved. Except as provided by the Copyright Act 1994, no part of this book may be reproduced, stored in or introduced into a retrieval system or transmitted in any form or by any means (electronic, mechanical, photocopying, recording or otherwise) without the prior written permission of both the copyright owner(s) and the publisher.

A catalogue record for this book is available from the National Library of New Zealand

Printed and bound in China by 1010 Printing Asia

ISBN: 978-1-99-101088-9

The publisher and the author gratefully acknowledge the assistance of Rod Donald Banks Peninsula Trust, Christchurch City Council, Lyttelton Port Company, Canterbury History Foundation and the Governors Bay Heritage Trust.

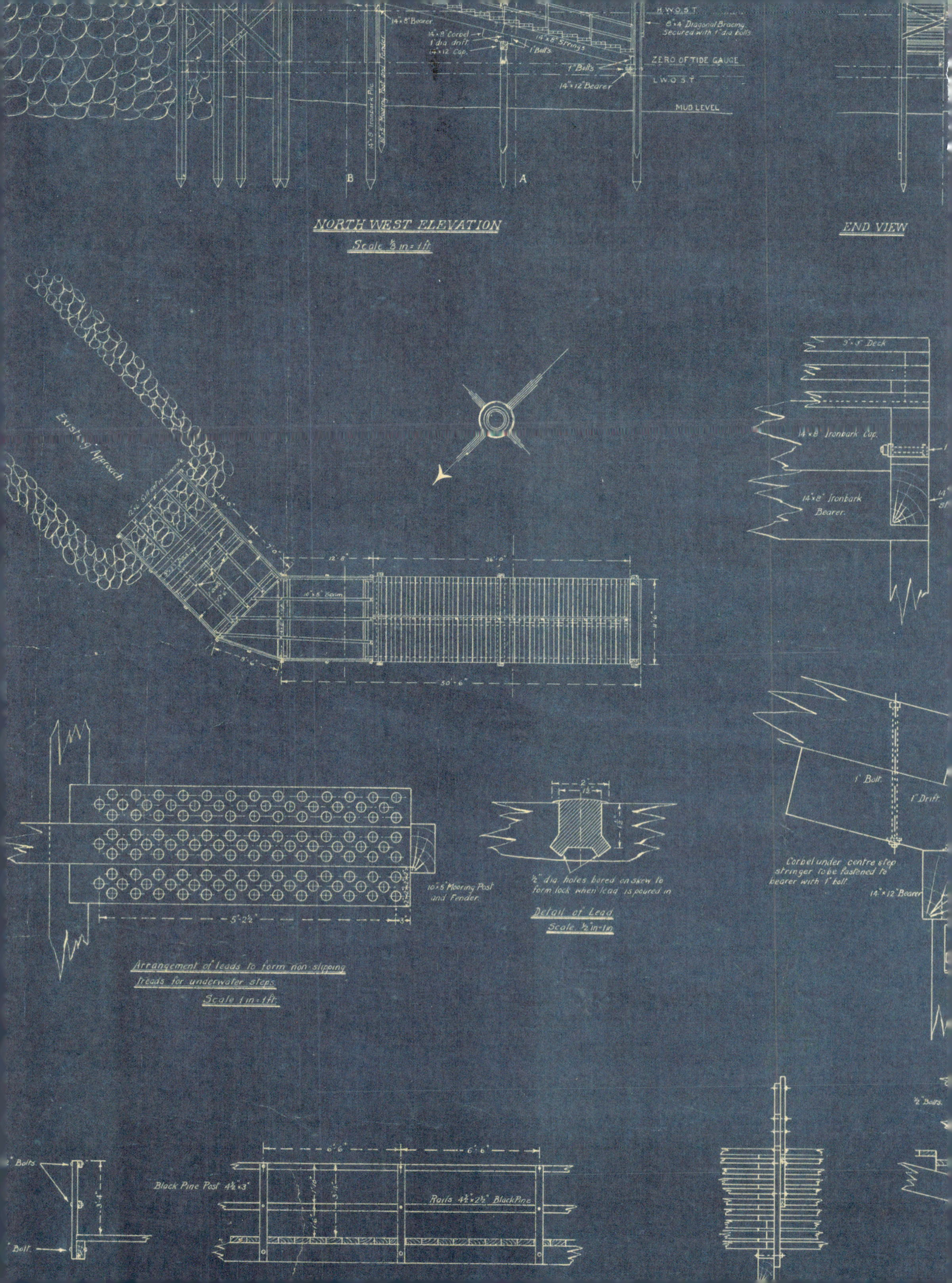
14"x8" Bearer
14"x8" Corbel
1" dia. drift
14"x12" Cap
14"x8" Strings
1" Bolts
H.W.O.S.T.
8"x4" Diagonal Bracing Secured with 1" dia. bolts
ZERO OF TIDE GAUGE
L.W.O.S.T.
MUD LEVEL
14"x12" Bearer
B
A
NORTH WEST ELEVATION
Scale 1/8 in = 1 ft
END VIEW
Existing Approach
12'8"
36'0"
50'6"
9"x3" Deck
14"x8" Ironbark Cap.
14"x8" Ironbark Bearer.
1" Bolt.
1" Drift.
Corbel under centre step stringer to be fastened to bearer with 1" bolt.
14"x12" Bearer
10"x5" Mooring Post and Fender.
5'2½"
Arrangement of leads to form non-slipping treads for underwater steps.
Scale 1 in = 1 ft
½" dia. holes bored on skew to form lock when lead is poured in
Detail of Lead
Scale ½ in = 1 in
Black Pine Post 4½"x3"
Rails 4½"x2½" Black Pine
6'6"
½" Bolts
Bolts
Bolt